A GENERAL SURVEY OF THE HISTORY

OF THE CANON

OF THE NEW TESTAMENT

A GENERAL SURVEY OF THE HISTORY

OF THE CANON

OF THE NEW TESTAMENT

BY

BROOKE FOSS WESTCOTT D.D.
LATE FELLOW OF TRINITY COLLEGE, CAMBRIDGE.

SIXTH EDITION.

Eugene, Oregon

Εὐλόγως ὁ διδάσκαλος ἡμῶν ἔλεγεν·

ΓΙΝΕϹΘΕ ΤΡΑΠΕΖΙΤΑΙ ΔΟΚΙΜΟΙ.

Wipf and Stock Publishers
199 W 8th Ave, Suite 3
Eugene, OR 97401

A General Survey of the History of the Canon of the New Testament
By Westcott, B. F.
ISBN: 1-59752-239-2
Publication date 6/8/2005
Previously published by Macmillan and Co., 1889

TO THE RIGHT REVEREND

JAMES PRINCE LEE D.D.

LORD BISHOP OF MANCHESTER

AND LATE

HEAD MASTER OF KING EDWARD'S SCHOOL

BIRMINGHAM,

This Essay is inscribed,

WITH SINCERE AFFECTION AND GRATITUDE,

BY HIS FORMER PUPIL.

July 1855.

PREFACE.

MY object in the present Essay has been to deal with the New Testament as a whole, and that on purely historical grounds. The separate books of which it is composed are considered not individually, but as claiming to be parts of the Apostolic heritage of Christians. And thus reserving for another occasion the inquiry into their mutual relations and essential unity, I have endeavoured to connect the history of the New Testament Canon with the growth and consolidation of the Catholic Church, and to point out the relation existing between the amount of evidence for the authenticity of its component parts, and the whole mass of Christian literature. However imperfectly this design has been carried out, I cannot but hope that such a method of inquiry will convey both the truest notion of the connexion of the written Word with the living body of Christ, and the surest conviction of its divine authority. Hitherto the co-existence of several types of Apostolic doctrine in the first age and of various parties in Christendom for several generations afterwards has been quoted to prove that our Bible as well as our Faith is a mere compromise. But while I acknowledge most willingly the great merit of the Tübingen School in pointing out with marked distinctness the characteristics of the different books of the New Testament, and their connexion with special sides of Christian doctrine and with various eras in the Christian Church, it seems to me almost inexplicable that they should not have found in those writings the explanation instead of the result of the divisions which are traceable to the Apostolic times.

To lay claim to candour is only to profess in other words that I have sought to fulfil the part of an historian and not of a controversialist. No one will be more grieved than myself if I have misrepresented or omitted any point of real importance; and those who know the extent and intricacy of the ground to be travelled over will readily pardon less serious errors. But candour will not I trust be mistaken for indifference: for I have no sympathy with those who are prepared to sacrifice with apparent satisfaction each debated position at the first assault. Truth is indeed dearer than early faith, but he can love truth little who knows no other love. If then I have ever spoken coldly of Holy Scripture, it is because I have wished to limit my present statements to the just consequences of the evidence brought forward. But history is not our only guide; for while internal criticism cannot usurp the place of history, it has its proper field; and as feeling cannot decide on facts, so neither can testimony convey that sense of the manifold wisdom of the Apostolic words which is I believe the sure blessing of those who seek rightly to penetrate into their meaning.

Whatever obligations I owe to previous writers are I hope in all cases duly acknowledged. That they are fewer than might have been expected is a necessary result of the change which was required in the treatment of the subject owing to the form of modern controversy; and the same change will free me from the necessity of discharging the unwelcome office of a critic. Yet it would be ungrateful not to bear witness to the accuracy and fulness of Lardner's ' Credibility'; for, however imperfect it may be in the view which it gives of the earliest period of Christian literature, it is, unless I am mistaken, more complete and trustworthy than any work which has been written since on the same subject.

There is however one great drawback to the study of Christian antiquity, so serious that I cannot but allude to it. The present state of the text, at least of the early Greek Fathers, is altogether unworthy of an age which has done so much to restore to classic writers their ancient beauty; and yet even in intellect Origen has few rivals. But it is perhaps as unreasonable as it is easy to complain; and I have done nothing more than follow Manuscript authority as far as I could in giving the different catalogues of the New Testament. I can only regret that I have not done so throughout; for—to take one example—the text of the Canons given in Mansi, as far as my experience goes, is utterly untrustworthy, while the materials for determining a good one are abundant and easily accessible.

During the slow progress of the Essay through the press several works have appeared of which I have been able to make little or no use. All that I wished to say on the Roman and African Churches was printed before I saw Milman's *Latin Christianity;* and of the second edition of Bunsen's *Hippolytus and his Age* I have only been able to use partially the *Analecta Ante-Nicæna*. It is however a great satisfaction to me to find that Dr Milman maintains that the early Roman Church was essentially Greek; a view which I believe to be as true as it is important, notwithstanding the remarks of his Dublin reviewer.

It only remains for me to acknowledge how much I owe to the kind help of friends in consulting books which were not within reach. And I have further to offer my sincere thanks to the Rev. W. Cureton, Canon of Westminster, to the Rev. Dr Burgess of Blackburn, to Dr Tregelles of Plymouth, and to Mr T. Ellis of the British Museum, for valuable information relative to Syriac Manuscripts; and likewise to the Rev. H. O. Coxe of the Bodleian Library for consulting several Greek Manuscripts of the Canons contained in that collection.

HARROW,
July, 1855.

NOTICE TO THE SECOND EDITION.

DURING the eleven years which have elapsed since the first edition of this *History of the New Testament Canon* was published, the subject with which it deals has been brought under frequent discussion. It is therefore with real thankfulness that I can feel that the positions which I occupied at first have in every case, as far as I can judge, remained unshaken. On the first appearance of the book a favourable critic remarked that I had 'conceded to opponents more than I *need* 'have done' in the conduct of the inquiry. Perhaps it was so then, but I felt sure that I had not conceded more than I *ought*, and therefore no further concessions remain to be made now. The lesson even in this narrow field is not without value. Every one admits that Truth has nothing to fear from the fullest inquiry into each portion of the realm which she claims for her inheritance; but it is hard to carry the admission into practice. And so reticence begets suspicion, and suspicion hardens into distrust and disbelief, which would never have grown up, if a candid exposition of difficulties and defects in evidence had been made in the first instance by one who did not hold them to be insuperable.

It will be found that the whole Essay has been carefully revised. Very much has been added from sources either new or neglected by me before. By an enlargement of Appendix D I have given the documentary evidence for the Canon of the whole Bible, furnishing in this way the original texts of the principal passages which are given only in a translation in the *Bible in the Church*. In the task of revision I found valuable help in Credner's posthumous *Geschichte des Neutestamentlichen Kanon* (Berlin 1860), though the unfinished work is at best only an inadequate expression of his judgment.

My thanks are due to Dr Tregelles for a fac-simile of his tracing of the Muratorian Canon, and to many other friends for corrections and additions, of whom I may be allowed to name specially the Rev. F. J. A. Hort. To the Rev. Hilton Bothamley my obligations are still greater. He not only revised the proofs and verified almost all the references, but also furnished me with constant and valuable suggestions which have contributed in no small degree to whatever superiority in accuracy and arrangement the new edition has over the old.

B. F. W.

HARROW,
July 9, 1866.

PREFACE TO THE FOURTH EDITION.

IN revising this Edition of my Essay I have had the help of an elaborate and continuous criticism on the earlier part of it by the anonymous author of *Supernatural Religion*[1]. It is, I think, impossible to value too highly the privilege of being able to regard a complicated line of evidence from another point of sight : to see difficulties as they are actually experienced and not as they are anticipated, or imagined : to realise the importance of details in a new position which are insignificant in the old one. And before I proceed to offer some necessary remarks upon the arguments of my critic, I wish to acknowledge most fully the obligation under which I lie to him. He has called my attention to several omissions, to one or two errors of detail, to many imperfections of language, which may have misled others, since they have misled him. These various faults and defects

[1] [My references are made to the *first* edition. This, however, will cause no difficulty. In the *second* edition Vol. I. coincides (as far as I have observed) page for page with the *first* edition from p. 217 onwards, 5 being subtracted from the number of the original page. In Vol. II. I have not observed any difference of page or line. The 'revision' must have been singularly hasty, for numerous misprints are kept unchanged: *e.g.*, "Hegesippus in the second half of the *eleventh* century" (i. 218); '*Dial.* 103, 105, thrice 107' (for 105 thrice,) (i. 291); Ναξωραῖος, Ναξιραῖος (i. 309 n.), &c.; nor have I noticed that any errors other than clerical have been corrected.].

I have endeavoured to remove or remedy; and I trust that each objection has been fairly met, as each has certainly been fairly considered.

On two points of some interest, but on two only, I am inclined to modify the statements which I made before. A fresh consideration of the actual circumstances in which Papias was placed, and of the fragmentary notices of his writings which remain, leads me to think that I have conceded too much to the supposition of his anti-Pauline tendencies. I have, however, left what I originally wrote with some very slight changes. On the other hand, I do not now think that the evidence on which I relied before is sufficient to prove beyond reasonable doubt that the Valentinian quotations in the *Treatise against Heresies* can be referred to Valentinus himself. In this case, therefore, I have re-written the paragraph which deals with the debateable facts, though, on the whole, I am still disposed to maintain my former opinion.

So far I am indebted to the criticisms of my learned opponent for many improvements in detail in the course of the Essay; but my chief obligation is of a different kind. I owe to him a more complete conviction than I could otherwise have had of the soundness of the conclusions which I have maintained. He has stated objections, which I knew before only through foreign books, with the clear, calm vigour of an English-speaking advocate, and the objections, even when thus stated, seem to me to be conclusively answered by the replies which have been given to them by anticipation. As to this, however, each student must judge for himself from the facts which lie before him.

The wide acceptance which the work appears to have met with will also in the end, as I believe, render another service to the truth. It will lead many to investigate the early history of Christianity for themselves; and if so, it will serve at once to establish the importance of close historical investigation for the understanding of our faith, and also to illustrate the utter hopelessness of a historical investigation which deals only with literary fragments and leaves out of account the continuity and power of life.

Still, however widely I may differ from my critic both as to method and results, in one thing at least I am wholly at one with him. I heartily accept his proposition (what Christian will not?) that in relation to the present subject, Truth, whatever it may be, 'is the only 'object worthy of desire or capable of satisfying a 'rational mind;' and, this being so, I do not know that I can make a better return for the service which I have received, than by pointing out some cases, more or less serious, in which he has fallen into error.

In this connexion I may perhaps express my surprise that a writer who is quite capable of thinking for himself should have considered it worth while to burden his pages with lists of names and writings, arranged, for the most part, alphabetically, which have in very many cases no value whatever for a scholar, while they can only oppress the general reader with a vague feeling that all 'profound' critics are on one side. The questions to be discussed must be decided by evidence and by argument and not by authority. Even if it were otherwise, the real authority, in this way of presenting it, bears no exact relation to the apparent authority. Writers are quoted as holding on independent grounds an opinion which is involved in their characteristic assumptions. And more than this, the references are not unfrequently actually misleading. One example will shew that I do not speak too strongly. The following passage occurs Vol. i. p. 273 :

'It has been demonstrated that Ignatius was not sent to Rome 'at all, but suffered martyrdom in Antioch itself on the 20th of 'December, A.D. 115,[8] when he was condemned to be cast to wild 'beasts in the amphitheatre, in consequence of the fanatical ex-'citement produced by the earthquake which took place on the '13th of that month.[4]'

The references in support of these statements are the following :

[8] Baur, *Urspr. d. Episc.* Tüb. Zeitschr. f. Theol. 1838, H. 3, p. 155 anm. ; Bretschneider, *Probabilia,* &c. p. 185 ; Bleek, *Einl. N. T.,* p. 144; Guericke, *H'buch,* K. G. I. p. 148; Hagenbach, *K. G.,* I. p. 113 f.; Davidson, *Introd. N. T.,* I. p. 19; Mayerhoff, *Einl. petr. Schr.,* p. 79; Scholten, *Die ält. Zeugnisse,* p. 40, p. 50 f.; Volkmar, *Der Ursprung,* p. 52 ; *H'buch Einl. Apocr.,* I. p. 121 f., p. 136.

[4] Volkmar, *H'buch Einl. Apocr.,* I. p. 121 ff., 136 f.; *Der Ursprung,* p. 52 ff. ; Baur, *Ursp. d. Episc.* Tüb. Zeitschr. f. Th. 1838, H. 3, p. 149 f. ; *Gesch. chr. Kirche,* 1863, I. p. 440, anm. 1; Davidson, *Introd. N. T.,* I. p. 19 ; Scholten, *Die ält. Zeugnisse,* p. 51 f. ; cf. Francke, *Zur Gesch. Trajans,* u. s. w. 1840, p. 253 f. ; Hilgenfeld, *Die ap. Väter,* p. 214.

Such an array of authorities, drawn from different schools, cannot but appear overwhelming; and the fact that about half of them are quoted twice over emphasizes the implied precision of their testimony as to the two points affirmed. I can therefore hardly be wrong in supposing that any ordinary reader would believe that if he could turn to the passages specified, he would find in each some elements, or at least some authoritative confirmation, of the 'demonstration' (1) of the place and date of the death of Ignatius [references (3)], and (2) of the circumstances and occasion of it [references (4)]. As very few English readers can be expected to have access to the works in question, it may be worth while to set down in order what the student would find in place of the 'demonstration,' and the general agreement in its validity which he is led to expect.

i. References (3).

1. Baur, *Urspr. d. Episc.* Tüb. Zeitschr. 1838, ii. 3, p. 155 anm. In this note, which is too long to quote, there is nothing, so far as I see, in any way bearing upon the history except a passing supposition 'wenn......Ignatius 'im J. 116 an ihn [Polycarp]......schrieb......'

2. Bretschneider, *Probabilia* x. p. 185. 'Pergamus 'ad Ignatium *qui circa annum cxvi obiisse dicitur.*'

3. Bleek, *Einl. N. T.* p. 144 [p. 142 ed. 1862] '...... 'In den Briefen des Ignatius Bischofes von Antiochien, 'der unter Trajan gegen 115 *zu Rom* als Märtyrer 'starb.'

4. Guericke, *Handb. K. G.* i. p. 148 [p. 177 ed. 3, 1838, the edition which I have used]. 'Ignatius, Bischoff 'von Antiochien (Euseb. *H. E.* iii. 36), *welcher* wegen 'seines standhaften Bekenntnisses Christi *unter Trajan* '115 *nach Rom geführt, und hier* 116 *im Colosseum von* '*Löwen zerrissen wurde* (vgl. § 23, 1)' [where the same statement is repeated].

5. Hagenbach, *K. G.* i. 113 f. [I have not been able to see the book referred to, but in his Lectures *Die christliche Kirche der drei ersten Jahrhunderte*, 1853 (pp. 122 ff.), Hagenbach mentions the difficulty which has been felt as to the execution at Rome, while an execution at Antioch might have been simpler and more impressive, and then quotes Gieseler's solution, and passes on with 'Wie dem auch sei'.]

6. Davidson, *Introd. N. T.* i. p. 19. 'All [the 'Epistles of Ignatius] are posterior to Ignatius himself, 'who was not thrown to the wild beasts in the amphi-

'theatre at Rome by command of Trajan, but at Antioch
'on December 20, A.D. 115. The Epistles were written
'after 150 A.D.' [For these peremptory statements no
evidence and no authority whatever is adduced.]
    7. Mayerhoff, *Einl. Petr. Schr.* p. 79. '......Ignatius,
'*der spätestens* 117 *zu Rom den Märtyrertod litt*.......'
    8. Scholten, *Die ält. Zeugnisse* p. 40, mentions 115
as the year of Ignatius' death: p. 50 f. The Ignatian
letters are rejected partly 'weil sie eine Märtyrer-reise
'des Ignatius nach Rom melden, deren schon früher
'erkanntes ungeschichtliches Wesen durch Volkmar's
'nicht ungegründete Vermuthung um so wahrschein-
'licher wird. Darnach scheint nämlich Ignatius nicht zu
'Rom auf Befehl des sanftmüthigen Trajans, sondern zu
'Antiochia selbst, in Folge eines am dreizehnten Decem-
'ber 115 eingetretenen Erdbebens, als Opfer eines aber-
'gläubischen Volkswahns am zwanzigsten December
'dieses Jahres im Amphitheater den wilden Thieren zur
'Beute überliefert worden zu sein.'
    9. Volkmar, *Der Ursprung*, p. 52. [p. 52 ff.] [This
book I have not been able to consult, but from secondary
references I gather that it repeats the arguments given
under the next reference.]
    10. Volkmar, *Handb. Einl. Apocr.* p. 121 f., p. 136.
'Ein Haupt der Gemeinde zu Antiochia, Ignatius, wurde
'während Trajan dortselbst überwinterte, am 20. De-
'zember den Thieren vorgeworfen, in Folge der durch
'das Erdbeben vom 13. Dezember 115 gegen die ἄθεοι
'erweckten Volkswuth, ein Opfer zugleich der Siegesfeste
'des Parthicus, welche die Judith-Erzählung (i. 16) an-
'deutet, Dio (c. 24 f. vgl. c. 10) voraussetzt...' [I do not
quote the arguments with which I am not now concerned.]
    If now these authorities are placed in connexion with

the statements under (3) which they are naturally supposed to confirm, it will be seen that three only of the nine writers lend any support to them: Volkmar (9, 10) and his two followers, one English, Davidson (6), and one Dutch, Scholten (8); and that one only (Volkmar) offers any arguments in support of them. Baur (1) occupies a negative position. Bleek (3), Guericke (4), Hagenbach, doubtfully (5), and Mayerhoff (7) *affirm* the martyrdom at Rome, the fact which the text *denies;* for it must be remembered that the references are made (apparently) in support of a definite fact which is said to have been 'demonstrated.'

  ii. References (4).
  1. Volkmar: see above.
  2. Baur, *Ursprung d. Episc.* Tüb. Zeitschr. 1838, ii. H. 3, p. 149 f. In this passage Baur discusses generally the historical character of the Martyrdom, which he considers, as a whole, to be 'doubtful and incredible.' To establish this result he notices the relation of Christianity to the Empire in the time of Trajan, which he regards as inconsistent with the condemnation of Ignatius; and the improbable circumstances of the journey. The personal characteristics, the letters, the history of Ignatius, are, in his opinion, all a mere creation of the imagination. The utmost he allows is that he may have suffered martyrdom (p. 169).
  3. Baur, *Gesch. chr. Kirche*, 1863, i. p. 440, anm. 1. 'Die Verurtheilung ad bestias und die Abführung dazu 'nach Rom......mag auch unter Trajan nichts zu un-'gewöhnliches gewesen sein, aber.....bleibt die Geschichte 'seines Märtyrerthums auch nach der Vertheidigung 'derselben von Lipsius......höchst unwahrscheinlich. Das 'Factische ist wohl nur dass Ignatius im J. 115, als Trajan 'in Antiochien überwinterte, in Folge des Erdbebens in

'diesem Jahr, in Antiochien selbst als ein Opfer der 'Volkswuth zum Märtyrer wurde.'
4. Davidson : see above.
5. Scholten : see above.
6. Francke, *Zur Gesch. Trajan's,* 1840 [1837] p. 253 f. [A discussion of the date of the beginning of Trajan's Parthian war, which he fixes in A.D. 115, but he decides nothing directly as to the time of Ignatius' martyrdom.]
7. Hilgenfeld, *Die ap. Väter,* p. 214 [pp. 210 ff.]. Hilgenfeld points out the objections to the narrative in the Acts of the Martyrdom, the origin of which he refers to the period between Eusebius and Jerome: setting aside this detailed narrative he considers the historical character of the general statements in the letters. The mode of punishment by a provincial governor causes some difficulty : 'bedenklicher,' he continues, 'ist jedenfalls der andre Punct, die Versendung 'nach Rom.' Why was the punishment not carried out at Antioch ? Would it be likely that under an Emperor like Trajan a prisoner like Ignatius would be sent to Rome to fight in the amphitheatre ? The circumstances of the journey as described are most improbable. The account of the persecution itself is beset by difficulties. Having set out these objections he leaves the question, casting doubt (like Baur) upon the whole history, and gives no support to the bold affirmation of a martyrdom 'at Antioch, on December 20, A.D. 115.'

In this case, therefore, again, Volkmar alone offers any arguments in support of the statement in the text; and the final result of the references is, that the alleged 'demonstration' is, at the most, what Scholten calls 'a not groundless conjecture[1].'

[1] It may be worth while to add that in spite of the profuse display

It seems quite needless to multiply comments on these results. Any one who will candidly consider this analysis will, I believe, agree with me in thinking that such a style of annotation, which runs through the whole work, is justly characterized as frivolous and misleading. It suggests the notion that the contents of a commonplace book have been emptied into the margin without careful collation and sifting. But it should be remembered in adopting such a process, if I may for once borrow the vigorous language of the author, that 'a good strong assertion becomes a power-'ful argument, since few readers have the means of 'verifying its correctness' (ii. 66).

The text of the Essay is not unfrequently deformed by similar blemishes, which I can only refer to haste and impatience of revision. But from whatever source they spring such errors detract greatly from the value of the author's judgment. It is difficult, for example, to see how a writer with any clear views on the principles of textual criticism could either write or allow to stand even at the interval of eight hundred pages the two following statements: (1) 'The episode of the angel 'who was said to descend at certain seasons and trouble 'the water of the pool of Bethesda......may be mentioned 'here in passing, although the passage is not found in 'the older MSS. of the fourth Gospel (John v. 3, 4) and '*it was certainly* ['probably' p. 113, ed. 2] *a late interpo-* '*lation*' (i. 103). (2) 'The words which most pointedly 'relate the miraculous phenomena characterizing the 'pool do not appear in the oldest MSS. and are con-'sequently rejected......[John v. 3, 4, is quoted]. We 'must believe, however, that this passage did originally

of learning in connexion with Ignatius, I do not see even in the second edition any reference to the full and elaborate work of Zahn.

'belong to the text, and has from an early period been 'omitted from MSS. on account of the difficulty it 'presents; and one of the reasons which points to this 'is the fact that verse 7, which is not questioned and has 'the authority of all the codices, absolutely implies the 'existence of the previous words, without which it has 'no sense' (ii. 421). No contradiction could be more complete or more peremptory. On the other hand no critical problem could be more simple; yet all principles of solution appear to be lost in the medium through which it is regarded.

It would scarcely be worth while to refer to the startling mistranslations of Greek and Latin which occur from time to time, if the author did not most justly insist on the necessity of rigorous exactness[1]. Many of these may be due as much to want of care as to want of scholarship. Sometimes, however, they lead to serious consequences; and in one place an inattention to grammar has led the author to charge those who do not feel at liberty to disregard the fundamental laws of oblique construction with 'a falsification of the text' (ii. 329, f.).

It follows almost as a necessary consequence that a want of grammatical accuracy leads to a want of accuracy in statement. The author of *Supernatural Religion*

---

[1] Two examples from Greek and two from Latin will suffice: ii. 31... ἔφη 'Ο πονηρός ἐστιν ὁ πειράζων, ὁ καὶ αὐτὸν πειράσας..."he said, 'The evil 'one is the tempter, who also tempted 'himself'," as if ὁ καὶ αὐτὸν π. were part of the quotation. ii. 46 ἐπεὶ οὖν ἔδει ἀποκαλυφθῆναι, φησίν, ἡμᾶς τὰ τέκνα τοῦ θεοῦ περὶ ὧν ἐστέναξεν, φησίν, ἡ κτίσις καὶ ὤδινεν, ἀπεκδεχομένη τὴν ἀποκάλυψιν...' when there- 'fore it was necessary to reveal, he 'says, us, who are children of God, in 'expectation of which revelation, he 'says, the creature groaneth and tra- 'vaileth...' ii. 100, Marcion, aufer etiam... 'Marcion also *removes*...' ii. 99, Nam ex iis commentatoribus quos habemus, Lucam videtur Marcion elegisse quem læderet. 'For of the *Commentators* whom we possess, Marcion 'seems to have selected Luke, which '*he mutilates.*' Such blunders ought not to have been made, and certainly not to have been passed over in the most cursory revision of the work. Can any one seriously have supposed that Bp. Thirlwall could have so set grammar at defiance?

PREFACE TO THE FOURTH EDITION. xxiii

strives, I cannot doubt, to be fair, but in spite of an ostentation of justice he falls into errors of fact far more frequently than an accurate scholar (as I believe) could do. Some of these errors I have had occasion to notice in the body of my essay (*e.g.* pp. 60 n. 1, 70 n. 2, 86 n. 4, 150 n. 4, 166 n. 1, &c.); and not to dwell now on isolated passages, a few continuous sentences will illustrate the fault of which I speak.

We read, i. p. 426, 'Eusebius informs us that Papias 'narrated from the Gospel according to the Hebrews a 'story regarding a woman accused before the Lord of 'many sins. The same writer likewise states that Hege-'sippus, who came to Rome and commenced his public 'career under Anicetus, quoted from the same Gospel. 'The evidence of this "ancient and apostolic" man is very 'important, and although he evidently attaches great 'value to tradition, knew of no Canonical Scriptures 'of the New Testament, and, like Justin, rejected the 'Apostle Paul, he still regarded the Gospel according to 'the Hebrews with respect, and made use of no other. 'The best critics consider that this Gospel was the 'evangelical work used by the author of the Clementine 'Homilies.'

Now of these seven or eight statements, which are made without any reserve, only one is supported by any direct evidence. One is at direct variance with the authority quoted; and the rest are mere conjectures of a small group of critics who are assumed to have a monopoly of right judgment. It is true that Eusebius says that Hegesippus quoted the Gospel to the Hebrews, and this is all in the paragraph which I can allow to be true. Eusebius does *not* say that Papias narrated the history in question '*from* the Gospel accord-'ing to the Hebrews' (see p. 71 n. 1). There is absolutely no evidence to shew that Justin rejected the Apostle Paul, or that Hegesippus rejected him, or that Hegesippus made use of no other Gospel than that according to the Hebrews, or that he knew of no canonical Scriptures of the New Testament (see pp. 167 ff. 205 ff.).

The Gospel according to the Hebrews becomes frequently elsewhere the occasion of remarkable assertions. For example, ii. 167: 'The Gospel according to 'the Hebrews...was made use of by all the Apostolic 'Fathers, by pseudo-Ignatius, Polycarp, Papias, Hege-'sippus, Justin Martyr, and at least employed along 'with our Gospels by Clement of Alexandria, Origen 'and Jerome, whilst Eusebius is in doubt whether to 'place it in the second class among the Antilegomena 'with the Apocalypse, or, in the first, amongst the 'Homologomena (sic)[1].' Here again definite statements are made for which partly I know no foundation of any kind, and partly only precarious conjectures. It is apparently quite an original assertion that Barnabas and Hermas (for if these are not meant, 'all the Apostolic 'Fathers' must be a periphrasis for Clement of Rome) and Polycarp used this Gospel: Papias, as we have shewn, if we may trust Eusebius, certainly did not use it: and there is nothing to shew that Clement of Rome or Justin Martyr did. If it is implied (and nothing less will serve the argument) that 'Clement of Alexandria, 'Origen, and Jerome' placed it on the same footing as the four Gospels, the statement is palpably false. And Eusebius neither states nor implies that he had ever any thoughts of placing it in 'the first class.'

We may take an illustration of another kind. It is

[1] The reference in the next sentence to the Gospel of Peter as used 'in the Church of Rhosse' (sic, and again p. 161) seems to be rather a recollection of some French critic than of Eusebius ('Ρωσσός, *H. E.* vi. 12).

PREFACE TO THE FOURTH EDITION. xxv

stated by anticipation (i. 244), as the result to be afterwards established, 'that all the early writers avoid our 'Gospels, if they knew them at all, and systematically 'make use of other works.' Now I submit that even if the author had established all which he afterwards asserts, this statement would convey a perfectly false impression to the reader. Is it true that 'all the early writers' make use of Apocryphal Gospels? We read afterwards: '[The Shepherd of Hermas] has no quotations from the 'Old or New Testament' (i. 262): and again of the evangelic references of Polycarp, 'in no case is there 'any written source indicated from which these passages 'are derived' (i. 286): of the Epistle to Diognetus, 'it is 'admitted that it does not contain a single direct quo- 'tation from any evangelical work' (ii. 40): of Dionysius of Corinth, on the supposition that he referred to Gospels, 'we have no indication whatever what evan- 'gelical works were in the Bishop's mind' (ii. 167): of Melito, that he might have been 'passed over alto- 'gether,' so far as any references to the Gospels are concerned (ii. 172, 181): of the fragments of Claudius Apollinaris, in which the Canonical Gospels are referred to, that 'there is exceedingly slight reason for attri- 'buting these fragments to him' (ii. 191). The phrase 'all the early writers' must be considerably modified when six out of the fifteen orthodox patristic authorities are set aside. But still further, is it fair to convey the belief that we are in a position to say anything whatever from the evidence of their writings of the 'systematic' usage of any one of the writers examined except Justin Martyr and (perhaps) the author of the Clementine Homilies? The fragments and fragmentary notices of the other writers, if considered apart from their connexion with the life of the Church, are too

C. *c*

meagre to allow us to draw any conclusion as to their habits of quotation[1].

At first sight it must seem strange that a writer so learned, and in design so just, as the author of *Supernatural Religion* can make such statements as I have quoted, but it is not difficult to see the reason. He is far more familiar, unless I am mistaken, with some modern German and Dutch speculations on the Gospels and early Church history, than with the New Testament itself[2]

---

[1] Sometimes the author shews unconsciously that his mode of argument proves too much. Thus when he has noticed the fact that 'the 'pseudo-Ignatius' does not refer (by name) to St John he adds in a note: 'Indeed in the universally repu-'diated Epistles, beyond the fact 'that two are addressed to John... 'the only mention of him is...' (ii. 430). But I can hardly suppose that he would argue from this that the writer of these confessedly late Epistles did not know St John as 'the 'disciple whom Jesus loved' and as the author of the fourth Gospel.

[2] One or two examples of grave inaccuracy as to the letter of the New Testament may be given to justify my statement:

(*a*) As to *contents*. 'The assump-'tion that the disciple thus indicated 'is John rests principally on the fact 'that...and also that he *only once* 'distinguishes John the Baptist by 'the appellation ὁ βαπτιστής...' (ii. 423). St John *never* uses the phrase *John the Baptist*.

'There is no instance whatever 'that we can remember, in which 'a writer [of the New Testament] 'claims to have himself performed 'a miracle' (i. 191). Can the writer have forgotten Rom. xv. 19; 2 Cor. xii. 12?

(*b*) As to *text*. 'This census was 'first made...Luke ii. 2' (i. 311). The true reading is without doubt αὕτη ἀπογραφὴ πρώτη ἐγένετο, which cannot be so translated [nor indeed can the common reading]. (Marcion reads in Luke xi. 2) 'ἐλθέτω τὸ ἅγιον πνεῦ-'μά σου ἐφ' ἡμᾶς instead of ἁγια-'σθήτω τὸ ὄνομά σου. The former is 'recognized to be the true original 'reading...We are therefore indebted 'to Marcion for the correct version 'even of "the Lord's Prayer."' (ii. 126.) The reading of Marcion is most uncertain, and on the other hand it is known that the words in question were substituted (*e.g.* by Gregory of Nyssa) for ἐλθέτω ἡ βασιλεία σου.

(*c*) As to *interpretation*. The natural fear of Martha (John xi. 39) lends no support whatever to the statement that the Evangelist describes 'the restoration to life of a 'decomposed human body' (i. 42, cf. 37). 'The reading of Luke,' τὸ γεννώμενον ἅγιον κληθήσεται υἱὸς θεοῦ, translated 'that holy thing 'which shall be born of thee shall be 'called...' is said (ii. 67) to 'present 'an important variation' from the reading of Basilides τὸ γεννώμενον ἐκ σοῦ ἅγιον κληθήσεται, translated 'the 'thing begotten of thee shall be called 'holy,' as if there were any difficulty in taking ἅγιον as the predicate in St Luke.

The whole discussion on the internal character of the Gospel of St John (ii. 415 ff.) abounds with errors of this kind, and is, I must not shrink from saying, more inaccurate and

and the writings of the Fathers. Hence it is that he gives plausible conjectures as certain facts. Thus, without one word of caution, and (as I think) in direct contradiction to the evidence, he says that 'Ebionitic 'Gnosticism' was 'once the purest form of primitive 'Christianity' (ii. 4), that 'John as well as Peter belonged 'to the Ebionitic party' (ii. 407), that 'Justin Martyr 'became a convert to Christianity strongly tinged with 'Judaism' (i. 289), that 'it is clear that Paul is referred to 'in *Apoc.* ii. 2' (ii. 408), and so on. He has consequently little patience even to attempt to understand the position of those from whom he differs. Their opinions are set down in perfect sincerity as 'absurd' and 'pre- 'posterous,' when, as I must still believe, the 'absurdity' lies in the attempt to construct a history of the Christian Church out of a few isolated fragments interpreted by a false assumption as to the character of the Gospel of Christ[1].

This fault appears to me to characterize the fatal defect—for so I must call it—of the critical investigations of the author of *Supernatural Religion*. They are, to sum up all in a word, wholly unhistorical. They are conducted without any regard to the specific nature of the evidence which is available; without any realization of the facts of the Christian life; and, I will venture to add, without any clear recognition of the historical problem which is under discussion. I will now endea-

---

superficial (if possible) even than Scholten's, on which it seems to be based. Any one who will examine the paragraphs on the 'great many 'geographical errors' supposed to be committed by St John (pp. 419—422) with the help of such a *Commentary* as Meyer's; or the entire chapter side by side with Mr Sanday's singularly calm and convincing discussion of *The authorship of the Fourth Gospel*, will see, I think, that I have not spoken too strongly.

[1] Much that is boldly said to be 'impossible,' as to the structure of a historical document, appears to me to be quite natural: *e.g.* ii. pp. 439 f.; 459.

vour to justify, as briefly as I can, these three general counts of accusation.

I. It is obvious that nothing can be more precarious than an argument drawn from silence, unless there is a very strong presumption that the witness would have mentioned the fact, which he fails to notice, if he had been acquainted with it. This presumption must arise, in the case under consideration, from what is known of the circumstances of the several early Fathers and of the occasions on which they wrote. When, for example, it is said that 'it is a significant fact that Justin Martyr, 'who attacks Marcion's system, never brings any ac-'cusation against him of mutilating or falsifying any 'Gospel......' (ii. 143), it is clear that the 'significance' of the fact depends wholly upon the nature and frequency of Justin's references to Marcion. Now I do not think that any reader of this passage would obtain a just impression of the fact from it, or that he would rate the significance of the fact very highly if he was aware that Justin refers to Marcion (if I am correct) twice only, and then in such a way that he could not, without a total disregard of the subject in hand, have made any allusion to his views on the written Gospels. Or, again, when we read that the variation of Justin's Evangelic references from the readings of our Gospels is 'a phenomenon elsewhere 'unparalleled in those times' (i. 374), I am obliged to ask where, outside of Justin's own works, can we find a parallel either in point of time, or in point of style and substance: I can think of none. Once more: when it is asserted that Justin 'knows nothing of the star guiding '[the magi]...' because he says simply that 'a star rose 'in heaven at the time of Christ's birth......' (i. 319), I can hardly believe that the same conclusion would hold of the writer of the well-known Epiphany hymn, 'Earth

PREFACE TO THE FOURTH EDITION.   xxix

'hath many a noble city,' who, in describing at length the visit of the wise men, tells us no more than Justin as to the phenomenon of the star[1].

The argument in favour of a negative conclusion from the absence of positive evidence is invalid when this absence is directly or reasonably explained by the scope or usage of the writer; or by the character of the passage from which the conclusion is drawn. When the explanation is direct the controversy is at an end: in the other cases the issue remains more or less in suspense. Not to dwell on these doubtful cases I will notice two instructive examples in which our author has neglected to take account of the usage and the scope of the writer, from whose evidence he consequently deduces results which are (as I believe) false, and which certainly are not established as he supposes.

1. It is unquestionable that the Evangelic references of Justin are anonymous, and that they do not agree verbally with the text of our Gospels. The conclusions to be drawn from these two facts must depend upon the character of Justin's writing. From the first the author of *Supernatural Religion* affirms (i. 303) 'that the infer-'ence can not only be (*sic*) that [Justin] attached small 'importance to the Memoirs, but also, that he was 'actually ignorant of the author's name, and that his 'Gospel had no more definite superscription.' But I have shewn (pp. 17, ff) that anonymous citation is the constant rule of Apologists. The silence of Justin as to the names of the Evangelists suggests no more that he

---

[1] The phrase 'knows nothing of' appears to be used as synonymous with 'does not mention' (i. 168, 313, 335, 337, ii. 450, 455, 464). The usage is open to serious misconstruction, for I can hardly suppose that the author would argue that the writer of the Fourth Gospel was ignorant of Christian Baptism, though in his sense he 'knows nothing' of the Sacraments.

was ignorant of them than does the like silence of Origen and Eusebius in corresponding works. As to the second fact it is argued, that the supposition that these variations spring from a free handling of Evangelic materials is to imagine 'a phenomenon which is else-'where unparalleled in those times' (i. 374)[1]. But as I

---

[1] While these pages have been passing through the press I have had occasion to collect the references to the New Testament in Chrysostom's treatise *On the Priesthood*. The result is an instructive illustration of the phenomena of free quotation in all times. Speaking roughly, about one half of Chrysostom's quotations contain variations from the Apostolic texts; and these variations include cases (1) of repeated variation, (2) of the combination of distinct passages, and (3) of coincidence with 'the ' Ebionitic Gospel.' It will be worth while to set these down as an illustrative commentary on the corresponding variations of Justin Martyr.

1. *Repeated variations.* John xxi. 15 (16, 17). Lib. II. 1 § 82 [ὁ χριστός]...διαλεγόμενος Πέτρε, φησίν, φιλεῖς με; and again § 90 Πέτρε γάρ φησι φιλεῖς με πλεῖον τούτων· This substitution of Πέτρε for Σίμων Ἰωάννου (Ἰωνᾶ) is (as far as I know) quite unsupported by other authorities. The φιλεῖς too (in § 90 at least) is an error for ἀγαπᾷς derived from v. 17.

1 Cor. ii. 11. Lib. II. 2 § 102 οὐδεὶς γὰρ οἶδε τὰ τοῦ ἀνθρώπου εἰ μή... Lib. III. 14 § 267 ἐπειδὴ τὰ τοῦ ἀνθρώπου οὐδεὶς οἶδεν εἰ μή... This substitution of οὐδεὶς for τίς γάρ or τίς γὰρ ἀνθρώπων is again (as far as I know) peculiar to Chrysostom.

Hebr. xiii. 17. Lib. III. 18 § 338 πείθεσθε...καὶ ὑπείκετε, ὅτι αὐτοί... ἀποδώσοντες. Lib. VI. 1 § 497 τὸ γὰρ Πείθεσθε...καὶ ὑπείκετε, ὅτι αὐτοί ...ἀποδώσοντες. The substitution of ὅτι αὐτοί for αὐτοὶ γάρ is not noticed in Tischendorf's last edition of the New Testament.

2. *Combinations.* Lib. II. 2 § 98 ...ὑποδεικνύει τοὺς ἐχθροὺς ὧδέ πως λέγων· φανερὰ δέ ἐστι τὰ τῆς σαρκὸς ἔργα, ἅτινά ἐστι, πορνεία, μοιχεία, ἀκαθαρσία,...θυμοί, ἐριθεῖαι (Gal. v. 19), καταλαλιαί, ψιθυρισμοί, φυσιώσεις, ἀκαταστασίαι (2 Cor. xii. 20), καὶ ἕτερα τούτων πλείονα. The words of one Epistle are added to the words of another without any mark of separation, the words common to both forming the transition.

Lib. II. 5 § 141 ἐν τούτῳ, φησίν [ὁ χριστός], γνώσονται οἱ ἄνθρωποι, ὅτι ἐμοί ἐστε μαθηταί, ἐὰν ἀγαπᾶτε ἀλλήλους. The words are a free combination of John xiii. 35 and xv. 12.

Lib. IV. 1 § 361...ἀκούσας τοῦ χριστοῦ λέγοντος ὅτι εἰ μὴ ἦλθον καὶ ἐλάλησα αὐτοῖς ἁμαρτίαν οὐκ εἶχον· καὶ εἰ μὴ τὰ σημεῖα ἐποίουν ἐν αὐτοῖς ἃ μηδεὶς ἄλλος ἐποίησεν ἁμαρτίαν οὐκ εἶχον. John xvi. 22, 24. Perhaps the second verse is a distinct quotation, but even in that case the variations in text are most striking.

3. *Alleged Ebionitic readings.* By a most singular accident (shall I say?) Chrysostom refers to John iii. 5, using both the characteristic words which are found in Justin and the Clementines : Εἰ γὰρ οὐ δύναταί τις εἰσελθεῖν εἰς τὴν βασιλείαν τῶν οὐρανῶν ἐὰν μὴ δι' ὕδατος καὶ πνεύματος ἀναγεννηθῇ (Lib. III. 5 § 187). Comp. p. 150 and note.

The parallels between the forms of variation in Chrysostom and Justin are thus seen to be complete in crucial instances. No one can doubt that Chrysostom used the Gospels and the Epistles of St Paul as having

have already said, Justin stands alone; and the only possible parallel must be from his procedure in a similar case. Such a parallel is actually found. Justin's quotations from the LXX. exhibit exactly the same kind of variations as his Evangelic references. This parallelism of manner (see pp. 172 f.) has been carefully exhibited by Prof. Norton and Semisch, and not overlooked by Credner, but I do not see that the author of *Supernatural Religion* has given any attention to it.

2. The conclusions which the author builds on the evidence of Eusebius are even less warranted by an exact consideration of the design of the historian than the deductions which he makes from the method of Justin. Eusebius states distinctly[1] that he proposes to record any use of *controverted* books—books on which opinion had been once divided—but he makes no such promise as to the use of the *acknowledged* books. As to these he proposes only to notice any details of special interest. It follows as a natural consequence that he has recorded every trace known to him of the use of the *Gospel according to the Hebrews*—as a 'controverted' book in the larger sense—while he does not, and could not, according to his plan, record the simple quotation of the Canonical Gospels as universally 'acknowledged' (comp. pp. 231 f.). As far as this fact is apprehended—and it seems to me to be quite undeniable—the whole fabric of the argument, or rather assertion, which the author of *Supernatural Religion* makes as to the 'exclusive' and 'earlier' use of the Apocryphal Gospels by the first Fathers at once collapses. We meet with distinct mention of the '*Gospel according to the Hebrews* long before we hear any-

that exclusive divine authority which we attribute to them now. His freedom, therefore, more than justifies the freedom which we have claimed for Justin.
[1] See pp. 231 f.

'thing of our Gospels' from the nature of the case, because the use of it by a Christian Father was something exceptional and to be noted[1]. Such statements, therefore, as 'Eusebius who never fails to enumerate the works of 'the New Testament to which the Fathers refer...' (i. 483); and 'Eusebius [makes no mention] of any reference [to 'any writing of the New Testament] in the Epistles [of 'Dionysius of Corinth] which have perished, which he 'certainly would not have omitted to do had they 'contained any' (ii. 164); and 'it is certain that had 'Dionysius mentioned books of the New Testament, 'Eusebius would as usual have stated the fact' (ii. 166); and, once again, 'the care with which Eusebius searches 'for every trace of the use of the books of the New 'Testament in early writers, and his anxiety to produce 'any evidence concerning the authenticity, render his 'silence upon the subject almost as important as his 'distinct utterance when speaking of such a man as 'Hegesippus' (i. 437 f.), are wholly incorrect. Eusebius neither does nor was likely to do anything of the kind here supposed. He definitely promised to do and does something very different. He collects notices of the use of *disputed* books. It necessarily follows that the conclusions which are based upon the complete misunderstanding of his evidence that 'Hegesippus made exclusive 'use of the Gospel according to the Hebrews' (i. 419: cf. 438 ff.); and that 'it is certain that had he [Hegesippus] 'mentioned our Gospels, and we may say particularly 'the fourth, the fact would have been recorded by Euse-'bius' (ii. 320); and that 'many (?) Apocryphal Gospels 'are known to have been exclusively used by dis-

---

[1] The same remark applies to the historical relation of Marcion's Gospel to St Luke (ii. 134, 139). The author justly points out (ii. 86 f.) that scholars like Hilgenfeld and Volkmar, whom he generally follows, decide that Marcion's Gospel was dependent on St Luke.

'tinguished contemporaries of Justin' (i. 299), are mere assertions not justified in the least degree by the only evidence brought forward in support of them, nor, as far as I know, by any evidence that anywhere exists.

II. That such assertions can be made without conscious unfairness, which I do not for a moment believe to exist in the writer whom I have quoted, springs from persistent forgetfulness of the fact that Christian literature is from the first one product of the Christian life: that the Christian Society, the Church, has lived continuously since the great day of Pentecost: that fragmentary writings must be always referred to this central truth for their due appreciation. Just those details which are most original and most singular will always occupy undue prominence among literary monuments. The work of an isolated thinker, such as was the author of the Clementines, may occupy perhaps more space than all the remains of earlier and contemporary Christian literature, but it would be idle to suppose that it therefore reflects the current belief. The great stream flows on, but what we observe and portray is that which varies its wide and even surface. The example of Eusebius which we have just noticed shews most instructively how exceptional phenomena naturally occupy a chief place in a history. No one thinks it necessary to chronicle what is the normal state of things.

Now when we bear this obvious fact in mind and take account of the extent and character of Christian literature up to the last quarter of the second century (comp. pp. 19 ff., 63 ff.), it becomes at once clear that we cannot hope to construct out of this by itself or primarily an idea of the contemporary Christian Society. But on the contrary if there is at that later date a fairly wide-spread and clear view of the constitution and opinions of the

Church, it is reasonable to examine the earlier and fragmentary records with this view as the standard of reference, unless it can be shewn that some convulsion interrupted the continuity of the development. If, then, there can be no doubt that at this time our Gospels were regarded as we regard them now, that there is no trace of any conflict after which they gained the position which they then occupied; if their acceptance and use adequately explain the varieties of opinion which are found: then nothing short of the most certain facts can be sufficient to justify us in believing that suddenly, in a space of about five-and-twenty years, the old Gospels were set aside and new books, actually unknown before, completely and permanently usurped their place in the estimation of Christian teachers. I find it quite impossible to realize how such a revolution could have been accomplished simultaneously, as far as we can tell, throughout Christendom. I have indeed endeavoured to shew how and why the idea of a New Testament, co-ordinate with the Old Testament, was slowly fashioned: how tradition and writings based on tradition were for some time current: how one or other book, which was afterwards accepted as canonical, had at first only a partial acceptance; but I see no evidence to shew that the universal consent which acknowledged the four Gospels as possessed of unique authority, when from the character of Christian literature such a consent could first be shewn, can be otherwise explained, as a historical fact, than by a general coincidence of traditional usage.

It is perhaps due to the natural temperament of German scholars, and still more to the circumstances of their civil life, that they should neglect what I may venture to call the vital relations of literature. They treat books, for the most part, as if they belonged wholly to the region of speculation, and were not products and reflections of social activity. In place of the full variety and manifold conflicts of life, in place of the inconsistencies, the imperfections, the inconsequences of opinions, they offer us an almost endless variety of ingenious and complete theories. They have, I will be bold to say, if I may speak generally, and with a full recognition of compensating merit, an inadequate sense of proportion, and very little power of realizing the actual course of events. In this respect I am surprised that the author of *Supernatural Religion* has completely surrendered himself to their guidance. St Paul's doctrine of the Person and Work of the Lord—the Catholic Church in Europe, Asia, Africa, in the last quarter of the second century, are facts. We must so interpret the century between as to give a full account of both[1].

III. There is, however, great danger lest we should lose sight of the real point at issue by diverging to a discussion on the canonicity of the four Gospels. For Christians the Gospels have their special religious significance; but for others they are simply records of particular facts. The truth of the facts is in this latter case the one question to be settled, and not any theory which may be or may have been held as to any books in which the facts are narrated. Historic testimony is limited to proving the existence of a belief that such and such events took place. The extent, the character, the effects of this belief influence those who consider it, and turn them to belief more or less definite as the case may be.

---

[1] Perhaps I may remark here how little the author has apprehended what Christianity professes to be. For example: 'It is quite true that 'a decided step beyond the doctrine 'of Philo is made when the Logos is 'represented as σὰρξ ἐγένετο in the 'person of Jesus, but this argument 'is equally applicable to the Jewish 'doctrine of Wisdom, and that step 'had already been taken before the 'composition of the Gospel' (ii. 415).

In this respect, then, the first three (Synoptic) Gospels are much more than three isolated histories. They represent, as is shewn by their structure, a common basis, common materials, treated in special ways. They evidently contain only a very small selection from the words and works of Christ, and yet their contents are included broadly in one outline. Their substance is evidently much older than their form.

Nor is this all. The common contents of the Synoptic Gospels include, to speak generally, all that is known from other sources of the Life of the Lord. The most careful search is not able to produce more than very few and unimportant additions to the sayings of Christ and to the details of His work from uncanonical records. On the other hand, any one who will examine the summary which I have given of the Evangelic references in the Apostolic Fathers and Justin Martyr will be struck by the extent and variety of the correspondences which they offer with the facts of the canonical history.

The phenomenon is most remarkable and contrary to all that might have been expected. The Lord was attended during His ministry by numerous disciples who must have retained lively recollections of countless scenes of His manifold labours. It would have been natural, to judge from common experience, that these should have spoken to others of what they had seen and heard, and that in this way a great variety of distinct accounts should have been formed. The only explanation of the narrow and definite limit within which the Evangelic history (exclusive of St John's Gospel) is confined seems to be that a collection of representative words and works was made by an authoritative body, such as the Twelve, at a very early date, and that this, which formed the basis of popular teaching, gained exclusive currency, receiving only subordinate additions and modifications.

This Apostolic Gospel—the oral basis, as I have endeavoured to shew elsewhere, of the Synoptic narratives—dates unquestionably from the very beginning of the Christian Society. One argument alone is sufficient to establish the fact. There can be no doubt that there existed in the Church from the first a Jewish party, which gradually became isolated as the organization of the faith advanced. The Church was never Ebionitic, but in the first stage of its formation that which was potentially Ebionitic was not distinguished from that which was potentially Catholic. As soon as these differences were developed common action became impossible. The selection of Evangelic memorials which found general acceptance among all sections of Christians in the second stage of the history of the Church, must therefore have been formed in the first. And, in fact, universal tradition affirms the closest resemblance between the Ebionitic Gospel, by whatever name it was called owing to later revisions, and the Canonical St Matthew. In this way the substance of the Synoptic records is clearly carried up to the age of the Apostles.

If, therefore, it were admitted that the author of *Supernatural Religion* is right in supposing that Justin derived his knowledge of the words and works of Christ from *the Gospel according to the Hebrews*, I cannot see that his particular object would be furthered by the concession. He allows—it would be impossible to do otherwise—that this Gospel bore the closest resemblance in contents and language to our Synoptic Gospels. We read, that is, substantially what Justin believed. His record and ours alike reflect the primitive Apostolic message. The history which we have received is that on which the Christian Church was founded, and which was universally held by Christians as true from the first.

There is yet another point of great importance which requires to be noticed. The Synoptic narratives present the common materials in the simplest and most original form. Any one who has carefully examined Justin's parallels with the text of our Gospels cannot fail to have noticed that the peculiarities of Justin often bear the marks of paraphrase and interpretation. No writer would say that, as a whole, from whatever source they may be derived, they exhibit an older recension of (for example) the Gospel of St Matthew, which still in its present form is probably the latest of the three Synoptic Gospels. So again, the few fragments of the 'Ebionitic' Gospels which remain offer obvious marks of a later revision and embellishment of common narratives. Our first three canonical Gospels, in a word, not only give the Apostolic Gospel, but give it in a form which is certainly purer than that in which it was found in other documents of very early date. Exactly in proportion as it can be shewn that *the Gospel to the Hebrews* is early, it is shewn by a comparison of their texts that our Gospels are earlier.

This argument receives a striking illustration from the history of the text of the Gospels. It will probably have been observed by the reader that a small group of very ancient authorities, D (codex Bezæ), several manuscripts of the Old Latin (*e.g. e, k*) and the Old (Cureton's) Syriac, offer frequent coincidences with readings found (or supposed to be found) in uncanonical Gospels. These readings, from their wide distribution, cannot be later than the last quarter of the second century; and

PREFACE TO THE FOURTH EDITION. xxxix

when they are examined together they are found certainly to be not genuine, but interpolations of the original texts. In other words, the readings in MSS. of the Canonical Gospels which offer the most striking coincidences with the apocryphal narratives are proved to be both later than the true readings, and intrinsically less likely to be authentic. Thus the history of the canonical texts themselves enables us to realize, at least on one side, the history of the apocryphal Gospels, and establishes the superior antiquity of the Synoptists.

The Gospel of St John stands on an entirely different footing. It is not a recension of the common Apostolic Gospel, but a distinct personal record, an individual testimony added to the collective testimony, a review of the historic work of Christ made in the light of individual experience and with a full knowledge of the contents of the general message. St John could not indeed have been ignorant of what I have called (as I believe rightly) the Apostolic Gospel; but, while this is so, it is uncertain whether he had seen the Synoptic representations of this oral Gospel; and, in spite of confident assertions to the contrary, I know of no evidence whatever sufficient to raise even a fair presumption that he used either these or any other documents in the composition of his own record. This, however, is not the place to enter on a discussion of the apostolicity of the fourth Gospel, though it was necessary to indicate sharply the peculiar position which it occupies in the history of the Gospels; for the apprehension of the fact goes far to explain the character of the external evidence by which it is attested.

There is still one other feature in *Supernatural Religion* which I feel bound to notice. The author, expressing in this respect the general spirit of the school which he represents, assumes for himself and those who think with him a monopoly of 'profound' learning, of critical sagacity, and of the love of truth. Scholars who maintain the Apostolic authority of the Gospels are represented as advocates often insincere and constantly unscrupulous. It is either insinuated or stated that their object is simply to obtain a verdict, and not to assist in bringing to light the real facts of the case. If they state anything which appears to tell against them, the confession is extorted from unwilling witnesses. They are 'obliged to admit' (i. pp. 339 n., 421) what apparently they would gladly conceal: '...for dog-'matic and other foregone conclusions [they] profess 'belief in the Apostolic authorship of [St Matthew's] 'Gospel, although in doing so they wilfully ignore the 'facts...' (i. 485): views which appear to me to be reasonable and obvious 'are adopted simply from the 'necessities of a divine defending an unsubstantial 'theory' (i. 394): they 'attempt to exclude,' with singular short-sightedness as it must be allowed, instances which they know there is 'great inconvenience 'in producing' (i. 395): and sometimes (how could such men do otherwise?) they fall before 'temptations which 'are too strong for an apologist' (ii. 45): unfairness is so truly their characteristic that it wins for them the credit of 'cleverness' and 'discretion' (i. 474 n.).

'Apologists' are no doubt liable to error. They have sometimes (to their sorrow) to confess that they have overrated the strict force of the evidence by which their views are supported in detail. But this is not an exceptional fault into which they only fall. Moreover they hold a position as definite as that of sceptics. They interpret doubtful passages in accordance with the general facts of the life of the Church. They do

PREFACE TO THE FOURTH EDITION. xli

not think that it is necessary to cease to be Christians in order to judge of the meaning of Christian documents. On the other hand, and this is a fact which is usually overlooked, a critic who starts with the affirmation that miracles are incredible, an affirmation which can only be logically defended on the assumption either that there is no God, or that it is not to be believed that He reveals Himself, cannot approach the examination of records, which are records of miracles, with an unbiassed mind. He has to explain away the staple of their contents. He has decided beforehand that whatever else they may be they are not true. Such an antecedent decision is obviously more fatal to a dispassionate inquiry than the 'orthodox' belief that miracles are credible, and that the accounts which the Evangelists have given may, so far as they are histories, be examined by the ordinary laws of historical investigation. And not to insist further on this fundamental difference of standing between the 'apologist' and the sceptic, which appears to me to be wholly in favour of the 'apologist,' if such an acquaintance as I have been able to make of the literature of the special subject of my Essay justifies me in expressing an opinion, I cannot say that sceptics are more free from 'foregone conclu-'sions' than apologists, more patient in seeking to understand adverse positions, more accurate in scholarship, more guarded in inference, more modest in assertion. It would indeed be grievous if they were. For the Christian, Light and Truth, from whatever source they seem to flow, are identified with the Lord whom he is pledged to serve. To watch the Light as it slowly spreads over the sky till the day dawns—to gather reverently each fragment of Truth till the whole sum is completed in perfect knowledge—is the office to which he is called. So far as he yields to the desire of obtaining at any cost a temporary advantage, he violates the law of his personal devotion. He has all to gain by a clearer and deeper insight into the foundations and structure of his faith, unless he has believed in vain.

It only remains for me to return my hearty thanks to many friends for corrections and suggestions. I desire especially to acknowledge the great kindness of Dr Ceriani, of Milan, who placed at my disposal the results of a fresh collation of the Muratorian Canon which he made, comparing the original manuscript twice, letter by letter, with the facsimile of Dr Tregelles.

B. F. W.

HUNSTANTON,
September 1, 1874.

NOTICE TO THE FIFTH EDITION.

IN revising the present Edition I have had the advantage of considering many important essays which have been published during the last six years upon the subjects with which I have dealt. Among these I wish to name especially Bp. Lightfoot's contributions to the *Contemporary Review*, Dr Sanday's *Gospels in the Second Century*, and Dr Abbot's *Authorship of the Fourth Gospel*. My work was completed before I had the opportunity of seeing Dr Charteris' *Canonicity*.

In one particular of some importance I have felt able after a fresh consideration of the evidence to speak more confidently than in former editions. There is, I think, no reasonable doubt that the writings of Justin Martyr shew that he was acquainted with the Gospel of

St John. On another point of interest additional evidence has been made available. The Latin Version of the Armenian translation of the Commentary of Ephraem Syrus on the *Diatessaron* of Tatian has confirmed beyond question, as it seems, what I had ventured to present as most probable before.

It is unlikely that I shall ever again be able to revise what now stands written; but in looking back over the work which has been spread over thirty years I cannot but remember with the deepest thankfulness that every fresh piece of documentary evidence which has been discovered in the interval has gone to confirm the conclusions which I sought to establish from the first. Our errors and misunderstandings as to the earliest ages of Christendom spring, I believe, most commonly from neglecting the life which underlies the fragmentary records. The testimonies which can be gathered from the meagre remains of a limited literature are the signs of the life of the Church and not the measure of it. It is true of the first centuries, as it is true of the present century, that we cannot understand the history of Christianity unless we recognise the action of the Holy Spirit through the Christian Society. It is through the active belief that He speaks and acts still as He spoke and acted then, not as we should expect beforehand, that we can yet 'win our souls in patience.'

DIVINITY SCHOOL, CAMBRIDGE,
April 30*th*, 1881.

NOTICE TO THE SIXTH EDITION.

WITH the exception of a note on *The Teaching of the Twelve Apostles* and a few corrections this Edition is a reprint of the last.

The following additional references may be most conveniently given here:

p. 31 note 2; p. 40 note 3. Comp. Bp Lightfoot's *Apostolic Fathers*, Part ii. vol. 1, p. 30 'His (Ignatius') Martyrdom may with a high degree of probability be placed within a few years of A.D. 110, before or after.' *Id.* pp. 629 ff., where M. Waddington's date of Polycarp's Martyrdom is defended at length.

p. 63. Compare Wohlenberg, *Die Lehre der zwölf Apostel in ihrem Verhältniss zum N. T. lichen Schriftthum* (1888. *Classical Review*, pp. 286 f.).

p. 77. Compare Harnack, *Patres Apost. Papiæ fragmenta*, pp. 101 ff.

pp. 83 ff. For the early Apologists compare Harnack, *Texte u. Untersuchungen d. alt. christ. Literatur*, i. 1, 2 (1882). A translation of the Armenian fragment of Aristides is given pp. 110 ff.

p. 197. Compare *De Aleatoribus*, § 2 (Harnack, *Texte u. Untersuch.* v. 1, 68. 1888).

p. 220. Compare Harnack, *a. a. o.* i. (1) 254 ff.

p. 228. On the Commentary on the Gospels which has been attributed to Theophilus see Zahn, *Forschungen zur Gesch. d. N.T.lichen Kanon's*, II. Theil (1882), and Harnack, *Texte u. Untersuchungen...* i. 4 (1883).

p. 262. Compare Zahn, *Gesch. d. N.T.lichen Kanon's*, pp. 103 ff. for the use of the words *testamentum* and *instrumentum*.

p. 322. Compare Zahn, *Forschungen...* I. Theil. *Tatian's Diatessaron*, (1881); and Rev. S. Hemphill, *The Diatessaron of Tatian...* now first edited in an English form... 1888.

p. 342. Compare Zahn, *Forschungen...* III. Theil. *Supplementum Clementinum*.

pp. 378, 380. Compare Prof. Gwynn's *Hippolytus and his Heads against Caius* (Hermathena, vi. 1888); and Rev. J. H. Kennedy, *Part of the Commentary of S. Hippolytus on Daniel* (1888).

p. 399. Compare Bonwetsch, *Gesch. d. Montanismus* 1881; and Zahn, *Gesch. d. N.T.lichen K.* Einleitung.

p. 512. Compare Zahn, *Gesch. d. N.T. lichen Kanon's*, § 7.

With the passages of Zahn's History the criticisms of Harnack in his Essay *Das N. T. um das Jahr* 200 (1889) must be compared.

There is a growing danger, I think, lest we should lose the sense of the fulness of the life of the early Christian Society in the controversial handling of the literary fragments which, as I have already said, imperfectly indicate, but do not measure it.

B. F. W.

CAMBRIDGE,
March 1, 1889.

CONTENTS.

	Page
INTRODUCTION	1—15
A general view of the difficulties which affected the formation and proof of the Canon	1—4

i. The *Formation* of the Canon was impeded by:

1. Defective means of communication	4
2. The existence of a traditional Rule of doctrine	5
But the Canon was generally recognised at the close of the second century	6

ii. The *Proof* of the Canon is affected by:

1. The uncritical character of the early Fathers	8
2. The casual nature of their evidence	10
3. The fragmentary state of early Christian literature	11
The Canon rests on the combined judgment of the Churches	12

FIRST PERIOD. A.D. 70—170.

CHAPTER I.

THE AGE OF THE APOSTOLIC FATHERS.

A.D. 70—120.

The general character of the Sub-Apostolic age conservative and yet transitional	19
The epistolary character of its literature	20
Its relation to the history of the Canon	*ib.*

SECTION I. *The relation of the Apostolic Fathers to the teaching of the Apostles.*

Page

§ 1. *CLEMENT of Rome.*
His legendary history and office 22
His *first Epistle* in relation to St PAUL, St JAMES, and St JOHN 25
The view which it gives of the position of the Christian Church 26

§ 2. *IGNATIUS.*
The general characteristics of the Ignatian Epistles common to all the shorter Epistles and consistent with the position of Ignatius 28
Their connexion with the teaching of St PAUL as to *Judaism* (p. 33), and to the *Church* (p. 34); and with St JOHN . . 35

§ 3. *POLYCARP.*
His Epistle eminently Scriptural (p. 36). Its connexion with St PETER, and with the *Pastoral Epistles* 37
The special value of Polycarp's testimony 40

§ 4. *BARNABAS.*
The *Epistle of Barnabas* genuine, but not Apostolic or Canonical 41
Its relation to the Epistle to the Hebrews, in regard to the mystical interpretation of Scripture (p. 43), and to the Mosaic Dispensation 45

SECTION II. *The relation of the Apostolic Fathers to the Canon of the New Testament.*

How far their testimony was limited by their position . . . 47
Their testimony to
 (α) The Books of the New Testament, both explicit and incidental 48
 Peculiar value of this anonymous evidence . . . 49
 Free references of CLEMENT and POLYCARP . . . 49 f.
 They do not witness so much to written Gospels (p. 52), as to the great facts of Christ's Life 53
 (β) The authority of the Apostolic Writings . . . 54
 Modified both by their position and by the gradual recognition of the Doctrine of Inspiration 55
 Still they all definitely place themselves below the Apostles 57
 Note (1). *On the Evangelic Words contained in the Apostolic Fathers* 60
 Note (2). *On the Teaching of the Twelve Apostles* . . 63

CHAPTER II.

THE AGE OF THE GREEK APOLOGISTS.

A.D. 120—170.

	Page
The wide range of Christian literature during this period	64
Justin Martyr the true representative of the age	65
The work of the Apologists twofold, to determine the relations of Christianity to Heathendom, and to Judaism	66
This latter work to be distinguished from the conflicts of the Apostolic age	67
Christian literature still wholly Greek; the effect of this	68

§ 1. *PAPIAS.*

His date (p. 69). The character of Hierapolis (p. 70). The true purpose of his *Enarrations* (p. 71).
His testimony to the Gospels of St MATTHEW (p. 73), St MARK (p. 74), St JOHN; to the *Catholic Epistles*, and to the *Apocalypse* 77
How it is that he does not allude to the Pauline writings . 78
[The *Martyrdom of Ignatius*, p. 80, n. 1.]

§ 2. *The Elders quoted by Irenæus* 80

§ 3. *The Evangelists in the reign of Trajan* 82

§ 4. *The Athenian Apologists* 83
QUADRATUS (p. 84) and *ARISTIDES* 85

§ 5. *The Letter to Diognetus.*

Its authorship (p. 86), compound character (p. 87), and date . 88
Its testimony to the teaching of St PAUL and St JOHN (p. 90), to the *Synoptic Gospels*, and to other parts of the New Testament 91
The 'Gnostic' element in the concluding fragment . . . 92

§ 6. *The Jewish Apologists* 93
The Dialogue of Jason and Papiscus: ARISTO of Pella its supposed author 94
AGRIPPA CASTOR 95

§ 7. *JUSTIN MARTYR.*

	Page
Some account of the studies, labours, and writings of Justin	96
A general account of the relation of his books to the Gospels	99

I. The general coincidence of Justin's Evangelic quotations with our Gospels, (1) in facts (p. 101): *e.g.* (a) The Infancy (p. 102), (β) the Mission of John Baptist (p. 103); (γ) the Passion (p. 104); and (2) in the account of our Lord's teaching (p. 106), both in language and in substance 107

II. Justin's special quotations from the *Memoirs of the Apostles* 109
The quotations in the Apology (p. 111), and in the Dialogue 113
Coincidences with St MATTHEW, St MARK, and St LUKE 114
Justin's description of the Memoirs compared with Tertullian's description of the Gospels (p. 114); the substance of what he quotes from, and says of them 116
Objections to the identification of the Memoirs with the Gospels:

   1. No mention of their writers' names 117
      Yet the Gospels are often referred to anonymously (p. 118), as are also the Prophets 120
   2. The quotations differ from the Canonical Text 122
      Yet their character agrees with that of Justin's Old Testament quotations (p. 123); in which he both combines (p. 123) and adapts Texts [Note A, p. 173] . 124
      Probable reasons for many of these variations [Note B, p. 175] 126
      His repeated quotations 127
      The identification justified by an examination
      (α) Of the express quotations from the Memoirs . 131
      (β) Of the repetitions of the same peculiar reading . 137
      These various readings may be classed as synonymous phrases (p. 139), glosses (p. 143), and combinations, whether of words (p. 145), or of forms (p. 146); and are illustrated by the text of certain Manuscripts, *e.g.*
      Codex D [Note C, p. 176] 149
      (γ) Of the coincidences with Heretical Gospels . 151
      The differences from them are far more numerous and striking [Note D, p. 179] 158

   3. The coincidences of Justin's narrative with Apocryphal Traditions 158

	Page
The *Voice* (p. 159), and *Fire* at the Baptism (p. 160); and other facts and words (p. 161), which are to be explained as exaggerations or glosses	163
Summary of Justin's testimony (p. 165), in connexion with the Muratorian Canon and Irenæus (p. 167). How far he witnesses to the *Gospel of St John* and to *the Apocalypse* (p. 168); and to the writings of St Paul (p. 169), especially in quotations from the Old Testament	170
The testimony of the doubtful works attributed to Justin	171

§ 8. *The Second Epistle of Clement.*

A Homily	179
A Gentile writing	180
The peculiarity of its use of Scripture	181
Apocryphal quotations	184

[The two *Epistles to Virgins*, p. 186 n.]

§ 9. DIONYSIUS of Corinth, and PINYTUS.

What Dionysius says of the preservation of Christian writings; and how it bears on the New Testament	188
His direct reference to the New Testament Scriptures (p. 191), and coincidences of language with different parts	192
Pinytus refers to the Epistle to the Hebrews	ib.

§ 10. HERMAS.

The condition of the Church of Rome at the middle of the second century	193
Its character represented by the *Shepherd*	196
The history of the book (p. 196), its character (p. 198), in relation to St JAMES (p. 199); and its connexion with other books of Scripture	200
The Christology of Hermas in connexion with that of St JOHN (p. 203). He is falsely accused of Ebionism	204

§ 11. HEGESIPPUS.

The supposed Ebionism of Hegesippus (p. 205), opposed to the testimony of Eusebius	206
The character of his Memoirs in connexion with the Gospels (p. 207), and with Apocryphal books	209

§ 12. *The Muratorian Fragment*—

MELITO—CLAUDIUS APOLLINARIS.

The date of the Muratorian Canon (p. 212), its character (p. 213), and its testimony to the Gospels (p. 214), to the Acts (p. 216), to the Epistles of St Paul (*ib.*), and to the disputed

	Page
Catholic Epistles (p. 218). Its omissions, which however admit of an explanation	219
Melito implies the existence of a New Testament, and illustrates the extent of early Christian thought	221
His Treatise on Faith [His *Clavis*, 226 n.]	224
Claudius Apollinaris shews that the Gospels were generally recognised	227
THEOPHILUS	228
ATHENAGORAS	229
Summary	230
Note. On the Patristic references to books of the New Testament collected by Eusebius	231

CHAPTER III.

THE EARLY VERSIONS OF THE NEW TESTAMENT.

How far they help to determine the Canon 235

§ 1. *The Peshito.*

Its language, and probable origin (p. 236). Syrian traditions on the subject 239
The difficulty of deciding these questions from the want of an early Syriac literature (p. 240). Other Syriac Versions (p. 242 n.). The Syrian Canon 244

§ 2. *The Old Latin Version.*

The Roman Church originally Greek (p. 248), while Africa was the home of Latin Christian literature (p. 249), of which the *Vetus Latina* is the oldest specimen 250
The existence of such a version proved from Tertullian (p. 251). Augustine's testimony on the subject (p. 253), supported by existing documents 255
The quotations in the Latin Version of Irenæus (p. 256). The Canon of the *Vetus Latina* coincides with that of Muratori 258
The Manuscripts in which it is now found . . . . *ib.*
How far its influence can be traced in the present Vulgate . 263
Application of this argument to the language of 2 Peter (p. 265), St James (p. 266), the Epistle to the Hebrews . . . 265
The importance of the combined testimony of these early Versions 267

CHAPTER IV.

THE EARLY HERETICS.

                                                                                   Page

The early heretics made no attack on the New Testament (p. 270) on historical grounds, as their adversaries remarked (p. 271), and though their testimony is partial it is progressive   272

§ 1. *The Heretical teachers of the Apostolic Age.*
    SIMON MAGUS, and the *Great Announcement* . . . 273
    MENANDER (p. 276), and *CERINTHUS* (*ib.*). Cerinthus acquainted with the writings of the New Testament (*ib.*). How the *Apocalypse* came to be ascribed to him (p. 277), and thence the other writings of St John 279
    The importance of early heretical teaching in relation to the New Testament as a link between it and later speculations 280

§ 2. *The Ophites and Ebionites.*
    The rise of early sects (p. 282). The Ophites (*ib.*), the Peratici and Sethiani (p. 283), of Hippolytus. What writings the Ebionites received (p. 284). The testimony of the Clementines 285
    Note. *The corresponding quotations of Justin Martyr and the Clementines* 289

§ 3. *BASILIDES and ISIDORUS.*
    The position (p. 292) and date of Basilides (p. 293). What books he used (p. 294); what he is said to have rejected . 296

§ 4. *CARPOCRATES* 296

§ 5. *VALENTINUS.*
    He received the same books as Catholic Christians (p. 298); but is said to have introduced verbal alterations (p. 300), and to have used another Gospel 301
    Other Gnostic Gospels 302

§ 6. *HERACLEON.*
    His Commentaries; the books they recognise . . . 304

§ 7. *PTOLEMÆUS* 306

§ 8. *The Marcosians.*
    They used Apocryphal writings (p. 308), but also the Gospels (p. 309), and the writings of St Paul 310

§ 9. *MARCION.*
 The Canon of Marcion the earliest known 312
 His position (p. 312), and date (p. 313). What books he
 received [Note, p. 317] 314
 The text of his edition (p. 314), and the principles by which
 he was guided 317

§ 10. *TATIAN.*
 The relation of Tatian to Marcion (p. 319). His importance . 320
 What Scriptures he recognises . . . . . . *ib.*
 An account of his *Diatessaron* 322

  General Summary of the First Part.
 i. The direct evidence fragmentary; but wide, unaffected, uniform, and comprehensive 327
 ii. The authenticity of the Canon a key to the history of the
  early Church 329
 Still (1) partial doubts remained as to certain books, (2) the
  evidence is mainly anonymous, and (3) the idea of a Canon
  was implied rather than expressed 330

SECOND PERIOD. A.D. 170—303.

CHAPTER I.

THE CANON OF THE ACKNOWLEDGED BOOKS.

Three stages in the advance of Christianity (p. 335). How they
 are connected (p. 336), and the bearing of this on the his-
 tory of the Canon 337
On what grounds the Canon of acknowledged Books rests . 338
The testimony of (i) the *Gallican* Church, The *Epistle of the
 Churches of Vienne and Lyons* (p. 339), *IRENÆUS* . 340
 ii. The *Alexandrine* Church, *PANTÆUS* (p. 342), *CLE-
  MENT* 343
 iii. The *African* Church,—*TERTULLIAN* . . . 344
All these writers appeal to antiquity (p. 346), and recognise a
 collection of sacred books 348
The Canon of the acknowledged Books formed by general
 consent 349

CHAPTER II.

THE TESTIMONY OF THE CHURCHES TO THE DISPUTED BOOKS.

	Page
The question of the disputed books essentially historical (p. 351), a Deutero-Canon no solution of the problem	352
A summary of the evidence up to this point	353

§ 1. *The Alexandrine Church,—CLEMENT* (p. 354). *ORIGEN* (p. 358): his catalogues (*ib.*), and isolated testimonies in Greek (p. 362) and in Latin texts (p. 363). *DIONYSIUS* (p. 366). Later Alexandrine writers 368
The Egyptian Versions 369

§ 2. *The Latin Churches of Africa.*
As to the Epistle to the Hebrews (p. 371), the Catholic Epistles (p. 372), the Apocalypse 373
The Latin Canon defective, yet free from Apocryphal additions 375

§ 3. *The Church of Rome.*
   i. Latin writers,—*MINUCIUS FELIX, NOVATUS* . 377
   ii. Greek writers,—*DIONYSIUS, CAIUS* (p. 378), *HIPPOLYTUS* 380

§ 4. *The Churches of Asia Minor.*
   1. *Ephesus. POLYCRATES* (p. 381), *APOLLONIUS* . 382
   2. *Smyrna. IRENÆUS* 383
   3. *PONTUS. GREGORY* of Neo-Cæsarea (p. 385). *FIRMILIAN, METHODIUS* 386
The Asiatic Canon defective 388

§ 5. *The Churches of Syria.*
   1. *Antioch. THEOPHILUS* (p. 389), *SERAPION* (p. 390), *PAUL* of Samosata (p. 391), *MALCHION* (392), *DOROTHEUS* and *LUCIAN* 392
   2. *Cæsarea. PAMPHILUS* 393

CHAPTER III.

THE TESTIMONY OF HERETICAL AND APOCRYPHAL WRITINGS.

	Page
General connexion of the forms of heresy with the New Testament	397
1. Controversies on the person of Christ	398
2. *Montanism*	390
3. *Manichæism* (p. 400). Use of Apocryphal Books by the Manichees	402
The testimony of Apocryphal writings. The *Sibylline Oracles*, and the *Testaments of the Twelve Patriarchs*	403
The testimony of heathen writers. CELSUS, PORPHYRY	404

General Summary of the Second Part.

The work of this period to construct, not define	405
The results of the former period confirmed by it	407

THIRD PERIOD. A.D. 303—397.

CHAPTER I.

THE AGE OF DIOCLETIAN.

The persecution of Diocletian directed against the Christian books (p. 411), its results	412
i. In *Africa*. The *Donatists*	413
ii. In *Syria*. *EUSEBIUS*	414
The importance of his testimony	425

CHAPTER II.

THE AGE OF COUNCILS.

CONSTANTINE'S zeal for Holy Scripture (p. 426). The Scripture as a rule of controversy accepted on all sides	428
The use of Scripture at the Council of Nicæa	429

[ULFILAS, 429 n.]
[Greek MSS. AB ℵ, 430 n.]

		Page
The Synods which followed this Council:		

i. The *Synod of Laodicea* 431
    The last Laodicene Canon (p. 432). Evidence as to its authenticity from (1) Greek manuscripts (p. 434), (2) Versions—Latin (p. 435), and Syriac (p. 436), (3) Systematic Arrangements of the Canons (*ib.*) Result 437

ii. The third *Council of Carthage*.
    The Canon of the New Testament ratified there . . . 439
    How this Canon is supported by the testimony of Churches.

    i. The Churches of *Syria*.
        1. *Antioch*. CHRYSOSTOM (p. 441). THEODORE of Mopsuestia (p. 442). THEODORET 443
        2. *Nisibis*. JUNILIUS. EBED JESU . . . . *ib.*
        3. *Edessa*. EPHREM SYRUS 444
        JOHANNES DAMASCENUS . . . . . . *ib.*

    ii. The Churches of *Asia Minor*.
        GREGORY of Nazianzus. AMPHILOCHIUS 445
        GREGORY of Nyssa and BASIL 446
        ANDREW and ARETHAS 447

    iii. The Church of *Jerusalem*.
        CYRIL. EPIPHANIUS . . . . *ib.*

    iv. The Church of *Alexandria*.
        ATHANASIUS. CYRIL. ISIDORE. DIDYMUS (p. 448).
        COSMAS. EUTHALIUS. PSEUDO-DIONYSIUS . . 449

    v. The Church of *Constantinople*.
        CASSIAN (p. 449). LEONTIUS 450
        NICEPHORUS. PHOTIUS. ŒCUMENIUS. THEOPHYLACT *ib.*

    vi. The Churches of the West.
        Doubts as to the Epistle to the Hebrews 451
        The Canon of JEROME . . . . *ib.*
        AMBROSE. RUFINUS. PHILASTRIUS. AUGUSTINE . 454

The mediæval view of the Canon.
    ALFRIC (p. 456). The *Epistle to the Laodicenes* (p. 458).
    HUGO of St Victor (p. 462). JOHN of Salisbury . 464
    [R. Pecock, 466 n.]

CHAPTER III.

THE SIXTEENTH CENTURY.

	Page
Various elements combined in the discussions on the Bible	468
The debate guided by feeling more than criticism	469

§ 1. *The Roman Church.*

    Cardinal XIMENES (p. 470). ERASMUS (p. 471). Cardinal CAIETAN (p. 475). CATHARINUS (p. 476). The *Council of Trent* (*ib.*). Its decree on the Canon of Scripture (p. 477). SIXTUS SENENSIS 479

§ 2. *The Saxon School of Reformers.*

    LUTHER (p. 480). KARLSTADT 484

§ 3. *The Swiss School of Reformers.*

    ZWINGLI (p. 487). ŒCOLAMPADIUS (*ib.*). CALVIN (p. 488). BEZA (p. 490). The Reformed *Confessions* (p. 491). The Swiss *Declaration* of 1675 494

§ 4. *The Arminian School.*

    GROTIUS 495

§ 5. *The English Church.*

    TYNDALE (p. 497). The English Articles (p. 498). The opinions of the English Reformers: JEWEL; BULLINGER; WHITAKER; FULKE 499

    Conclusion 500

APPENDICES.

App. A.	*On the history of the word* Κανών	50
App. B.	*On the use of Apocryphal Writings in the early Church*	512
App. C.	*The Muratorian Fragment on the Canon.*	521
App. D.	*The chief Catalogues of the books of the Bible during the first Eight Centuries*	539
App. E.	*The Apocryphal Epistle to the Laodicenes*	580
INDEX I.	*List of the authorities quoted in reference to the Canon of the New Testament*	585
INDEX II.	*A Synopsis of the Historical Evidence for the Books of the New Testament*	588

The truth of our Religion, like the truth of common matters, is to be judged by all the evidence taken together.

BP. BUTLER.

<small>Introduction.

A general History of the Canon distinct from a particular history of the Books.</small>

A GENERAL survey of the History of the Canon forms a necessary part of an Introduction to the writings of the New Testament. A full examination of the objections which have been raised against particular Books, a detailed account of the external evidence by which they are severally supported, an accurate estimate of the internal proofs of their authenticity, are indeed most needful; but, besides all this, it seems no less important to gain a wide and connected prospect of the history of the whole collection of the New Testament Scriptures, to trace the gradual recognition of a written Apostolic rule as authoritative and divine, to observe the gradual equalization of 'the Gospel and Epistles' with 'the Law and the Prophets,' to notice the predominance of partial, though not exclusive, views in different Churches, till they were all harmonized in a universal Creed, and witnessed by a completed Canon[1]. For this purpose we must frequently assume results which have been obtained elsewhere; but what is lost in fulness will be gained in clearness. A continuous though rapid survey of the field on which we are engaged will bring out more prominently some of its great features, whose true effect is lost in the details of a minute investigation.

---

[1] By 'the Canon' I understand the collection of books which constitute the original written Rule of the Christian Faith. For the history of the word see Appendix A.

With this view it will be necessary to take into account the intellectual and doctrinal development which was realized in the early Church. The books which are the divine record of Apostolic doctrine cannot be fitly considered apart from the societies in which the doctrine was embodied. A mere series of quotations can convey only an inadequate notion of the real extent and importance of the early testimonies to the genuineness and authority of the New Testament. Something must be known of the nature and object of the first Christian literature—of the possible frequency of Scriptural references in such fragments of it as survive—of the circumstances and relations of the primitive Churches, before it is fair to assign any negative value to the silence or ignorance of individual witnesses, or to decide on the positive worth of the evidence which can be brought forward.

Introduction.
Range of the inquiry.

The question of the Canon of Holy Scripture has assumed at the present day a new position in Theology. The Bible can no longer be regarded merely as a common storehouse of controversial weapons, or an acknowledged exception to the rules of literary criticism. Modern scholars, from various motives, have distinguished its constituent parts, and shewn in what way each was related to the peculiar circumstances of its origin. Christianity has gained by the issue; for it is an unspeakable advantage that the Books of the New Testament are now seen to be organically united with the lives of the Apostles: that they are recognised as living monuments, reared in the midst of struggles within and without by men who had seen Christ, stamped with the character of their age, and inscribed with the dialect which they spoke: that they are felt to be a *product* as well as a *source* of spiritual life. Their true harmony can only be realized after a perception of their distinct pecu-

Especially necessary in relation to modern views.

liarities. It cannot be too often repeated, that the history of the formation of the whole Canon involves little less than the history of the building of the Catholic Church.

The common difficulties which beset any inquiry into remote and intricate events are in this case unusually great, since they are strengthened by the most familiar influences of our daily life. It is always a hard matter to lay aside the habits of thought and observation which are suggested by present circumstances; and yet this is as essential to a just idea of any period as a full view of its external characteristics. It is not enough to have the facts before us unless we regard them from the right point of sight; otherwise the prospect, however wide, must at least be confused. Our powers are indeed admirably suited to criticise whatever falls within their immediate range; but they need a careful adjustment when they are directed to a more distant field. Moreover, remote objects are often surrounded by an atmosphere different from our own, and it is possible that they may be grouped together according to peculiar laws and subject to special influences. This is certainly true of the primitive Church; and the differences which separate modern Christendom from ancient Jerusalem or Alexandria or Rome, morally and materially, are only the more important, because they are frequently concealed by the transference of old words to new ideas.

A little reflection will shew how seriously these difficulties have influenced our notions of early Christendom; for the negative conclusions of some modern schools of criticism have found acceptance chiefly through a general forgetfulness of the conditions of its history. These must be determined by the characteristics of the age, which necessarily modify the form of our inquiry, and limit the extent of our resources. The results which are obtained

It is hard to realize the conditions of the problem.

Introduction.

i. The Formation of the Canon was impeded by

(1) defective means of communication,

from an examination of the records of the ante-Nicene Church, as long as they are compared with what might be expected at present, appear meagre and inadequate; but in relation to their proper sources they are singularly fertile. This will be seen more clearly from the examination of one or two particulars, which bear directly upon the *formation* and *proof* of the Canon.

I. It cannot be denied that the Canon was fixed gradually. The condition of society and the internal relations of the Church presented obstacles to the immediate and absolute determination of the question, which are disregarded now, only because they have ceased to exist. The tradition which represents St John as fixing the contents of the New Testament betrays the spirit of a later age[1].

1. It is almost impossible for any one whose ideas of communication are suggested by the railway and the printing-press to understand how far mere material hinderances must have prevented a speedy and unanimous settlement of the Canon. The means of intercourse were slow and precarious. The multiplication of manuscripts in remote provinces was tedious and costly[2]. The common meeting-point of Christians was destroyed by the fall of Jerusalem, and from that time national Churches

---

[1] This tradition rests upon a misunderstanding of what Eusebius says of the relation of St John's Gospel to the former three (*Hist. Eccl.* III. 24; cf. VI. 14. Hieron. *De Virr. Ill.* 9). The earliest trace of the narrative of Eusebius occurs in the Muratorian fragment (see App. C).

[2] This fact however has been frequently exaggerated. The circulation of the New Testament Scriptures was probably far greater than is commonly supposed. Mr Norton has made some interesting calculations, which tend to shew that as many as 60,000 copies of the Gospels were circulated among Christians at the end of the second century. *Genuineness of the Gospels*, I. pp. 28—34 (Ed. 2, 1847). Whether the data on which this conclusion rests are sound or not, it is certain that the production of large and cheap editions of books at Rome was usual. Compare W. A. Schmidt, *Geschichte der Denk- und Glaubensfreiheit im ersten Jahrhundert...des Christenthums* (Berlin, 1847), c. v.

grew up around their separate centres, enjoying in a great measure the freedom of individual development, and exhibiting, often in exaggerated forms, peculiar tendencies of doctrine or ritual. As a natural consequence, the circulation of some books of the New Testament for a while depended, more or less, on their supposed connexion with specific forms of Christianity; and the range of other books was limited either by their original destination or by the nature of their contents.

This fact, which has been frequently neglected in Church histories, has given some colour to the pictures which have been drawn of the early divisions of Christians. Yet the separation was not the result of fundamental differences in doctrine, but rather of temporary influences. It was not widened by time, but gradually disappeared. It did not cut off mutual intercourse, but vanished as intercourse grew more easy and frequent. The common Creed is not a compromise of principles, but a combination of the essential types of Christian truth which were preserved in different Churches[1]. The New Testament is not an incongruous collection of writings of the Apostolic age, but the sum of the treasures of Apostolic teaching stored up in various places. The same circumstances at first retarded the formation, and then confirmed the claims of the Catholic Church and of the Canon of Scripture.

2. The formal declaration of the Canon was not by any means an immediate and necessary consequence of its practical settlement. As long as the traditional rule of Apostolic doctrine was generally held in the Church, there was no need to confirm it by the written Rule. The dogmatic and constant use of the New Testament was not made necessary by the terms of controversy or the wants

Introduction. which tended to individualize Churches,

though not to disunite them;

and also (2) by the existence of a traditional Rule of Doctrine,

---

[1] A faint sense of this is shewn in the late tradition which assigned the different Clauses in the Creed to separate Apostles.

of the congregation. Most of the first heretics impugned the authority of Apostles, and for them their writings had no weight. Most of the first Christians felt so practically the depth and fulness of the Old Testament Scriptures, that they continued to seek and find in them that comfort and instruction of which popular rules of interpretation have deprived us.

But in the course of time a change came over the condition of the Church. As soon as the immediate disciples of the Apostles had passed away, it was felt that the tradition of the Apostolic teaching had lost its direct authority. Heretics arose who claimed to be possessed of other traditionary rules derived in succession from St Peter or St Paul[1], and it was only possible to try their authenticity by documents beyond the reach of change or corruption. Dissensions arose within the Church itself, and the appeal to the written word of the Apostles became natural and decisive. And thus the practical belief of the primitive age was first definitely expressed when the Church had gained a permanent position, and a fixed literature.

From the close of the second century the history of the Canon is simple, and its proof clear. It is allowed even by those who have reduced the genuine Apostolic works to the narrowest limits, that from the time of Irenæus the New Testament was composed essentially of the same books which we receive at present, and that they were regarded with the same reverence as is now shewn to them[2]. Before that time there is more or less

---

[1] Clem. Alex. *Str.* VII. 17, § 106, κάτω δὲ περὶ τοὺς Ἀδριανοῦ τοῦ βασιλέως χρόνους οἱ τὰς αἱρέσεις ἐπινοήσαντες γεγόνασι καὶ μέχρι γε τῆς Ἀντωνίνου τοῦ πρεσβυτέρου διέτειναν ἡλικίας καθάπερ ὁ Βασιλείδης, κἂν Γλαυκίαν ἐπιγράφηται διδάσκαλον, ὡς αὐχοῦσιν αὐτοί, τὸν Πέτρου ἑρμηνέα· ὡσαύτως δὲ καὶ Οὐαλεντῖνον Θεοδάδι ἀκηκοέναι φέρουσιν, γνώριμος δ' οὗτος γεγόνει Παύλου. Cf. [Hipp.] *adv. Hæreses*, VII. 20, where we must read Ματθίου (Clem. Al. *Str.* VII. 17, § 108).

[2] It will be well once for all to give

difficulty in making out the details of the question, and the critic's chief endeavour must be to shew how much can be determined from the first, and how exactly that

a general view of the opinion of the most advanced critics of Tübingen on the canonical books of the New Testament, and their relation to early Christian literature. According to Schwegler they may be arranged as follows:

i. Genuine and Apostolic.
  1. Ebionitic:
     The APOCALYPSE.
  2. Pauline:
     Epp. to the CORINTHIANS i. ii.
     Ep. to ROMANS (capp. i—xiv.)
     Ep. to GALATIANS.

ii. Original sources of the Gospels:
  1. Ebionitic. *The Gospel according to the Hebrews.*
     St MATTHEW, a revision of this (A.C. 130—134. Baur, *Kan. Evv.* s. 609, anm.).
  2. Pauline. *The Gospel adopted by Marcion.* (Probably: Schwegler, *Nachap. Zeit.* i. 284.)
     St LUKE.

iii. Supposititious writings forged for party purposes.
  1. Ebionitic;
  (a) Conciliatory:
     Ep. of St JAMES (c. 150 A.C. Schwegler, I. s. 443).
     The Clementine Homilies.
     The Apostolical Constitutions.
     Clement, Ep. ii.
  (β) Neutral:
     St MARK (late; after St Matthew: Baur, 561).
     2 Ep. St PETER (c. 200 A.C. Schwegler, I. 495).
     Ep. St JUDE (late, *id.* 521).
     Clementine Recognitions.

  2. Pauline:
  (a) Apologetic:
     1 Ep. PETER (c. 115 A.C. Schwegler, II. 3).
     Κήρυγμα Πέτρου.
  (β) Conciliatory:
     St LUKE (c. 100 A.C. Schwegler, II. 72).
     The ACTS (same date, *id.* s. 115).
     Ep. to ROMANS, capp. xv., xvi. (same date, *id.* s. 123).
     Ep. to PHILIPPIANS (c. 130? *id.* s. 133).
     Clement, Ep. i.
  (γ) Constructive (Katholisirend):
     The PASTORAL *Epistles* (130 —150 A.C. Schwegler, II. 138).
     Ep. of Polycarp.
     Epp. of Ignatius.

  3. A peculiar Asiatic development:
     Ep. to HEBREWS (c. 100 A.C. Schwegler, II. 309).
     Ep. to COLOSSIANS (a little later, *id.* s. 289).
     Ep. to EPHESIANS (a little later, *id.* s. 291).
     Gospel and Epistles (?) of St JOHN (c. 150 A.C. Schwegler, *id.* s. 169; Baur, 350 ff.).

It will be at once evident how much critical sagacity lies at the base of this arrangement, apart from its historic impossibility. The Epistles to the THESSALONIANS and to PHILEMON are rejected, but Schwegler does not give any explanation of their origin.

[Schwegler's theory has been variously modified by later writers of the Tübingen school, but it still remains the most complete embodiment of the spirit of the school, in which relation alone we have to deal with it.]

Introduction.	coincides with the clearer view which is afterwards gained.
ii. *The* Proof *of the Canon is rendered more difficult*	II. Here however we are again beset with peculiar difficulties. The proof of the Canon is embarrassed both by the general characteristics of the age in which it was fixed, and by the particular form of the evidence on which it first depends.
(1) *by the uncritical character of the first two centuries,*	1. The spirit of the ancient world was essentially uncritical. It is unfair to speak as if Christian writers were in any way specially distinguished by a want of sagacity or research. The science of history is altogether of modern date; and the Fathers do not seem to have been more or less credulous or uninformed than their pagan contemporaries[1]. Their testimony must be tried according to the standard of their age. We must be content to ground our conclusions on such evidence as the case admits, and to interpret it according to its proper laws.
shewn in the use of Apocryphal books,	One important example will illustrate the application of these principles. As soon as the Christian Church had gained a firm footing in the Roman Empire it required what might be called an educational literature; and an attempt was made at an early period to supply the want by books which received in a certain degree the sanction of the Church. When this sanction was once granted, it became necessarily difficult to define its extent and duration. The ecclesiastical writings of the Old Testament furnished a precedent and an excuse for a similar appendix to the Christian Scriptures. Both classes seem to have been formed from the same motive: both found their readiest acceptance at Alexandria. 'Apocryphal'

[1] *E. g.* Clement's name is invariably coupled with the legend of the Phœnix (c. xxv.), but it does not appear that Tacitus' credit is weakened by the fact that he introduces the same story among the most tragic incidents (*An.* VI. 28).

writings were added to manuscripts of the New Testament, and read in churches; and the practice thus begun continued for a long time. The *Epistle of Barnabas* was still read among the 'Apocryphal Scriptures' in the time of Jerome; a translation of the *Shepherd* of Hermas is found in a MS. of the Latin Bible as late as the fifteenth century[1]; the spurious *Epistle to the Laodicenes* is found very commonly in English copies of the Vulgate from the ninth century downwards; and an important catalogue of the Apocrypha of the New Testament is added to the Canon of Scripture subjoined to the *Chronographia* of Nicephorus, published in the ninth century.

At first sight this mixture of different classes of books appears startling; but the Church of England follows the same principle with regard to the Apocrypha of the Old Testament. They are allowed to have an ecclesiastical use, but not a canonical authority. They are profitable for instruction—for elementary teaching ($\sigma\tau o\iota\chi\epsilon\iota\omega\sigma\iota\varsigma$ $\epsilon\iota\sigma\alpha\gamma\omega\gamma\iota\kappa\eta$) as is said[2] of the *Shepherd* of Hermas—but not for the proof of doctrine. And it was in this spirit that Apocrypha of the New Testament were admitted with reserve in many Christian Churches. 'They ought to be 'read,' it was said, 'though they cannot be regarded as 'Apostolic or prophetic[3].' And evidence is not wanting to shew that the ancient Church exercised a jealous watch lest supposititious writings should usurp undue influence. The presbyter who sought to recommend the story of Thecla by the name of St Paul was degraded from his office[4].

Introduction.

which was adopted with restrictions by the Church, but

---

[1] Anger, *Synopsis Evangg.* p. xxiv. In this MS. it stands between the Psalms and Proverbs. In the very remarkable Latin MS. known as g^1 (Bibl. Imp. Paris. S. Germ. Lat. 86) it follows the Epistle to the Hebrews.
[2] Euseb. *H. E.* III. 3.
[3] *Fragm. Murat. de Canone*, s. f., speaking of Hermas.
[4] Tertull. *de Bapt.* c. 15.

But the first Christian writers—and here again the parallel with our own divines still holds—did not always shew individually the caution and judgment of the Church. They quote ecclesiastical books from time to time as if they were canonical: the analogy of the faith was to them a sufficient warrant for their immediate use. As soon however as a practical interest attached to the question of the Canon their judgment was clear and unanimous. When it became necessary to determine what 'super-'fluous' books might be yielded to the Roman inquisitor[1] without the charge of apostasy, the Apocryphal writings sunk at once into their proper place. There was no change of opinion here; but that definite enunciation of it which was not called forth by any critical feeling within was conceded at last to a necessity from without. The true meaning of the earliest witnesses is brought out by the later comment[2].

2. This fact suggests a second difficulty by which the subject is affected: the earliest testimonies to the Canon are simply incidental. Now even if the ante-Nicene Fathers had been gifted with an active spirit of criticism—if their works had been left to us entire—if the custom of formal reference had prevailed from the first—it would still be impossible to determine the contents of the New Testament absolutely on merely casual evidence. Antecedently there is no reason to suppose that we shall be able to obtain a perfect view of the judgment of the Church on the Canon from the Scriptural references contained in the current theological literature of any particular period. The experience of our own day teaches us that books of Holy Scripture, if not whole classes of

---

[1] In the persecution of Diocletian. See below, Part iii. c. 1.

[2] See Appendix B. *On the use of Apocryphal writings in the early Church.*

books, may be suffered to fall into disuse from having little connexion with the popular views of religion. As a general rule, quotations have a value positively, but not negatively: they may shew that a writing was received as authoritative, but it cannot fairly be argued from this fact alone that another which is not quoted was unknown or rejected as apocryphal.

Introduction.

Still, though the use of Scripture is in a great degree dependent on the character of the controversies of the day, the argument from quotations obtains a new weight in connexion with formal catalogues of the New Testament. It is impossible not to admit that a general coincidence of the range of patristic references with the limits elsewhere assigned to the Canon confirms and settles them. And in this way the history of the Canon can be carried up to times when catalogues could not have been published, but existed only implicitly in the practice of the Churches.

which must be combined with later catalogues:

3. The track however which we have to follow is often obscure and broken. The evidence of the earliest Christian writers is not only uncritical and casual: it is also fragmentary. A few letters of consolation and warning, two or three Apologies addressed to Heathen, a controversy with a Jew, a Vision, and a scanty gleaning of fragments of lost works, comprise all Christian literature[1] up to the middle of the second century. And the Fathers of the next age were little fitted by their work to collect the records of their times. Christianity had not yet become a history, but was still a life. In such a case it is obviously unreasonable to expect that multiplicity of evidence and circumstantial detail which may be brought to bear upon questions of modern date.

and (3) by its fragmentary character.

[1] To these may perhaps be added *tines* and the *Apostolical Canons* and the original elements of the *Clemen- Constitutions*.

With our present resources there must be many unoccupied spots in the history of the Church, which give room for the erection of hypotheses, plausible though false. But this follows from the nature of the ground: and the hypotheses are tenable only so long as they are viewed without relation to the great lines of our defence. The strength of negative criticism lies in ignoring the existence of a Christian society from the Apostolic age, strong in discipline, clear in faith, and jealous of innovation.

It is then to the Church, as 'a witness and keeper of 'holy writ,' that we must look both for the formation and the proof of the Canon. The written Rule of Christendom must rest finally on the general confession of the Church, and not on the independent opinions of its members. Private testimony in itself is only of secondary importance: its chief value lies in the fact that it is a natural expression of the current opinion of the time.

It is impossible to insist on this too often or too earnestly. Isolated quotations may be in themselves unsatisfactory, but as embodying the tradition of the Church, generally known and acknowledged, they are of inestimable worth. To make use of a book as authoritative, to assume that it is Apostolic, to quote it as inspired, without preface or comment, is not to hazard a new or independent opinion, but to follow an unquestioned judgment. It is unreasonable to treat our authorities as mere pieces or weights, which may be skilfully manœuvred or combined, and to forget that they are Christian men speaking to fellow Christians, as members of one body, and believers in one Creed[1]. The extent of the Canon, like the order of the Sacraments, was settled

---

[1] This is very well argued by Thiersch in his *Versuch zur Herstellung des historischen Standpuncts für die Kritik der N. T. Schriften*, ss. 305 ff.; and in his answer to Baur, *Einige Worte über die Aechtheit der N. T. Schriften*. Erlangen, 1846.

by common usage, and thus the testimony of Christians becomes the testimony of the Church. *Introduction.*

There is however still another way in which we may discern from the earliest time the general belief of Christians respecting the Canon. The practical convictions of great masses find their peculiar expression in popular language and customs. Words and rites thus possess a weight and authority quite distinct from the casual references or deliberate judgments of individuals, so far as they convey the judgment of the many. If then it can be shewn that the earliest forms of Christian doctrine and phraseology exactly correspond with the different elements preserved in the Canonical writings, and that tradition preserves no trace of opinions not recognised in the Scriptures, and that the Scriptures consecrate no belief which is not seen embodied in Christian life; it will be reasonable to conclude that the coincidence implies a common source: that the written books and the traditional words equally represent the general sum of essential Apostolic teaching: and in proportion as the correspondences are more subtle and intricate, this proof of the authenticity of our books will be more convincing[1]. *and popular language and rites.*

Such appear to be the characteristics and conditions of the evidence by which the Canon must be determined. When these are clearly seen and impartially taken into account, it will be possible, and possible only then, to arrive at a fair conclusion upon it. It is equally unreasonable to prejudge the question either way, for it ought *Recapitulation.*

[1] This will explain how much truth there is in the common statement that doctrine was the test of Canonicity. It is just as incorrect to say that the doctrine of the Church was originally drawn from Scripture, as to say that Scripture was limited by Apostolic tradition. The Canon of Scripture and the 'Canon of Truth' were alike independent, but necessarily coincided in their contents as long as they both retained their original purity.

Introduction.

to be submitted to a just and searching criticism. But if it can be shewn that the Epistles were first recognised exactly in those districts in which they would naturally be first known; that from the earliest mention of them they are assumed to be received by Churches, and not recommended only by private authority; that the Canon as we receive it now was fixed in a period of strife and controversy; that it was generally received on all sides; that even those who separated from the Church and cast aside the authority of the New Testament Scriptures did not deny their authenticity: if it can be shewn that the four Gospels include, with the most trifling exceptions[1], all that has been preserved of the Life and Teaching of Christ, and that they adequately explain what is known of the other forms in which these were represented: if it can be shewn that the first references to the Canonical Books are perfectly accordant with the express decisions of a later period; and that there is no trace of the general reception of any other books: if it can be shewn that the earliest forms of Christian doctrine and phraseology exactly correspond with the different elements preserved in the New Testament; it will surely follow that a belief in the authority of the books of the New Testament so widely spread throughout the Christian body, so deeply rooted in the inmost consciousness of the Christian Church, so perfectly accordant with all the facts which we do know, can only be explained by admitting that they are genuine and Apostolic, a written Rule of Christian Faith and Life.

The whole history of the formation of the Canon of the New Testament may be divided into three periods. Of these the first extends to the time of Hegesippus

[1] These are collected in the *Introduction to the Study of the Gospels*, Ap. C.

(A.D. 70—170); the second to the persecution of Diocletian (A.D. 170—303); and the last to the third Council of Carthage (A.D. 303—397). Later speculations on the question in part belong more properly to special introductions to the different books, and in part are merely the perpetuation of old doubts. But each of these periods marks some real step in the progress of the work. The first includes the period of the separate circulation and gradual collection of the Sacred Writings: the second completes the history of their separation from the mass of ecclesiastical literature: the third comprises the formal ratification of the current belief by the authority of councils.

Something has been already said of the various difficulties which beset the inquiry, especially during the first period. An examination of the testimony of Fathers, Heretics, and Biblical Versions, will next shew how far it can be brought to a satisfactory issue.

FIRST PERIOD.

HISTORY OF THE CANON OF THE NEW TESTAMENT TO THE TIME OF HEGESIPPUS.

A.D. 70—170.

Φόβος νόμογ ᾄΔεται καὶ προφητῶν χάρις ΓινώςκετΑι καὶ
εὐαΓΓελίων πίςτις ἵΔργται καὶ ἀποςτόλων παράΔοςις φγλάς-
ςεται καὶ ἐκκληςίας χάρις ςκιρτᾷ.

Ep. ad Diognetum.

CHAPTER I.

THE AGE OF THE APOSTOLIC FATHERS.

A.D. 70—120.

Heaven lies about us in our infancy.
                              WORDSWORTH.

THE condition of the Church immediately after the Apostolic age was not such as to create or require a literature of its own. Men were full of that anxious expectation which always betokens some critical change in the world; but the elements of the new life were not yet combined and brought into vigorous operation[1]. There was nothing either within or without to call into premature activity the powers and resources which were still latent in the depths of Christian truth. The authoritative teaching of Apostles was fresh in the memories of their hearers. That first era of controversy, in which words are fitted to the ideas for which they are afterwards substituted, had not yet passed by. The struggle between Christianity and Paganism had not yet assumed the form of an internecine war[2]. The times were conservative, not creative.

Chap. i.
The sub-apostolic age conservative,

---

[1] The well-known passages of Virgil (*Ecl.* IV.), Tacitus (*Hist.* V. 13), and Suetonius (*Vesp.* c. 4), express this feeling in memorable words. *Percrebuerat Oriente toto*, says the last writer, *vetus et constans opinio esse in fatis ut eo tempore Judæâ profecti rerum potirentur.* The year of which he speaks is A.D. 67, the most probable date of the martyrdom of St Paul.

[2] Christianity as yet appeared to strangers only as a form of Judaism, even where St Paul preached, and consequently was a *religio licita*. Cf. Gieseler, *Kirchengeschichte*, I. 106, and his references.

Chap. i. and transitional.

But in virtue of this conservatism the sub-apostolic age, though distinguished, was not divided from that which preceded it. It was natural that a break should intervene between the inspired Scriptures and the spontaneous literature of Christianity, between the teaching of Apostles and the teaching of philosophers; but it was no less natural that the interval should not be one of total silence. Some echoes of the last age still lived: some voices of the next already found expression. In this way the writings of the Apostolic Fathers are at once a tradition and a prophecy. By tone and manner they are united to the Scriptures; for their authors seem to instruct, and not to argue; and at the same time they prepare us by frequent exaggerations for the one sided systems of the following age.

Its literature all epistolary.

The form of the earliest Christian literature explains its origin and object. The writings of the first Fathers are not essays, or histories, or apologies, but letters[1]. They were not impelled to write by any literary motive, nor even by the pious desire of shielding their faith from the attacks of its enemies. An intense feeling of a new fellowship in Christ overpowered all other claims. As members of a great household—as fathers or brethren—they spoke to one another words of counsel and warning, and so found a natural utterance for the faith and hope and love which seemed to them the sum of Christian life.

The evidence of the Apostolic Fathers for the Canon

With regard to the History of the Canon the Apostolic Fathers occupy an important place, undesignedly it may be, but not therefore the less surely. Their evidence indeed is stamped with the characteristics of their position,

direct and

and implies more than it expresses; but even directly they say much. Within the compass of a few brief letters they

[1] Cf. Möhler, *Patrologie*, s. 50.

I.]   THE AGE OF THE APOSTOLIC FATHERS.   21

shew that the writings of the Apostles were regarded from the first as invested with singular authority, as the true expression, if not the original source, of Christian doctrine and Christian practice. And more than this: they prove that it is unnecessary to have recourse to later influences to explain the existence of peculiar forms of Christianity which were coeval with its reception in the world. In a word, they mark the beginnings of a written Canon, and establish the permanence of the elements of the Catholic faith.

Chap. i.

indirect,

The latter point must be examined with care; for it is very needful to notice the proofs of the continuity of the representative forms of Christian doctrine at a time when it has been supposed to have undergone strange changes. Many have rightly perceived that the reception of the Canon implies the existence of one Catholic Church; and conversely, if we can shew that the distinct constituents of Catholicity were found in Christendom from the first age, we confirm the authenticity of those books which severally suggest and sanction them. It is true that these different types of teaching are at times arbitrarily expanded in the uncanonical writings without any regard to their relative importance, but still they are essentially unchanged; and by the help of patristic deductions we may see in what way the natural tendencies which give rise to opposing heresies are always intrinsically recognised in the teaching of the universal Church. The elements of Holy Scripture are so tempered that though truly distinct they combine harmoniously; elsewhere the same elements are disproportionately developed, and in the end mutually exclude each other[1].

in their preservation of the Apostolic types of doctrine

though often in an exaggerated form.

[1] In studying the writings of the early Fathers much help may be gained from the following works (in addition to the Church histories), by which I have sought to try and to correct my own views: ROTHE (R.) *Die Anfänge d. Christlichen Kirche* ...1837. MÖHLER (J. A.) *Patrologie,*

Chap. i.

SECT. I. THE RELATION OF THE APOSTOLIC FATHERS
TO THE TEACHING OF THE APOSTLES.

§ 1. *Clement of Rome.*

The legendary history of Clement.

The history of Clement of Rome is invested with a mythic dignity, which is without example in the ante-Nicene Church[1]. The events of his life have become so strangely involved in consequence of the religious romances which bear his name, that they must remain in inextricable confusion; and even apart from this, there can be little doubt that traditions which belong to very different men were soon united to confirm the dignity of the successor of St Peter[2]. There is however no reason to question the belief that he was an immediate disciple of the Apostles, and overseer of the Church of Rome[3]; but beyond this all is doubtful[4]. It is uncertain whether he was of Jewish or heathen descent[5]: he is called at one

Regensburg, 1840. SCHLIEMANN (A.) *Die Clementinen*, Hamburg, 1844. DORNER (J. A.) *Die Lehre von der Person Christi*, Stuttgart, 1845—53. SCHWEGLER (A.) *Das nachapostolische Zeitalter*, Tübingen, 1846. LECHLER (G. V.) *Das apostolische und nachapostolische Zeitalter*, Haarlem, 1851, 2te Aufl. 1857. RITSCHL, *Die Entstehung der altkatholischen Kirche*, 2te Aufl., Bonn. 1857. HILGENFELD (A.) *Die apostolischen Väter*, Halle, 1853. REUSS (E.) *Histoire de la Théologie Chrétienne au Siècle Apostolique*, 2me Éd. 1860. LANGE (J. P.) *Das apostolische Zeitalter*...1854. DONALDSON (J.) *A Critical History of Christian Literature and Doctrine*...Vol. I. 1865. LIGHTFOOT (Bp.) *Ignatius*, 1885.

[1] Cf. Schliemann, 118 ff.

[2] For instance, he was identified with Flavius Clemens, a cousin of Domitian, who was martyred at Rome. Schliemann, 109. Compare Lightfoot, *Clement of Rome*, pp. 264 ff., for the connexion of Clement with the imperial household.

[3] Iren. *c. Haer.* III. 3 (Euseb. *H. E.* v. 6), τρίτῳ τόπῳ ἀπὸ τῶν ἀποστόλων τὴν ἐπισκοπὴν (of the Roman Church) κληροῦται Κλήμης, ὁ καὶ ἑωρακὼς τοὺς μακαρίους ἀποστόλους καὶ συμβεβληκὼς αὐτοῖς καὶ ἔτι ἔναυλον τὸ κήρυγμα τῶν ἀποστόλων καὶ τὴν παράδοσιν πρὸ ὀφθαλμῶν ἔχων οὐ μόνος, ἔτι γὰρ πολλοὶ ὑπελείποντο τότε ὑπὸ τῶν ἀποστόλων δεδιδαγμένοι. The passage is a singular testimony to the intense vividness of the impression produced by the Apostolic preaching and to the multiplicity of personal evidence by which it was attested.

[4] The various traditions are discussed with great candour in Donaldson, I. pp. 90 ff.

[5] The former alternative seems to be supported by his Epistle not so

time the disciple of St Paul, and again of St Peter[1]: the order of his episcopate at Rome is disputed[2]; and yet, notwithstanding these ambiguities, it is evident that he exercised a powerful and lasting influence. In fact, he lost his individuality through the general acknowledgment of his representative character in the history of the Church.

Writings which were assigned to the authorship of Clement gained a wide circulation in the East and West. Two *Epistles to Virgins* were published in a Syriac translation under his name by Wetstein[3]. The Clementines, in spite of their tendency, remain entire, to represent the unorthodox literature of the first ages[4]. The Canons and Constitutions which claim his authority became part of the law-book of Christians[5]. Two Greek epistles, professing to be his, are appended to one of the earliest manuscripts of the Bible in existence[6].

The historical position of Clement is illustrated by the much by the manner in which he speaks of the Patriarchs as '*our* Fathers' (cc. 4, 31, 55) as by his familiar knowledge of the Old Testament in the LXX version: the latter is adopted in the Clementines, and maintained by Hefele, *Patrr. App.* xix. ff. Comp. Lightfoot, *l. c.* pp. 263 f., who concludes that Clement was of 'Jewish or proselyte parentage.'

[1] The former opinion is grounded on Phil. iv. 3 (cf. Jacobson, *ad Clem. vit.* not. b); the latter is found in the Clementines, and, from them, in Origen, *Philoc.* c. 23, and later writers. Schliemann, 120.

[2] The chief authorities are quoted by Hefele, *l. c.*

[3] Cf. Jacobson, *ad Clem. R. vit.* note l. Möhler, ss. 67 sqq. Möhler defends their authenticity, which Neander thinks possible (*Ch. H.* II. 441). The quotations from the New Testament which they contain shew that they were certainly written early, but, as far as I can judge, considerably after Clement's genuine Epistle. These quotations are examined below, ch. II. § 8 f.

[4] Schliemann gives a very full account of them: 50 ff. (the *Homilies*); 265 ff. (the *Recognitions*).

[5] Cf. Bunsen's *Hippolytus* III. 145 sqq. (the *Canons*); II. 220 sqq., and App. (the *Constitutions*).

[6] See App. B. In addition to the letters of Clement, the *Cod. Alex.* contains also three beautiful Christian hymns, one of which is the Greek original of the *Gloria in excelsis* of our own Liturgy. Cf. Bunsen, *Hippolytus*, III. 133 sqq. Their existence in the MS. proves no more than their *ecclesiastical* use. It should be added that the two epistles of Clement precede the addition of the books contained in the MS. while the Psalms of Solomon follow this total. See App. D. xii.

Chap. i.
His traditional office.

early traditions which fixed upon him as the author of the Epistle to the Hebrews[1], and of the Acts of the Apostles[2]. Subsequently he is charged with a two-fold office: he appears as the mediator between the followers of St Paul and St Peter, and as the lawgiver of the Church. Thus his testimony becomes of singular value, as that of a man to whom the first Christian society assigned its organization and its catholicity.

The relation of the first Epistle to the Canonical Books,

The first Greek Epistle alone can be confidently pronounced genuine[3]. The relation of this to our Canonical Books is full of interest. In its style, in its doctrine, and in its theory of Church government, it confirms the genuineness of disputed books of the New Testament[4].

(a) in style,

The language of the Epistle of St Peter has been supposed to be inconsistent with the distinctive characteristics of the Apostle. Now, according to the most probable accounts, Clement was a follower of St Peter; and the tone of his Epistle agrees with that of his master in exhibiting the influence of St Paul. This influence extends to peculiarities of language. Sometimes Clement uses words

---

[1] On the authority of Origen, ap. Euseb. *H.E.* VI. 25.
[2] Photius (quoted by Credner, *Einleit.* 271) mentions this tradition.
[3] Schwegler—following some earlier writers—has called in question the genuineness of the letter without any good ground (*Nachap. Zeit.* II. 125 sqq.). He has been answered by Bunsen, Ritschl, and others. Cf. Lechler, *Apost. Zeit.* 309 n.
   Its integrity appears to be as unquestionable as its genuineness. Few critics of any school would endorse the statement: 'there can be no 'doubt that the Epistle is much inter-'polated.' (*Supernat. Rel.* I. 227.) At the close of c. 57 a lacuna occurs in the MS. 'One leaf, and one leaf 'only of the MS. has disappeared.' (Lightfoot, *The Epistles of Clement*, pp. 166, 23.)
   The second *Epistle* is probably part of a homily, but this writing will be examined afterwards.
   [The discovery of a second MS. of the complete text of the 'Epistles' at Constantinople, and of a Syriac version of them, now in the University Library at Cambridge, confirms the above statements. See Lightfoot, *l. c.*, 1880.]
[4] The date of Clement's letter is disputed, for it depends on the order of his Episcopate. Hefele (p. xxxv.) places it at the close of the persecution of Nero (A.D. 68—70). The later date (circ. 95) seems more probable.

found only in St Peter's Epistles: more frequently those common to St Peter and St Paul; while his verbal coincidences with St Paul are both numerous and striking[1].

Again, the Epistle of Clement takes up a catholic position in the statement of doctrine, which shews that the supplementary views contained in the New Testament had in his time been placed in contrast, and now required to be combined. The theory of justification is stated in its antithetical fulness. The same examples are used as in the Canonical Epistles, and the teaching of St Paul and St James is coincidently affirmed. 'Through 'faith and hospitality (διὰ πίστιν καὶ φιλοξενίαν) a son was 'given to Abraham in old age, and by obedience (δι' 'ὑπακοῆς) he offered him a sacrifice to God.' 'Through 'faith and hospitality Rahab was saved (ἐσώθη[2]).' 'We 'are not justified by ourselves (δι' ἑαυτῶν)...nor by works 'which we have wrought in holiness of heart, but by our 'faith (διὰ τῆς πίστεως), by which Almighty God justified 'all from the beginning of the world[3].' Shortly afterwards Clement adds in the spirit of St James 'Let us then 'work from our whole heart the work of righteousness[4].' And the same tenor of thought reappears in the con-

Chap. i.

(β) *in doctrine,*

influence of St Paul.—

St JAMES—

---

[1] The following examples, which are taken from among many that I have noticed, will illustrate the extent and character of this connexion:
(α) Coincidence with St Peter in words not elsewhere found in the Epp. or PP. App.: ἀγαθοποιΐα—ἀδελφότης—ποίμνιον. (Perhaps no more.)
(β) With St Peter and St Paul: ἀγαθὴ συνείδησις—ἁγιασμός—εἰλικρινής—εὐσέβεια—εὐπρόσδεκτος—ταπεινοφροσύνη—ὑπακοή—ὑποφέρειν—φιλαδελφία—φιλοξενία, φιλόξενος.
(γ) With St Paul: ἀμεταμέλητος—ἐγκρατεύεσθαι

—λειτουργός, λειτουργία, λειτουργεῖν—μακαρισμός—οἰκτιρμοί—πολιτεία, πολιτεύειν (used by Polyc.)—σεμνός, σεμνότης—χρηστεύεσθαι.
(δ) Peculiar to Clement: αἰκία — ἀλλοιοῦν — ἀπόνοια — βούλησις — ἱκετεύειν —καλλονή—μιαρός—μυσαρός—παμμεγεθής—παναγίος—πανάρετος.

[2] cc. x., xii. Cf. Lightfoot, *Ep. to Galatians*, pp. 151 ff. c. xi. διὰ φιλοξενίαν καὶ εὐσέβειαν Λὼτ ἐσώθη.

[3] c. xxxii. The distinction suggested between the *final cause* and the *instrument* by the double use of διά is very interesting.

[4] c. xxxiii. 1 John ii. 2.

26   THE AGE OF THE APOSTOLIC FATHERS.   [PART

Chap. i.

St John—

Epistle to the Hebrews—

(γ) *in discipline,*

in matters of government, and of

tinual reference to the fear of God as instrumental in the accomplishment of these good works[1]. In other passages it is possible to trace the beginnings of modes of thought which are characteristic of St John. 'The blood of Christ gained for the whole world 'the offer of the grace of repentance[2].' 'Through Him 'we look steadfastly on the heights of heaven; through 'Him we view as in a glass (ἐνοπτριζόμεθα) His spotless 'and most excellent visage; through Him the eyes 'of our heart were opened; through Him our dull 'and darkened understanding is quickened with new 'vigour on turning to His marvellous light[3].' The allusions to the Epistle to the Hebrews are numerous though silent, and such as to shew that the language of the Epistle was transfused into Clement's mind[4].

And yet more than this: the Epistle of Clement proves the existence of a definite constitution and a fixed service in the Church. And this will explain why he was selected as the representative of that principle of organization which seems to have been naturally developed in every Roman society. A systematic constitution, as well as a Catholic Creed, had a necessary connexion with that form of mind whose whole life was law. Thus Clement refers to 'episcopal' jurisdiction as an institution of the Apostles, who are said to have appointed those 'who were

---

[1] cc. iii., xix., xxi., &c. Cf. Schliemann, s. 414. Herm. *Past.* Mand. vii. (p. 363).

[2] c. vii. ὑπήνεγκεν· the use of the word is remarkable. Cf. Lightfoot *in loc.*

[3] c. xxxvi. Nothing but the original can fully convey the exquisite beauty of the last words: ἡ ἀσύνετος καὶ ἐσκοτωμένη διάνοια ἡμῶν ἀναθάλλει εἰς τὸ θαυμαστὸν αὐτοῦ φῶς. Our understanding is like a flower in a sunless cavern till the light of God falls on it.

[4] The most remarkable of these allusions occurs directly after the passage just quoted (c. xxxvi.): ὃς σύνης αὐτοῦ τοσούτῳ μείζων ἐστὶν ἀγγέλων ὅσῳ διαφορώτερον ὄνομα κεκληρονόμηκεν, κ.τ.λ. Cf. Hebr. i. 3 ff. Other unquestionable parallels occur in c. xvii. (Hebr. xi. 37), c. xliii. (Hebr. iii. 5), &c. On Clement's references to the Lord's words, see p. 60.

'the firstfruits of their labours in each state as officers '(ἐπισκόπους καὶ διακόνους) for the ordering of the future 'Church[1].' At the same time earnest warnings are given against 'division and parties[2],' which, as we see from the Pastoral Epistles, arose as soon as the rules of ecclesiastical discipline were drawn closer. But this is not all; for the times of the 'offerings and services' of Christians are referred to the authority of the Lord Himself, who 'com-'manded that they should not be made at random, or in a 'disorderly manner, but at fixed seasons and hours[3].' It is possible that this is only a transference of the laws of the Jewish synagogue, which were sanctioned by the observance of our Saviour, to the Christian Church; as is indeed made probable by the parallel which Clement institutes between the Levitical and Christian priesthood[4]; but all that needs to be particularly remarked is that such phraseology is clearly of a date subsequent to the Pastoral Epistles[5]. The polity recognised by St Paul had advanced to a further stage of development at the time when Clement wrote.

Chap. i.

ritual.

The kind of testimony to the New Testament which is thus obtained is beyond all suspicion of design; and, admitting the genuineness of the record, above all contradiction. The Christian Church, as Clement describes it, exhibits a fusion of elements which must have existed separately at no distant period. Tradition ascribes to him expressly the task of definitely combining what was left still disunited by the Apostles; and we find that the very elements which he recognised are exactly those,

The peculiar value of this kind of testimony.

---

[1] c. xlii.
[2] c. xliv.
[3] c. xl.
[4] Id.
[5] The newly-discovered portion of the first Epistle consists in the main of a prayer, which probably represents the form and gives some of the language of the earliest unwritten liturgies. Comp. Lightfoot, *l. c.* pp. 269 ff.

Chap. i.

without any omission or increase, which are preserved to us in the New Testament as stamped with Apostolic authority[1]. The other Fathers of the first age, as will be seen, represent more or less clearly some special form of Christian teaching; but Clement places them all side by side. They witness to the independent weight of parts of the Canon: he ratifies generally the claims of the whole.

§ 2. *Ignatius.*

The peculiarities of the Ignatian letters

The letters which bear the name of Ignatius are distinguished among the writings of the Apostolic Fathers by a character of which no exact type can be found in the New Testament. They bear the stamp of a mind fully imbued with the doctrine of St Paul, but at the same time exhibit a spirit of order and organization foreign to the first stage of Christian society. In them 'the Catholic Church[2]' is recognised as an outward body

---

[1] The Apostles were charged with the enunciation of principles, and not with their combination. They had to do with essence, and not with form. But after the destruction of Jerusalem an outward framework was required for Christian truth: and the arranging of this according to Apostolic rules was left to the successors of the Apostles.

[2] The phrase occurs for the first time in Ignatius, *ad Smyrn.* viii. ὅπου ἂν φανῇ ὁ ἐπίσκοπος ἐκεῖ τὸ πλῆθος ἔστω, ὥσπερ ὅπου ἂν ᾖ Χριστὸς Ἰησοῦς ἐκεῖ ἡ καθολικὴ ἐκκλησία. The context deals with the principle of unity centred in the bishop in each Church. What the bishop is to the individual Church, that is Christ to the 'universal' Church. Where 'Christ Jesus' is (and the fulness of the title is not without significance) there is the 'universal' Church. His Presence is the one test of Catholicity.

In the *Martyrdom of Polycarp*, which was written in the name of the Church of *Smyrna* (A.D. 167), the phrase is found with somewhat greater latitude of meaning. This appears in the Salutation: ἡ ἐκκλησία τοῦ θεοῦ ἡ παροικοῦσα Σμύρναν τῇ ἐκκλησίᾳ τοῦ θεοῦ τῇ παροικούσῃ ἐν Φιλομηλίῳ καὶ πάσαις ταῖς κατὰ πάντα τόπον τῆς ἁγίας καὶ καθολικῆς ἐκκλησίας παροικίαις ἔλεος εἰρήνη καὶ ἀγάπη· and again in the combination...τῆς κατὰ τὴν οἰκουμένην καθολικῆς ἐκκλησίας (cc. viii., xix.); and still more in the title given to Polycarp as ἐπίσκοπος τῆς ἐν Σμύρνῃ καθολικῆς ἐκκλησίας (c. xvi.), where the word καθολικῆς is exchanged for *sanctae* in the old Latin Version.

In these passages there is a tendency towards two distinct conceptions of that Catholicity of which

IGNATIUS.

of Christ made up of many members. The image which St Paul had sketched is there realized and filled up with startling boldness. The Church polity of the Pastoral Epistles seems dim and uncertain when compared with the rigid definitions of these later writings. But in this lies their force as witnesses to our Canon. They presuppose those Epistles of St Paul which have seemed most liable to attack; and on the other hand they exhibit exactly that form of doctrine into which the

Chap. i.

explicable by the image which St Paul applies to the Church (Eph. vi.),

the Presence of Christ is the essential sign, the one external and regarding the extension of the Church throughout the whole world, the other internal and marking a characteristic of each part of the Society in itself. Speaking broadly, we may say that we can find in them the germs of the *local* and *dogmatic* ideas of catholicity which at a later time were well explained by Cyril of Jerusalem: καθολικὴ μὲν οὖν καλεῖται [ἡ ἐκκλησία] διὰ τὸ κατὰ πάσης εἶναι τῆς οἰκουμένης ἀπὸ περάτων γῆς ἕως περάτων· καὶ διὰ τὸ διδάσκειν καθολικῶς καὶ ἀνελλειπῶς ἅπαντα τὰ εἰς γνῶσιν ἀνθρώπων ἐλθεῖν ὀφείλοντα δόγματα... (*Catech.* xviii. § 11).

These two ideas though finally divergent are capable of being traced back to the same source; or rather they were necessarily evolved in due succession by the historic progress of Christianity, through its claim to universality. At first the Christian Church was contemplated in contrast with the Jewish Church: a society with no limits of race or nation in contrast with one confined to a chosen people. And next a contrast arose between Christian societies themselves, as this claimed to follow the teaching of one Apostle and that of another, while a third treasured up with equal reverence all the various forms of Apostolic teaching. The true Church was Catholic as opposed equally to what was special and to what was partial.

As the opposition between Christianity and Judaism became less keen, the universal extension of the Christian Church was interpreted in a merely local sense, and 'catholic' became practically synonymous with locally universal, in which sense the title is constantly interpreted by Augustine, as for instance: Ipsa est enim ecclesia catholica; unde καθολικὴ Græce appellatur, quod per totum orbem terrarum diffunditur. *Epist.* lii. 1. Comp. cxl. 43.

But it is in the sense of universal as opposed to partial that the term 'Catholic' is of vital importance in the history of the Church. In this respect Catholicity is the ecclesiastical correlative to the whole sum of the Holy Scriptures, Old and New, and the protest against all exclusiveness, whether of Ebionites, or Marcionites, or Donatists—the earliest types of legalism, rationalism, and puritanism, if we may venture to translate the names into general terms. It may be added that it is remarkable that the epithet 'Catholic,' which in later times the Latin Church has appropriated to herself, is not applied to the Church in the Western Creeds till the 7th (or perhaps the 6th) century. On the other hand it is found almost universally in the Eastern Creeds (Heurtley, *Harm. Symbol.* p. 143). Pearson has given a very rich collection of passages illustrating the usage of the word: *On the Creed*, Art. ix.

Chap. i.
and suitable to the position of Ignatius.

principles of St Paul would naturally be reduced by a vigorous and logical teacher presiding over the central Church of Gentile Christendom, 'the anti-pole of Jeru-'salem,' and there brought into contact with the two rival parties within the Church, as well as with the different heresies which had been detected and condemned by St John[1].

One general character marks all the shorter Epistles,

It is unnecessary to enter here into the controversy which has been raised about the Ignatian Epistles[2]. If any part of them be accepted as genuine, our argument holds good: for it is drawn from their general character. After they have been reduced within the narrowest limits which are justified by historical criticism, they still shew a clear and vivid individuality, a character which, however different from the popular idea of a disciple of St John, appears to be not unsuited to the early Bishop of Antioch. Its very distinctness has suggested doubts of its authenticity; but even at the first view it seems to be one far more likely to have been imitated than invented. The exaggerations of the copy bring out more clearly the traits of the original. It would have been

and it could not easily have been invented in a later age,

difficult, if not impossible, for a later writer to have imagined Ignatius, as he appears in the letters, zealous against Docetic heresies, Jewish traditions, and individual schism: keenly alive to the very dangers, and those only, with which he must have contended at Antioch.

however easily imitated.

But when the character was once portrayed it offered a

---

[1] Cf. Dorner, I. 144 sqq.
[2] Hefele gives a fair summary of the controversy. It is but right to confess that the more carefully I have studied the shorter recension the more firmly I am convinced that it proceeds entirely from one mind and one pen. The most startling peculiarities are those which spring most directly from the position of Ignatius. A careful and minute examination of the language of all the Epistles would I believe bring the question of their unity at least to a satisfactory close. But this would carry us far beyond the limits of our Essay. [Bp. Lightfoot has now established this conclusion beyond reasonable doubt. 1887.]

tempting model for imitation. The style and opinions of Ignatius are clear and trenchant. He was at an early time looked upon as the representative of ecclesiastical order and doctrine in its technical details, different in this from Clement, whose name, as we have seen, symbolised the union of the different elements contained in the Apostolic teaching. The one appears in tradition as systematizing the Catholic Church which the other has constructed[1].

The traditional aspect of these two great teachers harmonizes with their real historical position. The letter of Clement falls within the Apostolic age; and Ignatius was martyred in the reign of Trajan[2]. So that his letters probably come next in date among the remains of the earliest Christian literature. A comparison of the writings themselves would lead to the same conclusion. The letters of Ignatius could not naturally have preceded that of Clement, while they follow it in a legitimate sequence, and form a new stage, so to speak, in the building of the Christian Church. This may be clearly seen in the different modes by which they enforce the necessity of an organised ministry. Clement appeals to the analogy of the Levitical priesthood; Ignatius insists on the idea of a Christian body.

The circumstances under which Ignatius wrote, on his way from Antioch to Rome, necessarily impressed

This character moreover suits the historical position of Ignatius; and A.D. 107.

his letters, though marked by influences of his time,

---

[1] Popular traditions frequently embody a character with singular beauty in some one trait. Thus Ignatius is said to have instituted the custom of singing hymns antiphonally 'from a vision of angels whom 'he saw thus singing to the Holy 'Trinity' (Socr. *H. E.* VI. 8). Cf. Bingham, *Orig. Eccles.* IV. 434.

[2] Pearson, followed by many later writers, fixed Ignatius' martyrdom in 116. Hefele and Möhler prefer the earlier date. The latest and most thorough investigation of the question by Zahn (*Ignatius von Antiochien*, Gotha, 1873), shews that if the date of the Acta (107 A.D.) be set aside (so Zahn), there is absolutely no evidence to determine at what point between 107—117 A.D. the martyrdom is to be placed. On an assertion that he was martyred at Antioch, Dec. 20, 115, A.D., see the Preface.

Chap. i. his letters with a peculiar character. It has been argued that they are unlike the last words of a Christian martyr, written on the very road to death: it should be said that they are unlike the words of any other martyr than Ignatius. They are indeed the parting charge of one who was conscious that he was called away at a crisis in the history of the Church. As long as an Apostle lived *old things had not yet passed away;* but on the death of St John it seemed that the 'last times[1]' were at hand, though in one sense, according to his promise, Christ had then come, and a new age of the world had begun. The perils which beset this transition from Apostolic to Episcopal government, in the midst of heresies within and persecutions without, might well explain warmer language than that of Ignatius. He wrote with earnest vehemence because he believed that episcopacy was the bond of unity, and unity the safety of the Church[2].

form a last step in the development of the doctrine of the Church.

In this way the letters of Ignatius complete the history of one feature of Christianity. The Epistles of St Paul to the Ephesians, his Pastoral Epistles, and the Epistles of Clement and Ignatius, when taken together, mark a harmonious progression in the development of the idea of a Church. The first are creative and the last constructive. In the Epistle to the Ephesians the great mystery of the Christian Society is set forth under two images, which include the essential truths of all later speculations. It is the Body of Christ in virtue of the one life which it derives from *Him who is its Head;* and it is the Temple of God, so far as it is built up in various

---

[1] *Ad Eph.* xi.

[2] This feeling is expressed with touching simplicity in the Epistle to the Romans, which, as is well known, is most free from hierarchical views. Μνημονεύετε ἐν τῇ προσευχῇ ὑμῶν τῆς ἐν Συρίᾳ ἐκκλησίας, ἥτις ἀντὶ ἐμοῦ ποιμένι τῷ Θεῷ χρῆται. Μόνος αὐτὴν Ἰησοῦς Χριστὸς ἐπισκοπήσει καὶ ἡ ὑμῶν ἀγάπη (c. ix.). The passage is omitted in the Syriac Version.

I.]   IGNATIUS.   33

ages and of various elements on the foundations which   Chap. i.
Christ laid, and of which He is *the corner-stone*. In the
Pastoral Epistles this teaching is realised in the outlines
of a visible society. In the later writings the great principles of Scripture are reduced to a system, and expanded with logical ingenuity. But when this connexion
is traced by the help of an undesigned commentary in
writings fragmentary, occasional, and inartificial, it surely
follows that a series of books so intimately united must
indeed have been the original expressions of the successive forms of Christian thought which they exhibit.

Though the Ignatian letters witness to three chief   *The connexion of*
types of Apostolic teaching, one type stands forth in *the Ignatian letters with*
them with peculiar prominence. The image of St Paul   *the New Testament,*
is stamped alike upon their language and their doctrine. *and especially with*
The references to the New Testament are almost ex-   *St PAUL, in reference to*
clusively confined to his writings. Familiar words and *Judaism,*
phrases shew that he was a model continually before
the writer's eyes; and in one place this is expressly
affirmed[1].

The controversy against Jewish practices is conducted
as sternly as in the Epistle to the Galatians, though its
form shews that it belongs to a later epoch. Christianity
is distinguished by a new name (Χριστιανισμός[2]) as a
system contrasted with Judaism. Judaism ('Ιουδαϊσμός)

---

[1] The only coincidences which I have noticed between the language of St John and Ignatius consist in the frequent use of ἀγάπη, ἀγαπᾶν, and ὁ οὐρανός, while St Paul and Clement generally use οἱ οὐρανοί.
The words common to St Paul and Ignatius only are very numerous, e.g. ἀδόκιμος——ἀναψύχειν——ἀπερίσπαστος—ἔκτρωμα—ἑνότης—θηριομαχεῖν—'Ιουδαϊσμός—ὀναίμην—οἰκονομία (met.)—φυσιοῦν.
Those peculiar to Ignatius are still more numerous: e.g. ἁγιοφόρος—ἀμέριστος—ἀντίψυχον—compounds of ἄξιος, as ἀξιόθεος, ἀξιομακάριστος—ἀποδιυλίζεσθαι — δροσίζεσθαι — ἐνοῦν, ἕνωσις—compounds of θεός, as θεοδρόμος, θεοφόρος—κακοτεχνία—φάρμακον. The references are made to all the shorter Epistles without distinction, whether contained in the Syriac or not.

[2] *Ad Rom.* c. iii. &c. This new name likewise comes from Antioch. Cf. Acts xi. 26.

C.   D

is 'an evil leaven that has grown old and sour¹.' 'To 'use the name of Jesus Christ and yet observe Jewish 'customs is unnatural (ἄτοπον²).' 'To live according to 'Judaism is to confess that we have not received grace³.' At the same time, like St Paul, Ignatius regards Christianity as the completion, and not the negation, of the Old Testament. The prophets 'lived according to Jesus 'Christ,...being inspired by His grace, to the end that 'those who disbelieve should be convinced that it is one 'God who manifested Himself [both in times past and 'now] through Jesus Christ His Son, who is His Word, 'having proceeded from Silence⁴,' from which some have held that Thought and Word were evolved as successive forms of the Divine Being, and 'who in all things well-'pleased Him that sent Him⁵.'

the Church. The Ignatian doctrine of the unity of the Church, which in its construction shews the mind of St Peter, is really based upon the cardinal passage of St Paul⁶. Christians individually are members of Christ, who is their great Spiritual Head. And conversely, the Church universal, and each Church in particular, represents the body of Christ, and its history must so far set forth an image of the life of Christ in its spirit and its form. As a consequence of this view the Bishop in the earthly and typical Church is not only a representation of Christ,

---

¹ *Ad Magn.* x.
² Ibid.
³ *Ad Magn.* viii.
⁴ Dr Lightfoot has shewn (*Journ. of Philology*, i. pp. 53 ff. 1868) that the words ἀΐδιος and οὐκ in the common texts are an interpolation.
⁵ *Ad Magn.* viii. The reference to Silence (Σιγή), which forms an important element in Valentinianism, was a serious objection to the authenticity of the Ignatian letters till the discovery of the 'Treatise against Heresies.' Now it appears that the same phraseology was used in the 'Great Announcement,' an authoritative exposition of the doctrines of the Simonians, and consequently it must have been current in Ignatius' time (Hipp. *adv. Hær.* VI. 18). Cf. Bunsen, *Hippolytus*, I. 57 ff., whose opinion on the subject however seems improbable.
⁶ Eph. v. 23 sqq.

IGNATIUS. 35

whom 'we must regard as Christ Himself[1],' and 'a par-
'taker of the judgment of Christ, even as Christ was of
'the judgment of the Father[2],' while the Church is united
to Christ as He is united to the Father[3]: but also—and
in this lies the most remarkable peculiarity of his system
—the relation of the Church as a living whole to its different officers corresponds in some sense to that of Christ
Himself, of whom it is an image, to the Father on the
one hand, and on the other to the Apostles. On earth
the Bishop is the centre of unity in each society, as the
Father is the 'Bishop of all[4].' Believers are subject to
the Bishop as to God's grace, and to the presbytery as
to Christ's law[5]; since the Bishop, as he ventures to say in
another place, 'presides as representative of God, and the
'presbyters as representatives of the Apostolic Council[6].'

Chap. i.

The Ignatian writings, as might be expected, are not
without traces of the influence of St John. The circumstances in which he was placed required a special enunciation of Pauline doctrine; but this is not so expressed as
to exclude the parallel lines of Christian thought. Love
is 'the stamp of the Christian[7].' 'Faith is the beginning,
'and love the end of life[8].' 'Faith is our guide upward
'(ἀναγωγεύς), but love is the road that leads to God[9].'
'The Word is the manifestation of God[10],' 'the door (θύρα)
'by which we come to the Father[11],' 'and without Him
'we have not the principle of true life[12].' 'The Spirit
'(πνεῦμα) is not led astray, as being from God. For it
'knoweth whence it cometh and whither it goeth, and
'testeth (ἐλέγχει) that which is hidden[13].' The true meat

Connexion with St John.

---

[1] *Ad Eph.* vi.
[2] *Ad Eph.* iii.
[3] *Ad Eph.* v.
[4] *Ad Magn.* iii.
[5] *Ad Magn.* ii.   [6] *Ad Magn.* vi.
[7] *Ad Magn.* v.   [8] *Ad Eph.* xiv.
[9] *Ad Eph.* ix. (So Syr.)
[10] *Ad Magn.* viii. (quoted above).
[11] *Ad Philad.* ix. Cf. John x. 7.
[12] *Ad Trall.* ix.: οὗ χωρὶς τὸ ἀληθινὸν ζῆν οὐκ ἔχομεν. Cf. *ad Eph.* iii.: 'I. X. τὸ ἀδιάκριτον ἡμῶν ζῆν...
[13] *Ad Philad.* vii. Comp. John iii. 8; xvi. 8.

D 2

Chap. i.

of the Christian is the 'bread of God, the bread of 'heaven, the bread of life, which is the flesh of Jesus 'Christ,' and his drink is 'Christ's blood, which is love 'incorruptible[1].' He has no love of this life; 'his love 'has been crucified, and he has in him no burning passion 'for the world, but living water [as the spring of a new 'life] speaking within him, and bidding him come to his 'Father[2].' Meanwhile his enemy is the enemy of his Master, even 'the ruler of this age[3].'

These passages, it must be repeated, are not brought forward as proofs of the use of the writings of St John, but as proofs of the currency of the modes of thought of St John. They indicate at least that phraseology and lines of reflection which are preserved for us in the characteristic teaching of the fourth Gospel were familiar to the writer of the Ignatian Epistles. Different readers will estimate the value of the coincidences differently; but if once the Christian society be recognised as possessed of a continuous life, they cannot be disregarded[4].

§ 3. *Polycarp.*

The scriptural character of Polycarp's epistle

The short epistle of Polycarp contains far more references to the writings of the New Testament than any other work of the first age; and still, with one exception,

---

[1] *Ad Rom.* vii. The Syriac text though shorter gives the same sense. Cf. John vi. 32, 51, 53.

[2] *Ad Rom. l. c.* The last clause is wanting in the Syriac, yet the boldness of the metaphor seems to be in Ignatius' manner. Πῦρ φιλόϋλον, 'fiery passion for the material world,' which forms a good contrast with ὕδωρ ζῶν, 'living water,' is certainly, I think, the true reading. Cf. John iv. 13; vii. 38.

[3] *Ad Rom. l.c.:* ὁ ἄρχων τοῦ αἰῶνος τούτου. Cf. John xii. 31; xvi. 11 : ὁ ἄρχων τοῦ κόσμου τούτου· and see 1 Cor. ii. 6, 8.

[4] It is scarcely necessary to say that Philo's doctrine of the Word is wholly dissociated from Messianic expectations. The apprehension of the Truth ὁ λόγος σὰρξ ἐγένετο—'the 'mere application to an individual 'of a theory which had long occu- 'pied the Hebrew mind' as it has been called with startling want of spiritual discernment—was the greatest step ever taken in religious thought.

all the phrases which he borrows are inwoven into the texture of his letter without any sign of quotation. In other cases it is possible to assign verbal coincidences to accident; but Polycarp's use of scriptural language is so frequent that it is wholly unreasonable to doubt that he was acquainted with the chief parts of our Canon; and the mode in which this familiarity is shewn serves to justify the conclusion that the scriptural language of other books in which it occurs more scantily implies a similar knowledge of the Apostolic writings[1].

illustrates the early method of quotation.

A scriptural tone naturally involves a catholicity of spirit. Polycarp is second only to Clement among the early Fathers in the breadth of Apostolic teaching embraced in his epistle[2]. The influence of St Peter, St John, and St Paul, may be traced in his doctrine. In one sentence he has naturally united[3] the watchwords, so to say, of the three Apostles, where he speaks of Christians being 'built ' up into the *faith* given to them, *which is the mother of us* '*all* (cf. Gal. iv. 26), *hope* following after, *love* towards God ' and Christ and towards our neighbour preceding.' But the peculiar similarity of this epistle to that of St Peter was a matter of remark even in early times[4]. It would be curious to inquire how this happens; for though the disciple of St John reflects from time to time the burning

Its connexion with the New Testament, and especially with

St PETER *and*

---

[1] The authenticity of Polycarp's Epistle stands quite unshaken. Cf. Schliemann, s. 418 anm.; Jacobson, *ad vit. Polyc.* note q. Schwegler, II. 154 sqq., has added no fresh force to the old objections. Donaldson however, following Daillé and Bunsen, rejects c. xiii. as an interpolation, on grounds which appear to be insufficient. See Jacobson *ad loc.* On the evidence of Polycarp generally see Bp. Lightfoot, *Cont. Rev.*, May, 1875.
The fragments of 'Polycarp's Responsions' given by Feuardentius in his notes on Irenæus (III. 3) cannot, I think, be genuine. Is anything known of the MS. Catena from which they were taken?

[2] The similarity between parts of the Epistles of Clement and Polycarp is very striking. The passages are printed at length by Hefele, *Proleg.* p. XXVII. sqq. In single words the likeness is not less remarkable.

[3] Schwegler, II. 157. Polyc. *ad Phil.* c. iii. Compare Jacobson's note.

[4] Euseb. *H. E.* IV. 14.

38 THE AGE OF THE APOSTOLIC FATHERS. [PART

Chap. i.

zeal of his master[1]; though in writing to the Church most beloved by St Paul he recalls the features of their 'glorious' founder; still he exhibits more frequently the tone of St Peter, when he spoke at the last as the expounder of the Christian law. Whatever may be the explanation of this, the fact is in itself important; for it confirms and defines what has been already remarked as to the mutual influences which appear to have ultimately modified the writings of St Peter and St Paul. The style of St Peter, it is well known, is most akin to that of the later epistles of St Paul; and in full harmony with this, the letter of Polycarp, while it echoes so many familiar phrases of the First Epistle of St Peter, shews scarcely less likeness to the Pastoral Epistles of St Paul[2]. It can scarcely be an ac-

the Pastoral Epistles.

---

[1] The famous passage, c. vii. *init.* in connexion with Iren. III. 3 (Euseb. IV. 14), will occur to every one. The words of Irenæus deserve to be transcribed, as they carry on a generation later the power of the Apostolic life already noticed in Irenæus' account of Clement (supr. p. 22, n. 3). καὶ Πολύκαρπος δὲ οὐ μόνον ὑπὸ ἀποστόλων μαθητευθεὶς καὶ συναναστραφεὶς πολλοῖς τοῖς τὸν Χριστὸν ἑωρακόσιν ἀλλὰ καὶ ὑπὸ ἀποστόλων κατασταθεὶς εἰς τὴν Ἀσίαν ἐν τῇ ἐν Σμύρνῃ ἐκκλησίᾳ ἐπίσκοπος, ὃν καὶ ἡμεῖς ἑωράκαμεν ἐν τῇ πρώτῃ ἡμῶν ἡλικίᾳ, ἐπιπολὺ γὰρ παρέμεινε καὶ πάνυ γηραλέος ἐνδόξως καὶ ἐπιφανέστατα μαρτυρήσας ἐξῆλθε τοῦ βίου, ταῦτα διδάξας ἀεὶ ἃ καὶ παρὰ τῶν ἀποστόλων ἔμαθεν, ἃ καὶ ἡ ἐκκλησία παραδίδωσιν, ἃ καὶ μόνα ἐστὶν ἀληθῆ. Μαρτυροῦσιν τούτοις αἱ κατὰ τὴν Ἀσίαν ἐκκλησίαι πᾶσαι, κ.τ.λ. The perpetuity of Apostolic doctrine in its fulness is an implicit testimony to the authority of the New Testament as a whole.

To complete the testimony the words of Tertullian may be added: Hoc enim modo ecclesiæ Apostolicæ census suos deferunt, sicut Smyrnæ-orum ecclesia Polycarpum ab Johanne conlocatum refert, sicut Romanorum Clementem a Petro ordinatum edit, proinde utique et cæteræ exhibent quos Apostoli in episcopatum constitutos Apostolici seminis traduces habeant (*De Præscr. Hær.* 32).

[2] The following passages from St Peter may be noticed: 1 Pet. i. 8 (c. 1); i. 13 (c. ii.); i. 21 (c. ii.); iii. 9 (c. ii.); ii. 11 (c. v.); iv. 7 (c. vii.); ii. 22, 24 (c. viii.).

We may perhaps compare also the notices of St Paul found in 2 Pet. iii. 15; Polyc. c. iii.

As to the Pastoral Epistles, see c. iv. (1 Tim. vi. 10, 7); c. v. (2 Tim. ii. 12); c. xii. (1 Tim. ii. 2).

The inscriptions of the epistles of the Apostolic Fathers are not without special significance. Polycarp writes ἔλεος ὑμῖν καὶ εἰρήνη· in the New Testament ἔλεος occurs in the salutations of 1 and 2 Tim., 2 John, and Jude. Ignatius, with one exception (*ad Philad.*), says πλεῖστα χαίρειν. Cf. James i. 1. Clement, in the name of the Church of Rome, uses the common salutation of St Paul χάρις καὶ εἰρήνη.

cident that it does so; and at any rate it follows that a peculiar representation of Christian doctrine, which has been held in our own time to belong to the middle of the second century, was familiarly recognised in its double form, without one mark of doubt, almost within the verge of the Apostolic age[1]. Unless we admit the authenticity of the Pastoral Epistles and of the First Epistle of St Peter, the general tone and language of the Epistle of Polycarp are wholly inexplicable[2].

The dangers which impressed on the Ignatian letters their peculiar character have given some traits to that of Polycarp. He too insists on the necessity 'of turning 'away from false teaching to the word handed down 'from the first[3].' The true historic presence and work of the Lord, on which Ignatius insists with emphatic earnestness in combating the error of the Docetæ, forms the centre of the teaching of Polycarp. 'For whoever,' he affirms in the spirit and almost in the words of St John, 'does not confess that Jesus Christ has come in 'the flesh is Antichrist: and whoever does not confess 'the testimony of the cross is of the devil; and whoever 'perverts the oracles of the Lord to his own lusts and 'says that there is neither resurrection nor judgment, 'this man is the firstborn of Satan[4].' 'Christians,' he says elsewhere, 'are to be subject to the priests and deacons,

Chap. i.

Relation to Ignatian letters.

---

[1] The epistle of Polycarp was written shortly after the martyrdom of Ignatius, and its date consequently depends on that. Cf. cc. ix., xiii., and Jacobson's note on the last passage, which removes Lücke's objection.

[2] Among the peculiarities of Polycarp's language are the following: he has in common with St Paul only ἀποπλανᾶν — ἀρραβών — ἀφιλάργυρος — τὸ καλόν—ματαιολογία—προνοεῖν. Of his coincidences with St Peter, which consist in whole phrases and not in single words, we have already spoken. The following words are not found elsewhere in the Apostolic Fathers nor at all in the New Testament except in St Peter's and St Paul's Epistle, ἀνακόπτεσθαι — ψευδάδελφος — ψευδοδιδασκαλία——μεθοδεύειν (μεθοδεία, St Paul)—ἀπότομος (ἀποτομία, St Paul).

[3] c. vii.

[4] c. vii. The words might seem a condemnation of the characteristic errors of our own age.

'as to God and Christ¹.' Fasting had already become a part of the discipline of the Church².

In one respect the testimony of Polycarp is more important than that of any other of the Apostolic Fathers. Like his Master, he lived to unite two ages³. He had listened to St John, and he became himself the teacher of Irenæus. In an age of convulsion and change he stands at Smyrna and Rome as a type of the changeless truths of Christianity. In his extreme age he still taught 'that 'which he had learned from the Apostles, and which con- 'tinued to be the tradition of the Church⁴.' And in the next generation his teaching was confirmed by all the Churches in Asia⁵. Thus the zeal of Polycarp watches over the whole of the most critical period of the history of Christianity. His words are the witnesses of the second age⁶.

§ 4. *Barnabas.*

The arguments which have been urged against the claims of the Epistle of Barnabas to be considered as a

---

¹ c. v.
² c. vii.
³ His death is variously placed from 147—178. The recent investigations of M. Waddington as to the date of the Proconsulship of L. Statius Quadratus, under whom Polycarp suffered, fix the true date [Febr. 24] 155·6 A.D. The meeting of Polycarp with Anicetus will therefore fall in 154 A.D. Comp. Lipsius, *Der Märtyrer-tod Polycarp's*, Hilgenfeld's *Zeitschrift*, vii. 2, pp. 188 ff.
⁴ Iren. III. 3. 4.
⁵ Iren. *l. c.*
⁶ In the account of his martyrdom he is described as one 'who proved 'himself in our times an apostolic 'and prophetic teacher and bishop of 'the Catholic Church in Smyrna. 'For every word which he uttered 'from his mouth both was accom- 'plished and will be accomplished' (ὧν [scil. τῶν ἐκλεκτῶν] εἷς...γεγόνει ὁ ...Πολύκαρπος, ἐν τοῖς καθ' ἡμᾶς χρόνοις διδάσκαλος ἀποστολικὸς καὶ προφητικὸς γενόμενος, ἐπίσκοπός [τε] τῆς ἐν Σμύρνῃ καθολικῆς ἐκκλησίας... *Eccles. Smyr. Epist.* c. xvi.). It is obvious that the epithet 'apostolic' is explained by 'in our times,' and 'prophetic' by the last clause of the quotation. It might have been unnecessary to notice this but for Credner's strange theory: *Gesch. d. Kan.* 67 ff.

The authenticity of this narrative of the martyrdom has been called in question (see especially Donaldson, pp. 101 ff.), but there seems to be no sufficient reason for doubting its general truthfulness.

work of the first age cannot overbalance the direct historical testimony by which it is supported. It is quoted frequently, and with respect, by Clement and Origen. Eusebius speaks of it as a book well known, and commonly circulated (φερομένη), though he classes it with the books whose Canonicity was questioned or denied[1]. In Jerome's time it was still read among the Apocryphal Scriptures. It follows the Apocalypse in the Sinaitic manuscript of the Greek Bible. In the Stichometria of Nicephorus it is classed with the Antilegomena.

But while the antiquity of the Epistle is firmly established, its Apostolicity is more than questionable. A writing bearing the name of Barnabas, and known to be of the Apostolic age, might very naturally be attributed to the 'Apostle' in default of any other tradition; and the supposed connexion of Barnabas of Cyprus with Alexandria[2], where the letter first gained credit, would render the hypothesis more natural. Clement and Jerome identify the author with the fellow-labourer of St Paul; but on the other hand Origen and Eusebius are silent on this point. From its contents it seems unlikely that it was written by a companion of Apostles, and a Levite[3]. In addition to this, it is probable that Barnabas died before A.D. 62[4]; and the letter contains not only an allusion to the destruction of the Jewish Temple[5], but also affirms the abrogation of the Sabbath, and the general celebration of the Lord's Day[6], which seems to shew that it could not have been written before the beginning of the

but not Apostolic

---

[1] *H. E.* III. 25; VI. 14.
[2] Clem. *Hom.* I. 9, 13; II. 4.
[3] Hefele, *Das Sendschreiben des Apostels Barnabas*, ss. 166 ff.
[4] Hefele, ss. 37, 159.
[5] c. xvi.: διὰ γὰρ τὸ πολεμεῖν αὐτοὺς καθῃρέθη [ὁ ναὸς] ὑπὸ τῶν ἐχθρῶν νῦν, καὶ αὐτοὶ καὶ οἱ τῶν ἐχθρῶν ὑπηρέ- ται ἀνοικοδομήσουσιν αὐτόν. Hefele's punctuation (ἐχθρῶν· νῦν κ.τ.λ.) cannot, I think, stand. The writer calls attention to the *present* desolation of the Temple.
[6] c. xv. *ad fin.*: διὸ καὶ ἄγομεν τὴν ἡμέραν τὴν ὀγδόην εἰς εὐφροσύνην, κ.τ.λ. Cf. Ign. *ad Magn.* ix.

second century[1]. From these and similar reasons Hefele rightly, as it seems, decides that the Epistle is not to be attributed to Barnabas the Apostle; but at the same time he attaches undue importance to the conclusion as it affects the integrity of the Canon. Jerome evidently looked upon the Epistle as an authentic writing of 'him 'who was ordained with St Paul,' and yet he classed it with the Apocrypha. It is an arbitrary assumption that a work of this Barnabas would necessarily be Canonical. There is no reason to believe that he received his appointment to the Apostolate directly from our Lord, as the Twelve did, and afterwards St Paul; and those who regard the Canon merely as a collection of works stamped with Apostolic authority can scarcely find any other limit to its contents than that which is fixed by the strictest use of the Apostolic title[2].

Moreover there is no ground for supposing that every writing of an Apostle would have found a place in the Canon of the Christian Church. It is scarcely possible but that some Apostolic writings have perished, and yet we believe that the Bible is none the less complete. There is no essential difference between a selection of records, and a selection of facts, taken within a given range. The same Divine Power which watched over the fragmentary recital of the acts and words of the Lord and His disciples, so that nothing should be wanting which it concerns us to know, acted (as far as we can see) in like manner in preserving for our perpetual instruction those among the writings of the Apostles which had an abiding signi-

[1] Mr Cunningham in his *Dissertation* on the Epistle (Cambridge, 1877) inclines to follow Ewald and Weizsäcker in assigning a very early date to the Epistle 'not many years later than Vespasian' (p. xxxvi), and on the whole this view appears to be right.

[2] Möhler, I find with the greatest satisfaction, uses exactly the same argument as to the supposed necessary Canonicity of an authentic letter of the Apostle Barnabas (*Patrol.* 88).

ficance. The Bible is for us the sum of prophetic and apostolic literature, but that is not its essential characteristic. It contains 'all that concerns Christ' in the same sense in which the Gospel contains all the teaching of Christ. The completeness in each case is not absolute, but relative to the work which is to be accomplished.

Chap. i.

But while the Epistle of Barnabas has no claims to canonical authority, as a monument of the first Christian age it is full of interest. Among the writings of the Apostolic Fathers it holds the same place as the Epistle to the Hebrews in the New Testament. There is at least so much similarity between them as to render a contrast possible, and thus to illustrate and confirm the true theory of Scriptural Inspiration. Both Epistles are constructed, so to speak, out of Old Testament materials; and yet the mode of selection and arrangement is widely different. Both exhibit characteristic principles of the Alexandrine school; but in the one case they are modified, as it were, by an instinctive sense of their due relation to the whole system of Christianity; in the other they are subjected to no restraint, and usurp an independent and absolute authority.

Its relation to the Epistle to the Hebrews

The mystical interpretations of the Old Testament found in the Epistle to the Hebrews are marked by a kind of reserve. The author shews an evident consciousness that this kind of teaching is not suited to all, but requires mature powers alike in the instructor and in the taught[1]. As if to transfer his readers to a more spiritual atmosphere, though this is but one aspect of the motive which seems to have ruled his choice, he takes his illustrations from the Tabernacle, and not from the Temple. The transitory resting-place which was fashioned according to the command of God, and not the permanent

in regard to the mystical interpretation of Scripture, and

[1] Hebr. v. 11 sqq.

'house' which was reared according to the design of man, was chosen as the figure of higher and divine truths. Those types which are pursued in detail are taken from the salient points of the Jewish ritual, and serve to awaken attention, without creating any difficulties in the way of those who are naturally disinclined to what are called mystical speculations. It is otherwise in the Epistle of Barnabas. In that the subtlest interpretations are addressed to promiscuous readers—to 'sons and daughters'—and the highest value is definitely affixed to them[1]. In parts there is an evident straining after novelty wholly alien from the calm and conscious strength of an Apostle; and the details of his explanations are full of the rudest errors[2]. In the one Epistle we have to do with a method of interpretation clear and broad; in the other we have an application of the method, at times ingenious and beautiful, and then again arbitrary and incongruous. The single point of direct connexion between the two Epistles illustrates their respective characters. Both speak of the rest of God on the seventh day; but in the Epistle to the Hebrews this rest, not yet realised by man, though prepared for him from the foundation of the world, is made a motive for earnest and watchful efforts, and nothing more is defined as to the time of its approach. Barnabas on the contrary, having spoken of the promise, determines the date of its fulfilment. The six days of the creation furnish a measure, and so he accepts the old tradition, current even in Etruria, which fixed the con-

---

[1] c. ix. *ad fin.*: οὐδεὶς γνησιώτερον ἔμαθεν ἀπ' ἐμοῦ λόγον, ἀλλ' [οἶδα] ὅτι ἄξιοί ἐστε ὑμεῖς. Barnabas has been speaking of the mystical interpretation of the 318 members of Abraham's household as prefiguring Jesus (IH′ = 18) together with the Cross (T′ = 300).

[2] c. x. Yet the passages are quoted by Clement of Alexandria. Cf. Hefele, *Das Sendschreiben, u. s. w.*, s. 86 anm.

summation of all things at the end of six thousand years from the creation[1].

the Mosaical Dispensation.

But yet more than this: the general spirit of the Epistle of Barnabas is different from that of the Epistle to the Hebrews. In the latter it is shewn that there lies a deep meaning for us under the history and the law of Israel. The old Covenant was real, though not 'faultless,' and its ordinances were 'patterns of the things in heaven,' though not the heavenly things themselves[2]. But in the former it is assumed throughout that the Law was from its first institution misunderstood by the Jews. The first covenant was broken by reason of their idolatry, and the second became a stumblingblock to them in spite of the teaching of the Prophets[3]. Fasts, feasts, and sacrifices, were required by God only in a spiritual sense[4]. Even circumcision, as they practised it, was not the seal of God's covenant, but rather the work of an evil spirit, who induced them to substitute that for the circumcision of the heart[5]. The Jewish Sabbath was not according to God's will: their temple was a delusion[6]. Judaism is

---

[1] Heb. iv., Barn. xv. The Etrurian tradition is so remarkable that it deserves to be quoted. 'An able 'writer among them [the Etrurians] 'compiled a history: God, he said, 'the Maker of all things providen- 'tially appointed twelve periods of a 'thousand years for the duration of 'all His creatures, and distributed 'them to the twelve so-called dispen- 'sations (οἶκοι). In the first period '(χιλιάς) He made the heaven and 'the earth. In the second the visible 'firmament, and called it heaven. 'In the third the sea and all the wa- 'ters in the earth. In the fourth the 'great lights (φωστῆρας), the sun and 'moon and the stars. In the fifth 'all living-fowls and creeping things 'and four-footed beasts in the air and 'on the earth and in the waters. In 'the sixth man. It appears then that 'the first six periods passed away 'before the formation (διάπλασις) of 'man; and that during the remaining 'six the race of man will continue 'so that the whole time up to the 'consummation of all things extends 'to twelve thousand years' (Suidas, s. v. Τυρρηνία). The conception of the gradual progress of creation in each period, so that man is the final result of the sixth, is remarkable. A trace of the same tradition is preserved by Servius *ad Virg. Ecl.* ix. 47.

[2] Hebr. viii. 7 ; x. 23.
[3] Barn. c. xiv.
[4] Barn. cc. ii., iii.
[5] c. ix.
[6] cc. xv., xvi.

made a mere riddle, of which Christianity is the answer. It had in itself no value, not even as the slave (παιδαγωγός) which guards us in infancy from outward dangers, till we are placed under the true teacher's care[1]. Each symbolic act is emptied of its real meaning, because it is deprived of the sacramental character with which God invested it. The worth of the Law, as one great instrument in the education of the world, is disregarded: the true idea of revelation, as a gradual manifestation of God's glory, is violated: the harmonious subordination of the parts of the divine scheme of redemption is destroyed. On such principles it is not enough that the sum of all future growth should be implicitly contained in the seed: that the vital principle which inspires the first and the last should be the same: that the identity of essence should be indicated by the identity of life: but all must be perfect according to some arbitrary and stereotyped standard. Against this doctrine, which is the germ of all heresy, the Holy Scriptures ever consistently protest. Their catholicity is the constant mark of their divine origin; and the undesigned harmony which results from every possible combination of their different parts is the surest pledge of their absolute truth[2].

[1] Gal. iii. 24.
[2] The language of Barnabas is more remarkable for peculiar words than for coincidences with any parts of the New Testament. He has (ἀνακαινίζειν)—ἐνέργημα—ζωοποιεῖσθαι, in common with St Paul; and among his peculiarities may be noticed ἀκεραιοσύνη—δίγνωμος—δίγλωσσος—διπλοκαρδία—θρασύτης—παναμάρτητος — (πλάσμα), ἀναπλάσσεσθαι — προφανεροῦσθαι — συλλήπτωρ —ὑπεραγαπᾶν.

On *The Teaching of the Apostles* see Note (2) at the end of the Chapter.

SECT. II. THE RELATION OF THE APOSTOLIC FATHERS TO THE CANON OF THE NEW TESTAMENT.

The testimony of the Apostolic Fathers is not however confined to the recognition of the several types of Christianity which are preserved in the Canonical Scriptures: they confirm the genuineness and authority of the books themselves. That they do not appeal to the Apostolic writings more frequently and more distinctly springs from the very nature of their position. Those who had heard the living voice of Apostles were unlikely to appeal to their written words. We have an instinct which always makes us prefer any personal connexion to the more remote relationship of books. Thus Papias tells us that he sought to learn from every quarter the traditions of those who had conversed with the elders, thinking that he should not profit so much by the narratives of books as by the living and abiding voice of the Lord's disciples. And still Papias affirmed the exact accuracy of the Gospel of St Mark, and quoted testimonies (μαρτυρίαι) from the Catholic Epistles of St Peter and St John[1]. So again Irenæus in earnest language records with what joy he listened to the words of Polycarp, when he told of his intercourse with those who had seen the Lord; and how those who had been with Christ spoke of His mighty works and teaching. And still all was according to the Scriptures (πάντα σύμφωνα ταῖς γραφαῖς); so that the charm lay not in the novelty of the narrative, but in its vital union with the fact[2].

The testimony of the Apostolic Fathers to the New Testament.

How far modified by the 'Apostolic tradition.'

---

[1] See pp. 74 ff.
[2] Iren. *Ep. ad Flor.* ap. Euseb. *H. E.* v. 20. Compare the passage of Irenæus (III. 3. 4) quoted above, p. 38.

48 THE AGE OF THE APOSTOLIC FATHERS. [PART

Chap. i.
(a) *Their testimony to the Books of the New Testament*
(1) *explicit*,

In three instances[1] in which it was natural to expect a direct allusion to the Epistles of St Paul the references are as complete as possible. 'Take up the Epistle of 'the blessed Paul the Apostle,' is the charge of Clement to the Corinthians, '...... in truth he spiritually charged 'you concerning himself and Cephas and Apollos[2]......' 'Those who are borne by martyrdom to God,' Ignatius writes to the Ephesians, 'pass through your city; ye are 'initiated into mysteries (συμμύσται) with St Paul, the 'sanctified, the martyred, worthy of all blessing......who 'in every letter (ἐν πάσῃ ἐπιστολῇ) makes mention of 'you in Christ Jesus[3].' 'The blessed and glorious Paul,' says Polycarp to the Philippians, '......wrote letters 'to you, into which if ye look diligently, ye will be 'able to be built up to [the fulness of] the faith given 'to you[4].'

(2) *incidental*.

Elsewhere in the Apostolic Fathers there are clear traces of a knowledge of the Epistles of St Paul to the Romans, 1 and 2 Corinthians, Galatians, Ephesians, Philippians, and 1 and 2 Timothy, of the Epistle to the Hebrews, of the Epistle of St James, the first Epistle of St Peter, and the first Epistle of St John. The allusions to the Epistles of St Paul to the Thessalonians, Colossians, to Titus, and Philemon, and to 2 Peter, are very uncertain; and there are, I believe, no coincidences of language with the Epistles of Jude, and 2 and 3 John[5].

---

[1] The subject of Ignatius' letter to the Romans explains the absence of any direct allusion to St Paul's Epistle. The mention of St Peter and St Paul (c. iv.) however is worthy of notice.
[2] Clem. c. xlvii.
[3] *Ad Ephes.* c. xii. The reference in συμμύσται to Eph. v. 32 seems clear when we remember the whole tenor of Ignatius' letter. The phrase ἐν πάσῃ ἐπιστολῇ is best taken as a (not unnatural) hyperbole. Comp. Bp. Lightfoot *ad loc.* The passage is not found in the Syriac.
[4] Polyc. c. iii.
[5] The following table will be found useful and interesting as shewing how far each writer makes use of other books of the New Testament than the Gospels:
CLEMENT. Romans (c. xxxv.); 1 Corinthians (c. xlvii.); Ephe-

It is true that these incidental references are with one exception anonymous. The words of Scripture are inwrought into the texture of the books, and not parcelled out into formal quotations. They are not arranged with argumentative effect, but used as the natural expression of Christian truths. Now this use of the Holy Scriptures shews at least that they were even then widely known, and therefore guarded by a host of witnesses; that their language was transferred into the common dialect; that it was as familiar to those first Christians as to us who use it as unconsciously as they did in writing or in conversation. Two passages of Clement will sufficiently illustrate the statements which have been made. No one, as far as I know, has ever questioned the genuineness of the chapters from which they are taken, or doubted the reality of the references to Apostolic writings which they contain. Clement had referred the Corinthians to St Paul's Epistle[1]. Not long afterwards he goes on to speak of love (ἀγάπη) in the following terms: 'Love uniteth '(κολλᾷ) us to God: *love covereth a multitude of sins* '(1 Pet. iv. 8): *love* supporteth (ἀνέχεται not στέγει) *all* '*things* (1 Cor. xiii. 7), *suffereth long* in all things (1 Cor. 'xiii. 4): there is nothing vulgar in love, nothing proud: 'love hath no divisions (σχίσμα), love is not factious,

Chap. i.
The peculiar value of this anonymous evidence.

The freedom of the references of CLEMENT, *and*

sians (c. xlvi.); 1 Timothy? (c. vii.); Titus? (c. ii.); Hebrews (cc. xvii., xxxvi. &c.); James (c. x. &c.).
IGNATIUS. 1 Corinthians (*ad Ephes.* xviii.); Ephesians (*ad Ephes.* xii.); Philippians? (*ad Philad.* viii.); 1 Thessalonians? (*ad Ephes.* x.); Philemon? (*ad Ephes.* c. ii. &c.).
POLYCARP. Acts ii. 24 (c. i.); Romans (c. vi.); 1 Corinthians (c. xi.); 2 Corinthians (cc. ii., vi.); Galatians (cc. iii., xii.); Ephesians? (c. xii.); Philip-

pians (c. iii., xi.); 1 Thessalonians? (cc. ii., iv.); 2 Thessalonians? (c. xi.); 1 Timothy (c. iv.); 2 Timothy (c. v.); 1 Peter (cc. i., ii. &c.); 1 John (c. vii.); 2 Peter iii. 15 (c. iii.) (?).
BARNABAS. Eph.? (c. vi.); 1 Timothy? (c. xii.); 2 Timothy? (c. vii.). Cf. Hefele, ss. 230— 240. Cunningham, pp. xciv. ff. The Evangelic references are examined below, pp. 60 ff.
[1] c. xlvii.

'love doeth all things in concord[1].' The language of St Paul is evidently floating before the writer's eyes, and yet he deliberately avoids reproducing it. He clothes the Pauline thoughts in words of his own, and adds a cognate phrase of St Peter. Nothing would have been easier, or even more plausible, than to deny the reference to 1 Corinthians if it had been established only by the coincidences of words. The second passage is no less instructive. Clement has occasion to speak of Jesus Christ as 'the High Priest of our offerings: the cham-'pion and helper of our infirmity.' 'Through Him,' he says, '... the Lord (δεσπότης) wished us to taste 'immortal knowledge *who being the brightness* of His 'greatness (Hebr. i. 3) is *so much* greater *than angels* '*as He hath by inheritance obtained a more excellent name* '(i. 4); for it is written thus, *who maketh His angels* '*spirits, and His ministers a flame of fire* (i. 7). But in 'the case of His *Son* the Lord spake thus, *Thou art my* '*Son, this day have I begotten Thee* (i. 5): ask of me and 'I will give thee nations for thine inheritance, and the 'utmost parts of the earth for thy possession. And again, 'He saith unto Him, *Sit on my right hand until I make* '*thine enemies thy footstool*' (i. 13). Here there are, as it will be seen, compressions, omissions, transpositions, substitutions, and yet no one could with reason doubt that Hebrews i., as we read it, was clearly present to the writer's mind[2].

This free adaptation of the Apostolic language by Clement will enable us to give its true weight to a passage in which Polycarp uses the language of 1 John[3],

---

[1] c. xlix. The free use made of 1 Cor. xii. in c. xxxvii. ought to be compared with this reminiscence.
[2] Dr Sanday has examined the character of the quotations in early Christian Fathers generally with great care in c. ii. of *The Gospels in the Second Century* (Cambridge, 1876).
[3] The strange notion that Poly-

I.] THEIR RELATION TO THE CANON. 51

'Every one that *doth not confess that Jesus Christ hath* *come in the flesh is antichrist;* and whoever does not 'confess the testimony of the cross is of the devil.' The agreement with 1 John iv. 3 is complete in the essential thoughts, and the form of Polycarp's sentence appears to be based upon 2 John 7[1].

The general style of the writers with whom we are dealing goes far to establish the validity of these silent and incomplete quotations. For it will be readily admitted that if the quotations from the Old Testament in the Apostolic Fathers were uniformly explicit and exact, this mode of argument would lose much of its force. But with the exception of Barnabas it does not appear that they have made a single reference by name to any one of the books of the Old Testament[2]; and Barnabas perhaps quotes a passage from St Matthew with the technical formula 'as it is written[3].' Clement uses the general formula 'It is written,' or even more frequently 'God

Chap. i.

illustrated by the quotations from the Old Testament.

carp 'contradicted the statements of the fourth Gospel' when he 'contended that Christian festival should be celebrated on the 14th Nisan' will be noticed when we speak of Claudius Apollinaris.

[1] 1 John iv. 3, πᾶν πνεῦμα ὃ ὁμολογεῖ Ἰησοῦν Χριστὸν ἐν σαρκὶ ἐληλυθότα, ἐκ τοῦ Θεοῦ ἐστίν· καὶ πᾶν πνεῦμα ὃ μὴ ὁμολογεῖ τὸν Ἰησοῦν ἐκ τοῦ Θεοῦ οὐκ ἔστιν, καὶ τοῦτό ἐστιν τὸ τοῦ ἀντιχρίστου... 2 John 7, οἱ μὴ ὁμολογοῦντες Ἰησοῦν Χριστὸν ἐρχόμενον ἐν σαρκί· οὗτός ἐστιν...ὁ ἀντίχριστος. Yet it may be observed that there is good authority for ἐληλυθέναι in 1 John iv. 3. The author of *Supern. Relig.* gives (ii. p. 268) a good example of the facility with which similar phrases are mixed up when he quotes as ' 1 John iv. 3' the mixed reading which is given by א only, καὶ πᾶν πνεῦμα ὃ μὴ ὁμολογεῖ Ἰησοῦν κύριον ἐν σαρκὶ ἐληλυθότα ἐκ τοῦ Θεοῦ οὐκ ἔστιν, καὶ τοῦτο κ.τ.λ. Is this also taken from an apocryphal writing?

[2] Barn. Ep. c. x.: λέγει αὐτοῖς [Μωσῆς] ἐν τῷ Δευτερονομίῳ. Elsewhere Barnabas mentions the writer's name: c. iv. *Daniel;* c. xii. *David, Esaias;* c. vi., x., xii. *Moses.*

[3] Barn. iv. Matt. xxii. 14. The reading of *Cod. Sinaiticus* (ὡς γέγραπται) removes the doubt which naturally attached to the Latin Version *sicut scriptum est,* and thus this quotation from St Matthew, if indeed it is a quotation, is the earliest direct example of the use of a book of the New Testament as Holy Scripture.

In the second 'Epistle' of Clement there is the same explicitness of reference as in Barnabas, c. iii. *Esaias;* c. vi. *Ezechiel.* So likewise a passage of St Matthew's Gospel is called γραφή (c. ii.). The fact is worth notice. On the other hand it is just to add

E 2

saith,' or simply 'One saith[1].' The two quotations from the Old Testament in Ignatius are simply preceded by 'It is written.' In the Greek text of Polycarp there is no mark of quotation at all[2]; and Clement sometimes introduces the language of the Old Testament into his argument without any mark of distinction[3]. Exactness of quotation was foreign to the spirit of the writing.

How far it can be applied to the Gospels.

Nothing has been said hitherto of the coincidences between the Apostolic Fathers and the Canonical Gospels. From the nature of the case casual coincidences of language cannot be brought forward in the same manner to prove the use of a history as of a letter. The same facts and words, especially if they be recent and striking, may be preserved in several narratives. References in the sub-apostolic age to the discourses or actions of our Lord as we find them recorded in the Gospels shew, so far as they go, that what the Gospels relate was then held to be true; but it does not necessarily follow that they were already in use, and were the actual source of the passages in question. On the contrary, the mode in which Clement[4] refers to our Lord's teaching, 'the Lord said,' not 'saith,' seems to imply that he was indebted to tradition, and not to any written accounts, for words most closely resembling those which are still found in our Gospels. The main testimony of the Apostolic Fathers is therefore to the substance, and not to the authenticity of the Gospels.

---

that the proverbial form of the saying ('Many are called but few chosen') is such as to admit of the supposition that it may have been derived by Barnabas from some older book than St Matthew.

[1] c. xxvi. (Job) &c., lii. (David), cannot be considered exceptions to the rule.

[2] The reading of the Latin Version in c. xi. *sicut Paulus docet* seems to be less open to suspicion than that in c. xii. *ut his scripturis dictum est* (Ps. iv. 5; Eph. iv. 26), which is at least quite alien from Polycarp's manner.

[3] E.g. cc. xxvii., liv. So also Ignatius *ad Trall.* viii.

[4] cc. xiii., xlvi. (εἶπεν), compared with Acts xx. 35. The past tense in Ignat. *ad Smyr.* iii. appears to be of a different kind.

I.] THEIR RELATION TO THE CANON. 53

And in this respect they have an important work to do. They witness that the great outlines of the life and teaching of our Lord were familiarly known to all from the first: they prove that Christianity rests truly on a historic basis.

Chap. i.

The 'Gospel' which the Fathers announce includes all the articles of the ancient Creeds[1]. Christ, we read, our God, the Word, the Lord and Creator of the World, who was with the Father before time began[2], humbled Himself, and came down from heaven, and was manifested in the flesh, and was born of the Virgin Mary, of the race of David according to the flesh; and a star of exceeding brightness appeared at His birth[3]. Afterwards He was baptized by John, *to fulfil all righteousness;* and then, speaking His Father's message, He invited not the righteous, but sinners, to come to Him[4]. Perfume was poured *over His head,* an emblem of the immortality which He breathed on the Church[5]. At length, under Herod and Pontius Pilate He was crucified, and vinegar and gall were offered Him to drink[6]. But on the first day of the week He rose from the dead, the first-fruits of the grave; and many prophets were raised by Him for whom they had waited. After His resurrection He ate with His disciples, and shewed them that He was not an incorporeal spirit[7]. And He ascended into heaven,

The great features of Christ's life familiarly known.

---

[1] On the use of oral and written Gospels in the first age, compare Gieseler, *Ueber die Entstehung u. s. w.* ss. 149 sqq. *Introduction to the Study of the Gospels,* pp. 154 ff.

[2] Ign. *ad Rom.* inscr., c. iii.; *ad Ephes.* inscr.; *ad Magnes.* viii.: Barn. v.: Ign. *ad Magnes.* vi.

[3] Clem. xvi.: Ign. *ad Magnes.* vii.: Barn. xii.: Ign. *ad Smyr.* i.; *ad Trall.* ix.; *ad Ephes.* xix.: Ign. *ad Ephes.* xx.; *id.* xix. (of especial interest).

[4] Ign. *ad Smyr.* i. The words which are parallel with St Matthew, ἵνα πληρωθῇ πᾶσα δικαιοσύνη ὑπ' αὐτοῦ, appear to have been wanting in the Ebionite Gospel: Hieron. *adv. Pelag.* iii. 2. *Ad Rom.* viii.: Barn. v.

[5] Eph. xvii. the words ἐπὶ τῆς κεφαλῆς connect the reference with Matt. xxvi. 7 (true reading).

[6] Ign. *ad Magnes.* xi.; *ad Trall.* ix.; *ad Smyr.* i.: Barn. vii.

[7] Barn. xv.: Ign. *ad Magnes.* ix.:

and sat down on the right hand of the Father, and thence He shall come to judge the quick and the dead[1].

Such, in their own words, is the testimony of the earliest Fathers to the life of the Saviour. Round these facts their doctrines are grouped; on the truth of the Incarnation and the Passion and the Resurrection of Christ their hopes were grounded[2].

(β) Testimony to the authority of Apostolic writings

If the extent of the evidence of the Apostolic Fathers to the books of the New Testament is exactly what might be expected from men who had seen the Apostles, who had heard them, and who had treasured up their writings as the genuine records of their teaching, the character of their evidence is equally in accordance with their peculiar position. It will be readily seen that we cannot expect

modified by

Clem. xxiv.: Polyc. ii.: Ign. *ad Magnes.* ix.; *ad Smyr.* iii.
[1] Barn. xv.: Polyc. ii.: Barn. vii.: Polyc. ii. Barnabas (*l.c.*) appears at first sight to place the Ascension also on a Sunday; but it is more likely that he regarded the Manifestation and Ascension of the Risen Christ as simply additional moments in the story of the Resurrection.
There are also numerous references to discourses of our Lord which are recorded in the Gospels:
CLEMENT.
  c. xiii. Comp. Matt. v. 7; vi. 14; vii. 2, 12, and parallels.
  c. xlvi. Comp. Matt. xxvi. 24 and parallels.
IGNATIUS.
  ad Eph. v. Matt. xviii. 19.
  id. vi. Matt. x. 40.
  ad Trall. xi. Matt. xv. 13.
  ad Rom. vii. Cf. John xvi. 11.
  id. Cf. John iv. 14; vii. 38.
  id. Cf. John vi. 51.
  ad Philad. vii. Cf. John iii. 8.
  ad Smyrn. vi. Matt. xix. 12.
  ad Polyc. i. Matt. viii. 17.
  id. ii. Matt. x. 16.

POLYCARP.
  c. ii. Matt. vii. 1; vi. 14; v. 7; Luke vi. 38, 40. Matt. v. 10.
  c. vii. Matt. vi. 13; xxvi. 41; Mark xiv. 38.
  c. v. Cf. Matt. xx. 28.
  c. vi. Cf. Matt. vi. 12, 14.
BARNABAS.
  c. iv. Matt. xxii. 14.
  c. v. Matt. ix. 13.
These parallels together with supposed references to sayings of the Lord not contained in the Canonical Gospels are examined in a Note at the end of the Chapter: pp. 60 ff. Compare *Introd. to the Study of the Gospels*, App. C. Gieseler, *Ueber die Entstehung der schrift. Evv.* ss. 147 ff.
[2] Cf. Ign. *ad Philad.* viii. It is very worthy of notice that there are no references to the miracles of our Lord in the Apostolic Fathers. All miracles are implicitly included in the Incarnation and Resurrection of Christ. Compare Note at the end of the Chapter.

I.] THEIR RELATION TO THE CANON. 55

to find in the first age the New Testament quoted as authoritative in the same manner as the Old Testament. There could not indeed be any occasion for an appeal to the testimony of the Gospels when the history of the faith was still within the memory of many; and most of the Epistles were of little use in controversy, for the earliest heretics denied the Apostleship of St Paul. The Old Testament, on the contrary, was common ground; and the ancient system of biblical interpretation furnished the Christian with ready arms. When these failed it was enough for him to appeal to the Death and Resurrection of Christ, which were at once the sum and the proof of his faith. 'I have heard some say,' Ignatius writes, '*Unless I find in the ancients* [*the writers of the* '*Old Testament*] *I believe not in the Gospel*, and when I '*said to them It is written* [*in the Prophets that Christ* '*should suffer and rise again*], they replied [*That must be* '*proved;*] *the question lies before us*. But to me,' he adds, 'Jesus Christ is [the substance of all] records; my 'inviolable records are His Cross and Death and Resur-'rection, and the Faith through Him[1].'

It cannot however be denied that the idea of the Inspiration of the New Testament, in the sense in which it is maintained now, was the growth of time. When St Paul spoke[2] of *the Holy Scriptures* of the Old Testament as *able to make wise unto salvation through faith which is in Christ Jesus*, he expressed what was the practical belief of the first century of the Christian

Chap. i.

(1) *the circumstances of the time, and*

(2) *the gradual perception of the co-ordinate authority of a new Testament with the Old Testament,*

---

[1] *Ad Philad.* viii. The passage is beset with many difficulties, but the translation which I have ventured to give seems to remove many of them. Προκεῖσθαι is continually used of a question in debate: Plat. *Euthyd.* 279 D, καταγέλαστον δήπου ὃ πάλαι πρόκειται τοῦτο πάλιν προ- τιθέναι. *Resp.* VII. 533 E, etc. If in place of ἐν τοῖς ἀρχαίοις we read ἐν τοῖς ἀρχείοις according to Voss' conjecture the sense would be unchanged. The sudden burst of feeling (ἐμοὶ δέ κ.τ.λ.) is characteristic of Ignatius.

[2] 2 Tim. iii. 15.

Church. The Old Testament was for two or three generations a complete Bible both doctrinally and historically when interpreted in the light of the Gospel. Many of the most farsighted teachers, we may believe, prepared the way for the formation of a collection of Apostolic Writings co-ordinate with the writings of the Prophets, but the result to which they looked forward was achieved gradually, even as the Old Testament itself was formed by slow degrees[1]. Distance is a necessary condition if we are to estimate rightly any object of vast proportions. The history of any period will furnish illustrations of this truth; and the teaching of God through man appears to be always subject to the common laws of human life and thought. If it be true that a prophet is not received in his own country, it is equally true that he is not received in his own age. The sense of his power is vague even when it is deepest. Years must elapse before we can feel that the words of one who talked with men were indeed the words of God.

which followed from the relation of the Apostles to their first successors.

The successors of the Apostles did not, we admit, recognise that the written histories of the Lord and the scattered epistles of His first disciples would form a sure and sufficient source and test of doctrine when the current tradition had grown indistinct or corrupt. Conscious of a life in the Christian body, and realising the power of its Head, in a way impossible now, they did not feel that the Apostles were providentially charged to express once for all in their *writings* the essential forms of Christianity, even as the Prophets had foreshadowed them. The position which they held did not command that comprehensive view of the nature and

---

[1] Comp. *The Bible in the Church*, Ap. A.

fortunes of the Christian Church by which the idea is suggested and confirmed. But they had certainly an indistinct perception that their work was essentially different from that of their predecessors. They declined to perpetuate their title, though they may have retained their office. They attributed to them power and wisdom to which they themselves made no claim. Without having any exact sense of the completeness of the Christian Scriptures, they still drew a line between them and their own writings. As if by some providential instinct, each one of those teachers who stood nearest to the writers of the New Testament contrasted his writings with theirs, and definitely placed himself on a lower level. The fact is most significant; for it shews in what way the formation of the Canon was an act of the intuition of the Church, derived from no reasoning, but realised in the course of its natural growth as one of the first results of its self-consciousness.

Still the Apostolic Fathers separate the Apostles from themselves.

Clement, the earliest of the Fathers, does not even write in his own name to the Church of Corinth, but simply as the representative of the Church of Rome. He lays aside the individual authority of an Apostle, and the Epistle was well named in the next age that of the Romans to the Corinthians[1]. He apologizes in some measure for the tone of reproof which he himself uses, and at the same time refers his readers to the Epistle of the blessed Paul, who wrote to them 'spiritually,' and certainly with the fullest consciousness of absolute and unsparing authority[2].

[1] Clem. Alex. *Str.* v. 12. § 81. Elsewhere however it is quoted in the same work as the Epistle of Clement, *Str.* I. 7. § 38; VI. 3. § 65; and even of Clement *the Apostle*: *Str.* IV. 17. § 107.
[2] c. vii. 'These injunctions we give, beloved, not only admonishing you, but putting ourselves also in mind [of our duty]; for we are in the same arena (ἐν τῷ αὐτῷ σκάμματι), and the same conflict is laid upon us [as upon you].' c. xlvii. 'Take up the Epistle of

Polycarp, in like manner, who had listened to the words of the loved disciple, still says afterwards that 'neither he nor any like him is able to attain fully to '(κατακολουθῆσαι) the wisdom of the blessed and 'glorious Paul¹.'

Ignatius, who, if we receive the testimony of the writings attributed to him, seems very little likely to have disparaged the power of his office, still twice disclaims in memorable words the idea that he wished to impose his commands like Peter and Paul: they were 'Apostles, while I,' he adds, 'am a condemned man' (κατάκριτος²).

Barnabas again twice reminds his readers that he speaks as one of them, not as a teacher, but as a member of Christ's Church³.

One passage of the Ignatian Epistles still remains to be noticed. In this there appears to be an indication that when they were written there was a recognised collection of Christian books. Ignatius speaks of himself as 'having fled to the Gospel as to the flesh of Jesus, and 'to the Apostles as to the presbytery of the Church. Yea,' he continues, 'and let us love the prophets also, because 'they also preached unto the Gospel⁴.' The juxtaposition of prophets (i.e. the prophetic writings of the Old Testament) with the Gospel and the Apostles is harsh and unnatural unless these also are represented by writings.

'the blessed Paul the Apostle. What 'did he write first to you at the be-'ginning of the Gospel? In very 'truth he gave you spiritual injunc-'tions about himself and Cephas and 'Apollos...'
¹ c. iii.
² *Ad Rom.* iv.: Οὐχ ὡς Πέτρος καὶ Παῦλος διατάσσομαι ὑμῖν· ἐκεῖνοι ἀπόστολοι, ἐγὼ κατάκριτος· ἐκεῖνοι ἐλεύθεροι, ἐγὼ δὲ μέχρι νῦν δοῦλος. Ἀλλ' ἐὰν πάθω ἀπελεύθερος Ἰησοῦ, καὶ ἀναστήσομαι ἐν αὐτῷ ἐλεύθερος. Cf. *ad Trall.* c. iii. [Eph. xii.] The word was doubtless suggested by his actual condition, but it must have a spiritual meaning too.
³ c. i.: οὐχ ὡς διδάσκαλος ἀλλ' ὡς εἷς ἐξ ὑμῶν. Cf. c. iv.
⁴ *Ad Philad.* c. v.

I.]   THEIR RELATION TO THE CANON.   59

And in the conception of Ignatius the Epistles would represent the teaching of the Apostles just as the Gospel represented the historic, human, Presence of Jesus (not Christ). But at the same time it will be observed that the writer uses the word 'Gospel' and not 'Gospels.' The substance of the records was as yet considered in its unity and not in its variety.

It would be easy to say much more on the Apostolic Fathers, but enough perhaps has been said already to shew the value of their writings as a commentary on the Apostolic age[1]. They illustrate alike the language and the doctrines of the New Testament. They prove that Christianity was Catholic from the very first, uniting a variety of forms in one faith. They shew that the great facts of the Gospel-narrative and the substance of the Apostolic letters formed the basis and moulded the expression of the common creed. They recognise the fitness of a Canon, and indicate the limits within which it must be fixed. And their evidence is the more important when it is remembered that they speak to us from four great centres of the ancient Church—from Antioch and Alexandria, from Ephesus and Rome. One Church alone is silent. The Christians of Jerusalem contribute nothing to this written portraiture of the age. The peculiarities of their belief were borrowed from a conventional system destined to pass away, and did not embody the permanent characteristics of any particular type of Apostolic doctrine. The Jewish Church at Pella was an accommodation, if we may use the word, and not a form of Christianity. How far its principles

Chap. i.

General Summary of their testimony.

Its great local extent and importance.

---

[1] It is perhaps the commentary of a childlike age; but Möhler has admirably said 'auch in den geisti-'gen Aeusserungen des Kindes ist 'der Keim aller möglichen Wissen-'schaften schon enthalten.' (*Patrol.* 51.)

Chap. i. influenced the Church of the next age will be seen in the following Chapter¹.

¹ Papias perhaps might have been noticed in this Chapter, but I believe that he belongs properly to the next generation. The testimony to the Gospel of St Mark which he quotes from the presbyter John must however be considered as drawn from the Apostolic age. It will be convenient to notice this when speaking of Papias (c. ii. § 1).

NOTE (1) TO PAGE 54.

ON THE EVANGELIC WORDS CONTAINED IN THE APOSTOLIC FATHERS.

It has been said (p. 52), that the Evangelic words and facts referred to in the Apostolic Fathers may have been derived from oral tradition, like the corresponding references in the Apostolic Epistles. The student will be able to draw his own conclusion as to the source from which the Evangelic words were derived if the evidence is briefly placed before him. The references to the words of the Lord are:

i. CLEMENT. i. (a) CLEMENT, c. xiii. μεμνημένοι τῶν λόγων τοῦ κυρίου Ἰησοῦ οὓς ἐλάλησεν διδάσκων ἐπιείκειαν καὶ μακροθυμίαν· οὕτως γὰρ εἶπεν :

ἐλεᾶτε ἵνα ἐλεηθῆτε.

ἀφίετε ἵνα ἀφεθῇ ὑμῖν.

ὡς ποιεῖτε, οὕτω ποιηθήσεται ὑμῖν.

ὡς δίδοτε, οὕτως δοθήσεται ὑμῖν.

ὡς κρίνετε, οὕτως κριθήσεται ὑμῖν.

ὡς χρηστεύεσθε, οὕτως χρηστευθήσεται ὑμῖν.

ᾧ μέτρῳ μετρεῖτε, ἐν αὐτῷ μετρηθήσεται ὑμῖν.

Now if this passage be compared with the parallels in St Matthew (v. 7; vi. 14; vii. 2, 12) and St Luke (vi. 31, 36, 37, 38; iv. 38), it will, I think, be felt that the markedly symmetrical form of Clement's version indicates a free and yet deliberate handling of the contents of the Gospels. It is in style later than our Gospels, whether it was shaped by Clement or at an earlier time. The use of χρηστός, χρηστεύομαι is interesting because the word χρηστός occurs in combination with οἰκτίρμων in Just. *Ap.* i. 15; *Dial.* 96. See below, chap. ii.

(β) CLEMENT, c. xlvi. μνησθῆτε τῶν λόγων Ἰησοῦ τοῦ κυρίου ἡμῶν· εἶπεν γάρ· οὐαὶ τῷ ἀνθρώπῳ ἐκείνῳ· καλὸν ἦν αὐτῷ εἰ οὐκ ἐγεννήθη, ἢ ἕνα τῶν ἐκλεκτῶν μου σκανδαλίσαι· κρεῖττον ἦν αὐτῷ περιτεθῆναι μύλον καὶ καταποντισθῆναι εἰς τὴν θάλασσαν, ἢ ἕνα τῶν μικρῶν μου σκανδαλίσαι.

The parallels are Matt. xxvi. 24; Mark xiv. 21, and Matt. xviii. 6, 7; Mark ix. 42; Luke xvii. 1, 2. The words may be a recollection of our Gospels. Comp. Lightfoot, *l.c.*

But it has been argued that the words in c. xiii. (and the same applies to xlvi.) are introduced 'with a remark implying a well-known record... and in a way suggesting careful and precise quotation of the very words' (*Supern. Rel.* i. 230 f.). Clement's words are (as we have seen), 'remembering the words of the Lord Jesus which He spake...for thus He said...' (μεμνημένοι τῶν λόγων τοῦ κυρίου Ἰησοῦ...οὕτως γὰρ εἶπεν). Now the corresponding words in the passage of the Acts, xx. 35, are 'you ought...to remember the words of the Lord Jesus that He Himself said' (δεῖ...μνημονεύειν τῶν λόγων τοῦ κυρίου Ἰησοῦ ὅτι αὐτὸς εἶπεν), and I can see no reason for referring the quotation assigned to St Paul in this latter passage to any 'well-known record.' Moreover in the context of Clement the contrast between the 'words of the Lord Jesus' and 'that which is written' (1 Sam. ii. 10; Jerem. ix. 23, 24), appears to be marked; and both are included in the phrase 'the command and the injunctions,' which follows. Some difficulty has been felt as to the source of the reference in c. xliv, καὶ οἱ ἀπόστολοι ἡμῶν ἔγνωσαν διὰ τοῦ κυρίου ἡμῶν Ἰησοῦ Χριστοῦ, ὅτι ἔρις ἔσται ἐπὶ τοῦ ὀνόματος τῆς ἐπισκοπῆς. Yet the words seem to be a very natural deduction from such sayings of the Lord as are preserved in Matt. xxiii. 8 ff.; xx. 20 ff. Perhaps they point to the origin of the traditional saying in Justin *Dial.* 35. See below.

(γ) In c. xv. Clement quotes a passage from Isaiah (xxix. 13) in a form different from that of the LXX. and like that in which it is found in St Mark vii. 6 (comp. Matt. xv. 8) with the single difference of ἄπεστιν for ἀπέχει. The passage is just one of those general statements which easily become moulded orally into a traditional form, and it appears to be quite insufficient to shew that Clement was dependent for it on the text of St Mark.

ii. IGNATIUS. (a) The one saying directly attributed to the Lord in the Ignatian Epistles occurs in *ad Smyrn.* iii. ὅτε πρὸς τοὺς περὶ Πέτρον ἦλθεν ἔφη αὐτοῖς· Λάβετε, ψηλαφήσατέ με, καὶ ἴδετε ὅτι οὐκ εἰμὶ δαιμόνιον ἀσώματον. This saying, which was found in part in the *Doctrine of Peter*, and the *Nazarean Gospel* (comp. *Introd. to the Study of the Gospels*, App. C. 16), is in all probability a traditional (and later) form of the words recorded in Luke xxiv. 39[1].

(β) There are several coincidences with Evangelic words which deserve to be mentioned:
ad Eph. v. || Matt. xviii. 19.
id. vi. || Matt. x. 40 (a general correspondence in sense).
ad Trall. xi. οὗτοι γὰρ οὐκ εἰσὶ φυτεία πατρός || Matt. xv. 13, πᾶσα φυτεία ἣν οὐκ ἐφύτευσεν ὁ πατήρ μου...
[*ad Rom.* vi. || Matt. xvi. 26 (an interpolation)].
ad Rom. vii. ὁ ἄρχων τοῦ αἰῶνος τούτου διαρπάσαι με βούλεται. Cf. John xvi. 11.
id. ὕδωρ ζῶν... Cf. John iv. 14; vii. 38.
id. ἄρτον θεοῦ...ὅς ἐστι σὰρξ Ἰησοῦ Χριστοῦ. Cf. John vi. 51. It is, I think, quite impossible to understand the Ignatian passage without presupposing a knowledge of the discourse recorded by St John.
ad Philad. vii. τὸ πνεῦμα...οἶδεν...πόθεν ἔρχεται καὶ ποῦ ὑπάγει καὶ τὰ κρυπτὰ ἐλέγχει. Cf. John iii. 8 (an apparent use of familiar words in a different connexion).

---

[1] I am at a loss to understand how any one who looks at the connexion in *ad Philad.* vii. can suppose that in the words 'The 'Spirit proclaimed, saying thus: Without the 'Bishop do nothing, &c.' we have 'an apo-'cryphal writing quoted as Holy Scripture' (*Supernat. Rel.* p. 278). The contrast throughout is between the natural knowledge (κατὰ σάρκα) of Ignatius and the divine Spirit by which he was moved. Ἐκραύγασα...τῷ ἐπισκόπῳ προσέχετε...μάρτυς δέ μοι ἐν ᾧ δέδεμαι ὅτι ἀπὸ σαρκὸς ἀνθρωπίνης οὐκ ἔγνων· τὸ δὲ πνεῦμα ἐκήρυσσεν λέγων τάδε· χωρὶς τοῦ ἐπισκόπου μηδὲν ποιεῖτε κ.τ.λ.

62 THE AGE OF THE APOSTOLIC FATHERS. [PART

Chap. i.

ad Smyrn. vi. ὁ χωρῶν χωρείτω. ‖ Matt. xix. 12, ὁ δυνάμενος χωρεῖν χωρείτω.
ad Polyc. i. πάντων τὰς νόσους βάσταζε ‖ Matt. viii. 17, αὐτὸς...τὰς νόσους ἐβάστασεν.
id. ii. φρόνιμος γίνου ὡς ὄφις ἐν ἅπασιν καὶ ἀκέραιος ὡς ἡ περιστερά ‖ Matt. x. 16, γίνεσθε φρόνιμοι ὡς οἱ ὄφεις καὶ ἀκέραιοι ὡς αἱ περιστεραί.

iii. POLY-
CARP.

iii. (*a*) POLYCARP, c. ii. μνημονεύοντες ὧν εἶπεν ὁ κύριος διδάσκων· μὴ κρίνετε ἵνα μὴ κριθῆτε.
ἀφίετε καὶ ἀφεθήσεται.ὑμῖν.
ἐλεεῖτε ἵνα ἐλεηθῆτε.
ᾧ μέτρῳ μετρεῖτε, ἀντιμετρηθήσεται ὑμῖν.
καὶ ὅτι μακάριοι οἱ πτωχοὶ καὶ οἱ διωκόμενοι ἕνεκεν δικαιοσύνης, ὅτι αὐτῶν ἐστὶν ἡ βασιλεία τοῦ θεοῦ.

The parallels in our Gospels are Matt. vii. 1; vi. 14 (Luke vi. 37); v. 7; Luke vi. 38 (Matt. vii. 2); Luke vi. 20 (Matt. v. 3); Matt. v. 10. The last clauses are evidently compressed in quotation from whatever source they may have been derived. The first clauses have points of resemblance with Clement's quotation (see p. 60), and more especially the introductory clause, so that Polycarp's words are probably influenced by Clement's. But at any rate the differences in order and phraseology in Clement's and Polycarp's quotations, shew conclusively that they were not derived from any one record different from our Gospels.

c. vii. αἰτούμενος τὸν παντεπόπτην θεὸν μὴ εἰσενεγκεῖν ἡμᾶς εἰς πειρασμόν, καθὼς εἶπεν ὁ κύριος· τὸ μὲν πνεῦμα πρόθυμον ἡ δὲ σὰρξ ἀσθενής ‖ Matt. vi. 13; xxvi. 41; Mark xiv. 38.

(*β*) Two coincidences of language may be noticed:
c. v. κατὰ τὴν ἀλήθειαν τοῦ κυρίου ὃς ἐγένετο διάκονος πάντων. Comp. Matt. xx. 28; Mark ix. 35.
c. vi. εἰ οὖν δεόμεθα τοῦ κυρίου ἵνα ἡμῖν ἀφῇ, ὀφείλομεν καὶ ἡμεῖς ἀφιέναι. Comp. Matt. vi. 12, 14; Luke xi. 4.

There are no supposed allusions to apocryphal writings in Polycarp.

iv. BARNA-
BAS.

iv. BARNABAS, c. iv. προσέχωμεν μήποτε ὡς γέγραπται πολλοὶ κλητοὶ ὀλίγοι δὲ ἐκλεκτοὶ εὑρεθῶμεν. ‖ Matt. xxii. 14. It is possible that this proverbial phrase introduced by the form of scriptural quotation 'it is written' may have been referred by the writer (rightly or wrongly) to some scripture of the Old Testament.

The question as to its source is beset by much difficulty. Dr Sanday, *l.c.* 71 ff., and Mr Cunningham, *l.c.* lxxxvi. f., both incline to refer the quotation to St Matthew.

c. v. τοὺς ἰδίους ἀποστόλους...ἐξελέξατο ὄντας ὑπὲρ πᾶσαν ἁμαρτίαν ἀνομωτέρους, ἵνα δείξῃ ὅτι οὐκ ἦλθε καλέσαι δικαίους ἀλλὰ ἁμαρτωλούς. ‖ Matt. ix. 13; Mark ii. 17 (εἰς μετάνοιαν is an addition in the texts of the Gospels and of Barnabas).

Other parallels have been noticed: c. iv. (Matt. xxv. 5 ff.); c. v. (Matt. xxvi. 31). Comp. Hefele, s. 233. The clause (Luke vi. 30) in c. xix. is probably an interpolation; and it seems most likely that the reference to the brazen serpent as a type of Christ was derived directly from the Old Testament, or at least not from John iii.

(c. xii.)

BARNABAS has been supposed to refer to two sayings of our Lord which are not found in our Gospels.

(*a*) c. iv. Sicut dicit filius Dei: Resistamus omni iniquitati et odio habeamus eam.

So the words stood in the Latin version; but the Greek text of ℵ reads ώς πρέπει υἱοῖς θεοῦ, so that there can be no doubt that the first clause is a corruption of *sicut decet filios Dei*. The quotation therefore disappears though Reuss still refers to the verse as an apocryphal saying of Christ (*Hist. du Canon*, 26 n.).

(β) c. vii. οὕτω, φησί, οἱ θέλοντές με ἰδεῖν καὶ ἄψασθαί μου τῆς βασιλείας ὀφείλουσι θλιβέντες καὶ παθόντες λαβεῖν με.

These words appear to be a free reminiscence of the saying contained in Matt. xvi. 24, compared with Acts xiv. 22. No trace of them, as far as I know, occurs elsewhere.

In the passage, c. vi. λέγει κύριος· ἰδοὺ ποιήσω τὰ ἔσχατα ὡς τὰ πρῶτα, the context, no less than the phrase λέγει κύριος, shews that the reference is to some passage of the Old Testament: *e.g.* Ezek. xxxvi. 11.

An examination of these passages will confirm what has been said generally, pp. 51 f. The result may be briefly summed up in the following propositions:

1. No Evangelic reference in the Apostolic Fathers can be referred certainly to a written record.

2. It appears most probable from the form of the quotations that they were derived from oral tradition.

3. No quotation contains any element which is not substantially preserved in our Gospels.

4. When the text given differs from the text of our Gospels, it represents a later form of the Evangelic tradition.

5. The text of St Matthew corresponds more nearly than the other synoptic texts with the quotations and references as a whole.

Chap. i.

NOTE (2).

ON THE 'TEACHING OF THE TWELVE APOSTLES.'

The 'Teaching of the Twelve Apostles[1]' offers several points of peculiar interest in regard to the history of the writings of the New Testament; but their exact significance depends in a great measure upon the view which is taken of the document itself. There can, I think, be little doubt that the two parts of which it consists, 'The two ways' (cc. i.—vi.), and the brief 'Manual of Christian Practice' (cc. vii.—xvi.), are distinct in origin. The first part appears to be an adaptation of an earlier Jewish 'rule'[2]; and the latter an appendix which was added to this particular revision of the Jewish tract, or traditional lesson. This Christian revision of 'The two ways' and the Manual appear to belong in their original form to the first century; but it seems to be no less clear, that the work has undergone some revision, and it is extremely difficult to fix the date of the present text, though it belongs substantially to the earliest post-apostolic age.

The document composed of two distinct elements.

[1] Διδαχὴ τῶν δώδεκα ἀποστόλων with a secondary title Διδαχὴ κυρίου διὰ τῶν δώδεκα ἀποστόλων τοῖς ἔθνεσιν. The Manual was first published by Philoth. Bryennios Abp of Nicomedia in 1883. A full account of the extensive literature which has been called out by it is given in Dr Schaff's edition (New York, Edinburgh), 1885. It appears to have been known in various forms to [Clement of Alexandria], Eusebius (infr. p. 419), Athanasius (p. 555, Ap. D, xiv), Nicephorus (p. 562, Ap. D. xix). Comp. Rufinus p. 570, Ap. D, xxv; *Codd. Baroc. Coislin*, p. 559, Ap. D. xvii.
[2] Comp. Dr Taylor, *The Teaching of the Twelve Apostles*, Lect. i. 1886.

Chap. i.

Biblical quotations.

The document contains two express quotations from the Old Testament, both in the latter part[1]; and in the same part there are four distinct references to a written Gospel[2]. One phrase, also found verbally in St Matthew, is quoted with the words 'the Lord hath said'[3]. With these exceptions words which we find in Scripture are silently incorporated into the writing without any mark that they are borrowed from written sources[4].

The extent of the witness to Apostolic writings.

If the references to the written Gospel are supposed to form part of the original document, they are the earliest witness to an authoritative Evangelic text. But their form and the manner of their introduction make it likely that they belong to a later revision, when they were added as explanatory notes to statements which were at first made generally[5]. But, however this may be, the Evangelic words, which certainly belong to the earliest elements of the writings, contain coincidences of language with peculiarities of the Gospels of St Matthew and St Luke[6]. There are also some striking resemblances in the Eucharistic prayers to forms of expression characteristic of St John. Other phrases recal sentences in the Epistles of St Jude, St Peter, and St Paul[7]; and while it is not possible to conclude from such parallelisms that the writer was acquainted with the Epistles, they indicate the substantial unity of early Christian tradition. It cannot be surprising from the character of the document that it contains no reference to any fact of the Lord's Life; the references are to 'Oracles of the Lord' in the narrower sense of the phrase.

The text of the Evangelic words.

The most interesting features in the text of the Evangelic parallels are (1) the form of the summary of the Law, and (2) the Doxology at the close of the Lord's Prayer. The summary: πρῶτον ἀγαπήσεις τὸν θεὸν τὸν ποιήσαντά σε· δεύτερον τὸν πλησίον σου ὡς σεαυτόν· πάντα δὲ ὅσα ἐὰν θελήσῃς μὴ γενέσθαι σοί, καὶ σὺ ἄλλῳ μὴ ποίει (c. i. 2) seems to be independent of and earlier than the Evangelic summary (Matt. xxii. 37; vii. 12). The *negative* form of the last clause is characteristically Jewish: the positive is no less characteristically the teaching of the Lord (comp. Dr Taylor, *l.c.* pp. 8 ff.). The Doxology ὅτι σοῦ ἐστιν ἡ δύναμις καὶ ἡ δόξα εἰς τοὺς αἰῶνας (c. vii. 2) is an important link in the history of the Liturgical addition to the text of

---

[1] c. xiv. 3 αὕτη γάρ ἐστιν ἡ ῥηθεῖσα ὑπὸ κυρίου [θυσία]· ἐν παντὶ τόπῳ...Mal. i. 11, 14.
c. xvi. 7 ὡς ἐρρέθη Ἥξει ὁ κύριος...Zech. xiv. 5.

[2] See note 5.

[3] c. ix. 5 περὶ τούτου εἴρηκεν ὁ κύριος Μὴ δῶτε τὸ ἅγιον τοῖς κυσί. Matt. vii. 6. The words are peculiar to St Matthew.

[4] The passage in c. iv. 5 appears to be borrowed from Ecclus. iv. 31. There are no other verbal coincidences with the Old Testament.

[5] c. viii. μηδὲ προσεύχεσθε ὡς οἱ ὑποκριταί· ἀλλ' [ὡς ἐκέλευσεν ὁ κύριος ἐν τῷ εὐαγγελίῳ] οὕτω προσεύχεσθε Πάτερ ἡμῶν... Comp. Matt. vi. 5, 9.
c. xi. περὶ δὲ τῶν ἀποστόλων καὶ προφητῶν [κατὰ τὸ δόγμα τοῦ εὐαγγελίου] οὕτω ποιήσατε...
c. xv. ἐλέγχετε δὲ ἀλλήλους μὴ ἐν ὀργῇ ἀλλ' ἐν εἰρήνῃ, [ὡς ἔχετε ἐν τῷ εὐαγγελίῳ] καὶ παντὶ ἀστοχοῦντι κατὰ τοῦ ἑτέρου, μηδεὶς λαλείτω... [τὰς δὲ εὐχὰς ὑμῶν καὶ τὰς ἐλεημοσύνας, καὶ πάσας τὰς πράξεις οὕτω ποιήσατε ὡς ἔχετε ἐν τῷ εὐαγγελίῳ τοῦ κυρίου ἡμῶν]. The corresponding clauses in the *Apostolical Constitutions* are (c. viii.) ὡς ὁ κύριος

ἡμῖν ἐν τῷ εὐαγγελίῳ διετάξατο (*Const. Ap.* vii. 24), and (c. xv.) πάντα τὰ προστεταγμένα ὑμῶν ὑπὸ τοῦ κυρίου φυλάξατε. The eleventh chapter is omitted in the *Constitutions*.

[6] *e.g.* c. iii. 7 ἴσθι πραΰς. ἐπεὶ οἱ πραεῖς κληρονομήσουσι τὴν γῆν. Matt. v. 5.
c. i. 5 παντὶ τῷ αἰτοῦντί σε δίδου καὶ μὴ ἀπαίτει. Lc. vi. 30.
See also for clear parallels with St Matthew i. 3, 4, 5; vii. 1; viii. 2; xi. 7; xiii. 1. In other cases there seem to be more or less certain references to Evangelic words: xiv. 2; xv. 4; xvi. 1, 3, 4, 5.
The writing agrees with the narrative of St Luke in placing the distribution of the Cup first: c. ix. 2. Comp. Lk. xxii. 14 f.

[7] c. ii. 7 οὓς μὲν ἐλέγξεις, περὶ δὲ ὧν προσεύξῃ, οὓς δὲ ἀγαπήσεις ὑπὲρ τὴν ψυχήν σου. Comp. Jude 22.
c. i. 4 ἀπέχε τῶν σαρκικῶν καὶ κοσμικῶν ἐπιθυμιῶν. Comp. 1 Pet. ii. 11.
c. iii. 1 φεῦγε ἀπὸ παντὸς πονηροῦ καὶ ἀπὸ παντὸς ὁμοίου αὐτοῦ. Comp. 1 Thess. v. 22. See also c. xvi. 4: 2 Thess. ii. 3 ff.; c. iv. 8: Rom. xv. 25; c. x. 16: 1 Cor. xvi. 22.

the Gospel. The *Teaching* contains six other Doxologies in Liturgical passages (1) σοὶ ἡ δόξα εἰς τοὺς αἰῶνας (ix. 2, 3; x. 2, 4); (2) σοῦ ἐστιν ἡ δόξα καὶ ἡ δύναμις διὰ Ἰησοῦ Χριστοῦ εἰς τοὺς αἰῶνας (ix. 4); and once again σοῦ ἐστιν ἡ δύναμις καὶ ἡ δόξα εἰς τοὺς αἰῶνας (x. 5), the same form as that added to the Lord's Prayer, occurs at the close of the Thanksgiving over the Bread (κλάσμα) in the Eucharist. The text of the Prayer has also two variations from St Matthew not found elsewhere: ὁ ἐν τῷ οὐρανῷ, τὴν ὀφειλήν (Matt. xviii. 32). This fact points to the conclusion that the Prayer itself was not originally taken from a written text of St Matthew. The text in the *Constitutions* (vii. 24) is conformed in these points to the text of St Matthew, and the Doxology is given there in its full form.

The adaptations of Evangelic language in viii. 1, xiv. 2, to later circumstances is also worthy of notice, as shewing how quickly usage obscured the original force of the Lord's words, how pure, to express the thought differently, the Gospels are from the admixture of foreign elements which from the earliest time affected the external tradition of their substance.

The command in St Matt. vi. 16 ὅταν δὲ νηστεύητε, μὴ γίνεσθε ὡς οἱ ὑποκριταί becomes c. viii. 1, αἱ δὲ νηστεῖαι ὑμῶν μὴ ἔστωσαν μετὰ τῶν ὑποκριτῶν. The moral direction, that is, as to the character of fasting is replaced by a formal direction as to the times of fasting, 'not on Mondays or Thursdays' (comp. Epiph. *Hær.* xvi. 1). And again an injunction moulded on Jewish practice in Matt. v. 23 f. is fitted to the Christian 'Sacrifice' in c. xiv. 2.

CHAPTER II.

THE AGE OF THE GREEK APOLOGISTS.

A.D. 120—170.

Οὐ σιωπῆς μόνον τὸ ἔργον, ἀλλὰ μεγέθους ἐστὶν ὁ Χριστιανισμός.

IGNATIUS.

Chap. ii.
The wide scope of the Christian Literature of this period

THE writings of the Apostolic age were all moulded in the same form, and derived from the same relation of Christian life. As they represented the mutual intercourse of believers, so they rested on the foundation of a common rule and shewed the peculiarities of a common dialect. The literature of the next age was widely different both in scope and character[1]. It included almost every form of prose composition—letters, chronicles, essays, apologies, visions, tales—and answered to the manifold bearings of Christianity on the world[2].

occasioned by the new relation of the Church to the Empire,

The Church had then to maintain its ground amid systematic persecution, organized heresies, and philosophic controversy. The name of the Christian had already become a by-word[3]; and it was evident that they were free alike from Jewish superstition and Gentile polytheism[4]: they were no longer sheltered by the old title of Jews, and it became needful that they

---

[1] Cf. Möhler, ss. 179 ff.

[2] It is probable that some of the Christian parts of the Sibylline Oracles (Libb. VI., VII.) also fall within this period. Cf. Friedlieb, *Oracula Sibyllina*, Einleit. ss. lxxi., lii.
Very little is known of the prophecies of Hystaspes. Cf. Lücke, *Comm. ü. d. Schriften des Ev. Johannes*, IV. I. ss. 45 f.

[3] Just. Mart. *Ap.* I. 4. (p. 10, n. 4. Otto.)

[4] *Ep. ad Diogn.* i.: ὁρῶ...ὑπερεσπουδακότα σε τὴν θεοσέβειαν τῶν Χριστιανῶν μαθεῖν...τίνι τε Θεῷ πεποιθότες, καὶ πῶς θρησκεύοντες...οὔτε τοὺς νομιζομένους ὑπὸ τῶν Ἑλλήνων θεοὺς λογίζονται, οὔτε τὴν Ἰουδαίων δεισιδαιμονίαν φυλάσσουσι...The whole passage is very interesting as shewing how the object and form of Christian worship, and the character of the Christian life, would strike a thoughtful man at the time.

should give an account of the faith for which they sought protection. The Apostolic tradition was insufficient to silence or condemn false teachers who had been trained in the schools of Athens or Alexandria; but now that truth was left to men it was upheld by wisdom. New champions were raised up to meet the emergency; and some of these did not scruple to maintain the doctrines of Christianity in the garb of philosophers.

Chap. ii. to Heresies, and to Philosophy.

But although the entire literature of the age was thus varied, the fragments of it which are left scarcely do more than witness to its extent. The letter to Diognetus, the Clementine homilies, the Testaments of the twelve Patriarchs, and some of the writings of Justin, alone survive in their original form. In addition to these there are two Latin translations of the Shepherd of Hermas as well as a large fragment of the original Greek, a Syriac translation of the Apology of Melito, and a series of precious quotations from lost books, preserved chiefly by the industry of Eusebius[1]. The *Exposition* of Papias, the Treatises of Justin and Agrippa Castor against Heresies, the numerous works of Melito with the exception of the Apology, the Chronicles of Hegesippus, have perished, and with them the most natural and direct sources of information on the history of this period of the Church.

The remains of it however are scanty.

It does not however seem to have been a mere accident which preserved the writings of Justin. As the Apologists were the truest representatives of the age, so was he in many respects the best type of the natural character of the Greek Apologist. For him philosophy was truth, reason a spiritual power, Christianity the fulness of both. The Apostolic Fathers exhibit their faith in its inherent energy; their successors shew in

Yet Justin represents the character of the Greek Apologist, and so of the age.

[1] Collected by Routh, *Reliquiæ Sacræ* (Ed. 2, Oxon. 1846).

what way it was the satisfaction of the deepest wants of humanity—the sum of all 'knowledge;' it was reserved for the Latin Apologists to apprehend its independent claims, and establish its right to supplant, as well as to fulfil what was partial and vague in earlier systems. The time was not ripe for this when Justin wrote, for there is a natural order in the development of truth. As Christianity was shewn to be the true completion of Judaism before the Church was divided from the synagogue; so it was well that it should be clearly set forth as the centre to which old philosophies converged before it was declared to supersede them. In each case the fulfilment and interpretation of the old was the groundwork and beginning of the new. The pledge of the future lay in the satisfaction of the past.

The first work of the period—the settlement of the relation of Christianity to Heathendom.

This then was one great work of the time, that Apologists should proclaim Christianity to be the Divine answer to the questionings of Heathendom, as well as the antitype to the Law, and the hope of the Prophets. To a great extent the task was independent of the direct use of Scripture. Those who discharged it had to deal with the thoughts, and not with the words of the Apostles—with the facts, and not with the records of Christ's life. Even the later Apologists abstained from quoting Scripture in their addresses to heathen; and the practice was still more alien from the object and position of the earliest[1]. The arguments of philosophy and history were brought forward first, that men might be gradually familiarized to the light; the use of Scripture was for a while deferred (*dilatæ paulisper divinæ lectiones*), that they might not be blinded by the sudden sight of its unclouded glory[2].

[1] Justin's use of the *prophecies* of the Old Testament is no exception to the rule; but this will be noticed in § 7.
[2] Lactant. *Instit.* v. 4.

I.] THE AGE OF THE GREEK APOLOGISTS. 67

The recognition of Christianity as a revelation which had not only a general, but also in some sense a special message for the heathen was co-ordinate with its final separation from the Mosaic ritual[1]. This separation was the second great work of the period. It is difficult to trace the progress of its consummation, though the result was the firm establishment of the Catholic Church. But by the immediate reaction which accompanied it one type of Apostolic Christianity was brought out with great clearness, without which the circle of its secondary developments would have been incomplete. The old party *of the Circumcision* once again rose up to check the revolution which was on the eve of accomplishment. Yet the conflict which was then carried on was not the repetition, but the sequel of that of the Apostolic age[2]. The great crisis out of which it sprang impressed it with a peculiar character. The Christians of Jerusalem had clung to their ancient law, till their national hopes seemed to be crushed for ever by the building of Ælia, and the establishment of a Gentile Church within the Holy City. Then at length men saw that they were

Chap. ii.

The second work of the period—the separation of Christianity from Judaism.

A reaction.

The crisis by which this was brought about.

[1] Just. Mart. *Ap.* I. 46: Οἱ μετὰ λόγου βιώσαντες Χριστιανοί εἰσι κἂν ἄθεοι ἐνομίσθησαν, οἷον ἐν Ἕλλησι μὲν Σωκράτης καὶ Ἡράκλειτος καὶ οἱ ὅμοιοι αὐτοῖς, ἐν βαρβάροις δὲ Ἀβραάμ...Cf. *Ap.* II. 13.

[2] Some modern writers have confounded together the different steps by which the distinctions of Jew and Gentile were removed in the Christian Church. Since it is of great importance to a right understanding of the early history of Christianity that they should be clearly distinguished, it may not be amiss to mention them here:

1. The admission of Gentiles (in the first instance εὐσεβεῖς) to the Christian Church. Acts x., xi.

2. The freedom of Gentile converts from the Ceremonial Law. Acts xv.

3. The indifference of the Ceremonial Law for Jewish converts. Gal. ii. 14—16; Acts xxi. 20—26.

4. The incompatibility of Judaism with Christianity.

The first three—that is the essential—principles are recognised in Scripture; the last, which introduces no new element, is evolved in the history of the Church. This is an instance of the true 'Development,' which organises, but does not create.

The first three stages are fully discussed by Bp Lightfoot, *Galatians*, Essay iii. pp. 276 ff.

already in the new age—*the world to come:* they saw that *the kingdom of heaven*, as distinguished from the typical kingdom of Israel, was now set up; and it seemed that the Gospel of St Paul was to be the common law of its citizens. Under the pressure of these circumstances the Judaizing party naturally made a last effort to regain their original power. It was only possible to maintain what had ceased to be national by asserting that it was universal. The discussions of the first age were thus reproduced in form, but they had a wider bearing. The struggle was not for independence but for dominion. The Gentile Christians no longer claimed tolerance, but supremacy. They had been established on an equality with the Jewish Church; but now, when they were on the point of becoming paramount, the spirit which had opposed St Paul was roused to its greatest activity.

Apart from heretical writings the effect of this movement may be traced under various forms in the contemporary literature. The orthodox members of the Hebrew Churches were not uninfluenced by the general movement which agitated the body to which they belonged. They were impelled to write, and their activity took a characteristic direction. As the Apologists represent the Greek element in the Church, so the Jewish is represented by the chroniclers Papias and Hegesippus. The tendency to that which is purely rational and ideal is thus contrasted with that towards the sensuous and the material[1].

In one respect however Christian literature still pre-

[1] The *Clementines* stand in a peculiar position as the embodiment of individual rather than popular opinion; and it is perhaps due to this fact that they have been preserved. The *Testaments of the Twelve Patri-archs* are in the main orthodox in doctrine and recognise the authority of St Paul, while they contain at the same time a very remarkable estimate of the priestly claims of Levi. See below.

served the same form as in the Apostolic age. It was wholly Greek: the work of the Latin churches was as yet to be wrought in silence[1]. It is the more important to notice this, because the permanent characteristics of the national literatures of Greece and Rome reappear with powerful effect in patristic writings. On the one side there is universality, freedom, large sympathy, deep feeling: on the other there is individuality, system, order, logic. The tendency of the one mind is towards truth, of the other towards law[2]. In the end, when the objects are the highest truth and the deepest law, they will achieve the same results, but the process will be different. This difference is not without its bearing on the history of the New Testament. From their very constitution Greek writers would be inclined in the first instance to witness, not to the Canon of Scripture, but to the substance of its teaching.

§ 1. *Papias*[3].

The first and last names of this period—Papias and of Hegesippus—belong to the early Christian chroniclers, who have been taken to represent the Judaizing party of the time. Papias, a friend of Polycarp, was Bishop of Hierapolis in Phrygia[4] in the early part of the second century. According to some accounts he was a disciple of the Apostle St John[5]; but Eusebius, who was ac-

---

[1] Of the *Greek* literature of the Italian Churches we shall speak hereafter.

[2] As a familiar instance of these characteristic differences we may refer to the marked distinction in form and tone between the Nicene Creed and the Latin Exposition of the Creed *Quicunque vult;* or between the Eastern and Western types of the same Creed (*Nicene Creed, Apostles' Creed*).

[3] Papias has been made the subject of exhaustive articles by Bp Lightfoot: *Contemporary Review*, Aug. 1867; Aug. Oct. 1875.

[4] This follows from Hieron. *de Virr. Ill.* 18; Papias...Hierapolitanus Episcopus *in Asia;* and also from a comparison of Euseb. *H. E.* III. 36, 39, 31.

[5] This is maintained by Routh, I. p. 22, sqq. On the other hand, cf. Davidson, *Introd.* I. 425, sqq.

Chap. ii.

The character of his See.

quainted with his writings, affirms that his teacher was the Presbyter and not the Apostle; and the same conclusion appears to follow from his own language[1].

A church was formed at Hierapolis in very early times[2]; and it afterwards became the residence of the Apostle Philip and his daughters[3], whose tomb was shewn there in the third century[4]. This fact seems to point to some close connexion with the churches of Judæa; but the city was also remarkable in another respect. The Epistle of St Paul to the neighbouring church of Colossæ proves that even in the Apostolic age the characteristic extravagance of the province—the home of the Galli and Corybantes—was already manifested in the corruption of Christianity; and it is not unreasonable to attribute the extreme Chiliasm of Papias to the same influence[5].

---

[1] Euseb. *H. E.* III. 39. 'I used 'to inquire,' he says, 'when I met 'any who had been acquainted with 'the Elders, of the teaching of the 'Elders—what Andrew or Peter said '(εἶπεν)...or John or Matthew...or 'any other of the Lord's disciples; as 'what Aristion and the Elder (Pres-'byter) John, the Lord's disciples, 'say (λέγουσιν).' The natural interpretation of these words can only be that the Apostles—Elders in the highest sense, 1 Pet. v. 1—were already dead when Papias began his investigations, and that he distinguished two of the name of John, one an Apostle, and another the Presbyter who was alive at that time. Dr Milligan has stated very ably all that can be urged in favour of identifying the Apostle and the Presbyter (*Journ. of Sac. Lit.* Oct. 1867), but his arguments fail to convince me.

[2] Coloss. iv. 13. See Bp Lightfoot, *l. c.* It is said that Papias suffered martyrdom (Steph. Gobar. ap. Cave, I. 29) at Pergamum in the time of Aurelius (A.D. 164), under whom Polycarp and Justin Martyr also suffered (*Chron. Alex. l. c.*); but this is more than doubtful. See Lightfoot, *Colossians*, p. 48, n.

His work was probably written at a late period of his life (c. 140—150), since he speaks of those who had been disciples of the Apostles as now dead. His inquiries were made some time before he wrote (ἀνέκρινον), and he had treasured up the tradition in his memory (καλῶς ἐμνημόνευσα). The necessity for such a work as his would not indeed be felt, as Rettig has well observed, till the first generation after the Apostles had passed away. Cf. Thiersch, *Versuch u. s. w.* s. 438.

[3] Euseb. *H. E.* III. 31. Cf. Routh, II. 25.

[4] Euseb. *H. E.* III. 31, on the authority of Caius.

[5] The peculiar form which this Chiliasm took is seen best in the narrative given on the authority of 'presbyters who saw John the dis-

Since he stood on the verge of the first age Papias naturally set a high value on the Evangelic traditions still current in the Church. These he preserved, as he tells us, with zeal and accuracy; and afterwards embodied them in five books, entitled 'An Exposition of 'Oracles of the Lord' (Λογίων κυριακῶν ἐξήγησις¹). There is however no reason to suppose that he intended to compose a Gospel; and the very name of his treatise implies the contrary. The traditions which he collected do not appear to have formed the staple of his book; but they were introduced as illustrative of his explanation. 'Moreover,' he says, 'I must tell you that I shall 'not scruple to place side by side with my interpreta-'tions all that I ever rightly learnt from the elders and 'rightly remembered, solemnly affirming that it is true².'

Chap. ii.
An account of his work.

His own description of it.

'ciple of the Lord' by Irenæus. 'The 'days will come,' thus they represented the Lord teaching, 'in which 'vines will spring up, each having 'ten thousand stems, and on one stem 'ten thousand branches, and on each 'branch ten thousand shoots, and on 'each shoot ten thousand clusters, 'and on each cluster ten thousand 'grapes, and each grape when pressed 'shall give five and twenty measures 'of wine. And when any of the saints 'shall have taken hold of one cluster, 'another shall cry out: I am a better 'cluster, take me, through me bless 'the Lord.'...'These things,' Irenæus goes on to say, 'Papias also tes-'tifies in the fourth of his books, and 'added moreover: these things are 'credible to believers. And when 'Judas the traitor believed not, and 'asked *How then will such produc-*'*tions be brought about by the Lord?* 'he relates that the Lord said, *They* '*shall see who shall come to those* '*times.*' (Iren. v. 33.) It is not difficult to see the true Evangelic element which lies at the bottom of this strange tradition.

¹ Pap. ap. Euseb. *H. E.* III. 39: οὐκ ὀκνήσω δέ σοι καὶ ὅσα ποτὲ παρὰ τῶν πρεσβυτέρων καλῶς ἔμαθον καὶ καλῶς ἐμνημόνευσα, συγκατατάξαι ταῖς ἑρμηνείαις, διαβεβαιούμενος ὑπὲρ αὐτῶν ἀλήθειαν, κ.τ.λ. It is important to notice that the title is without the definite article, just as Πράξεις ἀποστόλων.

² In accordance with this view of Papias' book we find him mentioned with Clement, Pantænus, and Ammonius, as 'one of the ancient In-'terpreters (ἐξηγητῶν) who agreed to 'understand the Hexaemeron as re-'ferring to Christ and the Church' (fr. ix., x.). Compare also Euseb. *H. E.* v. 8, with reference to Iren. IV. 27 and similar passages, ἐξηγήσεις αὐτοῦ [ἀποστολικοῦ τινὸς πρεσβυτέρου] θείων γραφῶν παρατίθεται.

The passage quoted by Irenæus from 'the Elders' (v. *ad f.*) may probably be taken as a specimen of his style of interpretation. '[At 'the time of the restoration of all 'things,] as the presbyters say, they 'who have been held worthy of life 'in heaven shall go thither, and

Chap. ii.
It was expository, and not narrative.

The apologetic tone of the sentence, its construction (δέ), the mention of his interpretations (αἱ ἑρμηνεῖαι), convey the idea that his reference to tradition might seem unnecessary to some, and that it was in fact only a secondary object:—in other words, they imply that there were already recognised records of the teaching of Christ which he sought to expound. For this purpose he might well go back to the Apostles themselves, and 'make it his business to inquire what they said,' believing 'that the information which he could draw from 'books was not so profitable as that which was pre-'served in a living tradition[1].'

'others shall enjoy the indulgence of
'Paradise, and others shall possess
'the splendour of the City; for every
'where the Saviour shall be seen as
'they who see Him shall be worthy.
'This distinction of dwelling, they
'taught, exists between those who
'brought forth a hundred-fold, and
'those who brought forth sixty-fold,
'and those who brought forth thirty-
'fold (Matt. xiii. 8)...and it was for
'this reason the Lord said that *in*
'*His Father's house* (ἐν τοῖς τοῦ Πα-
'τρός) *are many mansions* (John xiv.
'2).' Indeed, from the similar mode of introducing the story of the vine, which is afterwards referred to Papias (p. 70, note 5), it is reasonable to conjecture that this interpretation is one from Papias' *Exposition.* The passage changes from the direct to the oblique form; but no scholar, I imagine, would doubt for a moment that the second part, where I have marked the oblique construction by introducing 'they taught,' is a continuation of the quotation ὡς οἱ πρεσβύτεροι λέγουσι, τότε οἱ μὲν...χωρήσουσιν, οἱ δέ...οἱ δέ...εἶναι δὲ τὴν διαστολὴν ταύτην...τῶν...καρποφορούντων ὧν οἱ μέν...οἱ δέ...οἱ δέ...καὶ διὰ τοῦτο εἰρηκέναι τὸν Κύριον... I should not have thought it necessary to call attention to this obvious point if a critic had not quoted a number of passages with διὰ τοῦτο (propter hoc) and the *indicative* to shew that this *oblique* sentence is a comment of Irenæus.

This view which I have given of the object of the work of Papias is supported with illustrations by Bp Lightfoot (*Cont. Rev.* Aug. 1867, pp. 405, 6, *id.* Aug 1875, 399 ff.); and it is indeed surprising that the account of it should have received any other interpretation.

'The books' of which Papias speaks may have been some of the strange mystical commentaries current at very early times among the Simonians and Valentinians. See Lightfoot, *ll. cc.* There is not the slightest ground for supposing that he referred to our Gospels or records like them.

[1] Eusebius, *l. c.* gives some account of the traditional stories which he collected; among others he mentions that of 'a woman accused be-'fore our Lord of many sins,' generally identified with the disputed *pericope,* John vii. 53—viii. 11. It is not superfluous to observe that Eusebius does *not* say that Papias derived this narrative from the Gospel according to the Hebrews (*Supern. Rel.* I. p. 426), or that he used that Gospel

Papias, in other words, claimed for himself the office of expositor and not of historian. 'Oracles of the Lord' are presupposed as the basis of his work, and not for the first time set forth in it. So far, therefore, from it being possible to deduce from the object of Papias in undertaking the Exposition that he was unacquainted with any authoritative Evangelic records, his purpose seems to be unintelligible unless there were definite and familiar narrations which called for such illustration as could be provided. The fragments which remain can in fact be brought into a natural connexion with passages of our Gospels; and a careful consideration of the exact title shews the limit of the Exposition. It made no claim to completeness. It was 'an Exposition of Oracles 'of the Lord' and not 'of the Oracles of the Lord'— such a summary (τὰ λόγια) as, for instance, St Matthew composed.

Chap. ii.

This conclusion, which we have drawn from the apparent aim of Papias' work, is strongly confirmed by the direct testimony which he bears to our Gospels. It has been inferred already that some Gospel was current in his time; he tells us that the Gospels of St Matthew and St Mark were so. Of the former he says: 'Mat- 'thew composed the oracles in Hebrew; and each one 'interpreted them as he was able[1].' The form of the

Papias' testimony to the Gospels.

St Matthew.

at all. Indeed if Eusebius had known that Papias derived the narrative from this particular source, he would hardly have said 'a narrative which the Gos- 'pel according to the Hebrews con- 'tains' (ἱστορίαν...ἣν τὸ καθ' Ἑβραίους εὐαγγέλιον περιέχει). To these must be added the account of Judas (*fr.* iii. Routh).

[1] Euseb. *l. c.*: Ματθαῖος μὲν οὖν Ἑβραΐδι διαλέκτῳ τὰ λόγια συνεγράψατο· ἡρμήνευσε δ' αὐτὰ ὡς ἦν δυνατὸς ἕκαστος. It is difficult to give the full meaning of τὰ λόγια, τὰ κυ-

ριακὰ λόγια—the Gospel—the sum of the words and works of the Lord.

The sense, I believe, would be best expressed in this passage by the translation 'Matthew composed his *Gospel* in Hebrew,' giving to the word its necessary notion of scriptural authority. Cf. Acts vii. 38; Rom. iii. 2; Heb. v. 12; 1 Pet. iv. 11. Polyc. *ad Phil.* c. vii.; Clem. *ad Cor.* I. 19, 53.

Davidson (*Introd.* I. 65, sqq.) has reviewed the other interpretations of the word.

sentence (μὲν οὖν) would seem to introduce this statement as the result of some inquiry, and it may perhaps be referred to the presbyter John; but all that needs to be particularly remarked is that when Papias wrote, the Aramaic Gospel of St Matthew was already accessible to Greek readers: the time was then past when each one was his own interpreter[1].

The account which he gives of the Gospel of St Mark is full of interest: 'This also,' he writes, 'the Elder '[John] used to say. Mark, having become Peter's in-'terpreter, wrote accurately all that he remembered[2]; 'though he did not [record] in order that which was 'either said or done by Christ. For he neither heard 'the Lord, nor followed Him; but subsequently, as I

---

[1] It has been argued that this statement of Papias cannot be used to establish the authority of our Canonical St Matthew for two reasons: (1) Papias speaks only of a Hebrew Gospel; and (2) the description cannot apply to the present Gospel.
1. As to the first objection, it is enough to say that Eusebius, who had the full text of Papias before him, evidently understood the words to apply to the original form of our Greek Gospel; and that the long chain of writers who affirm the Hebrew original of St Matthew accept the present Greek text as apostolic without the least doubt. It is idle to conjecture how or by whom the translation or reproduction was made. That such a translation or reproduction would be almost inevitable is shewn by the experience of all writers in bilingual countries like Palestine. Comp. *Introd. to the Study of the Gospels*, p. 209, note.
2. It has been shewn that the use of τὰ λόγια for 'the Scriptures' generally is fully established; and I am not aware that λόγια can be used in the sense of λόγοι 'discourses.'
Comp. Lightfoot, *l. c.* 410 f.

The form of the sentence (ἡρμή-νευσε δέ) proves, as has been remarked above, that at the time when Papias wrote this necessity for private translation had ceased to exist. There was then, it is implied, an acknowledged representation of St Matthew's work.

[2] The ἐμνημόνευσεν here and ἀπε-μνημόνευσεν below are ambiguous. They may mean either 'remembered' or 'related.' In the latter case the sense would be that Mark 're-corded all that *Peter* related.' The change of subject would be abrupt, but is not unexampled. On the other hand, Papias uses the same word μνημονεύειν elsewhere in the sense 'to remember,' where there can be no doubt as to its meaning. It is perhaps worthy of notice that in the Clementine Recognitions St Peter himself is represented as fixing by diligent effort in his own mind the words of Christ: 'In consuetudine 'habui verba Domini mei, quæ ab 'ipso audieram, revocare ad memo-'riam...ut evigilans ad ea et singula 'quæque recolens ac retexens possim 'memoriter retinere.' (*Recogn.* ii. 1.) See p. 71, n. 1.

'said, [attached himself to] Peter, who used to frame 'his teaching to meet the [immediate] wants [of his 'hearers]; and not as making a connected narrative of 'the Lord's discourses. So Mark committed no error, 'as he wrote down some particulars just as he recalled 'them to mind. For he took heed to one thing—to 'omit none of the facts that he heard, and to state 'nothing falsely in [his narrative of] them¹.'

It has however been argued that the Gospel here described cannot be the Canonical Gospel of St Mark, since that shews at least as clear an order as the other Gospels. On this hypothesis we must seek for the original record of which John spoke in 'the Preaching 'of Peter' (κήρυγμα Πέτρου) or some similar work². In short, we must suppose that two different books were current under the same name in the times of Papias and Irenæus—that in the interval, which was less than fifty years, the older document had passed entirely into oblivion, or at least wholly lost its first title—that this substitution of the one book for the other was so secret that there is not the slightest trace of the time, the motive, the mode, of its accomplishment, and so complete that Irenæus, Tertullian, Clement, Origen, and Eusebius, applied to the later Gospel what was really only true of that which it had replaced³. And all this

Objection from his description of St Mark's Gospel.

Its consequences.

---

¹ Euseb. *l. c.*: καὶ τοῦτο ὁ πρεσβύτερος ἔλεγε· Μάρκος μὲν ἑρμηνευτὴς Πέτρου γενόμενος ὅσα ἐμνημόνευσεν ἀκριβῶς ἔγραψεν, οὐ μέντοι τάξει τὰ ὑπὸ τοῦ Χριστοῦ ἢ λεχθέντα ἢ πραχθέντα· οὔτε γὰρ ἤκουσε τοῦ Κυρίου οὔτε παρηκολούθησεν αὐτῷ. ὕστερον δὲ, ὡς ἔφην, Πέτρῳ, ὃς πρὸς τὰς χρείας ἐποιεῖτο τὰς διδασκαλίας, ἀλλ' οὐχ ὥσπερ σύνταξιν τῶν Κυριακῶν ποιούμενος λόγων· ὥστε οὐδὲν ἥμαρτε Μάρκος οὕτως ἔνια γράψας ὡς ἀπεμνημόνευσεν· ἑνὸς γὰρ ἐποιήσατο πρόνοιαν, τοῦ μηδὲν ὧν ἤκουσε παραλιπεῖν ἢ ψεύσασθαί τι ἐν αὐτοῖς.

Burton and Heinichen rightly read λόγων, for which Routh has λογίων. I do not think that λογίων could stand in such a sense. As the word occurs again directly, and was used in the title of Papias' book, the error was natural.

² Schwegler, I. 458 ff.; Baur, *Kritische Untersuchungen*, 538 f.

³ Iren. III. 1. 1; Tertull. *adv. Marc.* IV. 5; Clem. Alex. ap. Euseb.

Chap. ii.

How we must understand his words.

must be believed, because it is assumed that John could not have spoken of our present Gospel as not arranged 'in order.' But it would surely be far more reasonable to conclude that he was mistaken in his criticism than to admit an explanation burdened with such a series of improbabilities[1]. There is however another solution of the difficulty which seems preferable. The Gospel of St Mark is not a complete Life of Christ, but simply a memoir of 'some events' in it. It is not a chronological biography, but simply a collection of facts which seemed suited to the wants of a particular audience. St Mark had no personal acquaintance with the events which he recorded to enable him to place them in their natural order, but was wholly dependent on St Peter; and the special object of the Apostle excluded the idea of a complete narrative. The sequence observed in his teaching was moral, and not historical. That the arrangement of the other Synoptic Evangelists very nearly coincides with that of St Mark is nothing to the point: John does not say that it was otherwise. He merely shews, from the circumstances under which St Mark wrote, that his Gospel was necessarily neither chronological nor complete; and under similar conditions—as in the case of St Matthew[2]—it is reasonable to look for a like result[3].

H. E. II. 15, VI. 14; Orig. ap. Euseb. *H. E.* VI. 25, II. 15; Euseb. *H. E.* II. 15; *Dem. Evang.* III. 5.

[1] Cf. Davidson, *Introd.* I. 158 sq., who supposes that John was 'mistaken in his opinion.'

[2] Euseb. *H. E.* III. 24: Ματθαῖος μὲν γὰρ πρότερον Ἑβραίοις κηρύξας, ὡς ἔμελλεν καὶ ἐφ' ἑτέρους ἰέναι, πατρίῳ γλώττῃ γραφῇ παραδοὺς τὸ κατ' αὐτὸν εὐαγγέλιον, τὸ λεῖπον τῇ αὐτοῦ παρουσίᾳ τούτοις ἀφ' ὧν ἐστέλλετο διὰ τῆς γραφῆς ἀπεπλήρου. The written Gospel was the sum of the oral Gospel. The oral Gospel was not, as far as we can see, a Life of Christ, but a selection of representative events from it, suited in its great outlines to the general wants of the Church, and adapted by the several Apostles to the peculiar requirements of their special audiences —ἔνια, οὐ τάξει, πρὸς τὰς χρείας [τῶν ἀκουόντων]. *H. E.* III. 39.

[3] No conclusion can be drawn from Eusebius' silence as to express testi-

In addition to the Gospels of St Matthew and St Mark, Papias appears to have been acquainted with the Gospel of St John[1]. Eusebius also says explicitly that he quoted 'the former Epistle of John, and that of Peter likewise[2].' He maintained moreover 'the divine inspiration' of the Apocalypse, and commented at least upon part of it[3].

Chap. ii.
His testimony to St John's Gospel.
1 John.
1 Peter.
Apocalypse.

monies of Papias to the Gospel of St John. Compare Lightfoot, *Colossians*, Pref. pp. 50 ff.; and see note at the end of the chapter.

[1] In an argument prefixed to a Vatican MS. of the Gospel of St John (ixth cent.) the following passage occurs: 'Evangelium Johannis manifestatum et datum est ecclesiis ab Johanne adhuc in corpore constituto; sicut Papias nomine Hierapolitanus, discipulus Johannis carus, in exotericis, id est in extremis [externis] quinque libris retulit. Descripsit vero evangelium dictante Johanne recte. Verum Martion hæreticus, cum ab eo fuisset improbatus, abjectus est ab Johanne. Is vero scripta vel epistolas ad eum pertulerat a fratribus qui in Ponto fuerunt.' The text of the fragment is evidently corrupt, and it seems to have been made up of fragments imperfectly put together. But the main fact seems certainly to be based on direct knowledge of Papias' book which is rightly described (in...quinque libris). The general tenor of the account is like that given in the Muratorian Canon. Marcion, it will be remembered, was met by Polycarp (Euseb. *H. E.* IV. 14), who, like Papias, belonged to 'the School of St John.' The fact that Eusebius omits this statement about St John's Gospel must be taken in connexion with the other fact that he omits to notice the use which Papias made of the Apocalypse. The difficulty is the same in both cases. There is also an allusion to the Gospel of St John in the quotation from the 'Elders' found in Irenæus (Lib. v. ad f.), which may have been taken from Papias (fr. v. Routh, et nott.). Comp. p. 71, n. 2.

The Latin passage containing a reference to the Gospel which is published as a fragment of 'Papias' by Grabe and Routh (fr. xi.) is taken from the 'Dictionary' of a mediæval Papias quoted by Grabe upon the passage, and not from the present Papias. The 'Dictionary' exists in MS. both at Oxford and Cambridge. I am indebted to the kindness of a friend for this explanation of what seemed to be a strange forgery.

[2] Euseb. *H. E.* III. 39: κέχρηται μαρτυρίαις ἀπὸ τῆς Ἰωάννου προτέρας ἐπιστολῆς, καὶ τῆς Πέτρου ὁμοίως. The language of Eusebius is remarkable: ἡ Ἰωάννου προτέρα, and ἡ Πέτρου—not ἡ Ἰωάννου πρώτη and ἡ Πέτρου προτέρα, as in *H. E.* v. 8. Can he be quoting the titles which Papias gave to them? In the fragment on the Canon (see below, § 12) *two* Epistles only of St John are mentioned; and the very remarkable Latin MS. of the Epistles B. M. *Harl.* 1772, has in the first hand *Petri Epistola*, as the heading of the *First* Epistle, and no heading to the *Second* Epistle; but the capriciousness of the scribe in this respect makes the significance of the omission uncertain.

[3] περὶ τοῦ θεοπνεύστου τῆς βίβλου ὁ ἐν ἁγίοις Βασίλειος καὶ...καὶ Παπίας καὶ...ἐχέγγυοι πιστώσασθαι. Andreas,

Chap. ii.

But he makes no mention of the writings of St Paul *or* St Luke.

There is however one great chasm in his testimony. Though he was the friend of Polycarp, there is no direct evidence that he used any of the Pauline writings. It may be an accident that he omits all these—the Epistles of St Paul, the Gospel of St Luke, and the Acts of the Apostles[1]—and these alone of the acknowledged books of the New Testament. But the cause of the omission must perhaps be sought for deeper than this; and if the explanation offered be true, it will then be seen that the limited range of his evidence gives it an additional reality[2].

The distinction between the Jewish and Gentile Churches in the Apostolic age

As we gain a clearer and fuller view of the Apostolic age it becomes evident that the fusion between the Gentile and Judaizing Christians was far less perfect than we are at first inclined to suppose. Both classes indeed were essentially united by sharing in a common spiritual life, but the outward barriers which separated them had not yet been removed. The elder Apostles gave to Barnabas and Paul the right hand of fellowship, but at the same time they defined the limits of their teaching[3]. This division of missionary labour was no compromise, but a gracious accommodation to the needs of the time. As Christianity was apprehended more thoroughly the

Proleg. in Apoc. (fr. viii. Routh). A quotation from Papias occurs in Cramer's *Catena in Apoc.* xii. 9 (VIII. p. 360). τοῦτο καὶ πατέρων παράδοσις καὶ Παπίου διαδόχου τοῦ Εὐαγγελιστοῦ Ἰωάννου, οὗ καὶ ἡ προκειμένη ἀποκάλυψις, διαβεβαιοῖ.

[1] In his account of the fate of Judas Iscariot (Fragm. iii.) there is a remarkable divergence from the narrative in Matt. xxvii. 5 and Acts i. 18. But there is no sufficient reason to suppose that he confounded Philip the Deacon with the Apostle of the same name. Bp Lightfoot notices some slight indications of Papias' use of the writings of St Luke (*l. c.* p. 415), but I do not think that much stress can be laid on them. Indeed the textual phenomena of the Gospel of St Luke and the Acts, which point to two distinct and early recensions, are best explained by the supposition that these writings had a limited circulation at first about two distinct centres, as, for example, Antioch and Alexandria.

[2] I feel now less certain than before as to the neglect of the Pauline writings by Papias. The absence of reference to the Epistles of St Paul can be easily explained otherwise. Comp. Lightfoot, *Colossians*, 51 ff. [1874].

[3] Gal. ii. 7—9.

causes which necessitated the distinction lost their force; but the change was neither sudden nor abrupt. It would have been contrary to reason and analogy if differences recognised by the Apostles and based on national characteristics had either wholly disappeared at their death or had been at once magnified into schisms. If this were implied in the few but precious memorials of the first age, then it might well be suspected that they gave an unfaithful picture of the time; but on the contrary, just in proportion as we can trace in them each separate principle which existed from the first must it be felt that there is a truth and reality in the progress of the Church by which all the conditions of its development suggested by reason or experience are satisfied.

to be looked for also in the next.

It is in this way that the partial testimony of Papias furnishes a characteristic link in the history of Christianity. As far as can be conjectured from the scanty notices of his life, he was probably of Jewish descent, and constitutionally inclined to Judaizing views[1]. In such a man any positive reference to the teaching of St Paul was not to be expected. He could not condemn him, for he had been welcomed by the other Apostles as their fellow-labourer, and Polycarp had early rejoiced to recognise his claims: he could not feel bound to witness to his authority, for his sympathies were with 'the circumcision,' to whom St Paul was not sent[2]. He stands as the representative of 'the Twelve,' and witnesses to every book which the next generation com-

Papias was the representative of the Jewish Church.

The value of his evidence on this account.

[1] Euseb. *H. E.* III. 36: ἀνὴρ τὰ πάντα ὅτι μάλιστα λογιώτατος (*in all respects of the greatest erudition*) καὶ τῆς γραφῆς εἰδήμων. This disputed clause is quite consistent with what Eusebius says elsewhere (III. 39): σφόδρα γάρ τοι σμικρὸς ὢν τὸν νοῦν, ὡς ἂν ἐκ τῶν αὐτοῦ λόγων τεκμηράμε- νον εἰπεῖν, [ὁ Παπίας] φαίνεται. The recent addition, however, of a very ancient Syriac version to the authorities which omit the clause, turns the balance of evidence against its genuineness. Lightfoot, *l. c.* 408 n.
[2] Gal. ii. 9.

C. G

monly received in their name. His testimony is partial; but its very imperfection is not only capable of an exact explanation, but is also in itself a proof that the Christianity of the second age was a faithful reflexion of the teaching of the Apostles[1]. In his case even partiality did not degenerate into exclusiveness. The force of this distinction will be obvious from a memorable contrast. For the converse of the judgment of Papias was already formed by his contemporary Marcion, but with this difference, that while Papias passed in silence over the Pauline writings Marcion definitely excluded all except these from his Christian Canon[2].

§ 2. *The Elders quoted by Irenæus.*

The evidence of the second generation after the Apostles not confined to Papias.

Papias is not however the only representative of those who had been taught by the immediate disciples of the Apostles. Irenæus has preserved some anonymous fragments of the teaching of others who occupied the same position as the Bishop of Hierapolis; and the few sentences thus quoted contain numerous testimonies to books of the New Testament, and fill up that which is left wanting by his evidence[3]. Thus 'the elders, disci-

His testimony is

---

[1] In speaking of Papias as the first Chronicler of the Church, it would perhaps have been right to except the authors of the 'Martyrdom of Ignatius.' The substance at least of the narrative seems an authentic memorial of the time. The mention of 'the Apostle Paul' (c. ii.) by Ignatius admirably accords with his character; and the whole scene before Trajan could scarcely have been invented at a later time. The history contains coincidences of language with the Epistles of St Paul to the Romans (c. iii.), 1 and 2 Corinthians (c. ii), Galatians (c. ii.), and 1 Timothy (c. iv.). At the close of the first chapter there is also a remarkable similarity of metaphor with 2 Pet. i. 19. But the parallelism between many parts of the narrative with the Acts is still more worthy of notice, because, from the nature of the case, references to that book are comparatively rare in early writings. See especially chapp. iv., v.

[2] See chap. iv.

[3] They have been collected by Routh, *Reliquiæ Sacræ,* I. 47 sqq. Eusebius notices the quotations, but did not know their source (*H. E.* v. 8). It is clear that Irenæus appeals to several authorities; and it appears also that he quoted traditions as well

'ples of the Apostles,' as he tells us, speak of 'Paradise, *Chap. ii.*
'to which the Apostle Paul was carried, and there heard *completed by that of other 'Elders.'*
'words unutterable to us in our present state' (2 Cor.
xii. 4)¹. In another place he records the substance of
that which he had heard 'from an Elder who had heard
'those who had seen the Apostles and had learnt from
'them,' to the effect that 'the correction drawn from the
'Scriptures was sufficient for the ancients in those mat-
'ters which they did without the counsel of the Spirit.'
In the course of the argument, after instances from the
Old Testament, the Elder alludes to 'the Queen of the
'South' (Matt. xii. 42), the Parable of the Talents
(Matt. xxv. 27), the fate of the traitor (Matt. xxvi. 24),
the judgment of unbelievers (Matt. x. 15); and also
makes use of the Epistles to the Romans (as St Paul's),
to the Corinthians (the First by name), and to the
Ephesians, and probably to the First Epistle of St
Peter². In another place an Elder appears to allude to
the Gospels of St Matthew and St John³.

Thus each great division of the New Testament is *Thus this generation*
again found to be recognised in the simultaneous teach- *also wit-*

as writings: e.g. IV. 27 (45), *Audivi a quodam Presbytero, &c.* IV. 31 (49), Talia quædam enarrans de antiquis Presbyter reficiebat nos et dicebat, *&c.* The other forms of quotation are: ὑπὸ τοῦ κρείττονος ἡμῶν εἴρηται (I. Pref. 2)—ὁ κρείσσων (sic) ἡμῶν ἔφη (I. 13. 3)—quidam dixit superior nobis (III. 17. 4)—ex veteribus quidam ait (III. 23. 3)—senior Apostolorum discipulus disputabat (IV. 32. 1)—λέγουσιν οἱ πρεσβύτεροι τῶν Ἀποστόλων μαθηταί (V. 5. 1)—ἔφη τις τῶν προβεβηκότων (V. 17. 4)—quidam ante nos dixit (IV. 41. 2)—ὁ θεῖος πρεσβύτης καὶ κήρυξ τῆς ἀληθείας... ἐπιβεβόηκε...εἰπών (I. 15. 6). The last precedes some Iambic lines against Marcus: cf. Grabe, *in loc.*

¹ Iren. v. 5. 1; Fr. vii. (Routh).
² Iren. IV. 27 (45); Fr. v. (Routh). The oblique construction of the whole paragraph proves that Irenæus is giving accurately at least the general tenor of the Elder's statement; and the quotations form a necessary part of it, and cannot have been added for illustration. *E.g.* Non debemus ergo, inquit ille Senior, superbi esse ...sed ipsi timere...et ideo Paulum dixisse: *Si enim naturalibus ramis,* &c. (Rom. xi. 20, 21).
³ Iren. IV. 31 (49); Fr. vi. (Routh). The reference to St Matthew (xi. 19) is remarkable from being introduced by 'Inquit;' that to St John (viii. 56) is more uncertain. See also p. 71, n. 2.

G 2

ing of the Church. We have already traced in the disciples of the Apostles the existence of the characteristic peculiarities by which they were themselves marked; and we can now see that their writings still remained in the next generation to witness at once to the different forms and essential harmony of their teaching. Polycarp, who united by his life two great ages of the Church, reconciles in his own person the followers of St James and St Paul: he was the friend of Papias as well as the teacher of Irenæus[1].

Chap. ii. nesses to each great division of the New Testament.

§ 3. *The Evangelists in the reign of Trajan.*

The change in our point of sight.

Hitherto Christianity has been viewed in its inward construction: now it will be regarded in its outward conflicts. It is no longer 'a work for silence, but for 'might.' Truth was not only to be strengthened, consolidated, developed to its full proportions: it was charged to conquer the world. The preparation for the accomplishment of this charge was the work of the Apologists.

The early Evangelists said to have circulated written Gospels. A.D. 98— 117.

Before we consider their writings it is very worthy of notice that Eusebius introduces the mention of New Testament Scriptures into the striking description which he gives of the zeal of the first Christian missionaries. 'They discharged the work of Evangelists,' he says, speaking of the time of Trajan, 'zealously striving to 'preach Christ to those who were still wholly ignorant 'of Christianity (ὁ τῆς πίστεως λόγος), and to deliver to 'them the Scripture of the divine Gospels' (τὴν τῶν θείων εὐαγγελίων παραδιδόναι γραφήν[2]). The statement may not be in itself convincing as an argument; but it

---

[1] Compare Lightfoot, *l. c.* pp. 409 f.
[2] Euseb. *H. E.* III. 37.

THE ATHENIAN APOLOGISTS.

falls in with other traditions which affirm that the preaching of Christianity was even in the earliest times accompanied by the circulation of written Gospels; for these were at once the sum of the Apostolic message—the oral Gospel—and its representative[1]. Thus in the other glimpse which Eusebius gives of the labours of Evangelists—'men inspired with godly zeal to copy the pat-'tern of the Apostles'—the written word again appears. Pantænus towards the end of the second century penetrated 'even to the Indians; and there it is said that 'he found that the Gospel according to Matthew had 'anticipated his arrival among some there who were 'acquainted with Christ, to whom Bartholomew, one of 'the Apostles, had preached, and given on his departure '(καταλεῖψαι) the writing of Matthew in Hebrew let-'ters[2].'... The whole picture may not be original; but the several parts harmonize exactly together, and the general effect is that of reality and truth.

Thus Pantænus found the Gospel of St Matthew among some of the Indians, c. A.D. 180.

§ 4. *The Athenian Apologists.*

At the very time when the first Evangelists were extending the knowledge of Christianity, the earliest Apologists were busy in confirming its authority[3]. While Asia and Rome had each their proper task to do in the building of the Church, it was reserved for the countrymen of Socrates to undertake in the first instance the

The place and occasion of the first Apology.

---

[1] Euseb. *H. E.* III. 24: Ματθαῖος ...Ἑβραίοις κηρύξας...τὸ λεῖπον τῇ αὐτοῦ παρουσίᾳ τούτοις ἀφ' ὧν ἐστέλ-λετο διὰ τῆς γραφῆς ἀπεπλήρου. The traditions of the origin of the Gospels of St Mark and St Luke point to the same fact. See *Introduction to the Study of the Gospels*, pp. 167 ff.

[2] Euseb. *H. E.* V. 10. Cf. Heini-chen, *in loc.* and Add. Pantænus was at the head of the Catechetical School of Alexandria in the time of Commodus (Euseb. *H. E.* V. 9, 10); and his journey to India probably preceded his appointment to that office.

[3] Euseb. *H. E.* III. 37.

84   THE AGE OF THE GREEK APOLOGISTS.   [PART

Chap. ii.

A.D. 123—126.

c. A.D. 130.

The character of the Apology of Quadratus.

formal defence of its claims before the rulers of the world. The occasion of this new work arose out of the celebration of the Eleusinian mysteries—those immemorial rites which seem to have contained all that was deepest and truest in the old religion. During his first stay at Athens, Hadrian suffered himself to be initiated; and probably because the Emperor was thus pledged to the support of the national faith, the enemies of the Christians set on foot a persecution against them. On this, or perhaps rather on his second visit to the city, Quadratus, 'a disciple of the Apostles[1],' offered to him his Apology, which is said to have procured the well-known rescript to Minucius in favour of the Christians[2].

This Apology of Quadratus was generally current in the time of Eusebius, who himself possessed a copy of it; 'and one may see in it,' he says, 'clear proofs both 'of the intellect of the man and of his apostolic ortho-'doxy[3].' The single passage which he has preserved shews that Quadratus insisted rightly on the historic worth of Christianity. 'The works of our Saviour,' he argues, 'were ever present; for they were real: being 'the men who were healed: the men who were raised

---

[1] Hieron. *de Virr. Ill.* 19. It is disputed whether the *Apologist* was identical with the *Bishop* of the same name, who is said to have ' brought 'the Christians of Athens again to-'gether who had been scattered by 'persecution, and to have rekindled 'their faith' (Euseb. *H. E.* IV. 23). The narrative of Eusebius leaves the matter in uncertainty, but they were probably different. (Cf. *H. E.* III. 37; IV. 3, with IV. 23.) Jerome identifies them (*l. c.*; *Ep. ad Magn.* LXX. § 4), and Cave supports his view (*Hist. Litt.* I. an. 123). Cf. Routh, *Rel. Sacræ*, I. 72 sq.

[2] Cf. Routh, *l.c.* The details of the history are very obscure. If Jerome (*Ep. ad Magn. l. c.*) speaks with strict accuracy when he says ' Quadratus ...Adriano principi *Eleusinæ sacra invisenti* librum pro nostra religione tradidit,' the *Apology* must be placed at the time of Hadrian's first visit; otherwise it seems more likely that it should be referred to the second. Pearson (ap. Routh, p. 78) fixes the date on the authority of Eusebius (?) at 127. The rescript to Minucius is found in Just. *Ap.* I. lxviii. *ad f.* Euseb. *H. E.* IV. 9.

[3] *H. E.* IV. 3: ἐξ οὗ [συγγράμματος] κατιδεῖν ἐστὶ λαμπρὰ τεκμήρια τῆς τε τοῦ ἀνδρὸς διανοίας καὶ τῆς ἀποστολικῆς ὀρθοτομίας.

THE ATHENIAN APOLOGISTS.

'from the dead: who were not only seen at the moment
'when the miracles were wrought, but also [were seen
'continually like other men] being ever present; and
'that not only while the Saviour sojourned on earth, but
'also after His departure for a considerable time, so that
'some of them survived even to our times[1].'

A second 'Apology for the Faith,'—'a rationale of
'Christian doctrine'—was addressed to Hadrian by Aristides, 'a man of the greatest eloquence,' who likewise
was an Athenian, and probably wrote on the same occasion as Quadratus[2]. Eusebius and Jerome speak of the
book as still current in their time, but they do not appear to have read it. Jerome however adds that 'in the
'opinion of scholars it was a proof of the writer's ability;'
and this falls in with what he elsewhere says of its character, that it was constructed out of philosophic elements[3]. Aristides in fact, like Justin, was a philosopher;
and did not lay aside his former dress when he became
a Christian[4].

Marginal note: Chap. ii.
Marginal note: The Apology of Aristides.

[1] The original cannot be quoted too often: Τοῦ δὲ Σωτῆρος ἡμῶν τὰ ἔργα ἀεὶ παρῆν· ἀληθῆ γὰρ ἦν· οἱ θεραπευθέντες· οἱ ἀναστάντες ἐκ νεκρῶν· οἳ οὐκ ὤφθησαν μόνον θεραπευόμενοι καὶ ἀνιστάμενοι, ἀλλὰ καὶ ἀεὶ παρόντες· οὐδ' ἐπιδημοῦντος μόνον τοῦ Σωτῆρος, ἀλλὰ καὶ ἀπαλλαγέντος ἦσαν ἐπὶ χρόνον ἱκανόν, ὥστε καὶ εἰς τοὺς ἡμετέρους χρόνους τινὲς αὐτῶν ἀφίκοντο (Euseb. *H. E.* IV. 3). The repetition of ὁ Σωτὴρ absolutely is remarkable; in the New Testament and in the Apostolic Fathers it occurs only as a title. The usage of Quadratus clearly belongs to a later date. It appears again in the Letter to Diognetus (c. ix.), and very frequently in the fragment on the Resurrection appended to Justin's works (cc. ii., iv., v., &c.).

[2] Hieron. *de Virr. Ill*. 19: Volumen nostri dogmatis rationem continens. *Fragm. Martyrol.*, ap. Routh, p. 76: Aristides philosophus, vir eloquentissimus......If there were sufficient reason for the supposition that Quadratus himself suffered martyrdom in the time of Hadrian, the *Apology* of Aristides might be supposed to have been called forth at that time. The fragment published in an Armenian translation (1878) may be substantially genuine, but it contains no quotations from the N. T. The sermon on the penitent robber published with it is of much later date.

[3] Hieron. *l. c.*: Apud philologos ingenii ejus indicium est. *Ep. ad Magn.* LXX. § 4: Apologeticum pro Christianis obtulit contextum philosophorum sententiis, quem imitatus postea Justinus, et ipse philosophus.

[4] Hieron. *l. c.* Dorner (I. 180) says the same of Quadratus, but I cannot

86   THE AGE OF THE GREEK APOLOGISTS.   [PART

Chap. ii.
Both witness to the Catholic doctrine.

Nothing, it will be seen, can be drawn directly from these scanty notices in support of the Canon; but the position of the men gives importance even to the most general views of their doctrine. They represent the teaching of Gentile[1] Christendom in their generation, and witness to its soundness. Quadratus is said to have been eminently conspicuous for the gift of prophecy[2]; and yet he appealed with marked emphasis, not to any subjective evidence, but to the reality of Christ's works. Aristides investigated Christianity in the spirit of a philosopher; and yet he was as conspicuous for faith as for wisdom[3]. Their works were not only able, but in the opinion of competent judges they were orthodox.

§ 5. *The Letter to Diognetus.*

The Letter to Diognetus.

In addition to the meagre fragments just reviewed, one short work—the so-called Letter to Diognetus—has been preserved entire, or nearly so, to witness to the character of the earliest apologetic literature[4]. It differs however from the Apologies in this, that it was written in the first instance to satisfy an inquirer, not to conciliate an enemy. It is anonymous, resembling in form a speech much more than a letter, and there are no adequate means of determining its authorship. For a long time it was attributed to Justin Martyr; but it is

Not written by Justin, but

---

tell on what authority. Probably the names were interchanged.

[1] Yet Grabe's conjecture that the rule attributed to Quadratus in a Martyrology, ut nulla esca a Christianis repudiaretur quæ rationalis et humana est, was assigned to him by error, seems very plausible. Cf. Routh, I. p. 79.

[2] Euseb. *H. E.* III. 37; V. 17.

[3] Hieron. *ad Magn. l.c.*: Fide vir sapientiaque admirabilis. Another very remarkable testimony to the character of his teaching is found in the *Martyrolog. Rom.* (ap. Routh, p. 80): Quod Christus Jesus solus esset Deus præsente ipso Imperatore luculentissime peroravit.

[4] Like the Epistles of Clement it is at present found only in one ancient MS. Cf. Otto, *Just. Mart.* II., *Proleg.* xiv. xx. sqq. Stephens may have had access to another. [The Strasburg MS. was burnt in the war.]

equally alien in thought and style from his acknowledged writings; and the mainstay of such a hypothesis seems to be the pardonable desire not to leave a gem so precious without an owner[1]. Other names have been suggested; but in the absence of external evidence they serve only to express the character of the Essay. It is eloquent, but that is no sure sign that it was written by Apollos. It is opposed to Judaism, but that is no proof that it proceeded from Marcion[2]. It may be the work of Quadratus[3] or Aristides; but it is enough that we can regard it as the natural outpouring of a Greek heart holding converse with a Greek mind in the language of old philosophers[4].

Chap. ii.

purely Greek.

[1] The evidence on which we conclude that it cannot be Justin's is briefly this: (1) It is contained in no catalogue of his writings. (2) Justin's style is cumbrous, involved, and careless; while that of the Letter to Diognetus is simple, vigorous, and classical. (3) Justin regards idolatry, Judaism, even Christianity itself, from a different point of view. Idols, according to him, were really tenanted by spiritual powers (*Apol.* I. xii.), and were not mere stocks or stones (*ad Diogn.* ii.): the Mosaic Law was a fitting preparation for the Gospel (*Dial. c. Tr.* xliii.), and not an arbitrary system (*ad Diogn.* iv.): Christianity was the completion of that which was begun in men's hearts by the seminal word (*Ap.* II. xiii.), so that they were not even in appearance left uncared for by God before Christ came (*ad. Diogn.* viii.). The second ground is in itself decisive: the doctrinal differences can be more or less smoothed down by the comparison of other passages of Justin; *e.g. Ap.* I. ix.; *Dial. c. Tr.* xlvi. *ad fin.*

[2] Lumper (ap. Möhler, 165) and Galland (ap. Hefele, lxxix.) suggest Apollos. Bunsen in his *Analecta Ante-Nicæna*, I. 103 ff. publishes the first part as 'the lost early letter of Marcion,' but brings forward no satisfactory arguments in support of his opinion.

[3] Cf. Dorner, I. 178 *anm.*

[4] Doubts have been raised, wholly groundless, as I believe, to the authenticity of the first fragment or of the two fragments which form the letter. Dr Donaldson, after enumerating several difficulties and curious facts, says: '[*These*]...led me ' to suspect that the epistle to Diog-'netus might possibly be the pro-'duction of H. Stephanus himself... '[*But*]...one should be cautious in 'attributing a forgery to any one. ' I am inclined to think it more 'likely that some...Greeks...may have 'written the treatise...*But there is ' no sound basis for any theory with ' regard to this remarkable production.*' (*Hist. of Christian Liter.* II. p. 142.) This guarded statement becomes in the hands of a controversialist the following: '*Donaldson* considers it 'either a forgery by H. Stephanus, 'the first editor, or by Greeks who 'came over to Italy when Constanti-'nople was threatened by the Turks.' (*Supernat. Rel.* II. 39, n. 3.) I cannot think that Mr. Cotterill's arguments alter the state of the case.

Chap. ii.
The letter consists of two parts.

Their characteristics.

The date of the Letter to Diognetus.

The question of the authorship of the Letter being thus left in uncertainty, that of its integrity still remains. As it stands at present it consists of two parts (cc. i.—x.; xi., xii.) connected by no close coherence; and at the end of the first the manuscript marks the occurrence of a 'chasm[1].' The separation thus pointed out is fully established by internal evidence. The first part—the true Letter to Diognetus—is everywhere marked by the characteristics of Greece; the second by those of Alexandria. The one, so to speak, sets forth truth 'rationally,' and the other 'mystically.' The centre of the one is faith: of the other knowledge. The different manner in which they treat the ancient Covenant illustrates their mutual relation. The Mosaic institutions—sabbaths and circumcision and fasts—are at once set aside in the Letter to Diognetus as palpably ridiculous and worthless. In the concluding fragment, on the contrary, 'the fear of the law and the 'grace of the prophets' are united with 'the faith of the 'Gospels and the tradition of the Apostles' as contributing to the wealth of the Church[2].

Indications of the date of the writings are not wholly wanting. The address to Diognetus was composed after the faith of Christians had been tried by wide-spread

---

[1] Cf. Otto, II. p. 201, n. The words are: καὶ ὧδε ἐγκοπὴν εἶχε τὸ ἀντίγραφον.

[2] It is always impossible to convey by words any notion of the variations in tone and language and manner which are instinctively felt in comparing two cognate but separate books; and yet the distinction between the two parts of the 'Letter to Diognetus' seems to me to be shewn clearly by these subtle, but most real differences. In addition to this the argument is completed at the end of c. x. according to the plan laid down in c. i.; and the close of c. xi. seems to imply a different motive for writing. On the other hand it is quite wrong to insist on the fact that 'the second fragment addresses not one but many,' for the singular is used as often as the plural (c. xi.: ἣν χάριν μὴ λυπῶν ἐπιγνώσῃ. c. xii.: ἤτω σοι καρδία γνῶσις).

There may have been a formal conclusion after c. x., but even now the termination is not more abrupt than that to Justin's first Apology, and it expresses the same motive—a regard to future judgment (c. x. *ad*

persecution, which had not even at that time passed over[1]; and on the other hand a lively faith in Christ's speedy Presence (παρουσία) still lingered in the Church[2]. The first condition can hardly be satisfied before the reign of Trajan; and the second forbids us to bring the Letter down to a much later time. In full accordance with this, Christianity is spoken of as something 'recent;' Christians are a 'new class;' the Saviour has been only 'now' set forth[3].

Chap. ii.

c. 117 A.D.

The concluding fragment is more recent, but still, I believe, not later than the first half of the second century. The greater maturity of style and the definite reference to St Paul can be explained by the well-known activity of religious thought and the early advancement of Christian literature at Alexandria[4]. And everything else in the writing betokens an early date. The author speaks of himself as 'a disciple of Apostles and a teacher of Gentiles[5].' The Church, as he describes it, was still in its

The date of the concluding Fragment somewhat later.

---

fin.); Just. *Ap.* 1. lxviii. In c. vii. there is a lacuna. Cf. next note.

[1] c. vii.: [οὐχ ὁρᾷς] παραβαλλομένους θηρίοις... It is impossible to read the words without thinking of the martyrdom of Ignatius, which indeed may have suggested them.

Just before παραβαλλομένους there is a lacuna: οὐχ ὁρᾷς is introduced from the next sentence. The MS. has the note: οὕτως καὶ ἐν τῷ ἀντιγράφῳ εὗρον ἐγκοπὴν παλαιοτάτου ὄντος (Otto, II. p. 184, n.). It is quite unnecessary to alter the last words as Otto wishes. Cf. Jelf, *Gr. Gr.* § 710 c.

[2] c. vii.: ταῦτα τῆς παρουσίας αὐτοῦ δείγματα. The word, which is almost universally spread through the writings of the N. T., does not occur in this sense in the Apostolic Fathers, and its meaning here may be questioned. Justin speaks of the second παρουσία without alluding to its ap-

proach: *Dial. c. Tr.* cc. xxxi., xxxii.

[3] cc. i., ii., ix. This argument is of weight when connected with the others, though not so independently. Our view of the date of the Letter is not inconsistent with the belief that it was addressed to Diognetus the tutor of Marcus Aurelius. That prince openly adopted the dress and doctrines of the Stoics when twelve years old (133 A. D.); and if we place the Epistle at the close of the reign of Trajan (c. 117 A. D.) there is no difficulty in reconciling the dates.

[4] c. xii.: ὁ ἀπόστολος. The antagonism between the Serpent (ἡδονή) and Eve (αἴσθησις) was commented on by Philo, *Leg. Alleg.* II. §§ 18 sqq. Τὴν ὀφιομάχον οὖν γνώμην ἀντίταττε καὶ κάλλιστον ἀγῶνα τοῦτον διάθλησον...κατὰ τῆς τοὺς ἄλλους ἅπαντας νικώσης ἡδονῆς...(§ 26). Cf. Just. M. *Dial.* ch. c., and Otto *in loc.*

[5] c. xi. *init.*

Chap. ii.

Both parts shew a combination of the doctrine of St Paul and of St John.

first stage[1]. The sense of personal intercourse with the Word was fresh and deep. Revelation was not then wholly a thing of the Past[2].

In one respect the two parts of the book are united, inasmuch as they both exhibit a combination of the teaching of St Paul and St John. The love of God, it is said in the Letter to Diognetus, is the source of love in the Christian; who must needs 'love God who thus 'first loved him' (προαγαπήσαντα), and find an expression for this love by loving his neighbour, whereby he will be 'an imitator of God.' 'For God loved men, for 'whose sakes He made the world, to whom He sub-'jected all things that are in the earth,...unto (πρός) 'whom He sent His only-begotten Son, to whom He 'promised the kingdom in heaven (τὴν ἐν οὐρανῷ βασι-'λείαν), and will give it to those who love Him:' God's will is mercy; 'He sent His Son as wishing to save '(ὡς σώζων)...and not to condemn;' and as witnesses of this 'Christians dwell in the world, though they are not ' of the world[3].' So in the Conclusion we read that 'the 'Word Who was from the beginning,...at His appear-'ance, speaking boldly, manifested the mysteries of the

---

[1] c. xii. *ad fin.* ...σωτήριον δείκνυ-ται καὶ ἀπόστολοι συνετίζονται, καὶ τὸ κυρίου πάσχα προέρχεται, καὶ κλῆροι συνάγονται, καὶ μετὰ κόσμου ἁρμόζε-ται, καὶ διδάσκων ἁγίους ὁ Λόγος εὐ-φραίνεται, δι' οὗ Πατὴρ δοξάζεται. I have adopted the admirable emendation κλῆροι (1 Pet. v. 3) for κηροί, printed by Bunsen (*Hipp.* I. p. 192), though in p. 188 he seems to read καιροί. It does not appear on what authority Otto says Designantur *cerei* quibus Christiani potissimum tempore paschali utebantur; if it were so, κηροὶ συνάγονται would still be a marvellous expression. Cf. Bingham, *Orig. Eccles.* II. 461 sq. The phrase παράδοσις ἀποστόλων φυλάσ-σεται (c. xi.) is of no weight on the other side. Cf. 2 Thess. ii. 15; iii. 6; 1 Cor. xi. 2.

[2] The phrase already quoted (last note) 'the Lord's passover advances,' seems to point to the early Paschal controversy. If a special date must be fixed, I should be inclined to suggest some time between 140—150.

[3] c. x., vii., vi. Cf. 1 John iv. 19, 11; Eph. v. 1; John iii. 17; [James i. 12;] John xvii. 11, 16. I cannot call to mind a parallel to the phrase ἡ ἐν οὐρανῷ βασιλεία, which is very different from 'the kingdom' or 'the kingdom *of* heaven.'

I.] THE LETTER TO DIOGNETUS. 91

'Father to those who were judged faithful by Him[1].' And those again to whom the Word speaks 'from love 'of that which is revealed to them' share their knowledge with others. And this is the true knowledge which is inseparable from life; and not that false knowledge of which the Apostle says, *knowledge puffeth up, but love edifieth*[2]. The presence of the teaching of St John is here placed beyond all doubt[3]. There are however no direct references to the Gospels throughout the Letter, nor indeed any allusions to our Lord's discourses; and with regard to the Synoptic Evangelists, it is more difficult to trace the marks of their use. From time to time the writer to Diognetus appears to shew familiarity with their language; but this is all[4].

The influence of the other parts of the New Testament on the Letter is clearer. In the first part the presence of St Paul is even more discernible than that of St John. In addition to Pauline words and phrases[5],

Chap. ii.

How far the Synoptic Gospels are recognised in the Letter to Diognetus.

Other references to the New Testament in the Letter to Diognetus; and

---

[1] c. xi. οὗ χάριν ἀπέστειλε Λόγον ἵνα κόσμῳ φανῇ· ὃς ὑπὸ λαοῦ ἀτιμασθείς, διὰ ἀποστόλων κηρυχθείς, ὑπὸ ἐθνῶν ἐπιστεύθη. οὗτος ὁ ἀπ' ἀρχῆς, ὁ καινὸς φανείς......And a little before οἷς ἐφανέρωσεν ὁ Λόγος φανείς, παρρησία λαλῶν...οἱ πιστοὶ λογισθέντες ὑπ' αὐτοῦ ἔγνωσαν πατρὸς μυστήρια. The exact phrase παρρησία λαλεῖν is peculiar to St John among the writers of the New Testament with the exception of Mark viii. 32.

[2] cc. xi., xii. Cf. John i. 1, 18; 1 Cor. viii. 1. 'Ἐξ ἀγάπης τῶν ἀποκαλυφθέντων is a very note-worthy expression.

[3] I am unable to modify this conclusion after considering what has been urged against it (*Supernat. Rel.* II. pp. 357—370). Indeed I can only wonder that a writer who states that 'the Epistles of Paul chiefly

'[including apparently Colossians 'and Titus], together with the other 'canonical Epistles [including He-'brews, James], are the sources of the 'writer's inspiration' (p. 359), should think it worth while to dispute 'the 'presence of St John's *teaching*,' or, as has been said in a former page, 'a combination of the teaching of St 'Paul and St John' in this letter.

[4] Compare Matt. vi. 25—31; xix. 17, with cc. ix., viii.; and also Matt. v. 44; xix. 26, with cc. vi., ix.

[5] The following phrases may be noticed: ἀποδέχομαί τινά τινος (Acts) —τὸ ἀδύνατον τῆς ἡμετέρας φύσεως— τὸ τῆς θεοσεβείας μυστήριον—οἰκονομίαν πιστεύεσθαι—τεχνίτης καὶ δημιουργός (Ep. to Hebr.)—μιμητὴς Θεοῦ —κατὰ σάρκα ζῆν—καινὸς ἄνθρωπος.

Among the Pauline words are: παρεδρεύειν (1 Cor. ix. 13)—θεοσέ-

92   THE AGE OF THE GREEK APOLOGISTS.   [PART

Chap. ii.

in the concluding Fragment.

whole sections are constructed with manifest regard to passages in the Epistles to the Romans, Corinthians, and Galatians; and there are other coincidences of language more or less evident with the Acts, and with the Epistles to the Ephesians, Philippians, the First Epistle to Timothy, and the Epistle to Titus, and with the First Epistle of Peter[1]. In the concluding fragment there is, in addition to the references of St John, to the Gospels generally, and to the Epistles to the Corinthians already mentioned, an apparent reminiscence of a passage in the First Epistle to Timothy[2].

The 'Gnostic' element recognised in the concluding Fragment.

The conclusion of the Letter moreover has a further importance as marking the presence of a new element in the development of Christian philosophy. Knowledge (γνῶσις) is vindicated from its connexion with heresy, and welcomed as the highest expression of revealed truth. Believers are God's Paradise, bringing forth manifold fruits; and in them, as in Paradise of old, the tree of Knowledge is planted hard by the tree of Life; for it is not knowledge that killeth, but disobedience. Life cannot exist without knowledge; nor sure knowledge without true Life. Knowledge without the witness of Life is only the old deception of the serpent. The Christian's heart must be knowledge; and his Life must be true Reason. In other words, Christian wisdom must be the spring of action, and Christian life the

---

βεια—δεισιδαιμονία—χορηγεῖν—συνήθεια—προσδεόμενος—παραιτοῦμαι—πολιτεύομαι—ἀφθαρσία—ἐκλογή—ὁμολογουμένως—ὑπόστασις (Hebr.).

The peculiarities in the language of the Letter may be judged from these examples: ὑπερσπουδάζειν—προκατέχειν—ἐξομοιοῦσθαι—ἐγκαταστηρίζειν—ἀπερινόητος—παντοκτίστης—γεραίρειν—ψοφοδεής—μνησικακεῖν.

[1] Compare c. ix. with Rom. iii. 21—26, and Gal. iv. 4; and c. v. with 2 Cor. vi. 9, 10. The following references also are worthy of remark: c. iii., Acts xvii. 24, 25: c. ii., Eph. iv. 21—24: c. v., Phil. iii. 18 sqq.: c. iv., 1 Tim. iii. 16 : c. ix., Tit. iii. 4, and 1 Pet. iii. 18.

[2] Cf. 1 Tim. iii. 16 with c. xi.

THE JEWISH APOLOGISTS.

realisation of truth[1]. The groundwork of this teaching lies in the relation of the Word to man. The Incarnation of the Eternal Word is connected intimately with His Birth from time to time in the heart of believers[2]. The same Word which manifested the mysteries of the Father when He was shewn to the world is declared still to converse with whom He will[3]. The Word is still the teacher of the saints[4].

Chap. ii.

In this doctrine it is possible to trace the germs of later mysticism, but each false deduction is excluded by the plain recognition of the correlative objective truth. The test of knowledge is the presence of Life[5]; and the influence of the Word on the Christian is made to flow from His historical revelation to mankind[6].

How corrected.

§ 6. *The Jewish Apologists.*

The conclusion of the Letter to Diognetus offers a natural transition to the few relics of Apologetic writings derived apparently from Jewish authorship. It bears, as has been said, the impress of Alexandria, and was probably the work of a Jewish convert[7]. Coming from such a source it may be taken to shew the Catholic

The Letter to Diognetus a transition to the Judæo-Christian writings.

---

[1] c. xii.
[2] c. xi.: Οὗτος ὁ ἀπ' ἀρχῆς, ὁ καινὸς φανεὶς καὶ [παλαιὸς] εὑρεθεὶς καὶ πάντοτε νέος ἐν ἁγίων καρδίαις γεννώμενος.
[3] c. xi.: ...ἐπιγνώσῃ ἃ Λόγος ὁμιλεῖ δι' ὧν βούλεται ὅτε θέλει.
[4] c. xii.: διδάσκων ἁγίους ὁ Λόγος εὐφραίνεται.
It is to be remarked that the Word appears in both parts of the Letter rather as the correlative to Reason in man (ζωὴ δὲ λόγος ἀληθής, c. xii. ὁ Θεὸς...τὴν ἀλήθειαν καὶ τὸν Λόγον τὸν ἅγιον καὶ ἀπερινόητον ἀνθρώποις ἐνίδρυσε...c. vii.), than as the expression of the creative Will of God. Cf. Dorner, I. p. 411.
[5] Ὁ γὰρ νομίζων εἰδέναι τι ἄνευ γνώσεως ἀληθοῦς καὶ μαρτυρουμένης ὑπὸ τῆς ζωῆς οὐκ ἔγνω...c. xii.
[6] Εὐαγγελίων πίστις ἵδρυται...c. xi.
[7] This follows, I think, from the manner in which the Book of Genesis is allegorized. In later writers such interpretations became generally current. The contrast which the fragment offers to the Epistle of Barnabas is very instructive, as shewing the opposite extremes deducible from the same principles.

94   THE AGE OF THE GREEK APOLOGISTS.   [PART

Chap. ii.

spirit of one division of Jewish Christendom; but since it may seem that the freedom of thought which distinguished Alexandria was unlikely to foster Judaizing views, it becomes a matter of importance to inquire whether there be any early records of the Palestinian Church, their acknowledged source and centre. A notice of one such book,—the 'Dialogue between 'Jason and Papiscus,' has been preserved[1]. It appears to have had a wide popularity, and was translated into Latin in the third century[2]. Celsus, it is true, thought that it was fitter for pity than for ridicule; but Origen speaks highly of its dramatic skill[3]. It is uncertain whether it has been attributed rightly to Aristo of Pella; for that late belief may have arisen from its known connexion with the Church to which he belonged[4]. The general plan of the writer however is exactly characteristic of the position which a teacher at Pella may be supposed to have occupied. It was

The Dialogue of Jason and Papiscus.

Its character.

---

[1] Routh, I. 95—109.
[2] This is the date given by Cave. Others have placed it as late as the end of the fifth century. The translation was made by Celsus, and dedicated to Bishop Vigilius; but nothing can be determined as to their identity. The preface to the translation is appended to many editions of Cyprian. Cf. Routh, p. 109.
[3] Orig. c. Cels. IV. 52; Παπίσκου τινὸς καὶ Ἰάσονος ἀντιλογίαν ἔγνων (in the words of Celsus) οὐ γέλωτος ἀλλὰ μᾶλλον ἐλέους καὶ μίσους ἀξίαν. The book, as Origen allows, was more adapted in some parts for the simpler sort of men than for the educated: δυνάμενον μέν τι πρὸς τοὺς πολλοὺς καὶ ἁπλουστέρους πίστεως χάριν συμβαλέσθαι, οὐ μὴν οἷόν τε καὶ συνετωτέρους κινῆσαι (*l. c.*). Afterwards he adds: καίτοιγε οὐκ ἀγεννῶς οὐδ᾽ ἀπρεπῶς τῷ Ἰουδαϊκῷ προσώπῳ τοῦ ἑτέρου ἱσταμένου πρὸς τὸν λόγον.
[4] Origen and Jerome quote the Dialogue without mentioning the author's name; and it is not given in the preface of Celsus. Eusebius (*H. E.* IV. 6) quotes a passage from Aristo in reference to the Jewish rising under Bar-Cochba, but it seems at least doubtful whether this was taken from the Dialogue. Maximus (7th cent.) is the earliest writer who attributes the Dialogue to Aristo, adding: ἦν [διάλεξιν] Κλήμης ὁ Ἀλεξανδρεὺς ἐν ἕκτῳ βιβλίῳ τῶν Ὑποτυπώσεων τὸν ἅγιον Λουκᾶν φησὶν ἀναγράψαι. This tradition is probably due to the identification of Jason with the Jason mentioned in Acts xvii. 5. Of the Apology which Aristo is said to have offered to Hadrian (*Chron. Pasc.* 477, ap. Routh, p. 104, if the reading be correct) nothing is known.

his object to represent a *Hebrew Christian* convincing an *Alexandrine Jew* 'from the Old Testament Scrip-'tures (ἐκ τῶν Ἰουδαϊκῶν γραφῶν), shewing that the Mes-'sianic prophecies were applicable to Jesus[1].' To this end he apparently made frequent use of allegorical interpretations of Scripture; but it is more important to notice that he speaks of Jesus as the Son of God the Creator of the World[2]. The words, though few, are key-words of Christianity, and as the single expression of the early doctrine of the Church of Palestine they go far to expose the unreality of the hypothesis which exhibits it as Ebionitic. They do not prove anything as to the existence of a New Testament Canon; but as far as they have any meaning they tend to shew that no such divisions had place in the Church as have been supposed to render the existence of a Catholic Canon impossible[3].

Chap. ii.

Agrippa Castor introduces a new form of the Apology. Hitherto we have noticed in succession defences of Christianity addressed to persecutors, philosophers, and Jews; he maintained the truth against heretics. Nothing appears to be known of his history. He is said to have been a 'very learned man,' and was probably of Jewish descent[4]. Eusebius speaks of him as a

The writings of Agrippa Castor

---

[1] Pref. Cels. ap. Routh, p. 97; Orig. *l. c.*
[2] Orig. *l. c.*: Cels. Pref. *l. c.*: Hieron. *Quæst. Hebr.* II. 507 (ap. Routh, p. 95). In the last instance he reads in Gen. i. 1, In filio fecit Deus cœlum et terram. Cf. Routh, p. 100.
[3] The Dialogue was in circulation in the time of Celsus, and consequently the date of its composition cannot be placed long after the death of Hadrian.
It may be concluded from Origen's notice (*l. c.*) that the doctrine of the Resurrection of the body suggested some of Celsus' objections, probably in connexion with the Second Advent. The reference to 'a strange and memorable narrative' contained in one of the Christian books probably refers to the Dialogue (compare c. 53, p. 200 *init.* with c. 52 *init.*).
[4] Vir valde doctus. Hieron. *de Virr. Ill.* 21. His Jewish descent appears to follow from the fact that he charged Basilides with teaching 'indifference in eating meats offered

contemporary of Saturninus and Basilides, and adds that he was the most famous among the many writers of the 'time who defended the doctrine of the Apostles and the 'Church chiefly on philosophic principles' (λογικώτερον)[1]. In particular, he composed 'a most satisfactory (ἱκανώ-'τατος) refutation of Basilides,' in which he noticed his commentaries on the Gospel, and exposed the claims of certain supposititious (ἀνύπαρκτοι) prophets, whom he had used to support his doctrines. This slight fact shews that historical criticism was not wholly wanting in the Church when first it was required. It would not, as far as we can see, have been an easy matter to secure a reception for forgeries claiming to be authoritative, even at the beginning of the second century.

shew signs of historical criticism.

§ 7. *Justin Martyr.*

The comparative fulness of our knowledge of Justin.

The writings and character of Justin Martyr stand out in clear relief from the fragments and names which we have hitherto reviewed. Instead of interpreting isolated phrases we can now examine complete and continuous works: instead of painfully collecting a few dry details from tradition we can contemplate the image which a Christian himself has drawn of his own life and experience. Justin was of Greek descent, but his family had been settled for two generations in the Roman colony of Flavia Neapolis, which was founded in the time of Vespasian near the site of the ancient Sichem[2]. The date of his birth is uncertain, but it was probably at the close of the first century. He tells us that his countrymen generally were addicted to the

---

'to idols' (Euseb. *H.E.* IV. 7); yet see Just. M. *Dial.* c. 35. His controversy with Basilides probably indicates some connexion with Alexandria.
[1] Euseb. *l. c.*
[2] *Ap.* I. I.

errors of Simon Magus[1], but it appears that he himself escaped that delusion, and began his search for truth among the teachers of the old philosophic schools. First he applied to a Stoic[2]; but after some time he found that he learned nothing of God from him, and his master affirmed that such knowledge was unnecessary. Next he betook himself to a peripatetic, 'a shrewd man,' he adds, 'in his own opinion.' But before many days were over, the Philosopher was anxious to settle with his pupil the price of his lessons, that their intercourse might prove profitable to them both. So Justin thought that he was no philosopher at all; and still yearning (τῆς ψυχῆς ἔτι σπαργώσης) for knowledge he applied to a Pythagorean, who enjoyed a great reputation and prided himself on his wisdom. But a knowledge of Music, Astronomy and Geometry was the necessary passport to his lectures; and since he was not possessed of it, Justin, as he seemed near to the fulfilment of his hopes, was once again doomed to disappointment. He fared better however with a Platonist, his next teacher, and in his company he seemed to grow wiser every day. It was at that time—when 'in his folly,' as he says, 'he hoped soon to attain to a clear vision of God'—that, seeking calm and retirement by the sea-shore, he met an aged man, meek and venerable, who led him at length from Plato to the Prophets, from metaphysics to faith. 'Pray before all things,' were the last words of this new master, 'that the gates of light be opened 'to you; for [the truths of revelation] are not compre-

His own account of his philosophic studies.

---

[1] *Ap.* I. 26; Σχεδὸν πάντες μὲν Σαμαρεῖς ὀλίγοι δὲ καὶ ἐν ἄλλοις ἔθνεσιν ὡς τὸν πρῶτον θεὸν ἐκεῖνον (Simon) ὁμολογοῦντες [ἐκεῖνον] καὶ προσκυνοῦσι. Cf. *Dial.* c. 120. It is an instructive fact that Sadducæism also prevailed in Samaria. [Hipp.] *Adv. Hær.* IX. 29.

[2] The following account is given chiefly in a translation from his own striking narrative. *Dial.* c. 2 sqq.

'hensible by the eye or mind of man, unless God and 'His Christ give him understanding¹.'

'Immediately a fire was kindled in my soul,' Justin adds, 'and I was possessed with a love for the prophets 'and those men who are Christ's friends². And as I 'discussed his arguments with myself I found Christi-'anity to be the only philosophy that is sure and suited 'to man's wants (ἀσφαλῆ τε καὶ σύμφορον). Thus then, 'and for this cause, am I a philosopher.'

In the strength of his new conviction he travelled far and wide to spread the truth which he had found. In the public walk (*xystus*) at Ephesus he held a discussion with the Jew Trypho, proving from the Old Testament that Jesus was the Christ. At Rome he is said to have established a school where he endeavoured to satisfy the doubts of Greeks. Everywhere he appeared 'as an ambassador of the Divine Word in the guise of 'a philosopher³.'

His active spirit found frequent expression in writing. Eusebius has given a list of such books of his 'as 'had come to his own knowledge,' adding that there were besides 'very many other works which were widely 'circulated⁴.' Of the writings which now bear his name two Apologies and the Dialogue with Trypho are genuine beyond all doubt; the rest are either undoubtedly spurious or reasonably suspected⁵. But those three

---

[1] *Dial.* c. 7 *ad fin.*

[2] This phrase, in connexion with the phrase immediately below, βου-λοίμην ἄν...πάντας...μὴ ἀφίστασθαι τῶν τοῦ Σωτῆρος λόγων, seems to point to Christian Scriptures coordinate with the Old Testament. The nature of the first interview with Trypho precluded any more immediate mention of them at the time.

[3] Euseb. *H. E.* IV. 11. Cf. *Dial.*

c. 1. If the *Cohortatio ad Græcos* be Justin's we must add Alexandria to the cities which he visited (c. 13). Compare Semisch, *Denkwürd. Just.* ss. 2 ff.

Credner (*Beiträge*, I. 99) suggests Corinth as the place where the Dialogue took place, if it be historical.

[4] Euseb. *H. E.* IV. 18.

[5] There is I believe a difference of style and tone which distinguishes

books are invaluable so far as they combine to give a wide view of the relation of Christianity, not indeed to the Christian Church, but to heathendom and Judaism[1].

A general account of the relation of his books to the Gospel-narrative.

The evidence of Justin is thus invested with peculiar importance; and the difficulties by which it is perplexed, though they have been frequently exaggerated, are proportionately great. Since a general view of its chief features will render our inquiry into its extent and character easier and more intelligible, we may state by anticipation that his writings exhibit a mass of references to the Gospel-narrative; that they embrace the chief facts of our Lord's life, and many details of His teaching; that they were derived, at least frequently, from written records, which he affirms to rest upon Apostolic authority, and to be used in the public assemblies of Christians, though he does not mention the names of their authors. It is to be noticed further that these references generally coincide both in facts and substance with what has been related by the three Synoptic Evangelists (most commonly by St Matthew), that they preserve by implication peculiarities of each of the Gospels, that they nevertheless shew additions to the received narrative and remarkable variations from its text, which in some cases are both repeated by Justin and found also in other writings[2].

---

the two Apologies and the Dialogue from all the other works attributed to Justin. The question is of little importance for our present inquiry, since the Gospel-references are chiefly found in the former.

[1] The chronology of Justin's life is involved in considerable perplexity. After a complete examination of the evidence Mr Hort concludes that 'we may without fear of considerable 'error set down Justin's *First Apo-* '*logy* to 145 or better still to 146,

'and his death to 148. The *Second* '*Apology*, if really separate from the 'first, will then fall in 146 or '147, and the *Dialogue with Try-* '*phon* about the same time' (*Journal of Class. and Sacr. Philology*, III. 139).

[2] Compare Semisch, *Denkwürdigkeiten Justin's* (Hamburg, 1848); Credner, *Beiträge*, I. 92—267 (Halle, 1832); Schwegler, *D. nachapostolische Zeitalter*, I. 217—231. [Later Essays by Hilgenfeld, Ritschl, Volk-

100   THE AGE OF THE GREEK APOLOGISTS.   [PART

Chap. ii.

Various solutions of the problem arising therefrom.

Such are the various phenomena which must be explained and harmonized. At first the difficulties of the problem were hardly felt, and the testimony of Justin was quoted in support of our Gospels without doubt or justification. But when the whole question was fairly stated there came a reaction, and various new hypotheses were proposed as offering a better solution of it than the traditional belief. Some fancied that Justin made use of one or more of the original sources from which the Canonical Gospels were derived. Others, with greater precision, identified his Memoirs of the Apostles with the Gospel according to the Hebrews. Others again suggested that he made use of a Harmony or combined narrative constructed out of Catholic materials[1]. Further investigations shewed that these notions were untenable, and the old opinion had again gained currency, when Credner maintained with great sagacity and research that we must look for the peculiarities of his quotations in a Gospel according to St Peter, one of the oldest writings of the Church, which under various forms retained its influence among Jewish Christians even after the doctrine of St Paul had obtained general reception[2].

Their common ground to be examined.

In one respect all these theories are alike. They presuppose that Justin's quotations cannot be naturally

mar, and the author of *Supernatural Religion*, leave the main results of this chapter quite unchanged.]

[1] These various hypotheses are examined clearly and satisfactorily by Semisch, ss. 16—33.

[2] *Beiträge*, I. 266, &c. (This *Gospel according to Peter* is supposed by Credner to have been 'essentially 'identical with the *Diatessaron* of 'Tatian and the *Gospel according to* '*the Hebrews*' (*Gesch. d. N. T. Kanon*, 22). In the absence of satisfactory evidence it is impossible to examine seriously what is a mere conjecture. The early historic notices of the Gospel lend no support to the identification, and our knowledge of the contents of the Gospel is far too meagre to allow of any conclusion being drawn from internal evidence, especially as all the early Gospels were recensions (so to speak) of the original oral Gospel of the Apostolic age.

reconciled with a belief in his use of our Gospels[1]. This is their common basis; and instead of examining in detail the various schemes which have been built upon it, we may inquire whether it be itself sound.

The first thing that must strike any one who examines a complete collection of the passages in question is the general coincidence in range and contents with our Gospels. Nothing for instance furnished wider scope for Apocryphal narrative than the history of the Infancy of our Lord: nothing on the other hand could be more fatal to Ebionism—the prevailing heresy of the age, as we are told—than the early chapters of St Matthew and St Luke. Yet Justin's account of the Infancy is as free from legendary admixture as it is full of incidents recorded by the Evangelists. He does not appear to have known anything more than they

1. The general coincidence of Justin's quotations with our Gospels:
1. Coincidence in facts.

The *Gospel according to Peter* is expressly referred to by Eusebius as used at Rhossus in Cilicia in the time of Serapion (see below P. II. c. 2. § 5); and by Origen, *In Matt.* T. x. 17; and again by Eusebius, *H. E.* III. 3, without any hint of its identity with the better known *Gospel according to the Hebrews*. In the fifth century however Theodoret (*Hæret. Fab.* II. 2) speaks of the 'Nazarenes as 'Jews who hold Christ to be a just 'man and use the so-called *Gospel ac-'cording to Peter'*; but the testimony is too late, even if it were explicit, to establish the supposed identity from what is known of the Nazarene Gospel.

The passage of Justin, *Dial.* c. 106 (see p. 111, note 2), has I believe nothing to do with this *Gospel of Peter*. The fragments of the *Gospel according to the Hebrews* which have been preserved offer no remarkable parallels with Justin's citations. See below.

[1] Credner himself allows that Justin was *acquainted* with the Canonical Gospels of St Matthew, St Mark, and St Luke, though he used in preference (p. 267) the Gospel of St Peter. His acquaintance with the Gospel of St John he considers more doubtful. Credner's words are well worthy of notice: 'Justin kannte in 'der That, wie es auch kaum anders 'denkbar ist, unsere Evangelien... 'Nur allein über die Bekanntschaft 'Justin's mit dem Ev. des Johannes 'lässt sich, ausser der allgemeinen 'Analogie, nichts Bestimmtes nach- 'weisen' (*Beiträge*, I. 258). It was however unlikely that his conclusions should be allowed to remain so incomplete. Schwegler for instance says (I. 232): '...so hat er (Justin) 'ohne Zweifel die εὐαγγέλια κατὰ 'Ματθαῖον, Μάρκον, u. s. f., bei denen 'es überdiess eine Frage ist, ob sie 'damals schon existirten, nicht ge- 'kannt, sondern ausschliesslich das 'sogenannte Evangelium Petri...oder 'das mit demselben identische He- 'bräer-evangelium benützt...'

Chap. ii.

(a) His account of the Infancy.

knew; and he tells without suspicion what they have related.

He tells us that Christ was descended from Abraham through Jacob, Judah, Phares, Jesse, and David[1]—that the Angel Gabriel was sent to foretell His Birth to the Virgin Mary[2]—that this was a fulfilment of the prophecy of Isaiah (vii. 14[3])—that Joseph was forbidden in a vision to put away his espoused wife, when he was so minded[4]—that our Saviour's Birth at Bethlehem had been foretold by Micah[5]—that His parents went thither from Nazareth where they dwelt, in consequence of the enrolment under Cyrenius[6]—that as they could not find a lodging in the village they lodged in a cave close by it, where Christ was born, and laid by Mary in a manger[7]—that while there wise men from Arabia, guided by a

---

[1] *Dial.* c. 120. See c. 100, ἐξ ὧν κατάγει ἡ Μαρία τὸ γένος. Cf. c. 43. This interpretation of the genealogies was probably adopted early. Clement of Alexandria, for example, distinctly refers the genealogy in *St Matthew* to the V. Mary: ἐν τῷ κατὰ Ματθαῖον εὐαγγελίῳ ἡ ἀπὸ Ἀβραὰμ γενεαλογία μέχρι Μαρίας τῆς μητρὸς τοῦ Κυρίου πεπαίωται. The grounds on which this conclusion was based may have been false, but at least it is strange carelessness to quote Justin's acceptance of the conclusion as a proof that he used some other than the Canonical Gospels.

[2] *Dial.* c. 100; Luke i. 35, 38.

[3] *Ap.* I. 33; Matt. i. 23.

[4] *Dial.* c. 78; Matt. i. 18 sqq.

[5] *Ap.* I. 34; *Dial.* c. 78. Matt. ii. 5, 6. The quotation (Mic. v. 2) in Justin agrees verbally with that in St Matthew, with the exception that Justin omits τὸν Ἰσραήλ, and differs very widely from the LXX. Cf. Credner, *Beiträge*, II. 148 f.

[6] *Ap.* I. 34: ἐπὶ Κυρηνίου τοῦ ὑμετέρου ἐν Ἰουδαίᾳ πρώτου γενομένου ἐπιτρόπου. *Dial.* c. 78: ἀπογραφῆς οὔσης ἐν τῇ Ἰουδαίᾳ τότε πρώτης ἐπὶ Κυρηνίου. The agreement of these words with the true reading in Luke ii. 2 αὕτη ἀπογραφὴ πρώτη ἐγένετο is worthy of notice. Cf. Credner, *Beitr.* I. 232 f.

[7] *Dial.* c. 78:...Ἐπειδὴ Ἰωσὴφ οὐκ εἶχεν ἐν τῇ κώμῃ ἐκείνῃ που καταλῦσαι, ἐν σπηλαίῳ τινὶ σύνεγγυς τῆς κώμης κατέλυσε· καὶ τότε αὐτῶν ὄντων ἐκεῖ ἐτετόκει ἡ Μαρία τὸν Χριστὸν καὶ ἐν φάτνῃ αὐτὸν ἐτεθείκει, κ.τ.λ. Luke ii. 7:...ἀνέκλινεν αὐτὸν ἐν φάτνῃ (without the article) διότι οὐκ ἦν αὐτοῖς τόπος ἐν τῷ καταλύματι. The two accounts seem to be simply supplementary. Later Fathers (*e. g.* Orig. *c. Cels.* I. 51) speak of the Cave without any misgiving that they contradict St Luke: Epiphanius actually quotes him for the fact; ὁ Λουκᾶς λέγει...τὸν παῖδα ...καὶ κεῖσθαι ἐν φάτνῃ καὶ ἐν σπηλαίῳ διὰ τὸ μὴ εἶναι τόπον ἐν τῷ καταλύματι (*Hær.* 51, 9: p. 431). Thilo has collected the authorities on the question: *Cod. Apocr.* I. 381 sqq.

star, worshipped Him, and offered Him gold and frankincense and myrrh, and by revelation were commanded not to return to Herod to whom they had first come[1]—that He was called Jesus as the Saviour of His people[2]—that by the command of God His parents fled with Him to Egypt for fear of Herod, and remained there till Archelaus succeeded him[3]—that Herod being deceived by the wise men commanded the children of Bethlehem to be put to death, so that the prophecy of Jeremiah was fulfilled who spoke of Rachel weeping for her children[4]—that Jesus grew after the common manner of men, working as a carpenter, and so waited in obscurity thirty years more or less, till the coming of John the Baptist[5].

He tells us moreover that this John the son of Elizabeth came preaching by the Jordan the baptism of repentance, wearing a leathern girdle and a raiment of camel's hair, and eating only locusts and wild honey[6]—that men supposed that he was the Christ, to whom he

Chap. ii.

(β) *His account of the Mission of John the Baptist.*

---

[1] *Dial.* c. 78; Matt. ii. 11, 12. The repetition of the phrase ἀπὸ Ἀρραβίας (cc. 77, 78, 88, 102, 103, 106) is remarkable. The more specific term is evidently a gloss adopted to bring out the correspondence with prophecy as to the 'strength of Damascus.' Damascus was reckoned as part of Arabia (c. 78, p. 305 A).
[2] *Ap.* I. 33 ; Matt. i. 21.
[3] *Dial.* cc. 78, 103; Matt. ii. 13.
[4] *Dial.* c. 78; Matt. ii. 17, 18. There is a natural exaggeration in Justin's language which forms a remarkable contrast to St Matthew. 'Herod ordered,' he says, 'all the 'male children in Bethlehem without 'exception (πάντας ἁπλῶς τοὺς παῖδας 'τοὺς ἐν Βηθλεέμ) to be put to death.' Cf. c. 103. So again it is not unsignificant that he appeals to the prophecy (Jerem. xxxi. [xxxviii.] 15) in

a different manner. St Matthew says simply τότε ἐπληρώθη τὸ ῥηθέν· but he more definitely τοῦτο ἐπεπροφήτευτο μέλλειν γίνεσθαι. He transforms a typical event into a special prediction. In the Gospel they are markedly distinguished.
The quotation is verbally the same in Justin and St Matthew, differing widely from the LXX.
[5] *Dial.* c. 88; Luke ii. 40, iii. 23. Mark vi. 3. The explanation of the ὡσεὶ of St Luke is to be noticed.
[6] *Dial.* c. 88, cf. cc. 49, 84; Matt. iii. 1, 4; Luke i. 13; John i. 19 ff. The phrase Ἰωάννου καθεζομένου ἐπὶ τοῦ Ἰορδάνου, repeated by Justin (*Dial.* cc. 88, 51) is changed into καθεζομένου ἐπὶ τὸν Ἰορδάνην in c. 49. There can be no reason to think with Credner (p. 218) that Justin found the words in his Gospel.

Chap. ii.

answered *I am not the Christ, but a voice of one crying; for He that is mightier than I will soon come* (ἥξει), *whose sandals I am not worthy to bear*—that when Jesus descended into the Jordan to be baptized by him a fire was kindled in the river, and when He came up out of the water the Holy Spirit as a dove lighted upon Him, and a voice came from Heaven saying *Thou art my Son; this day have I begotten Thee*[1]—that immediately after His Baptism the devil came to Jesus and tempted Him, bidding Him at last to worship him[2]. He further adds that Christ Himself recognised John as the Elias who should precede Him, *to whom men had done whatsoever they listed;* and thus he relates how Herod put John into prison; and how the daughter of Herodias danced before the king on his birthday and pleased him, so that he promised to grant her anything she wished, and that she by her mother's desire asked for the head of John to be given her on a charger, and that so John was put to death[3].

(γ) *His account of the Passion.*

Henceforth, after speaking in general terms of the miracles of Christ, how *He healed all manner of sickness and disease*[4], Justin says little of the details of His Life till the last great events. Then he narrates Christ's triumphal entry into Jerusalem from Bethphage as a fulfilment of prophecy[5] the (second) cleansing of the Temple[6], the conspiracy against Him[7], the institution of the

---

[1] *Dial.* cc. 88, 103. Compare ii. 2. γ, below, for an explanation of the Apocryphal additions to the text of the Evangelists.
[2] *Dial.* cc. 103, 125. The order of the Temptations followed by Justin is therefore apparently that of St Matthew. Semisch, s. 99 *anm.*
[3] *Dial.* c. 49; Matt. xvii. 11—13.
[4] *Ap.* I. 31, 48; *Dial.* c. 69. Matt. iv. 23.
[5] *Ap.* I. 35; *Dial.* c. 53. The version of the prophecy is different in the two passages. The first part however in both agrees with the LXX. and differs from St Matthew; the last words on the contrary agree better with St Matthew than with the LXX. Cf. Semisch, ss. 117—119.
[6] *Dial.* c. 17.
[7] *Dial.* c. 104.

Eucharist *for the remembrance of Him*[1], the singing of the Psalm afterwards[2], the Agony at night on the Mount of Olives at which three of His disciples were present[3], the prayer[4], the bloody sweat[5], the arrest[6], the flight of the Apostles[7], the silence before Pilate[8], the remand to Herod[9], the Crucifixion, the division of Christ's raiment by lot[10], the signs and words of mockery of the bystanders[11], the Cry of Sorrow[12], the Last Words of Resignation[13], the Burial on the evening of the day of the Passion[14], the Resurrection on Sunday[15], the Appearance to the Apostles and disciples, how Christ opened to them the Scriptures[16], the calumnies of the Jews[17], the commission to the Apostles[18], the Ascension[19].

The same particularity, the same intertexture of the narratives of St Matthew and St Luke—for St Mark has few peculiar materials to contribute—the same occasional introduction of a minute trait or of higher colouring, characterize the great mass of Justin's references to the Gospel-history. These features are as distinctly marked in his account of the Passion as of the Nativity. There are some slight differences in detail, which will be noticed afterwards, but the broad resemblance remains unchanged. The incidents of the Gospel-narrative to which Justin refers appear to be exactly such as he might have derived

Chap. ii.

General character of this coincidence.

---

[1] *Ap.* I. 66. Cf. *Dial.* cc. 41, 70.
[2] *Dial.* c. 106.
[3] *Dial.* c. 99.
[4] *Ibid.*
[5] *Dial.* c. 103. Cf. *Ap.* I. 50; *Dial.* c. 53.
[6] *Dial.* c. 103. *Dial.* 103, οὐδεὶς γὰρ οὐδὲ μέχρις ἑνὸς ἀνθρώπου βοηθεῖν αὐτῷ ὡς ἀναμαρτήτῳ βοηθὸς ὑπῆρχε. The words are suggested by Ps. xxi. (xxii.) 12 οὐκ ἔστιν ὁ βοηθῶν, and I cannot see in them any 'contradiction' of the Gospels. Cf. Matt. xxvi. 56.
[7] *Dial.* c. 53.
[8] *Dial.* c. 102.
[9] *Dial.* c. 103; Luke xxiii. 7.
[10] *Dial.* c. 97. Cf. *Ap.* I. 35.
[11] *Ap.* I. 38; *Dial.* c. 101.
[12] *Dial.* c. 99.
[13] *Dial.* c. 105; Luke xxiii. 46.
[14] *Dial.* c. 97.
[15] *Ap.* I. 67.
[16] *Dial.* cc. 53, 106. *Ap.* I. 50.
[17] *Dial.* c. 108; Matt. xxviii. 13. See p. 150 ff.
[18] *Ap.* I. 61.
[19] *Dial.* 132; *Ap.* I. 46.

from the Synoptic Evangelists. His object is to give a general view of the substance of the Evangelic records; and not to reproduce exactly any one record. The variations in his quotations of the same passage absolutely exclude the latter supposition.

2. Coincidence in the quotations of our Lord's teaching.

The greater part however of Justin's references are made to the teaching of the Saviour, and not to His works. He spoke of Christianity as a power mighty in its enduring and godlike character. He spoke of Christ as Him of whom the prophets witnessed. But miracles —those transient signs of a Divine Presence—are almost unnoticed in comparison with the words which bear for ever the living stamp of their original source. This form of argument was in some degree imposed upon him by the position which he occupied; but to such a mind as his it was no less congenial than necessary. Whether he addressed Heathen or Jews, the fulfilment of prophecy furnished him with a striking outward proof of the claims of Christianity; and the moral teaching of Christ completed the impression by introducing an inward proof. It was enough if he could bring men to listen to the teaching of the Church. It was not his task to anticipate its office, or to do away with the discipline and duties of the catechumen. To forget this is to forget the very business of an Apologist. And yet the entire consistency of his writings with their proposed end has furnished an objection against the authenticity of St John's Gospel. For unless we put out of sight the purpose for which Justin wrote, can it be a matter of wonder that he makes few allusions to the 'spiritual Gospel'—that he exhibits few traces of those deep and mysterious revelations which our Lord vouchsafed under peculiar circumstances, for the conviction of His enemies, or for the confirmation of believing hearts? They were

How far Justin's quotations were limited by his position.

Relation to St John's Gospel.

I.] JUSTIN MARTYR. 107

of no weight as evidence, even as our Lord Himself said; and the time was not yet come when Justin could naturally unfold them to his hearers. The same cause which retarded the publication of St John's Gospel deferred the use of it. It was a spiritual supplement to the others—a light from heaven to kindle them into life: but it was necessary that the substance should exist, before the supplement could be added; it was necessary that the body should be fully formed, before the spirit, the highest life, could be infused into it.

It has been already shewn that the incidents in the Life of Christ which Justin mentions strikingly coincide with those narrated in the Gospels; the style and language of the quotations which he makes from Christ's teaching agree no less exactly with those of the Evangelists. He quotes frequently from memory[1]; he interweaves the words which we find at present separately given by St Matthew, St Mark, and St Luke[2]; he condenses, combines, transposes, the language of our Lord as they have recorded it[3]; he makes use of phrases characteristic of different Gospels[4]; yet, with very few exceptions, he preserves through all these changes the marked

Chap. ii.
John v. 47.

(a) *Coincidences in language.*

---

[1] This follows from the fact that his quotations of the same passage differ. See pp. 127 sqq.
[2] (a) Matthew and Luke: *Dial.* cc. 17, 51, 76; *Ap.* I. 19; (β) Matthew and Mark: *Ap.* I. 15.
[3] *E. g. Ap.* I. 15, 43; *Dial.* cc. 49, 77, 78, &c.
[4] (a) Words characteristic of St Matthew: *e.g.* βασιλεία τῶν οὐρανῶν—μαλακία—[ἵνα πληρωθῇ τὸ ῥηθέν, de Resurr. c. 4]—ὁ πατὴρ ὁ ἐν τοῖς οὐρανοῖς—ἐρρέθη—βρέχειν (impers.)—ἀνατέλλειν (act.).
(β) Words characteristic of St Luke: *e. g.* χάρις—εὐαγγελίζεσθαι—υἱὸς ὑψίστου.
(γ) Words characteristic of St John: *e. g.* τέκνα θεοῦ—προσκυνοῦμεν λόγῳ καὶ ἀληθείᾳ τιμῶντες—τὸ ὕδωρ τῆς ζωῆς—πηγὴ ὕδατος ζῶντος—φῶς. Credner's remark (*Beiträge,* I. p. 213) that there is no trace of the linguistic peculiarities of our Evangelists in Justin's quotations seems to me to be incorrect.

peculiarities of the New Testament phraseology without the admixture of any foreign element[1]. And more than this: though he omits the Parables[2], which are rather lessons of wisdom than laws of authority, he refers to parts of the whole series of our Lord's discourses given in the Synoptic Gospels; and attributes only two sayings to Him which are not substantially found there[3]. The first call to repentance[4], the Sermon on the Mount[5], the gathering from the East and West[6], the invitation to sinners[7], the description of the true fear[8], the charge to the Apostles[9], the charge to the Seventy[10], the mission of John[11], the revelation of the Father[12], the promise of the sign of Jonah[13], the prophecy of the Passion[14], the acknowledgement of Sonship[15], the teaching on the price of a soul[16], on marriage[17], on the goodness of God alone[18], on the tribute due to Cæsar[19], on the two commandments[20], the woes against the Scribes and Pharisees[21], the prophecy concerning false teachers[22], the denouncement of future punishment on the wicked[23], the

---

[1] The differences of language which I have noticed are the following: καινὸν ποιεῖτε (*Ap*. I. 15, *bis*)—δέρματα προβάτων (*Ap*. I. 16; *Dial*. c. 35; cf. Hebr. xi. 37)—σκολοπενδρῶν (*Dial*. c. 76)—ψευδαπόστολοι (*Dial*. c. 35) —δικαιοσύνην καὶ εὐσέβειαν πληροῦσθαι (*Dial*. c. 93)—αἱ κλεῖς (*Dial*. c. 17)—ἅμα (freq.). Credner (p. 260) quotes ἐπὶ τῷ ὀνόματι αὐτοῦ as a peculiarity, but surely without reason. Cf. Matt. xviii. 5, xxiv. 5; Mark ix. 39; Luke ix. 48, 49, xxi. 8.
[2] The only references to the Parables are, I believe, to that of the Sower and of the Talents (*Dial*. c. 125).
[3] *Dial*. c. 47: Διὸ καὶ ὁ ἡμέτερος κύριος Ἰησοῦς Χριστὸς εἶπεν· Ἐν οἷς ἂν ὑμᾶς καταλάβω, ἐν τούτοις καὶ κρινῶ (κρίνω, Credner). *Dial*. c. 35. See below, ii. 2. γ.
[4] *Dial*. c. 51; Matt. iv. 17.
[5] *Ap*. I. 15, 16; *Dial*. cc. 96, 105, 115, 133.
[6] *Dial*. c. 76.
[7] *Ap*. I. 15.   [8] *Ap*. I. 19.
[9] *Dial*. c. 82; Matt. x. 22.
[10] *Ap*. I. 16; Luke x. 16. *Dial*. c. 76; Luke x. 19.
[11] *Dial*. c. 51; Matt. xi. 12—15.
[12] *Ap*. I. 63; *Dial*. c. 100; Matt. xi. 27.
[13] *Dial*. c. 107.
[14] *Dial*. cc. 76, 100.
[15] *Dial*. c. 76.
[16] *Ap*. I. 15.
[17] *Ap*. I. 15; Matt. xix. 12. *Dial*. c. 81; Luke xx. 35, 36.
[18] *Ap*. I. 16; *Dial*. c. 101.
[19] *Ap*. I. 17.
[20] *Ap*. I. 16; *Dial*. c. 93.
[21] *Dial*. cc. 17, 112, 122.
[22] *Ap*. I. 16; *Dial*. cc. 35, 82.
[23] *Ap*. I. 16; *Dial*. c. 76. Cf. *Ap*. I. 17; Luke xii. 48.

teaching after the Resurrection[1]—are all clearly recognized, and quoted, if not always in the language of any one Evangelist, at least in the dialect of the New Testament. At present we do not offer any explanation of the peculiar form which Justin's quotations wear. It is sufficient to remark that both in range and tone, in substance and expression, they bear a general and striking likeness to the contents of our Gospels.

Up to this time it has been noticed that the quotations from the Gospel-history in the early Fathers are almost uniformly anonymous. The words of Christ were as a living voice in the Church, apart from any written record; and the great events of His Life were symbolized in its services. In Justin the old and new meet. He habitually represents Christ as speaking, and not the Evangelist as relating His discourses; but he also distinctly refers to histories, the famous *Memoirs of the Apostles*[2], in which he found written 'all things con-'cerning Jesus Christ.' These striking words mark the presence of a new age[3]. The written records were now regarded as the sufficient and complete source of knowledge with regard to the facts of the Gospel. Tradition, to which Papias still appealed, was by Justin definitely cast aside as a new source of information. The expression is casual, but on this account it presents only the more clearly the instinctive conviction of the Christian society to which Justin belonged.

The peculiar objects which Justin had in view in his

Chap. ii.

II. *Justin's special quotations from the* Memoirs *of the Apostles.*

The nature

---

[1] *Ap.* I. 61; *Dial.* c. 53.
[2] Τὰ 'Απομνημονεύματα τῶν 'Αποστόλων. Cf. p. 111, note 2. The title was probably adopted from that of Xenophon's well-known 'Απομνημονεύματα Σωκράτους, from which indeed the word had been already borrowed by several writers. In various forms it appears frequently in Ecclesiastical Greek. Euseb. *H. E.* III. 39; V. 8; VI. 25. It can scarcely be necessary to remark that the genitive may describe either the author or the subject.
[3] Cf. p. 112, n. 1.

extant writings did not suggest, even if they did not exclude, any minute description of these comprehensive records. It would have added nothing to the vivid picture of Christianity which he drew for the heathen to have quoted with exact precision the testimony of this or that Apostle, even if such a mode of quotation had been usual. One thing they might require to know, and that he tells them, that the words of Christ were still the text of Christian instruction, that the *Memoirs of the Apostles* were still read together with the writings of the Prophets in their weekly services[1]. The writings to which he appealed were not only complete in their contents but they were publicly attested. There was no room for interpolation of new facts or for the introduction of new documents into the use of the Christian Church. The heathen inquirer looked to the general character of Christianity, and on that point Justin satisfies him. So on the other hand the great difficulty in a controversy with a Jew was to shew that the humiliation and death of Christ were reconcileable with the Messianic prophecies. The chief facts were here confessed, the work of the Apologist was to harmonize the prediction and the fulfilment. In both cases his task was preparatory and not final, to lay the foundation of faith and not to build it up; and with this object it was enough for him to assert generally that the Memoirs which he quoted rested upon Apostolic authority[2].

The manner in which Justin alludes to these Memoirs of the Apostles in his first Apology and in his Dialogue with Trypho confirms what has been just said. If his mode of reference had not been modified by the nature of his subject, it would surely have been the same in both. As it is, there is a marked difference, and exactly such as

[1] *Ap.* I. 67.   [2] *Dial.* c. 103.

might have been expected. In the Apology, which contains nearly fifty allusions to the Gospel-history, he speaks only twice of the Apostolic authorship of his Memoirs, and in one other place mentions them generally[1]. In the Dialogue, which contains about seventy allusions, he quotes them ten times, directly or by implication, as *The Memoirs of the Apostles*, and in four other places as *The Memoirs*[2].

This difference is still more striking when examined closely. Every quotation of our Lord's words in the Apology is simply introduced by the phrases 'thus 'Christ said' or 'taught' or 'exhorted;' His words were their own witness. For the public events of His Life Justin refers to the Enrolment of Quirinus and the Acts of Pilate[3]. He quotes the 'Gospels' only when he must speak of things beyond the range of common history. Standing before a Roman emperor as the apologist of the Christians, he confines himself as far as possible to common ground; and if he is compelled for illustration

Chap. ii.

The quotations in the Apology.

---

[1] *Ap.* I. 66, 67, 33: cf. c. 61.
[2] It will be useful to give a classification of all the passages in which Justin quotes the *Memoirs*, with the forms of quotation. The following will suffice to explain and justify the statement in the text:
(a) Generally: τὰ ἀπομνημονεύματα τῶν ἀποστόλων. *Dial.* c. 100, γεγραμμένον ἐν τ. ἀπομν. τ. ἀπ. cc. 101, 103, 104, 106, γέγραπται ἐν τ. ἀπομν. τ. ἀπ. c. 102, ἐν τ. ἀπομν. τ. ἀπ. δεδήλωται. c. 106, ἐν τ. ἀπομν. τ. ἀπ. δηλοῦται γεγενημένον. c. 88, ἔγραψαν οἱ ἀπόστολοι.
(β) Specially: *Dial.* c. 106, γεγράφθαι ἐν· τοῖς ἀπομν. αὐτοῦ (*i. e.* Πέτρου) γεγενημένον. c. 103, [ἀπομνημονεύματα] ἅ φημι ὑπὸ τῶν ἀποστόλων αὐτοῦ καὶ τῶν ἐκείνοις παρακολουθησάντων συντετάχθαι. It is obvious that the article in both

cases describes the class to which the writers belonged. If the article in the first case 'refers the Memoirs 'to the collective body of the Apo-'stles'; what is 'the collective body' of the disciples?
(γ) τὰ ἀπομνημονεύματα. *Dial.* c. 105, ἀπὸ τ. ἀπομν. ἐμάθομεν. c. 105, ἐκ τ. ἀπομν. ἔμαθον. c. 105, 107, ἐν τοῖς ἀπομν. γέγραπται.
[3] *Ap.* I. 34: ὡς καὶ μαθεῖν δύνασθε ἐκ τῶν ἀπογραφῶν τῶν γενομένων ἐπὶ Κυρηνίου. c. 35: καὶ ταῦτα ὅτι γέγονε δύνασθε μαθεῖν ἐκ τῶν ἐπὶ Ποντίου Πιλάτου γενομένων ἄκτων. Whether Justin referred to the Apocryphal *Acts of Pilate* which we now have, or not, is of no importance: it is only necessary to remark the kind of evidence which he thought best suited to his design.

Chap. ii.

to quote the books of the Christians, he takes care to shew that they were recognised by the Church, and were no private documents of his own. Thus in speaking of the Annunciation he says: 'And the Angel of 'God sent to the Virgin at that season announced to 'her glad tidings, saying, *Behold thou shalt conceive of* '*the Holy Spirit, and bear a Son, and He shall be called* '*the Son of the Highest; and thou shalt call His name* *Jesus, for He shall save His people from their sins;* as 'those who have written Memoirs of all things con- 'cerning our Saviour Jesus Christ taught us, whom we 'believed, since also the Prophetic Spirit said that this 'would come to pass[1].' So again when explaining the celebration of the Eucharist he adds: 'The Apostles in 'the Memoirs made by them, which are called Gospels, 'handed down that it was thus enjoined on them[2]....'

---

[1] *Ap.* I. 33: ὡς οἱ ἀπομνημονεύ-σαντες πάντα τὰ περὶ τοῦ σωτῆρος ἡμῶν Ἰησοῦ Χριστοῦ ἐδίδαξαν κ.τ.λ. The phrase οἱ ἀπομνημονεύσαντες recals Tertullian's remarkable phrase 'Matthæus *commentator Evangelii*' (*de carne Christi* 22. Cf. *de resurr. carn.* 33), that is 'compiler of the 'Gospel' (commentarii). Credner (p. 129) raises a difficulty about the description. Where, he asks, is the written Gospel which could contain all? The quotation points to St Luke; and St Luke himself tells us that his Gospel contained an account *concerning* all things (περὶ πάντων) '*that Jesus began to do and* '*to teach*' (Acts i. 1). The coincidence is at least well worthy of notice. It removes the difficulty, even if it does not also point to the very source of Justin's language. Cf. supr. p. 109.

[2] *Ap.* I. 66: οἱ γὰρ ἀπόστολοι ἐν τοῖς γενομένοις ὑπ᾽ αὐτῶν ἀπομνημονεύμασιν, ἃ καλεῖται εὐαγγέλια, οὕτως παρέδωκαν ἐντετάλθαι αὐτοῖς... The conjecture that ἃ καλεῖται εὐαγγέλια is a gloss is very unfortunate. It could not be intended for the information of Christian readers; and a copyist would scarcely be likely to supply for the use of heathen what Justin had not thought fit to add. Credner's argument that if our Gospels were referred to Justin would have said ἃ καλεῖται τὰ τέσσαρα εὐαγγέλια (*Gesch. d. N. T. Kanon*, 107) is even more unhappy, and a singular instance of a want of apprehension of the circumstances of the writing. The use of the term 'Gospels' in this connexion is more important than might appear at first; for 'there is 'really no *proof* that in the time of 'Justin Martyr (with the possible ex-'ception of the Gospel according to 'the Hebrews) there was a single 'work, bearing the title of a Gospel, 'which as a *history of Christ's Minis-*'*try* came into competition with our 'present four Gospels....' Dr Abbot, *The authorship of the Fourth Gospel*, Boston, 1880, p. 16, and for the use

I.] JUSTIN MARTYR. 113

And once more, when describing the Christian Service he notices that 'the Memoirs of the Apostles or the writings 'of the Prophets are read, as long as the time admits[1].' There is no further mention of the Memoirs in the Apology. In the Dialogue the case was somewhat different. Trypho was himself acquainted with the Gospel[2] and Justin's language becomes proportionately more exact. The words of our Lord are still quoted very often simply as His words, without any acknowledgement of a written record; but from time to time, when reference is made to words which seem to be of more special moment, it is added that they are so 'written in 'the Gospel[3].' In one passage the contrast between the substance of Christ's teaching and the record of it is brought out very clearly. After speaking of the death of John the Baptist, Justin adds: 'Wherefore also our

Chap. ii.

The quotations in the Dialogue.

Coincidences with

---

of the plural, even without the article, for a reference to a passage in one Gospel: *ibid.* p. 98.

[1] *Ap.* I. 67.
[2] *Dial.* c. 10: τὰ ἐν τῷ λεγομένῳ εὐαγγελίῳ παραγγέλματα. The use of the singular, which recurs c. 100, is worthy of notice when compared with the plural *Ap.* I. 66 (see above p. 112, n. 2); but nothing can be more unreasonable than to conclude (Credner, *Gesch. d. N. T. Kanon*, § 10) that the reference is necessarily to a single history. Εὐαγγέλιον and *Evangelium* were used from the first with the same latitude as the *Gospel* with us. Thus Irenæus in the great passage where he treats of the characteristics and mystical types of the four Gospels says: ὁποία οὖν ἡ πραγματεία τοῦ υἱοῦ τοῦ θεοῦ, τοιαύτη καὶ τῶν ζώων (the Cherubim) ἡ μορφή· καὶ ὁποία ἡ τῶν ζώων μορφή, τοιοῦτος καὶ ὁ χαρακτὴρ τοῦ εὐαγγελίου. Τετράμορφα γὰρ τὰ ζῶα, τετράμορφον καὶ τὸ εὐαγγέλιον καὶ ἡ πραγματεία τοῦ κυρίου...τούτων δὲ οὕτως ἐχόντων μάταιοι πάντες...οἱ ἀθετοῦντες τὴν ἰδέαν τοῦ εὐαγγελίου καὶ εἴτε πλείονα εἴτε ἐλάττονα τῶν εἰρημένων παρεισφέροντες εὐαγγελίων πρόσωπα (Iren. III. 11. 8, 9). Whatever may be thought of the argument of Irenæus, his words shew clearly that our four Gospels might be referred to either as εὐαγγέλιον or εὐαγγέλια. Tertullian's language is of the same character: Nam sicut in veteribus...ita in Evangelio responsionem Domini ad Philippum tuentur (*adv. Prax.* 20). Of Theophilus Jerome says: Legi sub ejus nomine *in Evangelium Commentarios* (*de Virr. Ill.* s. v.). And once again Origen at the beginning of his *Commentary on St John* writes καὶ γὰρ τολμητέον εἰπεῖν πασῶν τῶν γραφῶν εἶναι ἀπαρχὴν τὸ εὐαγγέλιον. The singular occurs also in [Clem.] *Ep. Sec.* c. viii..λέγει ὁ κύριος ἐν τῷ εὐαγγελίῳ· and probably in *Mart. Polyc.* c. iv. οὐχ οὕτως διδάσκει τὸ εὐαγγέλιον the reference is to the written Gospel. See also pp. 58 f. and Dr Abbot, *l.c.* p. 22 n.

[3] Cf. below, p. 131 ff.

I 2

'Christ when on earth told those who said that Elias 'must come before Christ, *Elias indeed will come and* '*will restore all things; but I say to you that Elias came* '*already, and they knew him not, but did to him all that* '*they listed.* And it is written, *Then understood the* '*disciples that he spake to them concerning John the Bap-* '*tist*[1].' In another place it appears that Justin refers particularly to a passage in the Memoirs. 'The mention 'of the fact,' he says, 'that Christ changed the name of 'Peter one of the Apostles and that the event has been 'written in his (Peter's) Memoirs, together with His 'having changed the name of two other brethren who 'were sons of Zebedee to *Boanerges*, tended to signify 'that He was the same through whom the surname 'Israel was given to Jacob, and Joshua to Hoshea[2].' Now the surname given to James and John is only found at present in one of our Gospels, and there it is mentioned in immediate connexion with the change of Peter's name. That Gospel is the Gospel of St Mark, which by the universal voice of antiquity was referred to the authority of St Peter[3]. That Justin found also in his Memoirs facts at present peculiar to St Luke's narrative is equally clear: for he writes 'Jesus as He gave 'up His Spirit upon the cross said *Father, into Thy* '*hands I commend my Spirit:* even as I learned from 'the Memoirs this fact also[4].'

But this is not all: in his Apology Justin speaks of the Memoirs generally as written by the Apostles. In the Dialogue his words are more precise: 'In the Me- 'moirs, which I say were composed by the Apostles and 'those who followed them, [it is written] that *Sweat as*

---

[1] *Dial.* c. 49; Matt. xvii. 13; cf. p. 132.
[2] *Dial.* c. 106; Mark iii. 16, 17.
[3] Cf. pp. 74 f.
[4] *Dial.* c. 105; Luke xxiii. 46.

'*drops [of blood] streamed down* [Jesus] as He was pray- 'ing and saying *Let this cup if it be possible pass away* '*from me*¹.' The description, it will be seen, precedes the quotation of a passage found in St Luke, the follower of an Apostle, and not an Apostle himself. Some such fact as this is needed to explain why Justin distinguishes at this particular time the authorship of the records which he used. And no short account would apply more exactly to our present Gospels than that which he gives. Two of them were written by Apostles, two by their followers. There were many Apocryphal Gospels, but it is not known that any one of them bore the name of a follower of the Apostles. The application of Justin's words to our Gospels seems indeed absolutely necessary when they are compared with those of Tertullian, who says²: 'we lay down as a principle first that the Evan- 'gelic Instrument has Apostles for its authors, on whom 'this charge of publishing the Gospel was imposed by the 'Lord himself; that if [it includes the writings of] Apo- 'stolic men also, still they were not alone, but [wrote] 'with [the help of] Apostles and after [the teaching of] 'Apostles... In fine, John and Matthew out of the num-

Chap. ii.

compared with that of Tertullian.

¹ *Dial.* c. 103: ἐν τοῖς ἀπομνημονεύμασιν, ἅ φημι ὑπὸ τῶν ἀποστόλων αὐτοῦ καὶ τῶν ἐκείνοις παρακολουθησάντων (Luke i. 3) συντετάχθαι, [γέγραπται] ὅτι ἱδρὼς ὡσεὶ θρόμβοι κατεχεῖτο αὐτοῦ εὐχομένου καὶ λέγοντος Παρελθέτω εἰ δυνατὸν τὸ ποτήριον τοῦτο. Luke xxii. 44 (Matt. xxvi. 39). The omission of the word αἵματος was probably suggested by the passage in Psalm xxii. 14 which Justin is explaining (Semisch, p. 147). It cannot have arisen from any Docetic tendency, as the whole context shews. The entire pericope (vv. 43, 44) is omitted by very important authorities, but I cannot find that αἵματος alone is omitted elsewhere than in Justin. (Yet cf. Hipp. ap. Tischdf.) Cf. Griesbach, with Schulz's additions, and Tischdf. *ad loc.* Epiphanius (*adv. Hær.* II. 2. 59, quoted by Semisch) insists on the sweat only, though he quotes the verse at length.

² Tertull. *adv. Marc.* IV. 2: Constituimus imprimis evangelicum instrumentum *apostolos* autores habere, quibus hoc munus evangelii promulgandi ab ipso Domino sit impositum; si et *apostolicos*, non tamen solos sed cum apostolis et post apostolos... Denique nobis fidem ex apostolis Johannes et Matthæus insinuant, ex apostolicis Lucas et Marcus instaurant...

Chap. ii.

The substance of Justin's quotations from them.

'ber of the Apostles implant faith in us, Luke and 'Mark out of the number of their followers refresh it...'

In addition to these cardinal quotations from the Memoirs, Justin refers to them elsewhere in his Dialogue for facts and words from the Evangelic history. As the exact form of all these quotations will be examined afterwards as far as may be necessary, it will be sufficient now merely to shew by a general enumeration the extent of their coincidence with our Gospels[1]. They include an account of the Birth of our Lord from a Virgin[2], of the appearance of a Dove at His Baptism[3], of His Temptation[4], of the conspiracy of the wicked against Him[5], of the hymn which He sang with His disciples before His betrayal[6], of His silence before Pilate[7], of His Crucifixion at the Passover[8], of the mockery of His enemies[9]. So also Justin quotes from them His reproof of the righteousness of the Pharisees[10], and how He gave them only the sign of Jonah[11]; and proclaimed that He alone could reveal the Father to men[12].

A summary of all that Justin says of them.

This then is the sum of what Justin says of the Memoirs of the Apostles. They were many, and yet one[13]: they were called Gospels: they contained a record of all things concerning Jesus Christ: they were admitted by Christians generally: they were read in their public ser-

---

[1] It is interesting to compare this summary of special references with the list of all Justin's Evangelic references given already, pp. 102 ff.
[2] *Dial.* c. 105.
[3] *Dial.* c. 88.
[4] *Dial.* c. 103.
[5] *Dial.* c. 104.
[6] *Dial.* c. 106; Matt. xxvi. 30.
[7] *Dial.* c. 102; Matt. xxvii. 12 ff.; Mark xv. 3 ff.
[8] *Dial.* c. 111.
[9] *Dial.* c. 101; Matt. xxvii. 39—43.
[10] *Dial.* c. 105; Matt. v. 20.
[11] *Dial.* c. 107; Matt. xii. 38—41.
[12] *Dial.* c. 100; Matt. xi. 27.
[13] *Ap.* I. 66: ἃ καλεῖται εὐαγγέλια. *Dial.* c. 100: ἐν τῷ εὐαγγελίῳ γέγραπται. This view of the essential oneness of the Gospels explains very naturally the freedom with which different narratives were combined in quotation. Irenæus was apparently the first to recognise, however imperfectly, variety in this unity. See p. 113, n. 2. As the records were several so too were the writers: *Ap.* I. 33, p. 112, n. 1.

vices: they were of Apostolic authority, though not exclusively of Apostolic authorship: they were composed in part by Apostles and in part by their followers. And beyond this, we gather that they related facts only mentioned at present by one or other of the Evangelists: that thus they were intimately connected with each one of the Synoptic Gospels: that they contained nothing, as far as Justin expressly quotes them, which our Gospels do not now substantially contain. And if we go still further, and take in the whole mass of Justin's anonymous references to the life and teaching of Christ, the general effect is the same. The resemblance between the narratives is in the one case more exact, but in the other it is more extensive. Up to this point of our inquiry, and omitting for the moment all consideration of Justin's historical relation to the anonymous Roman Canon of Muratori[1] and to Irenæus, the identification of his Memoirs with our Gospels seems to be as reasonable as it is natural. But on the other hand it is said that there are fatal objections to this identification; that Justin nowhere mentions the Evangelists by name: that the text of his quotations differs materially from that of the Gospels: that he introduces apocryphal additions into his narrative. And each of these statements must be examined before the right weight can be assigned to these general coincidences between the Gospels and Memoirs in subject, language, and character, of which we have hitherto spoken.

It has been already shewn[2] that there were peculiar circumstances in Justin's case which rendered any definite quotation of the Evangelists unlikely and unsuitable, even if such a mode of quotation had been common at the time. But in fact when he referred to

[1] See below § 12.   [2] p. 110.

Chap. ii.

Objections to their identification with our Gospels.

(1) *The authors' names are not mentioned,*

but the Gospels are

118   THE AGE OF THE GREEK APOLOGISTS.   [PART

*Chap. ii.
constantly referred to anonymously by other writers.*

written records of Christ's life and words he made an advance beyond which the later Apologists rarely proceeded¹. *Tatian* his scholar has several allusions to passages contained in the Gospels of St Matthew and St John, but they are all anonymous². *Athenagoras* quotes the words of our Lord as they stand in St Matthew four times, and appears to allude to passages in St Mark and St John, but he nowhere mentions the name of an Evangelist³. *Theophilus* in his Books to Autolycus cites five or six precepts from 'the Gospel' or 'the Evangelic voice,' and once only mentions John as 'a man moved by the Holy Spirit,' quoting the prologue to his Gospel; though he elsewhere classes the Evangelists with the Prophets as all inspired by the same Spirit⁴. In *Hermias* and *Minucius Felix* there appears to be no reference at all to the Gospels. The usage of *Tertullian* is very remarkable. In his other books he quotes the Gospels continually, and mentions each of the Evangelists by name, though his references to the writers of the Gospels are rare; but in his Apology, while he gives a general view of Christ's life and teaching, and speaks of the Scriptures as the food and the comfort of the Christian⁵, he nowhere cites the Gospels, and scarcely exhibits any coincidence of language

---

¹ Cf. Norton, *Genuineness of the Gospels*, I. 137; Semisch, 83 ff.
² *Orat. c. Gr.* c. 30; Matt. xiii. 44. Cf. *Fragg.* i., ii.; Matt. vi. 24, 19; xxii. 30. *Orat.* c. 5; John i. 1: c. 4; John iv. 24: c. 13; John i. 5: c. 19; John i. 3.
³ *Ap.* p. 2; Matt. v. 39, 40: p. 11; Matt. v. 44, 45: p. 12; Matt. v. 46, 47: p. 36; Matt. v. 28: *Ap.* p. 37; Mark x. 6, 11: *Ap.* p. 12; John xvii. 3.
⁴ *Ad Autolycum*, III. § 12, p. 124: ἔτι μὴν καὶ περὶ δικαιοσύνης ἧς ὁ νόμος

εἴρηκεν ἀκόλουθα εὑρίσκεται καὶ τὰ τῶν προφητῶν καὶ τῶν εὐαγγελίων ἔχειν, διὰ τὸ τοὺς πάντας πνευματοφόρους ἑνὶ πνεύματι θεοῦ λελαληκέναι. If the commentaries attributed to him were genuine he wrote on the *four* Evangelists.
Cf. *ad Autol.* III. p. 126; Matt. v. 28, 32, 44, 46; vi. 3: *id.* II. p. 92; Luke xviii. 17: *id.* II. § 22, p. 100; John i. 1, 3.
⁵ *Ap.* cc. xxi. pp. 57 sqq.; xxxix. p. 93.

with them[1]. *Clement of Alexandria*, as is well known, investigated the relation of the Synoptic Gospels to St John, and his use of the words of Scripture is constant and extensive; and yet in his 'Exhortation to Gentiles,' while he quotes every Gospel, and all except St Mark repeatedly, he mentions St John alone by name, and that but once[2]. *Cyprian* in his address to Demetrian quotes words of our Lord as given by St Matthew and St John, but says nothing of the source from which he derived them[3]. The books of *Origen* against Celsus turned in a great measure on the criticism of the Gospels, for Celsus had diligently examined them to find objections to Christianity; and yet even there the common custom prevails. In the first book for instance our Lord's words are quoted from the text of our Gospels more than a dozen times anonymously, and only once, so far as I have observed, with the mention of the Gospel in which they were to be found[4]. At a still later time *Lactantius* blamed Cyprian for quoting Scripture in a controversy with a heathen[5], and though he shews in his Institutions an intimate acquaintance with the writings of the Evangelists he mentions only John by name, quoting the beginning of his Gospel[6]. *Arnobius* again makes no allusion to the Gospels; and *Eusebius*, to whose zeal we owe most of what is known of the history of the New Testament, though he quotes the Gospels eighteen times in his 'Introduction to Christian Evidences' (Præparatio Evangelica), yet always does so

---

[1] The only passage I have noticed is c. xxxi. (Matt. v. 44). The same is true of the imperfect book *ad Nationes*.
[2] *Protrep.* § 59.
[3] *Ad Demetr.* c. i.; Matt. vii. 6: c. xxiv.; John xvii. 3.
[4] c. lxiii.; Luke v. 8. He also quotes the Gospels of St John, St Luke and St Mark by name for facts, cc. li., lx., lxii.; and St Matthew three times as used by Celsus, cc. xxxiv., xxxviii., xl.
[5] *Instit.* v. 4.
[6] *Instit.* iv. 8.

120   THE AGE OF THE GREEK APOLOGISTS.   [PART

Chap. ii.

The custom of anonymous reference even still more extensive.

without naming the Evangelist of whose writings he makes use[1].

It would be easy to extend what has been said:—to shew that the words of 'the Apostle' are quoted scarcely less frequently than those of the Lord, without any more exact citation:—that this custom of indefinite reference is not confined to Apologetic writings, of which indeed it is peculiarly characteristic, but likewise traceable in many other cases:—that a habit which arose almost necessarily in an age of manuscript literature has not ceased even when the printing-press has left no material hindrances to occasion or excuse it; but this would lead us away from our subject, and it must be sufficiently clear that if Justin differs in any way from other similar writers as to the mode in which he introduces his Evangelic quotations, it is because he has described with unusual care the sources from which he drew them. He is not less but more explicit than later Apologists as to the writings from which he derives his accounts of the Lord's life and teaching.

The case of quotations from the Prophets.

Justin's method of quotation from the Old Testament may seem at first sight to create a difficulty. It has been calculated that he makes 197 citations with exact references to their source, and 117 indefinitely. But under any circumstances this fact would affect the peculiar estimation, and not the historical reception, of the New Testament books[2]. And since the same phenomenon occurs in writers like Clement of Alexandria and Cyprian, whose views on the inspiration and autho-

---

[1] Are we to suppose that Eusebius 'not only attached small importance 'to the [Memoirs] but also that he 'was actually ignorant of the author's 'name...,' the inference which, we are told (*Supernat. Rel.* I. 303), must be drawn from the fact that Justin mentions no author's name?

[2] In the Apostolic Fathers Scriptural quotations are almost universally anonymous. Cf. p. 52.

rity of the New Testament were most definite and full, its explanation must be sought for on other principles. As far as Justin is concerned, the search leads to a satisfactory conclusion. His quotations are, I believe, exclusively prophecies; and the purpose for which he introduces them required particularity of reference[1]. The proof of Christianity, even for the heathen, was to be derived, as he tells us, from the fulfilment of prophecy[2]. The gift of foretelling the future—for already in his time this was the common view of a prophet's work—was a certain mark of a divine power; and the antiquity of the Prophets invested them with a venerable dignity beyond all other poets or seers. To quote prophecy habitually without mentioning the Prophet's name would be to deprive it of half its value; and if it seem strange that Justin does not quote Evangelists like Prophets, it is no less worthy of notice that he does quote by name the single prophetic book of the New Testament. 'Moreover also among us a man named John, one of 'the Apostles of Christ, prophesied in a revelation made 'to him that those who have believed on our Christ shall 'spend a thousand years in Jerusalem[3]....' This reference to the Apocalypse appears to illustrate the difference which Justin makes between his quotations from the Prophecies and the Gospels; and it is sufficiently justified both by the usage of later writers and by the object which he had in view[4].

Justin refers to the Apocalypse of St John by name.

---

[1] e.g. *Ap.* I. 32: Μωυσῆς πρῶτος τῶν προφητῶν γενόμενος...καὶ 'Ησαΐας δὲ ἄλλος προφήτης...

[2] *Ap.* I. 14; and 30: τὴν ἀπόδειξιν ἤδη ποιησόμεθα οὐ τοῖς λέγουσι πιστεύοντες ἀλλὰ τοῖς προφητεύουσι πρὶν ἢ γενέσθαι κατ' ἀνάγκην πειθόμενοι...

[3] *Dial.* c. 81: ἐπειδὴ καὶ παρ' ἡμῖν ἀνήρ τις ᾧ ὄνομα 'Ιωάννης, εἷς τῶν ἀποστόλων τοῦ Χριστοῦ, ἐν ἀπο- καλύψει γενομένῃ αὐτῷ χίλια ἔτη ποιήσειν ἐν 'Ιερουσαλὴμ τοὺς τῷ ἡμετέρῳ Χριστῷ πιστεύσαντας προεφήτευσε... The constrained manner of this special reference in itself serves to explain why Justin did not mention the Christian writers more frequently.

[4] It is very remarkable that Justin makes no allusion to our Lord's prophecy of the destruction of Jerusa-

122   THE AGE OF THE GREEK APOLOGISTS.   [PART

Chap. ii.

(2) *The quotations differ from the canonical text.*

From Justin's indefiniteness of reference we next pass to his inexactness of quotation. Though it sounds like a paradox, it is no less true, that up to a certain point familiarity with a book causes it to be quoted inaccurately. The memory is trusted where otherwise the text would be transcribed, and the error thus originated becomes perhaps a tradition. In addition to this disturbing influence, which must have been at least as powerful in Justin's time as in our own and as fruitful of mistakes, the accuracy of Scriptural quotations varied according to a natural law derived from their subject-matter. In history the facts of the narrative seem of the first importance: in ethics the sense and spirit of the precept: in prophecy and doctrine the precise words of the Divine lesson. Conformably with this general rule Justin like the other Fathers may be expected to relate the events of Christ's life often in his own words, combining, arranging, modifying, as the occasion may require: like them he may be expected to change but rarely the language of the Gospels in citing Christ's teaching, though he transpose words and clauses: like them too, we may be allowed to believe, he would have quoted the language of the New Testament with scrupulous care in his polemical writings if they had been preserved to us. If this be a mere supposition, it must be remembered that we have no longer those books of his in which we might have expected to find critical accuracy.

Various degrees of accuracy in quotation.

The general character of Justin's quotations from the Old Testament.

But at the same time it is to be noticed that Justin appears to be remarkable for freedom, not only in his use of classical authors[1], but also in his treatment of the Old Testament, even in the Dialogue, in which it forms the

lem. It is quoted in the *Clementine Homilies* (*Hom.* III. 15; Credner, I. 291).

[1] Semisch has examined them in detail, pp. 232 ff. Examples may be found, *Ap.* I. 3 (Plat. *Resp.* v. p. 473 D); *Ap.* II. 10 (*Tim.* p. 28 c); *Ap.* II. 11 (Xen. *Mem.* II. 1).

real basis of his argument. In these cases his quotations are confessedly taken from books, whether by memory or reference; and the original text can be compared with his version of it. Here at least we can determine the limits of accuracy within which he confined himself; and when they have been once fixed they will serve as a standard. No greater accuracy is to be expected anywhere than in the use of the Prophecies; and a few characteristic examples of his mode of dealing with them as well as with the other writings of the Old Testament will shew what kind of variations we must be prepared to find in any references which he may make to the Gospel-narrative[1].

Chap. ii.

The first and most striking phenomenon in his quotations is the combination of detached texts, sometimes taken from different parts of the same book, and sometimes from different books. Thus when he is explaining the presence of the spirit of Elias in John the Baptist against Trypho's objection he says: 'Does it not seem to 'you that the same transference was made in the case of 'Joshua—when Moses was commanded to place his hands 'on Joshua (Numb. xxvii. 18), when God said to him '*And I will impart to him of the Spirit that is in thee*[2]*?*' (c. xi. 17). So again when shewing that the Word is the Messenger (ἄγγελος καὶ ἀπόστολος) of God he adds: 'And 'moreover this will be made clear from the writings of 'Moses. Now it is said in them thus: *The Angel of the 'Lord spake to Moses in a flame of fire out of the bush 'and said: I am That I Am* (ὁ ὤν), *the God of Abraham, 'the God of Isaac, the God of Jacob, the God of thy fathers. 'Go down to Egypt and lead forth my people*[3].' Passages

(a) Combination of different texts.

In the Dialogue.

In the Apology.

---

[1] See note A at the end of the quotation. Section.
[2] *Dial.* c. 49. The passage Numb. xi. 17 refers to the seventy elders. Credner appears to have omitted this
[3] *Ap.* i. 63. Exod. iii. 2, 14, 6, 10. 'These free quotations are adapted 'to the wants of heathen readers' (Credner, II. 58). By a reasonable

of different writers are combined even when the citation is made expressly from one. 'For Jeremiah cries thus,' we read, '*Woe to you, because ye forsook a living fountain, 'and digged for yourselves broken cisterns which will not be 'able to hold water* (Jerem. ii. 13). *Shall there be a wil-'derness [without water] where the Mount Sion is* (Isai. xvi. '1, LXX.), *because I gave to Jerusalem a bill of divorce in 'your sight*[1]*?*' (Jerem. iii. 8). The intertexture of various passages is sometimes still more complicated. 'What then 'the people of the Jews will say and do when they see 'Christ's advent in glory has been thus told in prophecy 'by Zacharias: *I will charge the four winds to gather 'together my children who have been scattered, I will 'charge the north wind to bring, and the south wind not 'to hinder* (cf. Zech. ii. 6; Isai. xliii. 5). *And then shall 'there be in Jerusalem a great lamentation, not a lamen-'tation of mouths and lips, but a lamentation of heart* '(Zech. xii. 11), *and they shall not rend their garments, 'but their minds* (Joel ii. 13). *They shall lament tribe to '.tribe* (Zech. xii. 12); *and then they shall look on him 'whom they pierced* (Zech. xii. 10), and say: *Why, O Lord, 'didst Thou make us to err from Thy way?* (Isai. lxiii. 17). '*The glory which our fathers blessed is turned to our re-'proach*[2]' (Isai. lxiv. 11).

The same cause which led Justin to combine various texts in other places led him to compress, to individualise,

adaptation these words become: 'These free quotations [from the 'Gospels] are adapted to the wants 'of Jewish [or heathen] readers.'
[1] *Dial.* c. 114. Credner (II. 246) remarks that Barnabas (c. xi.) connects the two former passages together; yet his text is wholly different from that of Justin. Cf. Semisch, 262 *anm.*
[2] *Ap.* I. 52. The clause ὄψονται

εἰς ὃν ἐξεκέντησαν is quoted in the *Dialogue* (c. 14) as from *Hosea*, ὄψεται ὁ λαὸς ὑμῶν καὶ γνωριεῖ εἰς ὃν ἐξεκέντησαν. The reading in the LXX. is ἐπιβλέψονται πρός με ἀνθ' ὧν κατωρχήσαντο, which arose from a double interchange of the Hebrew letters ר ד. The rendering which Justin gives occurs in John xix. 37, and also in Apoc. i. 7. Cf. Credner, pp. 293 ff.

to adapt, the exact words of Scripture for the better expression of his meaning; and at times he may appear to misuse the passages which he quotes. The extent to which this licence is carried will appear from the following examples.

In the Dialogue.

In speaking of the duty of proclaiming the truth which we know, and of the judgment which will fall on those who know and tell it not, he quotes the declaration of God by Ezechiel: '*I have placed thee as a watchman to* '*the house of Judah. Should the sinner sin, and thou not* '*testify to him, he indeed shall perish for his sin, but from* '*thee will I require his blood; but if thou testify to him,* '*thou shalt be blameless*' (Ezech. iii. 17—19). In this quotation only two phrases of the original text remain; but the remainder expresses the sense of the Prophet with conciseness and force[1]. Again, when referring to Plato's idea of the cruciform distribution of the principle of life through the universe[2], he says, 'This likewise he borrowed 'from Moses; for in the writings of Moses it is recorded 'that at that point of time when the Israelites came out 'of Egypt and were in the wilderness venomous beasts 'encountered them, vipers and asps and serpents of all 'kinds, which killed the people; and that by inspiration 'and impulse of God Moses took brass and made an image 'of a cross and set this on (ἐπί, dat.) the holy tabernacle, 'and said to the people: *Should you look on this image* '*and believe in it, you shall be saved.* And he has recorded 'that when this was done the serpents died, and so the 'people escaped death[3]' (Numb. xxi. 8, 9, sqq.). The de-

In the Apology.

---

[1] *Dial.* c. 82.
[2] Pl. *Tim.* p. 36 B: ταύτην οὖν τὴν ξύστασιν πᾶσαν διπλῆν κατὰ μῆκος σχίσας, μέσην πρὸς μέσην ἑκατέραν ἀλλήλαις οἷον (χ) προσβαλὼν κατέκαμψεν εἰς κύκλον... Justin's quotation of the passage is characteristic: 'Εχίασεν αὐτὸν [sc. τὸν υἱὸν τοῦ θεοῦ] ἐν τῷ παντί.
[3] *Ap.* I. 60. From the comparison of John iii. 15, I prefer to put the stop after ἐν αὐτῷ. Credner

tails of the fabrication of a cross rather than of a serpent, of the erection of the life-giving symbol on the tabernacle —that type of the outward world, of the address of Moses to the people, are due entirely to Justin's interpretation of the narrative. He gave what he thought to be the spirit and meaning of the passage, and in so doing has not preserved one significant word of the original text.

These variations in many cases must be errors of memory.

In many cases it is possible to explain these peculiarities of Justin's quotations by supposing that he intentionally deviated from the common text in order to bring out its meaning more clearly: in others he may have followed a traditional rendering or accommodation of scriptural language, such as are current at all times; but after every allowance has been made, a large residue of passages remains from which it is evident that the variations often spring from errors of memory. He quotes, for instance, the same passage in various forms; and that not only in different books, but even in the same book, and at short intervals. He ascribes texts to wrong authors; and that in the Dialogue as well as in the Apology, even when he shews in other places that he is not ignorant of their true source[1]. And once more: the variations are most remarkable and frequent in short passages: that is exactly in those for which it would seem superfluous to unroll the MS. and refer to the original text[2].

Application of Justin's

If then it be sufficiently made out that Justin dealt in

(p. 28) omits ἐν apparently by mistake. It will be observed that in the quotation each chief word is changed: προσβλέπειν is substituted for ἐπιβλέπειν, σώζεσθαι for ζῆν, and πιστεύειν is introduced as the condition of healing. These changes are also preserved in a general way in the second allusion to the passage, *Dial.* c. 94, which otherwise approaches more nearly to the LXX.

[1] In the *Apology:* Zephaniah for Zechariah (c. 35); Jeremiah for Daniel (c. 51); Isaiah for Jeremiah (c. 53). In the *Dialogue:* Jeremiah for Isaiah (c. 12); Hosea for Zechariah (c. 14); Zechariah for Malachi (c. 49). The first passage (Zech. ix. 9) is rightly quoted in *Dial.* c. 53; the next (Dan. vii. 13) rightly alluded to in *Dial.* c. 76. Cf. Semisch, 240 *anm.*

[2] See note B at the end of the Section.

this manner with the Old Testament, which was sanctioned in each *jot and tittle* by the authority of Christ himself, which was already inwrought into the Christian dialect by long and habitual use, which was familiarized to the Christian disputant by continual and minute controversy: —can it be expected that he should use the text of the Gospels with more scrupulous care? that he should in every case refer to his manuscript to ascertain the exact words of the record? that he should preserve them free from traditional details? that he should keep distinctly separate cognate accounts of the same event, complementary narratives of the same discourse? If he combined the words of Prophets to convey to the heathen a fuller notion of their divine wisdom, and often contented himself with the sense of Scripture even when he argued with a Jew, can it be a matter of surprise that to heathen and to Jews alike he sets forth rather the substance than the letter of those Christian writings which had for them no individual authority? In proportion as the idea of a New Testament Canon was less clear in his time, or at least less familiarly realized by ancient usage, than that of the Old Testament; in proportion as the Apostolic writings were invested with less objective worth for those whom he addressed; we may expect to find his quotations from the Evangelists more vague and imperfect and inaccurate than those from the Prophets. So far as it is not so, the fact implies that personal study had supplied the place of traditional knowledge, that what was wanting to the Christian Scriptures in the clearness of defined authority was made up by the sense of their individual value.

Evangelic quotations.

'It has been said that Justin's quotations are frequently made from memory[1]. This appears to be an

Justin's repeated quotations.

---

[1] The hypothesis that Justin quoted, is simply the supposition that so he did what any one in a similar position would do still. He was steeped

inevitable conclusion from the fact, that where he quotes a saying twice the quotations for the most part present differences greater or less. Such differences would have been impossible if in each case he had referred to his 'written Gospel.' The examples of repeated quotations which I have noticed are the following:

<table>
<tr><td>Apol. 15.</td><td>Dial. 96.</td></tr>
<tr><td>But be ye kind and pitiful (χρηστοὶ καὶ οἰκτίρμονες) as also your Father is kind and pitiful,

and He maketh His sun to rise upon sinners and just men and evil.</td><td>Be ye kind and pitiful (χρηστοὶ καὶ οἰκτίρμονες) as also your heavenly Father. For we see the Almighty God kind and pitiful,
making His sun to rise upon unthankful men and just, and raining upon holy men and evil...</td></tr>
</table>

The addition of χρηστός, which is not found in our texts, in both passages points to a various reading.

<table>
<tr><td>Apol. 15.</td><td>Dial. 133.</td></tr>
<tr><td>Pray for your enemies (τῶν ἐχθ. ὑμῶν),
and love those that hate you,
and bless those that curse you,
and pray for those that despitefully use you.</td><td>to pray even for enemies (τῶν ἐχθρ.),
and to love those that hate,
and to bless those that curse.</td></tr>
</table>

Here the coincidences of *pray for* for *love*, and of *love* for *do good to*, mark a different form (perhaps oral) of the precept from that found in our text. Compare pp. 142 f.

in the words of the Lord gathered from the Gospels and he brought them together as they rose before him in a connexion harmonious with his purpose. The aim of the Missionary or the Preacher is to convey the effect of that with which he is filled. No one, I imagine, supposes that Justin picked out phrases from his MS. any more than we ourselves pick out phrases from our printed Bibles when we link passage with passage.

Apol. 16.	*Dial.* 101.
When one came to him and said, Good Master, He answered saying, *No one is good except only God who made all things.*	When one said to him, Good Master, He answered, *Why callest thou me good? One is good, my Father which is in heaven.*

The difference here is complete.

Apol. 16.	*Dial.* 76.
But many shall say to me, Lord, Lord, did we not in Thy name eat and drink and *do mighty works?* And *then* I will say to them, Depart from me *Ye workers of iniquity.*	Many shall say to me *in that day*, Lord, Lord, did we not in Thy name eat and drink and *prophesy and cast out devils?* And I will say to them, Depart from me.

Here again the differences are remarkable.

Apol. 16.	*Apol.* 62.
Whoso heareth me *and doeth what I say* heareth Him that sent me.	He that heareth me heareth Him that sent me.

Apol. 16.	*Dial.* 35.
For many shall *come* (ἥξουσι) in my name clothed without *indeed* in sheep-skins, but *being* inwardly ravening wolves.	Many shall *come* (ἐλεύσονται) in my name clothed without in sheep-skins, but inwardly *they are* ravening wolves.

The coincidence of δέρματα προβάτων (sheep-skins) is remarkable and perhaps points to a distinct reading. Yet compare p. 141.

Apol. 63.	*Dial.* 100.
No man *knoweth* (ἔγνω) the Father, save the Son; nor the Son, save the Father and they to whom the Son reveals Him.	No man *cometh to know* (γινώσκει) the Father, save the Son; nor the Son, save the Father and they to whom the Son reveals Him.

Compare p. 134 n.

Dial. 17.	*Dial.* 112.
whited sepulchres, appearing fair without *but* full within of dead men's bones.	whited sepulchres, appearing fair without *and* full within of dead men's bones.

Dial. 76 (cf. c. 51).	*Dial.* 100.
The Son of Man must suffer many things and be rejected *by the Scribes and Pharisees,* and be crucified and on the third day rise again.	The Son of Man must suffer many things and be rejected *by the Pharisees and Scribes,* and be crucified and on the third day rise again.

The insertion of '*the Pharisees*' must be noticed. See p. 141.

Dial. 49.	*Dial.* 88.
But He that is stronger than I shall come (ἥξει), whose sandals I am not worthy to bear.	*For* He that is stronger than I shall come (ἥξει), whose sandals I am not worthy to bear.

The occurrence of ἥξει in both places seems to mark a true various reading. Compare pp. 143 ff.

A careful consideration of these crucial passages will, I believe, establish two conclusions which explain all the phenomena offered by Justin's quotations: the first is, that he quoted (often, at least,) from memory, and the second, that his Evangelic texts had several readings (like those of D, for example,) of which there are either few or no traces elsewhere.

I.] JUSTIN MARTYR. 131

To examine in detail the whole of Justin's quotations would be tedious and unnecessary. It will be enough to examine (1) those which are alleged by him as quotations, and those also which though anonymous are yet found repeated with the same variations either (2) in Justin's own writings or (3) in heretical books. It is evidently on these quotations that the decision hangs. If they be naturally reconcilable with Justin's use of the Canonical Gospels, the partial inaccuracy of the remainder can be of little moment. But if they be clearly derived from uncanonical sources, the general coincidence of the mass with our Gospels only shews that there was a wide uniformity in the Evangelic tradition.

In seven passages only, as far as I can discover[1], does Justin distinctly quote the Memoirs (γέγραπται); and in these passages, if anywhere, it is natural to expect that he will preserve the exact language of one of the Gospels which he used, just as in anonymous quotations we may conclude that he gives the substance of the common narrative[2]. The result of a first view of these pas-

Chap. ii.

How far Justin's quotations from the Gospel-narrative need be examined.

(a) *Express quotations from the Memoirs.*

---

[1] *Ap.* I. 66 (Luke xxii. 19, 20) and *Dial.* c. 103 (Luke xxii. 42—44) (cf. Matt. xxvi. 28) are not properly quotations of words, but concise narratives. The first runs as follows: οἱ γὰρ ἀπόστολοι ἐν τοῖς γενομένοις ὑπ' αὐτῶν ἀπομνημονεύμασιν, ἃ καλεῖται εὐαγγέλια, οὕτως παρέδωκαν ἐντετάλθαι αὐτοῖς· τὸν Ἰησοῦν λαβόντα ἄρτον εὐχαριστήσαντα εἰπεῖν· Τοῦτο ποιεῖτε εἰς τὴν ἀνάμνησίν μου· καὶ τὸ ποτήριον ὁμοίως λαβόντα καὶ εὐχαριστήσαντα εἰπεῖν· Τοῦτό ἐστι τὸ αἷμά μου· καὶ μόνοις αὐτοῖς μεταδοῦναι. The reference, it will be observed, is to 'the Gospels' (plural) and to 'the Apostles,' and the account is oblique. No more is told than is sufficient to establish the parallel with the Mithraic mysteries which he draws. The marvel is, not that Justin should have compressed the record, but that he should have told so much of a sacrament which was carefully kept from public knowledge. Comp. *Dial.* 70.

The second passage has been already noticed p. 115, n. 1.

Differences in detail supposed to have been derived by Justin from the *Memoirs* will be examined in the next division (3).

[2] The general moral teaching of the Lord which is epitomised in *Ap.* I. 15—17 is introduced by the following phrases τοσοῦτον εἶπεν—ταῦτα ἐδίδαξεν—ταῦτα ἔφη—οὕτως παρεκελεύσατο—ὡς ὁ Χριστὸς ἐμήνυσεν εἰπών—I venture to think that few will admit that words so introduced in the connexion in which they stand are "professedly literal quotations" from written documents (*Supernat.*

132   THE AGE OF THE GREEK APOLOGISTS.   [PART

sages is striking. Of the seven five agree verbally with the text of St Matthew or St Luke, exhibiting indeed three slight various readings not elsewhere found, but such as are easily explicable[1]: the sixth is a compressed

---

[1] The passages are these:

1. *Dial.* c. 103: οὗτος ὁ διάβολος ...ἐν τοῖς ἀπομνημονεύμασι τῶν ἀποστόλων γέγραπται προσελθὼν αὐτῷ καὶ πειράζων μέχρι τοῦ εἰπεῖν αὐτῷ Προσκύνησόν μοι· καὶ ἀποκρίνασθαι αὐτῷ τὸν Χριστόν· Ὕπαγε ὀπίσω μου σατανᾶ· κύριον τὸν θεόν σου προσκυνήσεις καὶ αὐτῷ μόνῳ λατρεύσεις = Matt. iv. 10. The addition ὀπίσω μου is supported by fairly good authority, though probably it is only a very early interpolation, as early as the time of Justin, like other readings of D *Syr. Vt.* and *Lat. Vt.* The form of the quotation explains the omission of γέγραπται γάρ, which Justin indeed elsewhere recognizes, c. 125: ἀποκρίνεται γὰρ αὐτῷ· Γέγραπται· κύριον τὸν θεόν κ.τ.λ. In the Clementine Homilies the answer assumes an entirely different complexion (*Hom.* VIII. 21): ἀποκρινάμενος οὖν ἔφη· Γέγραπται· Κύριον τὸν Θεόν σου φοβηθήσῃ καὶ αὐτῷ λατρεύσεις μόνον.

2. *Dial.* c. 105: ταῦτα εἰρηκέναι ἐν τοῖς ἀπομνημονεύμασι γέγραπται· Ἐὰν μὴ περισσεύσῃ ὑμῶν ἡ δικαιοσύνη πλεῖον τῶν γραμματέων καὶ Φαρισαίων, οὐ μὴ εἰσέλθητε εἰς τὴν βασιλείαν τῶν οὐρανῶν = Matt. v. 20. The transposition ὑμῶν ἡ δικ. is certainly correct. For Clement's variations in quoting this verse see Griesbach, *Symb. Crit.* II. 251.

3. *Dial.* c. 107: γέγραπται ἐν τοῖς ἀπομνημονεύμασιν ὅτι οἱ ἀπὸ τοῦ γένους ὑμῶν συζητοῦντες αὐτῷ ἔλεγον ὅτι Δεῖξον ἡμῖν σημεῖον. Καὶ ἀπε-

κρίνατο αὐτοῖς· Γενεὰ πονηρὰ καὶ μοιχαλὶς σημεῖον ἐπιζητεῖ, καὶ σημεῖον οὐ δοθήσεται αὐτοῖς εἰ μὴ τὸ σημεῖον Ἰωνᾶ = Matt. xii. [38], 39. The first part, as its form shews, is quoted freely; our Lord's answer differs from the text of St Matthew only in reading αὐτοῖς for αὐτῇ. Such a confusion of relatives with an antecedent like γενεά is very common. Cf. Luke x. 13 (καθήμενοι -αι); Acts ii. 3 (ἐκάθισεν -αν), Winer, *N. T. Gramm.* § 58. 4. b, p. 458 (ed. 6).

4. *Dial.* c. 49: ὁ ἡμέτερος Χριστὸς εἴρηκεν...'Ἠλίας μὲν ἐλεύσεται καὶ ἀποκαταστήσει πάντα· λέγω δὲ ὑμῖν ὅτι Ἠλίας ἤδη ἦλθε, καὶ οὐκ ἐπέγνωσαν αὐτὸν ἀλλ' ἐποίησαν αὐτῷ ὅσα ἠθέλησαν· καὶ γέγραπται ὅτι τότε συνῆκαν οἱ μαθηταὶ ὅτι περὶ Ἰωάννου τοῦ βαπτιστοῦ εἶπεν αὐτοῖς = Matt. xvii. 11—13. The express quotation (ver. 13) agrees exactly with the text of St Matthew, and Credner admits that it must have been taken from his Gospel (p. 237). In the other part the text of St Matthew has ἔρχεται (πρῶτον is certainly spurious), and ἐν αὐτῷ, but the preposition is omitted by ℵ D F U &c., see however Mark ix. 13. Credner insists (p. 219) on the variation ἐλεύσεσθαι (repeated again in the same chapter); with how much justice the various readings in Luke xxiii. 29 may shew. See also Gen. xviii. 14: ἀναστρέφω (*Dial.* c. 56); ἀποστρέψω (*Dial.* c. 126); ἀναστρέψω (LXX.). Cf. p. 140, and the next note. [This passage is inserted with some doubt on account of the use of γέγραπται.]

5. *Dial.* c. 105: καὶ γὰρ ἀποδιδοὺς τὸ πνεῦμα ἐπὶ τῷ σταυρῷ εἶπε· Πάτερ εἰς χεῖράς σου παρατίθεμαι τὸ πνεῦμά μου· ὡς καὶ ἐκ τῶν ἀπομνημονευμάτων καὶ τοῦτο ἔμα-

summary of words related by St Matthew: the seventh alone presents an important variation in the text of a verse, which is however otherwise very uncertain. Our inquiry is thus confined to the last two instances; and it must be seen whether their disagreement from the Synoptic Gospels is such as to outweigh the agreement of the remaining five.

The first passage occurs in the account which Justin gives of the Crucifixion as illustrating the prophecy in Psalm xxi.: 'Those who looked on Christ as He hung 'on the Cross shook their heads and pointed with their 'lips and sneering said in mockery these things which 'are also written in the Memoirs of His Apostles: *He* '*called Himself the Son of God; let Him come down* and '*walk; let God save Him*[1].' These exact words do not occur in our Gospels. In St Matthew the taunts are: *Thou that destroyest the Temple and buildest it in three days, save Thyself: if Thou art the Son of God, come down from the Cross...He saved others: Himself He cannot save. He is the King of Israel: let Him now come down from the Cross and we will believe on Him. He trusted on God: let Him deliver Him now if He will have Him; for He said, I am the Son of God.* St Mark gives a slight variation of one phrase: *Let the Christ, the King of Israel, come down from the Cross, that we may see and believe.* St Luke's quotation is shorter: *He saved*

Their disagreement.
Matt. xxvii.
39 sqq.
Mk. xv. 29 ff.
Luke xxiii.
35.

θον = Luke xxiii. 46. The quotation is verbally correct: παρατίθεμαι, not παραθήσομαι, is certainly the right reading.
  [1] *Dial.* c. 101: Οἱ θεωροῦντες αὐτὸν ἐσταυρωμένον καὶ κεφαλὰς ἕκαστος ἐκίνουν καὶ τὰ χείλη διέστρεφον καὶ τοῖς μυξωτῆρσιν ἐν ἀλλήλοις † διερινοῦντες † ἔλεγον εἰρωνευόμενοι ταῦτα ἃ καὶ ἐν τοῖς ἀπομνημονεύμασι τῶν ἀποστόλων αὐτοῦ γέγραπται. Υἱὸν θεοῦ ἑαυτὸν ἔλεγε, καταβὰς περιπα-

τείτω· σωσάτω αὐτὸν ὁ Θεός. The account in the *Apology* (I. 38) appears to prove that Justin gives only the substance of the Evangelic account: Σταυρωθέντος γὰρ αὐτοῦ ἐξέστρεφον τὰ χείλη καὶ ἐκίνουν τὰς κεφαλὰς λέγοντες· Ὁ νεκροὺς ἀναγείρας ῥυσάσθω ἑαυτόν. It is strange that in the quotation from the Psalm in *Dial. l. c.* the words σωσάτω αὐτὸν are omitted, though they are given in c. 98.

others; let Him save Himself, if this is the Christ of God, the Chosen. The peculiarity of Justin's phrase lies in the word '[let Him] *walk*[1].' No Manuscript or Father (so far as we know) has preserved any reading of the passage with this peculiarity; and if it appear that Justin's quotation is not deducible from our Gospels, due allowance being made for the object which he had in view, that is, to give a summary account of the record of the Evangelic narratives, its source must remain concealed.

The remaining passage is more remarkable. While interpreting the same Psalm xxi. Justin speaks of Christ as *dwelling in the holy place, as the praise of Israel,* to whom the mysterious blessings pronounced in old times to the Patriarchs belonged; and then he adds: 'Yea 'and it is written in the Gospel that he said : *All things* '*have been delivered to me by the Father; and no man* '*knoweth the Father except the Son, nor the Son except the* '*Father, and those to whomsoever the Son shall reveal* '*[the Father and Himself]*[2].' The last clause occurs again twice in the Apology, with the single variation that the verb is an aorist (ἔγνω) and not a present (γινώσκει)[3].

There are here three various readings to be noticed.

[1] It must be remarked that this word is not found in *Ap.* I. 38 where the taunt is said to be (ὡς μαθεῖν δύνασθε) Ὁ νεκροὺς ἀναγείρας ῥυσάσθω ἑαυτόν. Nothing, I think, could shew more clearly that Justin purposes to give only the substance of the narrative which he quotes.

[2] *Dial.* c. 100: καὶ ἐν τῷ εὐαγγελίῳ δὲ γέγραπται εἰπὼν [ὁ Χριστός·] Πάντα μοι παραδέδοται ὑπὸ τοῦ πατρός· καὶ οὐδεὶς γινώσκει τὸν πατέρα εἰ μὴ ὁ υἱός· οὐδὲ τὸν υἱὸν εἰ μὴ ὁ πατὴρ καὶ οἷς ἂν ὁ υἱὸς ἀποκαλύψῃ. The last word ἀποκαλύψῃ, as it has no immediate object, is I believe equivalent to 'makes a revelation,' *i.e.* of His own nature and of the nature of the Father. So I find Augustine takes the passage: *Quæst. Evv.* I. I.

[3] *Ap.* I. 63 (bis). Credner (I. 248 ff.) insists on the appearance of this reading ἔγνω, as if it were a mark of the influence of Gnostic documents on Justin's narrative. It is a sufficient answer that the reading is not only found in Marcion and the Clementines, but also repeatedly in Clement of Alexandria and Origen (Griesb. *Symb. Crit.* II. 271). Cf. Semisch, p. 367.

'*All things* have been delivered *to me* (παραδέδοται)' for '*all things* were (aor.) delivered *to me* (παρεδόθη)'—the transposition of the words *Father* and *Son*—the phrase '*those to whomsoever the Son shall reveal* [*Him*]' for '*he* '*to whomsoever the Son shall please to* [βούληται] *reveal* '[*Him*]'. Of these the first is not found in any authority in the text of St Matthew, but it occurs in a few copies of St Luke and is a common variation[1]; and the last is supported by Clement, Origen, and other Fathers, so that it cannot prove anything against Justin's use of the Canonical Gospels[2], while Justin himself in another place uses the present.

The transposition of the words still remains; and how little weight can be attached to that will appear upon an examination of the various forms in which the text is quoted by Fathers like Origen, Irenæus, and Epiphanius, who admitted our Gospels exclusively. It occurs in them, as will be seen from the table of readings, with almost every possible variation[3]. Irenæus in

Chap. ii.

---

[1] Cf. John vii. 39: δεδομένον, δοθέν. Abbot, *l. c.* pp. 92 f.
[2] Cf. Griesbach, *Symb. Crit. l. c.*
[3] The extent of the varieties of reading found in early orthodox authorities independent of Justin is shewn in the following scheme:

St Matt. xi. 27 οὐδεὶς ἐπιγινώσκει τὸν υἱὸν εἰ μὴ ὁ πατήρ οὐδὲ τὸν πατέρα τις (1)
Clem. *Strom.* I. § 178 ,, ἔγνω ,, ,, ,, ,, ,, ,, *om.* (2)
Orig. *c. Cels.* VI. 17 ,, ,, ,, ,, ,, ,, ,, ,, *om.* (3)
Orig. *c. Cels.* VII. 44 ,, ,, ,, ,, πατέρα ,, υἱὸς *om. om. om. om.* (4)
Clem. *Strom.* v. § 85 [οὐδεὶς] τὸν πατέρα ἔγνω ,, ,, *om. om. om. om.* (5)
Orig. *in Joh.* I. § 42 οὐδεὶς ἔγνω τὸν πατέρα ,, ,,
—— *in Joh.* XXXII. 18 ,, ,, υἱὸν ,, πατήρ
(1) ἐπιγινώσκει εἰ μὴ ὁ υἱὸς καὶ ᾧ ἐὰν βούληται ὁ υἱὸς ἀποκαλύψαι
(2) *om.* ,, ,, ,, ,, ἂν *om.* ,, ἀποκαλύψῃ
(3) *om.* ,, ,, ,, ,, ,, *om.* ,, ,, ,,
(4) *om. om. om. om. om.* ,, ,, *om.* ,, ,, ,,
(5) *om.* .... ,, ,, *om.* ,, ,, ,,
Compare also Clem. *Pæd.* I. § 20; *Strom.* VII. § 58. Orig. *in Joh.* XIII. § 25; XIX. § 1. From this evidence it is impossible not to believe that ἔγνω was found in some early MSS. of the Gospels.
Credner (I. p. 249) quotes from Irenæus (IV. 6. 1) 'et cui revelare *Pater* voluerit,' but I can find no authority for such a reading. The mistake at least shews how easy it is to misquote such a text.

136   THE AGE OF THE GREEK APOLOGISTS.   [PART

Chap. ii.   the course of one chapter quotes the verse first as it stands in the Canonical text; then in the same order, but with the last clause like Justin's; and once again altogether as he has given it, with the present (γινώσκει, *cognoscit*)¹; and in another place he gives the first clause as Justin with a 'past' (ἔγνω, *cognovit*)². Epiphanius likewise quotes the text seven times in the same order as Justin, and four times as it stands in the Gospels³. If indeed Justin's quotations were made from memory, no transposition could be more natural; and if we suppose that he copied the passage directly from a Manuscript, there is no difficulty in believing that he may have found it so written in a Manuscript of the Canonical St Matthew, since the variation is excluded by no internal improbability, while it is found elsewhere, and its origin is easily explicable⁴.

¹ Iren. IV. 6. 1   Nemo cognoscit filium nisi pater neque patrem quis (1)
—— IV. 6. 7   ,,   ,,   ,,   ,,   ,,   ,,   *om.* (2)
—— IV. 6. 3   ,,   ,,   patrem   ,,   filius   ,,   filium   *om.* (3)
Heretics ap. Iren. *l.c.*   ,,   cognovit   ,,   ,,   ,,   nec   ,,   *om.* (4)
Iren. II. 14.   ,,   ,,   ,,   ,,   ,,
Tertull. *c. Marc.* II. 27   ,,   ,,   ,,   ,,   ,,
—— *c. Marc.* IV. 25   scit   ,,   ,,   ,,
(1) cognoscit nisi filius et   cui   voluerit filius revelare
(2) *om.*   ,,   ,,   ,,   quibuscunque *om.*   ,,   revelaverit
(3) *om.*   ,,   pater ,,   ,,   *om.*   ,,   ,,
(4) *om.*   ,,   ,,   ,,   cui   *om.*   ,,   ,,
Compare note 4, below.

This variation is the more remarkable since in IV. 6. 1, Irenæus attributes the reading of Justin to those qui peritiores Apostolis volunt esse.
² Iren. II. 14. 7 : I can see nothing in this passage to indicate that Irenæus is using a reading which he rejects. So far is *novit* (*cognovit*) from being of a heretical stamp, that *novit* is the reading of the Old and Vulgate Latin, a few copies of the former only reading *cognoscit* (*agnoscit*). Augustine has both readings (*cognoscit, novit*).
³ Semisch, p. 369. *e.g. c. Hær.*

II. 2. 43 (p. 766 C); II. 1. 4 (p. 466 B).
⁴ Semisch has well remarked (p. 366) that the word πατρὸς immediately preceding may have led to the transposition.
To avoid repetition it may be well to give the passage as it stands in various heretical books, that Justin's independence of them may be at once evident.
(a) MARCION (*Dial. ap. Orig.* § 1, p. 283): οὐδεὶς ἔγνω τὸν πατέρα εἰ μὴ ὁ υἱός, οὐδὲ τὸν υἱόν τις γινώσκει εἰ μὴ ὁ πατήρ. The reading of the Marcionite interlocutor is apparently accept-

If the direct quotations which Justin makes from the Apostolic Memoirs supply no adequate proof that he used any books different from our Canonical Gospels, it remains to be seen whether there be anything in the character of his indefinite references to the substance of the Gospels which leads to such a conclusion: whether there be any stereotyped variations in his narrative which point to a written source; and any crucial coincidences with other documents which shew in what direction we must look for it.

It has been remarked already that a false quotation may become a tradition. Much more is it likely to reappear from association in a writer to whom it has once occurred by accident, or been suggested by peculiar influences. It must be shewn that there is something in the variation in the first instance which excludes the belief that it is merely a natural error, before any stress can be laid upon the fact of its repetition, which within certain limits is even to be expected. Erroneous readings continually recur in the works of Fathers who have preserved the true text in other passages where for some

Chap. ii.
(β) *Repetitions of the same variations from the Canonical text.*

Cases when the repetition of a reading becomes important.

ed in the argument. Directly afterwards however the words are given: οὐδεὶς γινώσκει τὸν υἱὸν εἰ μὴ ὁ πατήρ, and οὐδεὶς οἶδε τὸν υἱόν. These variations are found, it is to be remembered, in an argument between *Christians*.

(β) CLEMENTINES, *Hom.* XVII. 4: οὐδεὶς ἔγνω τὸν πατέρα εἰ μὴ ὁ υἱός, ὡς οὐδὲ τὸν υἱόν τις οἶδεν [εἶδεν, Cred. ?] εἰ μὴ ὁ πατὴρ καὶ οἷς ἂν βούληται [βούλεται, Cred., Cotel.] ὁ υἱὸς ἀποκαλύψαι. The text is repeated in the same words, *Hom.* XVIII. 4, 13, 20 (part). The difference of Justin's reading from this is clear and striking. Cf. *Recogn.* II. 47.

(γ) The MARCOSIANS, Iren. I. 20. 3: οὐδεὶς ἔγνω τὸν πατέρα εἰ μὴ ὁ υἱός, καὶ τὸν υἱὸν εἰ μὴ ὁ πατὴρ καὶ ᾧ ἂν ὁ

υἱὸς ἀποκαλύψῃ. Irenæus does not criticize the reading. This differs from Justin's by καί (for οὐδέ) and ᾧ (for οἷς). In the context παρεδόθη stands for Justin's παραδέδοται.

The case appears to me to be quite simple, and to call for no argument. Origen (to take one example) unquestionably used our Canonical Gospels as alone of authority; yet he several times agrees with Justin both (1) as to order and (2) as to the tense ἔγνω. Either then he found the reading which he quoted in manuscripts of St Matthew, or made an error of memory. What he did Justin may have done also. It must be remembered also that Justin reads γινώσκει in the one express quotation which he makes.

reason or other there seemed to be especial need for accuracy[1]. Justin himself has reproduced passages of the LXX. with persistent variations, of which no traces can be elsewhere found[2]. Unless then it can be made out that the recurrent readings in which he differs from the text of the Evangelists, whom he did not profess to quote, are more striking or more numerous than those found in the other Fathers, and in his own quotations from the Old Testament, the fact that there are corresponding variations in both cases serves only to shew that he treated the Gospels as they did, or as he himself treated the Prophets, and not that he was either unacquainted with their existence or ignorant of their peculiar claims.

The chief classes of various readings in MSS.

The real nature of the various readings of Justin's quotations will appear more clearly by a comparison with those found at present in Manuscripts of the New Testament. Errors of quotation often find a parallel in errors of copying; and even where they differ in extent they frequently coincide in principle. If we exclude mistakes in writing, differences in inflexion and orthography, adaptations for ecclesiastical reading, and intentional corrections, the remaining various readings in the Gospels may be divided generally into synonymous words and phrases, transpositions, marginal glosses, and combinations of parallel passages[3]. This classification will serve exactly for the recurrent variations in Justin;

Justin's readings to be examined

---

[1] See Semisch, pp. 330 sqq. Any critical commentary to the New Testament will furnish a crowd of instances. I intended to give a collection from Griesbach's *Symbolæ Criticæ*—only from Clement and Origen—but it proved too bulky.

[2] *e.g.* Isai. xlii. 6 sq. Credner, *Beiträge*, II. pp. 165, 213 sqq.

[3] This classification is given by Schulz in his third edition of the first volume of Griesbach's New Testament, pp. xxxviii. sqq. He has illustrated each class by a series of examples, which may be well compared with Justin's quotations. I cannot admit that the grounds of explanation proposed are 'purely imaginary.' They lie in the historical investigation of the text of the Gospels.

I.]   JUSTIN MARTYR.   139

and as it was made for an independent purpose it cannot seem to have been suggested by them, however nearly it explains their origin.

In the first group of passages which Justin quotes in his Apology from the 'Precepts of Christ' he says: 'Now concerning our affection (στέργειν) for all men He 'taught this: *If ye love them which love you* what strange 'thing do ye? *for the* fornicators do this...And to the 'end that we should communicate to those who need... 'He said: *Give to every one that asketh, and from him* '*that would borrow turn ye not away; for if ye lend to* '*them of whom ye hope to receive,* what strange thing do 'ye? this even the publicans do¹.' The whole form of the quotation, the context, the intertexture of the words of St Matthew and St Luke, shew that the quotation is made from memory. How then are we to regard the repetition of the phrase 'what strange thing do ye?' The corresponding words in St Luke in both cases are *what thank have ye?* in St Matthew, who has only the first passage, *what reward have ye?* This very diversity might occasion the new turn which Justin gives to the sentence; and the last words point to its source in the text of St Matthew: *If ye love them which love you, what*

*Chap. ii.
according to this classi-fication.*

1. Synony-mous phrases.

*First in-stance.
Luke vi. 32.*

---

¹ *Ap.* I. 15: Περὶ δὲ τοῦ στέργειν ἅπαντας ταῦτα ἐδίδαξεν· Εἰ ἀγαπᾶτε τοὺς ἀγαπῶντας ὑμᾶς, τί καινὸν ποιεῖτε; ('τίνα μισθὸν ἔχετε; *Mt.* ποία ὑμῖν χάρις ἐστίν; *Lc.*) Καὶ γὰρ οἱ πόρνοι (οἱ τελῶναι *Mt.* οἱ ἁμαρ-τωλοί *Lc.*) τοῦτο ποιοῦσιν (Luke vi. 32; Matt. v. 46)...Εἰς δὲ τὸ κοινων-εῖν τοῖς δεομένοις καὶ μηδὲν πρὸς δόξαν ποιεῖν ταῦτα ἔφη· Παντὶ τῷ αἰτοῦντι δίδοτε (δός *Mt.* δίδου *Lc.*) καὶ τὸν βου-λόμενον (θέλοντα *Mt.*) δανείσασθαι μὴ ἀποστραφῆτε (-ῇς *Mt.* the text of *Lc.* is here quite different). Εἰ γὰρ δανείζετε παρ᾽ ὧν ἐλπίζετε λαβεῖν, τί καινὸν ποιεῖτε; (*Mt.* omits this clause: *Lc. ut supra*) Τοῦτο καὶ οἱ τελῶναι ποιοῦσιν (Matt. v. 42; Luke vi. 30, 34). In all the quotations from Justin I have marked the *variations* from the text of the Gospels by *Ro-*man letters in the *Italicised* transla-tion, and in the original by spaced letters. If there appear to be any fair MS. authority for a reading which Justin gives I have not noticed it, unless it be of grave importance. For instance in the second passage λαβεῖν is read for ἀπολαβεῖν by אBL; and in the first τοῦτο for τὸ αὐτὸ by good Greek and (especially) Latin authori-ties.

Chap. ii.

reward have ye? Do not even the publicans the same? *And if ye salute your brethren only,* what remarkable thing do ye? *Do not even the heathen so*[1]? The change of the word (καινὸς for περισσὸς) which alone remains to be explained—if indeed it were not suggested by the common idiom[2]—falls in with the peculiar object of Justin's argument, who wished to shew the *reformation* wrought in men by Christ's teaching. The repetition of the phrase in two passages closely connected was almost inevitable.

Second instance.
Matt. vii. 17.

The recurrent readings in Justin offer another instance of the substitution of a synonymous phrase for the true text. He quotes our Lord as saying: '*Many 'shall come in my name* clothed without in sheep-skins '*but being inwardly ravening wolves*[3].' This quotation again is evidently a combination of two passages of St Matthew, and made from memory. The longer expression in Justin reads like a paraphrase of the words in the Gospel, and is illustrated by the single reference made to the verse by Clement, who speaks of the Prophetic Word as describing some men under the image

---

[1] Matt. v. 47: τί περισσὸν ποιεῖτε; In this verse we must read ἐθνικοὶ for τελῶναι, but τελῶναι is undoubtedly the right reading in the corresponding clause in ver. 46, and thus the connexion of the words is scarcely less striking than before. At the same time Justin *may* have read τελῶναι· the verse is not quoted by Clement, Origen, or Irenæus.

[2] The phrase καινὸν ποιεῖν occurs in Plato, *Resp.* III. 399 E. It is possible that περισσὸν ποιεῖν may be found elsewhere, but I doubt whether it would be used in the same sense; περισσὰ πράσσειν has a meaning altogether different.

[3] *Dial.* c. 35 (*Ap.* I. 16): Πολλοὶ ἐλεύσονται (ἥξουσιν *Ap.*) ἐπὶ τῷ ὀνόματί μου ἔξωθεν (+ μὲν *Ap.*) ἐνδεδυμένοι δέρματα προβάτων, ἔσωθεν δέ εἰσι (ὄντες *Ap.*) λύκοι ἅρπαγες (Matt. xxiv. 5; vii. 15). Immediately below (*Dial. l. c.*) Justin quotes, Προσέχετε ἀπὸ τῶν ψευδοπροφητῶν οἵτινες ἐλεύσονται (ἔρχονται *Mt.*) πρὸς ὑμᾶς ἔξωθεν, κ.τ.λ. (Matt. vii. 15: ἐν ἐνδύμασι προβάτων). The phrase ἐνδύμασι προβάτων is very strange, and though there is apparently no variation in the MSS. δέρμασι has been conjectured. Cf. Schulz, *in l.* Semisch has remarked that ἐνδεδυμένοι δέρματα shews traces of the text of St Matthew (p. 340).

of *wolves arrayed in sheep's fleeces*[1]. If Clement allowed himself this licence in quoting the passages, surely it cannot be denied to Justin.

In close connexion with these various readings is another passage in which Justin substitutes a special for a general word, and replaces a longer and more unusual enumeration of persons by a short and common one. 'Christ cried aloud before He was crucified, *The Son of* '*Man must suffer many things and be rejected* by (ὑπό) 'the scribes and Pharisees *and be* crucified and *on the* '*third day rise again*[2].' In another place the same words occur with the transposition of the titles '...by the Pha- 'risees and scribes.' Once again the text is given obliquely: '*Christ said that He must suffer many things* '*of* (ἀπό) the scribes and Pharisees *and be* crucified...' In this last instance the same preposition is used as in St Luke, and the two variations only remain constant— 'scribes and Pharisees' for 'elders and chief priests and 'scribes,' and 'crucified' for 'put to death[3].' Though these readings are not supported by any Manuscript authority, they are sufficiently explained by other Patristic quotations. The example of Origen shews the natural difficulty of recalling the exact words of such a passage. At one time he writes *The Son of Man must be rejected of* (ἀπό) *the chief priests and elders*...; again...*of the chief priests and* Pharisees *and scribes*...; again...*of the*

---

[1] Clem. Al. *Protr.* § 4: λύκοι κωδίοις προβάτων ἠμφιεσμένοι.
[2] *Dial.* c. 76: Ἐβόα γὰρ πρὸ τοῦ σταυρωθῆναι· Δεῖ τὸν υἱὸν τοῦ ἀνθρώπου πολλὰ παθεῖν καὶ ἀποδοκιμασθῆναι ὑπὸ (ἀπὸ *Lc.*) τῶν γραμματέων καὶ Φαρισαίων (πρεσβυτέρων καὶ ἀρχιερέων καὶ γραμματέων *Lc.*) καὶ σταυρωθῆναι (ἀποκτανθῆναι *Lc.*) καὶ τῇ τρίτῃ ἡμέρᾳ ἀναστῆναι. Cf. 100; 51: Luke ix. 22.
[3] In Matt. xvi. 21 παθεῖν ὑπό is read by D; in Mark viii. 31 it is supported by ℵ B C D (which however proceeds καὶ ἀπὸ τῶν ἀρχ.) &c. and must be received into the text; in Luke ix. 22 ἀπό is the reading of the majority of the MSS. From this note it will appear how little weight could be rested on the reading ὑπό in Justin, even if it were constant.

elders and chief priests and the scribes of the people[1]. In corresponding texts a similar confusion occurs both in Manuscripts and quotations[2]. The second variation is still less remarkable. Even in a later passage of St Luke the word 'crucified' is substituted for 'put to 'death,' and Irenæus twice repeats the same reading. *From that time He began to shew to His disciples that He must go to Jerusalem and suffer many things from* the priests and be rejected *and* crucified *and the third day rise again*[3]. *The Son of Man must suffer many things and be rejected and* crucified *and the third day rise again*[4]. It is scarcely too much to say that both these passages differ more from the original text than Justin's quotations, and have more important common variations; and yet no one will maintain that Irenæus was unacquainted with our Gospels, or used other records of Christ's life.

Another quotation of Justin's which may be classed under this same division is more instructive, as it shews the process by which these various readings were stereotyped. Prayer for enemies might well seem the most noble characteristic of Christian morality. 'Christ taught 'us to pray even for our enemies, saying *Be ye kind and* '*merciful, even as is your heavenly Father*[5].' 'We who 'used to hate one another...now pray for our enemies[6]...' The phrase as well as the idea was fixed in Justin's mind; and is it then strange that he quotes our Lord's teaching on the love of enemies elsewhere in this form: Pray

---

[1] Griesbach, *Symb. Crit.* p. 291. Luke ix. 22). The words *et reprobari* form no part of the text of St Matthew.
[2] See the various readings to Matt. xxvi. 3, 59; xxvii. 41.
[3] Iren. III. 18. 4: *Ex eo enim,* inquit, *cœpit demonstrare discentibus* (to his disciples) *quoniam oportet illum Hierosolymam ire et multa pati a* sacerdotibus et reprobari *et* crucifigi *et tertia die resurgere* (Matt. xvi. 21;
[4] *Id.* III. 16. 5: *Oportet enim,* inquit, *Filium hominis multa pati et reprobari et* crucifigi *et die tertio resurgere* (Luke ix. 22).
[5] *Dial.* c. 96. Comp. p. 128.
[6] *Ap.* I. 14.

for *your enemies*, and love *them that hate you*, and *bless them that curse you, and pray for them that despitefully use you*[1]? The repetition of the key-word *pray* points to the origin of the change; and the form and context of the quotation shew that it was not made directly from any written source. But here again there are considerable variations in the readings of the passage. In St Matthew it should stand thus: *Love your enemies, and pray for them that persecute you*. The remaining clauses appear to have been interpolated from St Luke. Origen quotes the text in this shorter form five times; and in the two remaining quotations he only substitutes *them that despitefully use you* from St Luke for *them that persecute you* in the last clause[2]. Irenæus gives the precept in another shape: '*Love your enemies, and* pray 'for them that hate you[3].' Still more in accordance with Justin's citation Tertullian says, 'It is enjoined 'on us to pray *to God* for our enemies, *and to bless our* '*persecutors*[4].' It would be useless to extend the inquiry further.

Transpositions are perhaps less likely to recur than new forms of expression; at least I have not noticed any repeated in Justin. One or two examples however shew the nature of a large class of glosses. Every scholar is familiar with what may be called the *prophetic* use of the present tense. In the intuition of the seer the future is already realised, not completely but incep-

Chap. ii.

2. *Transpositions.*

3. *Glosses.*

The prophetic use of the present tense.

---

[1] *Ap.* I. 15: Εὔχεσθε ὑπὲρ τῶν ἐχθρῶν ὑμῶν καὶ ἀγαπᾶτε τοὺς μισοῦντας ὑμᾶς (ἀγαπᾶτε τοὺς ἐχθροὺς ὑμῶν, καλῶς ποιεῖτε τοῖς μισοῦσιν ὑμᾶς *Lc.*) καὶ (om. *Lc.*) εὐλογεῖτε τοὺς καταρωμένους ὑμῖν καὶ εὔχεσθε (προσεύχεσθε *Mt.*, and *Lc.* omitting καὶ) ὑπὲρ (περὶ *Lc.*) τῶν ἐπηρεαζόντων ὑμᾶς (Luke vi. 27, 28. Cf. Matt. v. 44).

[2] Griesbach, *Symb. Crit.* II. pp. 253 sq.

[3] c. *Hær.* III. 18. 5: *Diligite inimicos vestros et orate pro eis qui vos oderunt.*

[4] *Ap.* 31: Præceptum est nobis ad redundantiam benignitatis etiam *pro inimicis Deum orare* et persecutoribus nostris bona precari.

tively: the action is seen to be already begun in the working of the causes which lead to its accomplishment. This is the deepest view of futurity, which regards it as the outgrowth of the present. But more frequently we break the connexion: future things are merely things separated by years or ages from ourselves; and this simple notion has a tendency to destroy the truer one. It is not then surprising that both in Manuscripts and quotations the clearly-defined future is confounded with the subtler present. Even in parallel passages of the Synoptic Gospels the change is sometimes found, being due to a slight alteration of the point of sight[1]. The most important instance in Justin occurs in his account of the testimony of John the Baptist: '*I indeed am bap-* '*tizing you with water unto repentance; but He that is* '*mightier than I* will come *whose shoes I am not worthy* '*to bear; He will baptize you with the Holy Ghost and* '*fire*[2]...' The whole quotation except the clause in question and the repetition of a pronoun agrees verbally with the text of St Matthew. This is the more remarkable because Clement gives the passage in a form differing from all the Evangelists[3], and Origen has quoted it with repeated variations, even after expressly comparing the words of the four Evangelists[4]. The series of changes

Instance of the interpretation of it in Justin.

[1] Matt. xxiv. 40; Luke xvii. 34 (where however παραλαμβάνεται and ἀφίεται are read by D K &c. though they retain the futures in ver. 35). Compare John xxi. 18, where D gives a present instead of οἴσει. Cf. Winer, *N. T. Grammatik*, § 40. 2. a (ed. 6).
[2] *Dial.* c. 49 (cf. c. 88): Ἐγὼ μὲν ὑμᾶς βαπτίζω ἐν ὕδατι εἰς μετάνοιαν· ἥξει δὲ (γὰρ c. 88) ὁ ἰσχυρότερός μου (ὁ δὲ ὀπίσω μου ἐρχόμενος ἰσχυρότερός μου ἐστίν *Mt.* ἔρχεται δὲ ὁ ἰσχυρότερός μου *Lc.*) οὗ οὐκ εἰμὶ ἱκανός ... πυρί· οὗ τὸ πτύον αὐτοῦ (om. *Mt.*, *Lc.*) ἐν τῇ χ...ἀσβέστῳ (Matt. iii. 11, 12; Luke iii. 16, 17). For the insertion of αὐτοῦ compare Mark vii. 25 (ℵ D Δ however omit the pronoun); Apoc. vii. 2. See Winer, § 22. 4. b.
[3] Clem. Alex. *Fragm.* § 25: ἐγὼ μὲν ὑμᾶς ὕδατι βαπτίζω, ἔρχεται δέ μου ὀπίσω ὁ βαπτίζων ὑμᾶς ἐν πνεύματι καὶ πυρί...τὸ γὰρ πτύον ἐν τῇ χειρὶ αὐτοῦ τοῦ διακαθᾶραι τὴν ἅλω καὶ συνάξει τὸν σῖτον εἰς τὴν ἀποθήκην (ἐπιθήκην Griesb.) τὸ δὲ... ἀσβέστῳ.
[4] *Comm. in Joan.* VI. 16. *Id.* VI.

involved in the reading of Justin can be traced exactly. In place of the phrase of St Matthew *but He that is coming is mightier than I*... St Mark and St Luke read *but He that is mightier than I is coming*... Now elsewhere Justin has represented this very verb *is coming* by two futures in different quotations of the same verse[1]. The fact that he uses two words shews that he intended in each case to give the sense of the original; and since one of them is the same as appears in the words of St John its true relation to the text of the Gospels is established[2].

The remaining instances of variations which are repeated occur in the combination of parallel texts. In the first given the coincidence is only partial: the differences of the two quotations from one another are at least as great as their common difference from the text of the Gospels. *Many shall say to me in that day,*—so Justin quotes our Lord's words,—*Lord, Lord, did we not in Thy name eat and drink and prophesy and cast out devils? And I will say to them, Depart from me.* In the Apology the passage runs thus: *Many shall say to me, Lord, Lord, did we not in Thy name eat and drink and do mighty works? And then will I say to them, Depart from me, ye workers of iniquity*[3]. It so

Chap. ii.

4. *Combination*
(a) *of words:*

26; ἐγὼ βαπτίζω ἐν ὕδατι, ὁ δὲ ἐρχόμενος μετ' ἐμὲ ἰσχυρότερός μου ἐστιν, αὐτὸς ὑμᾶς βαπτίσει ἐν πνεύματι ἁγίῳ. Cf. Griesb. *Symb. Crit.* II. 244, who seems to have confounded the Evangelist and the Baptist.

[1] Cf. p. 140, note 3: Matt. vii. 15.
[2] Good examples of 'glosses' occur *Apol.* I. 15 ἐκεῖ καὶ ὁ νοῦς τοῦ ἀνθρώπου for ἐκεῖ καὶ ἡ καρδία σου

(Matt. vi. 21). *Apol.* I. 16 λαμψάτω τὰ καλὰ ἔργα for· λαμψάτω φῶς (Matt. v. 16). *Apol.* I. 16 τότε ἐρῶ for τότε ὁμολογήσω (Matt. vii. 23), &c. Some of these may have been incorporated in Justin's text: some he may have introduced himself. In each of the cases quoted there can be no doubt which is the original reading.

[3] *Dial.* c. 76: πολλοὶ ἐροῦσί μοι τῇ ἡμέρᾳ ἐκείνῃ· Κύριε Κύριε οὐ
Apol. I. 16: πολλοὶ ἐροῦσί μοι .... Κύριε Κύριε οὐ
Matt. vii. 22, 23: πολλοὶ ἐροῦσίν μοι ἐν ἐκείνῃ τῇ ἡμέρᾳ· Κύριε Κύριε οὐ
D.   τῷ σῷ ὀνόματι ἐφάγομεν καὶ ἐπίομεν καὶ προεφητεύσαμεν καὶ ....

Chap. ii.

happens that Origen has quoted the same passage several times with considerable variations, but four times he combines the words of St Matthew and St Luke as Justin has done. *Many shall say to me in that day, Lord, Lord, did we not in Thy name eat and drink, and in Thy name cast out devils and do mighty works? And I will say to them, Depart from me, because ye are workers of unrighteousness*[1]. The parallel is as complete as can be required, and proves that Justin need not have had recourse to any Apocryphal book for the text which he has preserved. Indeed the very same insertions derived from St Luke xiii. 26, 27 are now found in Cureton's Syriac Version.

(b) of forms.

Sometimes a combination of different passages consists more in the intermixture of forms than of words. Of this Justin offers one good example. He twice quotes the woe pronounced against the false sanctity of the scribes and Pharisees with considerable variations, but in both cases preserves one remarkable difference from St Matthew whose words he uses. When exclaiming against the frivolous criticism of the Jewish doctors he asks, 'Shall they not rightly be called that which our 'Lord Jesus Christ said to them: *Whited sepulchres, 'without appearing beautiful and within full of dead*

A. τῷ σῷ ὀνόματι ἐφάγομεν καὶ ἐπίομεν ....
M. τῷ σῷ ὀνόματι .... ἐπροφητεύσαμεν καὶ τῷ σῷ ὀνόματι
D. δαιμόνια ἐξεβάλομεν; .... καὶ
A. .... καὶ.................. δυνάμεις......... ἐποιήσαμεν ; καὶ
M. δαιμόνια ἐξεβάλομεν καὶ τῷ σῷ ὀνόματι δυνάμεις πολλὰς ἐποιήσαμεν ; καὶ
D. ...... ἐρῶ   αὐτοῖς.. .... 'Αναχωρεῖτε ἀπ'
A. τότε ἐρῶ   αὐτοῖς................................... 'Αποχωρεῖτε ἀπ'
M. τότε ὁμολογήσω αὐτοῖς ὅτι οὐδέποτε ἔγνων ὑμᾶς, ἀποχωρεῖτε ἀπ'
D. ἐμοῦ.
A. ἐμοῦ ... ἐργάται   τῆς ἀνομίας.
M. ἐμοῦ οἱ ἐργαζόμενοι τὴν ἀνομίαν.
  See Luke xiii. 26, 27, from which the words peculiar to Justin's citation are derived.
  [1] Griesb. *Symb. Crit.* II. p. 262.

I.] JUSTIN MARTYR. 147

'*bones, paying tithe of mint but swallowing a camel, blind* '*guides*[1]?' 'Christ seemed no friend to you...when He '*cried, Woe to you, scribes and Pharisees, hypocrites, for* '*ye pay tithe of mint and rue but regard not the love of* '*God and judgment; whited sepulchres, without appearing* '*beautiful but within full of dead bones*[2].'
False teachers are no longer *like to whited sepulchres;* they *are* very sepulchres. The change is striking. If this be explained, the participial form of the sentence creates no new difficulty, but follows as a natural sequence. The text of St Matthew however offers no trace of its origin. There indeed in different authorities three different expressions of comparison—παρομοιάζετε, ὁμοιάζετε, ὅμοιοί ἐστε—are found, but none omit it. Clement and Irenæus give the passage with a very remarkable variation[3], but they agree with the Manuscripts in preserving the connexion. The Naassenes or Ophites, according to the *Treatise against Heresies* attributed to Hippolytus[4], quoted the saying in a form more similar to that of Justin but with an additional change: '*Ye are whited tombs*, [Christ] says, *full within of dead* '*bones*.' Here the passing characteristic is transformed into a substantive description. The clue to the solution

---

[1] *Dial.* cc. 112, 17. The passage common to both runs thus: τάφοι κεκονιαμένοι, ἔξωθεν φαινόμενοι ὡραῖοι καὶ ἔσωθεν (ἔσ. δὲ c. 17) γέμοντες ὀστέων νεκρῶν. The corresponding clause in Matt. xxiii. 27 is: ὅτι παρομοιάζετε τάφοις κεκονιαμένοις οἵτινες ἔξωθεν μὲν φαίνονται ὡραῖοι ἔσωθεν δὲ γέμουσιν ὀστέων νεκρῶν καὶ πάσης ἀκαθαρσίας. For παρομοιάζετε Lachmann reads ὁμοιάζετε with B. Clement (Griesb. *Symb. Crit.* II. 327) has ὅμοιοί ἐστε (*Pæd.* III. 9. 47).
[2] *Dial.* c. 17.
[3] Clem. *l. c.*: ἔξωθεν ὁ τάφος

φαίνεται ὡραῖος ἔνδον δὲ γέμει. ... Iren. IV. 18. 3: *A foris enim sepulcrum apparet formosum intus autem plenum est*...... The passage stands so also in D and d (*monumentum paretur decorum*).
[4] [Hipp.] *adv. Hær.* v. 8, p. 111 ed. Miller. Τοῦτο, φησίν, ἐστὶ τὸ εἰρημένον Τάφοι ἐστὲ κεκονιαμένοι γέμοντες, φησίν, ἔσωθεν ὀστέων νεκρῶν. I may add that though I have cited this Treatise for convenience sake under the name of Hippolytus, I am by no means satisfied that the question of its authorship has been finally settled.

Chap. ii.

of the difficulty which arises from these various modifications of the Lord's saying must be sought for in St Luke. He has not indeed a single word in common with Justin, but he has expressed the thought—at least according to very weighty evidence—in the same manner[1]: '*Woe to you, for* ye are unseen tombs, *and men when they walk over them know it not.*' Justin has thus clothed the living image of St Luke in the language of St Matthew.

General view of these variations:

These are all the quotations in Justin which exhibit any constant variation from the text of the Gospels[2]. In the few other cases of recurrent quotations the differences between the several texts are at least as important as their common divergence from the words of the Evangelist[3]. This fact alone is sufficient to shew that Justin did not exactly reproduce the narrative which he read, but made his references generally by memory, and that inaccurately. Under such circumstances the authority of the earliest of the Fathers, who are admitted on all sides to have made constant and special use of the Gospels, has been brought forward to justify the existence and recurrence of variations from the Canonical text; and though it would have been easy to have chosen more striking instances of their various readings, still by taking those only which are found in the very passages to which Justin also refers the parallel gains in

(a) on the supposition that the quotations were given from memory,

---

[1] Luke xi. 44: Οὐαὶ ὑμῖν ὅτι ἐστε [om. ὡς τὰ] μνημεῖα [om. τὰ] ἄδηλα καὶ οἱ ἄνθρωποι ἐπάνω περιπατοῦντες οὐκ οἴδασιν. So D a b c d, Syr. Crt. Lucif.; Griesbach marks the reading as worthy of notice.

[2] I have not noticed the variation in the reference to Luke x. 16: ὁ ἐμοῦ ἀκούων ἀκούει τοῦ ἀποστείλαντός με (*Apol.* I. 63. Cf. c. 16), because it is contained in several MSS.

and Versions: D a b d, Syrr., Arm., Æth., &c.

[3] The following passages may be compared: *Dial.* c. 96; *Apol.* I. 15 = Luke vi. 36; Matt. v. 45. For the repetition of χρηστοὶ καὶ οἰκτίρμονες compare Clem. *Strom.* II. 59. 100: ἐλεήμονες καὶ οἰκτίρμονες. *Dial.* c. 101; *Apol.* I. 16 = Matt. xix. 16, 17; Luke xviii. 18, 19.
Comp. pp. 127 ff.

direct force at least as much as it seemingly loses in point.

But even if it were not so: if it had seemed that recurrent variations could be naturally explained only by supposing that they were derived from an original written source, that written source might still have been a Manuscript of our Gospels. One very remarkable type of a class of early Manuscripts has been preserved in the *Codex Bezæ* (D)—the gift of the Reformer to the University of Cambridge—which contains verbal differences from the common text, and Apocryphal additions to it, no less remarkable than those which we here have to explain[1]. The frequent coincidences of the readings of this Manuscript with those of Justin must have been observed already; and if it had perished, as it might well have done, in the civil wars of France[2], many citations in Clement and Irenæus would have seemed as strange as his peculiarities[3]. We are arguing on premises only partly true, but it is none the less important to notice that up to this point there is nothing in Justin's quotations, supposing them to have been drawn immediately from a written source, which cannot be explained from what we know of the history of the text of our Gospels.

One or two examples given somewhat more in detail will place this statement in a clearer light. If the follow-

Chap. ii.

(b) *that they were taken from a MS.*

e.g. Codex Bezæ.

Examples of early readings

---

[1] See Note C at the end of the Section.
[2] Initio belli civilis apud Gallos an. MDLXII. ex cœnobio S. Irenæi Lugduni postquam ibi diu in pulvere jacuisset nactus est Beza... Mill, *Proleg. N. T.* 1268.
[3] The following examples will serve to confirm the statement:
Matt. xxiii. 26. ἔξωθεν ... Clem. *Pæd.* III. 9. 48; Iren. IV. 18. 3.

Luke xii. 11. φέρωσιν. Clem. Or. (Griesb. *Symb. Crit.* II. 377).
Luke xii. 27. οὔτε νήθει οὔτε ὑφαίνει. Clem. *Pæd.* II. 10. 102.
Luke xii. 38. τῇ ἑσπερινῇ φυλακῇ. Iren. V. 34. 2.
Luke xix. 26. προστίθεται. Clem. *Strom.* VII. 10, προστιθήσεται.
Cf. Hug, *Introduction*, I. § 22. It is needless to multiply instances.

ing phrase had been found in Justin: 'your Father 'knoweth what things ye have need of before *you open your mouth;*' it would have been urged with great show of reason that it could not have been derived from our St Matthew's Gospel: that the peculiar form of expression had an air of originality: that Justin had evidently taken it from an Apocryphal record. But the words stand in fact in the *Codex Bezæ* and one Latin copy in Matt. vi. 8. Or again if we had read in an early Father that Herod said to his servants on hearing of the fame of Jesus: *Can this be John the Baptist whom I beheaded?* it would have been pointed out that the sentence has points of similarity with our three Synoptic Gospels, and also marked points of difference from them: that its vividness and force bespeak a source earlier than those which these represent: that it must be a fragment of the primitive Gospel according to the Hebrews. So however Herod's words stand in Matt. xiv. 2 in *Codex Bezæ* and a number of old Latin authorities. Or to take another kind of illustration, could it be proved more triumphantly that an Apologist had made use of other records than the Canonical Gospels than by shewing that he had said that it was written in the Memoirs of the Apostles that the stone placed upon the sepulchre was one *which twenty men could scarcely roll?* Yet this addition is found at Luke xxiii. 53 in *Codex Bezæ*, in a copy of the old Latin and in an Egyptian version, so that the words undoubtedly formed part of a text of the Canonical St Luke in the last quarter of the second century at the latest.

Illustrations could be multiplied indefinitely. But these samples will be sufficient to establish the conclusion which has been drawn from the wide variations in copies of the Canonical Gospels during the second century. We are not at present concerned with the solution of the problems of textual criticism which such variations offer. It is enough to repeat in the presence of these facts that differences from the present text of the Gospels such as are found in Justin are wholly inadequate to prove that passages so differing could not have been taken from copies of our Gospels.

Chap. ii.

But it is said that some of Justin's quotations exhibit coincidences with fragments of heretical Gospels, which prove that he must have made use of them, if not exclusively, at least in addition to the writings of the Evangelists.

(γ) Coincidences with heretical Gospels.

One such passage has been already considered incidentally[1], and it has been shewn that the reading which Justin gives appears elsewhere in Catholic writers; and that in fact it may exhibit the original text. The remaining instances are neither many nor of great weight. The most important of them is the reference to our Lord's discourse with Nicodemus[2]: 'For Christ said *Except* ye be born again (ἀναγεννηθῆτε) ye shall *not enter into the kingdom of* heaven. But that *it is impossible for those who have been once born to enter into their mother's womb* is clear to all[3].' In the Clementines the passage reads: 'Thus sware our Prophet to us, saying *Verily I say unto you, except* ye be born again (ἀναγεν-'νηθῆτε) with living water into the name of the Father, 'Son, [and] Holy Spirit, ye shall *not enter into the kingdom of* heaven[4].' Both quotations differ from St John

Matt. xi. 27.

John iii. 3, 5.

---

[1] Cf. pp. 135 f.
[2] Cf. Semisch, § 25, pp. 189 ff.
[3] *Ap.* I. 61: καὶ γὰρ ὁ Χριστὸς εἶπεν· Ἂν μὴ ἀναγεννηθῆτε, οὐ μὴ εἰσέλθητε εἰς τὴν βασιλείαν τῶν οὐρανῶν. Ὅτι δὲ καὶ ἀδύνατον εἰς τὰς μήτρας τῶν τεκουσῶν τοὺς ἅπαξ †γενομένους ἐμβῆναι φανερὸν πᾶσίν ἐστι.
[4] *Hom.* XI. 26: οὕτως γὰρ ἡμῖν

ὤμοσεν ὁ προφήτης εἰπών· Ἀμὴν (+ἀμὴν *Joh.*) ὑμῖν λέγω (λ. σοι *Joh.*) ἐὰν μὴ ἀναγεννηθῆτε (τις γεννηθῇ *Joh.*) ὕδατι ζῶντι, εἰς ὄνομα πατρὸς, υἱοῦ, ἁγίου πνεύματος, οὐ μὴ εἰσέλθητε (οὐ δύναται εἰσελθεῖν *Joh.*) εἰς τὴν βασιλείαν τῶν οὐρανῶν (τοῦ Θεοῦ *Joh.*). See Matt. xviii. 3 (Schwegler, I. p. 218). Cf. *Recog.* VI. 9: Sic enim nobis cum sacramento

152   THE AGE OF THE GREEK APOLOGISTS.   [PART

Chap. ii.

in the use of the plural, in the word descriptive of the new birth, and in the phrase *ye shall not enter into the kingdom of heaven* instead of *he cannot enter into the kingdom of God;* but their variations from one another are not less striking, for the introduction of the phrase 'living water' and of the baptismal formula in the *Homily* is the most significant part of its variation from the text of St John[1].

If the familiar use of one phrase were in all cases a sufficient explanation of its substitution for another which is more strange, there would be little difficulty here. The whole class of words relative to the New Birth (ἀναγεννᾶσθαι, ἀναγέννησις) formed a part of the common technical language of Christians, and they occur repeatedly both in Justin and in the Clementines[2]. The phrase in the Gospel (γεννηθῆναι ἄνωθεν) on the other hand is not only peculiar but ambiguous[3]. Nor is this all: the passage as quoted in both cases is put

verus propheta testatus est dicens: Amen dico vobis, nisi quis *denuo renatus fuerit* (ἀναγεννηθῇ ἄνωθεν) ex aquâ, non introibit in regna *caelorum*. The natural confusion of the contents of the third and fifth verses in St John's record which is already seen in the passages quoted (*born again*, v. 3; *enter*, v. 5) is made still more puzzling by the reading of *Cod. Sinait.* in v. 5, εαν μη τισ εξ υδατοσ και πνσ γεννηθη ου δυναται ειδειν την βασιλιαν των ουρανων [τῶν οὐρανῶν is the original reading of ℵ and τοῦ θεοῦ the correction of ℵᵒ, and not *vice versa* as has been lately stated]. The use of ἀναγεννηθῆτε seems to me to point certainly to the γεννηθῆναι ἄνωθεν of v. 3.

Dr Hort calls my attention to the fact that the readings of the Old Latin Copies indicate conclusively that D also read ἀναγεννηθῆτε. It may be worth while referring to the familiar words in our Service for Baptism...'Christ saith, 'None can enter into the kingdom of 'God except he *be regenerate and born* 'anew of water and of the Holy Ghost,' where the phrase is rendered doubly. See also *Praef.* p. xxxii, n.

[1] The minute and cautious examination of the passage by Dr Abbot, *l. c.* pp. 29—41, goes very far to shew that Justin took the saying directly from St John. Even if the Lord's words were preserved in a traditional form it is hard to suppose that Nicodemus' difficulty would be. [See on the other hand Dr E. A. Abbott on *Justin's Use of St John's Gospel*, ii. pp. 24 ff. (from *Modern Review*, Oct. 1882).]

[2] The earliest examples of this Christian use of the words are 1 Pet. i. 3, 23: *Clem. Hom.* VII. 8; XI. 26 (immediately before the quotation); XI. 35; Justin, *Ap.* I. 61. Cf. Credner, *Beiträge*, I. p. 301 f.

[3] In saying this I must add that

in the form of a general address. If then the general formula was thus adapted from the Evangelist, one change might furnish occasion for the others. And it is not to be overlooked that Ephraem Syrus has given the words in a form which combines in equal proportions the peculiarities of St John and Justin[1]: '*Except a man* '*be* born again from above (ἀναγεννηθῇ ἄνωθεν) *he* shall '*not* see *the kingdom of* heaven.' So also in the *Apostolical Constitutions* the words are quoted thus: 'The 'Lord says *Except a man be born* (γεννηθῇ) *of water and* '*Spirit, he shall not enter into the kingdom of heaven*[2].' If these parallels are not sufficient to prove beyond doubt that the quotation of Justin is a reminiscence of St John, at least they indicate that it was not derived from any Apocryphal Gospel, but rather from some such tradition of our Lord's words as has preserved peculiar types of other texts[3]. Apocryphal Gospels were in fact only unauthorised collections of such traditionary materials; and it should be no matter of surprise if that which was recorded in them survived elsewhere as a current story or saying. The marvel is that early writers so constantly confined themselves within the circle of the Canonical narratives.

Chap. ii.

Coincidences with Apocryphal Gospels no proof of their use.

The next instance which is quoted as shewing a coincidence between Justin and the Clementine Gospel

Matt. v. 34, 37.

---

the context appears to be decisive in favour of the sense *denuo*.
   [1] *De Pœnit.* III. p. 183 (Semisch, p. 196): ἐὰν μή τις ἀναγεννηθῇ ἄνωθεν, οὐ μὴ ἴδῃ τὴν βασιλείαν τῶν οὐρανῶν. See also the reading of *Cod. Sinait.* given on p. 151, n. 4.
   [2] *Const. Apost.* VI. 15 (Semisch, *l. c.*): λέγει ὁ κύριος· ἐὰν μή τις γεννηθῇ ἐξ ὕδατος καὶ πνεύματος, οὐ μὴ εἰσέλθῃ εἰς τὴν βασιλείαν τῶν οὐρανῶν. For γεννηθῇ, the common reading is βαπτισθῇ which is probably a gloss on γενν. ἐξ ὕ. καὶ πν. No instance of βαπτίζειν ἔκ τινος occurs to me.
   [3] Schwegler (I. 218) has pointed out a passage in the Shepherd of Hermas which alludes to the same traditional saying: 'Necesse est, inquit [pastor], *ut per aquam habeant ascendere ut requiescant. Non poterant enim in regnum Dei aliter intrare*, quam ut deponerent mortalitatem prioris vitæ' (III. ix. 16). The latter clause, it will be seen, agrees with St John and not with Justin.

illustrates yet more clearly the existence of a traditional as well as of an Evangelic form of Christ's words. 'That we should not swear at all, but speak the truth 'always,' Justin says, 'Christ thus exhorted us: *Swear* '*not at all; but* let (ἔστω) *your yea be yea*: and your 'nay nay: *but what is more than these is of the evil one*[1].' In the text of St Matthew the corresponding words are *I say unto you Swear not at all...but* let your speech be Yea yea, Nay nay; *but what is more than these is of the evil one*. It so happens however that St James has referred to the same precept: *Before all things, my brethren, swear not, neither by the heaven neither by the earth neither by any other* (ἄλλος) *oath: but let* (ἤτω) *your yea be yea and your nay nay*[2]... Clement quotes the latter clause in this form as 'a maxim of the Lord[3];' and Epiphanius says that the Lord in the Gospel commands us '*Not to swear, neither by the heaven neither by the* '*earth neither by any other* (ἕτερος) *oath: but let* (ἤτω) 'your yea be yea and your nay nay: for *that which is* 'more (περισσότερον) *than these* is in its origin (ὑπάρχει) '*of the evil one*[4].' In the Clementine Homilies the words are: '[Our master] counselling us said: Let (ἔστω) your 'yea be yea and your nay nay; *but that which is more* '*than these is of the evil one*[5].' The differences of Epi-

---

[1] *Apol.* I. 16 (*Clem. Hom.* XIX. 2; Matt. v. 34, 37): περὶ δὲ τοῦ μὴ ὀμνύναι ὅλως τἀληθῆ δὲ λέγειν ἀεὶ οὕτως παρεκελεύσατο· μὴ ὀμόσητε ὅλως· ἔστω δὲ (+ὁ λόγος *Mt.*) ὑμῶν τὸ (om. *Mt.*) ναὶ ναὶ καὶ τὸ (om. καὶ τὸ *Mt.*) οὒ οὔ· τὸ δὲ περισσὸν τούτων ἐκ τοῦ πονηροῦ (+ἐστίν *Mt., Clem.*).
In *Clem. Hom.* III. 55 the passage stands: ἔστω ὑμῶν τὸ ναὶ ναί, τὸ οὒ οὔ· τὸ γὰρ κ.τ.λ.
[2] James v. 12: Πρὸ πάντων δέ, ἀδελφοί μου, μὴ ὀμνύετε μήτε τὸν οὐρανὸν μήτε τὴν γῆν μήτε ἄλλον τινὰ ὅρκον· ἤτω δὲ ὑμῶν τὸ ναὶ ναὶ καὶ τὸ οὒ οὔ, ἵνα μὴ ὑπὸ κρίσιν πέσητε.
[3] *Strom.* V. 14. 100: τὸ κυρίου ῥητόν· ἔστω (not ἤτω) ὑμῶν κ.τ.λ. Cf. Lib. VII. 11. 67, where the sentence is again quoted in a similar form: ἔσται ὑμῶν κ.τ.λ.
[4] Epiph. *adv. Haer.* I. 20. 6 (I. p. 44): [τοῦ κυρίου] ἐν τῷ εὐαγγελίῳ λέγοντος· μὴ ὀμνύναι μήτε τὸν οὐρανὸν μήτε τὴν γῆν μήτε ἕτερόν τινα ὅρκον· ἀλλ' ἤτω ὑμῶν τὸ ναὶ ναὶ καὶ τὸ οὒ οὔ· τὸ περισσότερον γὰρ τούτων ἐκ τοῦ πονηροῦ ὑπάρχει.
[5] *Hom.* XIX. 2: συμβουλεύων [ὁ

phanius from the text of St Matthew are thus greater than those of Justin; and the coincidence of Justin with the Clementines is confined to words found in St James, and quoted expressly by some Fathers as Christ's words. The many various readings of our Lord's words, when He limited the true application of the word 'good' to God only, are well known. It is recorded in different forms by the three Evangelists. Justin himself has quoted the passage twice, varying almost every word. It is brought forward repeatedly by other Fathers, with constant variations from the text of the Gospels. In the presence of these facts it would be impossible under any circumstances to lay great stress upon the coincidence of a few words in one of Justin's quotations with a reading recognised by the Marcosians[1] and the Ebionites. Yet the case is made still simpler when it is shewn that Catholic authority can be adduced for each word in which he agrees with those widely different sects. In the Apology the answer is given: '*No one is 'good save God* alone, who made all things[2].' In the Dialogue: '*Why callest thou me good? One is good*, 'my Father which is in heaven[3].' The Marcosians read

<small>Matt. xix. 17.
Mark x. 18.
Lu. xviii. 19.</small>

διδάσκαλος] εἴρηκεν· ἔστω ὑμῶν τὸ ναὶ ναὶ καὶ τὸ οὗ οὔ· τὸ δὲ περισσὸν τούτων ἐκ τοῦ πονηροῦ ἐστίν.

[1] We shall consider in another place (Ch. iv. § 8 and note) whether the passages quoted by Irenæus were corrupted by the Marcosians or simply misinterpreted.

[2] *Ap.* I. 16 (Mark x. 18; Luke xviii. 19): οὐδεὶς ἀγαθὸς εἰ μὴ μόνος (εἰς *Mc., Lc.*) ὁ (om. *Cod. Sinait.* in *Lc.*) Θεὸς ὁ ποιήσας τὰ πάντα (om. *Mc., Lc.*). In St Mark D d combine the former words, reading μόνος εἶς Θεός. Several other MSS. of the Old Latin give *solus* (Griesb. *l. c.*). The concluding words occur just before, and are to be considered as 'an addition of Justin's suggested by 'the circumstances of the time and 'his late controversy with Marcion' (Credner, I. 243). Such a concession takes away much of the force of Credner's other arguments. If Justin might add a clause to guard against a heresy, surely he might adapt the language of the Evangelists so as best to meet the wants of his readers.

[3] *Dial.* c. 101 (Marcos. ap. Iren. I. 20. 2): τί με λέγεις ἀγαθόν (Lc. xviii. 19); εἷς ἐστιν ἀγαθός (Mt. xix. 17 ὁ ἀγ.), ὁ πατήρ μου ὁ (om. μου ὁ Marcos.) ἐν τοῖς οὐρανοῖς.

156   THE AGE OF THE GREEK APOLOGISTS.   [PART

Chap. ii.

in their text: '*Why callest thou me good? One is good,* 'the Father in heaven.' In the Clementines the words are: '*Call me not good: for the Good is One, the Father 'which is in heaven*[1].' As to these quotations it is to be noticed that Epiphanius has connected the words of St Matthew and St Luke in a form similar to that found in the Marcosian Gospel and in Justin[2]. The last clause which is common to the three is the only remaining point of difference. Now not only are there traces of some addition to the text of St Matthew in several versions[3]: not only did Marcion and Clement and Origen recognise the words 'the Father[4];' but in one place Clement gives the whole sentence, '*No one is good except* 'my Father which is in heaven[5].' He has attached the last clause of Justin to the words of St Luke, exactly as in Epiphanius we find the last words of St Matthew added to the opening clauses of Justin.

Matt. xxv. 41.

The last instance which is quoted is not more important than those which have been examined[6]. After speak-

---

[1] *Hom.* XVIII. 3: μή με λέγε ἀγαθόν· ὁ γὰρ ἀγαθὸς εἷς ἐστιν, ὁ πατὴρ ὁ ἐν τοῖς οὐρανοῖς.
[2] Epiph. *adv. Hær.* LXIX. 19 (I. p. 742), 57 (I. p. 780), gives the words as quoted by the Arians: τί με λέγεις ἀγαθόν (*Mc., Lc.*); εἷς ἐστιν ἀγαθός (*Mt. ὁ ἀγ.*), ὁ Θεός. He makes no comment upon the form of the reading, but in the course of his argument quotes the words himself in the form in which they are found in St Mark and St Luke (*adv. Hær.* LXIX. 57, I. p. 781): τί με λέγεις ἀγαθόν; οὐδεὶς ἀγαθὸς εἰ μὴ εἷς, ὁ Θεός. If these quotations are compared with those given in the next note it will be obvious how little regard was paid to exactness of quotation in passages which were used very familiarly.
[3] It may be necessary to notice that the true text in St Matthew xix.

17 is simply τί με ἐρωτᾷς περὶ τοῦ ἀγαθοῦ; εἷς ἐστιν ὁ ἀγαθός.
[4] Marcion read (Epiph. *adv. Hær.* XLII. p. 315) μή με λέγετε ἀγαθόν· εἷς ἐστιν ἀγαθός, ὁ πατήρ. In the refutation (p. 339) his text is given: μή με λέγε ἀγαθόν· εἷς ἐστιν ἀγαθός, ὁ Θεὸς ὁ Πατήρ. For the passages of Clement (ὁ πατήρ) and Origen (ὁ Θεὸς ὁ πατήρ) see Griesb. *Symb. Crit.* II. pp. 305, 388.
[5] *Pæd.* I. 8. 72: διαρρήδην λέγει· οὐδεὶς ἀγαθὸς εἰ μὴ ὁ πατήρ μου ὁ ἐν τοῖς οὐρανοῖς. Semisch, p. 372. The passage has been overlooked by Griesbach.
[6] The connexion of *Dial.* c. 96 with *Hom.* III. 57 (Matt. v. 45) is noticed in Note D, p. 179. The reference to Luke xi. 52 in *Dial.* c. 17, where τὰς κλεῖς ἔχετε stands for ἤρατε τὴν κλεῖδα τῆς γνώσεως, is very different from that in *Hom.* III. 18,

JUSTIN MARTYR.

ing of those *sons of the kingdom who shall be cast into the outer darkness*, Justin quotes the condemnation of the wicked as pronounced by Christ in these words : 'Go ye 'into the outer darkness *which my Father prepared for* 'Satan *and his Angels*[1].' It occurs again in the same form in the Clementine Homilies. There are here two variations to be noticed—a change in the verb (ὑπάγειν for πορεύεσθαι), and the substitution of 'the outer darkness' for 'the eternal fire.' The first variation occurs elsewhere[2]: the naturalness of the second is shewn by the fact that in one Manuscript at least of St Matthew the original reading was *the outer fire*. And more than this: Clement of Alexandria has coupled the two images of 'the fire' and 'the 'outer darkness' in a passage which has a distinct reference to the words of St Matthew[3].

where the phrase is κρατοῦσι τὴν κλεῖν.

[1] *Dial.* c. 76 ; *Clem. Hom.* XIX. 2 ; Matt. xxv. 41: ὑπάγετε (+ ἀπ' ἐμοῦ Mt.) εἰς τὸ σκότος (πῦρ Mt.) τὸ ἐξώτερον (αἰώνιον Mt.) ὃ ἡτοίμασεν ὁ πατὴρ (+ μου Mt.) τῷ σατανᾷ (διαβόλῳ Mt., Clem.) καὶ τοῖς ἀγγέλοις αὐτοῦ.
Ὑπάγετε ἀπ' ἐμοῦ is found in ℵ; and the reading ὃ ἡτοίμασεν ὁ πατήρ μου is supported by D, 2 mss., MSS. of Old Lat., and many Fathers, so that we may suppose that it was early current in the Canonical Gospel. Irenæus again once omits ἀπ' ἐμοῦ (III. 23. 3); in two other places it is omitted by some manuscripts (IV. 33. 11 ; 40. 2); in the remaining place it appears to be read by all (IV. 28. 2). The omission of οἱ κατηράμενοι (or rather of κατηράμενοι, for the οἱ is probably spurious) does not require special notice.

[2] The Old Latin version of Irenæus has in the first two quotations *abite*, and in the last two *discedite* (Vulg.). The variation is not noticed by Lachmann. The words πορ.

and ὑπ. are confounded in Luke viii. 42.

[3] *Quis Div. Salv.* § 13 (Semisch, p. 377).
How easily such a passage might be altered may be seen from Epiphanius's quotation of the sentence of the just: δεῦτε ἐκ δεξιῶν μου οἱ εὐλογημένοι οἷς ὁ πατήρ μου ὁ οὐράνιος ἔθετο τὴν βασιλείαν πρὸ καταβολῆς κόσμου· ἐπείνασα γὰρ καὶ ἐδώκατέ μοι φαγεῖν· ἐδίψησα καὶ ἐποτίσατέ με· γυμνὸς καὶ περιεβάλετέ με (adv. Hær. LXI. 4). The whole form of the blessing is here changed.
Justin himself has introduced 'the eternal fire' into his reference to Matt. xiii. 42, 43, in *Ap*. I. 16.
Dr Abbot (*l. c.* pp. 101 ff.) has given a most instructive series of examples of the substitution of ὑπάγετε for πορεύεσθε and of τὸ σκότος τὸ ἐξώτερον for τὸ πῦρ τὸ αἰώνιον in patristic quotations of the passage.
Any one who has had the patience to go through the examination of these passages will be in a position to judge of the fairness of M. Reuss' statement: Toutefois il est remarqua-

Differences between Justin's citations and those in the Clementines.

It would be easy to shew that the differences of Justin's quotations from the Gospel-passages in the Clementines are both numerous and striking[1]. Their coincidences however are so few and of such a character as to lend no support to the belief that they belong to a common type. A comparison of all the passages which are found in both books places their independence beyond a doubt; but it is enough that important variations have been noticed in texts which exhibit the strongest resemblances. That the Apocryphal Gospels should exhibit points of partial resemblance to quotations made by memory from the written Gospels is most natural. They were not mere creations of the imagination, but narratives based on the original oral Gospel of which the written Gospel was the authoritative record. The same cause in both cases might lead to the introduction of a common word, a characteristic phrase, a supplementary trait. But there was this difference: in the one case these changes were limited only by the arbitrary rule of each particular sect; in the other they were restrained by an instinctive sense of Catholic truth, varying indeed in strength and susceptibility, but related to the bare individualism of heresy as the fulness of Scripture itself is related to the partial reflections of its teaching in the writings of a later age.

(3) Coincidences of Justin's narrative with Apocryphal Traditions.

The relation of Justin to the Apocryphal Gospels introduces the last objection which we have to notice. It is said that his quotations differ not only in language but also in substance from our Gospels: that he attributes sayings to our Lord which they do not contain, and nar-

ble que plusieurs des citations de Justin, dont le texte diffère du nôtre, se retrouvent *littéralment* (the italics are his own) dans d'autres ouvrages, par exemple dans les *Clémentines*... (*Hist. du Canon*...p. 56). It is impossible to exaggerate the mischief done by these vague, general statements, which produce a permanent impression wholly out of proportion with the minute element of truth which is hidden in them.

[1] See Note D at the end of the Section.

rates events which are either not mentioned by the Evangelists, or recorded by them with serious variations from his account. It is enough to answer that he never does so when he proposes to quote the Apostolic Memoirs. Like other early Fathers tradition had made him familiar with some few words of our Lord which are not embodied in the Gospels. Like them he may have been acquainted with details of His life treasured up by such as the elder of Ephesus[1] who might have heard St John. But whatever use he makes of this knowledge, he never refers to the Apostolic Memoirs for anything which is not substantially found in our Gospels[2].

Justin's account of the Baptism, which might seem an exception to this statement, really confirms and explains it. It is well known that there was a belief long current that the Heavenly Voice addressed our Lord in the words of the Psalm which have been ever applied to Him, *Thou art my Son; this day have I begotten Thee.* Augustine mentions the reading as current in his time[3]; and the words are found at present in the Codex Bezæ (D) and in the Old Latin Version[4]. Justin then might have found them in the manuscript of St Luke which he used; but the form of his reference is remarkable. When speaking of the Temptation he says: 'For the devil, of whom I just 'now spoke, as soon as [Christ] went up from the river

---

[1] *Dial.* c. 3: παλαιός τις πρεσβύτης.
[2] All the passages are given above, pp. 132 ff.
[3] August. *de Cons. Evv.* II. 14: Illud vero quod nonnulli codices habent secundum Lucam (iii. 22) hoc illâ voce sonuisse quod in Psalmo scriptum est *Filius meus es tu, ego hodie genui te;* quanquam in antiquioribus codicibus græcis non inveniri perhibeatur, tamen si aliquibus fide dignis exemplaribus confirmari possit, quid aliud... This, it will be remembered, is in a critical work; elsewhere he quotes the words as uttered at the Baptism without remark: *Enchiridion,* c. 14 [XLIX.]. Cf. *Lectt. Varr.* given in T. VI. p. xxiv. ed. Paris, 1837.
[4] Cf. Griesb. and Tischdf. *ad Luc.* iii. 22. The quotation of the words by Clement of Alexandria (*Pæd.* I. 25) is omitted in Griesbach's *Symbolæ Criticæ* (II. 363).

Chap. ii.

'Jordan—when the voice had been addressed to Him '*Thou art my Son, this day have I begotten Thee*—is de-'scribed in the Memoirs of the Apostles as having come to 'Him and tempted Him so far as to say to Him *Worship* '*me*[1].' The words which are definitely quoted form confessedly a part of the Evangelic text: and it does not appear from the construction of the sentence that Justin cites the Memoirs as his authority for the disputed clause[2].

The Fire kindled in the Jordan.

This apparent mixture of two narratives is still more noticeable in the passage in which Justin introduces the famous legend of the fire kindled in Jordan when Christ descended into the water. 'When Jesus came to the 'Jordan where John was baptizing, when He descended to 'the water both a fire was kindled in the Jordan, and the 'Apostles of our Christ Himself recorded that when He 'came up out of the water the Holy Spirit as a Dove 'lighted upon Him[3].' Here the contrast is complete.

---

[1] *Dial.* c. 103: καὶ γὰρ οὗτος ὁ διάβολος ἅμα τῷ ἀναβῆναι αὐτὸν ἀπὸ τοῦ ποταμοῦ τοῦ Ἰορδάνου τῆς φωνῆς αὐτῷ λεχθείσης Ὑιός μου εἶ σύ, ἐγὼ σήμερον γεγέννηκά σε· ἐν τοῖς ἀπομνημονεύμασι τῶν ἀποστόλων γέγραπται προσελθὼν αὐτῷ καὶ πειράζων μέχρι τοῦ εἰπεῖν αὐτῷ Προσκύνησόν μοι. The same words are quoted again (c. 88) without any reference to the Memoirs.

The words occurred in the Ebionite Gospel: Epiph. *adv. Hær.* xxx. 13. It is evident however that the narrative of the Baptism there given is made up from several traditions. That which it has in common with Justin must have been borrowed by both from some third source. Cf. Strauss, *Leben Jesu*, I. 378 (Ed. 2, quoted by Semisch, p. 407, n.).

[2] Nothing depends upon this view. The textual authorities shew that the words of Ps. ii. formed part of St Luke's Gospel in MSS. of the second century.

[3] *Dial.* c. 88: καὶ τότε ἐλθόντος τοῦ Ἰησοῦ ἐπὶ τὸν Ἰορδάνην ποταμὸν ἔνθα ὁ Ἰωάννης ἐβάπτιζε, κατελθόντος τοῦ Ἰησοῦ ἐπὶ τὸ ὕδωρ καὶ πῦρ ἀνήφθη ἐν τῷ Ἰορδάνῃ, καὶ ἀναδύντος αὐτοῦ ἀπὸ τοῦ ὕδατος ὡς περιστερὰν τὸ ἅγιον πνεῦμα ἐπιπτῆναι ἐπ᾽ αὐτὸν ἔγραψαν οἱ ἀπόστολοι αὐτοῦ τούτου τοῦ Χριστοῦ ἡμῶν. The conjectural emendation ἀνῆφθαι for ἀνήφθη destroys the contrast.

In the Ebionite Gospel (Epiph. *l. c.*) the legend is given differently: ὡς ἀνῆλθεν ἀπὸ τοῦ ὕδατος ἠνοίγησαν οἱ οὐρανοί...καὶ εὐθὺς περιέλαμψε τὸν τόπον φῶς μέγα. Comp. *Auct. de rebapt.* ap. Cypr. *Opp.* Otto (*ad loc.*) quotes a passage from 'a Syriac liturgy' which may indicate the origin of the tradition: Quo tempore adscendit ab aquis *sol inclinavit radios suos.* Justin appears to be the only Catholic writer who alludes to the appearance; unless the words of Juvencus *manifesta Dei præsentia claret* also refer

The witness of the Apostles is claimed for that which our Gospels relate; but Justin affirms on his own authority a fact which, however beautiful and significant in the symbolism of the East, is yet without any support from the Canonical history[1].

The remaining uncanonical details in Justin are either such facts and words as are known to have been current in tradition, or natural exaggerations, or glosses on the received text generally suggested by some Prophecy of the Old Testament.

He tells us that 'those who saw Christ's works said 'that they were a magic show; for they dared to call 'Him a magician and a deceiver of the people[2].' The Gospels have preserved the simplest form of this blasphemy and it survived even to the time of Augustine[3]. Again in St Mark our Lord is called *the Carpenter*. The reading indeed was obliterated in the Manuscripts used by Origen, for he denied that our Lord ' was ever Him-'self called a Carpenter in the Gospels current in the ' Churches[4];' but it is supported by almost all the authorities at present existing. The same pride or mistaken reverence which removed the word suppressed the tradition which it favoured; but it is characteristic of the earliest age that Justin speaks of 'the Carpenter's works

Chap. ii.

The remaining Apocryphal references in Justin.

Traditional facts.

Matt. xii. 24;
xxvii. 63;
John vii. 12.

Mark vi. 3.

---

[1] The details of the Transfiguration furnish an illustration of the passage. Light is the symbol of God's dwelling-place; Exod. xiv. 20; 1 Kings viii. 11; 1 Tim. vi. 16. Light is the outward mark of special to it. It is however to be observed that in Manuscripts of the Old Latin a g¹ a similar addition occurs: *et cum baptizaretur (Jesus* g¹) *lumen ingens circumfulsit* (*l. magnum fulgebat* g¹) *de aqua ita ut timerent omnes qui advenerant* (*q. congregati erant* g¹). Compare also the addition of k to Mark xvi. 4.

converse with Him; Exod. xxxiv. 30.

[2] *Dial.* c. 69: οἱ δὲ καὶ ταῦτα ὁρῶντες γινόμενα φαντασίαν μαγικὴν γίνεσθαι ἔλεγον· καὶ γὰρ μάγον εἶναι αὐτὸν ἐτόλμων λέγειν καὶ λαοπλάνον. Cf. *Ap.* I. 30, and Otto's notes.

[3] August. *de Cons. Evv.* I. 9: Christum propterea sapientissimum putant fuisse quia nescio quae illicita noverat....

[4] *c. Cels.* VI. 36: οὐδαμοῦ τῶν ἐν ταῖς ἐκκλησίαις φερομένων εὐαγγελίων τέκτων αὐτὸς ὁ Ἰησοῦς ἀναγέγραπται.

'which Christ wrought when among men, ploughs and
'yokes, by these both teaching the emblems of right-
'eousness and [enforcing] an active life¹.'

Traditional sayings.

In addition to these details Justin has recorded two sayings of our Lord not found in the Gospels. 'Our 'Lord Jesus Christ said: In whatsoever I find you, in 'this will I also judge you².' Clement of Alexandria has quoted the same sentence with slight variations, but without any distinct reference to its source³. In later times it was attributed to Ezekiel, or some Prophet of the Old Testament⁴; and though it was widely current, there is no evidence to shew that it was contained in any Apocryphal Gospel. It may have been contained in the *Gospel according to the Hebrews*⁵; but even if it were so, the tradition must have existed before the record, and may have survived independently of it. The same holds true of the other phrase, 'Christ said: 'There shall be schisms and heresies⁶.' If it were not for the mode in which Justin quotes them, the words might seem a short summary of our Lord's warnings against the false teachers and false prophets who should deceive many. In the Clementines the two prophecies

---

¹ *Dial.* c. 88: ταῦτα γὰρ τὰ τεκτονικὰ ἔργα εἰργάζετο ἐν ἀνθρώποις ὧν ἄροτρα καὶ ζυγά, διὰ τούτων καὶ τὰ τῆς δικαιοσύνης σύμβολα διδάσκων καὶ †ἐνεργῆ βίον. Otto refers to the Arabic *Gospel of the Infancy* (c. 38) and to the *Gospel of Thomas* (c. 13) for similar traditions. The latter narrative (ἐποίει ἄροτρα καὶ ζυγούς, said of Joseph) shews a remarkable coincidence of language with Justin.

The statement which Justin makes (*Dial.* 17, 108, quoted by Eusebius, *H.E.* IV. 18) as to emissaries sent out by the Jews to calumniate the Christians, does not belong to the Evangelic history.

² *Dial.* c. 47: ὁ ἡμέτερος κύριος Ἰησοῦς Χριστὸς εἶπεν· Ἐν οἷς ἂν ὑμᾶς καταλάβω ἐν τούτοις καὶ κρινῶ. Cf. Otto, *in loc.*

³ Clem. *Quis Div. Salv.* § 40.
⁴ Semisch, p. 394.
⁵ Cf. Credner, *Beiträge*, I. 247. *Introduction to the Study of the Gospels*, App. C, p. 426.
⁶ *Dial.* c. 35: εἶπε γὰρ...ἔσονται σχίσματα καὶ αἱρέσεις. Cf. 1 Cor. xi. 18, 19. The passage is quoted by Justin between Matt. xxiv. 5 (comp. vii. 15) and Matt. vii. 15, and distinguished from them.

are intermixed: 'There shall be, as the Lord said, false 'apostles, false prophets, heresies, lusts of rule¹.' Lactantius also affirms that 'both Christ Himself and His 'ambassadors foretold that many sects and heresies 'would arise...².'

Elsewhere Justin generalises the statements of the Gospels with what may seem natural exaggerations. 'Herod,' he says, 'commanded *all* the male children in 'Bethlehem to be slain *without exception*³;' yet he states in another place with more exactness that 'Herod slew 'all the male children who were born in Bethlehem 'about the time of Christ's birth⁴.' Again, when speaking of the calumnies of the Jews about the Resurrection, Justin not only gives the origin of the story as St Matthew does, but adds 'that they chose out men whom 'they sent *into the whole world* to announce the rise of 'a godless and lawless sect⁵;' a statement which explains the character of Christianity recorded in the Acts *that it is* everywhere *spoken against*.

Chap. ii.
Matt. vii. 15
xxiv. 5.

Exaggerations.

Acts xxviii. 22.

---

¹ *Hom.* XVI. 21: ἔσονται γάρ, ὡς ὁ Κύριος εἶπεν, ψευδαπόστολοι, ψευδεῖς προφῆται, αἱρέσεις, φιλαρχίαι. The word ψευδαπόστολοι occurs likewise in St Paul (2 Cor. xi. 13), in Hegesippus (Euseb. *H.E.* IV. 22), in Justin (*l. c.* ἀναστήσονται πολλοὶ ψευδόχριστοι καὶ ψευδαπόστολοι καὶ πολλοὺς τῶν πιστῶν πλανήσουσι), in Tertullian (*de Præscr. Hæret.* c. 4 quoted by Otto), and in other authors; so that it may point to some traditional version of our Lord's words. In *Dial.* 116 I can only see a reference to Zech. iñ. 4 ff. taken in connexion with the thought of Apoc. vii. 9.

² *Inst. Div.* IV. 30 (Semisch, p. 393): Ante omnia scire nos convenit et ipsum et legatos ejus prædixisse quod plurimæ sectæ et hæreses haberent existere quæ concordiam sancti corporis rumperent. Cf. Tertull. *l. c.* where the passage is apparently referred to the text of St Paul.

³ *Dial.* c. 78: πάντας ἁπλῶς τοὺς παῖδας τοὺς ἐν Βηθλεὲμ ἐκέλευσεν ἀναιρεθῆναι.

⁴ *Dial.* c. 103: ['Ηρώδου] ἀνελόντος πάντας τοὺς ἐν Βηθλεὲμ ἐκείνου τοῦ καιροῦ γεννηθέντας παῖδας. Origen quotes the passage with some variations: πάντα τὰ παιδία ἀνεῖλε τὰ ἐν Βηθλεὲμ καὶ ἐν (=πᾶσι) τοῖς ὁρίοις αὐτῆς ἀπὸ διετοῦς κ.τ.λ. Comm. *in Matt.* XVII. 11.

⁵ *Dial.* c. 108: ἄνδρας χειροτονήσαντες ἐκλεκτοὺς εἰς πᾶσαν τὴν οἰκουμένην ἐπέμψατε κηρύσσοντας ὅτι αἵρεσίς τις ἄθεος καὶ ἄνομος ἐγήγερται ἀπὸ Ἰησοῦ τινὸς Γαλιλαίου πλάνου...

More frequently he adds an interpretation to the text which he quotes; as when he says that Joseph 'was of Bethlehem,' as though that were his native village, but Nazareth only his dwelling-place[1]; or when he speaks of 'the magi from *Arabia*[2].' And this very commonly happens when the gloss is suggested by a Prophecy. Thus he alludes to the cave in which our Lord was born, because Isaiah had said *He shall dwell in a high cave of a strong rock*[3]. He speaks of the Star which rose in *heaven*, not mentioning *the East*[4], apparently because our Lord Himself is described as *the Day-spring* (ἀνατολή), *the Star of Jacob*. He tells us that the foal of the ass on which our Lord entered into Jerusalem was bound to a vine, as it was said of Judah that *he bound his foal unto the vine*[5]:—that 'there was 'no one not even one at hand to help Him [when 'betrayed] as being without sin,' even as David had prophesied in the Psalm[6]:—that the Jews when they mocked Him 'placed Him on a judgment-seat and said 'Judge for us,' as Isaiah had complained, '*they ask of me* '*now judgment*[7]:'—that 'His disciples who were with 'Him were scattered till He arose[8],'—that 'all His 'acquaintance departed from Him and denied Him[9],' referring to the prophecy of Zechariah quoted by St Matthew, and the picture of Christ's sufferings and loneliness in Isaiah.

Such is the analysis of Justin's quotations from the

---

[1] *Dial.* c. 78: ἀπογραφῆς οὔσης ἐν τῇ Ἰουδαίᾳ τότε πρώτης ἐπὶ Κυρηνίου ἀνεληλύθει ἀπὸ Ναζαρὲτ ἔνθα ᾤκει εἰς Βηθλεὲμ ὅθεν ἦν ἀναγράψασθαι.
[2] *Dial. l. c.* and c. 106.
[3] Cf. p. 102, note 7.
[4] *Dial.* c. 106; 78.
[5] *Ap.* I. 32. Justin interprets the prophecy in the same way in *Dial.* c. 53, without affirming this particular.
[6] *Dial.* c. 103.
[7] *Ap.* I. 35. Comp. Abbot *l. c.* p. 50, who inclines to follow Prof. Drummond's suggestion that Justin took ἐκάθισεν in John xix. 13 in an active sense (he *set* Him on the judgment seat).
[8] *Dial.* c. 53.
[9] *Ap.* I. 50.

Memoirs of the Apostles, of his various readings in Evangelic phrases, of his Apocryphal additions to the Gospel history. The process is long, but a full examination of all the passages in question is the best answer to objections which appear strong because isolated instances are taken as types of general laws; and the result to which it necessarily leads is full of strength and satisfaction for those who feel that the Catholic Church cannot have arisen from a mere fusion of discordant elements at the end of the second century, and who still look anxiously and candidly into every document and every fact which marks the characteristics of its form and the stages of its growth. The details of Justin's quotations shew us something of the manner in which the Scriptures, and especially the Gospels, were used by the first Christian teachers, something of the variations which existed in different copies (of which other traces still remain), something of the extent and character of the oral records of Christ's life; but they afford no ground for the belief that the Memoirs were anything but the Synoptic Gospels which we have, and they exhibit no trace of the use of any other Evangelic records. Justin lived at a period of transition from a traditional to a written Gospel, and his testimony is exactly fitted to the position which he held. He refers to books, but more frequently he appears to bring forward words which were currently circulated rather than what he had privately read. In both respects his witness to our Gospels is most important. For it has been shewn that his definite quotations from the Memoirs are so exactly accordant with the text of the Synoptists as it stands now, or as it was read at the close of the second century, that there can be no doubt that he was as well familiar with their writings as with the facts related in

Chap. ii.

The essential character of Justin's quotations.

No trace in Justin of the use of any written document other than our Gospels.

them. And the wide and minute agreement of his notices of the life and teaching of our Lord with what they record of it proves that his knowledge of the Gospel history was derived from a tradition which they had moulded and controlled, if not from the habitual and exclusive use of the books themselves[1].

His coincidences with Heretical or Apocryphal narratives have been proved to be not peculiar to him, but fragments of a wide-spread recension of the Canonical text. His simpler divergences from the received text have been illustrated by parallel examples of his quotations from the Septuagint and by recognised various readings in other authorities.

On a comprehensive view, all is seen to lead to the same conclusion. The lines which seemed at first to cross one another at random give a result perfectly complete and symmetrical when followed out in every case to their legitimate limit; and thus, even judging from a mere critical analysis, it appears to be a fact beyond doubt that Justin used the first three Gospels as we use them, as the authentic memoirs of Christ's life and work.

Justin's historical position

If we glance at his historical position we seem to gain the same result with equal certainty. He states that the Memoirs of the Apostles were read in the weekly services of the Church on the same footing as the writings of the Prophets; or in other words that they enjoyed the outward rank of Scripture. And since he speaks of their Ecclesiastical use without any restriction, it is na-

---

[1] The relation between Justin's quotations and our Gospels is so intimate that they cannot have been independent. The only alternative, namely that the Synoptic Gospels embodied the oral Gospel as it was current in Justin's time, apart from historical considerations, is excluded by the fact that the Evangelists exhibit the narrative in the simplest form. At the same time it is evident that the original oral Gospel could not have been so long preserved in its essential purity without the counter-check of written Gospels. The tradition and the record mutually illustrate and confirm one another.

tural to believe that he alludes to definite books, which were generally regarded in the same light, and which had acquired a firm place in the common life of Christians. He could not at any rate have been ignorant of the custom of the churches of Italy and Asia; and if his description were true of any churches it must have been true of those. Is it then possible to suppose that within twenty or thirty years after his death these Gospels should have been replaced by others similar and yet distinct[1]? that he should speak of one set of books as if they were permanently incorporated into the Christian services, and that those who might have been his scholars should speak in exactly the same terms of another collection as if they had had no rivals within the orthodox pale? that the substitution should have been effected in such a manner that no record of it has been preserved, while smaller analogous reforms have been duly chronicled[2]? The complication of historical difficulties in such a hypothesis is overwhelming; and the alternative is that which has already been justified on critical grounds, the belief that Justin in speaking of Apostolic Memoirs or Gospels meant the Gospels which were enumerated in the early anonymous Canon of Muratori, and whose mutual relations were eloquently expounded by Irenæus.

It appears then to be established both by external and internal evidence that Justin's 'Gospels' can be identified with those of St Matthew, St Mark and St Luke. His references to St John are more open to question; but this, as has been already remarked, fol-

---

[1] Cf. pp. 75 f.
[2] As for example when Serapion reproved certain in the church at Rhossus for the use of *the Gospel of St Peter* (Euseb. *H. E.* VI. 12); or when Theodoret substituted the Canonical Gospels for the Harmony of Tatian, of which he found 'above two hundred in the churches.'

lows from the character of the fourth Gospel. It was unlikely that he should quote its peculiar teaching in apologetic writings addressed to Jews and heathen. But at the same time he exhibits types of language and doctrine, which seem to mark the presence of St John's influence and the recognition of his authority[1].

and to the other books of the New Testament. The Apocalypse.

In addition to the Gospels the Apocalypse is the only book of the New Testament to which Justin alludes by name. Even that is not quoted, but appealed to generally as a proof of the existence of Prophetic power in the Christian Church[2]. But it cannot be concluded from his silence that Justin was either unacquainted with the Acts and the Epistles, or unwilling to make use of them. His controversy against Marcion is decisive as to his knowledge of the greater part of the books, and various Pauline forms of expression and teaching shew that the Apostle of the Gentiles had helped to mould

The writings of St Paul.

[1] Cf. pp. 106, 107, n. 4. Justin's acquaintance with the Valentinians proves (as I believe) that the Gospel could not have been unknown to him (*Dial.* c. 35; comp. *Ap.* I. 26).

A fresh examination of the parallels to the Gospel of St John in the writings of Justin leads me to speak more confidently than before as to his use of the Fourth Gospel.

In addition to the passage in *Ap.* I. c. 61 (John iii. 3—5) already noticed (pp. 151 f.), the following parallels are of importance: *Dial.* c. 88: John i. 20, 23. *Dial.* c. 29: John v. 17. *Dial.* c. 105: John i. 14 (18): iii. 16, 18. Comp. *fragm.* ap. Iren. IV. 6, 2. *Dial.* c. 49: John ix. Comp. *Clem. Hom.* XIX. 22. *Dial.* c. 100: John x. 18. *Dial.* c. 91: John iii. 17. *Ap.* I. 35: John xix. 13 (?) and more especially *Dial.* c. 123: 1 John iii. 1 (κληθῶμεν καὶ ἐσμέν). Comp. Abbot, *l. c.* pp. 41 ff. Lücke (*Comm. ü. d. Ev. Joh.* 34 ff.) has shewn the connexion between Justin's doctrine of the Logos and the Preface to St John's Gospel. Otto (p. 81) also calls attention to his doctrine of the Eucharist as related to John vi. Compare also Just. *Fragm.* XI. ed. Otto, with Otto's note.

It may be worth while to notice, since the contrary has been asserted, that Justin makes no mention at all of the Last Supper in *Dial.* III, still less does he contradict St John. Indeed his whole argument as to the correspondence of Christ and the Paschal lamb suggests that he, in agreement with St John, places the Crucifixion at the time of the sacrifice of the lamb, Nisan 14th.

[2] Cf. p. 121. *Ap.* I. 28: ὁ ἀρχηγέτης τῶν κακῶν δαιμόνων ὄφις καλεῖται καὶ σατανᾶς καὶ διάβολος coincides remarkably with Apoc. xx. 2. The other passage to which Otto refers (*a. a. O.* 1843, I. 42) *Dial.* c. 45, Apoc. xxi. 4, seems more uncertain.

both his faith and his language[1]. Thus he says 'We
'were *taught* that Christ is the *first-born* (πρωτότοκος) of
'God:' 'we have recognised Him as the first-born of
'God and before all creatures:' 'by the name of this
'very Son of God and *first-born of every creature* (πρω-
'τοτόκου πάσης κτίσεως)...every demon is overcome...'
'through Him God arranged (κοσμῆσαι) all things[2].'
Elsewhere he uses the example of Abraham to shew
that circumcision was for a sign and not for righteousness, 'since he, being in uncircumcision, for the sake of
'the faith with which he believed God was justified and
'blessed[3].' 'By faith (πίστει) we are cleansed through
'the blood of Christ and His death who died for this[4];'
'through whom we were called into the salvation pre-
'pared aforetime by our Father[5].' 'Christ was the
'passover who was sacrificed afterwards[6]:' 'who shall
'come with glory from the heavens, when also the
'man of the falling away—the man of lawlessness (c.
'32),—who speaketh strange things—blasphemous and
'daring (c. 32), even against the Most High, shall ex-
'ert his lawless daring against us Christians[7].' Else-

Chap. ii. Colossians.

Romans.

Corinthians.

2 Thessalonians.

---

[1] Otto, *a. a. O.* 1842, II. pp. 41 ff. The absence of all mention of the name of St Paul can create no difficulty when it is remembered that Justin speaks of St Peter as ἕνα τῶν ἀποστόλων, and of the sons of Zebedee as ἄλλους δύο ἀδελφούς. *Dial.* c. 106.

[2] *Ap.* I. 46; *Dial.* c. 100; *Ap.* II. 6; *Dial.* c. 85. Comp. c. 84, πρωτότοκον τῶν πάντων ποιημάτων; cf. Col. i. 15—17.

[3] *Dial.* c. 23: καὶ γὰρ αὐτὸς ὁ Ἀβραὰμ ἐν ἀκροβυστίᾳ ὢν διὰ τὴν πίστιν ἣν ἐπίστευσε τῷ θεῷ ἐδικαιώθη καὶ εὐλογήθη. The departure from the Pauline point of view is to be noticed; faith is here represented as the moving cause (διὰ *acc.*), and not as the instrumental (διὰ *gen.*) cause, or as the spring (ἐκ) of justification.

[4] *Dial.* c. 13.

[5] *Dial.* c. 131.

[6] *Dial.* c. 111; 1 Cor. v. 7: cf. Otto, *a. a. O.* 1843, I. 38 f. who refers to several other coincidences between the Epistles to the Corinthians and Justin. *Dial.* c. 14 ‖ 1 Cor. v. 8: *Ap.* I. 60 ‖ 1 Cor. ii. 4 f.

[7] *Dial.* c. 110 (cf. c. 32): δύο παρουσίαι αὐτοῦ κατηγγελμέναι εἰσί· μία μὲν ἐν ᾗ παθητὸς καὶ ἄδοξος καὶ ἄτιμος καὶ σταυρούμενος κεκήρυκται, ἡ δὲ δευτέρα ἐν ᾗ μετὰ δόξης ἀπὸ τῶν οὐρανῶν πάρεσται, ὅταν καὶ ὁ τῆς ἀποστασίας ἄνθρωπος ὁ καὶ εἰς τὸν ὕψιστον ἔξαλλα λαλῶν ἐπὶ τῆς γῆς ἄνομα τολμήσῃ εἰς ἡμᾶς τοὺς χριστιανούς. Comp. 2 Thess. ii. 3 ff.

170 THE AGE OF THE GREEK APOLOGISTS. [PART

Chap. ii. Hebrews.

Coincidences between Justin and St Paul in quotations from the Septuagint.

where he speaks of Christ as 'the Son and *Apostle* of 'God¹.'

The most remarkable coincidences between Justin and St Paul are found in their common quotations from the Septuagint. It is possible indeed that these may have been derived from some third source, or grounded on a traditional rendering of the words of the Old Testament; but in the absence of all evidence of such a fact it is more natural to believe that the arguments of St Paul and the readings which he adopted were at once incorporated into the mass of Christian evidences, and reproduced by Justin so far as they fell within the scope of his works. One example will explain the nature of the agreement. Speaking of the hatred which the Jews shewed to Christians, Justin says to them that it is not strange; 'for Elias also making intercession 'about you to God speaks thus: *Lord, they killed Thy* '*Prophets, and threw down Thy altars, and I was left* '*alone, and they are seeking my life.* And He answers 'him: *I have still seven thousand men who have not bent* '*knee to Baal*².' The passage agrees almost verbally with the citation of St Paul in the Epistle to the Romans, and differs widely from the text of the LXX. Similar examples occur in other citations common to

---

¹ *Ap.* I. 12, 63; cf. Hebr. iii. 1. The title is used nowhere else in the New Testament but in this passage of the Hebrews. Otto also quotes two other parallels to the language of the same Epistle: *Dial.* c. 13 ‖ Hebr. ix. 13 f.: c. 34 ‖ Hebr. viii. 7 f.
The references to the *Acts* are uncertain. Cf. *Ap.* I. 49 ‖ Acts xiii. 27, 48. Otto, *a. a. O.* Still more so those to the *Pastoral* and *Catholic Epistles.*

² Otto, *a. a. O.* 1843, I. pp. 36 ff. *Dial.* c. 39 = Rom. xi. 3. 1 Kings xix. 10, 14, 18. In the LXX. the text stands in ver. 10, ζηλῶν ἐζήλωκα τῷ Κυρίῳ παντοκράτορι ὅτι ἐγκατέλιπόν σε (τὴν διαθήκην σου v. 14, *v. l.* σε) οἱ υἱοὶ Ἰσραήλ· (v. 14 + καὶ) τὰ θυσιαστήριά σου κατέσκαψαν (καθεῖλαν v. 14) καὶ τοὺς προφήτας σου ἀπέκτειναν ἐν ῥομφαίᾳ, καὶ ὑπολέλειμμαι ἐγὼ μονώτατος καὶ ζητοῦσι τὴν ψυχήν μου λαβεῖν αὐτήν... v. 18: καταλείψεις ἐν Ἰσραὴλ ἑπτὰ χιλιάδας ἀνδρῶν, πάντα γόνατα ἃ οὐκ ὤκλασαν γόνυ τῷ Βάαλ...

Justin and the Epistles to the Galatians and the Ephesians[1]: and thus he appears to shew traces of the influence of all St Paul's Epistles with the exception of the Pastoral Epistles and those to the Philippians[2] and Philemon.

Chap. ii.

In the other writings commonly attributed to Justin besides the Apologies and Dialogue the references to the New Testament exhibit the same general range. In the fragment *On the Resurrection* there are allusions to words and actions of our Lord characteristic of each of the four Gospels[3] without any trace of Apocryphal traditions; and besides this there are coincidences of language with St Paul's First Epistle to the Corinthians, the Epistle to the Philippians, and the First to Timothy[4]. In the *Address* and *Exhortation to Greeks* there are apparently reminiscences of the Gospel of St John, of the Acts of the Apostles, and among the Epistles of St Paul of the First to the Corinthians and those to the Galatians and Colossians[5].

References to the New Testament in the fragment de Resurrec.;

the Oratio and Cohortatio ad Græcos.

A combination of these different results will give the

General result.

---

[1] These passages are:

Ap. I. 52 = Rom. xiv. 11.   Isai. xlv. 23.
Dial. c. 27 = Rom. iii. 12—17.   Ps. xiv. 3, 5, 10; cxxxix. 4.
— c. 95 = Gal. iii. 10.   Deut. xxvii. 26.
Deut. c. 96 = Dial. iii. 13.   Gal. xxi. 23.
— c. 39 = Eph. iv. 8.   Ps. lxviii. 18.

[2] The reference of *Dial.* c. 12 to Phil. iii. 3 is very uncertain.

[3] (α) St Matthew xxii. 29 (c. 9); 30 (c. 2); xxviii. 17 (c. 2).
(β) St Mark xvi. 19 (c. 9). This reference is uncertain, but the occurrence of the word ἀνελήφθη, and the connexion of the Ascension with the appearance after the Resurrection, point rather to the present conclusion of St Mark than to the Acts or to St Luke.
(γ) St Luke xxiv. 38, 39, 42 (c. 9).
(δ) St John xiv. 2, 3 (c. 9); xx. 25, 27 (c. 9); xi. 25 (cf. c. 1).

[4] 1 Cor. xv. 53 (c. 10). Philipp. iii. 20 (cc. 7, 9). 1 Tim. ii. 4 (c. 8).

[5] John viii. 44; *Cohort.* c. 21. Acts vii. 22; *Cohort.* c. 10. 1 Cor. iv. 20; *Cohort.* c. 35. 1 Cor. xii. 7—10; *Cohort.* c. 32. Galat. iv. 12, v. 20, 21; *Orat.* c. 5. Coloss. i. 16; *Cohort.* c. 15.

172 THE AGE OF THE GREEK APOLOGISTS. [PART

Chap. ii.

general conclusion of the whole section. And it will be found that the Catholic Epistles and the Epistles to Titus and Philemon alone of the writings of the New Testament have left no impression on the genuine or doubtful works of Justin Martyr.

Limits to the Evidence of Justin.

But the evidence of Justin so far as it is preserved stops short of the conclusions of the next generation. It establishes satisfactorily his acquaintance with the chief books of the New Testament Canon, and his habitual use of them within the range covered by his extant writings. But on the other hand it does not offer any clear indications of his recognition of a definite collection of Apostolic books parallel to the Old Testament and of equal authority with it. It is possible, and indeed likely, that this defect may be due in some degree to the nature of the subjects with which he deals. His object was to establish a conviction on the first elements of the faith and not to develope Christian truth. The coincidence of the facts of the Gospel with the ancient Prophecies of the Jews furnished him with arguments which he could not have drawn from the essential character of the Apostolic teaching. For the rest the words of Christ rather than the precepts of His disciples offered those broad maxims of Christian morality which could be presented with the greatest effect to readers who were at best very imperfectly acquainted with the nature of Evangelic doctrine.

How far he recognises a standard of Apostolic doctrine.

There are indeed traces of the recognition of an authoritative Apostolic doctrine in Justin, but it cannot be affirmed from the form of his language that he looked upon this as contained in a written New Testament. 'We have been commanded,' he says, 'by Christ Himself 'to obey not the teaching of men but those precepts 'which were proclaimed by the blessed Prophets and 'taught by Himself[1].' But this teaching of Christ was not strictly limited to His own words, as Justin explains in another passage: ' As [Abraham] believed on the voice 'of God *and it was reckoned to him for righteousness*, 'in the same way we also when we believed the voice 'of God which was spoken again by the Apostles of 'Christ, and the voice which was proclaimed to us by the 'Prophets, even to dying [for our belief], renounced all 'that is in the world[2].' Thus the words of the Apostles were in his view in some sense the words of Christ, and we are therefore justified in interpreting his language generally, so as to accord with the certain judgment of his immediate successors. His writings mark the era of transition from the oral to the written Rule[3]. His recognition of a New Testament was practical and not formal. As yet the circumstances of the Christian Church had not led to the final separation of the Canonical writings of the Apostles from others which claimed more or less directly to be stamped with their authority[4].

NOTE A: see page 123.

Norton has brought forward some good passages from the first *Apology* (Note E, § 2); and Semisch has carried out the investigation with considerable skill (pp. 239 ff.). Credner has collected Justin's quotations, and compared them elaborately with the MSS. of the LXX. It is superfluous to praise the care and ability by which his critical labours are always marked. The exact summary of Dr Sanday, *The Gospels in the Second Century*, pp. 41 ff. must be added to the earlier authorities.

The following Table of the more remarkable instances of the freedom of Justin's quotations from the Old Testament, where the variations cannot be

[1] *Dial*. c. 48.
[2] *Dial*. c. 119: ὃν γὰρ τρόπον ἐκεῖνος τῇ φωνῇ τοῦ θεοῦ ἐπίστευσε...καὶ ἡμεῖς τῇ φωνῇ τοῦ θεοῦ τῇ διά τε τῶν ἀποστόλων τοῦ Χριστοῦ λαληθείσῃ πάλιν καὶ τῇ διὰ τῶν προφητῶν κηρυχθείσῃ ἡμῖν πιστεύσαντες μέχρι τοῦ ἀποθνήσκειν πᾶσι τοῖς ἐν τῷ κόσμῳ ἀπεταξάμεθα. Thus the Christian Gospel is in some sense a ' republication ' of the Gospel of the Prophets, and an obvious analogy is suggested between the book of the Prophets in relation to the Lawgiver and that of the Apostles in relation to Christ.
[3] Compare pp. 52 f.
[4] Justin's scholar Tatian will be noticed below in Chap. iv. § 10.

174   THE AGE OF THE GREEK APOLOGISTS.   [PART

Chap. ii. explained on the supposition of differences in MSS., will be useful to those who wish to examine the question for themselves:

(a) Free quotations, giving the sense of the original text:

Gen. i. 1—3	*Apol.* I. 59
— iii. 15	*Dial.* c. 102
— vii. 16	— c. 127
— xi. 5	— —
— xvii. 14	— c. 10
Exod. iii. 2 &c.	*Apol.* I. 63
— xvii. 16	*Dial.* c. 49
— xx. 4	— c. 94
— xxxii. 6	— c. 20
2 Sam. vii. 14 sqq.	— c. 118
1 Kings xix. 14 sqq.	— c. 39
Job i. 6	— c. 79
Ezra vi. 21 (?)	— c. 72
Isai. i. 7	*Apol.* I. 47
— — 9	*Dial.* c. 55
— — 23	— c. 82
— iii. 16	— c. 27
— v. 25	— c. 133
— ix. 6	*Apol.* I. 35
— xxxv. 5 sqq.	— — 48. Cf. Matt. xi. 5.
— xlii. 16	*Dial.* c. 122
— liv. 9	— c. 138
— lix. 7, 8	— c. 27
— lxvi. 1	— c. 22
Jerem. vii. 21, 22	— —
— xxxi. 27	— c. 123
Ezek. iii. 17—19	— c. 82
— xiv. 20	— c. 45
— xxxvii. 7	*Apol.* I. 52
Hos. i. 9	*Dial.* c. 19
Joel ii. 28	— c. 87
Zech. ii. 6	*Apol.* I. 52
— xii. 10 sqq.	— —

(β) Adaptations of the text:

Gen. xxxv. 1	*Dial.* c. 60
Exod. iii. 5	*Apol.* I. 62
Numb. xxi. 8, 9	— — 60
— —	*Dial.* c. 94
Deut. xi. 16 sqq.	— c. 49
— xxi. 23	— c. 96. Cf. Gal. iii. 13.
— xxvii. 26	— c. 95. Cf. Gal. iii. 10.
— xxx. 15, 19	*Apol.* I. 44

(γ) Combinations of different passages:

1. Isai. xi. 1, 10 }
   Numb. xxiv. 17 }   *Apol.* I. 32
2. Psalm xxii. 17—19 }
   — iii. 5 }   — — 38

3. Isai. liii. 12 — lii. 13—liii. 8	*Apol.* I. 50	Chap. ii.
4. Zech. ii. 6 Isai. xliii. 5 Zech. xii. 11 sqq. Joel ii. 13 Isai. lxiii. 17 — lxiv. 11	*Apol.* I. 52	
5. Ezek. xxxvii. 7 Isai. xlv. 23	— —	
6. Exod. iii. 2, 14, 15	— 63	
7. Isai. vii. 10—16 — viii. 4 — vii. 16, 17	*Dial.* cc. 43, 66. Cf. c. 77.	
8. Jerem. ii. 13 Isai. xvi. 1 Jerem. iii. 8	— c. 114	

It will be noticed that the free quotations are found almost equally distributed in the *Apology* and the *Dialogue*, being chiefly short passages for which it was not unreasonable to trust to memory: that the adaptations are probably confined to the Pentateuch—the typical history of the establishment of Israel: that the combinations are almost peculiar to the first *Apology*, and consist of Prophecies fitted together according to the connexion of sense.

These passages will serve to illustrate the general principles of Justin's method of citation. In the following note will be found a table of the texts which he quotes more than once, from which may be seen the amount of verbal accuracy with which he contented himself.

NOTE B: see page 126.

A general view of the passages which Justin quotes more than once will give a better idea of the value of this argument than anything else. The following list is I believe fairly complete. The sign ∥ indicates agreement in the citations between which it stands;)(difference;)( )(difference from both the forms before given; v. l., vv. ll., mark the existence of one or more various readings apparently of less importance.

Gen. i. 1, 2 — *Ap.* I. 59 ∥ *Ap.* I. 64 v. l.
— iii. 22 — *Dial.* 62 ∥ *Dial.* 129
— xv. 6 — — 92. Cf. c. 119
— xviii. 1, 2 — — 56 ∥ *Dial.* 126 vv. ll.
— — 13, 14 sqq. — — 56 ∥ — 126 vv. ll.
— xix. 24 — — 56)(— 127. Cf. c. 129
— xxviii. 14 — — 58 ∥ — 120 v. l.
— xxxii. 24 — — 58. Cf. c. 126
— xlix. 10 — — 52 ∥ *Dial.* 120)(*Ap.* I. 32 (αὐτολεξεί), 54. Cf. Credner, *Beiträge*, II. pp. 51 sqq.
— — 11 — — 54. Cf. c. 76
Numb. xxiv. 17 — *Ap.* I. 32)(*Dial.* 106
Prov. viii. 21—25 — *Dial.* 61 ∥ — 129 vv. ll.

Chap. ii.	Ps. i. 3	Ap. I. 40 ‖ Dial. 86
	— ii. 7, 8	— — ‖ — 122
	— iii. 5	— 38)(— 96
	— xix. 2—5	— 40 ‖ — 64; 42 (ver. 4)
	— xxii. 16, 18	— 35)(Ap. I. 38)( )(Dial. 98
	— xxiv. 7	Dial. 36 ‖ Dial. 127)(c. 85)( )(Ap. I. 51
	— xlv. 6—17	Dial. 38 ‖ — 63 v. l.; 56 (vv. 6, 7); 86 (v. 7)
	— lxxii. 1—5, 17—19	Dial. 34)(— 64)( )(c. 121 (v. 17)
	— xcvi. 1—4	— 73. Cf. Ap. I. 41 (1 Chro. xvi. 26 ff.)
	— xcix. 1—7	— 37 ‖ Dial. 64 vv. ll.
	— cx. 1—3	— 32 ‖ Ap. I. 45 (but Ἰερ. for Σιών)
	Isai. i. 3	Ap. I. 37 (λαός μου) ‖ Ap. I. 63 v. l. (λαός με)
	— — 9	— 53)(Dial. 140. Cf. Dial. 55
	— — 16—20	— 44 ‖ Ap. I. 61 (omitting v. 19)
	— — 23	Dial. 82. Cf. c. 27
	— ii. 5, 6	— 135. Cf. c. 24
	— iii. 9, 10, 11	— 17 ‖ Dial. 133 v. l.; c. 136
	— v. 18—20	— ‖ — — v. l.;)(Ap. I. 49 (v. 20)
	— vi. 10	Dial. 12)(— — 33.
	— vii. 10—17 — viii. 4	— 43 ‖ — — 66 vv. ll.
	— xi. 1	Ap. I. 32 (cf. Numb. xxiv. 17))(Dial. 87
	— xxix. 13	Dial. 78)(Dial. 27)( )((c. 140 διαρρήδην)
	— — 14	Dial. 32)(— 78)( )(c. 38)( )( )(c. 123
	— xxxv. 4—6	Ap. I. 48)(— 69
	— xlii. 1—4	Dial. 123)(Dial. 135
	— lii. 15—liii. 1 sqq.	Ap. I. 50 ‖ — 13 vv. ll.
	— lv. 3—5	Dial. 12)(— 14
	— lvii. 1, 2	Ap. I. 48 ‖ — 16 vv. ll.
	— lxiv. 10—12	— 47)(— 25)(Ap. I. 52 (v. 11)
	— lxv. 1—3	Ap. I. 49)(— 24
	— lxvi. 1	— 37 ‖ — 22
	Ezek. xiv. 20	Dial. 45)(— 44)( )(c. 140
	Dan. vii. 13	Ap. I. 51)(— 31
	Micah v. 1, 2	— 34 ‖ — 78
	Zech. ii. 11	Dial. 115)(— 119
	Mal. i. 10—12	Dial. 28 ‖ — 41 vv. ll.

The only passage of any considerable length which exhibits continuous and important variations is Isai. xlii. 1—4. Cf. Credner, II. 210 sqq. It will be noticed that the number of texts repeated with verbal accuracy is very small.

NOTE C: see page 149.

Though I am by no means inclined to assent without reserve to the judgment of Bornemann on D, yet it seems to me to represent in important features a text of the Gospels, if not the most pure, yet the most widely current in the middle or at least towards the close of the second century. This is not the place to enter into a discussion of the extent of its agreement with the earliest Versions and Fathers. It is sufficient to have the result indicated which seems to follow from it. The MS. was probably written about A.D. 500—550, but it was copied from an older stichometrical MS., which in turn was based upon another older still. Compare Scrivener, *Bezæ Codex Cantab.* Introd. p. xxxiii.: Credner, *Beiträge*, 1. 465.

In Luke xv., to take a single chapter as an illustration of the statement in the text, the following readings are found only in D and d (the accompanying Latin version),

ver. 4. ὃς ἕξει.
7. οὐχ ἔχουσι χρείαν (order).
9. τὰς γείτονας καὶ φίλας (order).
13. ἑαυτοῦ τὸν βίον for τὴν οὐσίαν αὐτοῦ.
21. ὁ δὲ υἱὸς εἶπεν αὐτῷ (order).
23. ἐνέγκατε...καὶ θύσατε for φέρετε...θύσατε.
24. ἄρτι εὑρέθη.
27. τὸν σειτευτὸν μόσχον αὐτῷ (omitting however αὐτῷ *ad init.*).
[28. ἤρξατο (? παρακαλεῖν) *coepit rogare* Vulg.]
29. ἔριφον ἐξ αἰγῶν for ἔριφον (*haedum de capris* d.).
30. τῷ δὲ υἱῷ σου τῷ καφαγόντι (sic) πάντα μετὰ τῶν πορνῶν καὶ ἐλθόντι ἔθυσας τὸν σ. μ. Comp. the reading of e.

These readings it is to be remembered are found in a MS. of the Canonical Gospels. Is it then incredible that Justin's quotations were drawn directly from another, which need not have differed more from the common text? For other reasons it seems highly improbable that it was so, but not from the character of the variations which they consistently preserve.

The greater interpolations of D are well known. Examples may be found in Matt. xx. 28; Luke vi. 5; xvi. 8; Acts xv. 2; xviii. 26, 27; &c. Credner has examined many of the readings of D (*Beiträge*, 1. 452 ff.) but he has by no means exhausted the subject. See also Scrivener, *ib.* pp. xlviii. ff.

The peculiar readings of D are the best known and in many respects the most remarkable of those found in MSS. of the Canonical Gospels; but readings of a like character occur in considerable numbers in other of the most ancient Greek MSS., as for instance in *Cod. Sinait.* in 1 John, and in copies of the oldest Versions, as a e k of the *Vetus Latina*, and in the Curetonian Syriac, which happens to be the only copy of the *Vetus Syra* preserved to us.

Similar readings are also found in Greek and Latin MSS. of a much later date. Compare Scrivener, *Codex Augiensis*, pp. xl. ff. One of the most remarkable instances of a peculiar form of text in a detached narrative has been lately brought to light in a fragment of the ixth century discovered in the Library of Trin. Coll. Cambridge (Wᵈ). It was found by Mr White, the Assistant Librarian, in the binding of a MS. which came from Mount Athos. The little scraps of which it is made up when rightly fitted together give the text of Mark vii. 30 δαιμόνιον—viii. 16 ὅτι ἄρτους with the exception of a few words, and about six other isolated verses of the same Gospel (vii. 3, 7, 8; ix. 2, 7, 8, 9). The larger fragment is of great interest, and as it has not been published it may be well to give the text of the first paragraph (ch. vii. 31—37), which contains one of the very few passages peculiar to St Mark:

Και παλιν εξελθων απ[ο τω]
οριων Τυρου και Σιδ[ων]οσ
ηλθεν εισ την θαλα[σσ]αν
τησ Γαλιλαιασ ανα με[σο]ν
των οριων τησ Δ[εκαπολε]

178 THE AGE OF THE GREEK APOLOGISTS. [PART

Chap. ii.

ωσ + και φερουσιν αυτω
κωφον και μογγιλαλον
και παρεκαλουν αυτον
ιν............χειρασ + και (omitting either ταδ or αυτω)
επιλαβομενοσ αυτον απο
του οχλου κατ ιδιαν επτυ
σεν εισ τουσ δακτυλουσ αυ
του και εβαλεν εισ τα ωτα
του κωφου·˙και ηψατο
τησ γλωσσασ του μογγιλα
λου + κ[αι] αναβλεψασ ε[ισ] τον
ουνον [α]νεστεναξεν και
λεγει αυτω + εφφαθα ο εσ
τιν δ[ιαν]υχ[θ]ητι και δι | ευθεωσ
ηνοιχθησαν αυτου αι ακο
αι και του μογγιλαλου ελυ
............τησ γλ............(αυτου probably omitted)
ελαλη ορθωσ + και διεστειλατο
αυ[τ]οισ ινα μηδενι λεγωσιν
Οσο[ν δ]ε αυτοισ διεστελλετο
α[υτ]οι μαλλον περισσοτε
ρω[σ ε]κηρυσσον και παν
Τεσ [εξ]επλησσοντο λεγοντεσ
[καλ]ωσ παντα ποιει τουσ
κωφουσ ποιει ακουειν
και τουσ αλαλουσ λαλειν.

Thus we have in the space of seven verses, though there is no parallel narrative to disturb the text, the following readings in this Manuscript which are found *nowhere else:*

vii. 31. ἀπὸ τῶν ὁρίων.
    32. παρεκάλουν.
    33. ἔπτυσεν εἰς τοὺς δακτύλους αὐτοῦ καὶ ἔβαλεν εἰς τὰ ὦτα τοῦ κωφοῦ καὶ ἥψατο τῆς γλώσσας (sic) τοῦ μογγιλάλου.
    35. καὶ τοῦ μογγιλάλου.
    37. καὶ πάντες ἐξεπλήσσοντο.
    — πάντα ποιεῖ, τοὺς κ.

Nor are the peculiarities confined to this one narrative. In the remaining verses the following readings are found in this Manuscript alone:

[vii. 8. ἀφέντες—ἀνθρώπων omitted by homœoteleuton.]
viii. 1. συν[αχ]θέντος for ὄντος.
— 4. χορτάσαι ὧδε (order).
ix. 2. μεταμορφοῦται.
— 7. ἀγαπητὸς ὃν ἐξελεξάμην. (Cf. Luke ix. 35, not *Rec.*)

In addition to absolute peculiarities there are also about ten other readings which it gives in common with one or two other Manuscripts.
Of the peculiar readings one it will be observed contains a repetition of a peculiarity (vv. 33, 35, the emphatic τοῦ μογγιλάλου); and another (ix. 7) is an adaptation of a familiar biblical phrase to a new connexion. Thus we find within the compass of a few verses in a comparatively late MS. of the Canonical Gospels phenomena similar to those presented by the most remarkable of Justin's Evangelical quotations. All the fragments which

remain of the early variations of the text of the Gospels are full of instruction; but it is wholly needless to have recourse to unknown or uncanonical books for details which were probably introduced from tradition into our Canonical texts as soon as they were embodied in Apocryphal Gospels, if in fact they did ever find a place in the latter.

Chap. ii.

NOTE D: see page 156.

An examination of the following passages common to Justin and the Homilies will shew how their citations differ:

Matt. iv. 10	*Hom.* viii. 21	*Dial.* cc. 103; 125
— v. 39, 40	— xv. 5	*Apol.* I. 16
cf. Lu. vi. 29		
Matt. vi. 8	—	15
— vii. 15	— iii. 55	— 16; *Dial.* c. 35
— viii. 11	— xi. 35	*Dial.* c. 76
— x. 28	— vii. 4	*Apol.* I. 19
— xi. 27	— xviii. 3	— 63; *Dial.* c. 100
— xix. 16	— — 4	— 16; — c. 101
Luke vi. 36	— iii. 57	— 15; — c. 96
— xi. 52	— — 18	— 17
See Chap. iv.		

§ 8. *The Second Epistle of Clement.*

The so-called *Second Epistle of Clement* offers a remarkable example of the transitional view of the New Testament Scriptures which has been observed in Justin. The former part of it together with the *First Epistle* is found at the close of the Alexandrine MS. of the Greek Bible, where it is reckoned among the books of the New Testament. The recent discovery of the close of the work[1] places its character beyond doubt. It is a Homily (§§ 19, 20) and not a Letter. Its date is fixed most reasonably in the second quarter of the second century. In ancient times it seems to have been very little read and in itself it has little merit, but it is of great interest as the first example of its type of compo-

The Second Ep. of Clement *in the Alex. MS. probably a* Homily.

[1] Published first by Philoth. Bryennios at Constantinople in 1875. A Syriac translation of the two Epistles was shortly afterwards (1876) purchased at the sale of M. Mohl for the University Library at Cambridge.

sition. It may owe its connexion with the genuine Epistle of Clement to the fact that it was probably addressed to the Corinthian Church (§ 7), and, like Clement's Epistle, read there probably from time to time[1]. Eusebius is the earliest writer who mentions it, and he observes that it was 'not so well-known as the 'former one;' while from the tenour of his language it is evident that he questioned its genuineness[2]. Jerome distinctly states that 'it was rejected by the ancients,' though it is uncertain whether he had any independent evidence for his assertion[3]; at a later time Photius repeats the same statement, and adds some unfavourable criticisms on the character of the book[4].

A Gentile writing.

But however little claim the writing may have to the Canonical authority which was sometimes assigned to it in consideration of its supposed authorship[5], there can be no doubt that it was an early orthodox Christian composition of a date not much later than the middle of the second century. And it is of the greater interest because the writer is a Gentile and addressing Gentiles. The peculiarities of Justin's quotations have been connected more or less plausibly with his supposed Ebionitic connexions and tendencies; but no such explanation is admissible in this case. If it were allowable to assume the existence of any special tendency in the writer it would be towards *the Gospel of the Uncircumcision*; but on the contrary he speaks as the confident exponent of catholic

---

[1] Lightfoot, *Clement of Rome*, p. 306.
[2] Euseb. *H. E.* ·III. 38: ἰστέον δ' ὡς καὶ δευτέρα τις εἶναι λέγεται τοῦ Κλήμεντος ἐπιστολή· οὐ μὴν ἔθ' ὁμοίως τῇ προτέρᾳ καὶ ταύτην γνώριμον ἐπιστάμεθα, ὅτι μηδὲ καὶ τοὺς ἀρχαίους αὐτῇ κεχρημένους ἴσμεν.
[3] Hieron. *de Virr. Ill.* c. 13: Fertur et secunda ejus nomine epistola, quae a veteribus reprobatur.
[4] Photius, *Biblioth.* pp. 156, 163 (ed. Hoesch.).
[5] As in the *Cod. Alex.*, the *Apostolic Canons*, Can. 76 (85), Alexius Aristenus *ad Can. Apost. l. c.*, though not as some writers have said, in Johannes Damascenus, *de Fid. Orth.* IV. 17. See App. D, No. v.

truth, and his evidence may be received as the natural expression of the usage not of a party but of the age.

The chief scope of the Homily is an exhortation towards the perfection of Christian life. It is addressed to Christians, and therefore the fundamental doctrines of the faith are assumed. The importance of works is insisted on, not that they may earn salvation, but because Christ 'saved us' when 'He saw that we had no 'hope of salvation except that which comes from Him[1].' 'We must not think meanly of our salvation,' such is the opening of the discourse, 'we must think of Jesus 'Christ as God, as the Judge of quick and dead.' 'Our 'reward is [that He will confess us] if we confess Him 'through whom we were saved[2].' To quicken the perception of the need of this confession and to dwell on the necessity of holiness is the immediate purpose of the argument, as it must be with every preacher, but no phrase occurs which points to holiness as necessary otherwise than as the condition of realising salvation.

In support of his teaching the writer appeals to the Old Testament[3] and to the words of the Lord. Though the writings of the Apostles would have furnished him with almost every phrase which he needs, yet he never appeals to any one of them as of primary authority. And this silence was not due to ignorance and still less to any divergence from Apostolic doctrine. He was, as it appears, acquainted with the writings of St Paul, St James and St John[4], and he incorporates their thoughts

Chap. ii.

Its scope.

Use of Scripture.

---

[1] c. i.
[2] c. iii.
[3] The very remarkable anonymous reference (λέγει ὁ προφητικὸς λόγος, c. xi.) to some Apocryphal book of the Old Testament (? a *Book of Enoch*) is found also in Clem. *Ep.* I. 23, from which it may have been borrowed. The passage contains a striking coincidence with 2 Peter iii. 4.
[4] For ST PAUL see especially c. vii.: εἰς τοὺς φθαρτοὺς ἀγῶνας καταπλέουσιν πολλοὶ ἀλλ' οὐ πάντες στεφανοῦνται εἰ μὴ οἱ πολλὰ κοπιάσαντες καὶ καλῶς ἀγωνισάμενοι κ.τ.λ.

182   THE AGE OF THE GREEK APOLOGISTS.   [PART

Chap. ii.

and words into his Homily in a manner which shews that they had become his own. He speaks of the Scriptures generally (as it seems) under the title 'the Books and the Apostles' (c. xiv. τὰ βιβλία καὶ οἱ ἀπόστολοι), placing a kind of distinction between them. Up to his time the New Testament had no certain and defined existence as coordinate with the Old. The full extent of the teaching which it ratifies was received: the elements of which it consists were known and recognised: but its actual authority was not formally or consciously acknowledged, though the Gospel at least was quoted as 'Scripture,' and as part of 'the oracles of God' (c. xiii. τὰ λόγια τοῦ θεοῦ), and, as will be seen in the next section[1], the 'Scriptures of the Lord' were formed into a collection and distinguished from other Christian writings.

Quotations of the Lord's words.

The form of the quotations may have been influenced in part by the character of the writing. In a Homily it is more natural to quote the Gospels as the words of Christ than as the narrative of the Evangelist. But after due allowance has been made for this usage enough still remains to shew the freedom which was popularly allowed near the middle of the second century in dealing with Evangelic references and the influence still exercised by Apocryphal records. Of ten passages cited

as compared with 1 Cor. ix. 24. c. xix.: ἐσκοτίσμεθα τὴν διάνοιαν Eph. iv. 17 f. Comp. c. xiv.
c. ix.: δεῖ οὖν ἡμᾶς ὡς ναὸν Θεοῦ φυλάσσειν τὴν σάρκα.   1 Cor. iii. 16; vi. 19.
c. xi.   1 Cor. ii. 9; the Septuagint gives quite a different rendering. To these may be added c. i.: ἀποθέμενοι ἐκεῖνο ὃ περικείμεθα νέφος. Hebr. xii. 1.
For ST JAMES see c. xv.: μισθὸς οὐκ ἔστιν μικρὸς πλανωμένης ψυχὴν καὶ

ἀπολλυμένην ἀποστρέψαι εἰς τὸ σωθῆναι.   James v. 20.
For ST JOHN see c. ix.: εἰς Χριστὸς ὁ Κύριος ὁ σώσας ἡμᾶς ὦν μὲν τὸ πρῶτον πνεῦμα ἐγένετο σὰρξ καὶ οὕτως ἡμᾶς ἐκάλεσεν.   John i. 14.
c. xvii.: οὐαὶ ἡμῖν ὅτι σὺ ἦς καὶ οὐκ ᾔδειμεν καὶ οὐκ ἐπιστεύομεν.   John viii. 24, 28. Compare also the phrases ἔγνωμεν δι' αὐτοῦ τὸν πατέρα τῆς ἀληθείας (c. vi.).
[1] See page 191, n. 2.

from the Lord's teaching two only are referred to written sources. After quoting a passage of Isaiah with the same application of it as is made by St Paul[1], the writer continues, 'And moreover another Scripture saith *I 'came not to call righteous men but sinners*[2];' a saying which is exactly contained in St Matthew and St Mark. 'The Lord saith in the Gospel,' he adds in another place, 'If ye kept not that which is small who will give 'you that which is great? For I say unto you that he 'that is faithful in very little is faithful also in much[3].' Of this passage the last clause occurs verbally in St Luke xvi. 10, but the first part is not found in our Gospels. There is however some evidence to shew that it was once an alternative rendering of Luke xvi. 11, as it is quoted in the same form in the early Latin translation of Irenæus[4], though no Latin text of the Gospel at present preserves it. Of the anonymous quotations only one agrees verbally with our present Evangelic text, and that with St Luke[5]. Another passage, introduced by the remarkable words 'God saith,' appears also to be freely quoted from St Luke[6]. Two or perhaps three others are free renderings of sayings preserved by St Matthew. '[Christ] says Himself: *Him that* confesses

---

[1] Is. liv. 1: Gal. iv. 27. The passage is taken verbally from the LXX.
[2] c. ii.: καὶ ἑτέρα δὲ γραφὴ λέγει ὅτι οὐκ ἦλθον καλέσαι δικαίους ἀλλὰ ἁμαρτωλούς. The words occur Matt. ix. 13; Mark ii. 17. In the parallel passage of St Luke (v. 32) εἰς μετάνοιαν is added, in which form it is quoted in Barn. *Ep.* c. v., and Just. M. *Ap.* I. 15.
It will be remembered that a passage of St Matthew is quoted as 'Scripture' by Barnabas: see p. 62.
[3] c. viii.: λέγει γὰρ ὁ Κύριος ἐν τῷ εὐαγγελίῳ· Εἰ τὸ μικρὸν οὐκ ἐτηρή- σατε, τὸ μέγα τίς ὑμῖν δώσει; λέγω γὰρ ὑμῖν ὅτι ὁ πιστὸς ἐν ἐλαχίστῳ καὶ ἐν πολλῷ πιστός ἐστιν. On the use of τὸ εὐαγγέλιον see p. 113, n. 2.
[4] c. *Hær.* II. 34. 3.
[5] c. vi.: Luke xvi. 13, οὐδεὶς οἰκέτης δύναται δυσὶ κυρίοις δουλεύειν, and just afterwards θεῷ δουλεύειν καὶ μαμωνᾷ. In Matt. vi. 24 οἰκέτης is not found.
[6] c. xiii.: οὐ χάρις ὑμῖν εἰ ἀγαπᾶτε τοὺς ἀγαπῶντας ὑμᾶς, ἀλλὰ χάρις ὑμῖν εἰ ἀγαπᾶτε τοὺς ἐχθροὺς καὶ τοὺς μισοῦντας ὑμᾶς. Compare Luke vi. 32, 35.

184   THE AGE OF THE GREEK APOLOGISTS.   [PART

Chap. ii.

Apocryphal quotations.

'*me in the face of* men will I confess *in the face of* my
'Father[1].' '*For what* is the profit *if* a man *shall gain
'the whole world and lose his soul*[2]?' 'Let us not there-
'fore only call Him *Lord*, for this will not save us; for
'he says, *Not every one who saith to me Lord, Lord*, shall
'be saved, but he that doeth *righteousness*[3].'

The remaining four quotations are unquestionably
derived from Apocryphal sources so far as their form is
concerned, though they have points of close connexion
with the Canonical writings. 'For this reason the Lord
'said: Should you be gathered with me in my bosom,
'and not do my commandments, I will cast you away,
'and *will say to you*: Get you *from me: I know you not
'whence ye are, workers of* lawlessness[4].' 'The Lord
'says, Ye shall be as lambs *in the midst of wolves*. But
'Peter answering says to him: [What] then if the wolves
'should tear the lambs in pieces? Jesus said to Peter:
'Let not the lambs fear the wolves after their death;
'and fear ye not those who kill you and can do nothing
'[more] to you: but fear Him who after you are dead
'has power over soul and body to cast them into hell
'fire[5].' We have no data for ascertaining whence these

---

[1] c. iii.: λέγει δὲ καὶ αὐτὸς τὸν ὁμολογήσαντά με ἐνώπιον τῶν ἀνθρώπων ὁμολογήσω αὐτὸν ἐνώπιον τοῦ πατρός μου. Compare Matt. x. 32. No closer parallel is preserved.

[2] c. vi.: τί γὰρ τὸ ὄφελος ἐάν τις τὸν ὅλον κόσμον κερδήσῃ τὴν δὲ ψυχὴν ζημιωθῇ; Compare Matt. xvi. 26. The phrase τί [τὸ] ὄφελος is found in James ii. 14, 16, and 1 Cor. xv. 32.

[3] c. iv.:...λέγει γάρ· Οὐ πᾶς ὁ λέγων μοι Κύριε Κύριε σωθήσεται ἀλλὰ ὁ ποιῶν τὴν δικαιοσύνην. Compare Matt. vii. 21. No closer parallel is found.

[4] c. iv.:...ἐὰν ἦτε μετ' ἐμοῦ συνηγμένοι ἐν τῷ κόλπῳ μου καὶ μὴ ποιῆτε τὰς ἐντολάς μου, ἀποβαλῶ ὑμᾶς καὶ ἐρῶ ὑμῖν Ὑπάγετε ἀπ' ἐμοῦ· οὐκ οἶδα ὑμᾶς πόθεν ἐστὲ ἐργάται ἀνομίας. Compare Matt. vii. 23; Luke xiii. 27. The words are very variously quoted, but nowhere else in this form.

[5] c. v.: λέγει γὰρ ὁ Κύριος· Ἔσεσθε ὡς ἀρνία ἐν μέσῳ λύκων. Ἀποκριθεὶς δὲ ὁ Πέτρος αὐτῷ λέγει· Ἐὰν οὖν διασπαράξωσιν οἱ λύκοι τὰ ἀρνία; Εἶπεν ὁ Ἰησοῦς τῷ Πέτρῳ· Μὴ φοβείσθωσαν τὰ ἀρνία τοὺς λύκους μετὰ τὸ ἀποθανεῖν αὐτά· καὶ ὑμεῖς μὴ φοβεῖσθε τοὺς ἀποκτέννοντας ὑμᾶς καὶ μηδὲν ὑμῖν δυναμένους ποιεῖν· ἀλλὰ φοβεῖσθε τὸν μετὰ τὸ ἀποθανεῖν ὑμᾶς

passages were taken. Their length and style seem to indicate that they were derived from writings and not from oral tradition, but whether they were taken from any of the numerous Apocryphal Gospels, or from *Traditions* like those named after Mathias, or *Expositions* like that of Papias, is wholly unknown. The two quotations which are still left can be certainly connected with two Apocryphal Gospels, even if they were not immediately taken from them. 'The Lord said: My bre- 'thren are these who do the will of my Father[1].' The idea of the passage is contained in St Matthew, but the turn of expression, which is noticeable, recurs in a quotation made by Epiphanius from the 'Ebion- 'ites,' and it cannot be doubted that the writer of the Homily derived it from some such source. The remaining quotation is much more remarkable. 'The Lord 'Himself having been asked by some one When His 'kingdom will come? said, When the Two shall be One, 'and that which is Without as that which is Within, and 'the Male with the Female neither Male nor Female[2].' This passage Clement of Alexandria, who also quotes it, says 'was contained, as he believed, in the *Gospel according to the Egyptians*.'

It is however of comparatively little moment from what special source the sayings were derived, for there is no reason to believe that they were taken from any one

ἔχοντα ἐξουσίαν ψυχῆς καὶ σώματος τοῦ βαλεῖν εἰς γέενναν πυρός. Compare Matt. x. 16, 28; Luke x. 3; xii. 4, 5. No other trace of the conversation is preserved.

[1] c. ix.: εἶπεν ὁ Κύριος, 'Αδελφοί μου οὗτοί εἰσιν οἱ ποιοῦντες τὸ θέλημα τοῦ πατρός μου. Compare Matt. xii. 50. The passage quoted by Epiphanius from the Ebionites—it is not said from what exact source—is: οὗτοί εἰσιν οἱ ἀδελφοί μου καὶ ἡ μήτηρ

οἱ ποιοῦντες τὰ θελήματα τοῦ πατρός μου. For the plural τὰ θελήματα see Cod. B Mark iii. 35; and also Cod. ℵ Matt. vii. 21.

[2] c. xii.: ἐπερωτηθεὶς γὰρ αὐτὸς ὁ Κύριος ὑπό τινος πότε ἥξει αὐτοῦ ἡ βασιλεία εἶπεν,"Ὅταν ἔσται τὰ δύο ἕν, καὶ τὸ ἔξω ὡς τὸ ἔσω, καὶ τὸ ἄρσεν μετὰ τῆς θηλείας οὔτε ἄρσεν οὔτε θῆλυ. Compare Galat. iii. 28. Cf. *Introduction to the Study of the Gospels*, p. 427 n.

book[1]. The majority of the quotations are more like passages of the Canonical text than any other known record, and the two which are connected with other books are connected with books which appear to have been widely different in scope and character. No question therefore arises whether a Gospel was used which occupied the place of the Canonical Gospels. The phenomenon to be observed is that these were not regarded as the sole record of the teaching of the Lord. The feeling which led men to the words of Christ still survived even when the record of them had received the name of Scripture. It was not confined to any one party, but was common to all: to the Gentile no less than to the Jewish Churches. And it co-existed with that spirit which found its fitting expression in the next generation, and finally separated our four Gospels from all others both in popular use as well as in intrinsic and recognised authority[2].

[1] It may be noticed in particular XVII. 5; Just. *Ap.* I. 19. that they differ from corresponding c. vi.: Luke xvi. 13; *Clem. Recogn.* passages in the *Clementines.* Compare c. v.: Matt. x. 28; *Clem. Hom.* v. 9.

[2] The quotations which occur in the two *Epistles to Virgins* assigned to Clement, which are preserved in a Syriac translation, deserve more notice than they have received, and this will be the most convenient place for calling attention to them. The Epistles in question were first published by Wetstein as an Appendix to his New Testament in 1752. He found them in a Manuscript of the Syriac New Testament written at Mardin in 1469, which he obtained from Aleppo. The Manuscript contains all the books of the Syrian Canon with the Ecclesiastical Lections, and as an Appendix the remaining four Catholic Epistles (2 *Peter*, 2, 3, *John*, *Jude*) and the two *Epistles of Clement to Virgins* (Wetstein, *Proleg.* III. IV.). The *Apocalypse* is not contained in it. No other known Manuscript, as far as I am aware, contains the Epistles, so that like the two Greek Epistles they depend upon a single copy.

It would be impossible to enter into the question of the authenticity of the Epistles, which has found a zealous advocate in their latest editor, Card. Villecourt. They cannot I believe be much later than the middle of the second century, and it is hardly probable that they are much earlier. The picture of Christian life which they draw belongs to a very early age; and the comparison of the use made of Scripture in them with that made by

Clement in his genuine Epistle shews that a considerable interval is required for a satisfactory explanation of the difference of manner.

As in all the writings which have been examined hitherto so here the mass of quotations is anonymous; but it is hardly too much to say that whole paragraphs of these Epistles are a mosaic of Apostolic phrases. Some of the references to the Christian Scriptures however are more explicit, though no book of the New Testament (nor yet of the Old) is mentioned by name. Thus 'the divine Apostle' is cited for the condemnation in 2 Thess. iii. 11 ff., 1 Tim. v. 11[1]. The words in 2 Cor. xi. 29 are quoted as 'words of the Apostle[2];' and Rom. xiv. 15 and 1 Cor. viii. 12 as 'sayings of Paul[3].' 'It is written,' it is said again, 'of the Lord Jesus Christ, 'that when His disciples came and saw Him conversing apart near a well 'with the Samaritan woman, they wondered that He talked with a woman[4].' 'We *read*,' it is said in the same chapter, 'that women ministered to the 'Apostles and to Paul himself[5].' Other passages are quoted with the formulas applied to Scripture from 1 *Peter*, *James*, *Romans*, 1 *Corinthians*, *Colossians*, *Hebrews*, and 2 *Timothy*[6].

The anonymous quotations extend over a wider range and include passages from St Matthew, St Luke (*Ep.* I. 3, 6; II. 15), St John (*Ep.* I. 8, 13; II. 15), Acts (*Ep.* I. 9), 1 Peter, James, 1 John (*Ep.* II. 16), and probably from all the Epistles of St Paul, including Hebrews, except that to Philemon (for Titus see *Ep.* I. 4).

There are not however any quotations out of St Mark, 2 Peter, 2, 3 John, Jude, and the Apocalypse. This is by no means surprising with regard to St Mark. The comparative fewness of the Evangelic citations in the two Epistles and the small number of peculiarities in his Gospel render it extremely unlikely that any passage certainly derived from it should have been found. The same may be said, though with far less likelihood, of the shorter Catholic Epistles; but if the writer had been acquainted with the Apocalypse he could hardly have failed to quote such a passage as xiv. 4, which has the closest connexion with his argument.

In general it will be observed that (with the obviously accidental omission of St Mark and Philemon) quotations are made from every book included in the Syrian Canon and from these only. The fact is significant, and probably points to the country whence the Epistles derived their origin, though it is clear from internal evidence that they were originally written in Greek.

One indication of the early date of the Epistles may be noticed in addition to the anonymous form of the quotations. The enumeration of the primary authorities binding on the Christian is given in the form 'the Law 'and the Prophets and the Lord Jesus Christ[7],' just as it was given by Hegesippus, as we shall see afterwards. But while the formula witnesses to the antiquity of the record, the usage of the writer shews convincingly that it did not exclude the fullest recognition of the authority of St Paul and of the Three.

Compare Lardner's *Dissertation* (Works, Vol. XI. pp. 197 ff.); and Card. Villecourt's *Dissertatio Prævia* reprinted by Migne, *Patr. App.* I. 355 ff. Beelen, *S. Clementis Epp. ii. de Virginitate*, Lovanii, 1856.

Chap. ii.

[1] *Ep.* I. 10; II. 13.   [2] *Ep.* I. 12.   [3] *Ep.* II. 5.
[4] *Ep.* II. 15; John iv. 27.   [5] *Ibid.* Cf. Rom. xvi. 1, 2, &c.
[6] *Ep.* I. 11 (James iii. 2; 1 Peter iv. 11); I. 8 (Rom. viii. 9); I. 6 (1 Cor. iv. 16. Cf. c. 11 and *Ep.* II. 13); I. 11 (Coloss. iv. 6); I. 6 (Hebr. xiii. 7); I. 3 (2 Tim. iii. 5).
[7] *Ep.* I. 12.

§ 9. *Dionysius of Corinth and Pinytus.*

Connexion of Dionysius with Justin Martyr.

Ecclesiastical usage prepared the way to the recognition of the authority of the New Testament. It has been shewn from the testimony of Justin Martyr that the reading of *the Memoirs of the Apostles*[1] formed part of the weekly service of Christians: two fragments of Dionysius of Corinth throw light upon this usage. Dionysius appears to have been bishop of Corinth at the time of the martyrdom of Justin[2]: and the passages in question are taken from a letter to Soter bishop of Rome. His testimony is thus connected both chronologically and locally with that of Justin. There is no room left for the accomplishment of any such change in the organization of the Church as should cause their words to be applied to different customs.

c. 170—175 A.D.

His account of the preservation of Christian writings.

'To-day was the Lord's-Day [and] kept holy,' Dionysius writes to Soter, 'and we read your Letter; from 'the reading of which from time to time we shall be 'able to derive admonition, as we do from the former 'one written to us by the hand of Clement[3].' There are several points to be noticed here: it is implied that the public reading of Christian books was customary— that this custom was observed even in the case of those which laid no claim to Canonical authority—that it

---

[1] p. 113.
[2] Hieron. *de Virr. Ill.* c. 27: Claruit sub Impp. L. Antonino Vero et L. Aurelio Commodo. Routh (I. p. 177) fixes his death about 176, when Commodus began to reign jointly with his father.
[3] Euseb. *H. E.* IV. 23 (Routh, p. 180): Τὴν σήμερον οὖν Κυριακὴν ἁγίαν ἡμέραν διηγάγομεν, ἐν ᾗ ἀνέγνωμεν ὑμῶν τὴν ἐπιστολήν, ἣν ἕξομεν ἀεί ποτε ἀναγινώσκοντες νουθετεῖσθαι ὡς καὶ τὴν προτέραν ἡμῖν διὰ Κλήμεντος γραφεῖσαν. The plural pronoun (ὑμῶν) is to be noticed. Cf. p. 57, and n. 1.
The first clause is somewhat obscure. If Κυριακὴν be not a gloss, ἁγίαν ἡμέραν must be taken I think as a predicate, as I have translated it.

had been practised from the Apostolic age. Tertullian in a well-known passage[1] appeals to the copies of the Epistles still preserved by the Churches to which they were first written. The incidental reference of Dionysius shews that he is not using a mere rhetorical figure. If the Letter of the companion of Apostles was treasured up by those whom it reproved, it is past belief that the Churches of Ephesus or Colossæ or Philippi should have received, as Apostolic Letters addressed to themselves, writings which were not found in their own archives, and which were not attested by the tradition of those who had received them. The care which was extended to the Epistle of Clement would not have been refused to the Epistle of St Paul.

Dionysius it is true says nothing in this passage directly bearing on the writings of the New Testament; but in referring to the ecclesiastical use of Clement's Epistle he proved that the Corinthian Church must have retained throughout the doctrine of St Paul, to whose authority it gives the clearest witness. And not only this, but so far as the Epistle of Clement was found to be marked by a peculiarly Catholic character[2], the reception of that document is in itself a proof of the perpetuity of the complete form of faith which it exhibits. The Catholicity of the Corinthian Church is indeed expressly affirmed in another fragment. Just as Clement appealed to the labours of St Peter and St Paul, placing them in clear and intimate connexion[3], Dionysius describes the Churches of Rome and Corinth as their joint plantation. 'For both,' he says, 'having 'come to our city Corinth and planted us, taught the 'like doctrine.; and in like manner having also gone to

How far what he says bears upon the New Testament.

[1] *de Præscr. Hæret.* c. 36.   [3] Clem. *ad Cor.* I. 5.
[2] Cf. pp. 24 ff.: see also p. 207.

'Italy and taught together there, they were martyred at 'the same time¹.'

His testimony important from his intercourse with foreign Churches.

The intercourse of Dionysius with foreign Churches—his 'inspired industry' as it has been called²—gives an additional weight to his evidence. Besides writing to Rome, he addressed 'Catholic Letters' to Lacedæmon and Athens and Nicomedia, to Crete and to Pontus, for instruction in sound doctrine, for correction of discipline, for repression of heresy³. The glimpse thus given of the communication between the Churches shews their general agreement, and the character of Dionysius confirms their orthodoxy. There is no trace of any wide revolution in doctrine or government—nothing to support the notion that the Catholic Creed was the result of a convulsion in Christendom, and not the traditional embodiment of Apostolic teaching.

His direct reference to

There were indeed heresies actively at work, but their

---

[1] Euseb. *H. E.* II. 25 (Routh, *l.c.*): Ταῦτα (al. ταύτῃ) καὶ ὑμεῖς διὰ τῆς τοσαύτης νουθεσίας τὴν ἀπὸ Πέτρου καὶ Παύλου φυτείαν γεννηθεῖσαν Ῥωμαίων τε καὶ Κορινθίων συνεκεράσατε. καὶ γὰρ ἄμφω καὶ εἰς τὴν ἡμετέραν Κόρινθον φυτεύσαντες ἡμᾶς ὁμοίως ἐδίδαξαν· ὁμοίως δὲ καὶ εἰς τὴν Ἰταλίαν ὁμόσε διδάξαντες ἐμαρτύρησαν κατὰ τὸν αὐτὸν καιρόν. It is difficult to fix the exact sense of ὁμοίως and ὁμόσε in the last clause. I believe that ὁμοίως is to be taken with the whole sentence and not with διδάξαντες, and that ὁμόσε expresses simply 'to the same 'place.' Bishop Pearson's interpretation (Routh, p. 192) seems to rest on false analogies.

[2] Euseb. *H.E.* IV. 23: ἔνθεος φιλοπονία.

[3] Euseb. *l. c.* The description which Eusebius gives of the Letters accords with what might have been conjectured of the characteristic faults of the churches. Ἡ μὲν πρὸς Λακεδαιμονίους ὀρθοδοξίας κατηχητική, εἰρήνης τε καὶ ἑνώσεως ὑποθετική· ἡ δὲ πρὸς Ἀθηναίους διεργετικὴ πίστεως καὶ τῆς κατὰ τὸ εὐαγγέλιον πολιτείας ...ἄλλη δὲ...πρὸς Νικομηδέας φέρεται ἐν ᾗ τὴν Μαρκίωνος αἵρεσιν πολεμῶν τῷ τῆς ἀληθείας παρίσταται κανόνι... The Cretan Churches he warns against 'the perversion of heresy,' and cautions Pinytus bishop of Gnossus against imposing continence. The churches of Pontus—the home of Marcion—he urges to welcome those who came back to them after falling into wrong conversation or heretical deceit. From these casual traits we can form a picture of the early Church real and life-like, though differing as widely from that which represents it without natural defects as from that which deprives it of all historical unity. There is nothing to shew what 'the 'divine scriptures' were of which he added expositions in his letter to the Church at Amastris. Euseb. *l. c.*

progress was watched. Some of their leaders ventured to corrupt orthodox writings, but they were detected. 'When brethren urged me to write letters,' Dionysius says, 'I wrote them; and these the apostles of the devil 'have filled with tares, taking away some things and 'adding others, for whom the woe is appointed' (comp. Apoc. xxii. 18). 'It is not wonderful then that some 'have attempted to adulterate the Scriptures of the ' Lord (τῶν κυριακῶν γραφῶν), when they have formed 'the design of corrupting those which make no claims 'to their character (ταῖς οὐ τοιαύταις [sic] ἐπιβεβου-'λεύκασι)[1].' It is thus evident that 'the Scriptures of ' the Lord '—the writings of the New Testament[2]—were at this time collected, that they were distinguished from other books, that they were jealously guarded, that they had been corrupted for heretical purposes. The allusion in the last clause will be clear when it is remembered that Dionysius according to Eusebius 'warred against ' the heresy of Marcion, and defended the Rule of truth ' (παρίστασθαι κανόνι ἀληθείας)[3]. The Rule of Truth and

---

[1] Euseb. *l.c.*: 'Επιστολὰς γὰρ ἀδελφῶν ἀξιωσάντων με γράψαι ἔγραψα· καὶ ταύτας οἱ τοῦ διαβόλου ἀπόστολοι ζιζανίων γεγέμικαν, ἃ μὲν ἐξαιροῦντες ἃ δὲ προστιθέντες, οἷς τὸ οὐαὶ κεῖται. οὐ θαυμαστὸν ἄρα εἰ καὶ τῶν κυριακῶν ῥᾳδιουργῆσαί τινες [τινας Routh] ἐπιβέβληνται γραφῶν, ὁπότε καὶ ταῖς οὐ τοιαύταις ἐπιβεβουλεύκασι. It is mentioned that Bacchylides and Elpistus urged him to write to the churches of Pontus (Euseb. *l.c.*); it is then possible that he alludes to the corruption of this very letter by the Marcionites. The parallel thus becomes complete. The New Testament Scriptures and the letters of Dionysius were corrupted by the same men and for the same purpose.
[2] αἱ κυριακαὶ γραφαί form the correlative to αἱ Ἰουδαϊκαὶ γραφαί (comp. p. 95). The phrase is just one of those which naturally indicate a belief not expressly stated. Of course it is not affirmed that the collection here called αἱ κυριακαὶ γραφαί was identical with our 'New Testament,' but simply that the phrase shews that a collection of writings belonging to the New Testament existed. The whole usage of κυριακός in Christian writers is decisive against the application of the word to the Scriptures of the Old Testament in this connexion. The comparison of the title of the work of Papias λογίων κυριακῶν ἐξήγησις with this definite phrase αἱ κυριακαὶ γραφαί is full of interest.
[3] Cf. p. 190, note 3.

Chap. ii.	the Rule of Scripture, as has been said before, mutually imply and support each other.
Coincidences of language with separate books.	The language of Dionysius bears evident traces of his familiarity with the New Testament. The short fragment just quoted contains two obvious allusions, one
Mt. xiii. 24 ff. Apoc. xxii. 18, 19. 1 Th. ii. 11.	to the Gospel of St Matthew and one to the Apocalypse; and in another passage he adopts a phrase from St Paul's first Epistle to the Thessalonians[1].
Fragment of PINYTUS.	One sentence only has been preserved of an answer to his Letters, but that is marked by the same spiritual tone. The few words in which Pinytus asks for further instruction tend to shew that the familiar use of Apostolic language was a characteristic not of the man but
Heb. v. 12— 14.	of the age. He urges Dionysius to 'impart at some 'time more solid food, tenderly feeding the people com-'mitted to him with a Letter of riper instruction, lest by 'continually dwelling on milk-like teaching they should 'insensibly grow old without advancing beyond the 'teaching of babes[2].' The whole passage is built out of the Epistle to the Hebrews; and throughout the Letter, Eusebius adds, the orthodoxy of the faith of Pinytus was most accurately reflected.
The value of these fragments.	If our records be scanty, at least they have been found hitherto to be harmonious. It may seem of little importance to note passing coincidences with Scripture; and yet when it is observed that all the fragments which have been examined in this section do not amount to more than thirty lines, they prove more clearly than anything else could do how completely the words of the Apostles

---

[1] Euseb. *l.c.*:...τοὺς ἀνιόντας ἀδελ- φοὺς ὡς τέκνα πατὴρ φιλόστοργος (cf. Rom. xii. 10) παρακαλῶν.

[2] Euseb. *l. c.*:...ἀντιπαρακαλεῖ δὲ στερροτέρας ἤδη ποτὲ μεταδιδόναι τροφῆς τελειοτέροις γράμμασιν ἐσαῦθις τὸν ὑπ' αὐτῷ λαὸν ὑποθρέ- ψαντα, ὡς μὴ διατέλους τοῖς γαλα- κτώδεσιν ἐνδιατρίβοντες λόγοις τῇ νηπιώδει ἀγωγῇ λάθοιεν καταγηρά- σαντες. Cf. Hebr. v. 12—14.

were infused into the minds of Christians. They offer an exact parallel to modern usage in quoting the New Testament, and so far justify us in attributing our own views of the worth of the Apostolic Scriptures to the first Fathers; for as they treated them in the same manner as we do, they could hardly have rated them less highly.

Chap. ii.

§ 10. *Hermas.*

As we draw nearer to the close of this transitional period in the history of Christianity, it becomes of the utmost importance to notice every sign of the intercourse and harmony of the different Churches. In the absence of fuller records it is necessary to realise the connexion of isolated details by the help of such general laws as are discoverable upon a comparison of their relations. The task, however difficult, is not hopeless; and in proportion as the induction is more accurate and complete, the result will give a more trustworthy picture of the time. Even when a flood has covered the ordinary landmarks, an experienced eye can trace out the great features of the country in the few cliffs or currents which diversify the waters. This image will give a fair notion of the problem which must be solved by any real History of the Church of the second century. There is a fact here, a tendency there: and little is gained by describing the one or following the other, unless they are referred to the solid foundation which underlies and explains them.

A general view of the Church necessary to the right criticism of individual writers.

This is not the place to attempt to give any outline of the history of Christianity. But it is not the less necessary to regard the different elements which meet at each crisis in its course. For the moment Rome is

The condition of the Church of Rome at the middle of the second century.

our centre. The metropolis of the world becomes the natural meeting-place of Christians. There, at the middle of the second century[1], were to be found representatives of distant churches and of conflicting sects. At Rome Justin the Christian philosopher opened his school, and consecrated his teaching by his martyrdom. At Rome Polycarp the disciple of St John conferred with Anicetus on the celebration of Easter, and joined with him in celebrating the Eucharist[2]. At Rome Hegesippus a Hebrew Christian of Palestine completed, if he did not also commence, the first History of the Church. On the other side it was at Rome that Valentinus and Cerdo and Marcion sought to propagate their errors, and met the champions of orthodoxy. Nor was this all: while the attractions of the Imperial City were powerful in bringing together Christians from different lands, the liberality of the Roman Church extended its influence abroad. 'It has been your custom,' Dionysius of Corinth writes to Soter, 'from the first to confer 'manifold benefits on all the brethren, and to send sup-'plies to the many churches in every city...supporting 'moreover the brethren who are in the mines;...in this 'always preserving as Romans a custom handed down 'to you by your Roman forefathers[3].' Everything points

---

[1] The space might be limited even more exactly to the Episcopate of Anicetus (157—168 A.D.). Hegesippus came to Rome during that time, and Valentinus was then still alive (Euseb. *H. E.* IV. 22; Iren. ap. Euseb. *H. E.* IV. 11). The *Proverbs* of Xystus (c. 119 A. D.), published in a Syriac translation by Lagarde (*Anal. Syr.* 1—31), probably represent a still earlier activity in the Roman Church. It is difficult to say how far the book is genuine in its present form. Ewald (*Gött. Gel. Anz.*, 1859, pp. 261 ff., and *Gesch.* VII. 321 ff.) attributes the highest value to it, and places it among the most precious relics of early Christian literature. It contains no definite references to the New Testament, but shews certain traces of the influence of the thoughts and language of the Synoptic Gospels, of St James and of St John (especially Ep. i.). The influence of St Paul is less marked. Comp. Ewald *ll. cc.*

[2] Iren. ap. Euseb. *H. E.* v. 24.

[3] Dionys. ap. Euseb. *H. E.* IV. 23. Routh, I. p. 179.

to a constant intercourse between Christians which was both the source and the fruit of union. Heresy was at once recognised as such, and convicted by Apostolic tradition. The very differences of which we read are a proof of the essential agreement between the Churches. The dissensions of the East and West on the celebration of Easter have left a distinct impress on the records of Christianity; and it is clear that if the Churches had been divided by any graver differences of doctrine, much more if their faith had undergone a total revolution, some further traces of these momentous facts would have survived than can be found in the subtle disquisitions of critics. Once invest Christianity with life: let the men whose very personality seems to be lost in the fragments which bear their name be regarded as busy workers in one great empire, speaking a common language and connected by a common work: and the imaginary wars of Judaizing and Pauline factions within the Church vanish away. In each city the doctrine taught was 'that proclaimed by the Law, the Prophets 'and the Lord[1].'

These general remarks seem to be necessary before any satisfactory examination can be made of the writings of Hermas and Hegesippus, which are commonly brought forward as unanswerable proofs of the Ebionism of the Early Church, and therefore of the impossibility of the existence of any Catholic Canon of Holy Scripture. But even if it were to be admitted that those Fathers lean towards Ebionism, the general character of their age must fix some limit to the interpretation of their teaching. The real explanation of their peculiarities lies however somewhat deeper. While the true unity of the early Churches is to be most firmly main-

[1] Hegesippus ap. Euseb. *H. E.* IV. 22. Cf. p. 194, note 1.

tained, yet nothing can be more alien from the right conception of this unity than to represent them all as moulded in one type, or advanced according to one measure. The freedom of individual development is never destroyed by Catholicity. The Roman Church, in which we have seen collected an epitome of Christendom, had yet its own characteristic tendency towards form and order. Of this something has been said already in speaking of Clement[1]; but it appears in a simpler and yet maturer form in the *Shepherd of Hermas*, the next work which remains to witness of its progress.

This remarkable book—a threefold collection of Visions, Commandments and Parables—is commonly published among the writings of the Apostolic Fathers, and was for some time attributed to the Hermas saluted by St Paul. Evidence however both internal and external is decisive against a belief in its Apostolic date; and the mode in which this belief gained currency is an instructive example of the formation of a tradition. The earliest mention of the *Shepherd* is found in the Muratorian Fragment on the Canon to which we shall soon revert[2]. The anonymous author says: 'Hermas 'composed the *Shepherd* very lately in our times in 'the city of Rome, while the Bishop Pius his brother 'occupied the chair of the Roman Church[3].' The same statement is repeated in an early Latin poem against Marcion, and in a letter ascribed to Pius himself[4]. It

---

[1] Cp. p. 26.
[2] See below, § 12.
[3] Pastorem vero nuperrime temporibus nostris in urbe Roma Herma [Hermas] conscripsit, sedente [in] cathedrâ urbis Romæ ecclesiæ Pio episcopo fratre ejus. Et ideo legi eum quidem oportet: se publicare vero in ecclesiâ populo neque inter Prophetas completum [completo] numero neque inter Apostolos in finem temporum potest. The Fragment is given at length in App. C.
[4] Cf. Routh, I. p. 427; Hefele, p. lxxxii., where the authorities are given at length. The objections urged against this evidence by Dr Donaldson (*History of Christian Literature*, I. pp. 259 f.) simply rest on the fact that the Muratorian Fragment as well as

comes from the place at which the book was written, and dates from the age at which it appeared. There is no interval of time or separation of country to render it uncertain, or suggest that it was a conjecture. But the character of the book and its direct claims to inspiration gave it an importance which soon obscured its origin. The protest of the anonymous author just quoted shews that this was the case even in his time. 'It should therefore be read,' he adds, 'but it can never 'be publicly used in the Church either among the Pro-'phets...or the Apostles[1].' In the next generation Irenæus quotes with marked respect a passage which is found in the first of the Commandments, but he does not allude to Hermas by name, nor specify the book from which he derived it[2]. Clement of Alexandria mentions Hermas three times[3], but he does not distinguish

the poem is anonymous. It is difficult to see how this affects the authority of the statement if the Fragment is genuine. A contemporary Roman writer would be likely to know more about the authorship than Origen, who after all only offers his opinion as a conjecture. See page 198, note 1.
[1] Cf. p. 196, n. 3.
[2] Iren. (IV. 20) ap. Euseb. *H. E.* v. 8: καλῶς οὖν εἶπεν ἡ γραφὴ ἡ λέγουσα, Πρῶτον πάντων πίστευσον ὅτι εἷς ἐστὶν ὁ Θεὸς ὁ τὰ πάντα κτίσας, καὶ τὰ ἑξῆς (*Pastor, Mand.* i.). It may be reasonably supposed that Hermas here uses words sanctioned by common usage.
[3] *Str.* I. 17. 85; I. 29. 29; II. 1. 3. In three other places he quotes the book simply by the title of the *Shepherd: Str.* II. 12. 55; IV. 9. 67; VI. 6. 46.
The references which Tertullian makes to the book (*de Pudicitia*, cc. 10, 20) throw no direct light upon its date or authorship. He simply affirms that it was 'classed by *every*

'*council of the Churches* among the 'false and Apocryphal books.' The original text is important: Cederem tibi si scriptura Pastoris quæ sola mœchos amat divino instrumento meruisset incidi, si non ab omni concilio ecclesiarum etiam vestrarum inter apocrypha et falsa judicaretur, adultera et ipsa et inde patrona sociorum (*de Pud.* 10). Even if due allowance is made for the rhetorical character of the passage it is evident that the Canonicity of books was a question debated in Christian assemblies in Tertullian's time: that varieties of opinion on the Canon existed and were known to exist: that the Catholic Canon (etiam *vestrarum*) was more comprehensive than that of sects. In other words Marcion was but one out of many against whose arbitrary judgments the Church maintained with regard to Holy Scripture the whole truth. Compare *de Pudic.* 20: Et utique receptior apud ecclesias epistola Barnabæ (*i.e.* the *Epistle to the Hebrews*) illo apocrypho Pastore

198   THE AGE OF THE GREEK APOLOGISTS.   [PART

Chap. ii.

Origen first identifies its author with the Apostolic Hermas.

his name by any honorary title, and is wholly silent as to his date and position. The identification of the author of the *Shepherd* with his namesake in the Epistle to the Romans is due to Origen, and is in fact nothing more than a conjecture of his in his commentary on the passage in St Paul. 'I fancy,' he says, 'that that 'Hermas is the author of the tract which is called the '*Shepherd*, a writing which seems to me to be very use-'ful, and is, as I fancy, divinely inspired[1].' If there had been any historic evidence for the statement it could scarcely have escaped Origen's knowledge, and had he known any he would not have spoken as he does. When the conjecture was once made it satisfied curiosity and supplied the place of more certain information. But though it found acceptance, it acquired no new strength. Eusebius and Jerome, the next writers who repeat 'the 'report,' do not confirm it by any independent autho-rity[2]. It remained to the last a mere hypothesis, and cannot stand against the direct assertion of a contemporary.

The character of the Book.

Internal evidence alone is sufficient to prove that the *Shepherd* could not have been written in the Apostolic age. The whole tone and bearing shews that it is of the same date as Montanism: and the view which it opens of church discipline, government, and ordinances, can scarcely belong to an earlier period[3]. Theologically the

Its theological importance.

[1] Orig. *Comm. in Rom.* Lib. x. 31. Puto tamen quod Hermas iste sit scriptor libelli ejus qui Pastor appel-latur, quæ scriptura valde mihi utilis videtur et ut puto divinitus inspirata. He then goes on to explain the omis-sion of any remark upon his name, shewing that he is speaking from conjecture and not from knowledge. mœchorum. Here two disputed books are placed side by side, and a balance of external authority struck.

In § 24 he raises the question whether *Apelles* (Rom. xvi. 10) be not identical with *Apollos*. Cf. *Hom. in Luc.* xxv.

[2] Euseb. *H. E.* III. 5 (φασίν). Hieron. *de Virr. Ill.* c. 10 (asserunt).

[3] The following appear to be some of the weightiest proofs of its late date:

(a) The teaching on penitence (*Vis.* iii. 7; *Mand.* iv. 1; *Sim.* vii.), and fasting (*Sim.* v.). The allusions

book is of the highest value, as shewing in what way Christianity was endangered by the influence of Jewish principles as distinguished from Jewish forms. The peril arose not from the recollection of the old but from the organization of the new: its centre was not at Jerusalem but at Rome. At Jerusalem Christian doctrine was grafted on the Jewish ritual; but at Rome a Judaizing spirit was busy in moulding a substitute for the Mosaic system[1]. The one error was necessarily of short continuance: the other must continue to try the Church even to the end. This 'legal' view of Christianity is not without a Scriptural basis; but here again the contrast between the harmonious subordination of the elements of Scripture and the partial exaggerations of early patristic writings is most apparent. The *Shepherd* bears the same relation to the Epistle of St James as the Epistle of Barnabas to that to the Hebrews[2].

<small>*Chap. ii.*</small>

<small>*Legal in tone, but not Judaizing.*</small>

<small>*Relation to the Epistle of St James*</small>

---

to *stationes* (*Sim.* v. 1), and *subintroductæ* (*Sim.* ix. 11).

(β) The account of the Orders in the Church (*Vis.* iii. 5).

(γ) The teaching on Baptism (*Sim.* ix. 16) as necessary even for the Patriarchs. The revival in Mormonism of this belief is one of many singular coincidences with early errors which that system exhibits.

The direct historical data are few. The Church had endured much persecution (*Vis.* iii. 2), which was not yet over, and was conducted deliberately and not merely in popular outbursts (*Vis.* iii. 6; *Vis.* iv.; *Sim.* ix. 28). The Apostles were already dead (*Sim.* ix. 16). It is uncertain whether the introduction of 'Clemens and Grapte' (*Vis.* ii. 4) is part of the fiction of the book, or spiritually symbolic. Origen (*Philoc.* I. 11) interprets it in the latter sense.

[1] Hermas uses the number twelve to symbolize the universality of the Church—the spiritual Israel. τὰ ὄρη ταῦτα τὰ δώδεκα φυλαί εἰσιν αἱ κατοικοῦσαι ὅλον τὸν κόσμον (*Sim.* ix. 17). The common Latin text gives Duodecim montes...duodecim sunt gentes, and the repeated δώδεκα might easily have fallen out of the Greek text; but the word is not found in *Cod. Palat.* The passage itself points to the true interpretation of Apoc. vii.

I have given the Greek text of the quotations from the *Shepherd*. The discovery of the *Codex Sinaiticus* has placed the substantial authenticity of Simonides' copy beyond all reasonable doubt. Dr Donaldson's arguments (1. p. 399) prove too much, for *Cod. Sinait.* dates from a period *within* 'the first five centuries of the Christian era.'

[2] Cf. p. 44. The Epistle of St James, as has been often noticed, is remarkable for allusions to nature, and so also is the writing of Hermas; he says at the opening of his Visions: ἐδόξαζον τὰς κτίσεις τοῦ

Chap. ii.

The idea of a Christian Law lies at the bottom of them both: but according to St James it is a law of liberty, centering in man's deliverance from corruption within and ceremonial without; while Hermas rather looks for its essence in the rites of the outward Church. Both St James and Hermas insist on the necessity of works; but the one regards them as the practical expression of a personal faith, while the other finds in them an intrinsic value and recognises the possibility of supererogatory virtue[1]. Still throughout the *Shepherd* the Lawgiver is Christ and not Moses. It contains no allusion to the institutions of Judaism, even while insisting on ascetic observances. And so far from exhibiting the predominance of Ebionism in the Church, it is a protest against it; inasmuch as it is an attempt to satisfy by a purely legal view of the Gospel itself the feelings to which Ebionism appealed. It consists as it were of a system of Christian ethics based on ecclesiastical ideas.

Scriptural allusions.

The *Shepherd* contains no definite quotation from either Old or New Testament. The single reference by name is to a phrase in an obscure Apocryphal book *Eldad and Modat*, which is found in an ironical sentence apparently directed against the misuse made of it[2]. The

Θεοῦ ὅτι μεγάλαι καὶ δύναται καὶ εὐπρεπεῖς εἰσίν. The beauty of language and conception in many parts of the *Shepherd* has never been sufficiently appreciated. Much of it may be compared with the *Pilgrim's Progress*, and higher praise than this cannot be given to a book of its kind.

[1] *Sim.* v. 3: ἐάν γέ τι ἀγαθὸν ποιήσῃς ἐκτὸς τῆς ἐντολῆς τοῦ Θεοῦ σεαυτῷ περιποιήσῃ δόξαν περισσοτέραν καὶ ἔσῃ ἐνδοξότερος παρὰ τῷ Θεῷ οὗ ἔμελλες εἶναι. Cf. *Mand.* iv. 4, in connexion with 1 Cor. vii. 39, 40.

[2] *Vis.* ii. 3: 'Ερεῖς δὲ Μαξίμῳ, 'Ιδοὺ θλῖψις ἔρχεται· ἐάν σοι φανῇ

πάλιν ἀρνῆσαι (l. ἀρνήσαι)· ἐγγὺς κύριος τοῖς ἐπιστρεφομένοις, ὡς γέγραπται ἐν τῷ 'Ελδὰδ καὶ Μωδὰτ τοῖς προφητεύσασιν ἐν τῇ ἐρήμῳ τῷ λαῷ. So *Cod. Sinait.* The reading Μαξίμῳ is also given by *Cod. Palat.*, and there can be no doubt that it is correct. In form the message corresponds with the commissions to Clement and Grapte which follow in the next section, and it is very hard to see how any difficulty could have been found in the reading. The sense of the passage seems to be: You may if you please deny Christ again in persecution, vainly relying

scope of the writer gave no opportunity for the direct application of Scripture. He claims to receive a divine message, and to record the words of Angels. His knowledge of the New Testament can then only be shewn by passing coincidences of language, and these do in fact occur throughout the book. The allusions to the Epistle of St James[1] and to the Apocalypse[2] are naturally most frequent, since the one is most closely connected with the *Shepherd* by its tone, and the other by its form. The numerous paraphrases of our Lord's words prove that Hermas was familiar with some records of His teaching[3]. That these were no other than our Gospels is at least rendered probable by the fact that he makes no reference to any Apocryphal narrative: and the opinion is confirmed by probable allusions to St Mark[4], St John[5] and the Acts[6]. In several places also St John's teaching on 'the Truth' lies at the ground of Hermas' words[7]; and the parallels with the First Epistle of St Peter are well worthy of notice[8]. The relation of

Chap. ii.

St James. Apocalypse.

The Gospels.

St John. *The* Acts.

1 Peter. *The relation of Hermas to St Paul.*

on general promises of repentance. Cf. Numb. xi. 26, 27.
[1] The coincidences of Hermas with St James are too numerous to be enumerated at length. Whole sections of the *Shepherd* are framed with evident recollection of St James's Epistle: e.g. *Vis.* iii. 9; *Mand.* ii., ix., xi.; *Sim.* v. 4. Of the shorter passages one or two examples will suffice: *Mand.* iii. 1 = James iv. 5, *Mand.* xii. 5, 6 = James iv. 7, 12; *Sim.* viii. 6 = James ii. 7.
[2] The symbolism of the Apocalypse reappears in the *Shepherd*. The Church is represented under the figure of a woman (Apoc. xii. 1; *Vis.* ii. 4), a bride (Apoc. xxi. 2; *Vis.* iv. 2): her enemy is a great beast (Apoc. xii. 4; *Vis.* iv. 2). The account of the building the tower (*Vis.* iii. 5) and of the array of those who entered into it (*Sim.* viii. 2, 3) is to be compared with Apoc. xxi. 14; vi. 11; vii. 9, 14.
[3] The Similitudes generally deserve to be accurately compared with the Gospel Parables. Cf. Matt. xiii. 5—8, with *Sim.* ix. 19, 20, 21; Matt. xiii. 31, 32, with *Sim.* viii. 3; Matt. xviii. 3, with *Sim.* ix. 29. Of other passages compare Matt. x. 33 with *Vis.* ii. 2.
[4] *Mand.* ii. 2 = Mk. iii. 29.
[5] See pp. 203 f.
[6] *Vis.* iv. 2 = Acts iv. 12.
[7] *Mand.* iii.: 'Ἀλήθειαν ἀγάπα:... ἵνα τὸ πνεῦμα ὃ θεὸς κατῴκισεν ἐν τῇ σαρκὶ ταύτῃ ἀληθὲς εὑρεθῇ...καὶ οὕτω δοξασθήσεται ὁμοῦ ὁ ἐν σοὶ κατοικῶν, ὅτι ὁ κύριος ἀληθινός ἐστιν ἐν παντὶ ῥήματι καὶ οὐδὲν παρ' αὐτῷ ψεῦδος. Comp. 1 John ii. 27; iv. 6. [James iv. 5.] Comp. *Sim.* ix. 12.
[8] *Vis.* iv. 3 = 1 Pet. i. 7; *Vis.* iv. 2 = 1 Pet. v. 7.

Chap. ii.

His doctrine of Faith.

Hermas to St Paul is interesting and important. His peculiar object, as well as perhaps his turn of mind, removed him from any close connexion with the Apostle; but their divergence has been strangely exaggerated. In addition to marked coincidences of language with the First Epistle to the Corinthians and with that to the Ephesians[1], Hermas distinctly recognises the great truth which is commonly regarded as the characteristic centre of St Paul's teaching. 'Faith,' he says, 'is the first of 'the seven virgins by which the Church is supported. 'She keeps it together by her power; and by her the 'elect of God are saved. Abstinence the second virgin 'is her daughter; and the rest are daughters one of the 'other. And when the Christian observes the works of 'their mother, he is able to live[2].' Clement of Alexandria paraphrasing the passage says: 'Faith precedes: Fear 'edifies: Love perfects[3].' Whatever may be Hermas' teaching on works, this passage alone is sufficient to prove that he assigned to Faith its true position in the Christian Economy. The Law, as he understands it, is implanted only in the minds of those who have believed[4].

Christology of Hermas

The view which Hermas gives of Christ's nature and

---

[1] *Sim.* v. 7 = 1 Cor. iii. 16, 17; *Sim.* ix. 13 = Eph. iv. 4; *Mand.* iii. (cf. *Mand.* x. 1) = Eph. iv. 30.

[2] *Vis.* iii. 8: ὁ πύργος (the symbol of the Church) ὑπὸ τούτων βαστάζεται κατ' ἐπιταγὴν τοῦ κυρίου· ἄκουε νῦν τὰς ἐνεργείας αὐτῶν. ἡ μὲν πρώτη αὐτῶν ἡ κρατοῦσα τὰς χεῖρας Πίστις καλεῖται· διὰ ταύτης (ταύτην Cod. Sinait.) σώζονται οἱ ἐκλεκτοὶ τοῦ θεοῦ. ἡ δὲ ἑτέρα ἡ περιεζωσμένη καὶ ἀνδριζομένη Ἐγκράτεια καλεῖται· αὕτη θυγάτηρ ἐστὶν τῆς Πίστεως ....αἱ δὲ ἕτεραι....πέντε....θυγατέρες ἀλλήλων εἰσί...ὅταν οὖν τὰ ἔργα τῆς μητρὸς αὐτῶν πάντα ποιήσῃς δύνασαι ζῆσαι. For the last clause *Cod. Palat.* gives *omnes poteris videre,* and the common text *omnia poteris cus-todire.* In the former *videre* is an obvious mistake for *vivere, omnes* being taken with *operas* (sic *Palat.*): the latter is a distinct reading.

[3] Clem. *Str.* II. 12: Προηγεῖται μὲν πίστις, φόβος δὲ οἰκοδομεῖ, τελειοῖ δὲ ἡ ἀγάπη.

[4] *Sim.* viii. 3: ὁ δὲ ἄγγελος ὁ μέγας καὶ ἔνδοξος Μιχαὴλ ὁ ἔχων τὴν ἐξουσίαν τούτου τοῦ λαοῦ καὶ διακυβερνῶν· οὗτος γάρ ἐστιν ὁ διδοὺς αὐτοῖς τὸν νόμον εἰς τὰς καρδίας τῶν πιστευόντων. ἐπισκέπτεται οὖν αὐτὸς οἷς ἔδωκεν εἰ ἄρα τετηρήκασιν αὐτόν.

There are apparent coincidences with *Hebrews*: *Vis.* ii. 3, 2 = Hebr. iii. 12; *Vis.* i. 1 f. = Hebr. xi. 13 ff.; xiii. 14.

work is no less harmonious with Apostolic doctrine, and it offers striking analogies to the Gospel of St John[1]. Not only did the Son 'appoint Angels to preserve each 'of those whom the Father gave to Him;' but 'He 'Himself toiled very much and suffered very much to 'cleanse our sins...And so when He Himself had 'cleansed the sins of the people, He shewed them the 'paths of life by giving them the Law which He re-'ceived from His Father[2].' He is 'a Rock higher than 'the mountains, able to hold the whole world, ancient, 'and yet having a new gate[3].' 'His name is great and 'infinite, and the whole world is supported by Him[4].' 'He is older than creation, so that He took counsel 'with the Father about the creation which He made[5]. 'He is the sole way of access to the Lord; and no one 'shall enter in unto Him otherwise than by His Son[6].'

Chap. ii. in connexion with St John.

[1] The general cogency of these analogies lies in the attribution to a historic Person of the functions of 'the Son' or of 'the Word.' Of such a doctrine I know no trace in pre-Christian times: though it is quite true that in parts of St Paul's Epistles and in the Epistle to the Hebrews this type of doctrine is found, derived (as I believe) from the teaching preserved for us by St John. It seems to be forgotten that the term 'the Word' is found only in two verses in St John's Gospel.

[2] *Sim.* v. 6: καὶ αὐτὸς τὰς ἁμαρτίας ἡμῶν ἐκαθάρισε πολλὰ κοπιάσας καὶ πολλοὺς κόπους ἠντληκώς.... αὐτὸς οὖν καθαρίσας τὰς ἁμαρτίας τοῦ λαοῦ ἔδειξεν αὐτοῖς τὰς τρίβους τῆς ζωῆς δοὺς αὐτοῖς τὸν νόμον ὃν ἔλαβε παρὰ τοῦ πατρὸς αὐτοῦ. The last clause is characteristic of the Lord's discourses in St John: *e.g.*, xv. 15.

[3] *Sim.* ix. 2: ἔδειξέ μοι πέτραν μεγάλην λευκὴν ἐκ τοῦ πεδίου ἀναβεβηκέναι· ἡ δὲ πέτρα ὑψηλοτέρα ἦν τῶν ὀρέων τετράγωνος ὥστε δύνασθαι ὅλον τὸν κόσμον χωρῆσαι (*sustinere* Int. Lat.) παλαιὰ δὲ ἦν ἡ πέτρα ἐκείνη πύλην ἐκκεκομμένην ἔχουσα· ὡς πρόσφατος δὲ ἐδόκει μοι εἶναι ἡ ἐκκόλαψις τῆς πύλης. ἡ δὲ πύλη οὕτως ἔστιλβεν ὑπὲρ τὸν ἥλιον ὥστε με θαυμάζειν ἐπὶ τῇ λαμπρότητι τῆς πύλης.

Sim. ix. 12: ἡ πέτρα, φησίν, αὕτη καὶ ἡ πύλη ὁ υἱὸς τοῦ θεοῦ ἐστί. Πῶς, φημί, κύριε, ἡ πέτρα παλαιά ἐστιν ἡ δὲ πύλη καινή; Ἄκουε, φησί, καὶ σύνιε ἀσύνετε. Ὁ μὲν υἱὸς τοῦ θεοῦ πάσης τῆς κτίσεως αὐτοῦ προγενέστερός ἐστιν, ὥστε σύμβουλον αὐτὸν γενέσθαι τῷ πατρὶ τῆς πτίσεως αὐτοῦ. διὰ τοῦτο καὶ παλαιός ἐστιν. Ἡ δὲ πύλη διὰ τί καινή, φημί, κύριε; Ὅτι, φησίν, ἐπ' ἐσχάτων τῶν ἡμερῶν τῆς συντελείας φανερὸς ἐγένετο, διὰ τοῦτο καινὴ ἐγένετο ἡ πύλη, ἵνα οἱ μέλλοντες σώζεσθαι δι' αὐτῆς εἰς τὴν βασιλείαν εἰσέλθωσι τοῦ θεοῦ.

[4] *Sim.* ix. 14: τὸ ὄνομα τοῦ υἱοῦ τοῦ θεοῦ μέγα ἐστὶ καὶ ἀχώρητον καὶ τὸν κόσμον ὅλον βαστάζει.

[5] *Sim.* ix. 12: quoted above.

[6] *Sim.* ix. 12: ἡ δὲ πύλη ὁ υἱὸς τοῦ θεοῦ ἐστίν· αὕτη μία εἴσοδός ἐστι πρὸς

To Hermas, that is to the Christian of these later times, He appears 'by the Spirit in the form of the Church[1].'

It would be difficult to find a more complete contrast to Ebionism than these passages afford. Hermas indeed could never have been charged with favouring such a heresy unless the manifold developments of Christian character had been forgotten. His tendency towards legalism—a tendency peculiar to no time and no dispensation—was first transformed into an adherence to Jewish legalism; this was next identified with Ebionism; and then it only remained to explain away such phrases as were irreconcileable with the doctrines which it was assumed that he must of necessity have held. True criticism reverses the process, and sets down every element of the problem before it attempts a solution. Then it is seen how truly the teaching of St Paul and St John is recognised in the *Shepherd*, though that of St James gives the tone to the whole. The personality of its author is clearly marked, but his peculiar opinions do not degenerate into heresy. The book is distinguished from the writings of the Apostles by the undue preponderance of one form of Christian truth; from those of heretics by the admission of all.

§ 11. *Hegesippus.*

The name of Hegesippus has become a watchword for those who find in early Church history a fatal

---

[1] *Sim.* ix. 1: ...ὅσα σοι ἔδειξε τὸ πνεῦμα τὸ λαλῆσαν μετὰ σοῦ ἐν μορφῇ τῆς 'Εκκλησίας· ἐκεῖνο γὰρ τὸ πνεῦμα ὁ υἱὸς τοῦ θεοῦ ἐστίν. τὸν κύριον. ἄλλως οὖν οὐδεὶς εἰσελεύσεται πρὸς αὐτὸν εἰ μὴ διὰ τοῦ υἱοῦ αὐτοῦ. The allusion to the words recorded by St John (xiv. 6) appears to me to be unmistakeable. The different turn of Acts iv. 12 will make this clearer. The conception is well worthy of notice. This is however not the place to enter into the details of Hermas' doctrine of the Trinity—especially of the relation of the Son to the Holy Spirit. Cf. Dorner, I. 195 ff.

chasm in the unity of Christian truth which is implied in Holy Scripture. It has been maintained that he is the representative and witness of the Ebionism of 'the 'Twelve' or rather of 'the Three,' the resolute opponent of St Paul[1]. Many circumstances lend plausibility to the statement. Every influence of birth and education likely to predispose to Ebionism is allowed to have existed in his case.

He was it appears of Hebrew descent[2], conversant with Jewish history, and a zealous collector of the early traditions of his Church. The well-known description which he gives of the martyrdom of St James the Just shews how highly he regarded ritual observances in a Jew, and with what simple reverence he dwelt on every detail which marked the zeal of the 'Bishop of the Cir-'cumcision[3].' It is probable that he felt that same devoted attachment to his nation which was characteristic of St Paul no less than of the latest Hebrew convert of our own time[4]; but of Ebionism as distinguished from the natural feelings of a Jew we find no trace in his views either of the Old Covenant or of the Person of Christ. There is not one word in the fragments of his own writings or in what others relate of him which indicates that he looked upon the Law as of universal obligation, or indeed as binding upon any after the destruction of the Temple. There is not one word which

---

[1] In this as in many other instances later critics have only revived an old controversy. Cf. Lumper, III. 117 ff.; Bull maintained the true view in answer to Zwicker.

[2] Euseb. *H. E.* IV. 22. Cf. p. 209, n. 1.

[3] Euseb. *H. E.* II. 23. Routh, I. 208 ff. The details however of his life are not all drawn from Nazaritic asceticism.

[4] It is strange that the conduct of St Paul is not more frequently taken as a commentary on his teaching. Apart from the testimonies in the Acts, St Paul himself says in an Epistle universally acknowledged that he *became as a Jew to the Jews* (1 Cor. ix. 20). The whole relation of the Church to the Synagogue in the Apostolic age requires a fresh investigation.

Eusebius' testimony to his orthodoxy.

implies that he differed from the Catholic view of 'Christ' the 'Saviour' and the 'Door' of access to God. The general tone of his language authorizes no such deductions; and what we know of his life excludes them.

It is not necessary however to determine his opinions by mere negations. Eusebius, who was acquainted with his writings, has given the fullest testimony to his Catholic doctrine by classing him with Dionysius, Pinytus, and Irenæus, among those 'champions of the truth[1]' whose 'orthodoxy and sound faith conformable to the 'Apostolic tradition was shewn by their writings[2].' Hegesippus in fact proves that the faith which we have already recognised in its essential features at Ephesus, Corinth, and Rome, was indeed the faith of Christendom.

His inquiries in foreign Churches. c. 155 A.D.

Not being content to examine the records of his native Church only, Hegesippus undertook a journey to Rome[3], and visiting many bishops on his way 'found 'everywhere the same doctrine[4].' Among other places he visited Corinth, where he was refreshed by the right principles (ὀρθὸς λόγος) in which the Church had continued up to the time of his visit[5]. What these 'right

---

[1] Euseb. *H. E.* IV. 7, 8: παρῆγεν εἰς μέσον ἡ ἀλήθεια πλείους ἑαυτῆς ὑπερμάχους...δι' ἐγγράφων ἀποδείξεων κατὰ τῶν ἀθέων αἱρέσεων στρατευομένους· ἐν τούτοις ἐγνωρίζετο Ἡγήσιππος.

[2] Euseb. *H. E.* IV. 21 : ὧν καὶ εἰς ἡμᾶς τῆς ἀποστολικῆς παραδόσεως ἡ τοῦ ὑγιοῦς πίστεως ἔγγραφος κατῆλθεν ὀρθοδοξία. On such a point the evidence of Eusebius is conclusive.

[3] This journey took place during the bishopric of Anicetus (157—168 A.D. Euseb. *H. E.* IV. 11), and Hegesippus appears to have continued at Rome till the time of Eleutherius (177—190 A.D.). The Paschal Chronicle fixes his death in the reign of Commodus (Lumper, III. 108). Jerome speaks of him (*de Virr. Ill.* 22) as *vicinus Apostolicorum temporum*, so rendering, as it appears, the phrase of Eusebius ἐπὶ τῆς πρώτης τῶν ἀποστόλων γενόμενος διαδοχῆς (*H. E.* II. 23). This would represent him as a younger contemporary of Polycarp.

[4] Euseb. *H. E.* IV. 22 : τὴν αὐτὴν παρὰ πάντων παρείληφε διδασκαλίαν.

[5] Euseb. *H. E.* IV. 22 : καὶ ἐπέμενεν ἡ Κορινθίων ἐν τῷ ὀρθῷ λόγῳ μέχρι Πρίμου ἐπισκοπεύοντος ἐν Κο-

'principles' were is evident from the fact that he found there the Epistle of Clement, which was still read in the public services[1]. The witness of Hegesippus is thus invested with new importance. He not only proves that there was one rule of faith in his time, but also that it had been preserved in unbroken succession from the first age[2]. His inquiries confirmed the fact which we have seen personified in the life of Polycarp, that from the time of St John to that of Irenæus the Creed of the Church was essentially unchanged.

Hegesippus embodied the results of his investigations in five books or Memoirs. These according to Jerome[3] formed a complete history of the Church from the death of our Lord to the time of their composition; but this statement is probably made from a misunderstanding of Eusebius, who says that Hegesippus 'wrote 'Memoirs in five books of the unerring tradition of the 'Apostolic message in a very simple style[4],' 'leaving 'in these,' as he adds in another place, 'a very full 'record of his own opinion[5].' It appears then that his object was theological rather than historical. He sought

The character of his Memoirs.

τος ἐν Κορίνθῳ· οἷς συνέμιξα πλέων εἰς 'Ρώμην καὶ συνδιέτριψα τοῖς Κορινθίοις ἡμέρας ἱκανάς· ἐν αἷς συνανεπάημεν τῷ ὀρθῷ λόγῳ.
[1] Euseb. *l.c.* Cf. *H. E.* III. 16; and p. 188. The Catholic character of Clement's Epistle, with the clear recognition of the Apostolic dignity of St Paul which it contains (see pp. 25, 26, 57), gives peculiar force to this casual testimony.
[2] Euseb. *l. c.*: ἐν ἑκάστῃ δὲ διαδοχῇ (in each episcopal succession) καὶ ἐν ἑκάστῃ πόλει οὕτως ἔχει ὡς ὁ νόμος κηρύττει καὶ οἱ προφῆται καὶ ὁ κύριος. This last phrase has been already noticed as occurring in the Syriac Epistles of Clement (p. 186), which alone shews the error of Cred-

ner's supposition that the use of κύριος precludes the Canonical authority of the Epistles, Gesch. d. N. T. Kanon, p. 35. Compare Bp. Lightfoot, *Galatians*, p. 311.
[3] *De Virr. Ill. l. c.*: ...omnes a passione Domini usque ad suam aetatem Ecclesiasticorum Actuum texens historias...
[4] Euseb. *H. E.* IV. 8: ἐν πέντε δὴ οὖν συγγράμμασιν οὗτος τὴν ἀπλανῆ παράδοσιν τοῦ ἀποστολικοῦ κηρύγματος ἁπλουστάτῃ συντάξει γραφῆς ὑπομνηματισάμενος...
[5] Euseb. *H. E.* IV. 22: ἐν πέντε τοῖς εἰς ἡμᾶς ἐλθοῦσιν ὑπομνήμασι τῆς ἰδίας γνώμης πληρεστάτην μνήμην καταλέλοιπεν.

Traces of scriptural language in the fragments which remain.

to make out the oneness and continuity of Apostolic doctrine; and to this end he recorded the succession of bishops in each Church, with such illustrative details as the subject required[1].

The compilation of such a book of Chronicles gave little opportunity for the quotation of Scripture or for the exposition of any views on Scripture; but in the absence of direct reference to the historical books of the New Testament it is interesting to observe the influence of their language on the fragments of Hegesippus which survive. There are forms of expression corresponding to passages in the Gospels of St Matthew and St Luke and in the Acts which can scarcely be attributed to chance[2]; and when he speaks of 'the Door 'of Jesus' in his account of the death of St James, there can be little doubt that he alludes to the language of our Lord recorded by St John[3].

---

[1] The arrangement of his Memoirs cannot have been purely chronological, for the account of the martyrdom of St James the Just is taken from the *fifth* book. There is no definite quotation from any earlier book.

[2] The chief passages occur in the account of the martyrdom of St James: Euseb. *H. E.* II. 23: ['Ο υἱὸς τοῦ ἀνθρώπου] κάθηται ἐν τῷ οὐρανῷ ἐκ δεξιῶν τῆς μεγάλης δυνάμεως καὶ μέλλει ἔρχεσθαι ἐπὶ τῶν νεφελῶν τοῦ οὐρανοῦ. Cf. Matt. xxvi. 64. For the variation καὶ μέλλει ἔρχεσθαι for ἐρχόμενον cf. p. 140, n. 3. Δίκαιος εἶ καὶ πρόσωπον οὐ λαμβάνεις. This phrase πρ. λαμ. only occurs in Luke xx. 21 and Gal. ii. 6. Μάρτυς οὗτος ἀληθὴς Ἰουδαίοις τε καὶ Ἕλλησι γεγένηται ὅτι Ἰησοῦς ὁ Χριστός ἐστι. Cf. Acts xx. 21. The last words of St James as recorded by Hegesippus are still more remarkable: ἤρξαντο λιθάζειν αὐτὸν ἐπεὶ καταβληθεὶς οὐκ ἀπέθανεν, ἀλλὰ στραφεὶς ἔθηκε τὰ γόνατα λέγων· Παρακαλῶ Κύριε θεὲ πάτερ ἄφες αὐτοῖς, οὐ γὰρ οἴδασι τί ποιοῦσιν. The last clause agrees verbally with Luke xxiii. 34. In the *Clementine Homilies* the text is given: Πάτερ, ἄφες αὐτοῖς τὰς ἁμαρτίας αὐτῶν, οὐ γὰρ οἴδασιν ἃ ποιοῦσιν (XI. 20). It is to be noticed that he refers to Herod's fear of Christ, recorded in Matt. ii., which chapter was not found in the *Ebionite* Gospel: see Euseb. *H. E.* III. 20.

[3] The sense of this difficult phrase seems to be 'the Door of which 'Jesus spoke.' The claim ' I am the 'Door' (John x. 7, 9) was that of exclusive right to admit into the fold of God; and it was easy to see how, when this claim was pressed, the question would arise: What then is the door of Jesus? The Greek admits equally this translation and the translation 'The Door *to* Jesus;' and whether the interpretation given be right or wrong, it is both intelligible and pertinent.

It has been supposed that He-

It appears however that Hegesippus did not exclusively use Canonical writings. As a historian he naturally sought for information from every source; and the Apocryphal Gospels were likely to contain many details suited to his purpose. It is not strange then that Eusebius says that 'he sets forth certain things 'from the Gospel according to the Hebrews and the 'Syriac [Gospel] and especially from the Hebrew lan-'guage; thus shewing that he was a Christian of He-'brew descent; and he mentions other facts moreover, 'as it was likely that he would do, from unwritten Jew-'ish tradition[1].' He went beyond the range of the

His use of Apocryphal books.

---

gesippus in a Fragment given in Photius, *Bibl.* 232, alludes to a passage in St Paul (1 Cor. ii. 9) as 'vainly said' and contrary to our Lord's words (Matt. xiii. 16). It is enough to answer that the passage in question is quoted by St Paul from the Old Testament (Isa. lxiv. 4, καθὼς γέγραπται), and that it is immediately followed by ἡμῖν δὲ ἀπεκάλυψεν κ.τ.λ. Hegesippus evidently refers to some sect (τοὺς ταῦτα φαμένους) who claimed for themselves the true and sole possession of spiritual mysteries. Cf. Routh, I. pp. 281, 282: Bp. Lightfoot, *Galatians*, p. 311 n. The quotation is said to have been found in the *Ascensio Esaiæ* and the *Apocalypsis Eliæ*. Cf. Routh, *l.c.*; Dorner, I. 228. It is very common in early Christian writings; and it has been supposed that it was incorporated in a very ancient, perhaps Apostolic, Christian Hymn.

The fact that Eusebius does not expressly quote Hegesippus as recognising the Pauline Epistles has been supposed to shew that he disallowed their authority. The argument is worthless. See note at the end of the Chapter.

In one passage Eusebius (*H.E.* III. 32) quoting Hegesippus freely

uses the phrase ἡ ψευδώνυμος γνῶσις (1 Tim. vi. 20), but it cannot be certain that the words stood so in the original text.

[1] Euseb. *H. E.* IV. 22: ἔκ τε τοῦ καθ' Ἑβραίους εὐαγγελίου καὶ τοῦ Συριακοῦ καὶ ἰδίως ἐκ τῆς Ἑβραΐδος διαλέκτου τινὰ τίθησιν, ἐμφαίνων ἐξ Ἑβραίων ἑαυτὸν πεπιστευκέναι· καὶ ἄλλα δὲ ὡς ἂν ἐξ Ἰουδαϊκῆς ἀγράφου παραδόσεως μνημονεύει. By τὸ Συριακὸν we must I think understand the Aramaic recension of the Gospel according to St Matthew. Melito, as Routh has observed, speaks of ὁ Σύρος καὶ ὁ Ἑβραῖος in reference to a reading in the LXX. where the natural meaning is the Syrian translation (translator) and the Hebrew original. There is nothing in the language of Eusebius to lend support to the conclusion that Hegesippus used only this Semitic Gospel, as even Reuss most strangely assumes (*Hist. du Canon*, 42). The reference to unwritten tradition points the other way. At any rate it is absolutely necessary in such a case to keep strictly within the lines of the evidence; and I do not know of any direct evidence whatever in support of the assertion that 'Hegesip-'pus made exclusive use of the 'Gospel according to the Hebrews'

Scriptures both of the Old and of the New Testament. Tradition helped him in one case, and unauthoritative writings in the other. But the language used by Eusebius distinctly implies that the Gospel according to the Hebrews was used by Hegesippus as a supplemental source, subsidiary to the Gospels. In doing this Hegesippus did not disallow the Canon, or cast aside all criticism; for in immediate connexion with the words last quoted we read that 'when determining about the so-'called Apocrypha he records that some of the books 'were forged in his own time by certain heretics[1].' There is indeed nothing to shew distinctly that he refers to the Apocryphal books of the New Testament, but there is nothing to limit his words to the Old; and when he speaks of the teaching of 'the Lord,' in the same manner as of 'the Law and of the Prophets[2],' he clearly implies the existence of some written record of its substance. No further direct evidence however remains to identify this with the sum of our Canonical books, unless we accept the conjecture of a distinguished scholar of our own day, who has gone so far as to assert that the anonymous Fragment which will be the subject of the next section is in fact a translation from 'the historical work 'of Hegesippus[3].'

(*Supernat. Rel.* I. 419, 438 f.). There is no direct evidence that he did use other Gospels than this—and I have given reasons why we cannot expect that there should be—but that is a very different thing. Comp. p. 163, n. 1.

[1] Euseb. *l. c.*: καὶ περὶ τῶν λεγομένων δὲ ἀποκρύφων διαλαμβάνων, ἐπὶ τῶν αὐτοῦ χρόνων πρός τινων αἱρετικῶν ἀναπεπλάσθαι τινὰ τούτων ἱστορεῖ. Elsewhere (v. 8, vi. 13) Eusebius mixes together the controverted books of the Old and New Testaments.

[2] Cf. p. 207, n. 2.

[3] Bunsen's *Hippolytus*, I. p. 314. The evidence of the *Clementines* is noticed below in Chap. IV. § 2.

§ 12. *The Muratorian Fragment on the Canon—Melito—Claudius Apollinaris.*

A notice of the Latin Fragment on the Canon, first published by Muratori in his *Antiquitates Italicæ*[1], forms a natural close to this part of our inquiry. This precious relic was discovered in the Ambrosian Library at Milan in a Manuscript of the seventh or eighth century, which originally belonged to Columban's great Monastery at Bobbio[2]. It is mutilated both at the beginning and end; and is disfigured throughout by remarkable barbarisms, due in part to the ignorance of the transcriber, and in part to the translator of the original text; for there can be little doubt that it is a version from the Greek. But notwithstanding these defects it is of the greatest interest and importance. Enough

General account of the Fragm. de Canone.

---

[1] *Antiquit. Ital. Med. Ævi*, III. 851 sqq. (Milan, 1740). The best edition of the Fragment is in Routh, *Rell. Sacræ*, I. 394 sqq. (ed. 1846), who obtained a fresh collation of the Manuscript. Credner has also examined it in his *Zur Geschichte des Kanons*, 71 sqq. (1847), and again in his posthumous *Geschichte des N. T. Kanon*, 1860, to which the editor (G. Volkmar) has added an Appendix of his own upon the text and interpretation of this 'Tractate' as he prefers to call it. The complete text and context of the Fragment is given in App. C. The edition by Dr Tregelles accompanied by a facsimile (Oxford, 1867) is in every way the most complete which has appeared, and is practically exhaustive. [The new monograph by F. H. Hesse (*Das Muratori'sche Fragment*, Giessen 1873) is still more elaborate and full than that of Dr Tregelles. The learned author, in his desire to leave no difficulty unsolved, has overlooked in many cases the actual conditions of the problem offered by a careless copy of an archetype already imperfect. I cannot see that he takes any account of the most instructive phenomena furnished by the Fragment of Ambrose. 1874.]

[2] Murat. *l. c.*: Adservat Ambrosiana Mediolanensis Bibliotheca membranaceum codicem e Bobiensi acceptum, cujus antiquitas pæne ad annos mille accedere mihi visa est. Scriptus enim fuit litteris majusculis et quadratis. Titulus præfixus omnia tribuit Joanni Chrysostomo, sed immerito. Mutilum in principio codicem deprehendi...Ex hoc ergo codice ego decerpsi fragmentum antiquissimum ad Canonem Divinarum Scripturarum spectans. A more complete description of the Manuscript is given in App. C.

Chap. ii.

remains to indicate the limits which its author assigned to the Canon; and the general sense is sufficiently clear to shew the authority which he claimed for it.

The date of its composition.

The date of the composition of the Fragment is given by the allusion made in it to Hermas, which has been already quoted. It claims to have been written by a contemporary of Pius, and cannot on that supposition be placed much later than 170 A. D.[1] Internal evidence fully confirms its claim to this high antiquity; and it may be regarded on the whole as a summary of the opinion of the Western Church on the Canon shortly after the middle of the second century[2]. Though it adds but little to what has been already obtained in detail from separate sources, yet by combination and contrast it gives a new effect to the general result. It serves to connect the isolated facts in which we have recognised different elements of the Canon; and by its accurate coincidence with these justifies the belief that it was confined approximately within the same limits from the first.

Different theories as to its authorship.

There is no sufficient evidence to determine the authorship of the Fragment. Muratori supposed that it was written by Caius the Roman Presbyter, and his opinion for a time found acceptance[3]. Another scholar confidently attributed it to Papias, and perhaps with as good reason[4]. Bunsen again affirms that it is a translation from Hegesippus[5]. But such guesses are barely in-

---

[1] Pastorem vero nuperrime temporibus nostris in urbe Roma Herma conscripsit, sedente cathedra urbis Romæ ecclesiæ Pio episcopo fratre ejus. Cf. p. 196. The date of the episcopate of Pius is variously given 127—142 and 142—157. The statement in the text of the Fragment is perfectly clear, definite, and consistent with its contents, and there can be no reason either to question its accuracy or to interpret it loosely.

[2] The Books it omits are noticed below, p. 219.

[3] Cf. Routh, I. p. 398 ff.

[4] [Simon de Magistris] *Daniel secundum LXX*...MDCCLXXII. *Dissert.* IV. pp. 467 ff.

[5] *Hippolytus and his Age*, I. p. 314.

genious; and the opinions of those who assign it to the fourth century, or doubt its authenticity altogether, scarcely deserve mention[1].

Probably a fragment of some Greek Apologetic work.

The exact character of the work to which the Fragment belonged is scarcely more certain than its authorship[2]. The form of composition is rather apologetic than historical, and it is not unlikely that it formed part of a Dialogue with some heretic[3], unless indeed, as seems probable, it is made up of detached pieces taken from different parts of a considerable work[4]. One point alone can be made out with tolerable certainty. The recurrence of Greek idioms appears conclusive as to the fact that it is a translation[5], and this agrees well with its

---

[1] Such is also the decision of Credner, a most impartial judge: *Zur Gesch. d. K.* p. 93.

[2] It is not necessary to enter into the theory of Credner, which has been also supported by Volkmar, that the Fragment is in fact a complete *Tractatus de Libris quos Ecclesia Catholica Apostolica recipit* (*Gesch. des N. T. Kanon*, 153). The internal character of the Fragment seems to me to be absolutely decisive against such a view; and it would be hardly possible to indicate the circumstances under which any Christian writer would have ventured to publish such a tract in such a form, while the substance of the Fragment would naturally fall within the scope of a discussion with some non-Catholic adversary. Happily little or nothing turns upon the view which is taken of the original form of the Fragment.

It may be well to add that, though the details of the text are obscure and in part corrupt, the general sense of the Fragment is perfectly clear, so far as concerns the reception or rejection of particular books.

[3] *e.g.* De quibus singulis necesse est a nobis disputari...Recipimus... Quidam ex nostris.

[4] Comp. p. 219.

[5] Hesse maintains at some length the originality of the Latin text (§§ 25—39). In such a case the judgment must depend on a perception of style, and not simply on isolated phrases. If the Fragment be thus studied as a whole, I can scarcely suppose that any one who has had much experience in Greek and Latin composition will question that the Latin text is a translation. Special arguments are more or less precarious, but the following deserve consideration. 1. The usage of the particles is rather Greek than Latin: *e. g. quibus tamen...et ita...; dominum tamen nec ipse...et iidem...ita et...non solum...sed et...sed et...; sed et principium; et Johannes enim.* 2. Some phrases appear to reflect a Greek form: *nihil differt credentium fidei* (οὐδὲν διαφέρει τῇ πίστει); *quæ recipi non potest* (ἃ παραλαμβάνεσθαι οὐ δυνατόν or οὐ δύναται); *finctæ ad hæresim* (πρὸς τὴν αἵρεσιν); *dicens in semetipso.* Perhaps the form *Spania* (Σπανία) for *Hispania* may be added. 3. The writing evidently emanated from Rome (profectionem Pauli ab

Chap. ii.

The testimony which it bears (a) to the Gospels, and

Roman origin, for Greek continued to be even at a later period the ordinary language of the Roman Church.

The Fragment commences with the last words of a sentence which evidently referred to the Gospel of St Mark[1]. The Gospel of St Luke, it is then said, stands third in order [in the Canon], having been written by 'Luke the physician' the companion of St Paul, who, not being himself an eye-witness, based his narrative on such information as he could obtain, beginning from the birth of John. The fourth place is given to the Gospel of St John 'a disciple of the Lord[2],' and the occasion of its composition is thus described: 'At the 'entreaties of his fellow-disciples and his bishops John 'said: *Fast with me for three days from this time, and* '*whatever shall be revealed to each of us* [whether it be 'favourable to my writing or not][3] *let us relate it to one* '*another.* On the same night it was revealed to Andrew 'one of the Apostles that John should relate all things 'in his own name, aided by the revision of all[4]' ... 'what

urbe), and there is no trace of any Latin writing at Rome as early as the Fragment (comp. Part ii. c. ii. § 3). It may be added that Hesse fixes the composition of the Fragment at Rome (§§ 43 ff.) some time 'before Irenæus, Clement, and Tertullian' (§ 48). The volume in which the Fragment is found contains among other pieces translations from Chrysostom.

[1] The Fragment is given at length in App. C, to which reference must be made for the original text of the passages here quoted, and for the necessary critical remarks.

[2] Credner insists on this title *disciple* when compared with the title *one of the Apostles* given to Andrew, as shewing that the writer of the Fragment distinguishes the '*disciple* 'John' the author of the Gospel and the first Epistle from the '*Apostle* 'John' the author of the Apocalypse

and the second and third Epistles (a. a. O. pp. 159 ff.). The title is probably borrowed from St John's own usage: vi. 3; xii. 4; xiii. 23; &c., and especially xix. 26 f.; xxi. 24. Nothing in the Fragment itself suggests a distinction between the Johns whom it names.

[3] In spite of Hesse's objections I can find no other sense in the words. The whole tenor of the passage appears to me to exclude the idea that each was to await revelations which should furnish the contents of the new gospel, whether in the way of a quickened memory (John xiv. 26), or a better understanding (John xvi. 13), Hesse, p. 91. The οἴδαμεν in St John xxi. 24 seems to point to 'the revision.'

[4] Cf. Routh, I. pp. 409 sq. 'The 'particulars as to the fast and the 'revelation of which Jerome says *ec-*

'wonder is it then that John brings forward each detail 'with so much emphasis even in his Epistles[1], saying of 'himself, *what we have seen with our eyes and heard with* '*our ears and our hands have handled, these things have* '*we written to you?* For so he professes that he was 'not only an eye-witness, but also a hearer, and more-'over a historian of all the wonderful works of the Lord 'in order[2].'

Though there is no trace of any reference to the Gospel of St Matthew, it is impossible not to believe that it occupied the first place among the four Gospels of the anonymous writer[3]. Assuming this, it is of importance to notice that he regards our Canonical Gospels as essentially one in purpose, contents, and inspiration. He draws no distinction between those which were written from personal knowledge, and those which rested on the teaching of others. He alludes to no doubt as to their authority, no limit as to their reception, no difference as to their usefulness. 'Though various ideas '(*principia*) are taught in each of the Gospels, it makes 'no difference to the faith of believers, since in all of 'them all things are declared by one sovereign Spirit[4]

Chap. ii.

1 John i. 1.

the importance of this testimony,

'*clesiastica narrat historia* (*De Virr.* '*Ill.* IX.) seem to be found in no 'extant writer except this Fragment.' Tregelles, p. 35. The passage in Jerome is important as indicating probably the general character of the book to which the Fragment belonged.

[1] Or *Epistle*, for the plural is used in post-classical writers (as Justin) for a single letter.

[2] The writer evidently refers the *scripsimus*—a reading which is still found in two at least of the most ancient Latin copies in 1 John i. 4— to the Gospel. He may have had a false reading and he may have been mistaken in his interpretation, but I see no justification for the statement that 'in his zeal [he] goes so far as 'to falsify a passage of the Epistle...' (*Supernat. Rel.* II. 385).

[3] As bearing upon the authorship of the Fragment it may be noticed that the order of the Gospels is not that of the *African* Church, in which according to the oldest authorities Matthew and John stood first. And if the Fragment was not of African origin it follows almost certainly that it was not originally written in Latin. There is no evidence of the existence of Christian Latin Literature out of Africa till about the close of the second century.

[4] Uno ac *principali* Spiritu. *Prin*-

'concerning the Nativity, the Passion, the Resurrection, 'the conversation [of our Lord] with His disciples, and 'His double Advent, first in humble guise, which has 'taken place, and afterwards in royal power, which is yet 'future[1].' This the earliest recognition of the distinctness and unity of the Gospels, of their origin as due to human care and Divine guidance, is as complete as any later testimony. The Fragment lends no support to the theory which supposes that they were gradually separated from the mass of similar books. Their peculiar position is clear and marked; and there is not the slightest hint that it was gained after a doubtful struggle or only at a late date. Admit that our Gospels were regarded from the first as authoritative records of Christ's Life even when they did not supersede the living record of Apostolic tradition, and then this new testimony explains and confirms the fragmentary notices which alone witness to the earlier belief: deny that it was so, and the language of one who had probably conversed with Polycarp at Rome becomes an unintelligible riddle. It would be necessary in that case to suppose that the Gospels had usurped a place during his lifetime to which before they had only made claim in common with other rivals, and yet he speaks of them as if they had always occupied it.

(β) *to the Acts,*

Next to the Gospels the book of the Acts is mentioned as containing a record by St Luke 'of those acts 'of all the Apostles which fell under his own notice.' That this was the rule which he prescribed to himself is

---

cipalis is used to translate ἡγεμονικός in Ps. li. 12 Vulg., and Iren. *c. Hær.* III. 11. 8 [bis].

[1] It is frequently asserted that we have in this passage, taken in connexion with the context, an 'apolo-'getic defence of the fourth Gospel, 'which necessarily implies antecedent 'denial of its authority and apostolic 'origin.' As far as I can see, the explanation applies equally to the four Gospels, and not to any one in particular.

shewn, it is added, by 'the omission of the martyrdom 'of Peter and the journey of Paul to Spain¹.'

Chap. ii.

Thirteen Epistles are attributed to St Paul; of these nine were addressed to Churches, and four to individual Christians. The first class suggests an analogy with the Apocalypse. As St John when writing for all Christendom wrote specially to seven Churches, so St Paul also 'wrote by name only to seven Churches, shewing thereby 'the unity of the Catholic Church, though he wrote 'twice to the Corinthians and Thessalonians for their 'correction².' The order in which these Epistles are enumerated is remarkable: 1 and 2 Corinthians, Ephesians, Philippians, Colossians, Galatians, 1 and 2 Thessalonians, Romans. This order may have been determined by a particular view of their contents, since it appears that the author attributed to St Paul a special purpose in each Epistle, saying that 'he wrote at greater length 'first to the Corinthians to forbid heretical schism; after-'wards to the Galatians to put a stop to circumcision; 'then to the Romans, according to the rule of the [Old 'Testament] Scriptures, shewing at the same time that 'Christ was the foundation of them³.' The second class includes all that are received now: 'an Epistle to Phile-'mon, one to Titus, and two to Timothy,' which though written only 'from personal feeling and affection, are 'still hallowed in the respect of the Catholic Church, for '(*or* in) the arrangement of ecclesiastical discipline.'

(γ) *to the Epistles of St Paul.*

At this point the Fragment diverges to spurious or

(δ) *to the disputed*

---

¹ This appears to be the sense of the clause, though the text is undoubtedly corrupt. See App. C. It may be observed that this is the first reference to the book of the Acts by name.

² Routh has a good note (I. pp. 416 sqq.) on the symbolism of the number *seven*.

³ It will be observed that the relative chronological order of these epistles is rightly given. Cf. Lightfoot, *Galatians*, 44 ff.
If the reading *ordinem* be adopted, the sense will be 'pointing out the 'rule—the consistent revelation—of 'the Old Testament, and at the same 'time that......'

disputed books, and the exact words are of importance. 'Moreover,' it is said, 'there is in circulation an Epistle 'to the Laodiceans, [and] another to the Alexandrians 'forged under the name of Paul bearing on the heresy of 'Marcion[1], and several others which cannot be received 'into the Catholic Church. For gall ought not to be 'mixed with honey. The Epistle of Jude however (*sane*) 'and two Epistles bearing the name of John[2] are re-'ceived in the Catholic [Church] (*or* are reckoned among 'the Catholic [Epistles])[3]. And the book of Wisdom 'written by the friends of Solomon in his honour [is 'acknowledged]. We receive moreover the Apocalypses 'of John and Peter only, which [latter] some of our body 'will not have read in the Church.'

After this mention is made of the Shepherd[4], and of the writings of Valentinus, Basilides, and others: and so the Fragment ends abruptly.

---

[1] Nothing is known of the *Epistle to the Alexandrians*. The attempt to identify it with that *to the Hebrews* is not supported by the slightest external evidence. The *Epistle to the Laodiceans* is also involved in great obscurity. The *Epistle to the Ephesians* bore that name in Marcion's collection of St Paul's Epistles, and the text may contain an inaccurate allusion to it. In Jerome's time there was an 'Epistle to the 'Laodiceans rejected by all.' Cf. Routh, I. pp. 420 sqq. The remarkable cento of Pauline phrases which is frequently found in Manuscripts of the Vulgate under this name was undoubtedly of Latin origin. The first evidence of its existence occurs in the *Speculum* published by Mai, and the Latin Manuscript of La Cava (viiith cent.), both of which recognise the spurious clause in 1 John v. 7. From the sixth century downward it is very commonly found in Manuscripts of the Vulgate, and seems to have been especially popular in the English Church. See below, Part III.

[2] Hesse rightly, as I now believe, objects to the rendering. 'John who 'has been mentioned above' (§ 234). The translation given will hold equally whether *superscripti* or *superscriptæ* be read.

[3] The reading of the Manuscript is *in Catholica*, and Routh (I. 425; III. 44) has shewn that Tertullian (*de Præscr. Hær.* 30) and later writers sometimes omit *ecclesia*. The context on the other hand favours the correction *in Catholicis*, and I find that it has been adopted by Bunsen (*Hippolytus*, II. 136), who first gave what is certainly the true connexion of the passage. I do not know whether there is any earlier instance of καθολικὴ ἐπιστολή than in a fragment of Apollonius (Euseb. *H. E.* v. 18), who was a contemporary of Tertullian.

[4] See page 196, note 3.

It will then be noticed that there is no special enumeration of the acknowledged Catholic Epistles—1 Peter and 1 John[1]: that the Epistle of St James, 2 Peter, and the Epistle to the Hebrews, are also omitted: but that with these exceptions every book in our New Testament Canon is acknowledged, and one book only added to it —the Apocalypse of St Peter—which it is said was not universally admitted.

Chap. ii. Its omissions.

The character of the omissions helps to explain them. The first Epistle of St John is quoted in an earlier part of the Fragment, though it is not mentioned in its proper place, either after the Acts of the Apostles, or after the Epistles of St Paul: there is no evidence that the First Epistle of St Peter was ever disputed, and it has been shewn that it was quoted by Polycarp and Papias: the Epistle to the Hebrews and that of St James were certainly known in the Roman Church, and they could scarcely have been altogether passed over in an enumeration of books in which the Epistle of St Jude, and even Apocryphal writings of heretics, found a place. The cause of the omissions cannot have been ignorance or doubt. It must be sought either in the character of the writing, or in the present condition of the text.

The true explanation of them.

The present form of the Fragment makes the idea of a chasm in it very probable; and more than this, the want of coherence between several parts seems to shew that it was not all continuous originally, but that it has been made up of three or four different passages from some unknown author, collected on the same principle as the quotations in Eusebius from Papias, Irenæus, Clement, and Origen[2]. On either supposition it is easy

---

[1] The context tends to shew that the '*two* Epistles of St John' are the Second and Third Epistles. Compare however p. 77, n. 2: Iren. *c.*

[2] *Hær.* III. 16. 8; and App. C.
The connexion appears to be broken in at least two places; but as the general sense of the text is

Chap. ii. to explain the omissions, and if it is urged that these explanations of the omissions in the Fragment are conjectural, it must be admitted at once that the objection is valid against their positive force. But on the other hand it is to be noticed that the position in the Christian Canon which was occupied by the books which are passed over calls for some explanation. The Epistle to the Hebrews for example is just that of which the earliest and most certain traces are found at Rome[1]. Any one who maintains the integrity of the text must be able to shew how it came to be left out in the enumeration[2].

The judgment of the writer not a new one.

One other point must be noted as to the general character of this Fragment. The writer speaks throughout of a received and general opinion. He does not suggest a novel theory about the Apostolic books, but states what was held to be certainly known. He does not hazard an individual judgment, but appeals to the practice of 'the Catholic Church.' There was not indeed complete unanimity with regard to all the writings claiming to be apostolical, but the frank recognition of the divergence of opinion on the *Revelation of Peter* gives weight to the assumed agreement as to the authority and use of the other books.

Melito witnesses to the existence of a Canon.

A fragment of Melito Bishop of Sardis in the time of Marcus Antoninus, who must have been for many years the contemporary of Polycarp, adds a trait which is

---

[1] See p. 24.

[2] It is not, I now think, possible to lay any stress on Bunsen's supposition that the reference to Proverbs (Wisdom) as written 'by the 'friends of Solomon' was occasioned by the mention of the Epistle to the Hebrews as written by the friend of St Paul; nor yet on the conjecture *in Catholicis* as implying a central group of 'Catholic' Epistles among which 2, 3 John and Jude were reckoned.

wanting in the Fragment on the Canon[1]. In that the books of the New Testament are spoken of as having individual authority, and being distinguished by ecclesiastical use; but nothing is said of them in their collected form, or in relation to the Jewish Scriptures. The words of Melito on the other hand are simple and casual, and yet their meaning can scarcely be mistaken. He writes to Onesimus a fellow-Christian, who had urged him 'to make selections for him from the Law and the 'Prophets concerning the Saviour and the Faith gene-'rally, and furthermore desired to learn the accurate 'account of the Old (παλαιῶν) Books;' 'having gone 'therefore to the East,' Melito says, 'and reached the spot 'where [each thing] was preached and done, and having 'learned accurately the Books of the Old Testament, I 'have sent a list of them.' The mention of 'the Old Books'—'the Books of the Old Testament,'—naturally implies a recognition of the New Books, of 'the Books of the New Testament,' a written antitype to the Old[2]. But there is little evidence in the fragment of Melito to shew what writings he would have included in the

[1] Melito presented an Apology to Marcus Antoninus after the death of Aurelius Verus (A.D. 169); and, as appears from a passage quoted by Eusebius (μετὰ τοῦ παιδός, IV. 26), at a time when Commodus was admitted to share the imperial power (A.D. 176). His treatise on the Passover probably belongs to an earlier date. The persecution 'in which 'Sagaris was martyred' (Euseb. l. c.) may have been that in which Polycarp also suffered (A.D. 156).

[2] Euseb. H. E. IV. 26. This appears to be the natural interpretation of phrases like μαθεῖν τὴν τῶν παλαιῶν βιβλίων ἐβουλήθης ἀκρίβειαν, and ἀκριβῶς μαθεῖν τὰ τῆς παλαιᾶς διαθήκης βιβλία. Unless these ancient books were contrasted with others there could be no meaning in the two complementary phrases. Reuss' remark is instructive: Eusèbe a transcrit la préface de cet ouvrage qui contient une énumération de tous les livres de l'ancienne Alliance et qui en parle de manière à faire voir que Méliton n'avait aucune idée d'une autre collection de livres sacrés (Hist. du Canon, 43). The point of the argument lies in the reference to 'the Books,' 'the Books of the Old Testament;' and its force will be felt by a comparison with Origen's words:...ἐκ τῶν πεπιστευμένων ἡμῖν εἶναι θείων γραφῶν τῆς τε λεγομένης παλαιᾶς διαθήκης καὶ τῆς καλουμένης καινῆς (De Princ. IV. 1). Comp. p. 191, n. 2, αἱ κυριακαὶ γραφαί.

new collection. He wrote a treatise on the Apocalypse, and the title of one of his essays is evidently borrowed from St Paul—'On the obedience of Faith.'

An 'Oration of Melito the philosopher who was in 'the presence of Antoninus Cæsar' has been preserved in a Syriac translation; and though if it be entire it is not the Apology with which Eusebius was acquainted, the general character of the writing leads to the belief that it is a genuine book of Melito of Sardis. Like other Apologies this Oration contains only indirect references to the Christian Scriptures. The allusions in it to the Gospels are extremely rare and, except so far as they shew the influence of St John's writings, of no special interest. But the conception of God as the 'Father 'and God of Truth[1],' the Absolute and Self-existent[2], 'Who is Himself Truth and His Word Truth[3],' as contrasted with the vanity of idols, is a remarkable proof of the manner in which the highest Christian doctrine was used in controversy with heathen adversaries. The coincidences with the Epistles are more numerous. Those with St James and 1 Peter are particularly worthy of notice[4]; and one passage offers a very remarkable resemblance to 2 Peter[5].

---

[1] Cureton, *Spicilegium Syriacum*, p. 42.
[2] *Id.* p. 41.
[3] *Id.* p. 45.
[4] 'Light without envy is given to 'all of us that we may see thereby' (*id.* p. 42). 'With [the Lord] there 'is no jealousy of giving the know-'ledge of Himself to them that seek 'it' (*id.* p. 48). Compare James i. 5 ff.
'When thou Cæsar shalt learn 'these things thyself and thy chil-'dren also with thee, thou wilt be-'queath to them an eternal inherit-'ance which fadeth not away' (*id.* p. 51). Compare 1 Peter i. 4.

[5] 'There was once a flood and a 'wind and the chosen men were de-'stroyed by a mighty north wind... 'at another time there was a flood of 'waters...So also it will be at the 'last time: there shall be a flood of 'fire, and the earth shall be burnt up 'together with its mountains, and 'men shall be burnt up together with 'their idols...and the sea together 'with its isles shall be burnt; and 'the just shall be delivered from the 'fury like their fellows in the Ark 'from the waters of the deluge' (*id.* pp. 50, 51). Compare 2 Peter iii. 5—7.

The first allusion in the quotation

MELITO OF SARDIS.

But the evidence which remains of the remarkable literary activity of Melito is more important than the direct bearing which the fragments of his books have upon the Christian Canon. The titles of his works which have been preserved by Eusebius—and he implies that the list is not complete—bear a striking witness to the energy of speculation within the Church in the second century. Scarcely any branch of theological inquiry was left untouched by him: and the variety of his treatises is a witness to the variety of Christian culture in his age. And more than this: it is a presumptive argument of the greatest force against the possibility of any revolution in the Creed and constitution of the Church, such as is supposed to have been effected in his time by a series of supposititious Apostolic writings. The character of his inquiries shews that the broad outlines of Christianity were already clearly defined. Morality, Ritual, Psychology, Dogma, had already become subjects for systematic treatment. Thus in addition to the books already quoted he wrote on Hospitality—on Easter, and on the Lord's day (περὶ κυριακῆς)—on the Church, on [Christian] Citizenship (περὶ πολιτείας) and Prophets, on Prophecy, on Truth, and on Baptism (περὶ λουτροῦ)—on the Creation (κτίσις) and Birth of Christ, on the nature of Man, and on the Soul and Body—on the Formation of the World (περὶ πλάσεως), and (according to one reading)

Chap. ii. His writings also illustrate the extent of early Christian thought.

is to the destruction of the tower of Babel, which is mentioned in similar terms in the *Sibylline Oracles*, III. 110 ff. In the same passage of the Sibyllines there is also a description of the future destruction of the world by fire: Καὶ πέσεται πολύμορφος ὅλος πόλος ἐν χθονὶ δίᾳ Καὶ πελάγει· ῥεύσει δὲ πυρὸς μαλεροῦ καταράκτης Ἀκάματος, φλέξει δὲ γαῖαν φλέξει δὲ θάλασσαν. In other passages the same final catastrophe is described in similar terms: II. 196 ff.; VII. 118 ff. &c., and it is impossible therefore to affirm that the reference in Melito is to 2 Peter and not rather to the Sibyllines or to the wide-spread tradition on which they rested. [Dr Tregelles' argument (*Can. Murat.* pp. 103—4) leaves me still unable to admit the certainty of the reference to 2 Peter. 1869.]

C. Q

Chap. ii.

A fragment of his Treatise On Faith.

on the Organs of sense—on the Interpretation of Scripture (ἡ κλείς)—on the Devil, and on the Incarnation[1] (περὶ ἐνσωμάτου θεοῦ).

Of these multifarious writings very few fragments remain in the original Greek, but the general tone of them is so decided in its theological character as to go far to establish the genuineness of those which are preserved in the Syriac translation. One of these said to be taken from the treatise *On Faith* is a very striking expansion of the early historic Creed of the Church, and deserves on every account to be quoted in full[2]. 'We 'have made collections from the Law and the Prophets 'relative to those things which have been declared re-'specting our Lord Jesus Christ[3], that we may prove to 'your love that He is perfect Reason, the Word of God; 'Who was begotten before the light; Who was Creator 'together with the Father; who was the Fashioner of

---

[1] Euseb. *H. E.* IV. 26. It may be well to add Dr Cureton's translation of the Syriac version of this passage, which differs in some places from the Greek: 'The treatises [of 'Melito] with which we have become 'acquainted are the following: On 'Easter two, and On Polity and On 'the Prophets; and another On the 'Church and another On the First 'Day of the Week; and again an-'other On the Faith of Man. (*i.e.* 'περὶ πίστεως, not περὶ φύσεως ἀν-'θρώπου) and another On his For-'mation; and again another On the 'hearing of the Ear of Faith; and 'besides these [one] On the Soul 'and Body; and again On Baptism 'and On the Truth and On the 'Faith; and On the Birth of Christ 'and On the word of his Prophecy; 'and again On the Soul and on the 'Body; and another On the love of 'Strangers, and On Satan and On 'the Revelation of John; and again 'another On God who put on the 'Body; and again another which he 'wrote to the Emperor Antoninus' (*Spicilegium Syriacum*, p. 57). Some of the variations are interesting, as in the clauses corresponding to ὁ περὶ ὑπακοῆς πίστεως [καὶ ὁ περὶ] αἰσθητηρίων and περὶ κτίσεως καὶ γενέσεως Χριστοῦ. One treatise (ἡ κλείς) is omitted, and one (περὶ ψυχῆς καὶ σώματος) reckoned twice.

[2] It should however be added that this fragment is attributed in an Armenian version and in a shorter Syriac version to Irenæus. Comp. Pitra, *Spicil. Solesm.* i. 3 ff.; ii., viii. and 59.

[3] The remarkable coincidence of these words with the fragment quoted by Eusebius (*H. E.* IV. 26) is a strong proof of the genuineness of the fragment: ἠξίωσας...γενέσθαι σοι ἐκλογὰς ἔκ τε τοῦ νόμου καὶ τῶν προφητῶν περὶ τοῦ Σωτῆ-ρος καὶ πάσης τῆς πίστεως ἡμῶν.

'man; Who was all in all; Who among the Patriarchs
'was Patriarch; Who in the law was the Law; among
'the priests Chief Priest; among kings Governor; among
'prophets the Prophet; among the Angels Archangel;
'in the Voice the Word; among spirits Spirit; in the
'Father the Son; in God God, the King for ever and
'ever. For this was He who was Pilot to Noah; Who
'conducted Abraham; Who was bound with Isaac;
'Who was in exile with Jacob; Who was sold with
'Joseph; Who was Captain with Moses; Who was the
'Divider of the inheritance with Jesus the son of Nun;
'Who in David and the Prophets foretold His own suf-
'ferings; Who was incarnate in the Virgin; Who was
'born at Bethlehem; Who was wrapped in swaddling
'clothes in the manger; Who was seen of shepherds;
'Who was glorified of Angels; Who was worshipped by
'the Magi; Who was pointed out by John; Who as-
'sembled the Apostles; Who preached the kingdom;
'Who healed the maimed; Who gave light to the blind;
'Who raised the dead; Who appeared in the Temple;
'Who was not believed on by the people; Who was be-
'trayed by Judas; Who was laid hold on by the Priests;
'Who was condemned by Pilate; Who was pierced in
'the flesh; Who was hanged upon the tree; Who was
'buried in the earth; Who rose from the dead; Who
'appeared to the Apostles; Who ascended to heaven;
'Who sitteth on the right hand of the Father; Who is
'the Rest of those that are departed, the Recoverer of
'those who are lost, the Light of those who are
'in darkness, the Deliverer of those who are cap-
'tives, the Finder of those who have gone astray,
'the Refuge of the afflicted, the Bridegroom of the
'Church, the Charioteer of the Cherubim, the Captain
'of the Angels, God who is of God, the Son who is

Chap. ii.

'of the Father, Jesus Christ, the King for ever and 'ever. Amen[1].'

No writer could state the fundamental truths of Christianity more unhesitatingly or refer to the contents of the Scriptures of the Old and New Testaments with more perfect confidence. The subject of the passage offers full scope for the exhibition of these characteristics, but they are also found in a greater or less degree in all the other fragments of Melito's writings which admit of similar expressions of faith. The fact is of great significance, for it explains what might have seemed to be a certain dryness in most of the quotations which have been hitherto made. This fragment is clearer in its witness to the doctrinal and devotional use of Holy Scripture than any which has been yet noticed, because it is taken from a treatise addressed to believers, and that upon their Faith. Elsewhere we have heard the language of the Church to those without: here we are enabled to listen to the familiar language of Christians one to another. For once we catch the clear accents of faith. No heathen audience keeps back the expression of divine mysteries. In place of the constrained language of the Apology we listen to the triumphant Hymn[2].

---

[1] Cureton, *Spicilegium Syriacum*, pp. 53, 54. Comp. Bp. Lightfoot, *C. R. l. c.* pp. 481 ff.

[2] This is not the place to discuss the genuineness of the Latin translation of the *Clavis* attributed to Melito, which has been at length (cf. Routh, I. pp. 141 ff.) published by J. B. Pitra in the *Spicilegium Solesmense*. It is enough to say that I cannot believe that in its present form it fairly represents the work of the Bishop of Sardis, even if it may possibly have been based upon it.

As far as I have observed, the four Gospels are simply quoted as *In Evangelio*, without any further addition. The Epistles generally as *In Apostolo*. The only books of the New Testament from which no quotations are found are *James, Jude, 2, 3 John*. The *Revelation* is quoted as *In Apocalypsi*, and a passage from 2 *Peter* (ii. 17) is quoted twice: *Clavis*, III. 14; IV. 25. The reference to 1 Peter ii. 5 is wrongly given by Pitra to 2 Peter ii. 5.

MELITO OF SARDIS.

The testimony of Melito finds a natural confirmation in a fragment of a contemporary writer[1], Claudius Apollinaris Bishop of Hierapolis[2]. When discussing the time for the celebration of Easter he writes: 'Some say that 'the Lord ate the lamb with His disciples on the 14th '(of Nisan), and suffered Himself on the great day of 'unleavened bread; and they state that Matthew's narra-'tive is in accordance with their view; while it follows 'that their view is at variance with the Law, and accord-'ing to them the Gospels seem to disagree[3].' The Gospels are evidently quoted as books certainly known and recognised and not as books emerging with difficulty

Chap. ii.

CLAUDIUS APOLLINARIS *also shews that the Gospels were a definite and recognised collection at that time.*

---

[1] Claudius Apollinaris also presented an Apology to Marcus Antoninus c. 174 A.D. Hieron. *de Virr. Ill.* c. 26. Cf. Euseb. *H. E.* IV. 26.

[2] There is not any sufficient ground for doubting the genuineness of these fragments 'On Easter' in the fact that Eusebius mentions no such book by Apollinaris. The words of Eusebius (*H. E.* IV. 27) are 'that 'there were many works of Apolli-'naris in circulation, of which he 'enumerates only those which had 'come into his own hands:' τοῦ δ' Ἀπολιναρίου πολλῶν παρὰ πολλοῖς σωζομένων τὰ εἰς ἡμᾶς ἐλθόντα ἐστὶ τάδε...The two fragments are preserved in the *Paschal* or *Alexandrine Chronicle* (viith cent.). Cf. Routh, I. pp. 167 sq. Lightfoot *l. c.* 486 ff.

[3] Claud. Apoll. fr. ap. Routh, I. p. 160: καὶ διηγοῦνται Ματθαῖον οὕτω λέγειν ὡς νενοήκασιν· ὅθεν ἀσύμφωνός τε τῷ νόμῳ ἡ νόησις αὐτῶν, καὶ στασιάζειν δοκεῖ κατ' αὐτοὺς τὰ εὐαγγέλια. It seems strange that the Asiatic 'Paschal Controversy' should still be urged against the Johannine authorship of the Fourth Gospel, which certainly was recognised by the Asiatic 'School of St John.' The peculiarity of the Asiatic Churches was that they observed the 14th of Nisan (*i. e.* the day of the month and not the day of the week) as their Paschal Festival. This was the centre of the controversy. Now St John fixes the Death of the Lord as the true Passover, on the 14th; and there is every reason to believe that the Christian Paschal Festival was originally the commemoration (as it naturally would be) of the Death of the Lord and not of the Last Supper or of the Resurrection. Nothing therefore can be a more baseless assertion than that Polycarp (or Claudius Apollinaris) 'contradicted the statements 'of the fourth Gospel' by 'contend-'ing that the Christian Festival 'should be celebrated on the 14th 'Nisan' (*Supernat. Rel.* II. 271. Comp. 198 f., 472 f.). Such an assertion involves two conclusions which not only cannot be proved but which are inherently most improbable: (1) that the early Paschal Controversy turned on the choice of one of two days of the month and not on the choice of the day of the week measured back from Easter Day (Sunday); and (2) that the original Paschal Festival was a commemoration of the Last Supper and not of the Crucifixion.

from a mass of competitors; a contradiction between them is treated as impossible; and it must be remembered that this testimony comes from the same place as that of Papias, and that no such interval had elapsed between the two Bishops as to allow of any organic change in the Church[1].

THEOPHILUS of Antioch.

Two other apologists, Theophilus of Antioch, and Athenagoras of Athens, close the list of writers who belong to this age of apologists. Theophilus was, as it appears from his own writings, a heathen by birth and a native of the East; and Eusebius adds that he was sixth bishop of Antioch in the time of Marcus Aurelius.

c. 186 A.D.

He wrote several books for the purpose of Christian instruction (κατηχητικά τινα βιβλία), and among them three books to Autolycus (στοιχειώδη συγγράμματα) in which he devotes himself to convincing a learned heathen friend of the truth of Christianity. The personal and special character of his design gave him greater freedom than his predecessors in dealing with the Christian Scriptures, and his references to them are proportionately wider in range and more explicit than those contained in the earlier apologists[2]. Thus he quotes the 'evangelic voice' from a passage in St Matthew[3], and mentions St John by name as one of 'those who were 'vessels of the Spirit' (πνευματοφόροι), adding words from the Prologue to his Gospel as a specimen of his teaching[4]. Elsewhere his writings shew clear traces of St

c. 182 A.D.

---

[1] A second fragment of Apollinaris is preserved, in which he makes an evident allusion to John xix. 34, and in such a way as to shew that the Gospel had become the subject of careful interpretation. He speaks of Christ as ὁ τὴν ἁγίαν πλευρὰν ἐκκεντηθείς, ὁ ἐκχέας ἐκ τῆς πλευρᾶς αὐτοῦ τὰ δύο πάλιν καθάρσια ὕδωρ καὶ αἷμα, λόγον καὶ πνεῦμα. Cf.

[1] John v. 6 note.
[2] Comp. p. 118.
[3] iii. 13 ‖ Matt. v. 28.
[4] ii. 22. This is the earliest quotation of St John's Gospel by name which has been preserved. It is further worthy of notice that in the context the original distinction between 'the sacred Scriptures' (*i.e.* the Old Testament), and 'the in-

Paul's Epistles to the Romans, 1, 2 Corinthians, Ephesians, Philippians, Colossians, 1 Timothy[1], and Titus; of the Epistle to the Hebrews and of the first Epistle of St Peter[2]. In a work now lost he used, according to Eusebius, 'testimonies from the Apocalypse[3];' and Jerome speaks of a harmony of 'the four Evangelists' which he composed[4].

Chap. ii.

The little that is certainly known of Athenagoras is derived from his own writings; neither Eusebius nor Jerome give any account of him. He was, according to the superscription of his Apology, an Athenian and a philosopher; and his Apology ($\pi\rho\epsilon\sigma\beta\epsilon\iota\alpha$ $\pi\epsilon\rho\iota$ $X\rho\iota\sigma\tau\iota\alpha\nu\hat{\omega}\nu$—*A mission about Christians*—the title is most remarkable) was addressed to M. Aurelius and his son Commodus[5]. In this there are certain though tacit references to the Gospels of St Matthew[6] and St John[7]; and to the Epistles of St Paul to the Romans, Corinthians (1) and Galatians. The coincidences of thought or language with St Luke's Gospel and 1 Timothy are more questionable. In his discourse *On the Resurrection*

ATHENAGORAS.

c. 176 A.D.

---

spired men' of later times still remains, though elsewhere (*e.g.* iii. 14) Theophilus calls utterances of the New Testament 'divine,' and refers to one and the same source 'the inspiration of the law, the prophets and the Gospel' (iii. 12).
There is a reference to St Luke's Gospel, ii. 13 || Luke xviii. 27. Compare also iii. 2 *init.* with Luke i. 2.

[1] iii. 14 ($\dot{o}$ $\theta\epsilon\hat{\iota}os$ $\lambda\acute{o}\gamma os$) || 1 Tim. ii. 2.
[2] ii. 25 || Hebr. v. 12; xii. 9; ii. 34 || 1 Pet. i. 18; iv. 3. The passage ii. 9 may be compared with 2 Pet. i. 20, 21, and also ii. 13 with 2 Pet. i. 19. The form of the opening of i. 2 recals James ii. 18; but these references are doubtful.
[3] Euseb. *H. E.* IV. 24.

[4] Hieron. *Ep.* 121 (*ad Algasiam*), § 6. Theophilus...quatuor Evangelistarum in unum opus dicta compingens...hæc in suis Commentariis est locutus... Comp. *Prol. in Matt.* Jerome speaks more doubtfully (sub nomine ejus), *de Virr. Ill.* cxxv.
[5] This seems to be certainly established as against the supposition that the persons addressed are M. Aurelius and Lucius Verus. See Donaldson, *Christian Literature*, III. 108 ff.; or Lardner, *Credibility*, II. 181; or Otto's *Prolegomena*, § VII.
[6] *e.g. Legat.* XI. || Matt. v. 44, 45. 'These,' he says, 'are the words in which we are reared and with which we are nourished' ($o\hat{\iota}$ $\lambda\acute{o}\gamma o\iota$ $o\hat{\iota}s$ $\dot{\epsilon}\nu\tau\rho\epsilon\phi\acute{o}\mu\epsilon\theta\alpha$).
[7] *Legat.* XII. || John xvii. 3; *id.* 10 || John i. 3; x. 30; xvii. 21 ff.

230   THE AGE OF THE GREEK APOLOGISTS.   [PART

Chap. ii.

Athenagoras refers to St Paul as 'the apostle,' using thoughts from the Epistles to the Corinthians[1]. This, however, is the only direct citation which he makes, and his silence is the more important, because there can be no question that he was acquainted at any rate with the other writings of St Paul[2].

Summary of results.

One section of our inquiry is now finished. We have examined all the evidence bearing on the history of the New Testament Canon which can be adduced from those who are recognised as Fathers of the Church during the period which has been marked out[3]. It has been shewn that up to this point one book alone of the New Testament remains unnoticed: one Apocryphal book alone, and that doubtfully, placed within the limits of the Canon. There is not, so far as I am aware, in any Christian writer during the period which we have examined either direct mention of or clear reference to the second Epistle of St Peter[4]; and the Apocalypse which bore his name partially usurped a place among the New Testament Scriptures. Nor is this all: it has been shewn also that the form of Christian doctrine current

---

[1] c. xviii.

[2] In one passage (*Legat.* XXXII.) Athenagoras appears to quote a traditional saying of the Lord (λέγοντος τοῦ λόγου) which is not found elsewhere. Comp. *Introd. to Study of the Gospels*, Ap. C. no. 6.

[3] TATIAN will be noticed in Chap. IV.

The beautiful letter of the Church of Smyrna giving an account of the martyrdom of Polycarp, written shortly after it (A.D. 156. Cf. *Mart. Polyc.* c. xviii.), contains several allusions to books of the New Testament: *e.g.* Matt. x. 23=c. iv.; Matt. xxvi. 55=c. vii.; Acts ix. 7= c. ix.; Acts xxi. 14=c. vii.; 1 Cor. ii. 9=c. ii.; Rom. xiii. 1, 7=c. x. n. 5.

And besides several Pauline words occur: ἐξαγοράζεσθαι, βραβεῖον, ὁ ἀψευδὴς Θεός. The doxology in c. xiv. is very noteworthy. While speaking of this letter I cannot but mention the admirable emendation by which Dr Wordsworth (Hippolytus, App.) has effectually explained the famous passage about the Dove in c. xvi. For περιστερὰ καὶ, by the change of one letter, and the omission of I before a II following, he gives the true reading περὶ στύρακα. On this narrative compare Bp. Lightfoot, *C. R.* Febr. 1876, pp. 473 ff.

[4] The reference in Melito is not however to be neglected, see p. 222.

throughout the Church, as represented by men most widely differing in national and personal characteristics, in books of the most varied aim and composition, is measured exactly by the Apostolic Canon. It has been shewn that this exact coincidence between the Scriptural rule and the traditional belief is more perfect and striking in proportion as we apprehend more clearly the differences which coexist in both. It has been shewn that the New Testament in its integrity gives an adequate explanation of the progress of Christianity in its distinct types, and that there is no reason to believe that at any subsequent time such a creative power was active in the Church as could have called forth writings like those which we receive as Apostolic. They are the rule and not the fruit of the Church's development[1].

But at present the argument is incomplete. It is still necessary to inquire how far a Canon was publicly recognised by national Churches as well as by individuals— how far it was accepted even by those who separated from the orthodox communion, and on what grounds they rejected any part of it. These points will form the subject of the next two chapters, in which we shall examine the most ancient Versions of the East and West, and the writings of the earliest heretics.

On the Patristic references to Books of the New Testament collected by Eusebius.

SINCE it has been confidently affirmed that the silence of Eusebius as to the use made by an early Father of a particular book of the New Testament is a positive proof that the Father in question was unacquainted with it, inasmuch as he 'never fails to enumerate the writers of the New Testa-

---

[1] Some further considerations on which have been obtained are given the incompleteness of the results at the end of Chap. IV.

'ment to which the Fathers refer[1],' it becomes necessary to call the attention of students to the general principles on which Eusebius made quotations of this kind. These he lays down quite plainly on the first occasion when he deals with the contents of the Canon. 'In the course of my his-'tory,' he says, 'I shall make it my object to indicate together with the 'successions [of bishops in the great sees] what ecclesiastical writers at 'the several times have made use of what books from among the contro-'verted, and what they have said about the canonical and acknowledged 'writings, and all (ὅσα) that they have said about those writings which 'are not such[2].' He sets before himself therefore two main objects, (1) to notice from his own reading the simple use of the Antilegomena, and (2) to collect details recorded by others as to the composition and history of all the books which have been used as having Scriptural authority. The second object is again subdivided. On the one hand Eusebius proposes to bring together special statements about the canonical books[3], and on the other to complete the treatment of his first object by a collection of all the facts (ὅσα) which he could gather about the disputed books, seeing that in this case there was greater need of evidence with a view to the final determination of their character. By natural consequence it follows (1) that Eusebius would necessarily pass over, as a general rule, all mere references to the acknowledged books (e.g. the *Gospel of St John*, and *the thirteen Epistles of St Paul*); and (2) that if a writer simply made use of an apocryphal Gospel (e.g. the *Gospel according to the Hebrews*) as well as of canonical books (e.g. the four Gospels), he would quote the testimony to the apocryphal book and leave the testimony to the canonical books unnoticed[4].

These are the principles which he lays down, and by these he is guided, so far as his desultory method allows him to be guided by a consistent plan, with one exception more apparent than real. The exception is that he notices from time to time the simple use of the acknowledged Catholic Epistles (1 Peter, 1 John); for the group of the Catholic Epistles was of very uncertain extent, and in this case it might seem worth while to notice one or two individual testimonies.

---

[1] *Supernat. Rel.* 1. p. 488. Comp. p. 437: 'The care with which Eusebius searches for 'every trace of the use of the books of the 'New Testament in early writers, and his 'anxiety to produce any evidence concern-'ing their authenticity, render his silence 'upon the subject almost as important as his 'distinct utterance when speaking of such a 'man as Hegesippus.' p. 438: 'It is cer-'tain that Eusebius...would not have neg-'lected to have availed himself of the evi-'dence of Hegesippus...had that writer 'furnished him with any opportunity, for 'there can be no doubt that he exclusively 'made use of the Gospel according to the 'Hebrews together with unwritten tradition.'

[2] Euseb. *H. E.* III. (comp. v. 7), προιούσης τῆς ἱστορίας προὔργου ποιήσομαι σὺν ταῖς διαδοχαῖς ὑποσημήνασθαι τίνες τῶν κατὰ χρόνους ἐκκλησιαστικῶν συγγραφέων ὁποίαις κέχρηνται τῶν ἀντιλεγομένων, τίνα τε περὶ τῶν ἐνδιαθήκων καὶ ὁμολογουμένων γραφῶν καὶ ὅσα περὶ τῶν μὴ τοιούτων αὐτοῖς εἴρηται. Comp. Part III. c. 1.

[3] This he expresses even more clearly, v. 8: 'I promised that I would set forth...the 'utterances of the ancient ecclesiastical 'presbyters and writers, in which they had 'handed down in writing *the traditions* '*concerning the canonical Scriptures that* '*have come to them* (τὰς περὶ τῶν ἐνδια-'θήκων γραφῶν εἰς αὐτοὺς κατελθούσας πα-'ραδόσεις).' Nothing can be clearer than that he does not propose to collect evidence of the mere use of the acknowledged books.

[4] The words in reference to the Pauline Epistles, which follow very shortly after those which have been quoted, perfectly illustrate the design of Eusebius as he explains it: 'The Epistles of Paul are obvious 'and clear, the fourteen. That however certain have rejected that to the Hebrews, 'affirming that it was controverted (ἀντι-'λέγεσθαι) as not being Paul's by the Roman '[Latin] Church it is not right to ignore. 'And as opportunity offers (κατὰ καιρόν) I 'shall set forth what has been said about this '[Epistle] by our predecessors.' The Epistle to the Hebrews occupies just the same relation to the other Epistles of St Paul as the *Antilegomena* generally to the *Homologumena*; and Eusebius proposes to collect evidence as to that only.

A few illustrations will make the method of Eusebius quite clear, and dispose of the improper deductions which have been made from his silence.

CLEMENT. Eusebius notices (III. 38) that there are in the first Epistle of Clement verbal coincidences with the *Epistle to the Hebrews* (a disputed book); but he takes no notice of the reference by name to St Paul's *Epistle to the Corinthians*, and the certain coincidences with St James and Romans.

IGNATIUS. He notices (III. 36) the strange (apocryphal) saying in *ad Smyrn.* iii.; but passes over the reference to St Paul, *ad Ephes.* xii.

POLYCARP. ' Polycarp,' he writes (IV. 14), 'has made use of some tes-'timonies from the former Epistle of Peter;' but he passes over the reference by name to St Paul's *Epistle to the Philippians*, and the certain coincidences with *Galatians*, &c.

JUSTIN. He notices (IV. 18) his explicit reference to the *Apocalypse* of St John, a controverted book.

THEOPHILUS OF ANTIOCH. 'He made use,' he says (IV. 24), 'of tes-'timonies from the *Apocalypse*;' but he is silent as to his quotations by name (ii. 22) from *the Gospel of St John*.

IRENÆUS. '[Irenæus] mentions,' so he writes (v. 26), '*the Epistle to 'the Hebrews* and the so-called *Wisdom of Solomon*, quoting phrases from 'them.' And again (V. 8) Eusebius quotes from Irenæus special details of the composition of the four Gospels and the Apocalypse, and then adds: 'He has moreover made mention of the *first Epistle of John*, introducing 'many testimonies from it, and likewise of the *former Epistle of Peter*. And 'he not only knows but receives the writing (γραφήν) of *the Shepherd*...and 'he has used certain phrases from the *Wisdom of Solomon*...' But Eusebius says nothing of the countless references in Irenæus to all the acknowledged books of the New Testament as inspired and authoritative Scripture.

CLEMENT OF ALEXANDRIA. Eusebius notices (VI. 13) that Clement quoted the *Wisdom of Solomon*, *Ecclesiasticus*, the *Epistle to the Hebrews*, *Barnabas*, *Clement*, and *Jude*; but again says nothing of his countless references to the acknowledged books of the New Testament.

ORIGEN. Eusebius quotes Origen's detailed account of the books of the Old and New Testament (*H. E.* VI. 25); but passes over all his cursory references to controverted as well as to acknowledged books.

These examples will shew how utterly unjustifiable it is to conclude from Eusebius' notices of Papias and Hegesippus that they rejected or did not use or were unacquainted with the acknowledged books of the New Testament. *Supernat. Rel.* II. 320 ff. The same mode of argument would prove that Irenæus (for example) knew nothing of St Paul's Epistles; and if the *Cod. Alex.* had lost a few more leaves, the silence of Clement of Rome (as attested by Eusebius' silence) would have been urged as a manifest proof that St Paul never wrote to the Corinthians.

The fact is that except in the case of the Catholic Epistles Eusebius never notices the mere use of any of the acknowledged books. His silence under this head shews only that he had not observed in the particular writer under examination details of interest concerning them.

This argument has been urged with overwhelming force by Bp. Lightfoot, *C. R.* 1875, pp. 169 ff.

CHAPTER III.

THE EARLY VERSIONS OF THE NEW TESTAMENT.

JAM totum Christi corpus loquitur omnium linguis: et quibus nondum loquitur loquetur.

AUGUSTINUS.

The difficulties which beset the inquiry into the earliest Versions.

IT is not easy to overrate the difficulties which beset any inquiry into the early Versions of the New Testament. In addition to those which impede all critical investigations into the original Greek text, there are others in this case scarcely less serious, which arise from comparatively scanty materials and vague or conflicting traditions. There is little illustrative literature; or, if there be more, it is imperfectly known. There is no long line of Fathers to witness to the completion and the use of the translations. And though it be true that these hindrances are chiefly felt when the attempt is made to settle or interpret their text, they are no less real and perplexing when we seek only to investigate their origin and earliest form. Versions of Scripture appear to be in the first instance almost necessarily of gradual growth. Ideas of translation familiarized to us by long experience formed no part of the primitive system. The history of the Septuagint is a memorable example of what might be expected to be the history of Versions of the New Testament. And so far as there is any proof of unity in these which is wanting in that, we are led to conclude that the Canon of the New Testament was more definitely fixed, that the books of which it was composed were more equally esteemed, than was the case with the Old Testament at the time when it was translated into Greek.

Two Versions only claim to be noticed in this first Period—the original Versions of the East and West—the Peshito and Old Latin, which, though variously revised, remain after sixteen centuries the authorised liturgical versions of the Syrian and Roman churches. At present we have only to do with their extent: the peculiarities of text which they offer being considered only as one mark of their date. And here some care must be taken lest our reasoning form a circle. The Canon which the Peshito exhibits has been used to fix the time at which it was made; and yet we shall quote the Peshito to help us in determining the Canon. The text of the Old Latin depends in many cases on individual quotations; and yet we shall use it as an independent authority. Nor is this without reason; for the age of the Peshito is indicated by numerous particulars, and if the exact form in which the Canon appears in it accords with what we learn from other fragmentary notices of the same date, the two lines of evidence mutually support and strengthen each other. And so if there be any ground for believing that the earliest Latin Fathers employed some particular Version of the books of the New Testament, then we may analyse their quotations, and endeavour to determine how many books were included in the translation, and how far the whole translation bears the marks of one hand. There is nothing of direct demonstrative force in the conclusions thus obtained, but they form part of a series, and give coherence and consistency to it.

Chap. iii.

How far they can be used in investigating the Canon.

§ 1. *The Peshito*[1].

The Peshito represents the vernacular dialect of Palestine in the Apostolic age.

The Peshito[2] or 'simple' Syriac, that is Aramæan, Version is assigned almost universally to the most remote Christian antiquity. The Syriac Christians of Malabar even now claim for it the right to be considered as an Eastern original of the New Testament[3]; and though their tradition is wholly unsupported by external evidence, it is not to a certain extent destitute of all plausibility. There can be no doubt that the so-called Syro-Chaldaic (Aramæan) was the vernacular language of the Jews of Palestine in the time of our Lord, however much it may have been superseded by Greek in the common business of life[4]. It was in this dialect, the 'Hebrew' of the New Testament[5], that the Gospel of St Matthew was originally written, if we believe the unanimous testimony of the Fathers; and it is not unnatural to look to the Peshito as likely to contain some traces of its first form[6]. The early tradition which was

---

[1] The chief original authorities on the Peshito which I have examined are: *Ni. Ti. Versiones Syriacæ. Simplex, Philoxeniana, et Hierosolymitana, denuo examinatæ à* J. G. C. ADLER. *Hafniæ*, MDCCLXXXIX. *Horæ Syriacæ*, auctore N. WISEMAN, S. T. D. Tom. 1. *Romæ*, MDCCCXXXVIII. J. WICHELHAUS, *De N. T. versione Syriacâ quam Peschitho vocant Libri* IV. *Halis*, 1850.

[2] This title seems to be best interpreted 'simple,' as implying the absence of any allegorical interpretations. Hug, *Introd.* § LXII.

[3] Etheridge's *Syrian Churches*, pp. 166 ff.

[4] Wiseman, *Horæ Syriacæ*, pp. 69 sqq.

[5] John v. 2; xix. 13, 17, 20; xx. 16. Acts xxi. 40; xxii. 2; xxvi. 14. Cf. Apoc. ix. 11; xvi. 16. The word 'Hebrew' is first applied to the language of the Old Testament in the Apocrypha (*Prol. Sir.*). In Josephus it is used both of the true Hebrew, and of the Aramæan. Davidson, *Biblical Criticism*, I. 9; Etheridge, *Horæ Aramaicæ*, p. 7. In the conclusion to the Book of Job in the LXX. 'Syriac' appears to be used for the true Hebrew. Dr Roberts' *Dissertations on the Gospels* (Ed. 2, London, 1863) contain much that is very valuable on the language of Palestine in the time of our Lord; but his arguments only shew that the country was bilingual.

[6] The history of this Syriac Version offers a remarkable parallel to that of the Latin, but with this difference, that of the Old Syriac one

current at Alexandria that the Epistle to the Hebrews was written in the same Aramaic language sprang, as it appears, from the knowledge that it was addressed to 'Hebrew' speaking believers. And though little stress can be laid on such facts, they serve to shew how intimately the Peshito was connected with the wants of some among the early Christians of Palestine.

The dialect of the Peshito, even as it stands now, represents in part at least that form of Aramaic which was current in Palestine[1]. In this respect it is like the Latin Vulgate, which, though revised, is marked by the provincialisms of Africa. Both versions appear to have had their origin in districts where their languages were spoken in impure dialects, and afterwards to have been corrected, and brought nearer to the classical standard. In the absence of an adequate supply of critical materials it is impossible to construct the history of these recensions in the Syriac; the analogy of the Latin is at present our only guide. But if a conjecture may be allowed, I think that the various facts of the case are adequately explained by supposing that Versions of separate books of the New Testament were first made and used in Palestine, perhaps within the Apostolic age, and that shortly

---

very imperfect copy only, the Curetonian Version of the Gospel, has been preserved. But this is sufficient to shew that the Old Syriac was related very nearly to the later revision of the Peshito, as the Old Latin was to the Hieronymian Latin. The materials are not perhaps yet sufficiently extensive or trustworthy to furnish a complete decision as to the relation in which the Old Syriac St Matthew stood to the original 'Hebrew' Gospel (compare *Introduction to the Study of Gospels*, ch. IV. 2. i.). Dr Cureton has pointed out some facts bearing upon the question in his Introduction; but in the main it was certainly translated from the Greek.

[1] Gregory Bar Hebræus says that there were three dialects of Syriac (Aramæan): the most elegant was that of Edessa: the most impure that current among the inhabitants of Palestine and Libanus. The Peshito was written in the latter (Wiseman, *l. c.* p. 106), which seems to have been specially marked by the occurrence of Greek words. The occurrence of *Latin* words in the Peshito may be illustrated by examples from Syrian writers (Wiseman, *l. c.* p. 119, note).

Chap. iii.

How this conjecture is supported.

afterwards these were collected, revised, and completed at Edessa[1].

Many circumstances combine to give support to this belief. The early condition of the Syrian Church, its wide extent and active vigour, lead us to expect that a Version of the Holy Scriptures into the common dialect could not have been long deferred; and the existence of an Aramaic Gospel was in itself likely to suggest the work[2]. Differences of style, no less than the very nature of the case, point to separate translations of different books; and at the same time a certain general uniformity of character bespeaks some subsequent revision[3]. I have ventured to specify the place at which I believe that this revision was made[4]. Whatever may be thought of the alleged intercourse of Abgarus with our Lord, Edessa itself is signalized in early church-history by many remarkable facts. It was called the

The historical importance of Edessa.

---

[1] In the present section when speaking of the Peshito I mean the translation of the New Testament, unless it be otherwise expressed. At the same time it may be remarked that the Old Testament Peshito is probably the work of a Christian, and of the same date. Cf. Davidson, *Biblical Criticism*, I. p. 247; Wichelhaus, p. 73.
   It is clear from the consideration of readings (*e.g.* John v. 27 f.) that the *text* of the Peshito underwent a decisive revision in the 4th century by comparison with the Antiochene Greek copies.

[2] The activity of thought in Western Syria at an early period is most remarkable. It was not only the source of ecclesiastical order, but also of Apocryphal books. As a compensation for the latter it produced the first Christian Commentaries, those of Theophilus and Serapion. Cf. Wichelhaus, p. 55.

[3] Hug, *Introduction*, § 66; Etheridge, *Horæ Aramaicæ*, p. 52. It is but fair to say that the Syrians attributed the work to one translator.
   The Gospels are probably the earliest as they are the closest translation.
   The Acts are more loosely translated (Wichelhaus, p. 86); but it is to be remembered that the text of the Acts presents more variations than any part of the New Testament.
   The Epistle to the Hebrews is probably the work of a separate translator. (Wichelhaus, pp. 86 ff.)

[4] That it was made at some place out of the Roman Empire is shewn in the translation of στρατιῶται by *Romans* in Acts xxiii. 23, 31. [Cf. Acts xxviii. 15: Appi*us* For*us*.] But this is not the case in the Gospels, which, as I have conjectured, were translated earlier, and in Palestine. Cf. Wichelhaus, pp. 78 ff.

THE PESHITO.

'Holy' and the 'Blessed' city[1]: its inhabitants were said to have been brought over by Thaddeus in a marvellous manner to the Christian Faith; and 'from that 'time forth,' Eusebius adds[2], 'the whole people of Edessa 'has continued to be devoted to the name of Christ '(τῇ τοῦ Χριστοῦ προσανάκειται προσηγορίᾳ), exhibiting 'no ordinary instance of the goodness of our Saviour.' In the second century it became the centre of an important Christian school; and long afterwards retained its pre-eminence among the cities of its province.

As might be expected tradition fixes on Edessa as the place whence the Peshito took its rise. Gregory Bar Hebræus[3], one of the most learned and accurate of Syrian writers, relates that the New Testament Peshito was 'made in the time of Thaddeus and Abgarus King of 'Edessa,' when, according to the universal opinion of ancient writers, the Apostle went to proclaim Christianity in Mesopotamia. This statement he repeats several times, and once on the authority of Jacob a deacon of Edessa in the fifth century. He tells us moreover that 'messengers were sent from Edessa to Palestine to trans- 'late the Sacred Books;' and though this statement refers especially to the Old Testament, it confirms what has been said of the Palestinian authorship of the Ver-

Chap. iii.

Syrian traditions as to the origin of the Peshito. Gregory Bar Hebræus.

Jacob of Edessa.

---

[1] *Horæ Syriacæ*, p. 101.
[2] Euseb. *H. E.* II. 1.
[3] The following testimonies from Gregory—inter suos ferme κριτικώτατος—are given by Wiseman: Quod vero spectat ad hanc Syriacam [Versionem V. Ti.] tres fuerunt sententiæ; prima quod tempore *Salomonis* et *Hiram* Regum conversa fuerit; secunda quod *Asa* sacerdos, quum ab Assyriâ missus fuit Samariam, eum transtulerit; tertia tandem quod diebus *Adæi* Apostoli et *Abgari* Regis Osrhoeni versa fuerit, quando etiam Novum

Testamentum eadem simplici forma traductum est. p. 90. Cf. Adler, p. 42.
Occidentales [Syri] duas habent versiones, Simplicem, quæ ex Hebraico in Syriacum translata est post adventum Domini Christi tempore *Adæi* Apostoli, vel ut alii dicunt tempore *Salomonis* filii Davidis et *Hiram*, et Figuratam...p. 94.
Jacobus Edessenus dicit interpretes illos qui missi sunt ab *Adai* Apostolo et *Abgaro* Rege Osrhoeno in Palæstinam, quique verterunt Libros Sacros ...p. 103.

C. R

sion. And it is worthy of notice that Gregory assumes the Apostolic origin of the New Testament Peshito as certain; for while he gives three hypotheses as to the date of the Old Testament Version he speaks of this as a known and acknowledged fact.

Want of early Syrian literature.

No other direct historical evidence remains to determine the date of the Peshito; and it is impossible to supply the deficiency by the help of quotations occurring in early Syriac writers. The only Syriac work of a very early date which has been as yet discovered is

Bardesanes. [Bardesanes'] Dialogue *On Fate* (or *The Book of the Laws of Countries*), of which Eusebius has preserved a considerable fragment in Greek[1]. This contains no express quotation from Scripture, and the adaptation of Scriptural language in the course of the argument is so free that no conclusion can be drawn from the few coincidences which may be pointed out as to the existence of a Syriac Version in the time of the writer. On the other hand the general character of the work is such as not to admit of definite citations of Scripture, and thus the absence of explicit references to the books of the New Testament does not prove that they did not then exist in Syriac. Moreover it is known that books were soon translated from Syriac into Greek, and while such an intercourse existed it is scarcely possible to believe that the Scriptures themselves remained untranslated. The same conclusion follows from the controversial writings of Bardesanes, which necessarily imply the existence of a Syriac Version of the Bible[2]. Tertullian's example

---

[1] The Syriac text with a translation is given by Dr Cureton, in his *Spicilegium Syriacum*, London, 1855. The Greek fragment occurs in Euseb. *Præp. Ev.* VI. 10. On *The Doctrine of Addai* see note, p. 247.

[2] Bardesanes—Valentinianæ sectæ primum discipulus...vir erat litterarum gnarus, qui etiam ad Antoninum epistolam scribere ausus est, multosque sermones contra Marcionitas atque simulacrorum cultum composuit (Moses Choren. ap. Wichelhaus, p. 57). Cf. Euseb. *H. E.* IV. 30.

may shew that he could hardly have refuted Marcion without the constant use of Scripture. And more than this, Eusebius tells us that Hegesippus 'made quota-'tions from the Gospel according to the Hebrews and 'the Syriac and especially from [writings in?] the Hebrew 'language, shewing thereby that he was a Christian of 'Hebrew descent[1].' This testimony is valuable as coming from the only early Greek writer likely to have been familiar with Syriac literature; and may we not see in the two Gospels thus mentioned two recensions of St Matthew—the one disfigured by Apocryphal traditions, and the other written in the dialect of Eastern Syria?

Chap. iii.

Hegesippus.

Ephraem Syrus, himself a deacon of Edessa, treats the Version in such a manner as to prove that it was already old in the fourth century. He quotes it as a book of established authority, calling it 'Our Version:' he speaks of the 'Translator' as one whose words were familiar[2]; and though the dialects of the East are proverbially permanent, his explanations shew that its language even in his time had become partially obsolete[3].

Ephraem Syrus.

---

[1] Euseb. *H. E.* IV. 22: ἔκ τε τοῦ καθ' Ἑβραίους εὐαγγελίου καὶ τοῦ Συριακοῦ καὶ ἰδίως ἐκ τῆς Ἑβραΐδος διαλέκτου τινὰ τίθησιν, ἐμφαίνων ἐξ Ἑβραίων ἑαυτὸν πεπιστευκέναι (quoted by Hug).

[2] *Horæ Syriacæ*, pp. 116, 117.

[3] It does not seem that the difference of the Edessene and Palestinian dialects alone can account for the obscurities which Ephraem seeks to remove. The instances quoted by Dr Wiseman are in accordance with his plan taken from the Old Testament; but in the absence of all indications of the contrary it seems fair to suppose that his remarks apply equally to the New Testament. Cf. Wichelhaus, p. 21.

In reference to the phraseology of the Peshito it is worthy of remark that *Episcopus* is preserved in one place only, Acts xx. 28. Elsewhere it is *kashisho* (presbyter), except in 1 Pet. ii. 25. The name of *deacon* is nowhere retained. Wichelhaus, p. 89.

The text of the Curetonian Gospels is in itself a sufficient proof of the extreme antiquity of the Syriac Version. This, as has been already remarked, offers a striking resemblance to that of the Old Latin, and cannot be later than the middle or close of the second century. It would be difficult to point out a more interesting subject for criticism than the respective relations of the Old Latin and Syriac Versions to the Latin and Syriac Vulgates. But at present it is almost untouched.

Chap. iii.
The Peshito received by all the Syrian sects.

Another circumstance serves to exhibit the venerable age of this Version. It was universally received by the different sects into which the Syrian Church was divided in the fourth century, and so has continued current even to the present time. All the Syrian Christians[1], whether belonging to the Nestorian, Jacobite, or Roman communion, conspire to hold the Peshito authoritative, and to use it in their public services. It must consequently have been established by familiar use before the first heresies arose, or it could not have remained without a rival. Numerous versions or revisions of the New Testament were indeed made afterwards, for Syriac literature is peculiarly rich in this branch of theological criticism; but no one ever supplanted the Peshito for ecclesiastical purposes[2]. Like the Latin Vulgate in the

---

[1] *Horæ Syriacæ*, p. 108.

[2] Dr Wiseman enumerates twelve Versions of the Old Testament. The most important for the criticism of the New Testament are the Philoxenian, the Harclean, and the Palestinian.

The Philoxenian derives its name from a bishop of Mabug or Hierapolis in Syria (A.D. 485—518), in whose time it was made by one Polycarp for the use of the Monophysites. Of this Version only fragments remain; and it is uncertain whether it included all the books of the New Testament. Adler, p. 48. Wiseman, p. 178, n. Adler supposes that an early Mediceo-Florentine Manuscript (A.D. 757) of the Gospels exhibits this recension, but he adds that it differs little from the Harclean. pp. 53—55.

Thomas Harclensis, poor Thomas as he calls himself, a monk of Alexandria in 616 A.D., revised the Philoxenian translation by the help of some Greek Manuscripts, and seems to have attempted for the Syriac Version what Origen accomplished for the Septuagint. The Oxford Manuscript of this Translation contains the *seven* catholic Epistles, but omits the Apocalypse. Adler, pp. 49 sq. Comp. G. H. Bernstein, *De Charklensi Ni. Ti. Translatione Syriaca Commentatio*, Vratisl. 1837.

The Palestinian Version exists in an Evangelistarium of proper lessons for the Sundays and Festivals of the year. It is remarkable that the pericope, John vii. 53—viii. 11, which is wanting in the other Syriac versions, is contained in this in a form which agrees with the text of Cod. D. The dialect in which it is written is very similar to that of the Jerusalem Talmud: and thus Adler, who first accurately examined it, gave it the name of the Jerusalem Version. Adler, pp. 140—145; 190, 191; 198—202. [This Version has been edited with a Latin translation by Con. F. Miniscalchi Erizzo, 1861—4.]

In addition to these Versions there is the Karkaphensian recension of the Peshito made by an uncertain Jacobite author (Wiseman, p. 212), chiefly remarkable for the singular order in which the books are arranged. The New Testament Canon is the same

I.] THE PESHITO. 243

Western Church, the Peshito became in the East the fixed and unalterable Rule of Scripture. *Chap. iii.*

The respect in which the Peshito was held was further shewn by the fact that it was taken as the basis of other Versions in the East. An Arabic and a Persian Version were made from it; but it is more important to notice that at the beginning of the fifth century (before the Council of Ephesus A.D. 431) an Armenian Version was commenced from the Syriac in the absence of Greek Manuscripts[1]. *and used as the basis of other translations, especially* *the Armenian.*

These indications of the antiquity of the Peshito do not indeed possess any conclusive authority, but they all tend in the same direction, and there is nothing on the other side to reverse or modify them. It is not improbable that fresh discoveries may throw a clearer light on early Syriac literature; and that more copious critical resources may serve to determine the date of the Peshito on philological grounds. But meanwhile there is no sufficient reason to desert the opinion which has obtained the sanction of the most competent scholars, that its formation is to be fixed within the first half of the second century. The text, even in its present revised form, exhibits remarkable agreement with the most ancient Greek Manuscripts and the earliest quotations. The very obscurity which hangs over its origin is a proof of its venerable age, because it shews that it grew up spontaneously among Christian congregations, and was not the result of any public labour. Had it been a work of late date, of the third or fourth century, it is scarcely *General result;* *confirmed by the text*

---

as that of the original Peshito, but the Acts and three Catholic epistles stand first as *one book;* the fourteen Epistles of St Paul follow next; and the four Gospels in the usual order come last (Wiseman, p. 217). This recension has been accurately examined by Dr Wiseman, *ll. cc.*

[1] See Dr Tregelles, in the *Dictionary of the Bible,* s.v. *Versions.*

Chap. iii.

The present state of the Version.

The Syrian Canon.

535 A.D.

possible that its history should have been so uncertain as it is[1].

The Version exists at present in two distinct classes of Manuscripts[2]. Some are written in the ancient Syrian letters, and others of Indian origin in the Nestorian character. The latter are comparatively of recent date, but remarkable for the variations from the common text which they exhibit. Still though these two families of Manuscripts represent different recensions they coincide as far as the Canon is concerned. Both omit the second and third Epistles of St John, the second Epistle of St Peter, the Epistle of St Jude, and the Apocalypse, but include all the other books as commonly received without any addition. This Canon seems to have been generally maintained in the Syrian Churches, and in those which depended on their authority[3]. It is reproduced in the Arabic Version of Erpenius, which was taken from the Peshito[4]: Cosmas, an Egyptian traveller

---

[1] J. B. Branca (1781), from a desire to raise the Vulgate above all rivalry, endeavoured to prove that the Peshito was made as late as the fourth century. Dr Wiseman has fully refuted him, pp. 110 sqq.

[2] Adler, p. 3.

[3] EPHRAEM SYRUS however, if we may trust his Greek works, admitted the *seven* Catholic Epistles and the Apocalypse: but in this he represents the Greek rather than the Syrian Church. Compare Part III. Chap. II. There is no trace of their reception by the Syrian Churches, or of their admission into Manuscripts of the Peshito till a very late date.

The Syriac Manuscripts in the British Museum offer a very instructive history of the Syrian Canon of the N. T. The earliest dated N. T. (Rich, 7157), A.D. 768, contains four Gospels, Acts, James, 1 Peter, 1 John, 13 Epistles of St Paul, Epistle to the Hebrews. An earlier copy of the (5th or) 6th century gives the same books in a different order, Gospels, Epistles of St Paul, Acts, James, 1 Peter, 1 John (Add. 14,470). The earliest Manuscript in which the disputed Epistles occur is dated A.D. 823 (Add. 14,623). In another Manuscript (Add. 14,473) the then generally received Epistles were written in the sixth century, and the remaining four were added in the eleventh or twelfth. The Apocalypse (with a Commentary) is found in a Manuscript dated 1088. For these particulars I am indebted to the kindness of Dr W. Wright [now Professor of Arabic at Cambridge] of the British Museum.

[4] Actus app. et epistulas Pauli, item Iacobi epistulam, priorem Petri et primam Iohannis, quemadmodum in ed. Erpeniana leguntur, e Syra Peschito fluxisse certum est. Reli-

of the sixth century, states that only three Catholic Epistles were received by the Syrians[1]. Junilius mentions two Catholic Epistles as undoubted—1 John, 1 Peter—while the remaining five were received 'by very 'many[2].' Dionysius Bar Salibi[3] in the twelfth century alludes to the absence of the second Epistle of St Peter from the ancient Syrian Version; Ebed-jesu[4] in the fourteenth century repeats the Canon of the Peshito; and the mutilation of the New Testament by the omission of the disputed books was one of the charges brought against the Christians of St Thomas at the Synod of Diamper[5].

Such then is the Canon of the Syrian Churches[6]. Its general agreement with our own is striking and important; and its omissions admit of easy explanation. The purely historic evidence for the second Epistle of St Peter must always appear inconclusive; for it does not seem to have been generally known before the end of the third century. The Apocalypse again rests chiefly on the authority of the Western Churches; and it is not surprising that the two shorter and private letters of St John should have been at first unknown in Mesopotamia. The omission of the Epistle of St Jude is perhaps more remarkable, when it is remembered that it was written in Palestine, and appears to be necessarily connected with that of St James. But these points will

Chap. iii.
c. 530.

† 1318 A.D.

1599 A.D.

The relation of the Canon to our own.

---

quos libros ibidem exhibitos, i.e. apocalypsin cum quattuor reliquis epp. cath. unde interpres hauserit, non satis constat, sed videntur originem Coptam habuisse. Tischendorf, *Proleg. N. T.* ed. 7, p. CCXXXVII.
  [1] Credner, *Zur Gesch. d. Kanons*, p. 105, n. See below, Part III. Chap. II.
  [2] App. D. No. IV. Credner, *l. c.*
  [3] Hug, § 64.
  [4] App. D. No. VI.

  [5] Adler, p. 35.
  [6] The order of the Books is the same as that in the best Greek Manuscripts: The four Gospels—the Acts —the Catholic Epistles—the Epistles of St Paul. In the Karkaphensian recension, as we have seen, the order is in part inverted; and Jacob of Edessa follows the same arrangement, placing the Gospels last. Wichelhaus, p. 84.

come under examination in another place. Meanwhile it is necessary to insist on the absence of all uncanonical books from this earliest Version. Many writings we know were current in the East under Apostolic titles, but no one received the sanction of the Church; and this fact alone is sufficient to shew that the Canon was not fixed without direct knowledge or careful criticism.

The Peshito is the earliest monument of Catholic Christianity.

There is still another aspect in which the Peshito claims our notice. Proceeding from a Church which in character and language seems to represent most truly the Palestinian element of the Apostolic age, it witnesses to something more than the authenticity of the New Testament Scriptures. It is in fact the earliest monument of Catholic Christianity. Here for the first time we see the different forms of Apostolic teaching which still served as the watchwords of heresy recognised by the East as constituent parts of a common faith. The closing words of St Peter had witnessed to the same truth; and though the Syrian Churches refused to acknowledge the testimony, they confirmed its substance in this collection of their sacred books. The contest between the Jewish and Gentile Churches had passed away. The 'enemy' and 'deceiver,' as St Paul was still called by the Ebionites, is acknowledged in this first Christian Bible to have independent power and authority as an Apostle of Christ. Henceforth the great Father of the Western Church stands side by side with St James, St Peter, and St John, the Pillars of the Church of Jerusalem[1].

2 Pet. iii. 15.

---

[1] The *Ancient Syriac Documents* edited by Dr Cureton and Dr W. Wright (London, 1864) do not throw any new light upon the Syrian Canon. The writings themselves cannot maintain the claim to Apostolic antiquity which has been set up for some of them. In their present form they contain numerous anonymous references to the substance of the Gospels, including St John (xiv. 26, pp. 25, 36), and to the Epistle to the Romans (i. 25, p. 37; viii. 35, p. 54; *id.* 18, p. 81); and perhaps to Apoc. xx. 12 (p. 9:

this is very doubtful). The strange passage (p. 56): 'One of the Doctors 'of the Church hath said: The scars indeed of my body—that I may come 'to the resurrection from the dead:' appears to be derived from Gal. vi. 17; Phil. iii. 11.

Some Evangelic passages are given in what may be a traditional form. Thus we read (p. 20) that the Lord said: 'Accept not anything from any 'man, and possess not anything in this world' (cf. Matt. x. 7—10). And the account of the Descent of the Holy Spirit (p. 25) is full of interest when compared with Acts ii.

One passage (p. 10) appears to preserve the addition in Luke xxiii. 48 which is found in *Syr. Curet.* and some Latin copies. It may be observed also that a reference is found (p. 8) to the famous saying 'Prove yourselves 'tried money-changers,' on which Dr Cureton quotes from Lagarde's *Didasc. Apost.* (p. 42): 'Be expert discerners (money-changers). It is requisite 'therefore that a bishop like a trier of silver should be a discerner of the 'bad and the good.'

Among the ordinances attributed to the Apostles is one which probably formed the basis of the corresponding passages in the Apostolic Canons and Constitutions; 'Except the Old Testament and the Prophets and the Gos-'pel and the Acts of their own [the Apostles] triumph let not anything 'be read in the pulpit of the Church' (p. 27. Comp. p. 15).

But this ordinance is afterwards modified by a remarkable paragraph in which a general review is given of the writings of the Apostles with the exception of St Paul (p. 32): 'They again (the immediate successors 'of the Apostles) at their deaths committed and delivered to their disciples 'after them everything which they had received from the Apostles: also 'what James had written from Jerusalem, and Simon from the city of 'Rome, and John from Ephesus, and Mark from Macedonia, and Judas 'Thomas from India; that the Epistles of an Apostle might be received 'and read in the Churches in every place, as those Triumphs of their Acts 'which Luke wrote are read, that by this the Apostles might be known 'and the Prophets and the Old Testament and the New: that one truth 'was preached by them all, that one Spirit spake in them all from one 'God, whom they had all worshipped and had all preached.' The omission of St Paul is made the more remarkable by the fact that in the distribution of the various countries among the Apostles no land is assigned to St Paul (Rome, Spain, and *Britain*, are given to St Peter), though he is afterwards mentioned casually in the same paragraph (p. 35).

The *Doctrine of Addai*, which has been published in a complete form by Dr Phillips (London, 1876) gives some further parallels with the N. T.: *e.g.* p. 4, John xx. 29; p. 79, John xvii. 4 f.; p. 41, Matt. xviii. 10.

The direction as to the reading of Sacred writings in the Church appears in a somewhat different and fuller form: 'But the Law and the Prophets 'and the Gospel, which ye read every day before the people, and the 'Epistles of Paul, which Simon Peter sent us from the city of Rome, and 'the Acts of the twelve Apostles, which John the son of Zebedee sent 'us from Ephesus, these books read ye in the Church of God, and with 'these read not others......' p. 44.

The reference to Tatian's *Diatessaron* which Dr Cureton detected by conjecture (p. 15) is now established beyond doubt (Phillips, p. 34 n.).

Chap. iii.

The Early Christian literature of Rome was Greek and not Latin.

§ 2. *The Old Latin Version*[1].

At first it seems natural to look to Italy as the centre of the Latin literature of Christianity, and the original source of that Latin Version of the Holy Scriptures which in a later form has become identified with the Church of Rome. Yet however plausible such a belief may be, it finds no support in history. Rome itself under the emperors was well described as a 'Greek city;' and Greek was its second language[2]. As far as we can learn, the mass of the poorer population—to which the great bulk of the early Christians everywhere belonged—was Greek either in descent or in speech. Among the names of the fifteen bishops of Rome up to the close of the second century, four only are Latin[3]; though in the next century the proportion is nearly reversed. When St Paul wrote to the Roman Church he wrote in Greek; and in the long list of salutations to its members with which the epistle is concluded only four genuine Latin names occur. Shortly afterwards Clement wrote to the Corinthians in Greek in the name of the Church of Rome; and at a later date we find the Bishop of Corinth writing in Greek to Soter the ninth in succession from Clement. Justin, Hermas, and according to the common opinion Tatian[4], published their Greek treatises at

---

[1] The best original investigation into the Old Latin Version is Wiseman's *Remarks on some parts of the controversy concerning* 1 John v. 7, originally printed in the Catholic Magazine, ii., iii., 1832, f., and republished at Rome, 1835.
  Lachmann has produced his arguments with some new illustrations: *Nov. Test.* I. p. IX. ff. Comp. *Dictionary of Bible*, s. v. *Vulgate*: and especially Ziegler, *Die Lat. Bibel-übersetzungen vor Hieronymus*, München, 1879.

[2] Cf. Wiseman, III. pp. 366 f. Bunsen's *Hippolytus* II. 123 sqq.

[3] Bunsen *l.c.* says 'two, Clement and Victor:' but probably Sixtus (Xystus, Euseb. *H. E.* IV. 4; cf. VII. 5) and certainly Pius should be included in the number.

[4] Otto, *Proleg.* p. xxxv. Lumper, *Hist. Patrum*, II. p. 321.

THE OLD LATIN.

Rome. The Apologies to the Roman emperors were in Greek. Modestus, Caius, and Asterius Urbanus, bear Latin names, and yet their writings were Greek. Even further west Greek was the common language of Christians. The churches of Vienne and Lyons used it in writing the history of their persecutions; and Irenæus, though 'he lived among the Gauls,' and confessed that he had grown unfamiliar with his native idiom, made it the vehicle of his Treatise against Heresies[1]. The first sermons which were preached at Rome were in Greek; and to the present time the services of the Church of Rome bear clear traces that Greek was at first the language of its Liturgy.

Greek was also used in Gaul.

Meanwhile however, though Greek continued to be the natural, if not the sole language of the Roman Church[2], the seeds of Latin Christianity were rapidly developing in Africa. Nothing is known in detail of the origin of the African churches. The Donatists classed them among 'those last which should be first;' and Augustine in his reply merely affirms that 'some barbarian 'nations embraced Christianity after Africa; so that it is 'certain that Africa was not the last to believe[3].' The concession implies that Africa was converted late, and after the Apostolic times: Tertullian adds that it re-

Africa is the true birthplace of the Latin literature of Christianity.

---

[1] c. *Hær.* I. Pref. 3: οὐκ ἐπιζη-τήσεις δὲ παρ' ἡμῶν τῶν ἐν Κελτοῖς διατριβόντων καὶ περὶ βάρβαρον διά-λεκτον τὸ πλεῖστον ἀσχολουμένων...

[2] Jerome speaks of Tertullian as the first Latin writer after Victor and Apollonius. Victor was an African by birth, and yet he appears to have used Greek in the Paschal controversy. Polycrates at least addressed him in Greek: Euseb. *H. E.* v. 24. It is disputed whether Apollonius' defence was in Greek or in Latin. If it were in Latin, as seems likely, the place of its delivery—the Senate —sufficiently explains the fact. Cf. Lumper, IV. 3.

[3] August. *c. Donat. Epist.* [*de Unit. Eccles.*] c. 37: De nobis inquiunt [Donatistæ] dictum est *Erunt primi qui erant novissimi.* Ad Africam enim Evangelium postmodum venit; et ideo nusquam litterarum apostolicarum scriptum est Africam credidisse... Augustine answers: ... nonnullæ barbaræ nationes etiam post Africam crediderunt; unde certum sit Africam in ordine credendi non esse novissimam.

ceived the Gospel from Rome. But the rapidity of the spread of Christianity in Africa compensated for the lateness of its introduction. At the close of the second century Christians were found in every place and of every rank. They who were but of yesterday, Tertullian says[1], already fill the Palace, the Senate, the Forum, and the Camp, and leave to the heathen their Temples only. To persecute the Christians was even then to decimate Carthage[2]. These fresh conquests of the Roman Church preserved their distinct nationality by the retention of their proper language. Carthage, the second Rome, escaped the Græcism of the first. In Africa Greek was no longer a current dialect. A peculiar form of Latin, vigorous, elastic, and copious, however far removed from the grace and elegance of a classical standard, fitly expressed the spirit of Tertullian. But though we speak of Tertullian as the first Latin Father, it must be noticed that he speaks of Latin as the language of his Church, and that his writings abound with Latin quotations of Scripture. He inherited an ecclesiastical dialect, if not an ecclesiastical literature. It is then to Africa that we must look for the first traces of the Latin 'Peshito,' the 'simple' Version of the West. And here a new difficulty arises. The Syrian Peshito has been preserved without any break in the succession in the keeping of the churches for whose use it was made. But no image of their former life, however faint, lingers at Carthage or Hippo. No church of Northern Africa, however corrupt, remains to testify to its ancient Bible. The Version was revised by a foreign scholar, and adopted by a foreign church, until at last its independent existence in its original form has

The Vetus Latina *is the oldest specimen of it.*

---

[1] *Apol.* I. 37. c. 200 A.D.   [2] *Ad Scap.* c. 5.

been questioned and even denied. Before any attempt is made to fix the date of its formation and the extent of its Canon, it will be necessary to shew that we are dealing with a reality, and not with a mere creation of a critic's fancy.

The language of Tertullian if candidly examined is conclusive on the point. A few quotations will prove that he distinctly recognised a current Latin Version, marked by a peculiar character, and in some cases unsatisfactory to one conversant with the original text.

'Reason,' he says, 'is called by the Greeks *Logos*, a 'word equivalent to *Sermo* in Latin. And so it is al-'ready customary for our countrymen to say, through a 'rude and simple translation (per simplicitatem interpre-'tationis), that the Word of Revelation (*sermo*) was in 'the beginning with God, while it is more correct to 'regard the rational word (*ratio*) as antecedent to this, 'because God in the beginning was not manifested in 'intercourse with man (*sermonalis*), but existed in self-'contemplation (*rationalis*)[1].' From this it appears that the Latin translation of St John's Gospel was already so generally circulated as to mould the popular dialect; and invested with sufficient authority to support a rendering capable of improvement. If there had been many

Tertullian affirms the existence of a Latin Version of the New Testament in his time.

John i. 1.

---

[1] *Adv. Prax.* c. 5: [Rationem] Græci λόγον dicunt, quo vocabulo etiam Sermonem appellamus. Ideoque jam in usu est nostrorum per simplicitatem interpretationis Sermonem dicere *in primordio apud Deum fuisse*, cum magis *Rationem* competat antiquiorem haberi: quia non sermonalis a principio, sed rationalis Deus etiam ante principium, et quia ipse quoque Sermo ratione consistens orem eam ut substantiam suam ostendat; tamen et sic nihil interest. It will be noticed that Tertullian uses the word *principium* (so Vulg.) and not *primordium*. He quotes the passage with that reading, so *adv. Hermog.* 20; *adv. Prax.* 13, 21. This is another mark of the independence of the current translation. The rendering of λόγος by *sermo* occurs in Cyprian, *Testim.* II. 3; but I am not aware that it is found in any existing Manuscript. It certainly does not occur in any of the typical representatives of the different classes of the Old Latin.

rival translations in use, it is scarcely probable that they would all have exhibited the same 'rudeness of style;' or that a writer like Tertullian would have apologized for an inaccuracy found in some one of them.

Again, when arguing to prove that a second marriage is only allowed to a woman who had lost her first husband before her conversion to the Christian faith, inasmuch as this second husband is indeed her first, he adds in reference to the passage of St Paul which he has quoted before: 'We must know that the phrase in the 'original Greek is *not* the same as that which has 'gained currency [among us] through a clever or simple 'perversion of two syllables: *If however her husband shall 'fall asleep*, as if it were said of the future...[1]' The connexion of this passage with the last is evident. An ambiguous translation had passed into common use, and must therefore have been supported by some recognised claim. That this was grounded on the general reception of the version in which it was found is implied in the language of Tertullian. The '*simple* rendering' and the '*simple* perversion' naturally refer to some literal Latin translation already circulated in Africa.

It is then a fact beyond doubt that a Latin translation of some of the books of the New Testament was

Chap. iii.

1 Cor. vii. 39.

This translation included a

---

[1] *De Monog.* c. 11: Sciamus plane non sic esse in Græco authentico, quomodo in usum exiit per duarum syllabarum aut callidam aut simplicem eversionem: *si autem dormierit vir ejus*, quasi de futuro sonet... The general meaning of Tertullian is clear, but it is difficult to see the force of his argument as applied to *dormierit:* that tense is commonly used to translate ἐάν with the *aor.* (yet comp. Tert. II. 393, *edamus*, with Vulg. *manducaverimus*). In an earlier part of the chapter he quotes: *si autem mortuus fuerit.* For κοιμηθῇ A, al. read ἀποθάνῃ. Is it possible that the reading of F G (κεκοιμηθη) is a confusion of κοιμηθῇ and κεκοίμηνται (cf. ἐὰν οἴδαμεν 1 John v. 15, &c.), and that Tertullian read the latter? If so, the 'eversio duarum syllabarum' (*dormiit, dormierit*) would be intelligible; otherwise we must I think read *dormiet*. The only variation which occurs in the Manuscripts is *dormitionem acceperit*. No authority which I have seen gives *dormiit*.

I.] THE OLD LATIN. 253

current in Africa in Tertullian's time, and sufficiently authorized by popular use to form the theological dialect of the country. It appears from another passage that this translation embraced a collection of the Christian Scriptures. 'We lay down,' he says, 'in the first place 'that the Evangelical Instrument—[the collection of the 'authoritative documents of the Gospel]—rests on Apo-'stolic authority[1].' The very name by which the collection was called witnessed to the 'simplicity' of the version. 'Marcion,' Tertullian writes just before, 'supposed 'that different gods were the authors of the two *Instru-*'*ments,*' or, as it is usual to speak, of the two *Testaments*[2]. The word *Testament* (διαθήκη) would naturally find a place in a 'simple' version; otherwise it is not easy to see how it could have supplanted the more usual term[3].

Chap. iii.
collection of Apostolic books.

Thus far then the evidence of Tertullian decidedly favours the belief that one Latin Version of the Holy Scriptures was popularly used in Africa. It has however been argued, from the language which Augustine uses about two centuries later with reference to the origin and multiplicity of the Latin Versions in his time, that this view of the unity and authority of the African Version is untenable. 'Every one,' he says, 'in the first times of 'the faith who gained possession of a Greek manuscript 'and fancied that he had any little acquaintance with 'both Greek and Latin ventured to translate it[4].' On

The statements of Augustine relative to the Latin Version.

---

[1] *Adv. Marc.* IV. 2.
[2] *Adv. Marc.* IV. 1: ...duos deos dividens, proinde diversos, alterum alterius *instrumenti*, vel, quod magis usui est dicere, *testamenti*...
[3] The phrase *Novum Testamentum* was used both of the Christian dispensation and of the records of it: *adv. Marc.* IV. 22; *adv. Prax.* 31.
Instrumentum is used in late Latin of public or official documents: *e.g.*

Instrumenta litis—*Instrumentum imperii* (Suet. *Vesp.* 8)—*Instrumenti publici auctoritas* (Suet. *Cal.* 8). It is a favourite word with Tertullian: *Apol.* I. 18, *Instrumentum litteraturæ*; *adv. Marc.* V. 2, *Instrumentum actorum*; *de Resurrec. Carnis,* 39, Apostolus *per totum pene instrumentum*; *de Spectac.* 5, *Instrumenta ethnicarum litterarum.*
[4] *De Doctr. Christ.* II. 16 (XI.):

such a question the general statement of Augustine is of little weight. It is not unlikely that he is simply giving what seemed to him to be the most natural explanation of the multiplicity of existing copies. Moreover the alterations by revisers would cover the kind of changes to which he refers[1]. But even if we admit that the first version included the work of different translators, yet the analogy of later times is sufficient to prove that the freedom of individual translation must have been soon limited by ecclesiastical use. The translations of separate books would be combined into a volume. Some recension of the popular text would be adopted in the public services of each Church, and this would naturally become the standard text of the district over which its influence extended[2]. Even if it be proved that new Latin Versions[3] agreeing more or less exactly with the African Version were made in Italy, Spain, and Gaul, as the congregations of Latin Christians increased in number and importance, that fact proves nothing against the existence of an African original. For if we call all these various Versions 'new,' we must limit the force of the word to a fresh revision and not to an independent translation of the whole. There is not the

Ut enim cuique primis fidei temporibus in manus venit codex græcus, et aliquantulum facultatis sibi utriusque linguæ habere videbatur, ausus est interpretari. This can only refer, I believe, to translation, and not to the interpolation of a translation already made. Lachmann's explanation of the passage (Pref. p. XIV.) is quite arbitrary, if I understand him. The Old Version arose out of private efforts, and was afterwards corrupted by private interpolations; but the two facts are to be kept distinct.

[1] Comp. *Retract.* I. 21. 3. His own study of the Bible was in an Italian and not in an African text.

Comp. Ziegler, *a. a. O.* 59.
[2] There is a clear trace of such an ecclesiastical recension in Aug. *de Cons. Evv.* II. 128 (LXVI.): Non autem ita se habet vel quod Joannes interponit, vel *codices Ecclesiastici interpretationis usitatæ.* He is speaking of the quotation (Zech. ix. 9) in Matt. xxi. 7, compared with John xii. 14, 15.
[3] The history of the English Versions may offer a parallel. The Version of Tyndale is related to those that followed it in the same way perhaps as the Vetus Latina to such recensions (or 'new Versions,' as they may be called) as the Itala.

slightest trace of the existence of *independent* Latin Versions; and the statements of Augustine are fully satisfied by supposing a series of ecclesiastical recensions of one fundamental text, which were in turn reproduced with variations and corrections in private Manuscripts. In this way there might well be said to be an 'infinite variety 'of Latin interpreters[1],' while a particular recension like the 'Itala' could be selected for general commendation[2].

Chap. iii.

The outline which I have roughly drawn is fully justified by the documents which exhibit the various forms of the Latin Version before the time of Jerome. They are all united by a certain generic character, and again subdivided by specific differences, which will be capable I believe of clear and accurate distinction as soon as the quotations of the early Latin Fathers shall have been carefully collated with existing Manuscripts[3]. The writings of Tertullian offer the true starting-point in the history of the Old Latin Text[4]. His manner of cita-

His evidence confirmed by existing documents.

---

[1] Aug. *de Doctr. Christ.* II. 16 (XI.). This was no less true of the Old than of the New Testament. Cf. Aug. *Epp.* LXXI. 6 (IV.); LXXXII. 35 (V.).

[2] Aug. *de Doctr. Christ.* II. 22 (XV.): In ipsis autem interpretationibus Itala cæteris præferatur; nam est verborum tenacior cum perspicuitate sententiæ. The last clause probably points to the character by which the *Itala* was distinguished from the *Africana*. If, as I believe, Tertullian's quotations exhibit the earliest form of the latter, 'clearness of expression' was certainly not one of its merits. The connexion of Augustine with Ambrose naturally explains his preference for the *Itala*. For the specific sense of *Itala* as equivalent geographically to *Langobardica*, see an interesting essay by Rev. J. Kenrick, *Theol. Rev.* July, 1874.

[3] A rough classification of Manuscripts is given in the *Dictionary of the Bible*, s. v. *Vulgate*.

[4] It will be evident I think that Tertullian has preserved the original text of the African version from a comparison of his readings in the following passages, taken from two books only, with those of the other authorities:

Acts iii. 19—21; *de Resurr. Carn.* 23 (IV. p. 255).
— xiii. 46; *de Fuga*, 6 (III. p. 183).
— xv. 28; *de Pudic.* 12 (IV. p. 394).
Rom. v. 3, 4; *c. Gnost.* 13 (II. p. 383).
— vi. 1—13; *de Pudic.* 17 (IV. p. 414).
— vi. 20—23; *de Resurr. Carn.* 47 (III. p. 303).
— vii. 2—6; *de Monog.* 13 (III. p. 163).

Chap. iii. tion is often loose, and he frequently exhibits various renderings of the same text, but even in such cases it is not difficult to determine the reading which he found in the current Version from that which he was himself inclined to substitute for it[1].

The history of the Vetus Latina cannot be traced further back than the time of Tertullian.

We have no means of tracing the history of the Version before the time of Tertullian; but its previous existence is attested by other contemporary evidence. The Latin translation of Irenæus was probably known to Tertullian[2]; and the Scriptural quotations which occur in it were evidently taken from some foreign source, and not rendered by the translator[3]. That this source was no other than a recension of the *Vetus Latina* appears from the coincidence of readings which it

Rom. viii. 35—39; *c. Gnost.* 13 (II. p. 383).
— xi. 33; *adv. Hermog.* 45 (II. p. 141).
— xii. 1; *de Resurr. Carn.* 47 (III. p. 306).
— xii. 10; *adv. Marc.* v. 14 (I. p. 439).
The remarkable readings in the other books are equally striking. The Version which Tertullian used was marked by the use of Greek words, as *machæra* (*adv. Marc.* IV. 29; *c. Gnost.* 13); *sophia* (*adv. Hermog.* 45); *choicus* (*de Resurr. Carn.* 49). Some peculiar words are of frequent occurrence, *e.g. tingo* (βαπτίζω)—*delinquentia* (ἁμαρτία).

[1] As a specimen of the text which Tertullian's quotations exhibit I have given his various readings in two chapters. The references are to the marginal pages of Semler's edition.
Matt. i. 1: *geniturae* (III 392) for *generationis*,
— — 16: *generavit* (*genuit*) Joseph virum Mariæ, *ex* (*de*) qua *nascitur* (*natus est*) Christus (III. 387).
— — 20: *nam* quod (quod *enim*)

...(*l. c.*).
Matt. i. 25: ecce virgo concipiet (so a b c) in utero et pariet filium (III. 381) cujus et *vocabitur* (Iren. 452 *vocabunt*) nomen Emmanuel...(II. 257).
Rom. i. 8: gratias agit Deo per *dominum nostrum* (*om.*) Jesum Christum (II. 261).
— — 16, 17: non enim *me pudet Evangelii* (*erubesco Evangelium*)...Judæo (*om.* primum with BG, al.) et Græco; *quia* justitia (justitia *enim*) ... (I. 431).
— — 18: *om. omnem, eorum.* (*l. c.*).
— — 20: invisibilia enim *ejus* (*ipsius*) *a conditione* (*creatura*) mundi *de factitamentis* (*per ea quae facta sunt*) intellecta *visuntur* (*conspiciuntur*) (IV. 250). Cf. II. 141: Invisibilia ejus ab *institutione* mundi *factis ejus* (so Hil.) conspiciuntur.

[2] Cf. Grabe, *Proleg. ad Iren.* II.
[3] (II. p. 36, ed. Stieren).
[3] Cf. Lachmann, *N. T.* Pref. p. x. f.

exhibits with the most trustworthy Manuscripts of the Version[1]. In other words the *Vetus Latina* is recognised in the first Latin literature of the Church: it can be traced back as far as the earliest records of Latin Christianity, and every circumstance connected with it indicates the most remote antiquity. But in the absence of further evidence we cannot attempt to fix more than the inferior limit of its date; and even that cannot be done with certainty, owing to the doubtful chronology of Tertullian's life. Briefly however the case may be stated thus. If the Version was, as has been seen, generally in use in Africa in his time, and had been in circulation sufficiently long to stereotype the meaning of particular phrases, we cannot allow less than twenty years for its publication and spread: and if we take into account its extension into Gaul and its reception there, that period will seem too short. Now the beginning of Tertullian's literary activity cannot be placed later than c. 190 A.D., and we shall thus obtain the date 170 A.D. as that be-

The inferior limit of its date.

---

[1] The relation of the text of Tertullian's quotations to that of the Latin Translation of Irenæus is very interesting, as may be seen from the following examples. The variations from the Vulgate (V) (Lachmann) are given in Italics:
Matt. i. 1. Generationis, Iren. 471, 505 (ed. Stieren): *Geniturœ*, Tert.
— — 20. Quod enim *habet in utero* (*ventre*), Iren. 505, 638: Quod in ea natum est, Tert.
— iii. 7, 8. Cf. Luke iii. 7: Progenies — fructum, Iren. 457: Genimina —— fructum (fructus, IV. 393), Tert. II. 95.
— — 12. *Palam habens* in manu ejus *ad emundandam* aream suam, Iren. 569: *Palam* (al. ventilabrum) in manu *portat ad purgandam*

aream suam, Tert. II. 4. Cf. III. 172.
Matt. iv. 3. Si *tu es* filius Dei, Iren. 576. Tert. II. 189. (As Vulg. Iren. 774; Tert. II. 199.)
— — 4. Non in pane *tantum* (c. tr.) *vivit*, Iren. 774; Non in solo pane (so a; tr. V.) *vivit*, Tert. II. 313.
— — 6. Iren. 775; Si *tu es* filius Dei, *dejice te hinc:* Scriptum est enim quod mandavit angelis suis (tr.) *super te, ut* te manibus suis *tollant, necubi* ad lapidem pedem tuum offendas (tr.), Tert. II. 189.
Tertullian and the Translator of Irenæus represent respectively, I believe, the original African and Gallic recensions of the *Vetus Latina*.

fore which the Version must have been made. How much more ancient it really is cannot yet be discovered. Not only is the character of the Version itself a proof of its extreme age; but the mutual relations of different parts of it shew that it was made originally by different hands; and if so, it is natural to conjecture that it was coeval with the introduction of Christianity into Africa, and the result of the spontaneous efforts of African Christians.

The Canon of the Vetus Latina coincided with that of the Muratorian Fragment.

The Canon of the Old Latin Version coincided I believe exactly with that of the Muratorian fragment. It contained the Four Gospels, the Acts, thirteen Epistles of St Paul, the three Catholic Epistles of St John, the first Epistle of St Peter, the Epistle of St Jude, and the Apocalypse. To these the Epistle to the Hebrews was added subsequently, but before the time of Tertullian, and without the author's name. There is no external evidence to shew that the Epistle of St James or the second Epistle of St Peter was included in the *Vetus Latina*. The earliest Latin testimonies to both of them, so far as I am aware, are those of Hilary, Jerome, and Rufinus in his Latin Version of Origen[1].

The Manuscripts of the Version of the Gospels,

The Manuscripts in which the Old Latin Version is found are few, but some of them are of great antiquity. In the Gospels Lachmann made use of four, of which one belongs to the fourth, and another to the fourth or fifth century[2]. To these Tischendorf has since added several others more or less perfect, ranging in date from the fifth to the eleventh century; and our own Libraries contain several other copies of great interest. The ver-

---

[1] It is impossible to lay any stress on the passage in Firmilian, ap. Cypr. *Ep.* LXXV. Even if Irenæus himself was acquainted with the Epistle of St James (*c. Hær.* V. I. 1), no argument can be built on the reference to prove the existence of the Epistle in a Latin Version.

[2] I have given a full list of these Manuscripts in the *Dictionary of the Bible*, s. v. *Vulgate*. A more complete list with the addition of recently discovered authorities is given by Ziegler, *a. a. O.* 107 ff.

sion of the Acts in addition to two (or three) fragmentary authorities, is contained in three Manuscripts of the sixth and eighth centuries, which however clearly represent originals of much earlier date. The Pauline Epistles are represented by several Manuscripts of the sixth and ninth centuries: but there is no Manuscript which gives the original form of the text of the Catholic Epistles. A fragment of the first Epistle of St John has been published[1]. The *Codex Bezæ* has alone preserved a fragment of the third Epistle of St John, which is found immediately before the Acts; and as it is expressly stated that the Acts follows, it appears that the Epistle of St Jude was either omitted or transposed. Two other early Manuscripts which contain respectively the Epistle of St James and fragments of the Epistle of St James and of the first Epistle of St Peter, give the text of the Italian recension and not of the *Vetus Latina*. There is no ante-Hieronymian Manuscript of the second Epistle of St Peter, of the Epistle of St Jude, or of the Apocalypse[2].

The evidence of Tertullian as to the Old Latin Canon may be taken to complete that which is derived directly from Manuscripts. His language leaves little doubt as to the position which the Epistle of St Jude and that to the Hebrews occupied in the African Church. The former he assigns directly to the Apostle Jude; and if so, its canonicity in the strictest sense was assured[3]. And since the reference is made without any limitation or expression of doubt, since it is indeed made in order to prove the authority of the Book of Enoch, as if the quotation by St Jude were decisive, it may be assumed that Tertullian found the book in the 'New Testament' of his Church.

[1] By L. Ziegler, 1876.
[2] Yet compare A. A. VanSittart, *Journal of Philology*, 1872, and Ziegler, s. III. n. 7.
[3] Tertull. *de Cult. Fœm.* c. 3.

Chap. iii.
the Epistle to the Hebrews,

On the other hand his single direct reference to the Epistle to the Hebrews leads to the opposite conclusion. After appealing to the testimony of the Apostles in support of his Montanist views of Christian discipline, and bringing forward passages from most of the Epistles of St Paul and from the Apocalypse and first Epistle of St John, he says[1], 'The discipline of the Apostles is 'thus clear and decisive. ... I wish however, though it be 'superfluous, to bring forward also the testimony of a 'companion of the Apostles, well fitted to confirm the 'discipline of his teachers on the point before us. For 'there is extant an Epistle to the Hebrews which bears 'the name of Barnabas. The writer has consequently 'adequate authority, as being one whom St Paul placed 'beside himself in the point of continence; and certainly 'the Epistle of Barnabas is more commonly received 'among the Churches than the Apocryphal Shepherd 'of adulterers.' He then quotes with very remarkable various readings[2] Hebr. vi. 4—8, and concludes by saying: 'One who had learnt from the Apostles, and had

1 Cor. ix. 6.

---

[1] Tertull. *de Pudic.* c. 20. See Part II. Chap. II. for the original, and p. 261.

[2] Tertull. *l. c.*: Impossibile est enim eos qui semel illuminati sunt (V. *tr.*) *et* donum coeleste gustaverunt (V. *tr.* gustav. *etiam* d. c), et *participaverunt* spiritum sanc*tum* (V. *participes sunt facti* sp. s.), *et* verbum dei *dulce* gustaverunt (V. *tr.* gustav. *nihilominus bonum* d. v.), *occidente jam aevo cum exciderint* (V. *virtutesque saeculi venturi et prolapsi sunt*) rursus *revocari in* poenitentiam (V. renovari r. *ad poen.*), *re*figentes cruci (V. *rursum* cruci figentes) *in semetipsos* (V. *sibi*met ipsis) filium dei et *dedecorantes* (V. *ostentui habentes*). Terra enim *quae bibit saepius* devenientem *in se humorem* (V. *saepe* ven. *super* se *bibens imbrem*) *et peperit* herbam *aptam his propter quos et* colitur (V. *generans* h. *opportunam illis a quibus* c.) benedictionem *dei consequitur* (V. *accipit* b. *a deo*); proferens autem spinas (V. + *ac tribulos*) reproba (V. + *est*) et male*dictioni* (V. male*dicto*) proxima, cujus *finis* in exustionem (V. c. *consummatio* in combustionem).

The number and character of the various readings perhaps justify the belief that the translation given was made by Tertullian himself. It is certainly independent of that preserved in the Vulgate and that in the Claromontane Manuscript.

It may be added that the quotations from the Epistle in Jerome's Latin Version of Origen's *Homilies on Isaiah*, e.g. *Hom.* vii. 1, are most remarkable.

'taught with the Apostles, knew this, that a second 'repentance was never promised by the Apostles to an 'adulterer or fornicator.' If the Epistle had formed part of the African Canon, it is impossible that Tertullian should have spoken thus: for the passage bore more directly on his argument than any other, and yet he introduces it only as a secondary testimony. The book was certainly received with respect; but still it could be compared with the Shepherd, which at least made no claim to Apostolicity. And it is by this mark that Tertullian distinguishes between the Epistle of St Jude and the Epistle [of Barnabas] to the Hebrews. The one was stamped with the mark of the Apostle: the other was neither that, nor yet supported by direct Apostolic sanction.

Tertullian quotes the Apocalypse very frequently, and ascribes it positively to St John, though he notices the objections of Marcion. The text of his quotations exhibits a general agreement with that of the Vulgate; and it is evident that the version of which he made use was not essentially different from that current in later times[1]. There is then every reason to believe that when he wrote, the book was generally circulated in Africa; and as the translation then received retained its hold on the Church, it is probable that it was supported by eccle-

---

[1] The following are some of the most important various readings:
Apoc. i. 6: *Regnum quoque nos et sacerdotes... de Exhort. Cast.* c. 7.
—— ii. 20—23; Jezebel quæ se prophæten dicit et *docet atque seducit* servos meos *ad* fornica*ndum* et *edendum* de idolothytis. Et largitus sum illi *spatium temporis* ut pœnitentiam *iniret, nec* vult *eam inire*

*nomine*fornicationis. Ecce *dabo* eam in lectum, et *mœchos ejus* cum *ipsa in* maximam *pressuram*, nisi pœnitentiam egerint *operum* ejus. *de Pudic.* c. 19.
Apoc. vii. 14: Hi sunt qui veniunt *ex illa pressura* magna, et laverunt *vestimentum* suum et *candidaverunt ipsum* in sanguine agni. *c. Gnost.* c. 12.

Chap. iii.

The general divisions of the New Testament according to Tertullian.

siastical use. In other words everything tends to shew that the Apocalypse was acknowledged in Africa from the earliest times as Canonical Scripture.

In two of his treatises Tertullian appears to give a general summary of the contents of the Latin New Testament of his time[1] In one[2] after quoting passages from the Old Testament he continues: 'This is enough 'from the *Prophetic Instrument:* I appeal now to the '*Gospels.*' Passages from St Matthew, St Luke, and St John follow in order. Afterwards comes a reference to the Apocalypse as contained in the *Instrument of John;* and then a general reference to the *Apostolic Instrument*[3]. The first quotations under this head are from the Acts, and then from most of the Epistles in the *Instrument [of Paul].* The omission of St Mark's Gospel shews that the enumeration is not complete; but the broad distinction of the different *Instruments* points to the existence of distinct groups of books, which may have been separately circulated. In another treatise, probably of a somewhat earlier date[4], Tertullian observes a similar arrangement. First he quotes the Gospels, or rather as he calls it 'the Gospel;' and then appeals to the *Apostolic Instrument* in which again he includes the Acts and the Epistles of St Paul. Afterwards 'not to dwell always on Paul' he notices the Apocalypse and first Epistle of St John, and speaks of a passage from the last chapter as 'the close of his 'writing.' And then it is, when he has noticed the 'dis-

1 John v. 16.

---

[1] This was first pointed out by Credner and Volkmar: Credner, *Geschichte d. N. T. Kanon,* pp. 171 ff.; 364 ff. Comp. Roensch, *Das N. T. Tertullian's,* 47 ff., 316 ff., 528 ff., 555 ff.

[2] *De Resurr. Carn.* cc. 33, 38, 39, 40. This treatise was written c. A.D. 207—10.

[3] c. 39: Resurrectionem Apostolica quoque Instrumenta testantur... Tunc et Apostolus [Paulus] per totum pene Instrumentum fidem hujus spei corroborare curavit. c. 40: Nihil autem mirum si et ex ipsius [Pauli] Instrumento captentur argumenta...

[4] *De Pudicitia,* cc. 6, 12, 19.

'cipline of the Apostles,' that he adds as it were over and above 'a testimony of a companion of the Apostles' taken from 'the Epistle of Barnabas to the Hebrews[1].' The absence of all mention of the first Epistle of St Peter is remarkable; and it has been supposed with some probability that he was not acquainted with it till the close of his life, and then only from the Greek.

Internal evidence is not wanting to confirm the conclusions drawn from other sources. The peculiarities of language in different parts of the Vulgate offer a most interesting field for inquiry. Jerome's revision may have done something to assimilate the style of the whole, yet sufficient traces of the original text remain to distinguish the hand of various translators. Indeed in the Epistles Jerome's work seems to have been most perfunctory, and to have consisted in little more than the selection and partial revision of some one copy. But however tempting it might be to prosecute the inquiry at length, it would be superfluous at present to do more than point out how far it bears on those books which we suppose not to have formed part of the original African Canon[2].

The second Epistle of St Peter offers the best opportunity for testing the worth of the investigation. If we suppose that it was at once received into the Canon like the first Epistle[3], it would in all probability have been

---

[1] c. 20: Disciplina igitur Apostolorum proprie quidem instruit...Volo tamen ex redundantia alicujus etiam comitis Apostolorum testimonium superducere... Comp. Pt. II. ch. II. and p. 246 f. Comp. H. Roensch, *Das N. T. Tertullian's*, 1871.

[2] F. P. Dutripon's *Concordantiæ Bibliorum Sacrorum Vulgatæ Editionis*, Parisiis, MDCCCLIII. (the dates on the title vary) appears to be complete and satisfactory so far as the Sixtine text is concerned, but it is impossible not to regret the absence of all reference to important various readings.

[3] It must however be noticed that the actual traces of the early use of 1 Peter in the Latin Churches are very scanty. There is not the least evidence to shew that its authority was ever disputed, but on the other hand it does not seem to have been much read. The Epistle is not mentioned in the Muratorian Canon, though no stress can be laid upon that fact. It is more strange that

translated by the same person, as seems to have been the case with the Gospel of St Luke and the Acts, though their connexion is less obvious; and while every allowance is made for the difference in style in the original Epistles, we must look for the same rendering of the same phrases. But when on the contrary it appears that the Latin text of the Epistle not only exhibits constant and remarkable differences from the text of other parts of the Vulgate, but also differs from the first Epistle in the rendering of words common to both: when it further appears that it differs no less clearly from the Epistle of St Jude (which was received in the African Church) in those parts which are almost identical in the Greek: then the supposition that it was admitted into the Canon at the same time with them becomes at once unnatural[1]. It is indeed possible that

[1] Tertullian quotes it only twice, and that too in writings which are more or less open to suspicion. In the treatise *c. Gnosticos* the references are long and explicit: c. 12: Cui potius [Christus] figuram vocis suæ declarasset quam cui effigiem gloriæ suæ mutavit, Petro, Jacobo, Johanni, et postea Paulo?...Petrus quidem ad Ponticos *quanta enim* inquit *gloria*, &c. 1 Peter ii. 20, 21; et rursus: 1 Peter iv. 12—16. Similarly there is a possible but tacit reference to 1 Peter ii. 22 in *c. Judæos* 10. The supposed reference in *de Exhort. Cast.* 1 will not hold; and that in *adv. Marc.* IV. 13 is most doubtful. The Epistle is constantly quoted by Cyprian, and under the title *ad Ponticos* in *Testim.* III. 36; and all the Catholic Epistles are contained in the *Claromontane Stichometry.* See App. D. No. XVI.

The following examples will confirm the statements made in the text:

I. Differences from the general renderings of the Vulgate:

κοινωνός, †*consors* (i. 4); ἐγκράτεια, †*abstinentia* (i. 6); πλεονάζειν, *superare* (i. 8); ἀργός, *vacuus* (*id.*); σπουδάζειν, *satagere* (i. 10; iii. 14; i. 15, *dare operam*); παρουσία, *præsentia* [of Christ] (i. 16); ἐπίγνωσις, *cognitio* (i. 2, 3, 8; ii. 20; cf. Rom. iii. 20?); ἀρχαῖος, ††*originalis* (ii. 5).

II. Differences from the renderings in 1 Peter:

πληθύνεσθαι, *adimpleri* (i. 2); *multiplicari* (1 Pet. i. 2). ἐπιθυμία, *concupiscentia* (i. 4; ii. 10; iii. 3); *desiderium* (1 Pet. i. 14; ii. 11; iv. 2, 3); so also 2 Pet. ii. 18. τηρεῖν, *reservare* (ii. 4, 9, 17; iii. 7); *conservare* (1 Pet. i. 4).

III. Differences from the translation of St Jude:

ἄλογος, ††*inrationabilis* (ii. 12); *mutus* (Jude 10). φθείρεσθαι, *perire* (*id.*); *corrumpi* (*id.*).

the two Epistles may have been received at the same time and yet have found different translators. The Epistle of St Jude and the second Epistle of St Peter may have been translated independently, and yet both have been admitted together into the Canon. But when the silence of Tertullian is viewed in connexion with the character of the version of the latter Epistle, the natural conclusion is that in his time it was as yet untranslated. The two lines of evidence mutually support each other.

of St James,

The translation of St James's Epistle has several peculiar renderings; but in this case no more can be said with confidence than that it was the work of a special translator. One or two words indeed appear to me to indicate that it was made later than the translations of the acknowledged books, but they cannot be urged as conclusive[1].

of the Epistle to the Hebrews.

The Latin text of the Epistle to the Hebrews exhibits the most remarkable phenomena. As it stands in the Vulgate it is marked by numerous singularities of language and inaccuracies of translation; but the readings of the Claromontane Manuscript are most in-

---

συνευωχεῖσθαι, *luxuriare vobiscum* (13); †† *convivari* (12).
δόξαι, *sectæ* (10); *majestas* (8).
ὁ ζόφος τοῦ σκότους, *caligo tenebrarum* (17); *procella tenebrarum* (13).
Words marked † occur nowhere else in the New Testament Vulgate: those marked †† occur nowhere else in the whole Vulgate.

[1] The following peculiarities may be noticed in the version of St James:
ἁπλῶς, †† *affluenter* (i. 5); ἁπλότης, *simplicitas* (2 Cor. viii. 2; ix. 11, &c.)
οἴεσθαι, *æstimare* (i. 7); *existimare* (Phil. i. 17).
ἀγαπητοί, *dilecti, dilectissimi* (i. 16, 19; ii. 5; so Hebr. vi. 9;

1 Cor. xv. 58); elsewhere *carissimi* (twenty times).
ἀτιμάζειν, † *exhonorare* (ii. 6); elsewhere *inhonorare, contumelia afficere.*
σώζειν, *salvare* (i. 21; v. 15, 20); generally *salvum facere, salvus esse* and *fieri.*
πληροῦν, *supplere* (ii. 23): elsewhere *implere, adimplere.*
ἁγνός, *pudicus* (iii. 17, so Phil. iv. 8): elsewhere *castus,* and once *sanctus.*
ἀποτίθεσθαι, *abjicere* (i. 21, so Rom. xiii. 12); elsewhere *deponere* (six times).
μακαρίζω, † *beatifico* (v. 11).
πολεμεῖν, † *belligero* (iv. 2).
οἰκτίρμων, † *miserator* (v. 11).

Chap. iii.

teresting and important. Sometimes the translator in his anxiety to preserve the letter of the original employs words of no authority: sometimes he adapts the Latin to the Greek form: sometimes he paraphrases a participial sentence to avoid the ambiguity of a literal rendering: and again sometimes he entirely perverts the meaning of the author by neglecting the secondary meanings of Greek words[1]. The translation was evidently made at a very early period; but it was not made by any of those whose work can be traced in other parts of the New Testament, and apparently it was not submitted to that revision which necessarily attended the habitual use of Scripture in the services of the Church. The Claromontane text of the Epistle to the Hebrews represents I believe more completely than any other Manuscript the simplest form of the *Vetus Latina;* but from the very fact that the text of this Epistle exhibits more marked peculiarities than are found in any of the Pauline Epistles, it follows that it occupies a peculiar position. In other words, internal evidence, as far as it reaches, confirms the belief that the Epistle to the Hebrews, though known in Africa as early perhaps as any other book of the New Testament, was not admitted at first into the African Canon. 'The custom of the Latins,' as Jerome said even in his time, 'received it not[2].'

The importance of the evidence of

Only a few words are needed to sum up the testimony of these most ancient Versions to our Canon of

---

[1] The Latin text of the Manuscript is almost incredibly corrupt, from the ignorance of the transcriber, who accommodated the terminations of the words, and often the words themselves, to his elementary conceptions of grammar. Still a reference to the readings in the following passages will justify the statements which I have made: i. 6, 10, 14; ii. 1—3, 15, 18; iii. 1; iv. 1, 3, 13; v. 11; vi. 8, 16; vii. 18; x. 33.

[2] It may be added that in the *Claromontane Stichometry* it is still called the *Epistle of Barnabas.* There cannot, I think, be any doubt as to the identification. The number of στίχοι serve to identify the book. See App. D. No. xx.

the New Testament. Their voice is one to which we cannot refuse to listen. They give the testimony of Churches, and not of individuals. They are sanctioned by public use, and not only supported by private criticism. Combined with the original Greek they represent the New Testament Scriptures as they were read throughout the whole of Christendom towards the close of the second century. Even to the present day they have maintained their place in the services of a vast majority of Christians, though the languages in which they were written only live now so far as they have supplied the materials for the construction of later dialects. They furnish a proof of the authority of the books which they contain, wide-spread, continuous, reaching to the utmost verge of our historic records. Their real weight is even greater than this; for when history first speaks of them it speaks as of that which was recognised as a heritage from an earlier period, which cannot have been long after the days of the Apostles.

the Early Versions.

Both Canons however are imperfect; but their very imperfection is not without its lesson. The Western Church has indeed as we believe under the guidance of Providence completed the sum of her treasures; but the East has clung hitherto to its earliest decision. Individual writers have accepted the full Canon of the West; but even Ephraem Syrus failed to influence the judgment of his Church. And can this element of fixity be without its influence on our estimate of the basis of the Syrian Canon? Can that which was guarded so jealously have been made without care? Can that which was received without hesitation by Churches which differed on grave doctrines have been formed originally without the sanction of some power from which it was felt that there was no appeal? The Canon fails in com-

The results of the imperfection of the Syrian Canon.

pleteness, but that is its single error. Succeeding ages registered their belief in the exclusive originative power of the first age, when they refused to change what that had determined. So far they witnessed to a great truth; but in practice that truth can only be realized by a perfect induction. And their error arose not from the principle of conservatism on which it rested, but from the imperfect data by which the sum of Apostolic teaching was determined.

The combined testimony of the two Versions.

To obtain a complete idea of the judgment of the Church we must combine the two Canons; and then it will be found that of the books which we receive one only, the second Epistle of St Peter, wants the earliest public sanction of ecclesiastical use as an Apostolic work. In other words, by enlarging our view so as to comprehend the whole of Christendom and unite the different lines of Apostolic tradition, we obtain with one exception a perfect New Testament, without the admixture of any foreign element. The testimony of Churches confirms and illustrates the testimony of Christians. There is but one difference. Individual writers vary in the degree of respect which they shew to Apocryphal writings, and the same is true also in a less degree of single Churches; but the voice of the Catholic Church definitely and unhesitatingly excluded them from the Canon. And in this decision as to the narrow limits which they fixed to the Canon, it appears that they were guided by local and direct knowledge. The Epistle to the Hebrews and the Epistle of St James were at once received in the Churches to which they were specially directed; and external circumstances help us to explain more exactly the facts of their history. The Epistle of St James was not only distinctly addressed to Jews, but as it seems was also written in Palestine. It cannot there-

An explanation of their incompleteness.

fore be surprising that the Latin Churches were for some time ignorant of its existence. The Epistle to the Hebrews on the contrary was probably written from Italy, though it was destined especially for Hebrew converts. And thus the letter was known in the Latin Churches, though they hesitated to admit it into the Canon, believing that it was not written by the hand of St Paul. The Apocalypse again was acknowledged from the earliest time in the scene of St John's labours : and the very indefiniteness of the addresses of the Epistle of St Jude and of the second Epistle of St Peter may have tended to retard and limit their spread.

These considerations however belong to another place; but it is in this way, by combination with collateral evidence internal and external, that the earliest Versions are proved to occupy an important position in the history of the Canon. A fuller investigation would I believe establish many interesting results, especially if pursued with a constant reference to the present state of the Greek text; but for our immediate purpose the general outline which has been given is sufficiently accurate and comprehensive. It is enough to shew that the Versions exhibit a Canon practically—that they sanction no Apocryphal book—that they speak with the voice of early Christendom—that they go back to a period so remote as to precede all historic records of the Churches in which they were used.

CHAPTER IV.

THE EARLY HERETICS.

Non periclitor dicere ipsas quoque Scripturas sic esse ex Dei voluntate dispositas ut hæreticis materias subministrarent.
TERTULLIANUS.

<small>Chap. iv.
The importance of the testimony of heretics to the Canon.</small>

THE New Testament recognises the existence of parties and heresies in the Christian society from its first origin; and conversely the earliest false teachers witness more or less clearly to the existence and reception of our Canonical Books. The authority of the collection of the Christian Scriptures rests necessarily on other proof, but still the acknowledgment of their authenticity in detail by conflicting sects confirms with independent weight the results which we have already obtained. It cannot be supposed that those who cast aside the teaching of the Church on other points would have been willing to uphold its judgment on Holy Scripture unless it had been supported by competent evidence. Custom and reverence might mould the belief of those within the Catholic communion, but separatists left themselves no positive ground for the reception of the Apostolic books but the testimony of history.

<small>*No attacks were made on the Canon.*</small>

Still further: even negatively the history of the ante-Nicene heresies establishes our general conclusions.

The first three centuries were marked by long and resolute struggles within and without the Church. Almost every point in the Christian Creed was canvassed and denied in turn. The power of Judaism, strong in widespread influence and sensuous attractions, first sought to confine Christianity within its own sphere, and then to embody itself in the new faith. The spirit of Gnosticism, keen, restless, and self-confident, seems to have exhausted every combination of Christianity and philosophy. Mani announced himself as divinely commissioned to reform and reinstate the whole fabric of *the faith once* (ἅπαξ) *delivered to the saints*. And still it cannot be shewn that the Canon of 'acknowledged' books was ever assailed on historic grounds up to the period of its final recognition. Different books, or classes of books, were rejected from time to time, but no attempt was made to justify the measure by outward testimony. A partial view of Christianity was substituted for its complete form, and the Scriptures were judged by an arbitrary standard of doctrine. The new systems were not based on any historical reconstruction of the Canon, but the contents of the Canon were limited by subjective systems of Christianity.

of the New Testament on historical grounds by early heretics.

This important fact did not escape the notice of the champions of Catholic truth. Irenæus, Tertullian, Origen, and later writers, insist much and earnestly on the fact that heretics sought to maintain their own doctrines from the Canonical books, fulfilling the very prophecy therein contained that *there must needs be heresies*. ' So ' great is the surety of the Gospels, that even the very ' heretics bear witness to them; so that each one of them ' taking the Gospels as his starting-point endeavours ' thereby to maintain his own teaching[1].' 'They pro-

The Fathers insist on this fact.

1 Cor. xi. 19.

---
[1] Iren. *c. Hær.* III. 11. 7.

'fess,' says Tertullian, 'to appeal to the Scriptures: 'they urge arguments from the Scriptures:' and then he adds indignantly, 'as if they could draw arguments 'about matters of faith from any other source than the 'records of faith[1].'

The testimony of heretics however is partial and yet

It has however been already noticed that they did not all accept the whole Canon. How far they really used our Scriptures as authoritative will appear in the course of our inquiry; at present I only call attention to the general truth that they recognised an authoritative written word, which either wholly or in part coincided with our own. And the very fact that they did make choice of certain books whereon to rest their teaching shews that the use of Scripture was not a mere concession to their opponents, but the expression of their own belief.

We have seen that even in the Catholic Church various tendencies and lines of belief are reflected in the special use made by different Fathers of groups of Apostolic writings. In heretical books the same result is found in an exaggerated form. In this as in everything else heresy is special, limited, partial, where the Church is general, wide, catholic. Differences which are exalted in the one into party characteristics and tests of communion or division are tolerated in the other as imperfect and isolated growths or possible springs of some future and beneficent development. The one will define everything sharply now, whether in criticism or dogma or discipline: the other is content to know that the end is not yet, and to believe that in the broad range of truth 'God fulfils Himself in many ways.'

---

[1] *De Præscr. Hær.* c. 14: Sed ipsi [non] possent de rebus fidei nisi ex de scripturis agunt et de scripturis litteris fidei. Cf. Lardner's *History* suadent! Aliunde scilicet suadere *of Heretics*, Bk. I. § 10.

But apart from this essential difference in the treatment of the whole subject, the character of the testimony of heretical writers to the books of the New Testament is strictly analogous to that of the Fathers in its progressive development. In the first age, an oral Gospel, so to speak, was everywhere current; and all who assumed the name of Christ sought to establish their doctrine by His traditional teaching. Controversies were conducted by arguments from the Old Testament Scriptures, or by appeals to general principles and known facts. The conception of a definite New Testament was wholly foreign to the time. And while it has been seen how little can be found in the scanty writings of the first age to prove the peculiar authority of the Gospels and the Epistles, those who seceded from the company of the Apostles necessarily refused to be ruled by their opinions.

Chap. iv. progressive.

§ 1. *The Heretical Teachers of the Apostolic Age. Simon Magus—Menander—Cerinthus.*

The earliest group of heretical teachers exhibits in striking contrast the two antagonistic principles of religious error. Mysticism on the one hand and Legalism on the other appear in clear conflict. By both the Work and Person of Christ are disparaged and set aside. In Simon Magus and Menander we may see the embodiment of the antichristian element of the Gentile world[1]: in Cerinthus the embodiment of the antichristian element of Judaism. Catholic truth seems to be the only explanation of their simultaneous appearance.

The fundamental antagonism in heresy from the first.

[1] It would be interesting to inquire how far the magical arts universally attributed to Simon and his followers admit of a physical explanation. In his school, if anywhere, we should look for an advanced knowledge of Nature.

274 THE EARLY HERETICS. [PART

Simon Magus invested with a representative character.

It has been shewn that among the Apostolic Fathers one, Clement of Rome, was invested by tradition with representative attributes analogous in a certain degree to his real character, by which he was raised to heroic proportions. In like manner among the false teachers of the age Simon Magus a Samaritan of Gittæ is invested by the common consent of all early writers with mysterious importance as the great heresiarch, the open enemy of the Apostles, inspired as it were by the Spirit of Evil to countermine the work of the Saviour, and to found a school of error in opposition to the Church of God. The story of his life has undoubtedly received many apocryphal embellishments; but, as in the case of Clement, it cannot but be that his acts and teaching offered some salient points to which they could fitly be attached. Till the recent discovery of the work 'against Heresies[1],' the history and doctrine of Simon Magus were commonly disregarded as being inextricably involved in fable; but there at length some surer ground is gained. While giving a general outline of his principles, Hippolytus has preserved several quotations from the *Great Announcement*[2], which was published under his name, and contained an account of the revelation with which he professed to be entrusted. The work itself cannot have been written by him, but it was probably compiled from his oral teaching by one of his

The witness to the books of the New Testament in the Great Announcement.

[1] [Origenis] *Philosophumena, sive omnium hæresium refutatio, e Cod. Par. ed.* E. Miller, Oxon. MDCCCLI. The work cannot be Origen's; and scholars generally agree to assign it to Hippolytus Bishop of Portus near Rome. I shall therefore quote it under his name; for though I think that the question of its authorship is not yet settled beyond all doubt, internal evidence proves that it must have been written by a contemporary of Hippolytus at Rome, if not by Hippolytus himself. Döllinger has presented the arguments in support of Hippolytus' claims in the most satisfactory form.

[2] Ἀπόφασις, Ἀπόφασις μεγάλη. [Hipp.] *adv. Hær.* VI. 9 sqq. 'Announcement' hardly conveys the force of the original word, which implies an official or authoritative declaration.

immediate followers[1]: at any rate the language of Hippolytus shews that in his time it was acknowledged as an authentic summary of the Simonian doctrine[2]. In the fragments which remain there are coincidences with words recorded in the Gospel of St Matthew[3], and probably with a passage in the Gospel of St John[4]. Reference is also made to the first Epistle to the Corinthians, in terms which prove that it was placed by the author on the same footing as the books of the Old Testament[5].

Chap. iv.

Not only did the Simonians make use of the Canonical books, but they ascribed the forgeries current among them to 'Christ and his disciples, in order to 'deceive those who loved Christ and his servants[6].' They recognised not only some of the elements of the New Testament, but also the principle on which it was formed. The writings of the Apostles were acknowledged to have a peculiar weight: Christians sought in them the confirmation of the teaching which they heard,

The Simonians recognised the authority of the Apostles.

---

[1] Bunsen suggests Menander (I. 54), apparently without any authority.
[2] He quotes it constantly with the words λέγει δὲ ὁ Σίμων, φησί.
[3] [Hipp.] *adv. Hær.* VI. 16 = Matt. iii. 10. The various readings are singular: ἐγγὺς γάρ που, φησίν, ἡ ἀξίνη παρὰ τὰς ῥίζας τοῦ δένδρου κ.τ.λ. Simon's description of Helen ([Hipp.] *adv. Hær.* VI. 19) as 'the strayed sheep' (τὸ πρόβατον τὸ πεπλανημένον) is an evident allusion to the parable in Luke xv. The substitution of πεπλανημένον for ἀπολωλός is to be noticed. Cf. Matt. xviii. 12, 13 (τὸ πλανώμενον...τοῖς μὴ πεπλανημένοις); Iren. *c. Hær.* I. 8. 4. Bunsen supposes that he combined the parable with the healing of the Syro-Phœnician's daughter. Cf. Uhlhorn, *Die Homilien*, u. s. w. p. 296.
[4] *id.* VI. 9: οἰκητήριον δὲ λέγει εἶναι τὸν ἄνθρωπον τοῦτον τὸν ἐξ αἱμάτων γεγενημένον (John i. 13) καὶ κατοικεῖν ἐν αὐτῷ τὴν ἀπέραντον δύναμιν ἣν ῥίζαν εἶναι τῶν ὅλων φησίν.
Bunsen (I. pp. 49, 55) considers the statement that Simon manifested himself to the Samaritans as the Father ([Hipp.] *adv. Hær.* VI. 19) to be a reference to John iv. 21—23.
[5] *adv. Hær.* VI. 13: τοῦτο ἐστί, φησί, τὸ εἰρημένον "Ἵνα μὴ σὺν τῷ κόσμῳ κατακριθῶμεν (1 Cor. xi. 32).
[6] *Constit. Apost.* VI. 16. 1: Οἴδαμεν γὰρ ὅτι οἱ περὶ Σίμωνα καὶ Κλεόβιον Ἰώδη συντάξαντες βιβλία ἐπ' ὀνόματι Χριστοῦ καὶ τῶν μαθητῶν αὐτοῦ περιφέρουσιν εἰς ἀπάτην ὑμῶν τῶν πεφιληκότων Χριστὸν καὶ ἡμᾶς τοὺς αὐτοῦ δούλους.

and the seeming authority of their sanction gained acceptance for that which was otherwise rejected.

Menander.

Menander, the scholar and fellow-countryman of Simon Magus, is said to have repeated and advanced his master's teaching. His doctrine of the Resurrection, in which he taught that those who 'were baptized into 'him died no more but continued to live in immortal 'youth[1],' reminds us of the error of *Hymenæus and Philetus who said that the Resurrection was past already;* otherwise I am not aware that anything which is known of his system points directly to the Scriptures.

Cerinthus.

His relation to Simon Magus.

While Simon Magus represents the intellectual and rationalistic element of Gnosticism, Cerinthus represents it under a ceremonial and partially Judaizing form. The one was a Samaritan, the natural enemy of Judaism; the other was 'trained in the teaching of the Egyptians[2],' among whom the interpretation of the Law had become a science. The traditional opponent of the one was St Peter; of the other St John; and this antagonism admirably expresses their relative position. St John however was not the only Apostle with whom Cerinthus came into conflict. Epiphanius[3] makes him one of those who headed the extreme Jewish party in their attacks on St Peter for eating with Gentiles, and on St Paul for polluting the temple. The statement in itself is plausible: an excessive devotion to the Law was a natural preparation for mere material views of Christianity.

His acquaintance with the New Testament.

Cerinthus was evidently acquainted with the substance of the Gospel history. He must have known the orthodox accounts of the parentage of our Lord.

---

[1] Iren. *c. Hær.* I. 23. 5: Resurrectionem enim per id quod est in eum baptisma accipere ejus discipulos, et ultra non posse mori, sed perseverare non senescentes et immortales.
[2] [Hipp.] *adv. Hær.* VII. 33.
[3] Epiph. *Hær.* XXVIII. 2—4.

He was familiar with the details of His Baptism, of His preaching, of His Miracles, of His death, and of His Resurrection[1]. 'The Cerinthians,' Epiphanius says, 'make use of St Matthew's Gospel[2] as the Ebionites do, 'on account of the human genealogy, though their copy 'is not entire....The Apostle Paul they entirely reject, 'on account of his opposition to circumcision.' But the chief importance of Cerinthus is in relation to St John. It has been said that he was the author of the Apocalypse, and even of all the books attributed to the Apostle. And on the other hand it is the popular belief that the fourth Gospel was written to refute his errors. The coincidence is singular, and it is necessary to consider on what grounds these assertions have been made.

The transition from Judaizing views to Chiliasm is very simple, and Cerinthus appears to have entertained Chiliastic opinions of the most extreme form. In the account which Eusebius gives of him this fact is dwelt upon as if it were the characteristic of his system. In the earliest ages of the Church the language of Chiliasm at least was generally current; but from the time of Origen it fell into discredit from the gross extravagances which it had occasioned. The reaction itself became extreme; and imagery in itself essentially scriptural

Chap. iv.

How the Apocalypse came to be attributed to him.

---

[1] [Hipp.] adv. Hær. l. c. Epiph. l. c. What Epiphanius says (Hær. XXVIII. 6) of Cerinthus' teaching Χριστὸν πεπονθέναι καὶ ἐσταυρῶσθαι μήπω δὲ ἐγηγέρθαι, μέλλειν δὲ ἀνίστασθαι ὅταν ἡ καθόλου γένηται νεκρῶν ἀνάστασις, is to be taken as describing Epiphanius' deductions from his teaching, and not as giving Cerinthus' dogmas.

[2] Epiph. Hær. XXVIII. 5: Χρῶνται γὰρ τῷ κατὰ Ματθαῖον εὐαγγελίῳ ἀπὸ μέρους καὶ οὐχὶ ὅλῳ διὰ τὴν γενεαλογίαν τὴν ἔνσαρκον. It is not known in what the mutilation of the Gospel consisted. But that he did not remove the whole of the first two chapters, as the Ebionites did, appears again from what Epiphanius says, Hær. XXX. 14: ὁ μὲν γὰρ Κήρινθος καὶ Καρποκρᾶς τῷ αὐτῷ χρώμενοι δῆθεν παρ' αὐτοῖς εὐαγγελίῳ ἀπὸ τῆς ἀρχῆς τοῦ κατὰ Ματθαῖον εὐαγγελίου διὰ τῆς γενεαλογίας βούλονται παριστᾶν ἐκ σπέρματος Ἰωσὴφ καὶ Μαρίας εἶναι τὸν Χριστόν.

and pure was confounded with the glosses by which it had been interpreted. The Apocalypse, though supported by the clearest early testimony, was now viewed with distrust. 'Some said that it was unintelligible 'and unconnected: that its title was false, for that it was 'not the work of John: that that was certainly not a 'revelation which was enwrapped in a gross and thick 'veil of ignorance[1].' The arguments are purely subjective and internal. There is not a hint of any historical evidence for the opinion. The doctrine of the book was false, and consequently it could not be Apostolic. It became then necessary to assign it to a new author. Cerinthus it appears had written revelations, and assumed the Apostolic style[2]: it is possible that he had directly imitated St John: he was distinguished for Chiliasm ; and thus the conclusion was prepared, that he was the writer of the Apocalypse, and that he had ascribed it to St John from the desire 'to affix a name ' of credit to his forgery;' to continue the quotation, 'for 'this was the principle of his teaching, that the king-'dom of Christ would be earthly, and consist in those 'things which he himself desired, being a man devoted 'to sensual enjoyments and wholly carnal.' The Chiliasm of Cerinthus is here distinctly brought forward as the ground of what can only be considered as a conjecture; and Dionysius, who gives the history of the conjecture at length, was unwilling to accept it as true.

That the ascription of the Apocalypse to Cerinthus was in fact a mere arbitrary hypothesis resting on doc-

---

[1] Dionys. Alex. ap. Euseb. *H. E.* III. 28, VII. 25.
[2] Theodor. *Fab. Hæret.* II. 3 (ap. Routh, II. 139). The famous fragment of Caius is ambiguous; ap. Euseb. *H. E.* III. 28. I may express my decided belief that Caius is not speaking of the Apocalypse of St John, but of books written by Cerinthus in imitation of it. The theology of the Apocalypse is wholly inconsistent with what we know of Cerinthus' views on the Person of Christ.

trinal grounds is further shewn by the extension which was afterwards given to it. A body of men whom Epiphanius calls by a convenient name, which he himself invented, Alogi, attributed not only the Apocalypse but also the Gospel and the writings of St John generally to Cerinthus[1] and this purely on internal grounds. It was found difficult to reconcile the fourth Gospel with the Synoptists, and forthwith it was pronounced an Apocryphal book. Some theory was necessary to account for its origin, and as one of the Apostle's writings had been already assigned to Cerinthus, this was placed in the same category, in spite of its doctrinal character. The Epistles could not be separated from the Gospel; and so this early essay in criticism was completed. One important deduction follows from it. It may fairly be concluded that the early date of the writings which bear St John's name was acknowledged; and thus when his authorship was set aside they were assigned to a contemporary of the Apostle, and not to any later writer.

The other works of St John also attributed to Cerinthus.

Nothing however can be more truly opposite to Cerinthianism than the theology of St John. The character of his Gospel was evidently influenced by prevailing errors; and though it is unnecessary to degrade it into a mere controversial work, it is impossible not to feel that it was written to satisfy some pressing want of the age, to meet some false philosophy which had already begun to fashion a peculiar dialect, and to offer a solution by the help of Christian ideas of some of the great problems of humanity. Cerinthus upheld a ceremonial system,

St John truly antagonistic to Cerinthianism.

---

[1] Epiph. *Hær.* LI. 3. The history of the sect (if it can be so called) is very obscure, but we have only to do with the fact, which is sufficiently supported by Epiphanius' authority. It is very probable that under this title Epiphanius simply wished to include all those who rejected St John's writings. See Credner [Volkmar], *Geschichte d. N. T. Kanon*, p. 185, anm.

and taught only a temporary union of God's Spirit with man. St John proclaimed that Judaism had passed away, and set forth clearly the manifestation of the Eternal Word in His historic Incarnation no less than in His union with the true believer. The teaching of St John is doubtless far deeper and wider than was needed to meet the errors of Cerinthus, but it has a natural connexion with the period in which he lived.

The importance of the teaching of these first heretics generally in relation to the New Testament.

This relation of the first heretics to the Apostles is of the utmost importance. Like the early Fathers, they witness to Catholic Truth rather than to the Catholic Scriptures: they exhibit the correlative errors as the Fathers embodied its constituent parts. The real personality of Simon Magus and Cerinthus is raised beyond all reasonable doubt. The general character of their doctrine can be determined with certainty. And when we find the marks of activity of speculation, depth of thought, and variety of judgment in false teachers, can it appear wonderful that in the writings of the Apostles there are analogous differences? If the books of the New Testament stood alone, we might marvel at their fulness and diversity; but when it is found that their characteristic differences are not only stereotyped in Catholic doctrine but implied in contemporary heresies, they fall as it were into a natural historic position. They are felt to belong to that Apostolic age in which every power of man seems to have been quickened with some spiritual energy. No long interval of time was then needed for the gradual evolution of the various forms of teaching which they preserve. Error sprung up with a titanic growth: truth came down full-formed from heaven to conquer it.

They form a link between the heresies

But when it is said that the perfect principles of Gnosticism may be detected in these earliest heretics, I do not by any means ignore the vast developments which they afterwards received. In one respect the teaching of the Simonians and Cerinthians furnishes an important link between Catholic doctrine and the later Gnosticism of Valentinus or Marcion. In these systems the phenomena of the world are explained by the assumption of a Dualism—more or less complete—of a fundamental opposition between powers of good and evil. The creation was removed farther and farther from God, till at last it was ascribed to His enemy. The cosmogony of Simon Magus[1] and of Cerinthus[2] occupies a mean position. In this the world is represented as the work of Angels, themselves the offspring of God, who were also the authors of the Jewish Law and the inspirers of the Prophets. Against such a form of Gnosticism the Epistle to the Hebrews and the Introduction to St John's Gospel speak with divine power; but of the later developments there is not a trace in the New Testament. If however we suppose that any parts of it, the Pastoral Epistles for instance, or the Epistle of St Jude, had been written after the Apostolic age, is it possible that no word should have betrayed a knowledge of the existence of such theories, when error was being combated with an intense feeling of its present danger? The books which claim to be Apostolic are by their very character the produce of the Apostolic age. Exactly in proportion as we take into account the whole

Chap. iv. alluded to in the Scriptures and later speculations.

[1] There is some confusion in the account given by Hippolytus. In the first part, where he refers to the *Great Announcement*, the cosmogony of Simon appears to be expressed in a physical form. Fire is the fundamental element of the universe. This I believe to be the original form of his theory. Afterwards in a passage nearly identical with the account of Irenæus we read of a creation by Angels, of an arbitrary Moral Law, of the secondary inspiration of the Prophets (*adv. Hær.* VI. 19: Iren. *c. Hær.* I. 23). Uhlhorn, wrongly I think, takes the opposite view of the relative dates of the two systems (*a. a. O.* 293).

[2] Epiph. *Hær.* XXVIII. 1, 2.

history of Christianity in its developments within and without the Church, we find more surely that it implies a complete New Testament as its foundation; that at no subsequent period was there an opportunity for the forgery of writings which are seen to be the sources and not the results of different systems of speculation.

§ 2. *The Ophites and Ebionites.*

The mixture of Christianity with earlier systems.

While Simon Magus appeared in some measure as the author of an organised counterfeit of Christianity, claiming to be himself an Incarnation of the Deity, and opposing magical powers to the Apostolic miracles, Christians elsewhere came into contact with existing speculative schools, and often survived the encounter only to become ranged with their former enemies. In this way sects arose which were not called by the name of any special founder but by some general title. Probably one of the earliest of these was the sect of the Naasseni, Ophites, or Serpent-worshippers. Hippolytus, professing to follow the order of time, places them in the first rank; and it is evident that their system was not a mere corruption of Christianity, but rather a more ancient creed into which some Christian ideas were infused. Consistently with this view Origen[1] speaks of Ophites who required all who entered their society to blaspheme Christ; the bitterness of which law may be best explained if we suppose that it was first framed against some Christianizing members of their own body.

The Ophites.

The Ophites described by Hippolytus.

The Christian Ophites whom Hippolytus describes appear to have been the first who assumed the title of Gnostics[2]. They professed to derive their doctrines

---

[1] *c. Cels.* VI. 28. σκοντες μόνοι τὰ βάθη γινώσκειν. Cf.
[2] *adv. Hær.* V. 6: μετὰ δὲ ταῦτα 1 Cor. ii. 10; Apoc. ii. 24. ἐπεκάλεσαν ἑαυτοὺς Γνωστικούς, φά-

through Mariamne from James the Lord's brother[1]; and thus the authorities which he quotes may be supposed to date from the age next succeeding that of the Apostles. Their whole system shews an intimate familiarity with the language of the New Testament Scriptures. The passages given from their books[2] contain clear references to the Gospels of St Matthew, St Luke, and St John; to the Epistles of St Paul to the Romans, the Corinthians (both Epistles), the Ephesians, and the Galatians; and probably to the Epistle to the Hebrews and the Apocalypse[3]. They made use also of the Gospel according to the Egyptians and of the Gospel of St Thomas[4].

Their testimony to the New Testament.

The Peratici and the Sethiani are placed by Hippolytus in close connexion with the Ophites. The passages of the esoteric doctrine (ἀπόρρητα μυστήρια) of the Peratici which he brings to light contain obvious references to the Gospel of St John, the first Epistle to the Corinth-

The Peratici *and* Sethiani.

---

[1] adv. Hær. v. 7.
[2] The description of their opinions is constantly prefaced by the words φασίν or φησί.
[3] The following list of references, which might be increased, will shew to what extent the Ophites made use of the New Testament Scriptures.
St Matthew xiii. 33, 44, [Hipp.] adv. Hær. p. 108; xiii. 3 sqq., p. 113; xxiii. 27, τάφοι ἐστὲ κεκονιαμένοι (cf. supr. p. 147), p. 111; vii. 21, p. 112; xxi. 31, p. 112; iii. 10, p. 113; vii. 6, p. 114; vii. 14, 13, p. 116.
St Luke xvii. 21, pp. 100, 108; xvii. 4, p. 102 (?); xviii. 19 + Matt. v. 45, p. 102, xi. 33, p. 103.
St John iv. 10, pp. 100, 121; x. 34 + Luke vi. 35, (Ps. lxxxii. 6) p. 106; iii. 6, p. 106; i. 3, 4, as Lachm. p. 107; ii. 1—12, p. 108; vi. 53 + xiii. 33; *id.*+ Matt. xx. 23, p. 109; v. 37, p. 109; x. 9, p. 111; iv. 21, 23, p. 117; vi. 44, p. 112; ix. 1, i. 9, p. 121.
Romans i. 20—23, &c. p. 99 (as St Paul's).
I Cor. ii. 13, 14, p. 112; x. 11, p. 113.
2 Cor. xii. 2, 4, p. 112.
Gal. iii. 28, &c. p. 92.
Eph. iii. 15, pp. 97, 105; v. 14, p. 104; iii. 5, p. 107; ii. 17, p. 111.
Heb. v. 11, p. 97.
Apoc. ii. 27, p. 104.
[4] Their use of the 'Gospel entitled according to the Egyptians' (p. 98) and that 'entitled according to Thomas' (p. 101) does not prove that they ascribed to those books Canonical authority. Generally indeed the references to the Gospels are to our Lord's words, and I believe in every case anonymous. The passage quoted from the Gospel of St Thomas is not found in any of the present recensions of it. Cf. Tischendorf, *Evv. Apocr.* Pref. p. xxxix.

ians, and that to the Colossians[1]. The writings of the Sethiani again allude to the Gospels of St Matthew and St John and two of the Epistles of St Paul[2].

The general testimony of the Ophitic system to the writings of St John.

Apart from these special references the whole system of the Ophites bears clear witness to the authenticity of St John's Gospel. Everything tends to prove that in them we see one of the earliest forms of heresy. A similar combination of Gentile mysticism with Jewish and Christian ideas troubled the Church of Colossæ even in St Paul's time. Irenæus himself speaks of the Ophites as the first source of the Valentinian school, the original 'hydra-head from which its manifold progeny 'was derived;' and yet even they far passed the limits which St John had fixed for Christian speculation, and thereby witness that they belonged to a later generation.

The Ebionites.

The Ophites, like Simon Magus, represent a system to which Gentile mysticism gave its predominating character: on the opposite side was ranged the famous sect of the Ebionites, by whom Judaism was made an essential part of Christian life. Like Cerinthus they received a mutilated recension of St Matthew's Gospel[3];

What books of the New Testament they received.

---

[1] St John iii. 17 (τὸ εἰρημένον, cf. Luke ix. 56), p. 125; iii. 14, p. 134; i. 1—4, p. 134 (wrongly divided by the editor?); viii. 44, p. 136; x. 7, p. 137. 1 Cor. xi. 32 (ἡ γραφή) p. 125. Col. ii. 9 (τὸ λεγόμενον) pp. 124, 315.

[2] Matt. x. 34, p. 146. John iii. 5, p. 141; iv. 14, p. 143; 2 Cor. v. 2, p. 143; Phil. ii. 6, 7, pp. 143, 318.

The account of the Ophites is concluded by a summary of the opinions of Justin a Gnostic. The use of Isaiah lxiv. 4 in his teaching (p. 158) fully justifies the conjecture which I proposed above in p. 208, n. 3, and I think it very likely that Hegesippus had him in view when he wrote. In the quotations made from his writings there are apparent references to Luke xxiii. 46, p. 157; John iv. 14, p. 158; xix. 26, *ib.* The use of Amen as an angelic name (p. 151) may point, as Bunsen observes, to Apoc. iii. 14.

[3] Iren. *c. Hær.* I. 26. 2: Solo eo quod est secundum Matthæum evangelio utuntur et Apostolum Paulum recusant, apostatam eum legis dicentes. Eusebius calls this Gospel that 'according to the Hebrews' (*H. E.* III. 27), and adds that the Ebionites 'made little account of the rest.'

This is not the proper place to enter on an accurate inquiry into the perplexed question of the various forms of St Matthew's Gospel. I believe like him they wholly rejected the authority and writings of St Paul; but nothing I believe is known of their judgment on the Catholic Epistles. They cannot however have received St John's Epistles; and his Gospel, though not specially mentioned, must be included among those of which 'they made no account.'

One remarkable product of the Ebionite School still remains to be noticed, the *Clementine Homilies*[1]. The writer of this singularly interesting book was a determined adversary of the teaching of St Paul; and there can be no doubt that St Paul himself is referred to as 'the enemy whose lawless and foolish teaching some of 'the Gentiles accepted' in opposition to the alleged preaching of St Peter[2]. Here then if anywhere we might expect to find clear traces of evangelic traditions different in character and contents from those preserved in the Canonical Gospels, if such traditions had been really current in the early Church. But the facts are entirely at variance with this natural expectation. There

Chap. iv.

The Clementine Homilies.

them to have been the following:
(a) The original *Aramæan* text.
  (1) A revision (?) of this included in the Peshito.
  (2) An interpolated text used by the Nazarenes, which contained the first two chapters, and is described by Jerome.
  (3) A mutilated and interpolated text used by the Ebionites.
(β) An [Apostolic] translation in Greek.

[1] I quote the Homilies only, because the Latin translation of the Recognitions has been modified by Rufinus. It may be noticed however that the passage in *Recogn.* I. 68 which limits the argument from Scripture to 'the 'Law and the Prophets' refers only to a discussion between Jews and Christians, and does not contain any determination of the *Christian* view on the subject, as some have supposed. It should be added that the book is the product of an isolated speculator and cannot be supposed to represent a considerable society. This fact has been strangely overlooked in the conclusions which have been hastily drawn from them. Comp. Lightfoot, *Galatians*, pp. 326 ff.

[2] *Ep. Petri ad Jac.* 2: τινὲς τῶν ἀπὸ ἐθνῶν τὸ δι' ἐμοῦ νόμιμον ἀπεδοκίμασαν κήρυγμα τοῦ ἐχθροῦ ἀνθρώπου ἄνομόν τινα καὶ φλυαρώδη προσηκάμενοι διδασκαλίαν. I am not aware that there is a clear reference to any of the Epistles of the New Testament in the Clementine writings. Dr Tregelles (*Canon Murat.* p. 89) has however pointed out a striking coincidence of language εἴπερ ἀληθῶς τῇ ἀληθείᾳ συνεργῆσαι θέλεις (*Hom.* XVII. 19) with 3 John 8.

are references to about eighty different words of the Lord, and of those, so far as I have noticed, there is not one which contains anything essentially divergent from our Gospels, and there are not more than three or four which are not contained substantially in our Gospels[1]. Of the remaining quotations many are unquestionably free reproductions of the document, whatever it may have been, with which the writer was most familiar; about ten agree very closely with the text of St Matthew[2], one with the text of St Mark[3], and one with the text of St John[4]. The remaining passages agree in sense but not in letter with parallels in our Gospels, and of these parallels about four-fifths occur in St Matthew[5].

---

[1] The references are given in the *Introd. to Study of the Gospels* App. D. III. The sayings not contained in the Gospels which appear to be authentic are: (1) γίνεσθε τραπεζῖται δόκιμοι (*Hom.* III. 50, &c.); (2) τὰ ἀγαθὰ ἐλθεῖν δεῖ. μακάριος δέ, φησίν, δι' οὗ ἔρχεται (*Hom.* XII. 29); (3) μὴ δότε πρόφασιν τῷ πονηρῷ (*Hom.* XIX. 2). Other sayings are more of the nature of glosses (1) ὁ πονηρός ἐστιν ὁ πειράζων (*Hom.* III. 55): (2) διὰ τί οὐ νοεῖτε τὸ εὔλογον τῶν γραφῶν (*Hom.* III. 50); (3) τὰ μυστήρια ἐμοὶ καὶ τοῖς υἱοῖς τοῦ οἴκου μου φυλάξατε. Comp. Is. xxiv. 16, LXX. Comp. *Hom.* XIX. 20.

Of facts not noticed in the Gospels I have only noted the name of the Syrophœnician woman (Justin, *Hom.* II. 19); for the astronomical deductions in II. 23, I. 6 f. can hardly be called facts.

[2] The passages which I have marked are: *Hom.* III. 51 ‖ Matt. v. 17; *Hom.* III. 52 ‖ Matt. xi. 28, xv. 13; *Hom.* III. 55 ‖ Matt. xxii. 32; *Hom.* VIII. 4 ‖ Matt. xii. 14; (*Hom.* XI. 33 ‖ Matt. xii. 42); *Hom.* XVIII. 15 ‖ Matt. xiii. 35; *Hom.* XIX. 2 ‖ Matt. vi. 13, xii. 26; *Hom.* XIX. 7 ‖ Matt. xii. 34.

[3] *Hom.* III. 57 ‖ Mark xii. 29. In *Hom.* XIX. 20 Διὸ καὶ τοῖς αὑτοῦ μαθηταῖς κατ' ἰδίαν ἐπέλυε τῆς τῶν οὐρανῶν βασιλείας μυστήρια we have one of the few phrases peculiar to St Mark iv. 34: κατ' ἰδίαν τοῖς ἰδίοις μαθηταῖς ἐπέλυεν πάντα. This is the only place where ἐπιλύω occurs in the Gospels. Cf. Uhlhorn, *Die Homilien*, u. s. w. 122.

[4] *Hom.* XIX. 22: "Ὅθεν καὶ [ὁ διδάσκ]αλος ἡμῶν περὶ τοῦ ἐκ γενετῆς πηροῦ καὶ ἀναβλέψαντος παρ' αὑτοῦ ἐξετά[ζ]ουσι τοῖς μαθηταῖς] εἰ οὗτος ἥμαρτεν ἢ οἱ γονεῖς αὑτοῦ ἵνα τυφλὸς γεννηθῇ ἀπεκρίνατο· οὔτε οὗτός τι ἥμαρτεν οὔτε οἱ γονεῖς αὑτοῦ, ἀλλ' ἵνα δι' αὑτοῦ φανερωθῇ ἡ δύναμις τοῦ Θεοῦ τῆς ἀγνοίας ἰωμένη τὰ ἁμαρτήματα. Cf. John ix. 1, sqq. Uhlhorn, 128 ff.

It may fairly be left for any reader to decide which is the earlier form of words ἵνα φανερωθῇ τὰ ἔργα τοῦ θεοῦ ἐν αὐτῷ (John ix. 3) or ἵνα δι' αὑτοῦ φανερωθῇ ἡ δύναμις τοῦ θεοῦ τῆς ἀγνοίας ἰωμένη τὰ ἁμαρτήματα.

[5] *Hom.* XVII. 5 contains a close summary of a parable peculiar to St Luke (xviii. 6 ff.). See also *Hom.* XI. 20 ‖ Luke xxiii. 34.

This is not the place to discuss the Clementine quotations at length. The writer was distinctly opposed to the Catholic Church, so that even if it could be shewn decisively that he used a Gospel which was not recognised by the Church, no conclusion could be drawn from that fact as to the coequal authority of such a document with the four Gospels in the Church itself. But the general summary just given shews that the quotations as a whole do establish one point of primary importance. They shew beyond the possibility of doubt that our Gospels preserve with practical completeness all that was known and believed of the Gospel history throughout the early Church. This is what we are really concerned to know. If the Clementines had exhibited a type of narrative or of discourses different from that of the Synoptists some perplexity might have arisen in determining which type was the earlier. As it is, they establish by unimpeachable evidence that those who rejected St Paul accepted a record of the Lord's teaching substantially agreeing with that of St Matthew[1].

Chap. iv. Complete harmony in substance.

The Clementine quotations supply yet another important conclusion. In thirteen cases these quotations correspond with quotations in Justin Martyr. Now of these corresponding quotations only three agree in differences from the canonical text, while the character of the two sets of quotations as wholes is markedly dissimilar It is impossible therefore to suppose that both

Difference of the Clementine Quotations from Justin's.

---

[1] The quotations in the *Clementine Homilies* have been examined with great care by Dr Sanday, *The Gospel in the Second Century* c. vi. Dr Sanday attaches far greater importance than I can do to their testimony, but he arrives substantially at the results which I have given: 'Either the 'Clementine writer quotes our pre- 'sent Gospels, or else he quotes some 'other composition later than them 'and which implies them.... The 'facts do not permit us to claim the 'exclusive use of the canonical Gos- 'pels. But that they were used, 'mediately or immediately, and to a 'greater or less degree, is, I believe, 'beyond question' (pp. 186 f.).

were derived from the same 'Petrine Gospel' without admitting a looseness of quotation in Justin and the author of the Homilies which if once admitted is sufficient to explain how Justin's quotations were derived from the canonical texts[1].

The true value of this anonymous evidence.

The evidence that has been collected from the documents of these primitive sects is necessarily somewhat vague. It would be more satisfactory to know the exact position of their authors and the precise date of their composition. It is just possible that Hippolytus made use of writings which were current in his own time without further examination, and transferred to the Apostolic age forms of thought and expression which had been the growth of two or even of three generations. However improbable this notion may be, it lessens the direct argumentative value of the evidence, though it leaves the moral impression unimpaired. But it cannot be denied that each fresh discovery of ancient records confirms the authenticity of the books of the New Testament, so far as it bears upon them. The earliest known teachers of heresy quote them generally as familiarly known to Christians: they shew that they place them on the same level as the Old Testament Scriptures by the forms of citation which they employ: they appeal to them as having authority with those whom they address; and since they used them in their private books, it is evident that they recognised their claims themselves[2].

[1] See Note at the end of the Section: p. 289.
[2] Eusebius in noticing the different translators of Scripture (*H. E.* VI. 17) mentions that SYMMACHUS (c. 200 A.D.) was an Ebionite. He then adds: 'And moreover notes '(ὑπομνήματα) of Symmachus are 'still extant (φέρεται) in which he 'appears to support the heresy which 'I have mentioned, directing his 'efforts to the Gospel of St Matthew.' The last phrase (πρὸς τὸ κατὰ Ματθαῖον ἀποτεινόμενος εὐαγγέλιον) is obscure; but if its meaning be that Symmachus exerted himself to shew

the superior authority of the Ebionitic text of the Gospel of St Matthew, it still offers a singular proof of the general reception of the Canonical Gospel of St Matthew, though Symmachus assailed it. But Ruffinus, Jerome, and, following them at a much later time, Nicephorus, supposed that Symmachus wrote Commentaries on St Matthew, and the Greek will bear that meaning. Hieron. *de Virr. Ill.* 34: [Symmachus] in Evangelium quoque κατὰ Ματθαῖον scripsit Commentarios, de quo et suum dogma firmare conatur.

NOTE TO PAGE 288.

THE CORRESPONDING QUOTATIONS OF JUSTIN MARTYR AND THE CLEMENTINE HOMILIES.

In the following note I have endeavoured to collect all the corresponding quotations of Justin Martyr and the Homilies. General statements on such points are apt to be misleading, and the student, with all the facts before him, can draw his own conclusions, or test the conclusions of others. I have not thought it worth while to print the corresponding texts in our Gospels, for the one point to be decided is whether Justin and the author of the Homilies used the same record, that record not being one of the Canonical Gospels.

Homilies.

1. VIII. 21 ἔφη· Γέγραπται Κύριον τὸν θεόν σου φοβηθήσῃ καὶ αὐτῷ λατρεύσεις μόνῳ.
Comp. Matt. iv. 10; Lu. iv. 8.

2. III. 55; XIX. 2 ἔφη "Εστω ὑμῶν τὸ ναὶ ναί, [καὶ] τὸ οὒ οὔ· τὸ δὲ [γὰρ] περισσὸν τούτων ἐκ τοῦ πονηροῦ ἐστίν.
See p. 154.

3. III. 57 γίνεσθε ἀγαθοὶ καὶ οἰκτίρμονες, ὡς ὁ πατήρ, ὁ ἐν τοῖς οὐρανοῖς, ὃς ἀνατέλλει τὸν ἥλιον ἐπ' ἀγαθοῖς καὶ πονηροῖς, καὶ φέρει τὸν ὑετὸν ἐπὶ δικαίοις καὶ ἀδίκοις.
Comp. Luke vi. 36. See p. 140.

4. III. 55 ἔφη· Οἶδε γὰρ ὁ πατὴρ ὑμῶν ὁ οὐράνιος ὅτι χρῄζετε τούτων ἁπάντων πρὶν αὐτὸν ἀξιώσετε.
Comp. Matt. vi. 8, 32.

5. XI. 35 ἔφη Πολλοὶ ἐλεύσονται πρός με ἐν ἐνδύμασι προβάτων, ἔσωθεν δέ εἰσι λύκοι ἅρπαγες· ἀπὸ τῶν καρπῶν αὐτῶν ἐπιγινώσκετε (-σεσθε) αὐτούς.
Comp. Matt. vii. 15.

Justin M.

Dial. 125 (103) ἀποκρίνεται...Γέγραπται Κύριον τὸν θεόν σου προσκυνήσεις καὶ αὐτῷ μόνῳ λατρεύσεις.

Apol. I. 16 ...ἔστω δὲ ὑμῶν τὸ ναί, ναί, καὶ τὸ οὒ οὔ· τὸ δὲ περισσὸν τούτων ἐκ τοῦ πονηροῦ.

Dial. 96; Cf. *Apol.* I. 15. Γίνεσθε χρηστοὶ καὶ οἰκτίρμονες ὡς καὶ ὁ πατὴρ ὑμῶν ὁ οὐράνιος· καὶ γάρ... ὁρῶμεν τὸν ἥλιον αὐτοῦ ἀνατέλλοντα ἐπὶ ἀχαρίστους καὶ δικαίους καὶ βρέχοντα ἐπὶ ὁσίους καὶ πονηρούς.

Apol. I. 15 οἶδε γὰρ ὁ πατὴρ ὑμῶν ὁ οὐράνιος ὅτι τούτων χρείαν ἔχετε.

Apol. I. 16; Cf. *Dial.* 35. πολλοὶ γὰρ ἥξουσιν ἐπὶ τῷ ὀνόματί μου, ἔξωθεν μὲν ἐνδεδυμένοι δέρματα προβάτων, ἔσωθεν δὲ ὄντες λύκοι ἅρπαγες· ἐκ τῶν ἔργων αὐτῶν ἐπιγνώσεσθε αὐτούς.

6. VIII. 4 μέμνημαι... εἰπόντος πολλοὶ ἐλεύσονται ἀπὸ ἀνατολῶν καὶ δυσμῶν ἄρκτου τε καὶ μεσημβρίας, καὶ ἀνακλιθήσονται εἰς κόλπους Ἀβραὰμ καὶ Ἰσαὰκ καὶ Ἰακώβ.
Comp. Matt. viii. 11.

Dial. 76...εἰπών, "Ἥξουσιν ἀπὸ ἀνατολῶν καὶ δυσμῶν καὶ ἀνακλιθήσονται μετὰ Ἀβραὰμ καὶ Ἰσαὰκ καὶ Ἰακὼβ ἐν τῇ βασιλείᾳ τῶν οὐρανῶν...

7. XVIII. 5 ...λέγων Μὴ φοβηθῆτε ἀπὸ τοῦ ἀποκτείνοντος τὸ σῶμα τῇ δὲ ψυχῇ μὴ δυναμένου τι ποιῆσαι· φοβήθητε δὲ τὸν δυνάμενον καὶ σῶμα καὶ ψυχὴν εἰς τὴν γέενναν τοῦ πυρὸς βαλεῖν. ναὶ λέγω ὑμῖν, τοῦτον φοβήθητε.
Comp. Luke xii. 4 f. Matt. x. 28.

Apol. I. 19 μὴ φοβεῖσθε τοὺς ἀναιροῦντας ὑμᾶς καὶ μετὰ ταῦτα μὴ δυναμένους τι ποιῆσαι, εἶπε· φοβήθητε δὲ τὸν μετὰ τὸ ἀποθανεῖν δυνάμενον καὶ ψυχὴν καὶ σῶμα εἰς γέενναν ἐμβαλεῖν.

8. XVIII. 4 λέγει· Οὐδεὶς ἔγνω τὸν πατέρα εἰ μὴ ὁ υἱός, ὡς οὐδὲ τὸν υἱόν τις οἶδεν εἰ μὴ ὁ πατὴρ καὶ οἷς ἂν βούληται ὁ υἱὸς ἀποκαλύψαι.
Comp. Matt. xi. 27.

Apol. I. 63; Cf. *Dial.* 100. οὐδεὶς ἔγνω τὸν πατέρα εἰ μὴ ὁ υἱός, οὐδὲ τὸν υἱὸν εἰ μὴ ὁ πατὴρ καὶ οἷς ἂν ἀποκαλύψῃ ὁ υἱός.

9. XVIII. 3 ...ἔφη Μή με λέγε ἀγαθόν· ὁ γὰρ ἀγαθὸς εἷς ἐστίν, ὁ πατὴρ ὁ ἐν τοῖς οὐρανοῖς.
Comp. Matt. xix. 16.

Dial. 101; Cf. *Apol.* I. 16 ...ἀπεκρίνατο Τί με λέγεις ἀγαθόν; εἷς ἐστὶν ἀγαθός, ὁ πατήρ μου ὁ ἐν τοῖς οὐρανοῖς.

10. XV. 5 δίκαιον ἔφασκεν εἶναι καὶ τῷ τύπτοντι αὐτοῦ τὴν σιαγόνα παρατιθέναι καὶ τὴν ἑτέραν· καὶ τῷ αἴροντι αὐτοῦ τὸ ἱμάτιον προσδιδόναι καὶ τὸ μαφόριον· ἀγγαρεύοντι δὲ μίλιον συναπέρχεσθαι δύο καὶ ὅσα τοιαῦτα.
Comp. Matt. v. 39, 40.

Apol. I. 16 ...ἔφη...Τῷ τύπτοντί σου τὴν σιαγόνα πάρεχε καὶ τὴν ἄλλην· καὶ τὸν αἴροντά σου τὸν χιτῶνα ἢ τὸ ἱμάτιον μὴ κωλύσῃς ...παντὶ δὲ ἀγγαρεύοντί σε μίλιον ἀκολούθησον δύο.

11. XIX. 2; Cf. *Hom.* XX. 9. ...εἰπεῖν ὑπέσχετο τοῖς ἀσεβέσιν Ὑπάγετε εἰς τὸ σκότος τὸ ἐξώτερον, ὃ ἡτοίμασεν ὁ πατὴρ τῷ διαβόλῳ καὶ τοῖς ἀγγέλοις αὐτοῦ.
Comp. Matt. xxv. 41.

Dial. 76 ...ἔφη ἐρεῖν Ὑπάγετε εἰς τὸ σκότος τὸ ἐξώτερον, ὃ ἡτοίμασεν ὁ πατὴρ τῷ σατανᾷ καὶ τοῖς ἀγγέλοις αὐτοῦ.

12. III. 18 ἀλλὰ ναί, φησίν, κρατοῦσι μὲν τὴν κλεῖν τοῖς δὲ βουλομένοις εἰσελθεῖν οὐ παρέχουσι.
Comp. Luke xi. 52.

Dial. 17 ...τοὺς κλεῖς ἔχετε...καὶ τοὺς εἰσερχομένους κωλύετε...

13. XI. 26 Ἀμὴν ὑμῖν λέγω Ἐὰν μὴ ἀναγεννηθῆτε ὕδατι ζῶντι εἰς ὄνομα πατρός, υἱοῦ, ἁγίου πνεύματος, οὐ μὴ εἰσέλθητε εἰς τὴν βασιλείαν τῶν οὐρανῶν.
Comp. John iii. 3 ff.

Apol. I. 61 εἶπεν Ἂν μὴ ἀναγεννηθῆτε οὐ μὴ εἰσέλθητε εἰς τὴν βασιλείαν τῶν οὐρανῶν.

Without entering into any detailed investigation I cannot but indicate the results to which these parallels lead. There are three cases (2, 11, 13) in which the Clementine quotation agrees more or less with Justin's quotation in a difference from our present Evangelic text. These coincidences have been already noticed (pp. 152 ff.). On the other hand the whole complexion of the corresponding quotations differs. A fair comparison of them, therefore, lends no support to the belief that Justin and the author of the Clementines quoted from the same source, that source not being one or other of the Canonical Gospels. Those who have assumed or asserted this conclusion can scarcely have considered the parallel quotations as a whole. It is indeed quite possible that the author of the Clementines quoted freely from "a Petrine Gospel" inserting phrases from the Canonical Gospels, just as Justin quoted freely from the Canonical Gospels inserting phrases from other forms of the Evangelic narrative. Into this question I do not enter[1]. All that is to be observed is that the Clementine quotations as a whole differ from Justin's (so far as there are materials for a comparison) at least as much as Justin's differ from the Canonical texts.

[1] It must be observed that the sayings which are quoted more than once in the Homilies are quoted almost always either in the same form or with very slight variations, differing greatly in this respect from Justin's quotations. The examples are: *Hom.* II. 51; III. 50; XVIII. 20. *Hom.* III. 55; XIX. 2. *Hom.* III. 60; III. 64. (*Hom.* XIX. 2; XX. 9.) The quotations are all such as would be likely to be stereotyped in form, even if they were not quoted directly from a written text. On the other hand compare *Hom.* VII. 4 (ἅπερ ἕκαστος ἑαυτῷ βούλεται καλά......) with *Hom.* XII. 32 (ὃ θέλει ἑαυτῷ......).

§ 3. *Basilides and Isidorus.*

The case however does not turn wholly on anonymous evidence. The account of Basilides given by Hippolytus is composed mainly of passages from his own writings which fully establish the inferences which have been hitherto drawn[1]. The mode in which the books of

BASILIDES. *The character of his testimony.*

[1] The conclusion that Hippolytus quotes directly from Basilides seems to me to be fully established by the following considerations.
(a) The works of Basilides (his Ἐξηγητικά) were well known. They were quoted (αὐταῖς λέξεσιν) by Clement of Alexandria and in the discussion of Archelaus and Manes (c. 270 A.D.), and probably by Origen, so that they may have been easily accessible to Hippolytus.
(β) The quotations of Hippolytus are clearly taken directly from some book. The author appears in the first person βούλομαι δεῖξαι, λέγω (*Philos.* VII. c. 20; λέγω c. 21).
(γ) The author whose exposition is quoted by 'he says' is identified (as I must think) with Basilides by necessary implication. At the close of the exposition we read ταῦτα μὲν οὖν ἐστιν ἃ καὶ Βασιλείδης μυθεύει σχολάσας κατὰ τὴν Αἴγυπτον (c. 27. At the end of Book VI. Hippolytus had said ἴδωμεν τί λέγει καὶ Βασιλείδης); and in the

the New Testament are treated in these fragments shews that there is no anachronism in supposing that the earliest heretics sought to recommend their doctrines by forced explanations of Apostolic language. And yet more than this: they contain the earliest undoubted instances in which the Old and New Testaments are placed on the same level: the Epistles of St Paul are called 'Scripture,' and quotations from them are introduced by the well-known form 'It is written[1].' If it seem strange that the first direct proofs of a belief in the Inspiration of the New Testament are derived from such a source, it may be remembered that it is more likely that the apologist of a suspicious system should support his argument by quotations from an authority acknowledged by his opponents, than that a Christian teacher writing to fellow-believers should insist on those

course of the exposition and in direct connexion with it φεύγει Βασιλείδης, καλεῖ τὸ τοιοῦτο Βασιλείδης, διῄρηται ὑπὸ Βασιλείδου, Βασιλείδης διασαφεῖ &c. Now inasmuch as Basilides had written on the subjects treated of, and his works were well known, nothing but the most cogent evidence could be sufficient to shew that this language is not to be understood in its plain and literal sense.

(δ) At the beginning of the account Hippolytus says: Ἴδωμεν οὖν πᾶς καταφανῶς Βασιλείδης ὁμοῦ καὶ Ἰσίδωρος καὶ πᾶς ὁ τούτων χόρος οὐχ ἁπλῶς καταψεύδεται... And so in fact the school is distinguished in the exposition from the founder: c. 20 τοῦτο [a doctrine quoted with φησί]... λαβόντες ἀπατῶσιν... So again in a passage evidently belonging to the later phase of the heresy (c. 26, p. 240) we have κατ' αὐτούς and φάσκουσι preceded and followed by the φησί, and so again c. 27 (p. 243).

(ε) If the forms of quotation γέγραπται and ἡ γραφή are remarkable as anticipatory of later usage, the phrase τὸ λεγόμενον ἐν τοῖς εὐαγγελίοις (John i. 9) is no less remarkable as a trace of an early mode of citation.

The arguments which are urged on the other side (e.g. Supernat. Rel. II. 41 ff.) appear to resolve themselves into the 'foregone conclusion' that Basilides could not have quoted the Scriptures of the New Testament. Nor can I admit that all 'learned criticism' belongs to the very able but very narrow School of Tübingen, so that a result which obtains their support can be said to be 'admitted.'

[1] [Hipp.] adv. Hær. VII. 26: ἡ γραφὴ λέγει· οὐκ ἐν διδακτοῖς ἀνθρωπίνης σοφίας λόγοις ἀλλ' ἐν διδακτοῖς πνεύματος (1 Cor. ii. 13), VII. 25: ὡς γέγραπται, φησί· καὶ ἡ κτίσις αὐτὴ συστενάζει, κ.τ.λ. Rom. viii. 22, &c.

I.] BASILIDES. 293

testimonies with which he might suppose his readers to be familiar.

Chap. iv.

Very little is known of the history of Basilides[1]. It seems that he was an Alexandrine, and probably of Jewish descent. He is said to have lived 'not long 'after the times of the Apostles[2],' and to have been a younger contemporary of Cerinthus, and a follower of Menander who was himself the successor of Simon Magus. Clement of Alexandria and Jerome fix the period of his activity in the time of Hadrian[3]; and he found a formidable antagonist in Agrippa Castor[4]. All these circumstances combine to place him in the generation next after the Apostolic age, and to shew that in point of antiquity he holds a rank intermediate between that of Clement of Rome and Polycarp.

His date.

Since Basilides lived on the verge of the Apostolic times it is not surprising that he made use of other sources of Christian doctrine besides the Canonical books. The belief in divine Inspiration was still fresh and real; and Eusebius relates that he set up imaginary prophets Barcabbas and Barcoph (Parchor)—'names to 'strike terror into the superstitious'—by whose writings he supported his peculiar views[5]. At the same time he

He made use of other books besides those included in the Canon of the New Testament.

---

[1]. *Saturninus* (or *Satornilus*) of Antioch is generally placed in close connexion with Basilides. He was a scholar of Menander, whose opinions he advanced. All the accounts of his doctrine appear to be derived from one source, and they contain nothing which bears on the history of the Canon. [Hipp.] *adv. Hær.* VII. 28; Iren. *c. Hær.* I. 24; Epiph. *Hær.* XXIII.

[2] *Archel. et Man. Disp.*, Routh, *Rell. Sacr.* V. p. 197 ...Basilides quidam......non longe post nostrorum Apostolorum tempora.... Cf. *ib.* I. p.

258. Euseb. *H. E.* IV. 7.

[3] Cf. Pearson, *Vind. Ign.* II. 7, ap. Lardner, VIII. 350.

[4] Cf. supra, p. 95.

[5] Eusebius appears to consider the prophecies as forgeries (*H. E.* IV. 7). They may however have been 'Oriental books which he met with 'in his journey into the East,' as Lardner suggests (VIII. 390). Isidorus wrote a commentary on the prophecy of Parchor, which gives authority to the conjecture: Clem. Alex. *Strom.* VI. 6. 53.

appealed to the authority of Glaucias who as he proudly affirmed was 'an interpreter of Peter[1];' and he also made use of certain 'Traditions of Matthias' which claimed to be grounded on 'private intercourse with the 'Saviour[2].' It appears moreover that he himself published a Gospel[3]—a 'Philosophy of Christianity' as it

---

[1] Clem. Alex. *Strom.* VII. 17. 106. The Catholic tradition, it will be remembered, gave the same title to St Mark.

[2] [Hipp.] *adv. Hær.* VII. 20: Βασιλείδης τοίνυν καὶ Ἰσίδωρος ὁ Βασιλείδου παῖς γνήσιος καὶ μαθητὴς φασὶν εἰρηκέναι Ματθίαν αὐτοῖς λόγους ἀποκρύφους οὓς ἤκουσε παρὰ τοῦ Σωτῆρος κατ᾿ ἰδίαν διδαχθείς. Miller corrects the manuscript reading Ματθίαν into Ματθαῖον, wrongly I believe. Cf. Clem. Alex. *Strom.* VII. 17. 108.

[3] The few notices of Basilides' Gospel or Commentaries are perplexing. Origen is the first who mentions a *Gospel* as written by him. *Hom.* i. *in Luc.*: Ausus fuit et Basilides scribere evangelium, et suo illud nomine titulare. This statement is repeated by Ambrose and Jerome, who cannot however be considered as independent witnesses. In another passage Origen has been supposed to allude to the Gospel of Basilides as identical with that of Marcion and Valentinus: ταῦτα δὲ εἴρηται πρὸς τοὺς ἀπὸ Οὐαλεντίνου καὶ Βασιλείδου καὶ τοὺς ἀπὸ Μαρκίωνος.— ἔχουσι γὰρ καὶ αὐτοὶ τὰς λέξεις (the quotations from the Old Testament in Luke x. 27) ἐν τῷ καθ᾿ ἑαυτοὺς εὐαγγελίῳ (Fr. 6 in Luc.). The last clause however need not refer to any besides the Marcionites.

I am not aware that there are any more references to the work of Basilides as a *Gospel*; but Agrippa Castor mentions 'four and twenty 'books (τέσσαρα πρὸς τοῖς [?] εἴκοσι) 'which he composed on the Gospel' (εἰς τὸ εὐαγγέλιον) (Euseb. *H. E.* IV.

7); Clement of Alexandria quotes several passages from the twenty-third book (*Strom.* IV. 12. 83 sqq.); and another quotation from the thirteenth book (*tractatus*) occurs at the end of the 'discussion between Archelaus and Manes' (Routh, V. p. 197); and perhaps another in Origen *Comm. in Rom.* V. 1. p. 549, Hæc Basilides non advertens de lege naturali debere intelligi ad ineptas et impias fabulas sermonem apostolicum traxit...'Dixit enim' inquit 'apostolus 'quia ego vivebam sine lege aliquando '(Rom. vii. 9) hoc est antequam in 'istud corpus venirem....' This confirms the other definite references to Apostolic books in a remarkable way.

There is nothing in the title inconsistent with the notion that it was based on our Gospels: (comp. Hieron. *de Virr. Ill.* Legi sub nomine ejus (Theophilus) *in Evangelium*...commentarios) though this may be thought unlikely on other grounds.

The character of the quotations from the Ἐξηγητικά shews that these Commentaries cannot have formed part of a Gospel in the common sense of the word, but it appears that Basilides attached a technical meaning to the term: Εὐαγγέλιον ἐστὶ κατ᾿ αὐτοὺς (the followers of Basilides) ἡ τῶν ὑπερκοσμίων γνῶσις, ὡς δεδήλωται, ἣν ὁ μέγας ἄρχων οὐκ ἠπίστατο. [Hipp.] *adv. Hær.* VII. 27; cf. 26. May we not then identify the Commentaries with the Gospel in this sense, and suppose that the ambiguity of the word led Origen into error?

Norton (II. p. 310) assumes that

BASILIDES.

would perhaps be called in our days—but he admitted the historic truth of all the facts contained in the Canonical Gospels[1], and used them as Scripture. For in spite of his peculiar opinions the testimony of Basilides to our 'acknowledged' books, as given by Hippolytus[2], is comprehensive and clear. In the few pages of his writings which remain there are certain references to the Gospels of St Luke and St John, and to the Epistles of St Paul to the Romans, Corinthians, Ephesians, and Colossians, to the contents of St Matthew, and possibly also to the first Epistle to Timothy[3]. In addition to this he appears to have used the first Epistle of St Peter[4]; and he must have admitted the Petrine type of doctrine through his connexion with Glaucias. And thus again, apart from the consideration of particular books, an Alexandrine heretic recognised simultaneously the teaching of St Paul, St Peter, and St John, while Polycarp was still at Smyrna, and Justin Martyr only a disciple of Plato. And the fact itself belongs to an earlier date; for this belief cannot have originated with him, and if we go back

What Canonical books he quotes.

---

the Homilies on Luke are not Origen's. In this I suppose he follows the rash conjecture of Erasmus. Huet, *Orig.* III. 3. 13. Redepenning, *Origenes*, II. 69.

[1] [Hipp.] *adv. Hær.* VII. 27: Γεγενημένης δὲ τῆς γενέσεως τῆς προδεδηλωμένης γέγονε πάντα ὁμοίως κατ' αὐτοὺς τὰ περὶ τοῦ Σωτῆρος ὡς ἐν τοῖς εὐαγγελίοις γέγραπται. He gave a mystical explanation of the Incarnation, quoting Luke i. 35 (*id.* § 26).

[2] See next note. Even if these are set aside there is no evidence to shew that Basilides 'ignored the Canonical Gospels altogether.'

[3] The following examples will be sufficient to shew his method of quotation:

St Luke i. 35, p. 241 (τὸ εἰρημένον). Comp. Sanday, *l.c.* 195 ff.

St John i. 9, p. 232 (τὸ λέγ. ἐν τοῖς εὐαγγ.); ii. 4, p. 242. For the plural see p. 112, n. 2.

Romans viii. 22, p. 238 (ὡς γέγραπται), p. 241; v. 13, 14 (*id.*). Cf. Orig. *Comm. in Rom.* c. 5.

1 Corinthians ii. 13, p. 240 (ἡ γραφή); xv. 8, p. 241.

2 Corinthians xii. 4, p. 241 (γέγραπται).

Ephesians i. 21, pp. 230, 239; iii. 3, p. 241.

Colossians i. 26, p. 238 (Eph. iii. 5).

St Matthew ii. 1 sqq. p. 243.

1 Tim. ii. 6, p. 232 (?) καιροὶ ἴδιοι.

[4] Clem. *Strom.* IV. 12. 83 (1 Pet. iv. 14—16), quoted by Kirchhofer, p. 416.

but one generation we are within the age of the Apostles.

On the other hand Basilides is said to have anticipated Marcion in the rejection of the Pastoral Epistles and of that to the Hebrews; but Clement intimates that these books were commonly condemned by those who 'fancied' that their opinions were characterized in them as 'false-named wisdom;' and there is no reason to suppose that this judgment was the result of any historical inquiry[1]. Jerome speaks of it as a piece of arbitrary dogmatism based on 'their heretical authority,' and unsustained by any definite arguments.

Isidorus the son of Basilides maintained the doctrine of his father; nor need we believe that he differed from him in his estimation of the Apostolic writings. Some fragments of his works have been preserved by Clement of Alexandria, but I have noticed nothing in them bearing on the books of the New Testament.

§ 4. *Carpocrates.*

The accounts of Carpocrates are very meagre, and all apparently come from one source. He was an Alexandrine, and a contemporary of Basilides[2]. Nothing is said directly of his views of the Apostolic writings; but it is mentioned incidentally that he held

---

[1] Hieron. *Pref. in Ep. ad Tit.*: Nonnullas [epistolas] integras repudiandas crediderunt: ad Timotheum videlicet utramque, ad Hebræos, et ad Titum. Et si quidem redderent causas cur eas Apostoli non putarent, tentaremus aliquid respondere et forsan satisfacere lectori. Nunc vero cum hæretica auctoritate pronuncient et dicant Illa epistola Pauli est, hæc non est; ea auctoritate repelli se pro veritate intelligant, qua ipsi non erubescunt falsa simulare.

Perhaps we may refer to this school the general statement of Clement, ὑπὸ ταύτης ἐλεγχόμενοι τῆς φωνῆς (1 Tim. vi. 20) οἱ ἀπὸ τῶν αἱρέσεων τὰς πρὸς Τιμόθεον ἀθετοῦσιν ἐπιστολάς (*Strom.* II. 11, § 52).

[2] Clem. Alex. *Strom.* III. 2. 5. Iren. *c. Hær.* I. 25.

the Apostles themselves—'Peter and Paul and the 'rest'—as nowise inferior to Christ Himself[1]. This opinion followed naturally from his views of the Person of Christ; but the close juxtaposition of St Peter and St Paul is worthy of notice.

From another passage in Irenæus it may be concluded that the Carpocratians received our Canonical Gospels, adapting them to their own doctrine by strange expositions. Thus they applied the parable of the man and his adversary to the relation of man to the devil, whose office they held it to be 'to convey the souls of 'the dead to the Prince of the world, who in turn gave 'them to an attendant spirit to imprison in another 'body, till they had been engaged in every act done in 'the world[2].'

The key-word of the system of Carpocrates in itself bore witness to the teaching of St Paul and St John. 'Men are saved,' he said, 'by *faith and love*[3];' but the corollary which he drew from this truth on the essential indifference of actions seems to shew that he did not combine the teaching of St James with that of the other Apostles[4].

The Carpocratians received our Gospels.

Matt. v. 25; Luke xii. 58.

Their system combined the teaching of St Paul and St John.

---

[1] Iren. *c. Hær.* I. 25. 2. [Hipp.] *adv. Hær.* VII. 31. Epiphanius (*Hær.* XXVII. 2) says Πέτρου καὶ Ἀνδρέου καὶ Παύλου. I do not know how to explain the special mention of St Andrew. His connexion with St Peter affords scarcely sufficient reason.

[2] Iren. *c. Hær.* I. 25. 4.

[3] Iren. *c. Hær.* I. 25. 5: διὰ πίστεως γὰρ καὶ ἀγάπης σώζεσθαι· τὰ δὲ λοιπὰ ἀδιάφορα ὄντα κατὰ τὴν δόξαν τῶν ἀνθρώπων πῆ μὲν ἀγαθὰ πῆ δὲ κακὰ νομίζεσθαι, οὐδενὸς φύσει κακοῦ ὑπάρχοντος.

[4] The fragments of *Epiphanes* (Clem. Alex. *Strom.* III. 2. 6 sqq.) the son of Carpocrates contain no direct scriptural quotations; but the whole argument on justice reads like a comment on Matt. v. 45. The passage in § 7, μὴ συνιεὶς τὸ τοῦ ἀποστόλου ῥητὸν λέγοντος· διὰ νόμου τὴν ἁμαρτίαν ἔγνων (Rom. vii. 7), is a remark of Clement's, συνιεὶς referring to φησὶν in the former sentence. It is necessary to notice this, as the words have been quoted as used by Epiphanes. Cf. Epiph. *Hær.* XXXII. 4.

§ 5. *Valentinus.*

The date of Valentinus.

Shortly after Basilides began to propagate his doctrines another system arose at Alexandria, which was the result of similar causes, and was moulded on a similar type. Its author Valentinus was like Basilides probably an Egyptian, and his writings betray a familiarity with Jewish opinions[1]. After the example of the Christian teachers of his age he went to Rome, which he chose as the centre of his labours. Irenæus relates that 'he came there during the episcopate of Hyginus, 'was at his full vigour in the time of Pius, and con-'tinued there till the time of Anicetus[2].' Thus he was at Rome when Polycarp came on his mission from the Eastern Church; and Marcion may have been among his hearers. His testimony is as venerable in point of age as that of Justin; and he is removed by one generation only from the time of St John.

He received the same books as Catholic Christians.

Just as Basilides claimed through Glaucias the authority of St Peter, Valentinus professed to follow the teaching of Theodas a disciple of St Paul[3]. The circumstance is important; for it shews that at the beginning of the second century, alike within and without the Church, the sanction of an Apostle was considered to be a sufficient proof of Christian doctrine; and Tertullian says that in this he differed from Marcion, that he at least professed to accept 'the whole Instrument,' perverting the interpretation where Marcion mutilated the text[4]. The few unquestionable fragments of Valen-

---

[1] Cf. Epiph. *Hær.* XXXI. 2. Massuet, *Diss.* I. I. I.
[2] Iren. *c. Hær.* III. 4. 3 (ap. Euseb. *H. E.* IV. 11).
[3] Clem. Alex. *Strom.* VII. 17. 106.
[4] Tertull. *de Præscr. Hæret.* 38: Alius manu scripturas, alius sensus expositione intervertit. Neque enim si Valentinus integro Instrumento uti videtur, non callidiore ingenio quam Marcion [manus intulit veritati?]. Marcion enim exserte et pa-

VALENTINUS.

tinus[1] contain but little which points to passages of Scripture[2]. If it were clear that the anonymous quotations in Hippolytus were derived from Valentinus himself[3] the list would be much enlarged, and include a citation of the Epistle to the Ephesians as 'Scripture,' and clear references to the Gospels of St Luke and St John, to 1 Corinthians[4], perhaps also to the Epistle to the Hebrews and the first Epistle of St John[5].

Iam machæra non stylo usus est: quoniam ad materiam suam cædem scripturarum confecit. Valentinus autem pepercit: quoniam non ad materiam scripturas, sed materiam ad scripturas excogitavit: et tamen plus abstulit et plus adjecit, auferens proprietates singulorum quoque verborum et adjiciens dispositiones non comparentium rerum. By *uti videtur* I understand that Tertullian describes the profession of Valentinus; not that he expresses any doubt as to the fact.

[1] Very little is known of the writings of Valentinus. Clement quotes Homilies and Letters; and in the Dialogue against Marcion a long passage is taken from his treatise 'On the Origin of Evil.'

[2] Clem. *Strom.* II. 20. 114. St Matt. v. 8; xix. 17. In the latter place the reading of Valentinus was probably εἶς ἐστὶν ἀγαθός, ὁ πατήρ· which is also given by Clement *Strom.* V. 64 (εἶς ἀγαθὸς ὁ πατήρ) and the remarkable Latin MS. *e*, which bears a remarkable resemblance to D. D itself reads simply εἶς ἐστὶν ἀγαθός. Clem. *Strom.* IV. 13. 92. Rom. i. 20.

[3] In the former editions of this essay I assigned these anonymous passages to Valentinus. If Valentinus 'heard' one 'who was acquainted with St Paul' (Clem. *l. c.*) internal evidence cannot be urged against the view. But a fresh and careful examination of the whole section of Hippolytus makes me feel that the evidence is so uncertain, that I cannot be sure in this case, as in the case of Basilides, that Hippolytus is quoting the words of the founder. I am therefore unwilling any longer to use an authority which can fairly be challenged. At the same time there is very much to be urged in favour of the opinion that the quotations are from Valentinus. In cc. 29—38 Hippolytus appears to deal with the opinions of Valentinus (τὰ τῷ Οὐαλεντίνῳ δοκοῦντα): in cc. 38—55 he deals with the opinions of the Valentinian school (οἱ ἀπὸ τῆς Οὐαλεντίνου σχολῆς). In the first great division he notices divergences of interpretation which had arisen on points of the Master's teaching among later Valentinians, but always goes back to 'he says.' In the second division he quotes constantly by name the authorities whom he uses. It further appears that he was acquainted with writings of Valentinus (c. 37 p. 198; c. 42 p. 203). .

I cannot but add that the whole system of Valentinus is unintelligible to me unless the Gospel of St John is presupposed. Can any one suppose that the Hebdomas of Valentinus, νοῦς, ἀλήθεια, λόγος, ζωή, ἄνθρωπος, ἐκκλησία, ὁ πατήρ, was earlier than St John's Gospel or independent of it when compared with that of Simon, νοῦς, ἐπίνοια, ὄνομα, φωνή, λογισμός, ἐνθύμησις, ὁ ἑστώς, στάς, στησόμενος ([Hipp.] *adv. Hær.* IV. 51)? Compare Sanday, *The Fourth Gospel*, pp. 8 ff.

[4] In vi. 35 (Rom. viii. 11) the true reading is, I believe, φασί and not φησί.

[5] The references are:
St Luke i. 35 (ἅγιον is a predi-

Chap. iv.
But he is said to have introduced verbal alterations,

But though no charge is brought against Valentinus of mutilating the Canon or the books of the New Testament, he is said to have introduced verbal alterations, 'correcting without hesitation' as well as 'introducing 'new explanations¹.' And his followers acted with greater boldness, if the words of Origen are to be taken strictly, in which he says that 'he knows none other who 'have altered the form (μεταχαράξαντας) of the Gospel 'besides the followers of Marcion, of Valentinus, and, as 'he believes, of Lucanus².' However this may be, the whole question belongs rather to the history of the text than to the history of the Canon; and the statement of Tertullian is fully satisfied by supposing that Valentinus employed a different recension from that of the *Vetus Latina*. But it is of consequence to remark that textual differences even in heretical writings attracted the notice of the early Fathers; and is it then possible that they would have neglected to notice graver differences as to the authority or reception of books of the New Testament if they had really existed? Their very silence is a proof of the general agreement of Christians on the Canon; a proof which gains irresistible strength when

---

cate); [Hipp.] *adv. Hær.* VI. 35 (τὸ εἰρημένον).
St John x. 8; *ib.* VI. 35.
1 Corinth. ii. 14; *ib.* VI. 34. xv. 8; cf. *ib.* 31.
Ephes. iii. 5; *ib.* VI. 35. iii. 14—18; *ib.* 34 (ἡ γραφή).
Hebr. xii. 22; cf. *ib.* VI. 30.
1 John iv. 8; cf. *ib.* VI. 29.
In an obscure passage (Clem. *Strom.* VI. 6. 52) Valentinus contrasts 'what 'is written in popular books (ταῖς 'δημοσίοις βίβλοις) with that which 'is written in the Church' (τὰ γεγρ. ἐν τῇ ἐκκλ.). By 'popular books' Clement understands 'either the 'Jewish or Gentile writings.' The antithesis seems to involve the idea of an ecclesiastical Canon.

¹ Tertull. *de Præscr. Hæret.* 30: Item Valentinus aliter exponens, et sine dubio emendans, hoc omnino quicquid emendat ut mendosum retro anterius fuisse demonstrat. The connexion of the passage requires the reading *anterius* for *alterius*. Cf. p. 298, note 4.

² Orig. *c. Cels.* II. 27. I have already given an explanation of the passage in which Origen has been supposed to connect the Gospel of Marcion with that of Valentinus: p. 294, n. 3.

combined with the natural testimony of heretical writings, and the partial exceptions by which it is occasionally limited.

Chap. iv.

The Valentinians however are said to have composed a new Gospel: 'casting aside all fear, and bringing for-'ward their own compositions, they boast that they have 'more Gospels than there really are. For they have 'advanced to such a pitch of daring as to entitle a book 'which was composed by them not long since the *Gospel* '*of Truth*, though it accords in no respect with the 'Gospels of the Apostles; so that the Gospel in fact 'cannot exist among them without blasphemy. For if 'that which they bring forward is the Gospel of Truth, 'and still is unlike those which are delivered to us by 'the Apostles—they who please can learn *how* from the 'writings themselves—it is shewn at once that that which 'is delivered to us by the Apostles is not the Gospel 'of Truth[1].' What then was this Gospel? If it had been a history of our Blessed Lord, and yet wholly at variance with the Canonical Gospels, it is evident that the Valentinians could not have received these—nor indeed any one of them—as they undoubtedly did. And here then a new light is thrown upon the character of some of the early Apocryphal Gospels, which has been in part anticipated by what was said of the Gospel of Basilides[2]. The Gospels of Basilides and Valentinus contained their systems of Christian doctrine, their views of 'the Gospel' philosophically and not historically[3].

and to have used another Gospel.

---

[1] Iren. *c. Hær.* III. 11. 9. In the last clause I have adopted the punctuation proposed by Mr Norton (II. 305). The common reading gives the same sense.

I believe that no mention of this Gospel occurs elsewhere, except in [Tert.] *de Præscr. Hæret.* c. 49. But I can see no reason for doubting the correctness of Irenæus' statement. The book may have been brought prominently under his notice without having had any permanent authority among the Valentinians.

[2] Cf. p. 294, n. 3.

[3] This common use of the word

The writers of these new Gospels in no way necessarily interfered with the old. They sought, as far as we can learn, to embody their spirit and furnish a key to their meaning, rather than to supersede their use. The Valentinians had *more* Gospels than the Catholic Church, since they accepted an authoritative doctrinal Gospel.

The titles of some of the other Gnostic Gospels confirm what has been said. Two are mentioned by Epiphanius in the account of those whom he calls 'Gnostics,' as if that were their specific name, the *Gospel of Eve* and the *Gospel of Perfection*. Neither of these could be historic accounts of the Life of Christ, and the slight description of their character which he adds illustrates the wide use of the word 'Gospel.' The first was an elementary account of Gnosticism, 'based on 'foolish visions and testimonies, called by the name of 'Eve, as though it had been revealed to her by the 'serpent[1].' The second was a 'seductive composition, no 'Gospel, but a consummation of woe[2].'

The analogy of the title of this *Gospel of Perfection* leaves little doubt as to the character of the *Gospel of Truth*. Puritan theology can furnish numerous similar occurs in Rev. xiv. 6, which passage has given rise in our own days to the strangest and most widespread Apocryphal 'Gospel'—that of the Mormonites—which the world has yet seen.

The 'Gospel of Marcion' may seem an exception, but it will be remembered that he called it the *Gospel of Christ*—Christianity, in other words, as seen in the life of Christ. Our Canonical Gospels recognise the human teacher by whom it is conveyed to us: εὐαγγέλιον Χριστοῦ κατὰ Ματθαῖον.

[1] Epiph. *Hær.* XXVI. 2: εἰς ὄνομα γὰρ αὐτῆς [Εὔας] δῆθεν ὡς εὑρούσης τὸ ὄνομα τῆς γνώσεως ἐξ ἀποκαλύ-ψεως τοῦ λαλήσαντος αὐτῇ ὄφεως σπορὰν ὑποτίθεντι...ὁρμῶνται δὲ ἀπὸ μωρῶν μαρτυριῶν καὶ ὀπτασιῶν...

In the next section Epiphanius quotes a passage from it containing a clear enunciation of Pantheism which is of great interest.

[2] Epiph. *l. c.*: ἐπίπλαστον εἰσάγουσιν ἀγώγιμόν τι ποίημα, ᾧ ποιητεύματι ἐπέθεντο ὄνομα, εὐαγγέλιον τελειώσεως τοῦτο φάσκοντες· καὶ ἀληθῶς οὐκ εὐαγγέλιον τοῦτο ἀλλὰ πένθους τελείωσις.

Mr Norton has insisted very justly on the fact that the Apocryphal Gospels were speculative or mystical treatises and not records of the Life of Christ: II. pp. 302 ff.

titles. And the partial currency of such a book among the Valentinians offers not the slightest presumption against their agreement with Catholic Christians on the exclusive claims of the four Gospels to be the records of Christ's life. These they took as the basis of their speculations; and by the help of Commentaries endeavoured to extract from them the principles which they maintained. But this will form the subject of the next section.

§ 6. *Heracleon.*

The history of Heracleon the great Valentinian commentator is full of uncertainty. Nothing is known of his country or parentage. Hippolytus classes him with Ptolemæus as belonging to the Italian school of Valentinians[1]; and we may conclude from this that he chose the West as the scene of his labours. Clement describes him as the most esteemed of his sect[2], and Origen says that 'he was reported to have been a 'familiar friend of Valentinus[3].' If we assume this statement to be true, his writings cannot well date later than the first half of the second century[4]; and he claims the title of the first commentator on the New Testament.

---

[1] [Hipp.] *adv. Hær.* VI. 35: καὶ γέγονεν ἐντεῦθεν ἡ διδασκαλία αὐτῶν διῃρημένη, καὶ καλεῖται ἡ μὲν ἀνατολική τις διδασκαλία κατ' αὐτοὺς ἡ δὲ Ἰταλιωτική. Οἱ μὲν ἀπὸ τῆς Ἰταλίας, ὧν ἐστὶν Ἡρακλέων καὶ Πτολεμαῖος, φασίν, κ.τ.λ. Clement of Alexandria made ἐπιτομαὶ ἐκ τῶν Θεοδότου καὶ τῆς ἀνατολικῆς καλουμένης διδασκαλίας.

[2] Clem. Alex. *Strom.* IV. 9. 73: ὁ τῆς Οὐαλεντίνου σχολῆς δοκιμώτατος.

[3] *Comm. in Joan.* Tom. II. § 8.

[4] Epiphanius indeed speaks of him as later than Marcus (*Hær.* XXXVI. 2). The exact chronology of the early heretics is very uncertain. In fact at least all those with whom we have to do at present must have been contemporaries. It is surprising that Irenæus mentions Heracleon only once in passing (II. 4. 1), since he was closely associated with Ptolemæus against whom the work of Irenæus was specially directed.

Chap. iv.

His Commentaries on the Gospels.

There is no evidence to determine how far the Commentaries of Heracleon extended. Fragments of his comments on the Gospels of St Luke and St John have been preserved by Clement of Alexandria and Origen. And the very existence of these fragments shews clearly the precariousness of our information on early Christian literature. Origen quotes his comments on St John repeatedly, but gives no hint that Heracleon had written anything else. Clement refers to his interpretation of a passage of St Luke and is silent as to the Commentary on St John[1]. Hippolytus makes no mention of either.

The allusions which they contain to the writings of the New Testament.

The fragments contain allusions to the Gospel of St Matthew, to the Epistles of St Paul to the Romans and the first to the Corinthians, and to the second Epistle to Timothy[2]; but the character of the comments themselves is the most striking testimony to the estimation in which the Apostolic writings were held. The sense of the Inspiration of the Evangelists—of some providential guidance by which they were led to select each fact in their history and each word in their narrative—is not more complete in Origen. The first Commentary on the New Testament exhibits the application of the same laws to its interpretation as were employed in the Old Testament. The slightest variation of language was

The doctrine of Inspiration which they imply.

---

[1] Clem. Alex. *Strom.* IV. 9. 73 sq. τοῦτον ἐξηγούμενος τὸν τόπον (i.e. Luke xii. 11 f.). Clement is a perfectly competent witness to the fact that Heracleon did comment on this passage of St Luke; but it cannot be certainly deduced from his words that Heracleon wrote a continuous Commentary on the Gospel. This is indeed unlikely. The second passage is commonly referred to his Commentary on St Luke (ap. Clem. Alex. Frag. *Eclog. Proph.* § 25): ἔνιοι δὲ ὥς φησιν Ἡρακλέων πυρὶ τὰ ὦτα τῶν σφραγιζομένων κατεσημήναντο οὕτως ἀκούσαντες τὸ ἀποστολικόν. Cf. Iren. *c. Hær.* I. 25. 6. The reference is to the 'baptism with fire' (Luke iii. 16).

[2] The references are:
St Matthew viii. 12; Orig. *in Joan.* Tom. XIII. § 59.
Romans xii. 1; Orig. *id.* § 25. i. 25; *id.* § 19.
1 Corinthians, Orig. *id.* § 59.
2 Timothy ii. 13; Clem. Alex. *Strom.* IV. *l. c.*

I.] HERACLEON. 305

held to be significant¹. Numbers were supposed to conceal hidden truths. The whole record was found to be pregnant with spiritual meaning, conveyed by the teaching of events in themselves real and instructive. It appears also that differences between the Gospels were felt, and an attempt made to reconcile them². And it must be noticed that authoritative spiritual teaching was not limited to our Lord's own words, but the remarks of the Evangelist also were received as possessing an inherent weight³.

Chap. iv.

The introduction of Commentaries implies the strongest belief in the authenticity and authority of the New Testament Scriptures; and this belief becomes more important when we notice the source from which they were derived. They took their rise among heretics, and not among Catholic Christians. Just as the earliest Fathers applied themselves to the Old Testament to bring out its real harmony with the Gospel, so heretics endeavoured to reconcile the Gospel with their own systems. Commentaries were made where the want for them was pressing. But unless the Gospels had been generally accepted the need for such works would not have been felt. Heracleon was forced to turn and

The rise of Commentaries among heretics.

---

¹ I cannot help quoting one criticism which seems to me far truer in principle than much which is commonly written on the prepositions of the New Testament. Writing on Luke xii. 8 he remarks: 'With good 'reason Christ says of those who con-'fess Him *in me* (ὁμολ. ἐν ἐμοί), but 'of those who deny Him *me* (ἀρν. με) 'only. For these even if they con-'fess Him with their voice deny Him, 'since they confess Him not in their 'action. But they alone make con-'fession *in* Him who live in the con-'fession and action that accords with 'Him; *in* whom also He makes con-'fession, having Himself embraced 'them, and being held fast by them' (Clem. Alex. *Strom.* IV. l. c.).

² Orig. *in Joan.* X. § 21: ὁ μέντοι γε Ἡρακλέων τὸ ἐν τρισὶ φησιν ἀντὶ τοῦ ἐν τρίτῃ...(John ii. 19).

³ A collection of the fragments of Heracleon is published (after Massuet) at the end of Stieren's edition of Irenæus; but much still is wanting to make the collection complete. His Commentary on the fourth chapter of St John will illustrate the statements in the text. Orig. *in Joan.* Tom. XIII. § 10 sqq.

X 2

modify much that he found in St John, which he would not have done if the book had not been received beyond all doubt[1]. And his evidence is the more valuable, because it appears that he had studied the history of the Apostles, and spoke of their lives with certainty[2].

Heracleon quoted also the Preaching of Peter.

In addition to the books of the New Testament Heracleon quoted the *Preaching of Peter*. In this he did no more than Clement of Alexandria and Gregory of Nazianzus; and Origen when he mentions the quotation does not venture to pronounce absolutely on the character of the book[3]. It is quite possible that it contained many genuine fragments of the Apostle's teaching; and the fact that it was used for illustration[4] affords no proof that it was placed on the same footing as the Canonical Scriptures.

§ 7. *Ptolemæus.*

The position of Ptolemæus.

Ptolemæus, like Heracleon, was a disciple of Valentinus, and is classed with him in the Italian as distinguished from the Eastern School[5]. Irenæus in his great work specially proposed to refute the errors of his followers; and it appears that he reduced the

---

[1] Thus to John i. 3 οὐδὲ ἕν he added τῶν ἐν τῷ κόσμῳ καὶ τῇ κτίσει (Orig. *in Joan.* II. § 8). He argued that John i. 18 contained the words of the Baptist, and not of the Evangelist (Orig. *in Joan.* Tom. VI. § 2); and in like manner he supposed that the words of Ps. lxix. 9 as used in John ii. 17 were applied not to our Lord but to 'the powers which He 'had ejected' (Orig. *in Joan.* X. 19). These forced interpretations were made from doctrinal motives, and in themselves sufficiently prove that St John's Gospel was no Gnostic work.

[2] Clem. Alex. *Strom.* IV. *l. c.:* οὐ γὰρ πάντες οἱ σωζόμενοι ὡμολόγησαν τὴν διὰ τῆς φωνῆς ὁμολογίαν καὶ ἐξῆλθον· ἐξ ὧν Ματθαῖος, Φίλιππος, Θωμᾶς, Λευΐς (i. e. *Thaddeus*), καὶ ἄλλοι πολλοί.

[3] *Comm. in Joan.* Tom. XIII. § 17 Cf. App. B.

[4] The quotation which Heracleon made was in illustration of our Lord's teaching on the true worship, John iv. 22. The passage in question is given by Clement, *Strom.* VI. 5. 40, 41.

[5] [Hipp.] *adv. Hær.* VI. 35. Tertullian [*adv. Val.* 4] places Ptolemæus before Heracleon.

Valentinian system to order and consistency, and presented it under its most attractive aspect.

Chap. iv.

Epiphanius has preserved an important letter which Ptolemæus addressed to an 'honourable sister Flora,' in which he maintains the composite and imperfect character of the Law. In proof of this doctrine he quoted words of our Lord recorded by St Matthew, the prologue to St John's Gospel, and passages from St Paul's Epistles to the Romans, the first to the Corinthians, and that to the Ephesians[1]. He appealed, it is true, to an esoteric rule of interpretation, but there is nothing to shew that he added to or subtracted from the Christian Scriptures. 'You will learn,' he says, 'by the gift of 'God in due course the origin and generation [of evil], 'when you are deemed worthy of the Apostolic tradition, 'which we also have received by due succession, while 'at the same time you measure all our statements by 'the teaching of the Saviour[2].'

His Letter to Flora.

Many other fragments of the teaching if not of the books of Ptolemæus have been preserved by Irenæus[3]; and though they are full of forced explanations of Scripture, they recognise even in their wildest theories the importance of every detail of narrative or doctrine. He found support for his doctrine in the Parables, the Miracles, and the facts of our Lord's life, as well as in the teaching of the Apostles. In the course of the exposition of his system quotations occur from the four Gospels, and from the Epistles of St Paul to the

Fragments of his teaching preserved by Irenæus.

---

[1] Epiph. *Hær.* XXXIII. 3 sqq.
[2] Epiph. *Hær.* XXXIII. 7: μαθήσει γὰρ θεοῦ διδόντος ἑξῆς καὶ τὴν τούτου ἀρχήν τε καὶ γέννησιν, ἀξιουμένη τῆς ἀποστολικῆς παραδόσεως ἣν ἐκ διαδοχῆς καὶ ἡμεῖς παρειλήφαμεν, μετὰ καὶ τοῦ κανονίσαι πάντας τοὺς λόγους τῇ τοῦ σωτῆρος διδασκαλίᾳ.

[3] Iren. *c. Hær.* I. 1 sqq. After the exposition of the Valentinian system is completed (I. 8. 5), the Latin Version adds: *et Ptolemæus quidem ita*. There is however nothing to correspond to these words in the Greek.

Romans, the first to the Corinthians, to the Galatians, Ephesians, and Colossians[1]. Two statements however which he makes are at variance with the Gospels: that our Lord's ministry was completed in a year; and that He continued for eighteen months with His disciples after His Resurrection. The first, which has found advocates in modern times[2], is remarkable because it is chiefly opposed to St John's Gospel, on which the Valentinians rested with most assurance: the second was held by Ptolemæus in common with the Ophites[3].

§ 8. *The Marcosians.*

The Marcosians made use of Apocryphal writings.

One sect of the Valentinians was distinguished by the use of Apocryphal writings. 'The Marcosians,' Irenæus writes, 'introduce with subtlety an unspeakable 'multitude of Apocryphal and spurious writings (γρα-'φαί), which they themselves forged, to confound the 'foolish, and those who know not the Scriptures (γράμ-'ματα) of truth[4].' In the absence of further evidence it is impossible to pronounce exactly on the character of these books: it is sufficient to know that they did not supplant the Canonical Scriptures. At the same time

---

[1] The following references may be noticed:
Matthew v. 18 (Iren. I. 3. 2); ix. 20 (I. 3. 3); x. 34 (I. 3. 5); xiii. 33 (I. 8. 3); xx. 1 (I. 3. 1); xxvii. 46 and xxvi. 38 (I. 8. 2).
Mark v. 31 (I. 3. 3); x. 21 (I. 3. 5).
Luke ii. 42 (I. 3. 2); iii. 17 (I. 3. 5); vi. 13 (I. 3. 2); viii. 41 (I. 8. 2); ix. 57 sqq. and xix. 5 (I. 8. 3).
John xii. 27 (var. lect. I. 8. 2); i. 1 sqq. (I. 8. 5).
Romans xi. 16 (I. 8. 3); xi. 36 (I. 3. 4).
1 Corinthians i. 18 (I. 3. 5); xi. 10 and xv. 8 (I. 8. 2); xv. 48 (I. 8. 3).
Galatians vi. 14 (I. 3. 5).
Ephesians i. 10 (I. 3. 4); iii. 21 (I. 3. 1); v. 13 (I. 8. 5); v. 32 (I. 8. 4).
Colossians i. 16 (I. 4. 5); ii. 9 and iii. 11 (I. 3. 4).

[2] In particular this opinion has been supported with very forcible arguments by Canon Browne, *Ordo Sæclorum*, pp. 80 ff.

[3] Iren. *c. Hær.* I. 3. 2, 3; cf. I. 30. 14.

[4] Iren. *c. Hær.* I. 20. 21. Among these was a Gospel of the Infancy, containing a similar story to that in the Gospel of Thomas, c. 6.

their appearance in this connexion is not without importance. Marcus the founder of the sect was probably a native of Syria[1]; and it is well known that Syria was fertile in those religious tales which are raised to too great importance by being named Gospels.

But whatever these Apocryphal writings may have been, the words of Irenæus shew that they were easily distinguishable from Holy Scripture; and the Marcosians themselves bear witness to the familiar use of our Gospels. The formularies which Marcus instituted contain references to the Gospel of St Matthew, and perhaps to the Epistle to the Ephesians[2]. The teaching of his followers offers coincidences with all four Gospels. These Gospel-quotations present remarkable various readings, but there is no reason to suppose that they were borrowed from any other source than the Canonical books. Irenæus evidently considered that they were taken thence; and while he accuses the Marcosians of 'adapting' certain passages of the Gospels to their views, the connexion shews that they tampered with the interpretation and not with the text[3].

But they admitted also the Canonical Gospels,

---

[1] This may be deduced from his use of Aramaic liturgical forms. Iren. *c. Hær.* I. 21. 3.

[2] Iren. *c. Hær.* I. 13. 3 (Matt. xviii. 10); I. 13. 2 (Eph. iii. 16, πληρῶσαι σου τὸν ἔσω ἄνθρωπον).

[3] The various readings are of considerable interest when taken in connexion with those of the Gospel-quotations of Justin. They are exactly of such a character as might arise from careless copying or quotation. In some respects also they are supported by other authority. I have given the passages at length (with the variations from the Gospels) that they may be compared with Justin (Iren. *c. Hær.* I. 20. 2 sqq.).

Matt. xi. 25 sqq.: ἐξομολογήσομαί (-οῦμαι. So Int. Lat.) σοι Πάτερ κύριε τῶν οὐρανῶν (τοῦ οὐρανοῦ) καὶ τῆς γῆς, ὅτι ἀπέκρυψας (ἔκρυψας ταῦτα. So Int. Lat.) ἀπὸ σοφῶν καὶ συνετῶν καὶ ἀπεκάλυψας αὐτὰ νηπίοις. Οὐὰ (ναὶ) ὁ Πατήρ μου (om.), ὅτι ἔμπροσθέν σου εὐδοκία μοι ἐγένετο (οὕτως ἐγ. εὐ. ἔμπρ. σου. *Ita Pater meus, quoniam in conspectu tuo placitum factum est. Int. Lat.*). Πάντα μοι παρεδόθη ὑπὸ τοῦ Πατρός μου· καὶ οὐδεὶς ἔγνω τὸν Πατέρα εἰ μὴ ὁ Υἱός, καὶ τὸν Υἱὸν εἰ μὴ ὁ Πατὴρ καὶ ᾧ ἂν ὁ Υἱὸς ἀποκαλύψῃ. For the last clause see p. 136, note 1.

Matt. xi. 28, 29: δεῦτε...ὑμᾶς·

310   THE EARLY HERETICS.   [PART

Chap. iv.
and the teaching of St Paul.

Besides quoting the Gospels the Marcosians referred generally to St Paul in support of their peculiar opinions. 'They said that Paul in express terms had 'frequently indicated *the redemption in Christ Jesus;* 'and that this was that doctrine which was variously 'and incongruously delivered by them[1].'

How far they recognised other parts of the New Testament.

The coincidences with the other parts of the New Testament are less certain. An allusion to the Deluge bears a marked similarity to the passage in the first Epistle of St Peter[2]; and among the titles of our Lord

καὶ μάθετε ἀπ' ἐμοῦ τὸν τῆς ἀληθείας Πατέρα κατηγγελκέναι. ὁ γὰρ οὐκ ᾔδεισαν, φησί, τοῦτο αὐτοῖς ὑπέσχετο διδάξειν. The last words shew that τὸν—κατηγγελκέναι formed no part of the quotation, which agrees verbally with St Matthew, omitting one clause.
Mark x. 18; Matt. xix. 16: τί με λέγεις ἀγαθόν (Mk.); εἷς ἐστὶν ἀγαθός (Mt.), ὁ Πατὴρ ἐν τοῖς οὐρανοῖς. Cf. p. 156. The passage is referred to by Ptolemæus thus (Epiph. *Hær.* XXXIII. 7): ἕνα γὰρ μόνον εἶναι ἀγαθὸν Θεὸν τὸν ἑαυτοῦ πατέρα ὁ σωτὴρ ἡμῶν ἀπεφήνατο. See Cod. D, Mark x. 18.
Matt. xxi. 23: ἐν ποίᾳ δυνάμει (ἐξουσίᾳ) τοῦτο (ταῦτα) ποιεῖς;
Mark x. 38: δύνασθε τὸ βάπτισμα βαπτισθῆναι ὃ ἐγὼ μέλλω βαπτίζεσθαι (βαπτίζομαι); Μέλλω βαπτ. answers to Matt. xx. 22, μέλλω πίνειν. Cf. p. 156.
Luke ii. 49: οὐκ οἴδατε (so D, al., Tert.: ᾔδειτε) ὅτι ἐν τοῖς τοῦ πατρός μου δεῖ με εἶναι;
Luke xii. 50: καὶ ἄλλο (om. both words) βάπτισμα (+δὲ) ἔχω βαπτισθῆναι, καὶ πάνυ ἐπείγομαι εἰς αὐτό (πῶς συνέχομαι ἕως ὅτου τελεσθῇ). This change is a good instance of an interpretative gloss.
Luke xix. 42: εἰ ἔγνως καὶ σὺ σήμερον (ἐν τῇ ἡμέρᾳ ταύτῃ) τὰ πρὸς εἰρήνην· ἐκρύβη δέ (νῦν δὲ ἐκρ.

ἀπὸ ὀφθαλμῶν) σου.
John xx. 24. Cf. Iren. I. 18. 3.
One passage causes me some perplexity. It stands thus in Iren. I. 20. 2: ἐν τῷ εἰρηκέναι Πολλάκις ἐπεθύμησα ἀκοῦσαι ἕνα τῶν λόγων τούτων καὶ οὐκ ἔσχον τὸν ἐροῦντα, ἐμφαίνοντός φασιν εἶναι διὰ τοῦ ἑνὸς τὸν ἀληθῶς ἕνα θεὸν ὃν οὐκ ἐγνώκεισαν. The Latin Version offers no various reading. Stieren supposes that the words are taken from an Apocryphal Gospel; but that is contrary to what Irenæus says. May we not change ἐπεθύμησα into ἐπεθύμησαν, and refer to Matt. xiii. 17? This emendation gives ἐγνώκεισαν a natural antecedent, and improves, unless I am mistaken, the connexion of the passage. [Dr Abbot points out that Mr Norton made the same emendation, reading also πολλοὶ καὶ for πολλάκις, and διὰ τοῦ ἐροῦντας for διὰ τοῦ ἑνός (*Authorship of the Fourth Gospel*, p. 96).]

[1] Iren. *c. Hær.* I. 21. 3. The phrase occurs in the Epistle of St Paul to the Romans (iii. 24), Ephesians (i. 7), and Colossians (i. 14). The words of the Marcosians may consequently be taken as a testimony to these Epistles.

[2] Iren. *c. Hær.* I. 18. 3; 1 Peter iii. 20. The recurrence of the same word διεσώθησαν makes the similarity more worthy of notice.

occurs *Alpha and Omega*, which they would appear to have borrowed from the Apocalypse[1]. Apart from this special coincidence, the whole reasoning of the Marcosians shews a clear resemblance to the characteristic symbolism of the Apocalypse, which is distinguished by the sanction that it gives to a belief in the deep meaning of letters and numbers. And this belief, though carried to an extravagant extent, lies at the bottom of the Marcosian speculations. The principle of interpretation is one which I cannot attempt to discuss, but it is again a matter of interest to trace the general agreement between the contents of the Canon and the bases on which heretical sects professed to build their systems. If we suppose that the 'acknowledged' books of the New Testament were in universal circulation and esteem, we find in them an adequate explanation of the manifold developments of heresy. In whatever direction the development extended, it can be traced to some starting point in the Apostolic writings[2].

---

[1] Iren. *c. Hær.* I. 14. 6; 15. 1. The allusion would be certain beyond doubt if διὰ τοῦτο φησὶν αὐτὸν α καὶ ω could be translated, as Stieren translates it,...*ipse se dicit* A *et* Ω. It is evident from the next sentence that φησὶν implies a quotation. Must we not read αὐτός, 'on this account (he says) he is...'? (Dr Hort has pointed out to me that the full phrase occurs in [Hipp.] *adv. Hær.* VI. 49: Καὶ διὰ τοῦτο δὲ φασὶν αὐτὸν λέγειν 'Ἐγὼ τὸ ἄλφα καὶ τὸ ω, κ.τ.λ.)

[2] At the end of the works of Clement of Alexandria is usually published a series of fragments entitled *Short Notes from the writings of Theodotus and the so-called Eastern School at the time of Valentinus* (ἐκ τῶν Θεοδότου καὶ τῆς ἀνατολικῆς διδασκαλίας κατὰ τοὺς Οὐαλεντίνου χρόνους ἐπιτομαί). The meaning of the phrase *Eastern School* has been explained already (cf. pp. 303, 306); and the testimony of these fragments may be considered as supplementary to that which has been obtained from the Valentinians of the West. But as I am not now able to enter on the discussion of the authorship and date of the fragments, it will be enough to give a general summary of the books of the New Testament to which they contain allusions. They are these: the Four Gospels; the Epistles of St Paul to the Romans, 1 Corinthians, Ephesians, Galatians, Philippians, Colossians, 1 Timothy; the First Epistle of St Peter.

Epiphanius in his article on Theodotus of Byzantium, who is commonly identified with the Clementine Theodotus, represents him (*Hær.*

§ 9. *Marcion.*

The first known Canon that of Marcion.

Hitherto the testimony of heretical writers to the New Testament has been confined to the recognition of detached parts by casual quotations or characteristic types of doctrine. Marcion on the contrary fixed a definite collection of Apostolic books as the foundation of his system. The Canon thus published is the first of which there is any record; and like the first Commentary and the first express recognition of the equality of the Old and New Testament Scriptures, it comes from without the Catholic Church, and not from within it[1].

The peculiar position of Marcion.

The position which Marcion occupies in the history of Christianity is in every way most striking. Himself the son of a Bishop of Sinope, it is said that he aspired to gain the 'first place' in the Church of Rome[2]. And though his father and the Roman presbyters refused him communion, he gained so many followers that in the time of Epiphanius they were spread throughout the world[3]. While other heretics proposed to extend or complete the Gospel, he claimed only to reproduce in its original simplicity the Gospel of St Paul[4]. But his

LIV.) as using the Gospels of St Matthew, St Luke, and St John; the Acts of the Apostles; the First Epistle to Timothy.

The passages are given at length by Kirchhofer, § 403 ff.

[1] It is a very significant fact that the first quotation of a book of the New Testament as Scripture, the first Commentary on an Apostolic writing, and the first known Canon of the New Testament, come from heretical authors. It is impossible to suppose that in these respects they suggested the Catholic view of the whole Bible instead of following it.

[2] Epiph. *Hær.* XLII. 1. What the προεδρία was is uncertain. Probably it implies only admission into the college of πρεσβύτεροι. Cf. Bingham, *Orig. Eccles.* I. p. 266. Massuet, *de Gnostic. reb.* § 135.

[3] Epiph. *l.c.* (Rome, Italy, Egypt, Palestine, Arabia, Syria, Cyprus, the Thebaid, and even Persia. The omission of Asia Minor is worthy of notice).

[4] Tert. *adv. Marc.* I. 20: Aiunt Marcionem non tam innovasse regulam separatione Legis et Evangelii quam retro adulteratam recurasse.

personal influence was great and lasting. He impressed his own character on his teaching, where others only lent their names to abstract systems of doctrine. If Polycarp called him 'the first-born of Satan,' we may believe that the title signalised his special energy; and the fact that he sought the recognition of a Catholic bishop shews the position which he claimed to fill.

The time of Marcion's arrival at Rome[1] cannot be fixed with certainty. Justin Martyr speaks of him as 'still teaching' when he wrote his first Apology, and from the wide spread of his doctrine then it is evident that some interval had elapsed since he had separated from the Church[2]. Consistently with this Epiphanius places that event shortly after the death of Hyginus; and Tertullian states it as an acknowledged fact that Marcion taught in the reign of Antoninus Pius, but with a note to the effect that he had taken no pains to inquire in what year he began to spread his heresy[3]. This approximate date however is sufficient to give an accurate notion of the historical place which he occupied. As the contemporary of Justin he united the age of Ignatius with that of Irenæus. He witnessed the consolidation of the Catholic Church; and his heresy was the final struggle of one element of Christianity against the whole truth. It was in fact the formal counterpart of Ebionism, naturally later in time than that, but no less naturally the result of a partial view of Apostolic teaching[4].

Chap. iv.

His date.

139—142 A.D.

---

[1] Petavius has discussed his date, *Animadv. in Epiph. Hær.* XLVI. (p. 83); and Massuet much more fully and exactly, *de Gnostic. reb.*§136. Cf. Volkmar, *Theol. Jahrb.* 1855, p. 270 f.
[2] Just. Mart. *Ap.* I. 26.
[3] Tert. *adv. Marc.* I. 19: Quoto quidem anno Antonini Majoris de Ponto suo exhalaverit aura canicularis non curavi investigare; de quo tamen constat, Antonianus hæreticus est, sub Pio impius.
[4] Marcion is commonly described as the scholar and successor of *Cerdo*. But it is impossible to determine how far Cerdo's views on the

Chap. iv.

The contents of his Canon.

Marcion professed to have introduced no innovation of doctrine, but merely to have restored that which had been corrupted. St Paul only, according to him, was the true Apostle; and Pauline writings alone were admitted into his Canon. This was divided into two parts, 'The Gospel' and 'The Apostolicon[1].' The Gospel was a recension of St Luke with numerous omissions and variations from the received text[2]. The Apostolicon contained ten Epistles of St Paul, excluding the Pastoral Epistles and that to the Hebrews[3].

The text of the Epistles.

Tertullian and Epiphanius agree in affirming that Marcion altered the text of the books which he received to suit his own views; and they quote many various readings in support of the assertion. Those which they cite from the Epistles are certainly insufficient to prove the point; and on the contrary they go far to shew that Marcion preserved without alteration the text which he found in his Manuscript. Of the seven readings noticed by Epiphanius, only two are unsupported by other authority; and it is altogether unlikely that Marcion changed other passages, when, as Epiphanius himself shews, he left untouched those which are most directly opposed to his system.

The text of the Gospel.

With the Gospel the case was different. The influence of oral tradition upon the form and use of the written Gospels was of long continuance. The personality of their authors was in some measure obscured by

---

Canon were identical with those of Marcion. The spurious additions to Tertullian's tract *de Præscr. Hæret.* (c. LI.) are of no independent authority.

[1] I have not noticed the title 'Apostolicon' or 'Apostolus' in Tertullian; but it occurs in Epiphanius, and in the Dialogue appended to Origen's works.

[2] Of the numerous essays on Marcion's Gospel the most important are by Ritschl (1846), Volkmar (1852), and Hilgenfeld (*Theol. Jahrb.* 1853), Sanday, *The Gospels in the Second Century*, c. VIII. and Appendix. See also *Introduction to the Study of the Gospels*, App. D. No. IV.

[3] See Note at the end of the Section.

the character of their work. The Gospel was felt to be Christ's Gospel—the name which Marcion ventured to apply to his own—and not the particular narration of any Evangelist. And such considerations as these will explain, though they do not justify, the liberty which Marcion allowed himself in dealing with the text of St Luke. There can be no doubt that St Luke's narrative lay at the basis of his Gospel; but it is not equally clear that all the changes which were introduced into it were due to Marcion himself[1]. Some of the omissions can be explained at once by his peculiar doctrines; but others are unlike arbitrary corrections, and must be considered as various readings of the greatest interest, dating as they do to a time anterior to all other authorities in our possession[2].

There is no evidence to shew on what grounds Marcion rejected the Acts and the Pastoral Epistles[3]. Their character is in itself sufficient to explain the fact; and there is nothing to indicate that his judgment was based on any historical objections to their authenticity.

Chap. iv.

The cause of the omissions.

[1] The main question is are we to consider the third Gospel an enlargement of the Gospel put forth by Marcion, or the foundation of it? And I venture to think that the evidence is decisive in favour of the second alternative. But at the same time textual authorities shew that there were two very early 'recensions' of St Luke's Gospel, and it is by no means unlikely that Marcion's copy represented a peculiar text.

This is not the place to enter in detail upon this question, but it may be worth while to notice that Tertullian does *not* say that Marcion removed Matt. xv. 24, 26 *from St Luke*. He simply challenges him to take away from the Gospel what was a well-known part of it (Marcion *aufer* [not *aufert*] etiam illud de Evangelio...*adv. Marc.* IV. 7). So too the reading in Luke v. 14, assumed by Epiphanius, is found in good early authorities though wrong. Thus neither the statement nor the inference in *Supernat. Rel.* II. pp. 100 f. is correct.

[2] Of the longer omissions the most remarkable is that of the parable of the Prodigal Son (Epiph. p. 338). The quotations from Marcion's Gospels are collected by Kirchhofer (pp. 366 ff.). Cf. *Introduction to the Study of the Gospels*, App. D. No. IV.

[3] In one passage Epiphanius (p. 321) according to the present text affirms that he acknowledged at least in part the fourteen Pauline Epistles; but there is evidently some corruption in the words.

Chap. iv.
The Acts.

The Pastoral Epistles.

In the Acts there is the clearest recognition of the teaching of St Peter as one constituent part of the Christian faith, while Marcion regarded it as essentially faulty; and so again, since he claimed to be the founder of a new line of bishops, it was obviously desirable to clear away the foundation of the Churches whose Apostolicity he denied. This may have been the reason why they were not found in his Canon; but it is unsatisfactory to conjecture where history is silent. And the mere fact that Marcion did not recognise the Epistles cannot be used as an argument against their Pauline origin, so long as the grounds of his decision are unknown.

The remaining books of the New Testament.

The rejection of the other books of the New Testament Canon was a necessary consequence of Marcion's principles[1]. The first Apostles according to him had an imperfect apprehension of the truth, and their writings necessarily partook of this imperfection. But it does not follow that he regarded them as unauthentic because he set them aside as unauthoritative[2].

---

[1] The Epistle to the Hebrews is a continuous vindication of the spiritual significance of the Mosaic Covenant which Marcion denied. Even supposing therefore that he was acquainted with the tradition that it was written by St Paul, he could not have accepted it as part of his Canon.

[2] Though Marcion only used St Luke's Gospel, it appears that he was acquainted with the others, and endeavoured to overthrow their authority, not by questioning their authenticity, but by shewing that those by whose authority they were published were reproved by St Paul (*adv. Marc.* IV. 3): Connititur ad destruendum statum eorum evangeliorum quæ propria et sub Apostolorum nomine eduntur, vel etiam Apostolicorum (St Mark), ut scilicet fidem quam illis adimit suo conferat. The rejection of St John's writings by Marcion is remarkable, because the Gospel is in its tendency essentially anti-Judaic. On the other hand this Gospel bears the mark of individuality so strongly as distinguished from the common form of Evangelic tradition that it could not have been taken to represent the typical Gospel of Christ. Nothing I believe is known of the grounds on which Marcion assailed the position of St John's or St Matthew's Gospel, and it is uncertain whether Tertullian in the passage quoted speaks from a knowledge of what Marcion may have written on the subject or simply from his own point of sight. Still I can see no

Apart from the important testimony which it bears to a large section of the New Testament writings, the Canon of Marcion is of importance as shewing the principle by which the New Testament was formed. Marcion accepted St Paul's writings as a final and decisive test of St Paul's teaching; in like manner the Catholic Church received the writings which were sanctioned by Apostolic authority as combining to convey the different elements of Christianity. There is indeed no evidence to shew that any definite Canon of the Apostolic writings was already published in Asia Minor when Marcion's appeared; but the minute and varied hints which have been already collected tend to prove that if it were not expressly fixed it was yet implicitly determined by the practice of the Church. And though undue weight must not be attached to the language of his adversaries, it is not to be forgotten that they always charge him with mutilating something which already existed, and not with endeavouring to impose a test which was not generally received.

Chap. iv. The principles on which the Canon was formed.

reason, in the absence of other evidence, to question the fact which he affirms.

The opinions of APELLES, a disciple of Marcion, upon the Books of the New Testament are vaguely described. He is said to have admitted 'such parts of the Gospels and 'the Apostle as pleased him' (τῶν εὐαγγελίων ἢ τοῦ ἀποστόλου τὰ ἀρέσκοντα αὐτῷ αἱρεῖται, [Hipp.] *adv.*

Hær. VII. 38). Dr Abbot points out to me that he seems to refer to John xx. 25 as well as to Luke xxiv. 39 in the words cited by Hippolytus (*l. c.*). Epiphanius in refuting his opinions quotes without reserve the Gospel of St John among other Scriptures (*Hær.* XLIV. 4). This however proves little, but from Origen (*in Joan.* XIX. 1) it is clear that St John's Gospel was used by some Marcionite schools.

NOTE: see page 314.

According to Tertullian the Epistles were arranged by Marcion (*adv. Marc.* v.) in the following order: Galatians, 1 and 2 Corinthians, Romans, 1 and 2 Thessalonians, Ephesians (Laodiceans), Colossians, Philippians, Philemon.

Epiphanius gives the same order, with the single exception that he transposes the last two (*Hær.* XLII. p. 373).

Tertullian expressly affirms the identity of the Epistles to the Laodiceans and to the Ephesians (*ib.* 17); and implies that Marcion prided himself on the restoration of the true title, *quasi et in isto diligentissimus explorator.* The language of Epiphanius is self-contradictory.

The statements of Tertullian and Epiphanius as to the Epistle to Philemon are at first sight opposed; but I believe that Epiphanius either used the word διαστρόφως loosely, or was misled by some author who applied it to the transposition and not to the corruption of the Epistle. He uses the same word of the Epistle to the Philippians, but Tertullian gives no hint that that Epistle was tampered with in an especial manner by Marcion. Cf. Epiph. *Hær.* XLII. pp. 373 f.; Tertull. *adv. Marc.* v. 20, 21. Again Epiphanius says (*ib.* p. 371) that the Epistles to the Thessalonians were 'distorted in like manner.'

Epiphanius notices the following readings as peculiar to Marcion:
Eph. v. 31, om. τῇ γυναικί. So Jerome.
Gal. v. 9, δολοῖ. So Lucif., al.
1 Cor. ix. 8, ὁ νόμος + Μωυσέως. See the following verse.
— x. 9, Χριστὸν for Κύριον. So DEFGKL, al.
— — 19, τί οὖν φημί; ὅτι ἱερόθυτόν τι ἔστιν ἢ εἰδωλόθυτόν τι ἔστιν; ἀλλ' ὅτι, κ.τ.λ. Cf. varr. lectt.
1 Cor. xiv. 19, διὰ τὸν νόμον for δ. τοῦ νοός μου. So Ambrst.
2 Cor. iv. 13, om. κατὰ τὸ γεγραμμένον.

The language of Tertullian is more general. Speaking of the Epistle to the Romans he says: Quantas autem foveas in ista vel maxime Epistola Marcion fecerit auferendo quæ voluit de nostri Instrumenti integritate parebit (*adv. Marc.* v. 13); but he does not enumerate any of these lacunæ, nor are they noticed by Epiphanius. In the next chapter, after quoting Rom. viii. 11, he adds Salio et hic amplissimum abruptum intercisæ scripturæ, and then passes to Rom. x. 2. Epiphanius says nothing of any omission here; and the language of Tertullian is at least ambiguous, especially when taken in connexion with his commentary on Rom. xi. 33. It appears however from Origen (*Comm. in Rom.* xvi. 25) that Marcion omitted the last two chapters of the Epistle.

In the Epistle to the Galatians it seems that there was some omission in the third chapter (Tert. *adv. Marc.* v. 3), but it is uncertain of what extent it was. In Gal. ii. 5 Marcion read οὐδέ, while Tertullian omitted the negative (*l. c.*).

The other variations mentioned by Tertullian are the following:
1 Cor. xv. 45, Κύριος for Ἀδάμ (2). Cf. varr. lectt.
2 Cor. iv. 4, Marcion was evidently right in his punctuation. *In quibus deus ævi hujus*...Nos contra, says Tertullian, sic distinguendum dicimus; *In quibus deus*, dehinc : *ævi hujus excæcavit mentes infidelium* (*adv. Marc.* v. 11).
Eph. ii. 15, om. αὐτοῦ.
— — 20, om. καὶ προφητῶν.
— iii. 9, om. ἐν.
— vi. 2, om ἥτις—end.
1 Thess. ii. 15 + ἰδίους (before προφήτας). So D*** E** KL, al.
2 Thess. i. 8, om. ἐν πυρὶ φλογός.

In addition to these various readings Jerome (*in loc.*) mentions the omission of καὶ Θεοῦ Πατρός in Gal. i. 1; and from the Dialogue (c. 5) it appears that the Marcionites read 1 Cor. xv. 38 sqq. with considerable differences from the common text.

TATIAN. *Chap. iv.*

The examination of these readings perhaps belongs rather to the history of the text than to the history of the Canon; but they are in themselves a proof of the minute and jealous attention paid to the N. T. Scriptures. If the text was watched carefully, the Canon cannot have been a matter of indifference.

§ 10. *Tatian.*

The history of Tatian throws an important light on that of Marcion[1]. Both were naturally restless, inquisitive, impetuous. They were subject to the same influences, and were probably resident for a while in the same city[2]. Both remained for some time within the Catholic Church, and then sought the satisfaction of their peculiar wants in a system of stricter discipline and sterner logic. Both abandoned the received Canon of Scripture; and their combined witness goes far to establish it in its integrity. They exhibit different phases of the same temper; and while they testify to the existence of a critical spirit among Christians of the second century, they point to a Catholic Church as the one centre from which their systems diverged.   *The relation of Tatian to Marcion.*

Tatian was an Assyrian by birth, and a pagan, but no less than his future master Justin an ardent student of philosophy. Like the most famous men of his age, he was attracted to Rome, and there he met Justin,—that 'most admirable man,' as he calls him—whose influence and experience could not fail to win one of such a character as Tatian's to the Christian faith. The hostility of Crescens tested the sincerity of his conversion; and after the death of Justin he devoted himself to carrying on the work which his master had begun. For a time his work was successfully accomplished, and Rhodon was among his scholars. But afterwards, in   *The eventfulness of his life.*

[1] On Tatian see especially Bp Lightfoot, *C. R.*, May, 1877, 1132 ff.   [2] Tat. *Orat.* c. 18; Just. *Ap.* i. 26.

320 THE EARLY HERETICS. [PART

Chap. iv.

consequence of his elevation, as Irenæus asserts, he introduced novelties of doctrine into his teaching; and at last returning to the East, placed himself at the head of the sect of the Encratites, combining the Valentinian doctrine of Æons with the asceticism of Marcion[1].

The consequent importance of his evidence.

The strange vicissitudes of Tatian's life, whose literary activity may be most probably placed in the third quarter of the second century, contribute to the value of his evidence. In part he continues the testimony of Justin, and in part he completes the Canon of Marcion. Doubts have been raised as to Justin's acquaintance with the writings of St Paul and St John; and yet we find his scholar using them without hesitation. Marcion is said to have rejected the Pastoral Epistles on critical grounds; and Tatian, who was not less ready to trust to his individual judgment, affirmed that the Epistle to Titus was most certainly the Apostle's writing.

The testimonies contained in his Address to Greeks.

The existing work of Tatian, his *Address to Greeks*, offers no scope for Scriptural quotations. There is abundant evidence to prove his deep reverence for the writings of the Old Testament, and yet only one anonymous quotation from it occurs in his *Address*[2]; but it is most worthy of notice that in the same work he makes clear references to the Gospel of St John, to a parable recorded by St Matthew, and probably to the Epistle of St Paul to the Romans and his first Epistle to the Corinthians, and to the Apocalypse[3]. The absence of more explicit testimony to the books of the New Testa-

---

[1] Tatian, *Orat.* cc. 42, 1, 35, 18, 19. Iren. *c. Hær.* I. 28. 1 (Euseb. *H. E.* IV. 29). Epiph. *Hær.* XLVI. Cf. Iren. *c. Hær.* III. 23. 8.

[2] *Orat.* c. 15; Ps. viii. 5. The quotation occurs in Heb. ii. 7; and it may be remarked that Tatian just before uses the word ἀπαύγασμα (Heb.

[3] St Matthew xiii. 44, *Orat.* c. 30. St John [i. 1, *Orat.* c. 5, this reference is not certain]; i. 3, c. 19; i. 5, c. 13; iv. 24, c. 4. Romans i. 20, c. 4; vii. 15, c. 11. 1 Corinthians iii. 16, ii. 14, c. 15. Apoc. xxi. sq. c. 20.

ment is to be accounted for by the style of his writing, and does not imply either ignorance or neglect of them. A few fragments and notices in other writers help to extend the evidence of Tatian. Eusebius relates on the authority of others that 'he dared to alter some of the 'expressions of the Apostle (Paul), correcting their style¹.' In this there is nothing to shew that Eusebius was aware of greater differences as to the contents of the New Testament between the Catholics and Tatian than might fall under the name of various readings; yet in this it appears that he was deceived. Jerome states expressly that Tatian rejected some of the Epistles of St Paul, though he maintained the authenticity of that to Titus². However this may be, it can be gathered from Clement of Alexandria, Irenæus, and Jerome, that he endeavoured to derive authority for his peculiar opinions from the Epistles to the Corinthians and Galatians, and perhaps from the Epistle to the Ephesians and the Gospel of St Matthew³. Nor is this all: the name of one out of 'the great multitude of his compositions' is not the least important element of his testimony: his Diatessaron is apparently the first recognition of a fourfold Gospel.

The obvious sense of the title of the book *Diates-*

Chap. iv.

and in his fragments.

The title Diatessaron.

---

¹ Euseb. *H. E.* IV. 29: τοῦ ἀποστόλου φασὶ τολμῆσαί τινας αὐτὸν μεταφράσαι φωνάς, ὡς ἐπιδιορθούμενον αὐτῶν τὴν τῆς φράσεως σύνταξιν.
² *Pref. in Tit.* (Fr. 11, Otto): Tatianus Encratitarum patriarches, qui et ipse nonnullas Pauli Epistolas repudiavit, hanc vel maxime (*i.e.* the Ep. to Titus) Apostoli pronuncian- dam credidit, parvi pendens Marcionis et aliorum qui cum eo in hac parte consentiunt assertionem.
It is probable that he rejected the Epistles to Timothy (cf. Otto *l. c.*), but there is no evidence to prove it. Many of the Encratites rejected St Paul altogether. Cf. p. 323, n. 1.
³ 1 Corinthians vii. 5; Clem. Alex. *Strom.* III. 12, 81 (ταὐτά φησιν τὸν ἀπόστολον ἐξηγούμενος) (fr. 1): xv. 22; Iren. III. 23. 8 (fr. 5).
Galatians vi. 8; Hieron. *Comm. in loc.* (fr. 3).
St Matthew vi. 19; xxii. 30; Clem. Alex. *Strom.* III. 12. 86 (fr. 2).
Ephesians iv. 24; Clem. Alex. *l. c.* 82 (fr. 8) (ὁ παλαιὸς ἀνὴρ καὶ ὁ καινός. These two last references are from an anonymous citation (τις) which has been commonly assigned to Tatian.

saron, 'the [Gospel] by the Four,' in the absence of all real external evidence in support of another view, must be allowed to have great weight. There can be no reasonable doubt that the name was given to the work by Tatian himself; and if the Diatessaron was not a compilation of four Gospels, what is the explanation of the number? If again these four Gospels were not those which we receive, what other four Gospels ever formed a collection which needed no further description than *the Four?* I am not aware that any answer has been given to these questions; and in connexion with the belief and assertions of early Fathers they are surely decisive as to the sources of Tatian's Diatessaron[1].

His Diatessaron. *The account of it given by Eusebius and*

For all that can be gathered from history falls in with the idea suggested by the title. The earliest mention of it[2] is found in Eusebius. 'Tatian,' he says, 'the former leader 'of the Encratites, having put together in some strange 'fashion a combination and collection of the Gospels, 'gave this the name of the *Diatessaron*, and the work is 'still partially current[3].' The words evidently imply

[1] Tatian's Diatessaron is said to have contained one important addition (Matt. xxvii. 49), which is however found in אBCLU, al. Cf. Tischendorf, *in loc.*

[2] No notice is taken of the Diatessaron in Otto's Edition of Tatian. The most exact account of it with which I am acquainted is that of Credner, *Beiträge*, I. pp. 437 ff. He endeavours to shew that the Diatessaron was in fact a form of the Petrine Gospel, and identical with that of Justin Martyr (p. 444). When he says (p. 48) that the Diatessaron is spoken of 'bald als *eine von ihm* 'selbst (Tatian) verfasste, *gottlose* 'Harmonie aus unsern vier Evange-'lien, bald als *eine eigene, selbständige* '*Schrift*,' I confess that I do not recognise his usual accuracy and candour. His further arguments do not add plausibility to his conclusion: *Gesch. des N. T. Kanon*, p. 22.

[3] Euseb. *H. E.* IV. 29: ὁ μέντοι γε πρότερος αὐτῶν ἀρχηγὸς ὁ Τατιανὸς συνάφειάν τινα καὶ συναγωγὴν οὐκ οἶδ' ὅπως τῶν εὐαγγελίων συνθεὶς τὸ διὰ τεσσάρων τοῦτο προσωνόμασεν· ὃ καὶ παρά τισιν εἰσέτι νῦν φέρεται. Eusebius may speak from hearsay; but he explicitly attributes the title of the book to Tatian himself, and makes no mention of any Apocryphal additions to the Evangelic narrative. The vague language of Epiphanius (p. 326, n. 1) cannot be fairly used to invalidate Eusebius' direct statement as to the authenticity of the title.

The term διὰ τεσσάρων was used in music to express the concord of the fourth (συλλαβή). This sense may throw some light upon the choice of the name.

that the Canonical Gospels formed the basis of Tatian's Harmony; and that this was the opinion of Eusebius is placed beyond all doubt by the preceding sentence, in which he states that 'the Severians who consolidated 'Tatian's heresy made use of the Law and the Prophets 'and the Gospels, while they spoke ill of the Apostle 'Paul, rejecting his Epistles, and refusing to receive the 'Acts of the Apostles[1].' Not very long afterwards Theodoret gives a more exact account of the character and common use of the book. 'Tatian also composed 'the Gospel called *Diatessaron*, removing the genealo-'gies, and all the other passages which shew that the 'Lord was born of David according to the flesh. This 'was used not only by the members of his party, but 'even by those who followed the Apostolic doctrine, as 'they did not perceive the evil design of the composition, 'but used the book in their simplicity for its conciseness. 'And I found also myself more than two hundred such 'books in our churches (*i.e.* in Syria), which had been 'received with respect; and having gathered all together, 'I caused them to be laid aside, and introduced in their 'place the Gospels of the four Evangelists[2].' From this

Chap. iv.

Theodoret.

---

[1] Euseb. *l. c.* Credner (p. 439) supposes that the term *Severiani* was merely a translation of ἐγκρατηταί. Origen (*c. Cels.* v. 65) mentions the Encratites among those who rejected the Epistles of St Paul. They received some Apocryphal books also: κέχρηνται δὲ γραφαῖς πρωτοτύπως (? πρωτοτύποις) ταῖς λεγομέναις Ἀνδρέου καὶ Ἰωάννου πράξεσιν καὶ Θωμᾶ καὶ ἀποκρύφοις τισί (Epiph. *Hær.* XLVII. 1).

[2] Theodor. *Hæret. Fab.* I. 20 (Credn. p. 442): οὗτος καὶ τὸ διὰ τεσσάρων καλούμενον συντέθεικεν εὐαγγέλιον, τὰς γενεαλογίας περικόψας καὶ τὰ ἄλλα ὅσα ἐκ σπέρματος Δαβὶδ κατὰ σάρκα γεγενημένον τὸν Κύριον δείκνυσιν. Ἐχρήσαντο δὲ τούτῳ οὐ μόνον οἱ τῆς ἐκείνου συμμορίας ἀλλὰ καὶ οἱ τοῖς ἀποστολικοῖς ἐπόμενοι δόγμασι, τὴν τῆς συνθήκης κακουργίαν οὐκ ἐγνωκότες, ἀλλ' ἁπλούστερον ὡς συντόμῳ τῷ βιβλίῳ χρησάμενοι. Εὗρον δὲ κἀγὼ πλείους ἢ διακοσίας βίβλους τοιαύτας ἐν ταῖς παρ' ἡμῖν ἐκκλησίαις τετιμημένας καὶ πάσας συναγαγὼν ἀπεθέμην καὶ τὰ τῶν τεττάρων εὐαγγελιστῶν ἀντεισήγαγον εὐαγγέλια. The technical sense of κακουργία (*malitia*) forbids us to lay any undue stress on the word.

The large number of copies is a striking indication of the wide circu-

statement it is clear that the *Diatessaron* was so orthodox as to enjoy a wide ecclesiastical popularity. The heretical character of the book was not evident upon the surface of it, and consisted rather in faults of defect than in erroneous teaching. Moreover Theodoret had certainly examined it, and he like earlier writers regarded it as a compilation from the four Gospels. He speaks of omissions (taking the Synoptists as his standard) which were at least in part natural in a Harmony, but notices no such Apocryphal additions as would have found place in any Gospel not derived from Canonical sources.

The Doctrine of Addai.

These testimonies receive a remarkable illustration from the 'Doctrine of Addai', an apocryphal Syriac work, written at Edessa or in the neighbourhood, dating in all probability from about the middle of the third century. In this it is said that the early converts of Edessa heard read with the Old Testament 'the New '[Testament] of the Diatessaron[1].' The name of the author is not mentioned; but that can be supplied with certainty from another witness of the same region. It is stated by Dionysius Bar Salibi, a writer of the close of the twelfth century, that Ephraem Syrus († 373), the celebrated Deacon of Edessa, wrote a commentary on the Diatessaron of Tatian, as he might naturally do if the work was in public use in his Church.

Ephraem's Commentary.

This work, or perhaps a series of extracts from it, is still preserved in an Armenian translation. The Armenian text was published as long since as 1836, but recently the work has been made generally accessible in a Latin translation[2]. The first passage commented

---

[1] Comp. Lightfoot, *l. c.* 1137; Abbot *l. c.* p. 53 n.

[2] Evangelii concordantis expositio lation of the Gospels, which this compilation partially supplanted in a special district.

...a sancto Ephraemo...in Latinum translata a R. P. Ioanne Baptista Aucher, Mechitarista, cujus versionem emendavit...Dr Georgius Moesinger, Professor studii biblici A. T. Salisburgi Venetiis, 1876.

upon is John i. 1, with which, as it appears from the evidence of Bar Salibi, Tatian's Harmony began. Then follow passages from the four Gospels, of which those taken from St Matthew and St John are in the main in the order of the Gospels: the quotations from St Luke are much transposed; from St Mark there are, as far as I have observed, only three (or four) quotations. The last passage discussed is Acts i. 4.

There is no reason for doubting the authenticity of this work, and the character of the text of the passages quoted is a very strong positive argument in favour of the belief that they were taken from Tatian's Harmony. In many cases it is undoubtedly difficult to speak confidently as to the reading which has passed through two, or rather three, translations, but some of those which are beyond question are readings which are supported only by authorities which are of the most ancient type[1].

Against this decisive evidence a vague statement of Epiphanius is quoted, who writes that Tatian 'is said to 'have been the author of the Harmony of the four 'Gospels which some call the Gospel according to the

---

[1] The following may be mentioned:
Matt. viii. 10, παρ' οὐδενί, p. 74.
— xi. 25, πάτερ τοῦ οὐρ. καὶ τῆς γῆς ('in græco dicit'), p. 116 f.
— xi. 27, οὐδεὶς οὔπιγ. πατέρα...οὐδὲ τὸν υἱόν...p. 117.
— xxi. 31, ὁ δεύτερος, p. 191.
— xxii. 23, λέγοντες, p. 193.
Luke i. 78, ἐπισκέψεται, p. 20.
— ii. 14, ἐν ἀνθρώποις εὐδοκίας, p. 27.
— ii. 26, χριστὸν κύριον, p. 226.
John i. 3, 4, ὃ γέγονεν ἐν αὐτῷ ζωὴ ἦν, p. 5.
— iii. 13, om. ὁ ὢν ἐν τῷ οὐρ. (appy) pp. 168, 187, 189.
— iv. 19, om. οὐ γὰρ σ. I. Σ. (perhaps) p. 140.

Other remarkable readings occur:
Matt. x. 1 (Luke x. 1) add *after his likeness*, pp. 90, 115.
— xviii. 20, add *where there is one there am I*, p. 165 ('consolatus est dicens.')

In John vii. 8 οὐ is read, and in v. 8 ἐν τῇ ἑορ. p. 167. Luke xxii. 43 f. is read p. 235. Compare Abbot *l. c.* p. 55 n.

'Hebrews[1].' But such a statement from such a man has practically no weight. There was a superficial resemblance between the two books in the omission of the genealogies; and Epiphanius does not appear to have had any opportunity of comparing them[2].

There is then abundant evidence to shew that Tatian's work was constructed out of our four Gospels[3]; and thus once again a heretical writer is the first to recognise explicitly an important fact in the history of the Canon. It must indeed have been evident to the reader throughout this chapter that the testimony of heretical writers to the books of the New Testament tends on the whole to give greater certainty and weight to that which is drawn from other sources. So far from obscuring or contravening the judgment of the Church generally, they offer material help in the interpretation of it. And this follows naturally from their position. As separatists they fixed the standard by which they were willing to be judged, wherever it differed from that which was commonly received. And all early controversy proceeds on this basis. The authority of the Apostolic Scriptures is everywhere assumed: this is the rule, and only exceptions from the rule are noticed in detail.

---

[1] Epiph. *Hær.* XLVI. 1 λέγεται δὲ τὸ διὰ τεσσάρων εὐαγγελίων ὑπ' αὐτοῦ γεγενῆσθαι ὅπερ κατὰ 'Εβραίους τινὲς καλοῦσι. Some may be inclined to change εὐαγγελίων into εὐαγγέλιον.

[2] Comp. Lightfoot, *l. c.* pp. 1141 ff.

The confusion of the Harmony of Tatian with that of Ammonius by some late Syrian writers (though Bar Salibi carefully distinguishes them) led to the assertion of Gregory Bar Hebræus that Ephraem commented on the Harmony of Ammonius. For the origin and extent of this error see Lightfoot, *l. c.* 1139 n.

[3] Victor of Capua (A.D. 545) says that Tatian's Harmony was called *Diapente;* but he evidently derived his information from Eusebius alone, and Eusebius records that Tatian called it *Diatessaron.* This blunder therefore lends no support to the notion that the *Gospel according to the Hebrews* was included in Tatian's work. Comp. Lightfoot, *l.c.* 1142 f.

A BRIEF summary of the results which have been obtained in the First Part of our inquiry will shew how far they satisfy that standard of reasonable completeness which was laid down at the outset. The conditions of the problem must be fairly considered, as well as the character of the solution; and it cannot be too often repeated that the period which has been examined is truly the dark age of Church-history. In the absence of all trustworthy guidance every step requires to be secured by painful investigation; and if I have entered into tedious details, it has been because I know that nothing can rightly be neglected which tends to throw light upon the growth of the Catholic Church. And the growth of the Catholic Church is the comprehensive fact of which the formation of the Canon is one element.

The evidence which has been collected is confessedly fragmentary both in character and substance. And that it must be so follows from the nature of the case. But when all the fragments are combined, the result exhibits the chief marks of complete trustworthiness.

First, it is of wide range both in time and place. Beginning with Clement of Rome the companion of St Paul an uninterrupted series of writers belonging to the chief Churches of Christendom witness with more or less fulness to the books of the New Testament. And though the evidence is thus extended, yet it is not without its points of connexion. Most of the writers who have been examined visited Rome: all of them might have been acquainted with Polycarp.

The character of the evidence is no less striking than its extent. The allusions to Scripture are perfectly natural. The quotations are prefaced by no apology

Conclusion.

The summary of the First Part.

i. *The direct evidence is fragmentary, but*

of wide range,

of unaffected simplicity,

Conclusion.

or explanation. The language of the books used was so familiar as to have become part of the common dialect. And when men speak without any clear intimation that the opinions which they express are peculiar to themselves, it is evident that they express the general judgment of their time. The various testimonies which have been collected thus unite in one; and that one is the general judgment of the Church.

of perfect uniformity,

This is further shewn by the uniform tendency of the evidence. It is always imperfect, but the different parts are always consistent. It is derived from men of the most different characters, and yet all that they say is strictly harmonious. Scarcely a fragment of the earliest Christian literature has been preserved which does not contain some passing allusion to the Apostolic writings; and yet in all there is no discrepancy. The influence of some common rule is the only natural explanation of this common consent. Nor is evidence altogether wanting to prove the existence of such a rule. The testimony of individuals is expressly confirmed by the testimony

and sustained both by the judgment of Churches and

of Churches. Two great versions were current in the East and West from the earliest times, and the Canons which they exhibit agree with remarkable exactness with the scattered and casual notices of ecclesiastical writers. And their common contents—the four Gospels, the Acts, thirteen Epistles of St Paul, the first general Epistles of St Peter and St John—constitute a Canon of acknowledged books. And this agreement of independent writers is not limited to those who were members of the

the practice of heretics.

same Catholic Church: the evidence of heretics is even more full and clear; and when they differed from the common opinion, doctrinal and not historical objections occasioned the difference.

One circumstance which at first sight appeared to embarrass the inquiry has been found in reality to give it life and consistency. A traditional word was current among Christians from the first coincidently with the written Word. It is difficult indeed to conceive that it should have been otherwise if we regard the Apostles as vitally connected with their age; but it is evident that the two might have been in many ways so related as to have produced an unfavourable impression as to the completeness of our present Canon. But now on the contrary the New Testament is found to include all the great elements which are elsewhere referred to Apostolic sources. Many imperfect narratives of our Lord's life were widely current, but the Canonical Gospels offer the types on which they were formed. In the first ages the New Testament may serve at once as the measure, and as the rule of tradition.

Conclusion.
The relation of Scripture and Tradition in regard to the Canon.

For the earliest evidence for the authenticity of the books of which it is composed is not confined to direct testimony. Perhaps that is still more convincing which springs from their peculiar characteristics as representing special types of Christian truth. No one probably will deny the existence of distinguishing features in the several forms of Apostolic teaching, and the history of the sub-apostolic age is the history of corresponding differences developed in early Christian writers, and in turn transformed into the germs of heresy. The ecclesiastical phase of the difference is in every case later than the scriptural; and thus, while I have spoken of the first century after the Apostles as the dark age of Church-history, the recognition of the great elements of the New Testament furnishes a satisfactory explanation of the progress of the Church during that critical period, which on the other hand

ii. *The authenticity of the Canon is a key to the history of the early Church.*

itself offers no place for the forgery of such books as are included in the Canon.

But while the evidence for the authenticity of the Canonical books of the New Testament is up to this point generally complete and satisfactory, it is not such as to remove every doubt to which the subject is liable. At present no trace has been found of the existence of the second Epistle of St Peter[1]. And the Epistles of St James and St Jude, the second and third Epistles of St John, the Epistle to the Hebrews, and the Apocalypse, were received only partially, though they were received exactly in those places in which their history was most likely to be known[2].

It is also to be noticed that the references to the books of the New Testament are for the most part anonymous. This, however, is the case not only in regard to the Gospels, where the words might have been derived from other sources, but also in regard to St Paul's Epistles, where the references are beyond question. If, therefore, parallelism of language, without explicit citation, is not sufficient to prove with absolute conclusiveness the use of the Canonical Gospels, the close correspondence in range, substance, and phraseology between the early evangelic quotations and the texts of the Synoptic Gospels, when taken in connexion with the practice of the Fathers in such of their earliest writings as are preserved, leaves no reasonable ground for doubting the habitual if not exclusive use of them.

---

[1] One coincidence in addition to that noticed in p. 222, n. 3, has been pointed out by Dr Tregelles (*Can. Murat.* p. 102) which deserves notice. The language of the well-known reference to St Paul in Polycarp's Epistle (c. 8) bears considerable resemblance to the corresponding passage in 2 Pet. iii. 15 (σοφία ἐπιστολαί), but in the absence of all other evidence it is impossible to insist on this.

[2] Perhaps the Epistle of St Jude forms an exception to this statement. But the history of the Epistle is extremely obscure.

CONCLUSION OF THE FIRST PART.

But while the universal usage of the Church which is laid open at the close of the second century must have been the result of a continuous custom and not of a revolution, the idea of a Canon itself found no public and authoritative expression except where it was required by the necessities of translation. During the first age and long afterwards the Catholic Church offered no determination of the limits and groundwork of the authoritative collection of sacred books. These questions were practically settled by that instinctive perception of truth, if it may not be called by a nobler name, which I believe can be recognised as presiding over the organization of the early Church. The Canon of Marcion may have been the first which was publicly proposed, but the general consent of earlier Catholic writers proves that within the Church there had been no need for pronouncing a judgment on a point which had not been brought into dispute. The formation of the Canon may have been gradual, but it was certainly undisturbed. It was a growth, and not a series of contests[1].

In the next part it will be seen to what extent this agreement as to the Catholic Canon was established at the end of the second century. And this will furnish in some degree a measure of what had been already settled. The opinions of Irenæus, Clement, and Tertullian, were formed by influences which were at work within the age of Polycarp; and it is wholly arbitrary to suppose that the later writers originated the principles which they organized.

Conclusion.

(3) *the idea of a Canon is implied rather than expressed.*

The result of the teaching of this period to be sought in the first generation of the next.

---

[1] The question of the Inspiration of the writers and writings of the New Testament does not belong to our present inquiry. The evidence on this point is collected in the *Introd. to the Study of the Gospels.* App. B.

SECOND PERIOD.

HISTORY OF THE CANON OF THE NEW TESTAMENT
FROM THE TIME OF HEGESIPPUS TO THE
PERSECUTION OF DIOCLETIAN.

A.D. 170—303.

Τοῖς πειθομενοις μὴ ἀνθρώπων εἶναι συγγράμματα τὰς ἱερὰς βίβλους ἀλλ' ἐξ ἐπιπνοίας τοῦ ἁγίου πνεύματος βουλήματι τοῦ πατρὸς τῶν ὅλων διὰ Ἰησοῦ Χριστοῦ ταύτας ἀναγεγράφθαι καὶ εἰς ἡμᾶς ἐληλυθέναι, τὰς φαινομένας ὁδοὺς ὑποδεικτέον, ἐχομένοις τοῦ κανόνος τῆς Ἰησοῦ Χριστοῦ κατὰ διαδοχὴν τῶν ἀποστόλων οὐρανίου ἐκκλησίας.

Origenes.

CHAPTER I.

THE CANON OF THE ACKNOWLEDGED BOOKS AT THE CLOSE OF THE SECOND CENTURY.

Communicamus cum Ecclesiis Apostolicis quod nulli doctrina diversa: hoc est testimonium veritatis.

TERTULLIANUS.

THE close of the second century marks a great change in the character and position of the Christian Church. It cannot be a mere accident that up to that time the remains of its literature are both unsystematic and fragmentary, a meagre collection of Letters, Apologies, and traditions, while afterwards Christian works ever occupy the foremost rank in genius as well as in spiritual power. The contrast really expresses the natural progress of Christianity. At first its work was in the main with the heart; and when that was filled, it next asserted its right over the intellect. And this conquest was necessarily gradual and slow. A Christian dialect could not be fixed at once; and the scientific aspect of the new doctrines could be determined only by the experience of many efforts to unite them with existing systems. It was thus that for a time philosophic views of Christianity were chiefly to be found without the Church, since the partial representation of its philosophic worth naturally preceded any adequate realization of it. And perhaps it is not difficult to see a fitness in that disposition of events which

Chap. i.
The three stages of the advance of Christianity.

committed the teaching of the Apostles to minds essentially receptive and conservative, that it might be inwrought into the life of men before it became the subject of subtle analysis. However this may be, it is impossible not to recognise the vast access of power which characterizes the works of Irenæus, Clement, and Tertullian, when compared with earlier writings, both in their scope and in their composition. In them Christianity asserts its second conquest: the easiest and yet the most perilous alone remained. It had won its way to the heart of the simple and to the judgment of the philosopher: it had still to claim the deference of the statesman. And each success brought its corresponding trial. When Wisdom (γνῶσις) was ranged with Truth it was not always contented to follow; and in after times the subjugation of the imperial government prepared the way for the corruption of the Church by material influences.

The connexion of the Fathers of the second period with their predecessors.

But though the Fathers of the close of the second century are thus prominently distinguished from those who preceded them, it must not be forgotten that they were trained by that earlier generation which they surpassed. They inherited the doctrines which it was their task to arrange and harmonize. They made no claims to any discoveries in Christianity, but with simple and earnest zeal appealed to the testimony of the Apostolic Church to confirm the truth of their writings. They never admitted the possibility of being separated from their forefathers; and if it has been shewn that the continuity of the Christian faith has hitherto suffered no break, from this point it is confessedly maintained without interruption. From Lyons, from Carthage, from Alexandria, one voice proceeds, the witness and herald of the truth.

In other words the Catholic Church was now externally established. Partial but not exclusive views of truth were outwardly harmonized. The barriers of local or traditional separation between different societies were broken down. The various sides of Christian doctrine, after the rude test of conflict and the still surer trial of life, were combined in one great whole. Henceforth complexity in faith was seen to be the condition of unity. The Christian body, if we may use such an image, awoke to the consciousness of what it was. No great change or revolution passed over it: no great mind moulded its creed or its fabric: history itself revealed the sublime truth of which it was itself the preparation and the witness.

With regard to the Canon of the New Testament this development of the Church is of the greatest importance. In the final establishment of outward Catholicity that which has been already recognised in practice finds a formal expression. As long as those lived who had seen the Apostles; as long as the teaching of the Apostles was fresh in men's minds; it was, as has been already seen, unlikely that their writings as distinguished from their words would be invested with any special importance. But traditions soon became manifold, while the books remained unchanged: a catholic Church was organized, and it was needful to determine the *Covenant* in which its laws were written: Christianity furnished subjects for the philosopher, and it was requisite to settle from what sources his premises might be taken. As soon as the want was felt, it was satisfied. As soon as an independent Christian literature arose in which it was reasonable to look for any definite recognition of the Apostolic writings, we find that recognition substantially clear and correct. With the exception of the Epistle to the Hebrews, the two shorter Epistles of St John, the second Epistle of St Peter, the Epistles of St James and St Jude, and the Apocalypse[1], all the other books of the New Testament are acknowledged as Apostolic and authoritative throughout the Church at the close of the second century. The evidence of the great Fathers by which the Church is represented varies in respect of these disputed books, but the Canon of the acknowledged books is established by their common consent. Thus the testimony on which it rests is not gathered from one quarter but from many, and those the most widely separated by position and character. It is given, not as a private opinion, but as an unquestioned fact: not as a late discovery, but as an original tradition.

The Canon of acknowledged books at the close of the second century.

From this point then it will be needless to accumulate testimonies to the Canonicity of the four Gospels, of the Acts, of the thirteen Epistles of St Paul, of the first Epistles of St John and St Peter. No one at present will deny that they occupied the same position in the estimation of Christians in the time of Irenæus as they hold now. But here one strange fact must be noticed: the authenticity of the Apocalypse, which is supported by the satisfactory testimony of early writers, was disputed for the first time in the Western Church in the course of the third century. In other words there was a critical spirit still alive among Christians which impelled them even then to test afresh the records on which their faith rested.

On what grounds it rested.

But before dismissing the Canon of the acknowledged books it will be well to revert once again at greater length to the manner in which it is recognised by Irenæus and his contemporaries. Their evidence, considered

---

[1] The position of the Apocalypse is anomalous. If it were not for its omission in the Peshito it would be up to this time an acknowledged Book.

in connexion with the circumstances under which it is given, will go far to establish the point to which our investigations have all tended, that the formation of a Canon was among the first instinctive acts of the Christian society: that it was at first imperfect as the organization of the Church was at first incomplete: that it attained its full proportions by a sure growth as the development of the Church itself was finally matured.

Nothing is known directly of the origin of the Gallican Church; but from several ritual peculiarities its foundation may be probably referred to teachers from Asia Minor[1], with which province it long maintained an intimate connexion. And thus Gaul owed its knowledge of Christianity to the same country from which in former times it had drawn its civilization: the Christian missionary completed the work of the Phocæan exile. However this may have been, the first notice of the Church shews its extent and constancy. In the seventeenth year of the reign of Antoninus Verus it was visited by a fierce persecution, of which Eusebius has preserved a most affecting narrative addressed by the Christians of Vienne and Lyons to 'the brethren in Asia 'and Phrygia who held the same faith and hope of re-'demption as themselves[2].' This narrative was written immediately after the events which it describes, and is everywhere penetrated by scriptural language and thought. It contains no reference by name to any book of the New Testament, but its coincidences of language with the Gospels of St Luke and St John, with the Acts of the Apostles, with the Epistles of St Paul to the

---

[1] Palmer's *Origines Liturgicæ*, I. pp. 155 sqq. Compare Stuart, *Book of Deer*, p. lviii.
[2] Euseb. *H. E.* v. 1.

Chap. i.

Romans, Corinthians (?), Ephesians, Philippians, and the first to Timothy, with the first catholic Epistles of St Peter and St John, and with the Apocalypse, are unequivocal[1]. In itself this fact would perhaps call for little notice after what has been said of the general reception of the acknowledged books at the close of the second century, but it becomes of importance as being the testimony of a Church, and one which was not without connexion with the Apostolic age even at the time of the persecution. In the same Church where Irenæus was a presbyter 'zealous for the covenant of Christ[2]' Pothinus was bishop, already ninety years old. Like Polycarp he was associated with the generation of St John, and must have been born before the books of the New Testament were all written. And how then can it be supposed with reason that forgeries came into use in his time which he must have been able to detect by his own knowledge? that they were received without suspicion or reserve in the Church over which he presided? that they were upheld by his hearers as the ancient heritage of Christians? It is possible to weaken the connexion of the facts by arbitrary hypotheses, but interpreted according to their natural meaning they tell of a Church united by its head with the times of St John to which the books of the New Testament, and the books of St John above all others, furnished the unaffected language of hope and resignation and triumph. And the testimony of Irenæus is the testimony of this Church. Nor was this the only point in which

IRENÆUS
the representative of the

---

[1] Euseb. *l. c.* The reference to Apoc. xxii. 11 is introduced by the words ἵνα ἡ γραφὴ πληρωθῇ.
I do not see that the supposed reference to the death of Zacharias which is related in the *Protevan-gelium* of St James can shew that the description of the character of Zacharias was borrowed from that writing.
[2] Euseb. *H. E.* v. 4.

he came in contact with the immediate disciples of the Apostles. It has been seen already that he recalled in his old age the teaching of Polycarp the disciple of St John; and his treatise *against Heresies* contains several references[1] to others who were closely connected with the Apostolic age. He stood forth to maintain no novelties, but to vindicate what had been believed of old. Those whom he quoted had borne witness to the New Testament Scriptures, and he only continued on a greater scale the usage which they had recognised. When he wished to win back Florinus once his fellow-disciple to the truth, he reminded him of the zeal and doctrine of Polycarp their common master, and how he spake of Christ's teaching and mighty works from the words of those who followed Him 'in all things harmo-'niously with the Scriptures[2].' And is it then possible that he who was taught of Polycarp was himself deceived as to the genuine writings of St John? Is it possible that he decided otherwise than his first master, when he speaks of the tradition of the Apostles by which the Canon of Scripture was determined[3]? He appeals to the known succession of teachers in the Churches of Rome, Smyrna, and Ephesus, who held fast up to his own time the doctrine which they had received from the first age; and is it possible that he used writings as genuine and authoritative which were not recognised by those who must have had unquestionable means of deciding on their Apostolic origin[4]?

Chap. i.

Church of Lyons.
c. 130—200 A.D.

---

[1] Cf. pp. 80 f.
[2] Iren. *Ep. ad Flor.* ap. Euseb. *H. E.* v. 20.
[3] Iren. *c. Hær.* IV. 33. 8: Agnitio (γνῶσις) vera est Apostolorum doctrina et antiquus Ecclesiæ status in universo mundo et character corporis Christi secundum successiones episcoporum quibus illi eam quæ in unoquoque loco est Ecclesiam tradiderunt; quæ pervenit usque ad nos custoditione sine fictione Scripturarum tractatio plenissima neque additamentum neque ablationem recipiens.
[4] Volkmar has endeavoured to

Chap. i.
ii. *The testimony of the Church of Alexandria.*

PANTÆNUS.

From Lyons we pass to Alexandria. The early history of the Egyptian Churches is not more certain than that of those in Gaul. Tradition indeed assigns the foundation of the Church of Alexandria to St Mark, but the best evidence of its antiquity is found in its state at the time of the earliest authentic record which remains of it. Towards the close of the second century, 'in the 'time of Commodus,' Pantænus 'presided over the school '(διατριβή) of the faithful there[1].' The school then was already in existence, however much it may have owed to one distinguished alike 'for secular learning and 'scriptural knowledge.' Indeed there is no absolute improbability in the statement of Jerome[2], who interprets the words of Eusebius 'that a school (διδασκαλεῖον)

shew that though Irenæus was acquainted with 1 Peter, yet he did not use it as authoritative Scripture (Credner, *Gesch. d. N. T. Kanon*, § 185). But his argument certainly breaks down. See for instance *c. Hær.* IV. 16. 5. Propter hoc ait Dominus (Matt. xii. 36)... Et propter hoc Petrus ait (1 Peter ii. 16)... On the use of the Epistle in the Latin Churches, see supra, p. 263, n. 3.

[1] Euseb. *H. E.* v. 10; Hieron. *De Virr. Ill.* 36. There is considerable confusion in the account given by Jerome of the relation of Pantænus to Clement. In his notice of Pantænus he says that he 'was sent into 'India by Demetrius bishop of Alex-'andria' who succeeded to the See in 289, and that 'he taught in the 'reigns of Severus and Caracalla' (*De Virr. Ill.* c. 36). Again in the account of Clement he says that Clement was set at the head of the Catechetical school 'after the death of Pantænus' (*id.* c. 38). Now Clement left Alexandria in 202—3 and Origen then entered on the charge of the School (Euseb. *H. E.* VI. 3); nor is there any evidence that Clement returned to Alexandria. It is therefore all but impossible to suppose that Clement first succeeded Pantænus in the reign of Caracalla, and that he was afterwards succeeded by Origen. Jerome's statement as to the time of the teaching of Pantænus has probably been misplaced, as the order of the notices shews. If this be admitted the narratives of Eusebius and Jerome can be reconciled. The mission to India by Demetrius was, if the fact is authentic, a special and second journey undertaken 'at the request of the 'Indians,' and not that which preceded the work of Pantænus in the Catechetical school. It may be added that the statement of Philippus Sidetes that Pantænus succeeded Clement is probably due to the false date of the labours of Pantænus 'under Severus and Caracalla.' It does not fall within our present scope to inquire into the Hebrew Gospel which Pantænus found among the 'Indians.' The mention of the fact shews that attention was directed to the sacred books.

[2] Routh, *Rell. Sacr.* I. 375.

'of the Holy Scriptures had existed there after ancient 'custom' as meaning that 'ecclesiastical teachers had 'always been there from the time of the Evangelist 'Mark.' Without insisting however on the Apostolic origin of the school itself, it seems not improbable that Pantænus was personally connected with some immediate disciples of the Apostles. Many contemporaries of Pothinus and Polycarp may have survived to declare the teaching of St John; and Photius in fact represents Pantænus as a hearer of the Apostles[1]. At any rate there is not the slightest ground for assuming any organic change in the doctrine of the Alexandrine Church between the age of the Apostles and Pantænus. Everything on the contrary bespeaks its unbroken continuity. And Clement, the second of our witnesses, was trained in the school of Pantænus. He speaks as the representative of a class devoted specially to the study of the Scriptures, and established in a city second to none for the advantages and encouragement which it offered to literary criticism. Like Irenæus, Clement appeals with decision and confidence to the judgment of those who had preceded him. His writings were no 'mere compositions wrought for display,' but contained a faint picture 'of the clear and vivid discourses, and of 'the blessed and truly estimable men whom it was his 'privilege to hear.' For though Alexandria was in itself the common meeting-place of the traditions of the East and West, Clement had sought them out in their proper sources. As far as can be gathered from the clause in which he describes his teachers, he had studied in Greece and Italy and various parts of the East under various masters from Cœle-Syria, from Egypt, and from Assyria, and also under a Hebrew in Palestine,

CLEMENT.
c. 165—220
A.D.

[1] *Cod.* 118, p. 160, ed. Hoesch.; Lumper, IV. 44; Routh, I. 377.

before he met with Pantænus. 'And these men,' he writes, 'preserving the true tradition of the blessed 'teaching directly from Peter and James, from John and 'Paul, the holy Apostles, son receiving it from father '(but few are they who are like their fathers), came by 'God's providence even to us, to deposit among us those 'seeds [of truth] which were derived from their ancestors 'and the Apostles[1].'

iii. The testimony of the African Church.

Of the African Church I have already spoken. The venerable relics of the Old Latin Version attest the early reception of the New Testament there, and the care with which it was studied. In themselves those fragments are incomplete, and often questionable; but they do not stand alone. The writings of Tertullian furnish an invaluable commentary on the conclusions which have been drawn from them[2]; and in turn his testimony is the judgment of his Church; an inheritance, and not a deduction.

---

[1] Clem. Alex. *Strom.* I.I.II (Euseb. *H. E.* v. 11): Ἤδη δὲ οὐ γραφὴ εἰς ἐπίδειξιν τετεχνασμένη ἥδε ἡ πραγματεία ἀλλά μοι ὑπομνήματα εἰς γῆρας θησαυρίζεται λήθης φάρμακον, εἴδωλον ἀτεχνῶς καὶ σκιογραφία τῶν ἐναργῶν καὶ ἐμψύχων ἐκείνων ὧν κατηξιώθην ἐπακοῦσαι λόγων τε καὶ ἀνδρῶν μακαρίων καὶ τῷ ὄντι ἀξιολόγων. τούτων ὁ μὲν ἐπὶ τῆς Ἑλλάδος ὁ Ἰωνικός, οἱ (Euseb. ὁ) δὲ ἐπὶ τῆς μεγάλης Ἑλλάδος, τῆς κοίλης θάτερος αὐτῶν Συρίας ἦν ὁ δὲ ἀπ' Αἰγύπτου· ἄλλοι δὲ ἀνὰ τὴν ἀνατολήν, καὶ ταύτης ὁ μὲν τῆς τῶν Ἀσσυρίων ὁ δὲ ἐν Παλαιστίνῃ Ἑβραῖος ἀνέκαθεν· ὑστάτῳ δὲ περιτυχὼν (δυνάμει δὲ οὗτος πρῶτος ἦν) ἀνεπαυσάμην ἐν Αἰγύπτῳ θηράσας λεληθότα. Σικελικῇ τῷ ὄντι ἡ μέλιττα, προφητικοῦ τε καὶ ἀποστολικοῦ λειμῶνος τὰ ἄνθη δρεπόμενος ἀκήρατόν τι γνώσεως χρῆμα ταῖς τῶν ἀκροωμένων ἐνεγέννησε ψυχαῖς. ἀλλ' οἱ μὲν τὴν ἀληθῆ τῆς μακαρίας σώζοντες δι-δασκαλίας παράδοσιν εὐθὺς ἀπὸ Πέτρου τε καὶ Ἰακώβου, Ἰωάννου τε καὶ Παύλου, τῶν ἁγίων ἀποστόλων, παῖς παρὰ πατρὸς ἐκδεχόμενος (ὀλίγοι δὲ οἱ πατράσιν ὅμοιοι), ἧκον δὴ σὺν θεῷ καὶ εἰς ἡμᾶς τὰ προγονικὰ ἐκεῖνα καὶ ἀποστολικὰ καταθησόμενοι σπέρματα. καὶ εὖ οἶδ' ὅτι ἀγαλλιάσονται, οὐχὶ τῇ ἐκφράσει ἡσθέντες λέγω τῇδε, μόνῃ δὲ τῇ κατὰ τὴν ὑποσημείωσιν τηρήσει. The passage is of great importance as shewing the intimate intercourse between different churches in Clement's time and the uniformity of their doctrine. The use of the prepositions is singularly exact and worthy of notice. I have changed Klotz's punctuation, which makes the passage unintelligible.

[2] Compare his sequence of quotations *De resurr. carnis*, 33 ff., *De pudicitia*, 6 ff., given above pp. 262 f.

Tertullian himself insists on this with characteristic energy. 'If,' he says, 'it is acknowledged that that is 'more true which is more ancient, that more ancient 'which is even from the beginning, that from the begin-'ning which is from the Apostles; it will in like manner 'assuredly be acknowledged that that has been derived 'by tradition from the Apostles which has been preserved 'inviolate in the Churches of the Apostles. Let us see 'what milk the Corinthians drank from Paul; to what 'rule the Galatians were recalled by his reproofs; what 'is read by the Philippians, the Thessalonians, the Ephe-'sians; what is the testimony of the Romans, who are 'nearest to us, to whom Peter and Paul left the Gospel, 'and that sealed by their own blood. We have more-'over Churches founded by John. For even if Marcion 'rejects his Apocalypse, still the succession of bishops [in 'the seven Churches] if traced to its source will rest on 'the authority of John. And the noble descent of other 'Churches is recognised in the same manner. I say then 'that among them, and not only among the Apostolic 'Churches, but among all the Churches which are united 'with them in Christian fellowship, that Gospel of Luke 'which we earnestly defend has been maintained from 'its first publication[1]. And 'the same authority of the

Chap. i.

TERTUL-
LIAN.
c. 160—240
A.D.

---

[1] *Adv. Marc.* IV. 5: In summa si constat id verius quod prius, id prius quod et ab initio, ab initio quod ab Apostolis: pariter utique constabit id esse ab Apostolis traditum quod apud ecclesias Apostolorum fuerit sacrosanctum. Videamus quod lac a Paulo Corinthii hauserint; ad quam regulam Galatæ sint recorrecti; quid legant Philippenses, Thessalonicen-ses, Ephesii; quid etiam Romani de proximo sonent, quibus evangelium et Petrus et Paulus sanguine quoque suo signatum reliquerunt. Habemus et Johannis alumnas ecclesias. Nam etsi Apocalypsim ejus Marcion re-spuit, ordo tamen episcoporum ad originem recensus in Johannem sta-bit auctorem. Sic et cæterarum ge-nerositas recognoscitur. Dico itaque apud illas, nec solas jam Apostolicas sed apud universas quæ illis de so-cietate sacramenti confœderantur, id evangelium Lucæ ab initio editionis suæ stare quod cummaxime tuemur. The clause *in Johannem stabit auc-torem* is commonly translated 'will 'shew it [the Apocalypse] to have

'Apostolic Churches will uphold the other Gospels
'which we have in due succession through them and
'according to their usage, I mean those of [the Apostles]
'Matthew and John: although that which was published
'by Mark may also be maintained to be Peter's, whose
'interpreter Mark was: for the narrative of Luke also
'is generally ascribed to Paul: [since] it is allowable that
'that which scholars publish should be regarded as their
'master's work.' 'These are for the most part the sum-
'mary arguments which we employ when we argue about
'the Gospels against heretics, maintaining both the order
'of time which sets aside the later works of forgers (pos-
'teritati falsariorum præscribenti), and the authority of
'Churches which upholds the tradition of the Apostles;
'because truth necessarily precedes forgery, and proceeds
'from them to whom it has been delivered[1].'

All appeal to antiquity.

The words of Tertullian sum up clearly and decisively what has been said before of the evidence of Irenæus and Clement. All the Fathers at the close of the second century agree in appealing to the testimony of antiquity as proving the authenticity of the books which they used as Christian Scriptures[2]. And the appeal was made at

---

'John for its author;' but it is evident that such a translation is quite out of place even if the words admit of it. Comp. *de Præscr. Hær.* 36.

[1] *Adv. Marc. l. c.* Cf. *ib.* IV. 2: Constituimus inprimis evangelicum instrumentum *Apostolos* auctores habere, quibus hoc munus evangelii promulgandi ab ipso Domino sit impositum; si et *Apostolicos*, non tamen solos sed cum Apostolis et post Apostolos; quoniam prædicatio discipulorum suspecta fieri posset de gloriæ studio si non assistat illi auctoritas magistrorum, immo Christi, quæ magistros Apostolos fecit.

[2] It is almost superfluous to give any references to the quotations from the acknowledged Books made by Irenæus, Clement, and Tertullian; but many of the following are worthy of notice on other grounds than merely as attesting the authenticity of the books.

(α) The Four *Gospels:*
  Iren. *c. Hær.* III. 11. 8; Clem. *Strom.* III. 13. 93; Tert. *adv. Marc.* IV. 2.

(β) The *Acts:*
  Iren. III. 15. 1; Clem. *Strom.* V. 12. 83; Tert. *adv. Marc.* V. 2. Compare the remarkable passage, *De Præscr. Hær.* 22.

(γ) The *Catholic Epistles:*
  1 John: Iren. III. 16. 8; Clem.

II.] AT THE CLOSE OF THE SECOND CENTURY. 347

a time when it was easy to try its worth. The links which connected them with the Apostolic age were few and known: and if they had not been continuous it would have been easy to expose the break. But their appeal was never gainsaid; and it still remains as a sure proof that no chasm separates the old and the new in the history of Christianity. Those great teachers are themselves an embodiment of the unity and progress of the faith.

This will appear in yet another light when it is noticed that Clement and Irenæus speak from opposite quarters of Christendom, and exactly from those in which we have found before no traces of the circulation of the Apostolic writings. They tell us what was the fulness of the doctrine on Scripture where the Churches had grown up in silence. They shew in what way the books of the New Testament were the natural help of Christian men, as well as the ready armoury of Christian advocates.

The evidence for the reception of the acknowledged

Chap. i.

The testimony is the same when its original sources cannot be traced.

Strom. II. 15. 66; Tert. adv. Prax. 25.
1 Peter: Iren. IV. 9. 2; Clem. Pæd. I. 6. 44; Tert. c. Gnost. 12. See however p. 263, n. 3.
(δ) The *Pauline Epistles:*
Romans: Iren. II. 22. 2; Clem. Strom. II. 21. 134.
1 Corinthians: Iren. I. 8. 2; Clem. Strom. I. 1. 10.
2 Corinthians: Iren. III. 7. 1; Clem. Strom. I. 1. 4.
Galatians: Iren. III. 7. 2; Clem. Strom. I. 8. 41.
Ephesians: Iren. I. 8. 5; Clem. Strom. III. 4. 28.
Philippians: Iren. I. 10. 1; Clem. Strom. I. 11. 53.
Colossians: Iren. III. 14. 1; Clem. Strom. I. 1. 15.

1 Thessalonians: Iren. V. 6. 1; Clem. Strom. I. 11. 53.
2 Thessalonians: Iren. V. 25. 1; Clem. Strom. V. 3. 17.
1 Timothy: Iren. I. Pref.; Clem. Strom. II. 11. 52.
2 Timothy: Iren. III. 14. 1; Clem. Strom. III. 6. 53.
Titus: Iren. I. 16. 3; Clem. Strom. I. 14. 59.
The Epistle to Philemon is nowhere quoted by Clement or Irenæus, but Tertullian, who examines the *thirteen* Pauline Epistles in the fifth book against Marcion, distinctly recognises it.
(ε) The *Apocalypse:*
Iren. V. 35. 2; Clem. Pæd. II. 10. 108; Tert. adv. Marc. III. 14.

Chap. i.

And it includes the notion of a definite collection of sacred books.

books of the New Testament at the close of the second century is made more complete by the general character which was assigned to them. Special causes hindered the universal circulation of the other books, but these were regarded throughout the Church as parts of an organic whole, correlative to the Old Testament, and of equal weight with it. They were considered to be not only Apostolic, but also authoritative. 'The Scriptures 'are perfect,' Irenæus says, 'inasmuch as they were ut-'tered by the word of God and His Spirit[1];' and what he understands by the Scriptures is evident from the course of his arguments, in which he makes use of the books of the Old and New Testaments without distinction. 'There could not,' he elsewhere argues, 'be either more 'than four Gospels or fewer.' That number was prefigured by types in the Mosaic ritual and by analogies in nature, so that all are 'vain and ignorant and daring 'besides who set at nought the fundamental notion (ἰδέα) 'of the Gospel[2].' Clement again recognises generally a collection of 'the Scriptures of the Lord,' under the title of 'the Gospel and the Apostle[3];' and this collective title shews that the books were regarded as essentially one. But this unity was produced by 'the harmony 'of the Law and the Prophets, and of the Apostles and 'the Gospels in the Church[4].' All alike proceeded from One Author: all were 'ratified by the authority of 'Almighty Power[5].' Tertullian marks the introduction of the phrase 'New Testament' as applied to the Evangelic Scriptures. 'If,' he says, 'I shall not clear up this

---

[1] Iren. *c. Hær.* II. 28. 2: Scripturæ quidem perfectæ sunt, quippe a Verbo Dei et Spiritu ejus dictæ.
[2] Iren. *c. Hær.* III. 11. 8 sq.
[3] *Strom.* VIII. 3. 14: σφᾶς γὰρ αὐτοὺς αἰχμαλωτίζειν...τό τε εὐαγγέλιον ὅ τε ἀπόστολος κελεύουσι. Elsewhere Clement uses the plural ἀπόστολοι. Cf. Reuss, pp. 125, 140.
[4] *Strom.* VI. 11. 88.
[5] *Strom.* IV. 1. 2.

II.] AT THE CLOSE OF THE SECOND CENTURY. 349

'point by investigations of the Old Scripture, I will take
'the proof of our interpretation from the New Testa-
'ment...For behold both in the Gospels and in the
'Apostles I observe a visible and an invisible God...¹.'

    The clear testimony of Irenæus, Clement, and Ter-
tullian—clear because their writings are of considerable
extent—finds complete support not only in the fragments
of earlier Fathers, but also in smaller contemporary
works. Athenagoras at Athens and Theophilus at
Antioch make use of the same books generally, and
treat them with the same respect². And from the close
of the second century, with the single exception of the
Apocalypse, the books thus acknowledged were always
received without doubt until subjective criticism ventured
to set aside the evidence of antiquity³.

    But it is necessary to repeat, what has been continu-
ally noticed during the course of our enquiry, that this
result was obtained gradually, spontaneously, silently⁴.
There is no evidence to shew that at any time the claims
of the Apostolic writings to be placed on an equal footing with those of the Old Testament, which formed
the first Christian Bible, were deliberately discussed and
admitted. The establishment of purely Gentile Churches,
unfamiliar with the Jewish Scriptures, led no doubt to
the collection of other books which answered more

Chap. i.

The testimony of the chief Fathers supported by collateral evidence.

The Canon of the acknowledged Books formed by practical consent, not by definite authority.

---

¹ *Adv. Prax.* 15: Si hunc articulum quæstionibus Scripturæ Veteris non expediam, de Novo Testamento sumam confirmationem nostræ interpretationis, ne quodcumque in Filium reputo in Patrem proinde defendas. Ecce enim et in Evangeliis et in Apostolis visibilem et invisibilem Deum deprehendo, sub manifesta et personali distinctione conditionis utriusque. *id.* c. 20: totum instrumentum utriusque Testamenti... *De Pudic.* 1: Pudicitia... trahit...disciplinam per instrumentum prædicationis et censuram per judicia ex utroque Testamento... Comp. p. 253 and notes.
² Compare pp. 228 ff.
³ The assaults of the Manichees on the books of the New Testament cannot be considered an exception to the truth of this statement. Something will be said about them hereafter.
⁴ Compare pp. 5 f., 12 f., 56 ff., 230, 327 ff.

directly to new religious wants. The controversies with Ebionites and Marcionites served soon after to quicken the sense of the loss which followed from the neglect of the records of the earlier or of the later revelation. There must also have been frequent interchange and comparison of the first Christian writings. But when full allowance is made for these occasional influences and essays in criticism, the fact remains that slow experience and spiritual instinct decided the practical judgment of the Church. Step by step the books which were stamped with Apostolic authority were separated from the mass of other works which contained the traditions or opinions of less authoritative teachers. Without controversy and without effort 'the Gospel and the Apostles' were recognised as inspired sources of truth in the same sense as 'the Law and the Prophets.' In both cases the judgment appeared as a natural manifestation of the life of the Christian body, and not as a logical consequence of definite principles. It was an inevitable consequence of this progressive and vital recognition of an Apostolic canon that some difference of opinion as to its exact limits should coexist with general agreement as to its contents, though no difference of opinion remained as to the religious authority of all the books admitted in it. Thus doubts existed in various Churches as to the completeness with which some books satisfied the criterion of Apostolicity which was made the final test of reception; and an examination of these doubts as to their ground and their prevalence, which forms the subject of the next Chapter, throws considerable light upon the mode and circumstances in which the contents of the New Testament were fixed.

CHAPTER II.

THE TESTIMONY OF THE CHURCHES TO THE DISPUTED BOOKS OF THE NEW TESTAMENT.

In Canonicis Scripturis Ecclesiarum Catholicarum quamplurium auctoritatem [indagator solertissimus] sequatur.

AUGUSTINUS.

SEVEN books of the New Testament, as is well known, have been received into the Canon on evidence less complete than that by which the others are supported[1]. In the controversy which has been raised about their claims to Apostolic authority much stress has been laid on their internal character. But such a method of reasoning is commonly inconclusive, and inferences are drawn on both sides with equal confidence. In every instance the result will be influenced by preconceived notions of the state of the early Church, and it is possible that an original source of information may be disparaged because it is independent. History must deliver its full testimony before internal criticism can find its proper use. And here the real question to be answered in the case of the disputed books is not Why we receive them? but Why should we not receive them? The general agreement of the Church in the fourth century is an antecedent proof of their claims; and it remains to be seen whether it is set aside by the more uncertain and frag-

Chap. ii.

The question of the disputed Books to be decided historically.

---

[1] The Epistles of James, Jude, 2 Peter, 2 and 3 John, to the Hebrews, and the Apocalypse.

mentary evidence of earlier generations. If on the contrary it can be proved, that the books were known from the first though not known universally; if any explanation can be given of their limited circulation; if it can be shewn that they were more generally received as they were more widely known: then it will appear that history has decided the matter; and this decision of history will be conclusive. The idea of forming the disputed books into a Deutero-canon of the New Testament (advocated by many Roman Catholics in spite of the Council of Trent, and by many of the early reformers[1]), though it appears plausible at first sight, is evidently either a mere confession that the question is incapable of solution, or a re-statement of it in other words. The second Epistle of St Peter is either an authentic work of the Apostle or a forgery; for in this case there can be no mean. And the Epistles of St James and St Jude and that to the Hebrews, if they are genuine, are Apostolic at least in the same sense as the Gospels of St Mark and St Luke and the Acts of the Apostles[2]. It involves a manifest confusion of ideas to compensate for a deficiency of historical proof by a lower standard of Canonicity. The extent of the divine authority of a book cannot be made to vary with the completeness of the proof of its genuineness. The genuineness must be admitted before the

---

[1] Even Augustine appears to have favoured this view: Tenebit igitur [Scripturarum indagator] hunc modum in Scripturis Canonicis ut eas quæ ab omnibus accipiuntur Ecclesiis Catholicis præponat iis quas quædam non accipiunt; in iis vero quæ non accipiuntur ab omnibus præponat eas quas plures gravioresque accipiunt iis quas pauciores minorisque auctoritatis Ecclesiæ tenent (*De Doctr. Chr.* II. 12). In spite of the authority however it is clear that such a statement can rest on no logical basis.

[2] I do not by any means intend to assert that every work of an Apostle or Apostolic writer as such would have formed part of the Canon; indeed I believe that many Apostolic writings may have been lost when they had wrought their purpose, but that these books have received the recognition of the Church in such a manner that if genuine they must be Canonical.

authority can have any positive value, which from its nature cannot admit of degrees; and till the genuineness be established the authority remains in abeyance.

The evidence which has been collected hitherto for the Apostolicity of the disputed books may be briefly summed up as follows. The Epistle to the Hebrews is certainly referred to by Clement of Rome, and probably by Justin Martyr; it is contained in the *Peshito*, though probably the version was made by a separate translator; but it is omitted in the fragmentary Canon of Muratori, and, as it appears, it was wanting also in the *Old Latin* version[1]. Except the opinion of Tertullian, which has been mentioned by anticipation, nothing has been found tending to determine its authorship. The Epistle of St James is referred to by Hermas and probably by Clement, and is included in the *Peshito* (according to some copies as the work of St James the Elder); but it is not found in the Muratorian Canon, nor in the *Old Latin*[2]. The Epistle of St Jude and probably the two shorter Epistles of St John are supported by the authority of the Muratorian Canon and of the *Old Latin* version; but they are not found in the *Peshito*[3]. The Apocalypse is distinctly mentioned by Justin as the work of the Apostle John, and Papias and Melito bear witness to its authority: it is included in the Muratorian Canon, but not in the *Peshito*[4]. No certain trace has yet been found of the second Epistle of St Peter[5].

From this general summary it will be seen that up to this time the Epistle of St James and that to the Hebrews rest principally on the authority of the Eastern (Syrian) Church: the second and third Epistles of St John and

---

[1] Cf. pp. 50, 170, 218, 238 n. 3, 260, 265 ff.
[2] Cf. pp. 48, 201, 218, 244, 265.
[3] Cf. pp. 218, 244, 258.
[4] Cf. pp. 77, 168, 218, 222, 244.
[5] Cf. pp. 223 n. 5, 330 n. 1.

the Epistle of St Jude on that of the Western Church: the Apocalypse on that of the Church of Asia Minor. It remains to inquire how far these lines of evidence are extended and confirmed in the great divisions of the Church up to the close of the third century[1].

§ 1. *The Alexandrine Church.*

The importance of the witness of the Alexandrine Church,

The testimony of the Alexandrine Church, as has been noticed already, is of the utmost importance, owing to the natural advantages of its position and the conspicuous eminence of its great teachers during the third century. Never perhaps have two such men as Clement and Origen contributed in successive generations to build up a Christian Church in wisdom and humility. No two fathers ever did more to vindicate the essential harmony of Christian truth with the lessons of history and the experience of men; and in spite of their many faults and exaggerations, perhaps no influence on the whole has been less productive of evil[2].

CLEMENT.
c. 165—220 A.D.

No catalogue of the Books of the New Testament occurs in the writings of Clement; but Eusebius has given a summary of his 'Hypotyposes' or 'Outlines' which serves in some measure to supply the defect[3]. 'Clement 'in his *Outlines*, to speak generally, has given concise 'explanations of all the Canonical Scriptures (πάσης τῆς 'ἐνδιαθήκου γραφῆς) without omitting the disputed books: 'I mean the Epistle of Jude and the remaining Catholic 'Epistles, as well as the Epistle of Barnabas and the so-

---

[1] On the partial use of Apocryphal or Ecclesiastical writings as of authority by different Fathers, see App. B.

[2] Athenagoras is sometimes classed with the Alexandrine school, but his writings contain no clear references to any of the disputed books. Cf. Lardner, Pt. II. c. 18, § 12; supr. pp. 229 f.

[3] The testimony of Pantænus (?) to the Epistle to the Hebrews as a work of St Paul is noticed on the following page.

'called Revelation of Peter. And moreover he says that 'the Epistle to the Hebrews is Paul's, but that it was 'written to the Hebrews in the Hebrew dialect, and that 'Luke having carefully (φιλοτίμως) translated it pub-'lished it for the use of the Greeks. And that it is 'owing to the fact that he translated it that the com-'plexion (χρῶτα) of this Epistle and that of the Acts 'is found to be the same. Further he remarks that it is 'natural that the phrase *Paul an Apostle* does not occur 'in the superscription, for in writing to Hebrews, who 'had conceived a prejudice against him and suspected 'him, he was very wise in not repelling them at the 'beginning by affixing his name. And then a little 'further on he (Clement) adds: And as the blessed 'presbyter (? Pantænus) before now used to say, since 'the Lord, as being the Apostle of the Almighty, was 'sent to the Hebrews, Paul through his modesty, inas-'much as he was sent to the Gentiles, does not inscribe 'himself Apostle of the Hebrews, both on account of 'the honour due to the Lord, and because it was a work 'of supererogation that he addressed an Epistle to the 'Hebrews also (ἐκ περιουσίας καὶ τοῖς Ἑβραίοις ἐπιστέλ-'λειν) since he was herald and Apostle of the Gentiles[1].' The testimony to the Pauline origin of the Epistle to the Hebrews which is contained in this passage is evidently of the greatest value. There can be little doubt that the 'blessed presbyter' was Pantænus; and thus the tradition is carried up almost to the Apostolic age. With regard to the other disputed books, the words of Eusebius imply some distinction between 'the Epistle of Jude and the 'Catholic Epistles,' and 'the Epistle of Barnabas and the 'Revelation of Peter.' But the whole statement is very loosely worded, and its true meaning must be sought by

[1] Euseb. *H. E.* VI. 14.

Chap. ii.

Hebr. iii. 1.

to the Epistle to the Hebrews,

to the Catholic Epistles.

comparison with other evidence. Fortunately this is not wanting. Photius after commenting very severely on the doctrinal character of the *Outlines* adds; 'Now the 'whole scope of the book consists in giving as it were in-'terpretations of Genesis, of Exodus, of the Psalms; of 'the Epistles of St Paul, and of the Catholic Epistles, 'and of Ecclesiasticus[1].' The last clause is very obscure; but whatever may be meant by it, it is evident that the detailed enumeration is most imperfect, for the *Outlines* certainly contained notes on the four Gospels. But if Clement had distinctly rejected any book which Photius held to be Canonical, or treated any Apocryphal book as part of Holy Scripture, it is likely that he would have mentioned the fact; and thus negatively his testimony modifies that of Eusebius, at least so far as that seems to imply that Clement treated the Epistle of Barnabas and the Revelation of Peter as Canonical. A third account of the *Outlines* further limits the statements of Eusebius and Photius. Cassiodorus, the chief minister of Theodoric, in his 'Introduction to the reading of Holy Scripture' says: 'Clement of Alexandria a presbyter, 'who is also called Stromateus, has made some com-'ments on the Canonical Epistles, that is to say on the 'first Epistle of St Peter, the first and second of St 'John, and the Epistle of St *James*, in pure and elegant 'language. Many things which he has said in them 'shew refinement, but some a want of caution: and we 'have caused his comments to be rendered into Latin, 'so that by the omission of some trifling details which

---

[1] Phot. *Cod.* 109. Bunsen, *Anal. Ante-Nic.* I. p. 165. For καὶ τῶν καθολικῶν καὶ τοῦ ἐκκλησιαστικοῦ (Bekk. ἐκκλησιαστοῦ) Bunsen prints καὶ τῶν καθ. καὶ τοῦ καθόλου τόμου 'Εκκλησιαστικοῦ. But surely ὁ καθόλου τόμος 'Εκκλησιαστικὸς is a marvellous phrase. The reference to the book of Ecclesiasticus in such a connexion, however perplexing, is not without parallel. Cf. pp. 218 ff., 384.

'might cause offence his teaching may be imbibed with 'greater security¹.' There can be little doubt that the Latin *Adumbrationes* which are given in the editions of Clement are the notes of which Cassiodorus speaks. There is however one discrepancy between the description and the *Adumbrationes*. These are written on the first Epistle of St Peter, the Epistle of St Jude (not St James), and the first two Epistles of St John; but in general character they answer to the idea which might be formed of the work, and Cassiodorus himself is by no means so accurate a writer that his testimony should be decisive². The *Adumbrationes* contain numerous references to Scripture, and expressly assign the Epistle to the Hebrews to St Paul³. The scattered testimonies which are gathered from the text of Clement's extant works recognise the same books. He makes several quotations from the Epistle to the Hebrews as St Paul's⁴, from the Epistle of St Jude⁵, and one among many others from the first Epistle of St John which implies the existence of a second⁶; while he uses the Apocalypse frequently, assigning it to the Apostle St John⁷; but he nowhere makes any reference to the Epistle of St James⁸. There can then be little doubt that the reading in Cassiodorus is false, and that 'Jude' should be substituted

---

[1] The passages are printed at length by Bunsen, *ib.* pp. 323 sqq.; and in the editions of Clement. Klotz, IV. pp. 52 sqq.
[2] It may be added that Cassiodorus omits Jude in his list of the books of the New Testament. See App. D.
[3] But it is added that it was translated by St Luke: Lucas quoque et Actus Apostolorum stylo exsecutus agnoscitur et Pauli ad Hebræos interpretatus epistolam. Cf. p. 355.
[4] Clem. Alex. *Strom.* VI. 8. 62:

Παῦλος...τοῖς Ἑβραίοις γράφων.
[5] *Strom.* III. 2. 11: ἐπὶ τούτων οἶμαι...προφητικῶς Ἰούδαν ἐν τῇ ἐπιστολῇ εἰρηκέναι.
[6] *Strom.* II. 15. 66: φαίνεται δὲ καὶ Ἰωάννης ἐν τῇ μείζονι ἐπιστολῇ τὰς διαφορὰς τῶν ἁμαρτιῶν ἐκδιδάσκων. Comp. p. 384, n. 1.
[7] *Pæd.* II. 12. 119. *Strom.* VI. 13. 107: ὥς φησιν ἐν τῇ ἀποκαλύψει ὁ Ἰωάννης.
[8] The instances commonly quoted are rightly set aside by Lardner, II. 22, § 8.

for 'James;' and thus the different lines of evidence are found to coincide exactly. Clement, it appears, recognised as Canonical all the books of the New Testament except the Epistle of St James, the second Epistle of St Peter, and the third Epistle of St John. And his silence as to these can prove no more than that he was unacquainted with them[1].

Origen completed nobly the work which Clement began. During a long life of labour and suffering he learnt more fully than any one who went before him the depth and wisdom of the Holy Scriptures; and his testimony to their divine claims is proportionately more complete and systematic. Eusebius has collected the chief passages in which he speaks on the subject of the Canon, and though much that he says refers to the Acknowledged Books, his evidence is too important to be omitted. Like the Fathers who preceded him, he professes only to repeat the teaching which he had received. 'In the first book of his Commentaries on 'Matthew,' Eusebius writes, 'preserving the rule of the 'Church, he testifies that he knows only four Gospels, 'writing to this effect: I have learnt by tradition con-'cerning the four Gospels, which alone are uncontroverted 'in the Church of God spread under heaven, that that 'according to Matthew, who was once a publican but 'afterwards an Apostle of Jesus Christ, was written first; '...that according to Mark second;...that according to 'Luke third;...that according to John last of all[2].'

'The same writer,' Eusebius continues, 'in the fifth

[1] Clement's use of the writings of the sub-apostolic Fathers (Clement of Rome, Hermas, Barnabas) and of certain Apocryphal books (the Gospels according to the Hebrews and the Egyptians, the Preaching and the Apocalypse of Peter, the Traditions of Mathias) will be considered in App. B. It is enough to notice that there is no evidence to shew that he attributed to them a decisive authority, as he did to the writings of the Apostles in the strictest sense.

[2] Euseb. *H. E.* VI. 25.

'book of his Commentaries on the Gospel of John says *Chap. ii.*
'this of the Epistles of the Apostles: Now he who was
'*made fit to be a minister of the new covenant, not of the
'letter but of the spirit*, Paul, who fully preached the
'Gospel from Jerusalem round about as far as Illyricum,
'did not even write to all the Churches which he taught,
'and sent moreover but few lines (στίχους) to those to
'which he wrote. Peter again, on whom the Church of
'Christ is built *against which the gates of hell shall not
'prevail*, has left behind one Epistle generally acknow-
'ledged; perhaps also a second, for it is a disputed ques-
'tion. Why need I speak about him who reclined upon
'the breast of Jesus, John, who has left behind a single
'Gospel, though he confesses that he could make so
'many as *not even the world could contain?* He wrote *John xxi. 25.*
'moreover the Apocalypse, having been commanded to *the Apocalypse;*
'keep silence, and not to write the voices of the seven *Apoc. x. 4.*
'thunders. He has left behind also one Epistle of very
'few lines: perhaps too (ἔστω δὲ καὶ δευτ.[1]) a second
'and third; for all do not allow that these are genuine;
'nevertheless both together do not contain a hundred
'lines.'

'In addition to these statements [Origen] thus dis- *the Epistle to the Hebrews.*
'cusses the Epistle to the Hebrews in his Homilies upon
'it: Every one who is competent to judge of differences
'of diction (φράσεων) would acknowledge that the style
'(χαρακτὴρ τῆς λέξεως) of the Epistle entitled to the
'Hebrews does not exhibit the Apostle's rudeness and
'simplicity in speech (τὸ ἐν λόγῳ ἰδιωτικόν), though he
'acknowledged himself to be *simple in his speech*, that is
'in his diction (τῇ φράσει), but it is more truly Greek in
'its composition (συνθέσει τῆς λέξεως). And again, that
'the thoughts (νοήματα) of the Epistle are wonderful,

[1] Comp. *Ep. ad Afric.* c. 14.

Chap. ii. 'and not second to the acknowledged writings of the
'Apostle, every one who pays attention to the reading
'of the Apostle's works would also grant to be true.
'And after other remarks he adds: If I were to express
'my own opinion I should say that the thoughts are
'the Apostle's, but the diction and composition that of
'some one who recorded from memory the Apostle's
'teaching, and as it were illustrated with a brief Com-
'mentary the sayings of his master (ἀπομνημονεύσαντος...
'καὶ ὡσπερεὶ σχολιογραφήσαντος). If then any Church
'hold this Epistle to be Paul's, we cannot find fault with
'it for so doing (εὐδοκιμείτω καὶ ἐπὶ τούτῳ); for it was
'not without good reason (οὐκ εἰκῆ) that the men of old
'time have handed it down as Paul's. But who it was
'who wrote the Epistle God only knows certainly. The
'account (ἱστορία) which has reached us is [manifold],
'some saying that Clement who became Bishop of Rome
'wrote it, while others assign it to Luke the author of
'the Gospel and the Acts[1].'

Much has been written since upon the subject with which Origen deals thus wisely, but not one step has been surely made beyond the limit which he fixes. Others have expounded the arguments on which he touches, but without adding anything to their real force. New conjectures have been made, more groundless than those which he mentions, but his practical conclusion remains unshaken. The Epistle though not St Paul's in the strictest sense is eminently Pauline; and from the time of Origen it was generally received as St Paul's in this wider view of authorship by the Alexandrine Church,

---

[1] Comp. Hier. *in Eph.* c. ii. 15 (p. 583): Nescio quid tale et in alia epistola (si quis tamen eam recipit)... Paulus subindicat (Hebr. xi. 39 f.); *in Is.* c. lvii. 13 f. (p. 677) de quo ad Hebræos loquitur qui scribit episto- lam (Hebr. xii. 22 f.). These phrases are probably due to Origen.

and thence in the fourth century by the great scholars of the West.

There still remain two passages in Rufinus' version[1] of the Homilies on Genesis and Joshua in which we find an incidental enumeration of the different authors and books of the New Testament. It is however impossible to insist on these as of primary authority. Rufinus, as is well known, was not content to render the simple words of Origen, but sought in several points to bring them into harmony with the current belief; and the comparison of some fragments of the Greek text of one of the Homilies with his rendering of it shews clearly that he has allowed himself in these the same licence as in his other translations[2]. Still there is something of Origen's manner throughout the pieces; and in his popular writings he quotes parts of the disputed books without hesitation.

The first passage is contained in a spiritual explanation[3] of the narrative concerning the wells which were opened by Isaac after the Philistines had stopped them, and the new wells which he made. Moses, Origen tells us, was one of the servants of Abraham who first opened the fountain of the Law. Such too were David and the Prophets. But the Jews closed up those sources of life, the Scriptures of the Old Testament, with earthly thoughts; and when the antitype of Isaac had sought to lay them open, the Philistines strove with him. 'So 'then he dug new wells; and so did his servants. 'Isaac's servants were Matthew, Mark, Luke, and John:

---

[1] There can be no doubt that he was the author of it. Cf. Huet, *Origen.* III. 2.
[2] For instance, he adds such phrases as Sanctus Apostolus, and translates ὡς οὐχ ἅγια τὰ Μωυσέως συγγράμματα by Scripta Mosis nihil in se divinæ sapientiæ nihilque operis sancti Spiritus continere (*Hom. in Gen.* II. 2).
[3] *Hom. in Gen.* XIII. 2. A different explanation of the wells is given *Select. in Gen.* VIII. p. 77 (ed. Lomm.).

'his servants are Peter, James, and Jude: his servant
'also is the Apostle Paul; who all dig wells of the New
'Testament. But those *who mind earthly things* strive
'ever for these also, and suffer not the new to be formed,
'nor the old to be cleansed. They gainsay the sources
'opened in the Gospel: they oppose those opened by
'the Apostles' (*Evangelicis puteis contradicunt: Apostolicis adversantur*).

From a Homily on Joshua.

The last quotation which I shall make is equally characteristic of Origen's style. He has been speaking of the walls of Jericho which fell down before the blasts of the trumpets of the priests. 'So too,' he says[1], 'our
'Lord, whose advent was typified by the son of Nun,
'when he came sent his Apostles as priests bearing
'well-wrought (*ductiles*) trumpets. Matthew first sound-
'ed the priestly trumpet in his Gospel. Mark also,
'Luke and John, each gave forth a strain on their
'priestly trumpets. Peter moreover sounds loudly on
'the twofold[2] trumpet of his Epistles: and so also James
'and Jude. Still the number is incomplete, and John
'gives forth the trumpet-sound in his Epistles and
'Apocalypse; and Luke while describing the Acts of the
'Apostles. Lastly however came he who said: *I think
'that God hath set forth us Apostles last of all*, and thun-
'dering on the fourteen trumpets of his Epistles threw
'down even to the ground the walls of Jericho, that
'is to say all the instruments of idolatry and the doc-
'trines of philosophers.'

Isolated testimonies to the several Books in the Greek Text.

Such appears to have been Origen's popular teaching on the Canon, in discourses which aimed at spiritual instruction rather than at critical accuracy; and it remains to be seen how far these general outlines are filled up

---

[1] *Hom. in Jos.* VII. 1. has a very remarkable reading, *ex*
[2] Duabus tubis. One Manuscript *tribus*.

in detail by special testimonies. The first place is naturally due to references contained in the Greek text of his writings; and it is indeed on these only that absolute reliance can be placed. It is evident then from this kind of evidence, no less than from all other, that like Clement he received the Apocalypse as an undoubted work of the Apostle St John[1]. Like Clement also he quotes the Epistle of St Jude several times, and expressly as the work of 'the Lord's brother;' but he implies in one place the existence of doubts as to its authority[2]. In addition to this he refers to the 'Epistle in circulation under the name of James[3];' but he nowhere I believe either quotes or mentions the second Epistle of St Peter[4], or the two shorter Epistles of St John. On the contrary, he quotes *the Epistle of Peter*[5] and *the Epistle of John*[6] in such a manner as at least to shew that the other Epistles were not familiarly known.

The Latin version of the Homilies supplies in part

Chap. ii.

The Apocalypse.

St JUDE.

St JAMES.

2 Peter
2 *and* 3 John.

In the Latin Version.

---

[1] *Comm. in Joan.* T. I. 14: φησὶν οὖν ἐν τῇ ἀποκαλύψει ὁ τοῦ Ζεβεδαίου Ἰωάννης.

[2] *Comm. in Matt.* T. X. 17 (Matt. xiii. 55, 56): καὶ Ἰούδας ἔγραψεν ἐπιστολὴν ὀλιγόστιχον μὲν πεπληρωμένην δὲ τῆς οὐρανίου χάριτος ἐρρωμένων λόγων...*id.* T. XVII. 30: εἰ δὲ καὶ τὴν Ἰούδα πρόσοιτό τις ἐπιστολήν...

[3] *Comm. in Joan.* T. XIX. 6: ὡς ἐν τῇ φερομένῃ Ἰακώβου ἐπιστολῇ ἀνέγνωμεν. Cf. T. XX. 10 (ὑπὸ τῶν προσδεχομένων τό· πίστις κ.τ.λ., James ii. 20). He once quotes it without further remark: ὡς παρὰ Ἰακώβῳ, *Select. in Ps.* xxx. T. XII. p. 129, but the authority of detached Scholia is questionable. On the other hand he does not quote James i. 17 when discussing at length the conception of God as Light. It may be concluded from one passage in his Commentaries on St Matthew (xiii. 55, 56),

in which he notices that the St Jude there mentioned was the author of the Epistle which bore his name, and St James the one to whom St Paul refers in Gal. i. 19, that he was not inclined to believe that the Epistle of St James was written by the Lord's brother.

[4] It is impossible to insist confidently on the doubtful reading. *Comm. in Matt.* T. XV. 27: ἀπὸ τῆς Πέτρου πρώτης ἐπιστολῆς. Πέτρου is apparently omitted in the Manuscripts. Yet see Acts ii. 27, αἱρέσεις ἐπεισάγοντες (2 Pet. ii. 1).

[5] *Select. in Ps.* iii. (T. XI. 420): κατὰ τὰ λεγόμενα ἐν τῇ καθολικῇ ἐπιστολῇ παρὰ τῷ Πέτρῳ. Cf. *Comm. in Joan.* T. VI. 18.

[6] *Comm. in Matt.* T. XVII. 19: τὸ ἀπὸ τοῦ Ἰωάννου καθολικῆς ἐπιστολῆς. *ib.* T. XV. 31: ἡ Ἰωάννου ἐπιστολή. Yet cf. p. 366, n. 3.

364   THE DISPUTED BOOKS OF THE CANON.   [PART

Chap. ii.
2 Peter.
St James.

what is wanting in the Greek Commentaries. It contains several distinct quotations of the second Epistle of St Peter[1], and of the Epistle of St James, who is described in one place as 'the brother of the Lord,' but generally only as 'the Apostle[2];' but even in this there is no reference to the shorter Epistles of St John.

The Epistle to the Hebrews.

The Epistle to the Hebrews is quoted continually both in the Greek and in the Latin text, sometimes as the work of St Paul, sometimes as the work of the Apostle, and sometimes without any special designation[3].

Summary of Origen's opinion on the New Testament Canon.

On the whole then there can be little doubt as to Origen's judgment on the New Testament Canon. He was acquainted with all the books which are received at present, and received as Apostolic all those which were recognised by Clement. The others he used, but with a certain reserve and hesitation, arising from a want of information as to their history, rather than from any positive grounds of suspicion[4].

---

[1] *Hom. in Levit.* IV. 4: Petrus dixit (2 Pet. i. 4). Cf. *Comm. in Rom.* IV. 9. *Hom. in Num.* XIII. 8: ut ait quodam in loco scriptura (2 Pet. ii. 16). Cf. *Comm.* XVIII. *s. f.* Thus also *de Princ.* II. 5. 3: Petrus in prima epistola...

[2] *Comm. in Rom.* IV. 8; James iv. 4.

[3] The passage quoted by Eusebius from a Homily on the Hebrews gives probably Origen's mature judgment on the authorship of the Epistle. In the earlier letter to Africanus he says, after quoting Hebr. xi. 37: ἀλλ' εἰκός τινα θλιβόμενον ἀπὸ τῆς εἰς ταῦτα ἀποδείξεως συγχρήσασθαι τῷ βουλεύματι τῶν ἀθετούντων τὴν ἐπιστολὴν ὡς οὐ Παύλῳ γεγραμμένην· πρὸς ὃν ἄλλων λόγων κατ' ἰδίαν χρήσομεν εἰς ἀπόδειξιν τοῦ εἶναι Παύλου τὴν ἐπιστολήν (T. XVIII. p. 31). Though the date of this letter is probably A.D. 240, the Homilies were not written till after 245.

[4] Origen's quotations from the sub-apostolic Fathers (Clement of Rome, Hermas, Barnabas) and Apocryphal Books (the Gospel according to the Hebrews, the Preaching of Peter, the Acts of Paul) will be noticed in App. B.

One famous passage in which Origen contrasts the Canonical Gospels with others deserves to be quoted. In commenting on Luke i. 1 he says 'The phrase *have taken in hand* im-'plies a tacit accusation of those 'who rushed hastily to write Gospels 'without the grace of the Holy 'Spirit. Matthew and Mark and 'Luke and John did not *take in* '*hand* to write their Gospels, but 'wrote them being full of the Holy 'Spirit......The Church has four 'Gospels, heresies very many, of 'which one is entitled *according to* '*the Egyptians*, another *according to* '*the twelve Apostles*......Four Gospels 'only are approved, out of which 'we must bring forth points of teach-

Clement divided the Christian books into two great divisions, *the Gospel* and *the Apostle* or *the Apostles*. Origen repeats the same classification[1]; but he also advanced a step further, and found that these were united in one whole as 'Divine Scriptures of the New 'Covenant[2],' written by the same Spirit as those before Christ's coming[3], and giving a testimony by which every word should be established[4].

Among the most distinguished scholars of Origen was Dionysius, who was promoted to the presidency of the Catechetical School about the year 231 A.D., and afterwards was chosen Bishop of Alexandria. During an active and troubled episcopate he maintained an intimate communication with Rome, Asia Minor, and Palestine; and in one place (referring to the schism of Novatus) he expresses his joy at 'the unity and love 'everywhere prevalent in all the districts of Syria, in 'Arabia, Mesopotamia, Pontus, and Bithynia,' and 'in 'all the churches of the East[5].' Important fragments of his letters still remain, which contain numerous refer-

Chap. ii.
as a whole.

DIONYSIUS.
248 A.D.

'ing under the person of our Lord
'and Saviour. There is I know a
'Gospel which is called *according to*
'*Thomas*, and [one] *according to Ma-*
'*thias;* and there are many others
'which we read, lest we should seem
'to be unacquainted with any point
'for the sake of those who think they
'possess some valuable knowledge if
'they are acquainted with them.
'But in all these we approve nothing
'else but that which the Church ap-
'proves, that is, four Gospels only as
'proper to be received' (*Hom.* I. *in
Luc.*). The passage may stand as a
complete explanation of his judgment
and his practice.

[1] Clem. *Strom.* VII. 3, 14; V. 5.
31; VI. 2. 88. Orig. *Hom. in Jerem.*
XXI. f. See p. 348.

[2] *De Princip.* IV. 1 (*Philoc.* c. 1):

...ἐκ τῶν πεπιστευμένων ἡμῖν εἶναι
θείων γραφῶν τῆς τε λεγομένης παλαιᾶς διαθήκης καὶ τῆς καλουμένης καινῆς...

[3] *De Princip.* IV. 16: οὐ μόνον δὲ περὶ τῶν πρὸ τῆς παρουσίας ταῦτα τὸ πνεῦμα ᾠκονόμησεν, ἀλλ' ἅτε τὸ αὐτὸ τυγχάνον καὶ ἀπὸ τοῦ ἑνὸς θεοῦ, τὸ ὅμοιον καὶ ἐπὶ τῶν εὐαγγελίων πεποίηκε καὶ ἐπὶ τῶν ἀποστόλων. Comp. *Comm. in Joh.* I. 15.

[4] *Hom. in Jerem.* I. The well-known reference of Origen to the Shepherd of Hermas (*Comm. in Rom.* xvi. 14. Cf. *Comm. in Matt.* T. XIV. 21) evidently expresses a private opinion on the book, and by no means places it on an equality with the Canonical Scriptures. Cf. App. B.

[5] Euseb. *H. E.* VI. 46; VII. 4, 5.

ences to the New Testament; and among other quotations he makes use of the Epistle to the Hebrews as St Paul's[1], of the Epistle of St James[2], and in his remarks on the Apocalypse mentions 'the second and third 'Epistles circulated as works of John' in such a way as to imply that he was inclined to receive them as authentic[3]. His criticism on the Apocalypse has been already noticed. He had weighed the objections which were brought against it, and found them insufficient to overthrow its Canonicity[4], though he believed that it was not the work of the Apostle, and admitted that it was full of difficulties which he was unable to explain. 'I will not 'deny,' he says, 'that the author of the Apocalypse was 'named John, for I fully allow (συναινῶ) that it is the work 'of some holy and inspired man (ἁγίου...τινὸς καὶ θεο- 'πνεύστου); but I should not easily concur in the belief 'that this John was the Apostle, the son of Zebedee, the 'brother of James, who wrote the Gospel and the Catho- 'lic Epistle.' And he then adds the grounds of his opinion: 'for I conclude from a comparison of the cha- 'racter of the writings, and from the form of the language, 'and the general construction of the book [of the Reve-

---

[1] Dion. ap. Euseb. *H. E.* VI. 41: τὴν ἁρπαγὴν τῶν ὑπαρχόντων ὁμοίως ἐκείνοις οἷς καὶ Παῦλος ἐμαρτύρησε μετὰ χαρᾶς προσεδέξαντο. Cf. Hebr. x. 54.

[2] *Comm. in Luc.* XXII. (Gallandi, *Bibl. Pp.* XIV. App. p. 117. Cf. Proleg. v.) ὁ γὰρ θεός, φησίν, ἀπείραστός ἐστι κακῶν. James i. 13.

[3] Dion. ap. Euseb. *H. E.* VII. 25: ἀλλ' οὐδὲ ἐν τῇ δευτέρᾳ φερομένῃ Ἰωάννου καὶ τρίτῃ καίτοι βραχείαις οὔσαις ἐπιστολαῖς ὁ Ἰωάννης ὀνομαστὶ πρόκειται ἀλλ' ἀνωνύμως ὁ πρεσβύτερος γέγραπται. Though the context implies that he held these letters to be St John's, yet he afterwards

speaks of 'his Epistle,' as if he had written but one (ἡ ἐπιστολή, ἡ καθολικὴ ἐπιστολή). This may serve to explain the similar usage of Origen. Cf. p. 363. This mode of speaking is most remarkably illustrated in the records of the seventh Council of Carthage (A. D. 256, Routh *Rell. Sacr.* III. p. 130), where the *second* Epistle of St John is thus quoted: Ioannes Apostolus in epistola sua posuit dicens (2 John 10, 11). In the fifth Council (Routh, p. 111) the first Epistle is quoted in the same words.

[4] Cf. pp. 277 f.

'lation] that [the John there mentioned] is not the 'same¹.' In this passage Dionysius makes no reference to any historical evidence in support of the opinion which he advocates, and consequently his objections gain no weight from his position. But the fact that he urged them is of great interest, as shewing the liberty which was still allowed in dealing with the Canon. He set forth the absolute authority of that which 'could be 'proved by demonstration and teaching of the Holy 'Scriptures²:' he regarded it as a worthy task even in small matters to 'harmonize the words of the Evangelists 'with judgment and good faith³:' he allowed the Apocalypse itself to be the work of an inspired man; but nevertheless he regarded the special authorship of the sacred books as a proper subject for critical inquiry⁴. And this is entirely consistent with the belief that the Canon was fixed practically by the common use of Christians, and not definitely marked out by any special investigation—that it was formed by instinct, and not by argument. Dionysius exercised a free judgment on Scripture within certain limits, but these limits themselves were already recognised.

It does not appear that the opinion of Dionysius on the authorship of the Apocalypse made any permanent

---

¹ Dion. ap. Euseb. *H. E. l. c.*: τεκμαίρομαι γὰρ ἔκ τε τοῦ ἤθους ἑκατέρων καὶ τοῦ τῶν λόγων εἴδους καὶ τῆς τοῦ βιβλίου διεξαγωγῆς λεγομένης μὴ τὸν αὐτὸν εἶναι. The whole passage is too long to quote, but will repay a careful perusal. I do not think there is any other piece of pure criticism in the early Fathers to compare with it for style and manner.

² Dion. ap. Euseb. *H. E.* VII. 24: ...τὰ ταῖς ἀποδείξεσι καὶ διδασκαλίαις τῶν ἁγίων γραφῶν συνιστανόμενα

καταδεχόμενοι.
³ Dion. *Ep. Canon.* (Routh, *Rell. Sacr.* III. p. 225): καὶ μηδὲ διαφωνεῖν μηδὲ ἐναντιοῦσθαι τοὺς εὐαγγελιστὰς πρὸς ἀλλήλους ὑπολάβωμεν, ἀλλ' εἰ καὶ μικρολογία τις εἶναι δόξει περὶ τὸ ζητούμενον...ἡμεῖς εὐγνωμόνως τὰ λεχθέντα καὶ πιστῶς ἁρμόσαι προθυμηθῶμεν. He is referring to the accounts of the Resurrection.

⁴ It must be noticed that Dionysius himself quoted the Apocalypse with respect: Euseb. *H. E.* VII. 10 *ad init.*

C. B B

Chap. ii.

265 A.D.

THEOGNOSTUS.

PETER MARTYR. 300 A.D.

Summary of the judgment of the Alexandrine Church.

impression on the Alexandrine Church; but indeed the few fragments of later writers by which it is represented contain very little that illustrates the history of the disputed books. In the meagre remains which survive of the writings of Pierius, Theonas[1] (the successor of Dionysius in the Episcopate), and Phileas, I have noticed nothing which bears upon it. Theognostus, who was at the head of the Catechetical School towards the close of the third century, makes use of the Epistle to the Hebrews as authoritative Scripture[2]; and Peter Martyr (the successor of Theonas) refers to it expressly as the work of the Apostle[3].

The testimony of the Alexandrine Church to the New Testament Canon is thus generally uniform and clear. In addition to the acknowledged books the Epistle to the Hebrews and the Apocalypse were received there as divine Scripture even by those who doubted their immediate Apostolic origin. The two shorter Epistles of St John were well known and commonly received[4]; but no one except Origen, so far as can be discovered now, was acquainted with the second

---

[1] One passage of his famous letter to Lucianus deserves to be quoted. As one step by which he was to bring his master to the faith it is said: laudabitur et interim *Evangelium Apostolusque* pro divinis oraculis (Routh, *Rell. Sacr.* III. p. 443). The common use of this collective term, as has been noticed before (p. 348), marks a period in the history of the Canon.

[2] Routh, *Rell. Sacr.* III. 409: ἐπὶ δὲ τοῖς γευσαμένοις τῆς οὐρανίου δωρεᾶς καὶ τελειωθεῖσιν οὐδεμία περιλείπεται συγγνώμης ἀπολογία καὶ παραίτησις (Hebr. vi. 4).

[3] Routh, *Rell. Sacr.* IV. 35: εἰ μή, ὡς λέγει ὁ ἀπόστολος, ἐπίλιποι δ' ἂν ἡμᾶς διηγουμένους ὁ χρόνος (Hebr. xi. 32). The succession of testimony does not end here. Alexander who became bishop about 313 A.D., and Athanasius who succeeded him (326—373 A.D.), both quote the Epistle as St Paul's. And Euthalius (*c.* 460 A.D.) only mentions the doubts which had been raised on the question to refute them (Credner, *Einleit.* II. 498 f.).

[4] Alexander, who has been mentioned above, in a letter preserved by Socrates quotes the second Epistle as the work of 'the Blessed 'John.' Socr. *H. E.* I. 6. 30. His testimony is valuable as indicating the tendency of the Alexandrine Church, which is clearly seen in later writers.

Epistle of St Peter, and it is doubtful whether he made use of it[1].

In speaking of the Alexandrine Canon it is impossible to omit all mention of the Egyptian versions, which even in their present state shew singular marks of agreement with the Alexandrine text; but further investigations are still required before any satisfactory results can be obtained as to their exact age or as to their original form and character[2]. Two versions into the dialects of Upper and Lower Egypt—the Thebaic (Sahidic) and Memphitic (Bahuric, often called Coptic)—date from the third century[3]. The few fragments of the Bashmuric

---

[1] In connexion with the Alexandrine Church it is convenient to notice JULIUS AFRICANUS, who wrote a famous letter to Origen (cf. p. 364, n. 3), and studied at Alexandria, and afterwards lived at Emmaus in Palestine (c. 220 A.D.). His method of reconciling the genealogies in St Matthew and St Luke is well known, and furnishes an important proof of the attention bestowed in his time on the criticism of the Apostolic Books. He speaks generally of 'all '[the writings] of the Old Testament' (ὅσα τῆς παλαιᾶς διαθήκης φέρεται, Routh, Rell. Sacr. II. p. 226), thus implying (as Melito had done before him) the existence of a written New Testament. It is uncertain from the language of Origen whether he received the Epistle to the Hebrews.

ANATOLIUS bishop of Laodicea c. 270 A.D. was likewise an Alexandrian, but there is nothing in the fragments of his Paschal Canons (Euseb. H. E. VII. 32) which bears on the history of the disputed books; he makes use however of 2 Cor. iii. 12 sqq., giving to κατοπτρίζεσθαι (ver. 18) the sense of 'beholding' and not 'reflecting.'

It may also be convenient to notice here the reference to the Canon of the Old and New Testaments in the APOSTOLICAL CONSTITUTIONS, II. 57, cf. 55. (See App. D.) The description of the New Testament is very incomplete and comprises only 'the Acts of the Apostles...the 'Epistles of Paul ... the Gospels of 'Matthew and John...and of Luke 'and Mark...' The enumeration, it must be added, is made with reference to the use of the books in public services; but still the omission of all the Catholic Epistles is remarkable, and there are no certain references to any of them in the text of the book itself. Compare however Lardner, IV. 352.

[2] By far the most complete account of these versions yet given is that by Dr Lightfoot in the second edition of Dr Scrivener's Plain Introduction, pp. 319 ff.

[3] 'We should probably not be exaggerating, if we placed one or both 'of the principal Egyptian Versions, 'the Memphitic and the Thebaic, 'or at least parts of them, before 'the close of the second century.' Lightfoot, l. c. p. 324. Dr Lightfoot suggests that the date 'of the completion or codification of the Memphitic version' may be fixed at the middle of the third century, when

version belong to a dialectic revision of the Thebaic. Of the Thebaic version considerable portions have been preserved, and among them parts of all the disputed books; but it is as yet impossible to decide how far they are derived from one source[1]. The Memphitic version offers a far more hopeful field for criticism. This has been published entire from ancient Manuscripts, and the store of these has not yet been exhausted. It is then not unreasonable to expect that some scholar will point out in this translation, as has been done in the Latin and Syriac, how far an older work underlies the printed text, and whether that can be attributed to one author. But till this has been determined no stress can be laid upon the evidence which the Version affords for the disputed Catholic Epistles[2]. One point however is clear. The Apocalypse had not a place among the Canonical books in the Memphitic version[3]. It appears also that it was not included in the Thebaic Canon[4]. The other books are arranged in the MSS. of the Memphitic version, and in systematic quotations from the Thebaic in the same way: (1) Gospels, (2) Pauline Epistles, (3) Catholic Epistles, (4) Acts[5]. In the Memphitic version the Gospels are found in their common order; but there are indications that at one time the Gospel of St John stood before that of St Matthew in the Thebaic version[6]. It is further worthy of notice that the position in the Manuscripts occupied by the Epistle to the Hebrews —before the Pastoral Epistles—is consistent with the

doubts were raised at Alexandria as to the authorship of the Apocalypse (*id.* p. 343).
[1] Lightfoot, *l. c.* pp. 354 ff.
[2] Though the Æthiopic Version belongs to the next century, I may notice that it contains the entire N. T.
[3] Lightfoot, *l. c.* p. 342.
[4] *id.* p. 351.
[5] *id.* pp. 343, 351.
[6] *id.* p. 351.

judgment of the Alexandrine Church, which received it as the work of St Paul[1].

§ 2. *The Latin Churches of Africa.*

At Alexandria, as has been said, the two streams of tradition from the East and from the West unite; but elsewhere they may be traced each in its separate course. On the one side we follow the Latin Churches of Africa: on the other the Greek Churches of Asia. And both again re-appear in close connexion at Rome, a second centre of Christendom, but widely different from the first.

In one respect the judgment of the Churches of North Africa materially differed from that of Alexandria on the New Testament Canon. The Alexandrine Fathers uniformly recognised the Epistle to the Hebrews as possessed of Apostolic authority, if not indeed as the work of St Paul. The early Latin Fathers with equal unanimity either exclude it from the Canon or ignore its existence. The evidence of Tertullian on this point is at once the earliest and the most complete. Though the teaching of the Epistle offered the most plausible support to the severe doctrines of Montanism, yet he nowhere quotes it but in one place, and then assigns it positively to Barnabas the companion of St Paul, placing its authority above that of the Shepherd of Hermas, but evidently below that of the Apostolic Epistles[2]. In

---

[1] It may be observed here that the Epistle to the Hebrews is placed in the same position in the [Eastern] Manuscripts ℵ A B C H and several others, and also by many of the Greek Fathers. Cf. Tisch. *in Heb.* i. 1. The [Western] Manuscripts D E F G, on the contrary, place the Pastoral Epistles after those to the Thessalonians. There are also traces of another order: In B capitulorum numeri tales appositi ut appareat eorum auctorem hanc [ad Hebr. ep.] post ep. ad Galatas collocasse. Lachm. *N. T.* II. 537.

[2] *De Pudic.* c. 20: Volo tamen ex redundantia alicujus etiam comitis Apostolorum testimonium superdu-

Cyprian again there is no reference to the Epistle; and on the contrary he implicitly denies that it was a work of St Paul. After enumerating many places in which the mystical number seven recurs in Holy Scripture, he adds: 'And the Apostle Paul who was mindful of this 'proper and definite number writes to *seven* Churches. 'And in the Apocalypse the Lord writes his divine com- 'mands and heavenly precepts to seven Churches and 'their Angels[1].' It will be remembered that the same reference to the symbolism of the number of the Epistles occurs in the Muratorian Canon[2]; and on the very con- fines of the Latin Church, Victorinus bishop of Petavium (Pettau) in Pannonia reproduces the same idea: 'There 'are,' he says, '...seven spirits...seven golden candle- 'sticks...seven Churches addressed by Paul, seven dea- 'cons[3]....' And even Jerome bears witness to the gene-

cere idoneum confirmandi de proximo jure disciplinam magistrorum. Exstat etiam Barnabæ titulus ad Hebræos: adeo satis auctorati viri ut quem Paulus juxta se constituerit in abstinentiæ tenore, 1 Cor. ix. Et utique receptior apud ecclesias epistola Barnabæ illo apocrypho Pastore mœchorum. Cf. p. 260 f., 263. The phrase *de proximo jure* clearly implies that the Apostles had the *primum jus*, to which an Apostolic man approached nearest. The reading adeo satis auctorati viri (for auctoritatis viro) is justified by the context and *de Cor. Mil.* 2: ...observationem...*satis auctoratam* consensus patrocinio. The substitution of *a Deo* for *adeo* seems to be quite unnecessary, and in fact opposed to the idea of the sanction of St Paul which follows.

The allusions to the Epistle which have been found in other parts of Tertullian's writings are very uncertain.

Dr Tregelles (*Can. Murat.* p. 95) calls attention to *De Anima* 50 (nec mors eorum reperta est) and *adv. Jud.* 2 (qui necdum mortem gustavit) as containing references to Hebr. xi. 5 (not Gen. v. 24); but no stress can be laid even on these passages. The mention of the Epistle to the Hebrews under the title of the Epistle of Barnabas in the Claromontane Stichometry (App. D. xx.) is a remarkable trace of the opinion held by Tertullian.

[1] *De Exhort. Mart.* 11 (*med.*): Apostolus Paulus qui hujus numeri legitimi et certi meminit ad septem ecclesias scribit. Et in Apocalypsi Dominus mandata sua divina et præcepta cœlestia ad septem ecclesias et eorum angelos scribit. Cf. *Testim.* 1. 20: Unde et Paulus septem ecclesiis scribit et Apocalypsis ecclesias septem ponit ut servetur septenarius numerus.

[2] Cf. p. 217.

[3] Vict. ap. Routh, *Rell. Sacr.* III. p. 459.

ral prevalence of the belief when he says: 'The Apostle 'Paul writes to seven Churches, for his eighth Epistle to 'the Hebrews is by most excluded from the number¹.' Generally indeed it may be stated that no Latin Father before Hilary quotes the Epistle as St Paul's; and his judgment and that of the writers who followed him was strongly influenced by the authority of Origen².

With regard to the disputed Catholic Epistles the earliest Latin Fathers offer little evidence. Tertullian once expressly quotes the Epistle of St Jude as authoritative and Apostolic³. But there is nothing in his writings to shew that he was acquainted with the Epistle of St James⁴, the second and third Epistles of St John⁵, or the second Epistle of St Peter. In Cyprian there is I believe no reference to any of the disputed Epistles. Like several earlier writers, he quotes the first Epistles of St Peter and St John so as to imply that he was not

Marginalia: Chap. ii. HILARY. †368. ii. *The* Epistles of St James, 2 Peter, 2 *and* 3 John, Jude. TERTULLIAN. CYPRIAN.

---

¹ Hieron. *ad Paul.* 50 (al. 103, IV. p. 574): Paulus Apostolus ad septem ecclesias scribit, octava enim ad Hebræos a plerisque extra numerum ponitur.

² The references in Lactantius are very uncertain, though the coincidences of argument are remarkable. *E.g.* Hebr. iii. 3—6; v. 5, 6; vii. 21, compared with Lact. *Instit.* IV. 14 *init.* (quoted by Lardner).

³ *De Hab. Muliebri* 3: ...Enoch apud Judam Apostolum testimonium possidet. This is the only reference which occurs.

⁴ The references given by Semler, adv. *Jud.* 2 (James ii. 23); *de Orat.* 8 (James i. 13) are quite unsatisfactory. The latter passage indeed seems to prove clearly that Tertullian did not know the Epistle, for otherwise he must have quoted it. The quotation *de Exhort. Cast.* 7, *non auditores legis justificabuntur a deo sed factores*, is from Rom. ii. 13, not from James i. 22.

The well-known passage *adv. Gnost.* 12 does not in itself necessarily shew more than that Tertullian did not attribute the Epistle to St James the Elder; but the omission of all reference to it there, when connected with the other facts, can leave little doubt that he was unacquainted with it.

⁵ The reference in the treatise against Marcion (IV. 16) is certainly to 1 John iv. 1, 2, and not to 2 John 7, though the Latin has not preserved the difference between ἐληλυθότα and ἐρχόμενον. Some difficulty has been felt about the phrase *Johannes in primore Epistola* (*de Pudic.* 19): but Tertullian is there contrasting the teaching of 1 John iii. 8, 9 with the passage *at the beginning of his Epistle:* 1 John i. 8. This sense of *primoris* is fully justified by Aul. Gell. 1. 18. 2: Varro in primore libro scripsit... Cf. nott. *in loc.*

Chap. ii.	familiarly acquainted with any other[1]; but a clause from the record of the seventh Council of Carthage, at which he was present, shews how little stress can be laid upon such language alone. For after that one bishop had referred to the first Epistle of St John as 'St John's
AURELIUS.	'Epistle' as though it were the only one, Aurelius bishop of Chullabi uses exactly the same words in quoting the second epistle[2]. At the same time however the entire absence of quotations from these Epistles in the writings of Cyprian, and (with the exception of the short Epistle to Philemon) from these Epistles only of all the books of the New Testament, leads to the conclusion that he was either ignorant of their existence or doubtful as to their authority. One other passage alone remains to be
Auct. Adv. Novat. Hæret.	noticed. The judgment of Tertullian on the Epistle of St Jude is confirmed by a passage in one of the contemporary treatises commonly appended to the works of Cyprian, in which it is quoted as Scripture[3]; and this reference completes I believe the sum of what can be gathered from early Latin writers on this class of the disputed books.
iii. *The Apocalypse.* TERTULLIAN.	But if the evidence for these Epistles be meagre, that for the Apocalypse is most complete. Tertullian quotes it continually as the work of the Evangelist St John, and nowhere implies any doubt of its authen-
CYPRIAN.	ticity[4]. Cyprian again makes constant use of it as Holy Scripture, though he does not expressly assign it to the
COMMODIAN.	authorship of the Evangelist St John[5]. Commodian[6]

[1] *De Exhort. Mar.* c. 9: Petrus in epistola sua... c. 10: Johannes in epistola sua...
[2] Cf. p. 366, n. 3.
[3] *Adv. Novat. Hæret.* p. xvii. ed. Baluz. (quoted by Lardner): sicut scriptum est: Jude 14, 15.
[4] *Adv. Marc.* III. 14: Apostolus Johannes in Apocalypsi...

[5] *De Opere et Eleem.* 14: Audi in Apocalypsi Domini tui vocem... So *adv. Novat. Hær.* p. ix.
[6] Commod. *Instr.* I. 41. He interprets Antichrist of Nero, who should rise again. The conjecture II. 1. 17, *operta Johannis*, is very uncertain,

and Lactantius[1] make several allusions to it; and, with the exception of the Gospel of St John, it is the only book of the New Testament which the latter writer quotes by name. From every quarter the testimony of the early Latin Fathers to the Apostolic authority of the Apocalypse is thus decided and unanimous[2].

It appears then that the Canon of the Latin Churches up to the beginning of the fourth century differed from our own by defect and not by addition. The Latin Fathers were in danger of bounding the limits of the Canon too straitly, as the Alexandrine Fathers were inclined to extend them too widely. But the same causes which kept them from acknowledging all the books which we receive preserved them also from the risk of confounding Apocryphal with Canonical writings. Notwithstanding the extent of Tertullian's works he refers only to two Apocryphal books; and one of these—the Shepherd of Hermas—he rejects with contempt[3]: the other—the Acts of Paul and Thecla—he declares to be a detected forgery[4]. In Cyprian, though he freely uses the Apocryphal books of the Old Testament, there is no trace of any Christian Apocryphal book; and in the tracts appended to his works there is a single condemnatory reference to the *Preaching of Paul*[5]. Lactantius also once alludes to the same book, but without attributing

---

[1] Lact. *Ep.* 42 f.; ...sicut docet Johannes in Revelatione.
[2] For the *Claromontane Stichometry*, see App. D. xx.
[3] Tert. *de Orat.* 12. Cf. *de Pudic.* 10: Sed cederem tibi si scriptura Pastoris quae sola moechos amat divino instrumento meruisset incidi, si non ab omni concilio ecclesiarum etiam vestrarum inter apocrypha et falsa judicaretur, adultera et ipsa et inde patrona sociorum.
[4] *De Bapt.* 17: ...sciant in Asia presbyterum qui eam scripturam [Acta Pauli et Theclae] construxit, quasi titulo Pauli de suo cumulans, convictum atque confessum id se amore Pauli fecisse, loco decessisse.
[5] *De Bapt.* 14: Est autem adulterini hujus immo internecini baptismatis si quis alius auctor tum etiam quidam ab eisdem ipsis haereticis propter hunc eundem errorem confictus liber qui inscribitur Pauli praedicatio. On the name see Routh, *Rell. Sacr.* v. 325.

to it any remarkable authority[1]; and elsewhere he quotes the words of the Heavenly Voice at our Lord's Baptism according to the reading of Justin Martyr[2]. But here the list ends; and on the other hand numerous passages in Tertullian, Cyprian, and Victorinus, shew that they regarded the books of the New Testament not only as a collection but as a whole; not thrown together by caprice or accident, but united by Divine Providence, and equal in authority with the Jewish Scriptures. The language of Tertullian has been quoted already; and both Cyprian and Victorinus found a certain fitness in a *fourfold* Gospel, as well as in the *seven* Churches addressed by St Paul, so that the very proportions of the Canon seemed to them to be fixed by a definite law[3]. Nor was this strange; for the Old and New Scriptures were in their judgment 'fountains of 'Divine fulness,' written by 'Prophets and Apostles full of 'the Holy Spirit,' before which 'all the tediousness and 'ambiguities of human discourse must be laid aside[4].'

§ 3. *The Church of Rome.*

In passing from Africa to Rome we come to the second meeting-point of the East and West; for it could not but happen that Rome soon became a great centre of the Christian world. A Latin Church grew up round the Greek Church, and the peculiarities of both were harmonized by that power of organization which ruled

---

[1] Lact. *Instit.* IV. 21: ...sed et futura aperuit illis omnia quæ Petrus et Paulus Romæ prædicaverunt, et ea prædicatio in memoriam scripta permansit...
[2] *Instit.* IV. 15: Tunc vox de cœlo audita est: Filius meus es tu; ego hodie genui te. Cf. p. 160.
[3] Cf. pp. 345 f., 372. Cypr. *Ep.* 73. 10: Ecclesia paradisi instar...
arbores rigat quatuor fluminibus, id est evangeliis... Victorinus (Routh, *Rell. Sacr.* III. 456): ...quatuor animalia ante thronum Dei quatuor evangelia... It is I think unnecessary to make any apology for the use of Cyprian's letters.
[4] Cypr. *de Orat. Dom.* 1; *de Exhort. Mart.* I. 4.

the Roman life. But the combination of the same elements at Alexandria and Rome was effected in different modes, and produced different results. The teaching of the East and West was united at Alexandria by the conscious operation of a spirit of eclecticism: at Rome by the silent pressure of events. The one combination was literary: the other practical. The one resulted in a theological code: the other in an ecclesiastical system. And though it would be out of place to dwell longer on these fundamental differences of Alexandria and Rome —the poles of Christendom in the third century—it is of importance to bear them in mind even in an investigation into the history of the New Testament.

The earliest memorials of the Latin Church of Rome are extremely small, and contain very little which bears on the history of the New Testament Canon. Nothing survives of the writings of Apollonius and Victor, the first Latin authors whose names have been preserved. The *Octavius* of Minucius Felix, like former Apologies, contains no quotations from the Christian Scriptures; and the two letters of Cornelius included in the works of Cyprian are scarcely more productive[1]. The treatises of Novatus, the unsuccessful rival of Cornelius, are alone of such character and extent as to call for the frequent use of the Apostolic writings; and they do in fact contain numerous quotations from most of the acknowledged books. But Novatus nowhere quotes any other Christian Scriptures; and the passing coincidences of thought and language with the Epistle to the Hebrews which occur in his essay *On the Trinity* are very uncertain[2];

i. *The* Latin *writers.*

APOLLONIUS.
VICTOR.
MINUCIUS FELIX.
CORNELIUS.
† 252.
NOVATUS.

---

[1] One quotation occurs from St Matthew v. 8; *Ep.* ap. Routh, *Rell. Sacr.* III. 18.

[2] *De Trin.* 26: Cum sedere [Christum] ad dexteram Patris et a prophetis et ab apostolis approbatur (Hebr. i. 3; but cf. Eph. i. 20; 1 Pet. iii. 22); *id.* 31: ...ut quamvis probet illum nativitas Filium, tamen morigera obedientia asserat illum

while those with the Epistle of St James and 2 Peter are barely worthy of notice[1]. It is also of importance to remark that while in the later stages of the Novatian controversy, when the Epistle to the Hebrews was generally acknowledged, it is said that the reading of that Epistle was omitted in some Churches from the danger of misunderstanding its teaching on repentance, no distinct reference to it is made by Novatus or by his immediate opponents, which could scarcely have been avoided if it had been held to be authoritative in their time.

ii. The Greek writers.

The preponderance of the Greek element in the Roman Church even during the third century, at least in a literary aspect, is clearly shewn by the writings of Caius, Hippolytus, and Dionysius. Of the first and last only fragments remain; and nothing more can be gathered from the slight remains of Dionysius than that he recognised a New as well as an Old Testament as a final source of truth[2]. Of Caius it is reported by Eusebius that in arguing against the 'new scriptures' of the Montanists he enumerated only thirteen Epistles of St Paul, omitting that to the Hebrews[3]. Whether he received all the remaining books of the New Testament is left in uncertainty; and in the case of the Apocalypse this is the more to be regretted, because in one obscure fragment he has been supposed to attribute its authorship to Cerinthus[4]. In close connexion with Caius must be noticed a group of writings which were once attributed

DIONYSIUS.
259—269 A.D.

CAIUS.
c. 213 A.D.

[1] Paternæ voluntatis ex quo est ministrum (Hebr. v. 8); *id. s. f.* (Hebr. v. 7); *id.* 16: sed væ est adjicientibus quomodo et detrahentibus positum (Apoc. xxii. 18, 19).
De Trin. 8 (2 Pet. ii. 5); *id.* 4 (James i. 17). The latter passage indeed seems to me to shew clearly that Novatus was *not* acquainted with the Epistle of St James.

[2] Dion. Rom. fr. (Routh, *Rell. Sacr.* III. 374): Τριάδα μὲν κηρυττομένην ὑπὸ τῆς θείας γραφῆς σαφῶς ἐπίστανται, τρεῖς δὲ Θεοὺς οὔτε παλαιὰν οὔτε καινὴν διαθήκην κηρύττουσαν.

[3] Euseb. *H. E.* VI. 20.

[4] ap. Euseb. *H. E.* III. 28. Cf. p. 278, n. 2.

II.] HIPPOLYTUS. 379

to him, but which are now, by almost universal consent, assigned to his contemporary Hippolytus. Of these the most important is the *Treatise against all Heresies*, to which frequent reference has been made already in examining the opinions of early heretics on the New Testament Canon. But apart from the testimony which it thus conveys I have noticed nothing in it which bears upon the history of the disputed Books. Of the *Little Labyrinth* and the *Treatise on the Universe* only fragments remain. In one passage of the former work a charge is brought against certain heretics of 'fearlessly 'tampering with the Divine Scriptures while they said 'that they had corrected them; so that if any one were 'to take the Manuscripts of their several teachers and 'compare them together he would find them widely dif-'ferent....And how daring this offence is even they must 'know; for either they do not believe that the Divine 'Scriptures were uttered by the Holy Spirit, and are 'unbelievers, or they hold that they are themselves 'wiser than the Holy Spirit. And what is this but the 'conduct of madmen? for they cannot deny that the 'daring act is their own, since the corrections are written 'by their hand; and they did not receive the Scrip-'tures in such a form from those by whom they were 'instructed; and they have it not in their power to shew 'the Manuscripts from which they transcribed their read-'ings[1].' This refers of course chiefly to the text of Scripture, and probably of the Old Testament, but it is no less an evidence of the vigilance with which the sacred writings were guarded, and of the divine authority which was attributed to their words. And elsewhere, in noticing the statement that a revolution in Christian doctrine had happened after the times of Victor, the

Chap. ii.

The Treatise against Heresies.

The Little Labyrinth.

[1] Euseb. *H. E.* v. 28. Routh, *Rell. Sacr.* II. 132 sq.

Chap. ii.

The treatise On the Universe.

Hippolytus. c. 220 A.D.

same author replies that the assertion 'would perhaps 'have been plausible if in the first place the Divine 'Scriptures had not opposed it, and next also the writ-'ings of brethren before the time of Victor[1]....' An appeal is thus made both to Scripture and to tradition, and the line between them is drawn distinctly. The peroration of the *Address to the Greeks on the Universe* has been well likened to the conclusion of a Christian *Gorgias*, painting in vivid and brilliant colours the scenes of Hades and the Last Judgment. Many passages from the New Testament are inwrought into the composition, but so as to lose much of their original character; and it is consequently impossible to point with confidence to the coincidences of thought which it offers with the Epistle of St Jude (or 2 Peter) and the Apocalypse[2]. The undoubted writings of Hippolytus contain quotations from all the acknowledged books except the Epistle to Philemon and the first Epistle of St John. Of the disputed books he uses the Apocalypse as an unquestionable work of the Apostle St John, and is said to have written a Commentary upon it[3]. On the other hand he is reported not to have included the Epistle to the Hebrews among the Epistles of St Paul[4]. But be-

---

[1] Euseb. *l. c.*; Routh, *Rell. Sacr.* II. 129.

[2] Bunsen, *Anal. Ante-Nic.* I. 393 sqq. The passages which seem most remarkable are the following:...ἐν τούτῳ τῷ χωρίῳ...ἀνάγκη σκότος διηνεκῶς τυγχάνειν· τοῦτο τὸ χωρίον ὡς φρούριον ἀπενεμήθη ψυχαῖς ἐφ' ᾧ κατεστάθησαν ἄγγελοι φρουροί...(Jude 6; 2 Pet. ii. 4) ἐν τούτῳ δὲ τῷ χωρίῳ ...λίμνη πυρὸς ἀσβεστοῦ...(Apoc. xx. 10 sq.). It may be observed that in a passage shortly after this where the common text is ἀλλὰ καὶ οὗ τὸν τῶν πατέρων χορὸν...ὁρῶσι... we must read καὶ οὗτοι τὸν τῶν π. χ. Bun-sen's emendation οὐ τὸν τ. π. χ. does not suit the description.

[3] *De Antichr.* 36. Cf. 29.

[4] Phot. *Cod.* 121 (Bunsen, *Anal.* I. 411). Dr Tregelles (*Can. Murat.* p. 95) points out two possible references to the epistle (*adv. Jud.* 3 || Hebr. xiii. 2. *In Sus. v.* 23 || Hebr. x. 31). The same scholar (*id.* p. 101) considers that the words of 2 Pet. ii. 22 'are interwoven' in the *Philosoph.* ix. 7, μετ' οὐ πολὺ δὲ ἐπὶ τὸν αὐτὸν βόρβορον ἀνεκυλίοντο. In a proverbial phrase I should hesitate in deciding on the source from which the words might be derived.

yond this there is nothing to shew his opinion upon the contents of the Canon[1].

From this then it appears that though there is not evidence to establish a complete view of the Roman Canon in the third century, some points can be ascertained with satisfactory certainty. By the Roman, as well as by the Alexandrine and African Churches, the Apocalypse was added to the acknowledged books; but like the African Church it did not receive the Epistle to the Hebrews among the writings of St Paul. Apart however from the evidence for particular books, it is evident that as a whole the Apostolic writings occupied at Rome, no less than elsewhere, a definite and distinguished place as an ultimate standard of doctrine.

Summary of the opinion of the Roman Church.

§ 4. *The Churches of Asia Minor.*

The great work of Irenæus written in the remote regions of Gaul and preserved for the most part only in a Latin translation is the sole considerable monument of the literature of the Churches of Asia Minor from the time of Polycarp to that of Gregory of Neo-Cæsarea or even of Basil. Still there is abundant proof of their zeal and activity. At Ephesus and Smyrna, in Pontus and Cappadocia, there were those who traced back a direct connexion with the Apostles, and witnessed to the continuity of the Faith.

Scanty literature of the Asiatic Churches.

During the Paschal controversy in the time of Victor, Polycrates bishop of Ephesus addressed a letter in the name of a vast multitude' of Asiatic bishops to the Roman Church, justifying their peculiar usage by the

1. *The Church of Ephesus. Polycrates. c. 196 A.D.*

---

[1] The supposed reference to 2 Pet. i. 21 in *de Antichr.* 2 is wholly uncertain. Nor is the phrase εἰς κρίσιν τηρουμένας (Hipp. *in Dan.* p. 158 Lagarde), a clearer trace of Jude 6, 2 Pet. ii. 4.

example of their predecessors[1]. 'For these all,' he says, 'observed the fourteenth day of the moon according to 'the Gospel, transgressing it in no respect, but following 'it according to the rule of faith[2].' Yet even this tradition was not enough: he had also 'conversed with bre-'thren from the whole world, and gone through all Holy 'Scripture[3],' and so at length he was not afraid to meet his opponents. Such was the relation of Scripture and tradition in the resting-place of St John within a century after his death: such the intimate union of Churches which were last blessed by the presence of an Apostle. Apollonius, who is stated on doubtful authority to have been also bishop of Ephesus[4], recognises a similar combination of arguments when he accuses Themison a follower of Montanus of 'speaking against the Lord, the 'Apostles, and the Holy Church,' while in the endeavour to recommend his doctrine 'he ventured in imitation of 'the Apostle to compose a Catholic Epistle[5].' In addition to these natural indications of the peculiar position occupied by the Christian Scriptures generally, Eusebius mentions that Apollonius 'made use of testimonies from 'the Apocalypse;' and this indeed would necessarily be

---

[1] Euseb. *H. E.* v. 24. The letter of Polycrates was written in his 65th year, and Victor died 197 A.D.; Polycrates then may have conversed with Polycarp and Justin Martyr. He appears to have been of a Christian family (ἑξήκοντα πέντε ἔτη ἔχων ἐν Κυρίῳ); and probably the episcopate had been hereditary in it (ἑπτὰ μὲν ἦσαν συγγενεῖς μου ἐπίσκοποι ἐγὼ δὲ ὄγδοος). At least every detail points to the unbroken unity of the Church.

[2] Euseb. *l. c.*: οὗτοι πάντες ἐτήρησαν τὴν ἡμέραν τῆς τεσσαρεσκαιδεκάτης τοῦ πάσχα κατὰ τὸ εὐαγγέλιον, μηδὲν παρεκβαίνοντες ἀλλὰ κατὰ τὸν κανόνα τῆς πίστεως ἀκολουθοῦν-τες. It may be added that Polycrates speaks of St John as ὁ ἐπὶ τὸ στῆθος τοῦ κυρίου ἀναπεσών (John xiii. 25; xxi. 20). Compare p. 227, n. 3.

[3] Euseb. *l. c.*:...συμβεβληκὼς τοῖς ἀπὸ τῆς οἰκουμένης ἀδελφοῖς καὶ πᾶσαν ἁγίαν γραφὴν διεληλυθώς...These last words I believe refer to the New Testament. Yet cf. Anatol. ap. Euseb. *H. E.* VII. 32.

[4] Routh, *Rell. Sacr.* I. p. 465.

[5] Apoll. ap. Euseb. *H. E.* v. 18: Θεμίσων...ἐτόλμησε μιμούμενος τὸν ἀπόστολον καθολικήν τινα συνταξάμενος ἐπιστολήν...βλασφημῆσαι δὲ εἰς τὸν Κύριον καὶ τοὺς ἀποστόλους καὶ τὴν ἁγίαν ἐκκλησίαν.

the case in a controversy with Montanist teachers, who affirmed that the site of the *heavenly Jerusalem* was no other than the little Phrygian town which was the centre of their sect[1].

It is uncertain at what time and under what circumstances Irenæus left Smyrna on his mission to Gaul. He was 'still a boy,' 'at the commencement of life,' when he listened to Polycarp 'in lower Asia;' but yet he was not too young to treasure up the words of his teacher, so that they became the comfort of his old age[2]. While a presbyter at Lyons he was commended by the Church there to Eleutherus bishop of Rome as 'zealous 'for the covenant of Christ:' and at a later time he continued to take a watchful regard of the 'sound ordi- 'nances of the Church' throughout Christendom. Eusebius[3] has collected some of his testimonies to the Books of the New Testament, but they extend only to the four Gospels, the Apocalypse, 1 John, and 1 Peter; for he makes no mention of his constant use of the Acts and of twelve Epistles of St Paul. It is however of more importance to notice that he has neglected to observe the quotations which Irenæus makes from 2 John, once citing a verse from it as though it were contained in the

Chap. ii.

2. *The Church of Smyrna.* IRENÆUS. *c.* 135—200 A.D.

c. 177 A.D.

His testimony to the Apocalypse.

2 John.

---

[1] Euseb. *l. c.*: κέχρηται δὲ καὶ μαρτυρίαις ἀπὸ τῆς Ἰωάννου Ἀποκαλύψεως. The description which Apollonius gives of Montanus—οὗτός ἐστιν...ὁ Πέπουζαν καὶ Τύμιον Ἱερουσαλὴμ ὀνομάσας (πόλεις δέ εἰσιν αὗται μικραὶ τῆς Φρυγίας) τοὺς πανταχόθεν ἐκεῖ συναγαγεῖν ἐθέλων—may remind us of a 'prophet' of our own times. Cf. Epiph. *Hær.* XLIX. 1: Χριστὸς ...ἀπεκάλυψέ μοι (a Montanist prophetess) τουτονὶ τὸν τόπον εἶναι ἅγιον καὶ ὧδε τὴν Ἱερουσαλὴμ ἐκ τοῦ οὐρανοῦ κατιέναι.
On the tradition which Apollonius mentions that the Apostles were commanded by our Lord to remain twelve years at Jerusalem, compare Clem. Alex. *Strom.* VI. 5. 43; Lumper, VII. 5 sqq.

[2] Euseb. *H. E.* v. 20. Cf. Iren. *c. Hær.* III. 3. 4 (Euseb. *H. E.* IV. 14). The date of Irenæus is much disputed, depending on that of Polycarp. I have given that which appears to be the most probable. Eleutherus was still bishop of Rome when he wrote his great Treatise *c. Hær.* (III. 3. 3).

[3] *H. E.* v. 8.

first Epistle¹. But in addition to the Apocalypse, which Irenæus uses continually as an unquestioned work of St John², this is the only disputed book which he certainly acknowledged as having Apostolic authority; and there are no anonymous references to the Epistle of St James³, 3 John, 2 Peter, or St Jude, on which any reliance can be placed. Some coincidences of language with the Epistle to the Hebrews are more striking; and in a later chapter Eusebius states that in a book now lost Irenæus 'mentions the Epistle to the Hebrews and the Wisdom 'of Solomon⁴.' Agreeably with this, the Epistle to the Hebrews appears to be quoted in the second Pfaffian fragment as the work of St Paul⁵; but on the other hand Photius classes Irenæus with Hippolytus as denying the Pauline authorship of the Epistle. And this last

---

¹ Iren. *c. Hær.* I. 16. 3: Ἰωάννης δὲ ὁ τοῦ Κυρίου μαθητής...2 John 11. In the same connexion it would have been natural to quote 2 Peter and Jude.
Ib. III. 16. 8: Johannes in prædicta epistola... (2 John 7, 8), after quoting 1 John ii. 18 sqq. Comp. Clem. Alex. quoted p. 357, n. 6. Is it possible that the second Epistle was looked upon as an appendix to the first? and may we thus explain the references to *two* Epistles of St John? The first Epistle, as is well known, was called *ad Parthos* by Augustine and some other Latin authorities; and the same title πρὸς Πάρθους is given to the second Epistle in one Greek Manuscript (62 Scholz). The Latin translation of Clement's *Outlines* (IV. 66) says: Secunda Johannis epistola quæ ad virgines (παρθένους) scripta simplicissima est. Jerome, it may be added, quotes names from the *third* Epistle as from the *second* (*De Nom. Hebr.*).

² Iren. *c. Hær.* IV. 20. 11: Joannes domini discipulus in Apocalypsi... Yet he never calls him an Apostle, though he identifies him (*in loc.*) with the *disciple whom Jesus loved*, John xiii. 25.

³ The supposed reference to James ii. 23 in IV. 16. 2, *credidit Deo et reputatum est illi ad justitiam, et amicus Dei vocatus est*, is one which from its form cannot be regarded as certain. It is evident that many quotations from the Old Testament were widely current in modified forms, as is the case still, so that the recurrence of a particular type of rendering or application in two writers probably shews nothing more than their dependence on a common source. Comp. p. 170.

⁴ Euseb. *H. E.* v. 26. Cf. p. 356, n. 1. Iren. *c. Hær.* II. 30. 9: Solus hic Deus invenitur qui omnia fecit... *verbo virtutis suæ* (Hebr. i. 3): *ib.* IV. 11. 4; cf. Hebr. x. 1, &c.: *ib.* v. 5. 1; cf. Hebr. xi. 5.

⁵ Iren. fr. 38 (p. 854): ὁ Παῦλος παρακαλεῖ ἡμᾶς (Rom. xii. 1)...καὶ πάλιν (Hebr. xiii. 15).

statement leads the way to the most probable conclusion: Irenæus was I believe acquainted with the Epistle, but he did not attribute it to St Paul[1].

One of the most distinguished converts of Origen was Gregory surnamed Thaumaturgus (the Wonder-Worker) bishop of Neo-Cæsarea (Niksar) in Pontus. His chief remaining work is an eloquent address delivered before his master when he was about to leave him. From its character it contains very little which bears upon the Canon, and nothing in regard to the disputed books. But in a fragment quoted from Gregory in a Catena there occurs a marked coincidence with the language of St James[2]; and Origen in a letter which he addressed to him uses among other texts one from the Epistle to the Hebrews[3]. From this, as well as from the mode in which Gregory treats the writings of the New Testament generally, it may be reasonably concluded that he accepted the same books as Origen, to whom indeed he owed his knowledge of the Scriptures. But in sending forth such a scholar to the confines of Asia Minor, Origen only repaid a benefit which he had received. When he had been forced to leave Egypt he found protection and honour at the hands of Alexander, originally a Cappadocian bishop, who was advanced to the chair of Jerusalem on the death of Narcissus, whom he had previously assisted in his episcopal work. Nor can these facts be without value in our inquiry. It is surely no

Chap. ii.

3. *The Church of Pontus.* GREGORY of Neo-Cæsarea.

The Epistle to the Hebrews.

Foreign Connexions of the North of Asia.

231 A.D.

---

[1] Eusebius (*H. E.* v. 8) noticed that Irenæus quoted the Shepherd of Hermas (*c. Hær.* IV. 20. 2) by the name of 'Scripture.' But several instances have been lately given which prove the lax use of the word; and a difference of private opinion, which is found also in the case of Origen, makes the general agreement of the Churches more conspicuous.

[2] *Cat. Vat.* ap. Ghisler. *Comm. in Ierem.* I. p. 831 : δῆλον γὰρ ὡς πᾶν ἀγαθὸν τέλειον θεόθεν ἔρχεται. James i. 17.

[3] *Ep. ad Greg.* 3 : ἵνα λέγῃς οὐ μόνον τὸ Μέτοχοι τοῦ Χριστοῦ γεγόναμεν· ἀλλὰ καὶ Μέτοχοι τοῦ Θεοῦ. Hebr. iii. 14.

386   THE DISPUTED BOOKS OF THE CANON.   [PART

Chap. ii. slight thing that casual notices shew that Christians the most widely separated were really joined together by close intercourse: that the Churches of remote provinces, whose existence and prosperity were first disclosed by the zeal of a Roman governor, are found about a century after in intimate connexion with Syria, Egypt, and Greece¹. And the evidence is yet incomplete; for among others who visited Origen during his sojourn in *Firmilian.* Syria was Firmilian bishop of Cæsarea in Cappadocia, the correspondent and advocate of Cyprian²; and thus for the moment an obscure corner of Asia becomes a meeting-point of Christians from every quarter, not only 'as if they lived in one country, but as dwelling 256 A.D. 'in one house³.' The single letter of Firmilian, which is preserved in a Latin translation among the letters of Cyprian, contains numerous allusions to the acknowledged books, and in one place he appears to refer to the second Epistle of St Peter. 'The blessed Apostles Peter 'and Paul,' he says, 'have anathematized heretics in 2 Peter ii. 'their Epistles, and warned us to avoid them⁴.'

But the influence of Origen was not dominant in all *Methodius.* parts of Asia Minor. Methodius a bishop of Lycia⁵ and †*c.* 311 A.D. afterwards of Tyre distinguished himself for animosity to his teaching, which Eusebius so far resented, if we

---

¹ Cf. Euseb. *H. E.* IV. 23: ἄλλη δ' ἐπιστολή τις αὐτοῦ [Διονυσίου] πρὸς Νικομηδέας φέρεται...
² Euseb. *H. E.* VI. 27.
³ Firm. *Ep.* 75 (Cypr.) § 1.
⁴ Firm. *Ep.* § 6: Adhuc etiam infamans Petrum et Paulum beatos Apostolos...qui in Epistolis suis hæreticos exsecrati sunt et ut eos evitemus monuerunt. In the same chapter Firmilian notices (as unimportant) ritual differences between the Roman and Eastern churches: circa celebrandos dies Paschæ et circa multa alia divinæ rei sacramenta...secundum quod in cæteris quoque plurimis provinciis multa pro locorum et nominum (?) diversitate variantur...
⁵ Socr. *H. E.* VI. 13:...Μεθόδιος τῆς ἐν Λυκίᾳ πόλεως λεγομένης Ὀλύμπου ἐπίσκοπος. Socrates (*l. c.*) alone mentions that Methodius recanted his censures on Origen; yet probably his words mean no more than that he expressed admiration for Origen's character, and not for his doctrine.

may believe the common explanation of his silence, as to omit all mention of him in his history, though his works were 'popularly read' in Jerome's time[1]. There is nothing however to indicate that the differences which separated Methodius from Origen extended either to the Interpretation or to the Canon of Scripture; and thus they give fresh value to his evidence by confirming its independence. Like earlier Fathers, Methodius found a mystical significance in the number of the Gospels[2]; and his writings abound with quotations from the acknowledged books. He also received the Apocalypse as a work of 'the blessed John' and as possessing undoubted authority[3]. Besides this, numerous coincidences of language shew that he was acquainted with the Epistle to the Hebrews; and though he does not directly attribute it to St Paul, he uses it with the same familiarity and respect as he exhibits towards the Pauline Epistles[4].

Chap. ii.

He received the Apocalypse and the Epistle to the Hebrews.

The heresy of Montanus, as has been seen already, occupied much of the attention of Asiatic writers at the beginning of the third century. The steady opposition which they offered to the pretensions of the new prophets is in itself a proof of the limits which they fixed to the presence of inspired teaching in the Church, and of their belief in the completeness of the Revelation made through the Apostles. In an anonymous fragment

Frag. Adv. Cataphrygas.

---

[1] Hieron. *de Virr. Ill.* 83.
[2] *Sympos. de Cast.* p. 391 D.
[3] *De Resurr.* p. 326 B: ἐπίστησον δὲ μήποτε καὶ ὁ μακάριος Ἰωάννης... Apoc. xx. 13. *Ib.* p. 328 D: πῶς δὴ ἔτι ὁ Χριστὸς πρωτότοκος εἶναι τῶν νεκρῶν ὑπὸ τῶν προφητῶν καὶ τῶν ἀποστόλων ᾄδεται; (Apoc. i. 5; Col. i. 18). Methodius is also mentioned by Andreas of Cæsarea with Papias, Irenæus, and Hippolytus, as a witness to the 'divine inspiration' of the Apocalypse (Routh, *Rell. Sacr.* I. 15). He interpreted much of it allegorically—εἰς τὴν ἐκκλησίαν καὶ τὰς παρθενούσας (*Sympos.* p. 388 A).
[4] *De Resurr.* p. 286 D. Hebr. xii. 5, &c. In the spurious tract on 'Symeon and Anna' it is quoted as 'the most divine Paul's' (p. 427 D). Methodius must be added to the many before him who quote Ps. ii. 7 as having been uttered at our Lord's Baptism (*Sympos.* p. 387 D). Cf. p. 160, n. 1.

Chap. ii.	which Eusebius has preserved from one of the many treatises on the subject this opinion finds a remarkable expression. For a long time, the writer says, I was disinclined to undertake the refutation of the opinions of multitudes '...through fear and careful regard lest I 'should seem in any way to some to add any new article 'or clause to the word of the New Covenant of the
Apoc. xxii. 18, 19.	'Gospel, which no one may add to or take from who 'has determined to live according to the simple Gos-'pel[1].' The coincidence of these words with the conclusion of the Apocalypse cannot but be apparent; and they seem to recognise a complete written standard of Christian truth.
The Canon of Asia Minor defective but	So far then there is no trace in the Asiatic Churches of the use of the Epistle of St Jude; and the use of the Epistle of St James and of the second Epistle of St Peter is at least very uncertain. Methodius alone undoubtedly employs the language of the Epistle to the Hebrews; but on the other hand the Apocalypse was recognised from the first as a work of the Apostle in the districts most immediately interested in its contents. The same may be said of the second Epistle of St John, and the slight value of merely negative evidence is shewn by the fact that no quotation from his third Epistle has yet been noticed, though its authenticity is necessarily connected with that of the second. But if the evidence for the New Testament Canon in the
free from Apocryphal additions.	Churches of Asia Minor be incomplete, it is pure and unmixed. The reference of Irenæus to the Shepherd of Hermas is the only passage with which I am acquainted

[1] Auct. *adv. Cataphr.* ap. Euseb. *H. E.* v. 16 (Routh, *Rell. Sacr.* II. p. 183 sqq.): δεδιὼς δὲ καὶ ἐξευλαβούμενος μή πη δόξω τισὶν ἐπισυγγράφειν ἢ ἐπιδιατάσσεσθαι (cf. Gal. iii. 15) τῷ τῆς τοῦ εὐαγγελίου καινῆς διαθήκης λόγῳ, ᾧ μήτε προσθεῖναι μήτ' ἀφελεῖν δυνατὸν τῷ κατὰ τὸ εὐαγγέλιον αὐτὸ πολιτεύεσθαι προῃρημένῳ.

which even appears to give authority to an uncanonical book[1]. Holy Scripture as a whole was recognised as a sure rule of doctrine. We acknowledge, said the Presbytery to Noetus, 'one Christ the Son of God, who suf-'fered as He suffered, who died as He died, who rose 'again, who ascended into heaven, who is on the right 'hand of the Father, who is coming to judge quick and 'dead. This we say, having learnt it from the divine 'Scriptures, and this also we know[2].'

§ 5. *The Churches of Syria.*

Nothing more than the names of the successors of Ignatius in the see of Antioch has been preserved till the time of Theophilus the sixth in descent from the Apostles. Of the works which he wrote, three books to Autolycus—*Elementary Evidences of Christianity*[3]—have been preserved entire; but the commentaries which bear his name are universally rejected as spurious. Eusebius has noticed that Theophilus quoted the Apocalypse in a treatise against Hermogenes[4]; and one passage in his extant writings has been supposed to refer to it[5]. The reference however is very uncertain; nor can much greater stress be laid on a passing coincidence with the language of the Epistle to the Hebrews[6]. The use which Theophilus makes of a metaphor which occurs in 2 Peter is much more worthy of notice[7]; and it is re-

Chap. ii.

1. *The Church of Antioch.*
THEOPHILUS.
c. 168—180 A.D.

The Apocalypse.

Peter

---

[1] The references to the Epistles of Clement (III. 2, § 3) and Polycarp (*id.* § 4) are different in character.
[2] Epiph. *Hær.* LVI. 1; Routh, *Rell. Sacr.* IV. p. 243. MILTIADES again, with whose country I am unacquainted, is said to have shewn 'great zeal about the Divine Ora-'cles' (Euseb. *H. E.* v. 17). Anatolius of Laodicea has been mentioned already, p. 369, n. 1.
[3] Euseb. *H. E.* IV. 24; τρία τὰ πρὸς Αὐτόλυκον στοιχειώδη φέρεται συγγράμματα.
[4] Euseb. *l. c.*
[5] Theoph. *ad Autol.* II. p. 104. Apoc. xii. 3 sqq.
[6] *Ad Autol.* II. p. 102. Hebr. xii. 9. Cf. Lardner, II. 20, 25 sqq.
[7] *Ad Autol.* II. c. 13 (p. 92): ἡ διάταξις οὖν τοῦ Θεοῦ τοῦτό ἐστιν, ὁ λόγος αὐτοῦ φαίνων ὥσπερ λύ-

Chap. ii.

SERAPION.
c. 190 A.D.

markable that he distinctly quotes the Gospel of St John as written by one of those 'who were moved by 'the Spirit[1].'

Serapion who was second in descent from Theophilus has left a very remarkable judgment on the *Gospel according to Peter*, which he found in use at Rhossus, a small town of Cilicia. 'We receive,' he says, when writing to the Church there[2], 'both Peter and the other 'Apostles as Christ; but as experienced men we reject 'the writings falsely inscribed with their names, since we 'know that we did not receive such from [our fathers. 'Still I allowed the book to be used,] for when I visited 'you I supposed that all were attached to the right 'faith; and as I had not thoroughly examined the 'Gospel which they brought forward under the name of 'Peter I said: If this is the only thing which seems to 'create petty jealousies (μικροψυχίαν) among you, let it 'be read. But now since I have learnt from what has 'been told me that their mind was covertly attached to 'some heresy (αἱρέσει τινὶ ἐνεφώλευεν) I shall be anxious 'to come to you again; so, brethren, expect me quickly. 'But we, brethren, having comprehended the nature of 'the heresy which Marcianus held—how he contradicted 'himself from failing to understand what he said you 'will learn from what has been written to you—were 'able to examine [the book] thoroughly having bor-'rowed it from others who commonly use (ἀσκησάντων) 'this very Gospel, that is from the successors of those 'who first sanctioned it, whom we call Docetæ (for 'most of [Marcianus'] opinions belong to their teach-'ing); and to find that the greater part of its contents

χνος ἐν οἰκήματι συνεχομένῳ ἐφώτισε τὴν ὑπ' οὐρανόν... Cf. 2 Pet. i. 19.

[1] *Ad Autol.* II. 22.

[2] Euseb. *H. E.* VI. 12. Routh, *Rell. Sacr.* I. 452 sqq.

'agrees with the right doctrine of the Saviour, though 'some new injunctions are added in it which we have 'subjoined for your benefit[1].' Something then may be learnt from this as to the authority and standard of the New Testament Scriptures at the close of the second century: the writings of the Apostles were to be received as the words of Christ: and those only were to be acknowledged as such which were supported by a certain tradition. Nor can the conduct of Serapion in allowing the public use of other writings be justly blamed. It does not appear that the *Gospel of Peter* superseded the Canonical Gospels; and it is well known that even the *Gospel of Nicodemus* maintained a place at Canterbury—'fixed to a pillar'—up to the time of Erasmus.

The seventh in succession from Serapion was Paul of Samosata, who was convicted of heresy on the accusation of his own clergy, and finally deposed by the civil authority of the heathen Emperor Aurelian. Nothing remains of his writings, but it is recorded that he endeavoured to maintain his opinions by the testimony of the Old and New Testaments, and his adversaries relied on the same books to refute him. A Synodical Epistle 'addressed to Paul by the orthodox bishops before his 'deposition' has been preserved[2], in which, in addition

PAUL of Samosata.

260—272 A.D.

[1] Euseb. *l. c.;* Routh, *Rell. Sacr.* I. 452 sqq. The text of the fragment is corrupt, and I have ventured to introduce some slight corrections by which the whole connexion appears to be improved. The middle sentence should I believe be read thus: ἡμεῖς δὲ ἀδελφοὶ καταλαβόμενοι ὁποίας ἦν αἱρέσεως ὁ Μαρκιανὸς (καὶ [ὡς] ἑαυτῷ ἠναντιοῦτο μὴ νοῶν ἃ ἐλάλει [om. ἃ] μαθήσεσθε ἐξ ὧν ὑμῖν ἐγράφη) ἐδυνήθημεν [om. γὰρ] παρ' ἄλλων τῶν ἀσκησάντων, κ.τ.λ. Many Manuscripts omit ἃ before μαθ., and the confusion of ΠΑΡ with ΓΑΡ is of constant occurrence. The changes of number—ἡμεῖς, ἐγώ, ἡμεῖς —seem to prove that the sentences (βραχεῖαι λέξεις Eusebius calls them) are not continuous. As far as I am aware, all follow Valesius in translating καταρξαμένων αὐτοῦ *qui Marciano praeiverunt;* but analogy supports the rendering which I have given.

[2] Doubts were raised as to the genuineness of this Epistle by Basnage, and repeated by Lardner and

392   THE DISPUTED BOOKS OF THE CANON.   [PART

Chap. ii.

The Epistle to the Hebrews.

MALCHION.

St Jude.

The School of Antioch.

DOROTHEUS. *c.* 290 A.D.

LUCIAN.

to many other quotations from the New Testament, the Epistle to the Hebrews is cited as the work of St Paul[1]. And in another letter addressed to the bishops of Alexandria and Rome by Malchion a presbyter of Antioch in the name of the 'bishops, priests, and deacons, of the 'neighbouring cities and nations, and of the Churches 'of God,' Paul is described, with a clear allusion to the Epistle of St Jude, as one who 'denied his God and 'Lord, and kept not the faith which he himself had 'formerly held[2].'

The first traces of the theological school of Antioch, which became in the fourth and fifth centuries a formidable rival to that of Alexandria, appear during the period of the controversy with Paul. Dorotheus a presbyter of the Church is described by Eusebius[3] as a man remarkably distinguished for secular learning, who 'in 'his zeal to understand the full beauty of the divine '[writings] studied the Hebrew language, so as to read 'and understand the original Hebrew Scriptures.' Lucian another presbyter of Antioch 'well trained in sacred 'studies[4]' devoted himself to a critical revision of the Greek text of the Bible. In carrying out this work it is said that he introduced useless corrections into the Gospels; and the copies which he had 'falsified' were pronounced Apocryphal in later times[5]. In the absence

---

Lumper; but Routh considers them of no weight (Lumper, XIII. 711 sqq.; Routh, *Rell. Sacr.* III. 321 sqq.). The question appears to depend altogether on the good faith of Turrianus, who first published the Epistle. The Epistle itself is almost made up of a collection of passages of Scripture.
   [1] *Ep.* ap. Routh, *Rell. Sacr.* III. 299: ... κατὰ τὸν ἀπόστολον ... καὶ πάλιν...καὶ περὶ Μωυσέως· Μείζονα πλοῦτον ἡγησάμενος τῶν Αἰγύπτου

θησαυρῶν τὸν ὀνειδισμὸν τοῦ Χριστοῦ (Heb. xi. 26). So again just before, Heb. iv. 15 is incorporated in the text of the Epistle.
   [2] *Ep.* ap. Euseb. *H. E.* VII. 30: ...τοῦ καὶ τὸν Θεὸν τὸν ἑαυτοῦ καὶ Κύριον ἀρνουμένου, καὶ τὴν πίστιν ἣν καὶ αὐτὸς πρότερον εἶχε μὴ φυλάξαντος. Cf. Jude 3, 4 (reading Θεόν).
   [3] Euseb. *H. E.* VII. 32.
   [4] Euseb. *H. E.* IX. 6: τοῖς ἱεροῖς μαθήμασι συγκεκροτημένος.
   [5] *Decret. Gelas.* VI. § 14: Evan-

of all evidence on the question it is impossible to determine in what respect his text differed from that commonly received; but it may be noticed that there is nothing to shew that he held any peculiar views on the Canon itself. Lucian died a martyr in the persecution of Maximinus; and Rufinus has preserved in a Latin translation a part of the defence which he addressed to the Emperor on his trial[1]. The fragment is of singular beauty, and contains several allusions to the Gospels and Acts; but it is more remarkable as containing an appeal to the physical phenomena connected with the Passion—to the darkness, said by Lucian to be recorded in heathen histories, to the rent rocks, and to the Holy Sepulchre, still to be seen in his time at Jerusalem[2].

Antioch was not the only place in Syria where the Christian Scriptures were made the subject of learned and laborious study. Pamphilus a Presbyter of Cæsarea, the friend of Eusebius and the apologist of Origen, was 'inflamed with so great a love of sacred literature that he 'copied with his own hand the chief part of the works of 'Origen,' which in the time of Jerome were still pre-

2. *The Church of Cæsarea.*

PAMPHILUS.
†309 A.D.

---

[1] gelia quæ falsavit Lucianus Apocrypha. Credner (*Zur Gesch. d. K.* s. 216) regards this as one of the additions to the original Decree of Gelasius (*c.* 500 A.D.) made at the time when it was republished in Spain under the name of Hormisdas (*c.* 700 —800 A.D.).

The next clause in the decree is: Evangelia quæ falsavit Isicius Apocrypha, § 15. This certainly refers to the recension of the New Testament published in Egypt by Hesychius at the close of the third century, which is classed by Jerome with that of Lucian; but nothing is known of its character. The speculations of Hug are quite unsatisfactory.

[1] The defence occurs in Rufinus' version of Eusebius (*H. E.* IX. 6). It is printed by Routh, *Rell. Sacr.* IV. 5 sqq.; and I see no reason to doubt its authenticity.

[2] Luc. ap. Routh, *Rell. Sacr.* IV. p. 6: Si minus adhuc creditur, adhibebo vobis etiam loci ipsius in quo res gesta est testimonium. Adstipulatur his [quæ dico] ipse in Hierosolymis locus, et Golgothana rupes sub patibuli onere disrupta: antrum quoque illud quod avulsis inferni januis corpus denuo reddidit animatum, quo purius inde ferretur ad cœlum... Requirite in annalibus vestris: invenietis temporibus l'ilati, Christo patiente, fugato sole interruptum tenebris diem. The rhetorical colouring of the passage cannot affect the facts affirmed.

served in the library which he founded[1]. This library at Cæsarea is frequently mentioned by ancient writers, and when it fell into decay towards the close of the fourth century, it was restored by the care of two bishops of the city. Its extent is shewn by the fact that Jerome found there a copy of the famous *Hebrew Gospel of St Matthew;* and memorials of it have been preserved to the present time. The Coislinian fragment of the Pauline Epistles (H), in which the Epistle to the Hebrews is placed before the Pastoral Epistles, contains a note stating that it was 'compared with the copy in the library of 'St Pamphilus at Cæsarea, written by his own hand[2].' Nor is this all. At the end of the edition of the Acts and of the [seven] Catholic Epistles published by Euthalius it is said that the book was 'compared with the 'accurate copies contained in the library of Eusebius 'Pamphilus[3] at Cæsarea;' and though it is not expressly stated that these copies were written by Pamphilus himself, yet it is probable that they were, from the fact that the summary of the contents of the Acts published under the name of Euthalius is a mere transcript of a work of Pamphilus[4]. If then this conjecture be right, it

---

[1] Hieron. *de Virr. Ill.* 75: Tanto bibliothecæ divinæ amore flagravit... The phrase 'bibliotheca divina' means I believe the collection of sacred Scriptures. Cf. Routh, *Rell. Sacr.* III. 488. As to Pamphilus' labours on the LXX. cf. Lardner, II. 59. 5.

[2] For the order of the Epistles in this Manuscript see Montfaucon, *Bibl. Coislin.* p. 253. Tischendorf, *N. T.* ed. 7, p. CLXXXIX.

[3] Zacagni, *Collec.* p. 513: ἀντεβλήθη δὲ τῶν πράξεων καὶ καθολικῶν ἐπιστολῶν τὸ βιβλίον πρὸς τὰ ἀκριβῆ ἀντίγραφα τῆς ἐν Καισαρείᾳ βιβλιοθήκης Εὐσεβίου τοῦ Παμφίλου. The last genitives are ambiguous, and may refer either to ἀντίγραφα or βιβλιοθήκης.

The summary of verses given at the end (p. 513) does not agree with numbers previously given; nor can I explain the phrase τὸ πρὸς ἐμαυτὸν στίχοι κζ΄. But these difficulties seem to shew that Euthalius did not compose the whole work, but in part transcribed it.

[4] Montf. *Bibl. Coislin.* p. 78. Routh, *Rell. Sacr.* III. 510 sq. The recurrence in the preface to this summary of a very remarkable phrase found in the subscription of the Manuscript of the Pauline Epistles copied from that of Pamphilus seems to be conclusive on the point:

may be inferred that the seven Catholic Epistles were formed into a collection at the close of the third century, and appended, as in later times, to the Acts of the Apostles. So much at least is certain, that Pamphilus, a man of wide learning and research, reckoned the Epistle to the Hebrews among the writings of St Paul, whether he regarded it as actually penned by the Apostle, or, like Origen, as the expression of his thoughts by another writer.

Though Pamphilus devoted his life to the study of the Holy Scriptures, he never assumed the office of a commentator; but Jerome's statement that 'he wrote "nothing except short letters to his friends" must be received with some reserve[1]. In addition to the Summary of the Acts already noticed, there can be no doubt that the commencement of an apology for Origen occupied his attention during his last confinement in prison. The first book, which bears his name, and was probably his work, has been preserved; and the quotations from Origen which it contains embrace distinct references to the Apocalypse as the work of St John[2], proving, if proof were necessary, that on this point Pamphilus followed his master's judgment.

Thus then in the Syrian Church[3] there are traces of a complete Canon of the New Testament at the beginning of the fourth century, and that free from all admix-

Chap. ii.

Pamphilus' Apology for Origen

recognises the Apocalypse.

The Syrian Canon complete.

εὐχῇ τῇ ὑπὲρ ἡμῶν τὴν συμπεριφορὰν κομιζόμενος. The summary as it occurs in Zacagni (pp. 428 sqq.) is introduced quite abruptly; and Zacagni's explanation of the allusion to the youth of the writer (Pref. p. 63) is unsatisfactory.
[1] Hieron. *adv. Ruf.* IV. p. 419. Cf. IV. p. 347: Date quodlibet aliud opus Pamphili; nusquam reperietis. Hoc unum est. Jerome is speaking of the Apology for Origen, but he was misled by the fact that Eusebius completed it.
[2] Pamph. *Apol.* VII.; Apoc. xx. 13, 6. I have not noticed any other references to the disputed books in the Apology.
[3] The Greek Syrian Church is of course not to be confounded with the native Syrian Church, which retained the Canon of the Peshito; cf. p. 244, and Part III. ch. ii.

ture of Apocryphal writings. The same district which first recognised a collection of Apostolic writings in the Peshito was among the first to complete that original Canon by the addition of the other works which we now receive[1]. And briefly it may be said that wherever the East and the West entered into a true union there the Canon is found perfect; while the absence or incompleteness of this union is the measure of the corresponding defects in the Canon.

This clearly appears on a summary of the results obtained in this chapter. At Alexandria and Cæsarea, where there was the closest intercourse between the Eastern and Western Churches, the Canon of the New Testament was fixed, even if with some reserve, as it stands at present. In the Latin Churches on the contrary no trace has yet been found of the use of the Epistle of St James, or of the second Epistle of St Peter; and the Epistle to the Hebrews was not accepted by them as the work of St Paul. But one of the disputed books was still received generally without distinction of East and West. With the single exception of Dionysius all direct testimony from Alexandria, Africa, Rome, and Carthage, witnesses to the Apostolic authority of the Apocalypse.

---

[1] One testimony from an Eastern Church has not yet been noticed. In the Acts of a Disputation between Archelaus Bishop of Caschar (or, as some conjecture, of Carrhæ) in Mesopotamia (? cf. Beausobre, *Hist. de Manich.* I. p. 143) and Manes there are several clear allusions to the Epistle to the Hebrews, though it is not quoted by name. *Disp. Arch. et Man.* ap. Routh, *Rell. Sacr.* v. p. 45, Hebr. vi. 8: p. 75, Hebr. viii. 13: p. 127, Hebr. i. 3: p. 149, Hebr. iii. 5, 6. The reference to 2 Pet. iii. 9 in p. 107, *non enim moratus est in promissionibus suis*, is very uncertain. We have these Acts however at present in a very unsatisfactory form, as they exist for the most part only in a Latin translation from the Greek, which was itself probably a translation from the Syriac.

CHAPTER III.

THE TESTIMONY OF HERETICAL AND APOCRYPHAL WRITINGS TO THE BOOKS OF THE NEW TESTAMENT.

Quodcunque adversus veritatem sapit hoc erit hæresis, etiam vetus consuetudo.
TERTULLIANUS.

THE controversies which agitated the Christian Church from the close of the second century to the commencement of the third shew practically, like those of the first age, what theological position was then occupied by the New Testament. The form of the old errors was changed, but their spirit gave life to new systems. Ebionism had sunk down into a mere tradition[1], but its principles were embodied in the Christian legalism of the Montanists. The same rationalistic tendencies which moved Marcion afterwards appeared in the questions raised on the Person of Christ from the time of Praxeas to that of Arius. And the Simonian counterfeit of Christianity found a partial parallel in the scheme of Mani, less wild, it is true, and more successful. But each great school of heresy did good service in the cause of the Christian Scriptures. The discussions on

Chap. iii. The testimony of heretical writers. The forms of heresy though changed still witness to the New Testament.

---

[1] Haxthausen (*Transcaucasia*, p. 140) mentions the existence of a sect of Judaizing Christians (Uriani) at present in Derbend on the Caspian. They have, as he heard, no knowledge of the Apostolic writings, but possess a Gospel written by Longinus the first teacher of their Church. It is to be hoped that some light may be thrown on this strange statement.

the Holy Trinity turned upon their right interpretation, so that their authority was a necessary postulate to the argument. The Montanists, while they appealed to the fresh outpouring of the Spirit, did not profess to supersede or dispense with the books which were commonly received. Even the Manichæans found the belief in their divine claims so strong that they could not set them aside as a whole, but were contented with questioning their integrity.

1. Controversies on the Person of Christ.

The controversies on the person of Christ first arose from a necessary reaction within the Church against the speculations of the Gnostics on the succession and orders of divine powers. The simple baptismal confession which became the popular rule of faith[1] contained no reference to the doctrine of the Word, and the unlearned stumbled at the 'mysterious dispensation' of the Holy Trinity. 'We are Monarchians,' they said, 'we acknowledge only 'one God[2].' This Monarchianism naturally assumed a double form, according as the unity of God was supposed to be rightly asserted by identifying the Son with the Father, or by denying His proper divinity. Praxeas and Theodotus stood forth at the same time at Rome as the champions of these antagonistic opinions. Praxeas seems to have retained his connexion with the Catholic Church; Theodotus was excommunicated. But though they differed thus widely in doctrine and fortune, both held alike the general opinion of Christians on the authority of the Apostolic writings. Tertullian who attacked Praxeas, with greater zeal perhaps because he had proved himself a formidable opponent of Montanism, urged against him various passages of the New

(a) Patripassian: Praxeas. c. 170 A.D.

---

[1] Tert. *de Virg. Vel.* 1: Regula quidem fidei una omnino est, sola immobilis et irreformabilis, credendi scilicet in unicum Deum...   [2] Tert. *adv. Prax.* 3.

Testament without hesitation or reserve, and answers an argument which he drew from the Apocalypse[1]. And though the followers of Theodotus were accused of 'tampering fearlessly with the Holy Scriptures,' it is evident that their corrections extended only to the text, and not to the Canon itself[2]. So likewise in the later stages of the Trinitarian controversy, with Hermogenes, Noetus, Vero, Beryllus, and Sabellius[3], on one side, and with Artemon and Paul of Samosata on the other, the Scriptures were always regarded as the common ground on which the questions at issue were to be settled.

Chap. iii.
(β) *Unitarian: Theodotus.*

In the midst of the discussions which were thus extending rapidly in the Church towards the close of the second century, it was natural that Christians should look around for some sure sign of God's presence among them, and for some abiding criterion of truth. The urgency of this want gave power and success to the teaching of Montanus. A strict discipline promised to serve as a mark of the elect; and prophecy was offered to solve the doubts of believers. But the relation of the new prophecies to the Apostolic teaching proves how completely the New Testament Scriptures were identified with the sources of Christian doctrine. Tertullian after he became a Montanist, no less than before, appeals to them as decisive. The outpouring of the Spirit, he says, was made in order to remove the ambiguities and parables by which the truth was obscured[4]; to illustrate

2. *Montanism.*

c. 170 A.D.

---

[1] *Adv. Prax.* 17: Interim hic mihi promotum sit responsum adversus id quod et de Apocalypsi Joannis proferunt. Apoc. i. 8.
[2] Cf. p. 375.
[3] Epiphanius (*Hær.* LXII. 2) says that Sabellius borrowed many points in his system from the *Gospel according to the Egyptians*. There is however nothing to shew that Sabellius placed it in rivalry with the Canonical Gospels. The opinions of the Alogi on the writings of St John have been noticed already, p. 279, and note 1.
[4] *De Resurr. Carn. s. f.:* ...Jam omnes retro ambiguitates et quas volunt parabolas aperta atque per-

and not to set aside the written Word[1]; to confirm and define what had been already given, and not to introduce anything strange or novel[2]. The ancient Scriptures still remained a treasure common to Montanist and Catholic alike[3]. Some there certainly were among the Montanists who were not content with this view of the position occupied by their prophets, but the exceptions are not sufficient to lessen the importance of the testimony which they bear generally to the Christian Scriptures[4].

The Montanists proposed to restore Christianity: the Manichæans ventured to reconstruct it. Montanus proclaimed the presence of the Paraclete: Mani himself claimed to personify Him, and to lay open that perfect knowledge of which St Paul had spoken. While assuming such a character it is more surprising that Mani received the Christian Scriptures in any sense than that he brought them to the test of a merely subjective standard. And it is an important symptom of the popular feeling of the time, that the Manichæans called in question the integrity and sometimes the authenticity of the Christian records, but not the authority of their writers. The grounds on which they did so are purely arbitrary, and their objections are simple assertions without any ex-

---

spicua totius sacramenti prædicatione [Spiritus Sanctus] discussit, per novam prophetiam de Paracleto inundantem; cujus si hauseris fontes nullam poteris sitire doctrinam: nullus te ardor exuret quæstionum... *De Virg. Vel.* 1: Quae est ergo Paracleti administratio nisi hæc, quod disciplina dirigitur, quod scripturæ revelantur, quod intellectus reformatur, quod ad meliora proficitur?

[1] *Adv. Prax.* 13: Nos enim qui et tempora et causas scripturarum per Dei gratiam inspicimus maxime

Paracleti non hominum discipuli...

[2] *De Monog.* 3: Nihil novi Paracletus inducit. Quod præmonuit, definit: quod sustinuit, exposcit.

[3] *De Monog.* 4: Evolvamus communia instrumenta scripturarum pristinarum.

[4] Cf. Euseb. *H. E.* VI. 20. It is probable that Caius excluded the Epistle to the Hebrews from the number of St Paul's Epistles in opposition to some Montanists (ἐπιστομίζων). Cf. Schwegler, *Montan.* 287 f.

ternal proof[1]. Probably they differed considerably among themselves in their estimation of the Canonical books[2]. Thus Augustine states that they rejected the Acts of the Apostles as inconsistent with their belief in the character assumed by Mani[3]; but this explanation is evidently insufficient, because the Montanists received the book in spite of a similar difficulty, and several writers use it without hesitation in their controversies with Manichæans[4]. Generally however he speaks of the Manichæans as admitting 'the New Testament,' 'the four Gospels, and the Epistles of Paul,' in which must be included that to the Hebrews[5]; but without insisting on this evidence, it is an important fact that they did not attempt to assail the Scriptures historically. On the contrary Augustine argues against them (and his reasoning gains force from his own conversion) that no writings can be proved genuine if the books received as Apostolic be not so: that every kind of evidence combines to establish their claims, the rejection of which must be followed by universal historical scepticism[6]: that they had been circulated in the lifetime of their professed authors: that they had been

---

[1] Cf. Beausobre, *Hist. de Manich.* I. pp. 297 sqq.

[2] Beausobre is probably right in supposing that they generally accepted the Canon of the Peshito (I. pp. 294 sq.); but I do not think that he is right in limiting (p. 292) the *Epistolæ Canonicæ* (Aug. *c. Faust.* XXII. 15) to the *Catholic* Epistles, though that is the later meaning of the phrase.

[3] *De Util. Cred.* 7 [III.]. The Acts was generally much less known in the East than the other books of the New Testament. Cf. Beausobre, *l. c.* p. 293.

[4] Cf. Lardner, II. 63. 4.

[5] Aug. *c. Faust.* II. 1; v. 1: *de Util. Cred.* 7 [III.]. For the Epistle to the Hebrews, cf. Epiph. *Hær.* LXVI. 74; supr. p. 396, n. 1; and, on the other hand, Beausobre, I. p. 292.

[6] Aug. *de Mor. Eccl. Cath.* 60 [XXIX.]: Consequetur omnium litterarum summa perversio, et omnium qui memoriæ mandati sunt librorum abolitio; si quod tanta populorum religione roboratum est, tanta hominum et temporum consensione firmatum, in hanc dubitationem inducitur, ut ne historiæ quidem vulgaris fidem possit gravitatemque obtinere.

C.   D D

received throughout the Church: that they were in the hands of all Christians: that they had been scrupulously guarded and attested from the age of the Apostles by an unbroken line of witnesses[1]. And thus the first critical assault on the authority of the New Testament called forth a noble assertion of its historic claims.

The use of Apocryphal books by the Manichees.

But while the Manichæans admitted the original authority of the Scriptures of the New Testament, they appealed to other books for the confirmation of their doctrines. When received into the Catholic Church they were required to abjure the use of numerous Apocryphal writings[2]; and a bishop of the fifth century did not scruple to assert that they had either 'invented or 'corrupted every Apocryphal book[3].' Without entering in detail into the parallels which the Apocryphal Gospels, Acts, Epistles, and Apocalypses, offer to the Canonical Scriptures, it is evident that as a whole, like false miracles and false prophecies, they presuppose some authentic collection which determined the shape and furthered the circulation of the copy. And that they are copies is evident from their internal character; so that in one respect at least they are instructive, as shewing what might have been expected from writings founded on tradition, even when shaped after an Apostolic pattern[4].

How these attest the Canon generally.

Other Apocryphal writings.

Besides the direct imitations of the Apostolic books there are two other Apocryphal writings which deserve

---

[1] Aug. *c. Faust.* XXXII. 19; XXXIII. 6.

[2] The whole formula (ap. Cotel. *Patr. Apost.* I. 537 sqq., referred to by Beausobre) is extremely interesting. The passage more directly bearing on our subject is: ἀναθεματίζω πάντα τὰ δόγματα καὶ συγγράμματα τοῦ Μάνεντος...καὶ πάσας τὰς Μανιχαϊκὰς βίβλους, οἷον τὸ νεκροποιὸν αὐτῶν εὐαγγέλιον, ὅπερ ζῶν κα- λοῦσι, καὶ τὸν θησαυρὸν τοῦ θανάτου, ὃν λέγουσι θησαυρὸν ζωῆς, καὶ τὴν καλουμένην μυστηρίων βίβλον...καὶ τὴν τῶν ἀποκρύφων, καὶ τὴν τῶν ἀπομνημονευμάτων...

[3] Turibius, quoted by Beausobre, I. p. 348.

[4] Beausobre (I. pp. 348 sqq.) has given a general review of their contents; and I have noticed them elsewhere.

notice because they represent no Canonical type, the *Testaments of the Twelve Patriarchs* and parts of the *Sibylline Oracles*. The Apostles were contented to recommend the Gospel to the Jews by the evidence of the Old Testament, to the heathen by the testimony of their own consciences, to both on the broad grounds of its own divine character. But it was natural that a succeeding generation should look for more distinct intimations of the Hope of the world than are to be found in the symbolism of a nation's history, or the indistinct confessions of hearts ill at rest. By what combination of fraud and enthusiasm the desire was gratified cannot be told, but the works which have been named represent the result[1]. In the *Testaments of the Twelve Patriarchs* and in some of the *Sibylline Oracles* the history of the Gospel is thrown into a prophetic form; and the general use made of the latter writings from the time of Justin Martyr downwards shews how little any other age than that of the Apostles was able to originate or even to reproduce the simple grandeur of the New Testament. Besides numerous allusions to the facts of the Gospels, and to very little else connected with the life of Christ[2], these Apocryphal books contain several references to the Gospel and first Epistle of St John, to the Acts, to the Epistles of St Paul and to the Apocalypse[3]. And

The Testaments of the Twelve Patriarchs.
The Sibylline Oracles.

---

[1] The Testaments of the Twelve Patriarchs are quoted by Origen (*Hom. in Jos.* xv. 6). Friedlieb has given a summary of the probable dates of the Sibylline Oracles (*Orac. Sibyll. Einl.* § 32).
[2] The fire in the Jordan at the Baptism of our Lord (cf. p. 160, n. 3) is the only fact which occurs to me. *Orac. Sibyll.* VI. 6. Cf. VII. 84.
[3] *Test. Levi*, § 14; John i. 9, viii. 12. *Benj.* § 3; John i. 29. *Jud.* § 20; John xv. 26. *Iss.* § 7; 1 John v. 16, 17. *Benj.* § 9; Acts ii. 3. *Reuben*, § 5; 1 Cor. vi. 18. *Levi*, § 3; Rom. xii. 1. § 6; 1 Thess. ii. 16. § 18; Hebr. vii. 22—24. *Dan*, § 5; Apoc. xxi., Eph. iv. 25. *Nephthalim*, § 4; Eph. ii. 17.
Mr Sinker, in his edition of the *Testaments* (1869), has given a very full table of the coincidences between the Testaments and the Apostolic books, but I do not think

404 THE TESTIMONY OF APOCRYPHAL WRITINGS. [PART

Chap. iii.

Testimony to St Paul.

one passage from the Testament of Benjamin expresses such a remarkable judgment on the mission and authority of St Paul as to deserve especial notice, particularly as the work itself comes from the hand of a Jewish Christian[1].

'I shall no longer,' the Patriarch says to his sons[2], 'be called a ravening wolf on account of your ravages, 'but a worker of the Lord, distributing goods to those 'who work that which is good. And there shall arise 'from my seed in after times one beloved of the Lord, 'hearing His voice, enlightening with new knowledge all 'the Gentiles,...and till the consummation of the ages 'shall he be in the congregations of the Gentiles, and 'among their princes, as a strain of music in the mouth 'of them all. And he shall be inscribed in the Holy 'Books, both his work and his word, and he shall be 'chosen of God for ever[3]....'

The evidence of the heathen opponents of Christianity.

In addition to other evidence that of the heathen opponents of Christianity must not be neglected. Celsus, the earliest and most formidable among them, lived towards the close of the second century, and he had sought his knowledge of the Christian system in Christian books.

CELSUS.

He quotes the 'writings of the disciples of Jesus' con-

that the references to James, 2 Peter, Jude are established.
 Orac. Sibyll. I. 125 sqq.; 2 Pet. ii. 5. Lib. II. 167 sqq.; 2 Thess. ii. 8—10. Lib. VIII. 190 sqq.; Apoc. ix. &c.
[1] Bp Lightfoot (*on Galatians*, pp. 299 ff.) has called attention to the remarkable combination in this book of Levitical views with a thankful acknowledgment of the admission of the Gentiles into the divine Covenant.
[2] *Test. Benj.* § 11.
[3] It is perhaps impossible to fix with precision the date of the *Pistis Sophia* (ed. Schwartze et Petermann, Berlin, 1851). Petermann describes it simply as ab Ophitâ quodam superiori scriptum (Pref. p. vii.). It contains numerous references to the Gospels of St Matthew, St Luke, and St John; and once quotes St Paul (Rom. xiii. 7, p. 294). The only Apocryphal saying which I noticed in it is the well-known phrase attributed to our Lord, 'Be ye wise money-changers' (p. 353); but of Philip it is said: iste est qui scribit res omnes quas Jesus dixit et quas fecit omnes (p. 69).

cerning His life as possessing unquestioned authority[1]; and that these were the four Canonical Gospels is proved both by the absence of all evidence to the contrary, and by the special facts which he brings forward[2]. And not only this, but both Celsus and Porphyry appear to have been acquainted with the Pauline Epistles[3]. In Porphyry at least the influence of the Apostolic teaching can be distinctly traced, for Christianity even in his time had done much to leaven the world which rejected it[4].

Chap. iii.

PORPHYRY.
† 304 A.D.

TO pass once again from these details to a wider view, it is evident that the results of the last three chapters confirm what was stated at the outset, that this

Conclusion.
The summary of the Second Period.

---

[1] Orig. *c. Cels.* II. 13, 74. In the latter passage the Jewish antagonist in Celsus' work says: Ταῦτα μὲν οὖν ὑμῖν ἐκ τῶν ὑμετέρων συγγραμμάτων ἐφ' οἷς οὐδενὸς ἄλλου μάρτυρος χρῄζομεν, αὐτοὶ γὰρ ἑαυτοῖς περιπίπτετε. Nothing could shew more clearly the authority of the Gospels. Exactly the same title (τὰ ἡμέτερα συγγράμματα) occurs in Justin Martyr, *Apol.* I. 28.

[2] The title of Celsus' book was Λόγος ἀληθής, and Origen has answered it at length. The following references will be sufficient: Matt. ii., Orig. *c. Cels.* I. 34; Mark vi. 3, *ib.* VI. 36 (where Origen had a false reading); Luke iii., *ib.* II. 32; John xix. 34, *ib.* II. 36. Celsus evidently considered that the different Gospels were incorrect revisions of one original; *ib.* II. 27: μετὰ ταῦτά τινας τῶν πιστευόντων φησὶν...μεταχαράττειν ἐκ τῆς πρώτης γραφῆς τὸ εὐαγγέλιον τριχῇ καὶ τετραχῇ καὶ πολλαχῇ καὶ μεταπλάττειν ἵν' ἔχοιεν πρὸς τοὺς ἐλέγχους ἀρνεῖσθαι. To which Origen replies: μεταχαράττοντας τὸ εὐαγγέλιον ἄλλους οὐκ οἶδα ἢ τοὺς ἀπὸ Μαρκίωνος καὶ τοὺς ἀπὸ Οὐαλεντίνου οἶμαι δὲ καὶ τοὺς ἀπὸ Λουκάνου. All

the facts which Origen quotes from Celsus are I believe contained in our Canonical Gospels; yet cf. Orig. *c. Cels.* II. 74.

[3] Orig. *c. Cels.* I. 9; cf. 1 Cor. iii. 19, 1 Pet. iii. 15. *ib.* v. 64; cf. Gal. vi. 14. Porphyr. ap. Hieron. *Comm. in Galat.* i. 15, 16 (T. IV. p. 233); II. 11 (*ib.* p. 244).

[4] Cf. Ullmann, *Stud. u. Krit.* V. 376 sqq. His beautiful *Letter to Marcella* (ed. Mai, Mediol. 1816), the climax of philosophic morality, offers nevertheless a complete contrast to the Christian doctrine of the dignity of man's body.

In other heathen writers there is little which bears on the Christian Scriptures. LUCIAN in his *True History* (II. 11 sqq.) gives a poor imitation of Apoc. xxi. But the striking description which ARISTIDES (*ad Plat.* II. T. II. pp. 398 sqq. Df.) draws of the Christians is well worthy of notice, especially when compared with Lucian's (*de Peregr.* II. 13). LONGINUS' testimony to the eloquence of 'Paul of Tarsus' (fr. 1, ed. Weiske) is generally considered spurious.

Conclusion. *Its work to construct, not to define; though*	second period in the History of the Canon offers a marked contrast to the first. It is characterized not so much by the antagonism of great principles as by the influence of great men. But their work was to construct and not to define. And thus the age was an age of research and thought, but at the same time it was an age of freedom. The fabric of Christian doctrine was not yet consolidated, though the elements which had existed at first separately were already combined. An era of speculation preceded an era of councils; for it was necessary that all the treasures of the Church should be regarded in their various aspects before they could be rightly arranged.
it was fertile in controversy,	There was however among Christians a keen and active perception of that 'one unchangeable rule of faith,' which was embodied in the practice of the Church and attested by the words of Scripture. Apologists for Christianity were followed by advocates of its ancient purity even in the most remote districts of the Roman world. In addition to the writers who have been mentioned already, Eusebius has preserved the names of many others 'from an innumerable crowd,' which in themselves form a striking monument of the energy of the Church. Philip in Crete, Bacchylus at Corinth, and Palmas in Pontus, defended the primitive Creed against the innovations of heresy[1]. And the list might be easily increased; but it is enough to shew that the energy of Christian life was not confined to the great centres of its action, or to the men who gave their character to its development. The whole body was instinct with a sense of truth and ready to maintain it.
which however did not	Yet even controversy failed to create a spirit of

---

[1] Euseb. *H. E.* IV. 23, 25, 28; V. 22, 23.

historical inquiry. Tertullian once alludes to synodal discussions on the Canon[1], but as a general rule it was assumed by Christian writers that the contents of the New Testament were known and acknowledged. Where differences existed on this point, as in the case of the Marcionites, no attempt was made to compose them by a critical investigation into the history of the sacred records. And in the Church itself no voice of authority interfered to remove the doubts which formerly existed, however much they were modified by usage and by the judgment of particular writers. The age was not only constructive but conservative; and thus the evidence for the New Testament Canon, which has been gathered from writers of the third century, differs from that of earlier date in fulness rather than in kind.

But the fulness of evidence for the acknowledged books, coming from every quarter of the Church and given with unhesitating simplicity, can surely be explained on no other ground than that it represented an original tradition or an instinctive judgment of Apostolic times. While on the other hand the books which were not universally received seem to have been in most cases rather unknown than rejected. The Apocalypse alone was made the subject of a controversy, and that purely on internal testimony[2]. For it is well worthy of notice that the disputed books (with the exception of the second Epistle of St Peter, the history of which is most obscure) are exactly those which make no direct claims to Apostolic authorship, so that they might have been excluded from the Canon even by some who did not

Conclusion.

create historic criticism.

Hence we gain no new results, but

the old are strongly confirmed, as regards the Acknowledged Books,

the Disputed Books, and

---

[1] Tert. *de Pudic.* 10. See supr. p. 375, n. 3.
[2] It is a satisfaction to find that the opinion which I have given on the testimonies of Caius and Dionysius (pp. 278, n. 2, 367) is confirmed by that of Münster in a special tract on the subject: *de Dionys. Alex. Judic. c. Apocal.* Hafniæ, 1826, pp. 35 sqq., 67 sqq.

Conclusion.
Apocryphal writings.

doubt their genuineness. In the meantime Apocryphal writings had passed almost out of notice, and no one can suppose that they were any longer confounded with the Apostolic books. Nothing more indeed was needed than that some practical crisis should give clear effect to the implicit opinion which was everywhere held; and this, as we shall see in the next chapter, was soon furnished by the interrogations of the last persecutor.

THIRD PERIOD.

HISTORY OF THE CANON OF THE NEW TESTAMENT FROM THE PERSECUTION OF DIOCLETIAN TO THE THIRD COUNCIL OF CARTHAGE.

A.D. 303—397.

Solis eis Scripturarum libris qui jam Canonici appellantur didici hunc timorem honoremque deferre ut nullum eorum auctorem scribendo aliquid errasse firmissime credam.

AUGUSTINUS.

CHAPTER I.

‘THE AGE OF DIOCLETIAN.

'Επληρώθη τὸ Πῦρ ἦλθον βαλεῖν ἐπὶ τὴν γῆν οὐκ ἀφανιστικὸν ἀλλὰ καθαρτικόν.

ATHANASIUS.

THOUGH we do not possess any public Acts of the Ante-Nicene Church relative to the Canon, yet the zeal of its enemies has in some degree supplied the deficiency. During the long period of repose which the Christians enjoyed after the edict of Gallienus, the character and claims of their sacred writings became more generally known[1], and offered a definite mark to their adversaries. Diocletian skilfully availed himself of this new point of attack. The earlier persecutors had sought to deprive the Church of its teachers: he endeavoured to destroy the writings which were the unfailing source of its faith. Hierocles proconsul of Bithynia is said to have originated and directed the persecution[2]; and his efforts were the more formidable because he was well acquainted with the history and doctrines of Christianity.

The first result of this persecution was to create dissensions within the Church itself. A large section of

Chap. i.
The persecution of Diocletian directed in part against the Christian Scriptures, and so
261 A.D.

303—311 A.D.

---

[1] Cf. Lact. *Instit.* v. 2: Alius [Hierocles]...quædam capita [Scripturæ Sacræ] quæ repugnare sibi videbantur exposuit, adeo multa, adeo intima enumerans, ut aliquando ex eadem disciplina fuisse videatur... præcipue tamen Paulum Petrumque laceravit...
[2] Lact. *Instit. l. c., de Mort. Persec.* 16.

Chap. i.

productive of dissensions among Christians which led necessarily

Christians availed themselves of the means of escape offered by lenient magistrates, and surrendered 'useless 'writings[1]' which satisfied the demands of their inquisitors. Others however viewed this conduct with reasonable jealousy, and branded as 'traitors' (*traditores*) those who submitted to the semblance of guilt to avoid the trials of persecution. And the differences which arose on the question became deep and permanent. For more than three hundred years the schism of the Donatists remained to witness to the intensity and bitterness of the controversy. But schism as well as persecution furthered the work of God. Henceforth the *Canonical* Scriptures were generally known by that distinctive title, even if it was not then first applied to them[2]. Both parties in the Church naturally combined to distinguish the sacred writings from all others. The stricter Christians required clear grounds for visiting the *traditores* with Ecclesiastical censure[3]; and the more pliant were anxious not to compromise their faith, while they were willing to purchase peace by obedience in that which seemed to be indifferent.

to a clearer determination of the Canonical Books.

But at least the outlines of a Canon must have existed before.

But though it is evident that an ecclesiastical Canon must have been formed before the close of the persecution of Diocletian, it is not to be concluded that no such Rule existed before. The original edict which enjoined that 'the Churches should be razed, and the Scriptures 'consumed by fire...[4]' is unhappily lost; and Christian writers describe its provisions in words intelligible and definite to themselves, but little likely to have been used

---

[1] Cf. Neander, *Ch. Hist.* I. p. 205. August. *Brev. Coll. Donat.* III. 25; c. *Cresc.* III. 30. Credner (*Zur Gesch. d. K.* s. 66) gives another interpretation to *scripturæ supervacuæ* in the Acts of Felix.

[2] Cf. App. A., Credner, *a. a. O.*

[3] *Concil. Arelat.* XIII.: De his qui scripturas sanctas tradidisse dicuntur...ut quicunque eorum *ex actis publicis* fuerit detectus...

[4] Euseb. *H. E.* VIII. 2.

by a heathen Emperor. There can however be no doubt that it contained an accurate description of the books to be surrendered, and the official records of two trials consequent upon it seem to have preserved the exact phrase which was employed. 'Bring forward,' the Roman commissioner said to the bishop Paul, 'the 'Scriptures of the Law.' And Cæcilian writing to another bishop Felix says, 'Ingentius inquired whether any 'Scriptures of your Law were burnt according to the 'sacred law[1].' Now whether this title was of Christian or heathen origin it evidently had a meaning sufficiently strict and clear for the purposes of a Roman court: in other words the books which the Christians called 'divine' and 'spiritualizing' (*deificæ*), which were publicly read in their assemblies and guarded with their most devoted care, were formed into a collection so well known that they could be described by a title scarcely more explicit than that by which it was afterwards called 'the Bible' (τὰ βιβλία).

And what then were the contents of that collection? The answer to this question must be sought for in the results of the persecution. No district suffered more severely than North Africa, where schism continued the ravages which persecution began. Donatus placed himself at the head of a party who opposed the appointment

---

[1] Acta ap. Mansi, *Concil.* II. 501 (Florent. 1759); August. T. IX. App. p. 29 (ed. Bened.): Felix Flamen perpetuus curator Paulo episcopo dixit: Proferte *scripturas legis*, et si quid aliud hic habetis, ut præceptum est, ut præcepto et jussioni parere possitis. Paulus episcopus dixit: Scripturas lectores habent, sed nos quod hic habemus damus. Afterwards the command is simply Proferte scripturas. *ib.* p. 509 (T. IX. App. p. 18): Cæcilianus parenti Felici salutem: Cum Ingentius collegam meum Augentium amicum suum conveniret et inquisisset anno duoviratus mei, an aliquæ *scripturæ legis vestræ* secundum sacram legem adustæ sint...(These passages are quoted by Credner, *a. a. O.*). A similar phrase occurs also in Augustine, *Ps. c. Donat.* T. IX. p. 3 B: Erant quidam traditores *librorum de sacra lege.* Cf. Commod. *Inst.* I. Pref. 6. On the relation of the words *lex, regula*, and κανών, see Credner, *l. c.*

Chap. i.

of Cæcilian to the see of Carthage on the ground that he had been ordained by Felix a traditor; and, in spite of the judgment of a Synod, confirmed by Constantine, the rupture became complete. The ground of the Donatist schism was thus the betrayal of the Canonical Scriptures, and the Canon of the Donatists will necessarily represent the strict judgment of the African Churches. Now Augustine allows that both Donatist and Catholic were alike 'bound by the authority of 'both Testaments[1],' and that they admitted alike the 'Canonical Scriptures[2].' 'And what are these,' he asks, 'but the Canonical Scriptures of the Law and the 'Prophets? To which are added the Gospels, the Apo-'stolic Epistles, the Acts of the Apostles, the Apoca-'lypse of John[3].' The only doubt which can be thrown on the completeness and purity of the Donatist Canon arises from the uncertain language of Augustine about the Epistle to the Hebrews, and no Donatist writing throws any light upon the point[4]. But with this uncertain exception the ordeal of persecution left the African Churches in possession of a perfect New Testament.

ii. Syria— Eusebius. c. 270—340 A.D.

From Africa we pass to Palestine. Among the witnesses of the persecution there was Eusebius the friend of Pamphilus, afterwards bishop of Cæsarea, and the historian of the early Church. 'I saw,' he says, 'with '"mine own eyes the houses of prayer thrown down and 'razed to their foundations, and the inspired and sacred

---

[1] August. *Ep.* cxxix. 3.
[2] Aug. *c. Cresc.* I. 37: Proferte certe...de Scripturis Canonicis [qua-rum nobis est communis auctoritas] ...The last clause, if it be of doubtful authority in this place, occurs without any variation at the end of the chapter.
[3] *De Unit. Eccles.* 51 [xix.].
[4] The only disputed books which Tichonius (Aug. *c. Ep. Parm.* T. ix. p. 11) quotes are, so far as I have noticed, the second Epistle of St John (Gallandi, *Bibl. Pp.* viii. p. 124), and the Apocalypse (*ib.* pp. 107, 122, 125, 128).

'Scriptures consigned to the fire in the open market-
'place¹.' Among such scenes he could not fail to learn
what books men held to be more precious than their
lives, and it is reasonable to look for the influence of
this early trial on his later opinions. But the great
fault of Eusebius is a want of independent judgment.
He writes under the influence of his last informant, and
consequently his narrative is often confused and inconsistent. This is the case in some degree with his statements on the Canon, though it is possible I believe to
ascertain his real judgment on the question, and to remove some of the discrepancies by which it is obscured.

His character.

The manner in which he approaches the subject
illustrates very well the desultory character of his work.
He records the succession of Linus to the see of Rome
'after the martyrdom of Peter and Paul,' and without
any further preface proceeds²: 'Of Peter then one
'Epistle, which is called his former Epistle, is generally
'acknowledged; of this also the ancient presbyters have
'made frequent use (κατακέχρηνται) in their writings as
'indisputably genuine (ἀναμφιλέκτῳ). But that which is
'circulated as his second Epistle we have received to be
'not Canonical (ἐνδιάθηκον); still as it appeared useful
'to many it has been diligently read (ἐσπουδάσθη) with
'the other scriptures. The Book of the Acts of Peter
'and the Gospel which bears his name, and the book
'entitled his Preaching, and his so-called Apocalypse,
'we know to have been in no wise included in the Ca-
'tholic³ scriptures by antiquity (οὐδ' ὅλως ἐν καθολικοῖς
'ἴσμεν παραδιδόμενα), because no ecclesiastical writer in

His first account of the Apostolic Canon.

Writings of St Peter and

---

¹ *H. E.* VIII. 2.
² *H. E.* III. 3. The title of the Chapter is: Περὶ τῶν ἐπιστολῶν τῶν ἀποστόλων, yet he makes no allusion to the Epistles of St John, and di- gresses to other writings.
³ i.e. *Canonical*. This use of the word καθολικός is illustrated by *Concil. Carthag.* XXIV. Int. Gr. (given in App. D).

Chap. i.

St PAUL.

The Shepherd *of* Hermas.

How he continues his narrative till he speaks of

'ancient times or in our own has made general use of
'(συνεχρήσατο) the testimonies to be drawn from them...
'So many are the works which bear the name of Peter,
'of which I recognize (ἔγνων) one Epistle only as genuine
'(γνησίαν) and acknowledged by the ancient presbyters.'

'Of Paul the fourteen epistles commonly received (αἱ
'δεκατέσσαρες) are at once manifest (πρόδηλοι) and clear.
'It is not however right to ignore the fact that some
'have rejected the Epistle to the Hebrews, asserting that
'it is gainsayed by the Church of Rome as not being
'Paul's...The Acts that bear his name I have not re-
'ceived as indisputably genuine.'

'Since the same Apostle in the salutations at the
'end of the Epistle to the Romans has made mention
'among others of Hermas, whose the Shepherd is said
'to be, it must be known that this book has been gain-
'sayed by some, and therefore could not be considered
'an acknowledged book, though it has been judged by
'others most necessary for those who particularly need
'elementary instruction in the faith (στοιχειώσεως εἰσα-
'γωγικῆς). In consequence of this we know that it
'has been formerly publicly read (δεδημοσιευμένον) in
'churches, and I have found that some of the most
'ancient writers have made use of it.'

'These remarks will help to point out (εἰς παράστα-
'σιν) the divine writings which are uncontrovertible
'(ἀναντιρρήτων) and those which are not acknowledged
'by all.'

After this Eusebius continues the thread of his history, relating at length the siege of Jerusalem, and the succession of bishops in the Apostolic sees, till he comes to speak of the reign of Trajan and of the last labours of the Apostle St John. While doing this he quotes from Clement the beautiful story of the young robber, and then goes on abruptly to enumerate 'the uncontroverted 'writings of the Apostle.' His Gospel is placed first as being fully recognised 'in all the churches under hea-'ven;' and so Eusebius proceeds to speak of the other Gospels, prefacing his criticism with some remarks on Apostolic gifts which illustrate his view of Inspiration[1]. 'Those inspired and truly divine men (θεσπέσιοι καὶ 'ἀληθῶς θεοπρεπεῖς), I mean the Apostles of Christ, hav-'ing been completely purified in their life, and adorned 'with every virtue in their souls, though still simple and 'illiterate in their speech (τὴν γλῶσσαν ἰδιωτεύοντες), yet 'trusting boldly to the divine and marvellous power given 'them by the Saviour, had not indeed either the know-'ledge or the design to commend the teaching of their 'Master by subtilty and rhetorical art, but using only 'the demonstration of the divine Spirit, who wrought 'with them, and the wonder-working power of Christ 'realized through them, proclaimed the knowledge of 'the kingdom of heaven over all the world (οἰκουμένην), 'giving little heed to the labour of written composition '(σπουδῆς τῆς περὶ τὸ λογογραφεῖν). And this they did 'as being wholly engaged (ἐξυπηρετούμενοι) in a greater 'and superhuman ministry. For example Paul who 'shewed himself the most powerful of all in the means 'of eloquence and the most able in thought has not com-'mitted to writing more than his very short letters, 'although he had countless mysteries to tell, as one who 'attained to a vision of things in the third heaven, and 'was caught up to the divine paradise itself, and was 'counted worthy to hear unspeakable words from those 'who had been transported thither. The rest of the 'immediate followers (φοιτηταί) of the Saviour, twelve 'Apostles and seventy disciples and innumerable others

Chap. i.

the writings of St JOHN,

and after general remarks on the Gospels,

[1] *H. E.* III. 24.

'besides, were in some degree blessed with the same
'privileges...still Matthew and John alone of all have left
'us an account [of their intercourse with the Lord]...'
After this Eusebius discusses the mutual relations of the
Gospels, promising a more special investigation in some
other place, a promise which, like many others, he left
unfulfilled. He then continues: 'Now of the writings of
'John, in addition to the Gospel, the former of his
'Epistles also has been acknowledged as undoubtedly
'genuine both by the writers of our own time and by
'those of antiquity; but the two remaining Epistles are
'disputed. Concerning the Apocalypse men's opinions
'even now are generally divided. This question how-
'ever shall be decided at a proper time by the testimony
'of antiquity[1].' There is nothing to shew that Eusebius
carried his intention into effect, and without further
break he proceeds[2]: 'But now we have arrived at this
'point, it is natural that we should give a summary cata-
'logue of the writings of the New Testament to which
'we have already alluded[3]. First then we must place the
'holy quaternion of the Gospels, which are followed by
'the account of the Acts of the Apostles. After this we
'must reckon the Epistles of Paul; and next to them
'we must maintain as genuine (κυρωτέον) the Epistle cir-
'culated (φερομένη) as the former[4] of John, and in like
'manner that of Peter. In addition to these books, if

sums up his opinions on the books of the New Testament.

(a) *The* Acknowledged *Books.*

---

[1] The scattered testimonies which he quotes from Justin (IV. 18), Theophilus (IV. 24), Irenæus (V. 8), Origen (VI. 25), and Dionysius (VII. 25), can scarcely be considered to satisfy this promise.

[2] *H. E.* III. 25.

[3] 'Ἀνακεφαλαιώσασθαι τὰς δηλωθείσας τῆς καινῆς διαθήκης γραφάς. It seems incredible that there should have been any difference of opinion as to the meaning of the phrase. Eusebius had mentioned before all the books of the New Testament which he here accepts: Four Gospels, III. 24; Acts, II. 22; fourteen Epistles of St Paul, III. 3; seven Catholic Epistles, II. 23 *ad fin.*; Apocalypse, III. 24.

[4] Προτέρα not πρώτη. Cf. pp. 77, n. 2; 384, n. 1.

'possibly such a view seem correct[1], we must place the
'Revelation of John, the judgments on which we shall
'set forth in due course. And these are regarded as
'generally received (ἐν ὁμολογουμένοις).

'Among the controverted books, which are neverthe-
'less well known and recognised by most[2], we class the
'Epistle circulated under the name of James, and that of
'Jude, as well as the second of Peter, and the so-called
'second and third of John, whether they really belong to
'the Evangelist, or possibly to another of the same name.

'We must rank as spurious (νόθοι) the account of the
'Acts of Paul, the book called the Shepherd, and the
'Revelation of Peter. And besides these the epistle cir-
'culated under the name of Barnabas, and the so-called
'Teachings of the Apostles; and moreover, as I said, the
'Apocalypse of John, if such an opinion seem correct (εἰ
'φανείη), which some, as I said, reject (ἀθετοῦσι), while
'others reckon it among the books generally received.
'We may add that some have reckoned in this division
'the Gospel according to the Hebrews, to which those
'Hebrews who have received [Jesus as] the Christ are
'especially attached[3]. All these then will belong to the
'class of controverted books[4].

Chap. i.

(β) *The* Disputed *Books:*
1. *Generally known.*

2. *Spurious.*

---

[1] Εἴ γε φανείη. The difference between this and εἰ φανείη below must not be left unnoticed.
[2] Γνωρίμων τοῖς πολλοῖς. Cf. *H. E.* III. 38. The word γνώριμος implies a familiar knowledge. It is a singular coincidence that Alex. Aphrod. (*de An.* 2, quoted by Stephens) uses it in connexion with another Eusebian word. Speaking of Time and Place he says: τὸ μὲν εἶναι γνώριμον καὶ ἀναμφίλεκτον.
[3] There is no question of this being placed in the first class, as is stated *Supern. Rel.* II. 167. See App. C.
[4] The complete omission of the first Epistle of Clement in this detailed enumeration is very instructive as marking the principles on which Eusebius made it. The *genuineness* of the Epistle was acknowledged, but it was not *Apostolic*. Thus it could not make any substantial claim to be included among the books of the Canon if Apostolicity was the final test of the authority of a book. On the other hand it may be noticed that Eusebius himself using popular language calls the Epistle a 'disputed book' elsewhere. See p. 421, n. 2.

Chap. i.
(γ) *Heretical Books.*

'It has been necessary for us to extend our catalogue 'to these, in spite of their ambiguous character (τούτων 'ὅμως τὸν κατάλογον πεποιήμεθα), having distinguished 'the writings which according to the ecclesiastical tra-'dition are true and genuine (ἀπλάστους), and generally 'acknowledged[1] and the others besides these, which, 'though they are not Canonical (ἐνδιαθήκους) but contro-'verted, are nevertheless constantly recognised (γιγνω-'σκομένας) by most of our ecclesiastical authorities (ἐκ-'κλησιαστικῶν), that we might be acquainted with these 'scriptures, and with those which are brought forward 'by heretics in the name of Apostles, whether it be 'as containing the Gospels of Peter and Thomas and 'Matthias, or also of others besides these, or as the Acts 'of Andrew and John and the other Apostles, which no 'one of the succession of ecclesiastical writers has any-'where deigned to quote. And further also the cha-'racter of their language (φράσεως) which varies from 'the Apostolic spirit (παρὰ τὸ ἦθος τὸ ἀποστολικὸν ἐν-'αλλάττει), and the sentiment and purpose of their con-'tents, which is utterly discordant with true orthodoxy, 'clearly prove that they are forgeries of heretics; whence 'we must not even class them among the spurious (νό-'θοις) books, but set them aside (παριτητέον) as every 'way monstrous and impious.'

This last passage must interpret the others.

This last passage in which Eusebius professes to sum up what he had previously said upon the subject, however imperfect and vague it may appear in some respects, forms the centre to which all his other statements on the books of the New Testament must be referred. Here, instead of quoting the authority of others, he

---

[1] Ἀνωμολογημένους. Ἀνομολογεῖ-σθαι differs from ὁμολογεῖσθαι in bringing out the notion of examination, inquiry, and judgment. Cf. *H. E.* III. 3, 24, 38; IV. 7.

writes in his own person, and implies I believe his own judgment on the disputed books[1]. In order to determine what this was, it will be necessary to analyse briefly the classification which he proposes. And at the outset it is evident, I think, that he divides all the writings which laid claim to Apostolic authority into three principal divisions—the Acknowledged, the Disputed, and the Heretical. But these words, it must be remembered, are used with reference to a particular object, and consequently in a modified sense[2]. That a book should be *Acknowledged* as Canonical, it was requisite that its authenticity should be undisputed, and that its author should have been possessed of Apostolic power; if it were supposed to fail in satisfying either of these conditions, then it was *Disputed*, however well it satisfied the other.

With regard to the first and last classes there can be little ambiguity as to the limits which Eusebius would set to them generally; the position of the Apocalypse (for a reason which will be shortly seen) being left in some uncertainty. But considerable doubt has been felt as to the exact extent and definition of the second class, though the words at the beginning and end of the paragraph in which the disputed books are enumerated,

Three classes of books distinguished in it, of which the

second class is again subdivided into two others.

---

[1] In treating of the Eusebian Canon, I can only give the conclusions at which I have arrived. The best separate essay on it which I know is that of Lücke (Berlin, 1816), which is not however by any means free from faults.

[2] Thus under different aspects the same book may be differently described. The first Epistle of Clement for instance is called *acknowledged*, when the question of genuineness only is at issue (Euseb. *H. E.* III. 16, 38); but *disputed*, with regard to Canonicity (*H. E.* VI. 13). See p. 419, n. 4.

Origen once adopts a triple division of books claiming Apostolic authority somewhat different (*Comm. in Joan.* XIII. 17): ......ἐξετάζοντες περὶ τοῦ βιβλίου [τοῦ κηρύγματος Πέτρου] πότερόν ποτε γνήσιόν ἐστιν ἢ νόθον ἢ μικτόν—a genuine work, a spurious work falsely inscribed with St Peter's name, or a work containing partly true records of St Peter's teaching, partly spurious additions to it.

clearly state that they were all included under one comprehensive title. Yet it does not therefore follow that all the books included in the second class were on the same footing; for on the contrary this class itself is subdivided into two other classes, containing respectively such books as were generally though not universally recognised, and such as Eusebius pronounced to be *Spurious*, that is deficient in one or other of the marks of an acknowledged book. There are traces even of a further subdivision; for this latter class again is made up of subordinate groups, determined, as it appears, by the common character which fixed their position: the first group, containing the Acts of Paul, the Shepherd, and the Apocalypse of Peter, was not genuine; the second, containing the Epistle of Barnabas[1] and the Doctrines of the Apostles, was not Apostolic. And if this view be correct the ambiguous statement as to the Apocalypse becomes intelligible, because it was undoubtedly a genuine work of John; and if that John were identical with the Apostle, then it satisfied both the conditions requisite to make it an *acknowledged* book: otherwise, like the letter of Barnabas, it was *spurious*[2].

---

[1] In speaking of Barnabas the companion of St Paul Eusebius takes no notice of the Epistle, and he nowhere attributes it to him (*H. E.* I. 12; II. 1; VI. 13). Cf. p. 40 f.

[2] Though Eusebius does not here use the word ἀπόκρυφος, yet as he elsewhere applies it (*H. E.* IV. 22 *ad fin.*) to the books fabricated by heretics, it will be well to trace its meaning briefly:

i. The original sense is clearly *set apart from sight* as distinguished from the simple *hidden* (κρυπτός), the notion of separation or removal being brought prominently forward. Cf. Sirac. xlii. 12 (9): θυγάτηρ πατρὶ ἀπόκρυφος ἀγρυπνία. Gen. xxiv. 43 (Aq.); Dan. xi. 43 (Theod.); Col. ii. 3; Mark iv. 22; Luke viii. 17: comp. Matt. xi. 25; xxv. 18; Luke x. 21; 1 Cor. ii. 7; Eph. iii. 9; Col. i. 26 (ἀποκρύπτειν opposed to φανεροῦν).

ii. From this sense various others branch out corresponding to the several motives which may occasion the concealment. As applied to books, concealment might be caused by their

(*a*) Esoteric value, as containing the secrets of a religion or an art. Cf. Ex. vii. 11, 22 (Symm.); Suid. in Pherecydes (quoted by Stephens): ἤσκησε δὲ ἑαυτὸν κτησάμενος τὰ Φοινίκων ἀπόκρυφα βιβλία. As such

According to this view of the passage then it appears that Eusebius received as 'Divine Scriptures' the Acknowledged books, adding to them the other books in our present Canon, and no others, on the authority of most writers, with this single exception, that he was undecided as to the authorship of the Apocalypse. It remains for us to inquire how far this general judgment is supported by the isolated notices of the different books scattered throughout his writings.

General view of his Canon of the New Testament, supported by isolated testimonies to

It will be noticed that in the general summary no special mention is made of the Epistle to the Hebrews, but in the first quotation it is expressly attributed to St Paul; and though Eusebius elsewhere speaks of it as among the Disputed books[1], numerous quotations prove that he regarded it as substantially St Paul's, even if it had been translated by St Luke, or (as he was more inclined to believe) by Clement of Rome[2]. With regard

the Epistle to the Hebrews,

heretics brought forward writings under the names of Prophets and Apostles; cf. Orig. *Comm. Scr. in Matt.* § 28.

(β) Mysterious or ambiguous character, as containing that which specially needs interpretation or correction from its difficulty or imperfection. Cf. Sirac. xxxix. 3, 7 (Xen. *Memor.* III. 5. 14; *Conv.* VIII. 11). In the first sense the word is applied to the Revelation by Gregory of Nyssa (*Orat. in Ordin. suam*, T. I. p. 876, ed. Par. 1615): ἤκουσα τοῦ εὐαγγελιστοῦ Ἰωάννου ἐν ἀποκρύφοις δι' αἰνίγματος λέγοντος...: and in the other commonly to the so-called *Apocrypha* of the Old Testament. Cf. Orig. *Prol. in Cant. s. f.*

(γ) In the last sense the word offered a contrast to δεδημοσιευμένος, and so came to be applied to books wholly set aside from the use of the Church. Thus it is first used by Irenæus, *c. Hær.* I. 20 (with some allusion probably to the claims made

by the writers of the books; cf. Clem. *Strom.* I. 15. 69): ἀμύθητον πλῆθος ἀποκρύφων καὶ νόθων γραφῶν ἃς αὐτοὶ ἔπλασαν παρεισφέρουσιν: Athanas. *Ep. Fest.* (κανονιζόμενα, ἀναγινωσκόμενα, ἀπόκρυφα); Cyril. *Catech.* IV. 36. Cf. Schleusner, *Lex. Vet. Test.* and Suicer s. v.; and Reuss, *Gesch. der Heil. Schrift.* § 318.

[1] *H. E.* VI. 13: Κέχρηται δ' [ὁ Κλήμης]...ταῖς ἀπὸ τῶν ἀντιλεγομένων γραφῶν μαρτυρίαις...καὶ τῆς πρὸς Ἑβραίους ἐπιστολῆς, τῆς τε Βαρνάβα καὶ Κλήμεντος καὶ Ἰούδα.

[2] *H. E.* III. 38. For his use of the Epistle, see *Eclog. Proph.* I. 20 (ed. Gaisf. Oxf. 1842): ὁ ἀπόστολος ...ἐν τῇ πρὸς Ἑβραίους συντάξει... φησίν· Hebr. i. 5. So *ib.* III. 23: ὁ θαυμάσιος ἀπόστολος· Hebr. iv. 14. *c. Marc. de Eccl. Theol.* I. 20: καὶ ἀρχιερέα δὲ αὐτὸν ὁ αὐτὸς ἀπόστολος [Παῦλος] ἀποκαλεῖ λέγων· Hebr. iv. 14; *c. Marc.* II. 1. *Comm. in Ps.* (ed. Montfaucon, Par. 1706) I. 175 sq., 248, &c.

Chap. i.

the Catholic Epistles of St James and St Jude,

and generally seven Catholic Epistles,

and to the Apocalypse.

to the Catholic Epistles, after speaking of the martyrdom of James the Just he says[1]: 'The first of the Epistles 'styled Catholic is said to be his. But I must remark 'that it is held to be spurious (νοθεύεται). Certainly not 'many old writers have mentioned it, nor yet the Epistle 'of Jude, which is also one of the seven, Epistles called 'Catholic. But nevertheless we know that these have 'been publicly used with the rest in most Churches.' This again is thoroughly consistent with his summary; for the allusion to the order of the Catholic Epistles, and to their definite number (seven), shews that even such as were disputed were distinguished from those which he likewise calls *disputed* when mentioning the opinions of others, but *spurious* when expressing his own. It is more important to insist on this testimony, because though Eusebius has made use of the Epistle of St James in many places[2], yet I am not aware that he ever quotes the Epistle of St Jude, the second Epistle of St Peter, or the two shorter Epistles of St John[3].

The Apocalypse alone remains; and with regard to this book, the same uncertainty as marks Eusebius' judgment on its Apostolicity characterizes his use of it, though he shews a certain inclination to abide by the testimony of antiquity. 'It is likely,' he says in one place, 'that the [vision of the] Apocalypse circulated 'under the name of John was seen by the second John '[the presbyter], unless any one be willing to believe 'that it was seen by the first [the Apostle][4];' and he

---

[1] *H. E.* II. 23.
[2] *Comm. in Ps.* I. p. 247: λέγει γοῦν ὁ ἱερὸς Ἀπόστολος· James v. 13. *ib.* p. 648: τῆς γραφῆς λεγούσης· Prov. xx. 13; James iv. 11. Cf. *ib.*
p. 446; *c. Marc. de Eccl. Theol.* II. 26; James iii. 2.
[3] On the contrary cf. *Theophania,* v. 30 (p. 323, Lee).
[4] *H. E.* III. 39.

quotes it (though rarely in respect of its importance) simply as the 'Apocalypse of John[1].'

From all this it is evident that the testimony of Eusebius marks a definite step in the history of the Canon, and exactly that which it was reasonable to expect from his position. The books of the New Testament were formed into distinct collections—'a quaternion of Gos-'pels,' 'fourteen Epistles of St Paul,' 'seven Catholic 'Epistles.' Both in the West and in the East the persecutor had wrought his work, and a New Testament rose complete from the fires which were kindled to consume it. That it rested on no authoritative decision is simply a proof that none was needed; and in the next chapter it will be seen that the Conciliar Canons introduced no innovations, but merely proposed to preserve the tradition which had been handed down.

Result of the chapter.

[1] Cf. *H. E.* III. 18. 29. *Eclog. Proph.* IV. 30: κατὰ τὸν 'Ιωάννην· Apoc. xiv. 6. Cf. *ib.* IV. 8; *Demonstr. Ev.* VIII. 2: κατὰ τὴν 'Αποκάλυ- ψιν 'Ιωάννου· Apoc. v. 5. No reference to it occurs however in his Commentaries on the Psalms and on Isaiah published by Montfaucon.

CHAPTER II.

THE AGE OF COUNCILS.

Non doctrina et sapientia, sed Domini auxilio pax Ecclesiæ reddita.
HIERONYMUS.

Chap. ii.
Constantine's zeal for the Holy Scriptures.

NO sooner was Constantine's imagination moved by the sign of the heavenly cross (if we may receive the account of Eusebius), than he 'devoted himself to 'the reading of the divine Scriptures,' seeking in them the interpretation of his vision[1]. And in after times he continued, at least with outward zeal, the study which he had thus begun. If his predecessors 'had commanded 'the Inspired Oracles to be consumed in the flames, he 'gave orders that they should be multiplied, and embel-'lished magnificently at the expense of the royal trea-'sury[2].' One of his first cares after the foundation of Constantinople, when a 'great multitude of men devoted 'themselves to the most holy Church,' was to charge Eusebius with 'preparing fifty copies of the divine 'Scriptures, of which he judged the preparation and the 'use to be most necessary for the purpose of the Church, 'written on prepared skins, by the help of skilful artists 'accurately acquainted with their craft[3].' 'For this ob-

---

[1] Euseb. *V. C.* I. 32.
[2] Euseb. *V. C.* III. 1.
[3] Euseb. *V. C.* IV. 36. In doing this Eusebius must naturally have fol- lowed the conclusions as to the Canon of the N. T. to which he has given expression in his History (see pp. 414 ff.), but no direct evidence on the

CONSTANTINE.

'ject,' he adds, 'orders have been issued to the Governor 'of the Province to furnish everything required for the 'work;' and authority was given to Eusebius to employ 'two public carriages for the speedy conveyal of the 'books when finished to the Emperor.' Everything was designed to give importance to the commission. And as the Emperor himself set an example to his subjects, 'studying the Bible in his palace' and 'giving himself 'up to the contemplation of the Inspired Oracles[1],' he was better able to persuade 'weak women and count-'less multitudes of men to receive rational support for 'rational souls by divine readings, in exchange for the 'mere support of the body[2].'

The public and private zeal of the Emperor necessarily exercised a powerful influence upon the Greek Church. The copies of the Greek Bible which he had caused to be prepared were for the use of the Churches of his new capital, and thus they formed a standard for ecclesiastical use. The effects of this were soon seen. The difference between the *Controverted* and *Acknowledged* Epistles was done away except as a matter of history. On the Apocalypse alone some doubts still remained. Some received and some rejected it. But on this a judgment clear and weighty was soon given by Athanasius[3] supported by the prescription of primitive tradition. In other respects the New Testament Canons of Eusebius and Athanasius coincide, and thenceforth the question was practically decided.

During the great controversies which agitated the

His influence.

The Scripture the rule

---

point has been preserved. It is therefore uncertain whether the Apocalypse was contained in Constantine's Bible or not. The later evidence from the Greek churches of the East points with fair distinctness to its omission (see below), though it may have been added as an Appendix like the Alexandrine Apocrypha of the Old Testament.

[1] Euseb. *V. C.* IV. 17.
[2] Euseb. *De Laud. Const.* XVII.
[3] See p. 448.

Church throughout his reign Constantine—'appointed 'by God as bishop in outward matters[1]'—remained faithful to the same great principle of the paramount authority of Scripture. A historian of the Council of Nicæa represents him as closing his address to the fathers assembled there in memorable words. 'Let us cherish 'peace and forbearance,' he says, 'for it would be truly 'disastrous that we should assail one another, particu-'larly when we are discussing divine matters, and pos-'sess the teaching of the most Holy Spirit committed 'to writing; for the books of the Evangelists and Apo-'stles and the utterances of the ancient Prophets clearly 'instruct us what we ought to think of the Divine Na-'ture. Let us then banish strife which genders conten-'tion, and take the solution of our questions from the 'inspired words[2].' Though we may admit that this speech is due to the pen of the historian[3], it is thoroughly consistent with phrases in Constantine's letters which are of unquestioned authenticity. Thus he charges Arius with teaching 'things contrary to the inspired Scriptures 'and the holy faith,' which faith was 'in truth the exact 'expression of the Divine Law[4].'

Holy Scriptures appealed to as authoritative by both sides during the Arian controversy, on other occasions, and

The criterion laid down by Constantine was also acknowledged by the leaders of the conflicting parties in the Church. Alexander was bishop of Alexandria at the time when the opinions of Arius, 'a presbyter in 'the city entrusted with the interpretation of the divine

---

[1] Euseb. *V. C.* IV. 24. Cf. Heinichen, *Exc. in loc.*
[2] Gelas. *Hist. Conc. Nic.* II. 7. Theodor. *H. E.* I. 7.
[3] Gelasius states (Pref.) that his work was composed during the persecutions of Basiliscus (475 A.D.). Photius has criticised the book, cc. 15, 88. Gelasius, in the printed text of the Councils (Migne, 85. 1300ª), quotes 1 Tim. iii. 16 as ὃ ἐφανερώθη, which would be very remarkable in an Eastern writer (*Hist.* II. 23). Dr Abbot informs me (referring to Berriman, *Crit. Diss. on* 1 *Tim.* iii. 16, Lond. 1741, pp. 180 ff.) that four Vatican MSS. of Gelasius read ὃς ἐφανερώθη.
[4] *Ep. Const.* ap. Gelas. *Hist. Conc. Nic.* II. 27. Socr. *H. E.* I. 6.

III.]   THE COUNCIL OF NICÆA.   429

'Scriptures[1],' first gained notoriety. He convened a Synod of many bishops of his province, by whom Arius was condemned from the 'testimony of the divine Scrip-'tures;' and among other passages which Alexander quoted, there occur several from the Epistle to the Hebrews (as the work of the Apostle Paul) and one from the second Epistle of the 'blessed John[2].' Arius on the other hand, when sending a copy of his Creed to the Emperor, adds: 'this is the faith which we have received 'from the holy Gospels, according to the Lord's words, 'as the Catholic Church and the Scriptures teach, which 'we believe in all things: God is our Judge both now 'and in the judgment to come[3].' The followers of Arius repeated the assertion of their master; and though some of them held the Epistle to the Hebrews to be uncanonical, that opinion was neither universal among them, nor peculiar to their sect[4].

The discussions which took place at Nicæa were in accordance with the principle thus laid down, if the history of Gelasius be trustworthy[5]. Scripture was the

Chap. ii.

Matt. xxviii. 19.

at the general Council of Nicæa. 325 A.D.

---

[1] Theodor. *H. E.* I. 2.
[2] *Ep. Alex.* ap. Gelas. *Hist. Conc. Nic.* II. 3 (Socr. *H. E.* I. 3). Hebr. i. 3; xiii. 8; ii. 10. 2 John 11. so also *Ep. Alex.* ap. Theodor. *H. E.* I. 4 (Mansi, *Concil.* II. p. 14): σύμφωνα γοῦν τούτοις βοᾷ καὶ ὁ μεγαλοφωνότατος Παῦλος φάσκων περὶ αὐτοῦ· Hebr. i. 2.
[3] *Ep. Arii ad Const. Imp.* (ap. Mansi, *Concil.* II. p. 464. Ed. Par. 1671).
[4] Theodor. *Pref. Ep. ad Hebr.* Epiph. *Hær.* LXIX. 37.
The famous Gothic Version of ULPHILAS, who is generally reputed to have been an Arian, contained 'all the Scriptures, except the books 'of the Kings,' which were omitted because they contained a history of wars likely to inflame the spirit of the Goths (Philostorg. II. p. 5). Sixtus Senensis however says: omnes divinas Scripturas in Gothicam linguam a se conversas tradidit et catholice explicavit (Massmann, p. 98). The version as it stands at present is clear and accurate, and shews no trace of Arianism (Massmann, *a. a. O.*). A great part of the Gospels and Pauline Epistles has been published: the former chiefly from the Codex Argenteus at Upsala; the latter from Italian Manuscripts. At present no traces of the Acts, the Catholic Epistles, or the Apocalypse, have been discovered. A supposed reference to the Epistle to the Hebrews is of doubtful cogency.
[5] *Hist. Conc. Nic.* II. 13—23.

source from which the champions and assailants of the orthodox faith derived their premises; and among other books, the Epistle to the Hebrews was quoted as written by St Paul, and the Catholic Epistles were recognised as a definite collection[1]. But neither in this nor in the following Councils were the Scriptures themselves ever the subjects of discussion. They underlie all controversy, as a sure foundation, known and immoveable[2].

Mansi, *Concil.* II. 175—223. Phæbadius (c. 359 A.D.) asserts the same fact.

[1] Gelas. *Hist. Conc. Nic.* II. 19; καθώς φησι καὶ ὁ Παῦλος τὸ σκεῦος τῆς ἐκλογῆς τοῖς Ἑβραίοις γράφων· Hebr. iv. 12. *ib. ἐν καθολικαῖς Ἰωάννης ὁ εὐαγγελιστὴς βοᾷ·* 1 John iii. 6. Cf. II. 22. For the Epistle to the Hebrews see also Sozom. *H. E.* I. 23.

[2] Jerome (*Pref. in Judith*, I. p. 1169) says: Quia hunc librum synodus Nicæna in numero sanctarum scripturarum legitur computasse, acquievi postulationi tuæ (to translate it). No reference to the book of Judith occurs in the records of the Council, as far as I am aware, and it can be only to some casual reference that Jerome alludes.

The holy Gospels were placed in the midst of the assembled fathers at Chalcedon, but though it is commonly stated that it was so at Nicæa also, I know of no proof of the circumstance.

The contents of the three great MSS. of the Greek Bible,—the Alexandrine (A), the Vatican (B), the Sinaitic (א)—which belong to this period may be noticed here, so far as the books of the New Testament are concerned.

1. The Alexandrine MS. has a table of contents, of which the portion with which we are concerned is as follows:

The New Testament:

Gospels, 4 (according to Matthew ...Mark...Luke...John);
Acts of Apostles;
Catholic Epistles, 7 (*James*, 1, 2 Peter, 1, 2, 3 *John, Jude*);
Epistles of Paul, 14 (*Romans*...2 *Thess., Hebrews,* 1 *Tim.* ...*Philem.*);
Apocalypse of John;
Clement's Epistle, 1;
Clement's Epistle, 2.
Together...? Books.
Psalms of Solomon, xviii.

From the arrangement of the books in the Old Testament, the insertion of the Epistles of Clement, and the omission of the *Shepherd*, it seems likely that this MS. represents a Syrian judgment in spite of the position of *Hebrews*.

2. The Vatican MS. ends *Hebrews* ix. 14. Up to that point it contains the same books of the New Testament as are enumerated in the Catalogue of the Alexandrine MS. and in the same order (but compare p. 371, n. 1); and it is impossible to say what other books were originally included in it.

3. The order in the Sinaitic MS. is different. This contains:

Four Gospels (Matthew, Mark, Luke, John);
Fourteen Epistles of St Paul (*Romans*...2 *Thess., Hebrews,* 1 *Tim.* ... *Philem.*);
Acts;
Seven Catholic Epistles (*James*, 1, 2 *Peter,* 1, 2, 3 *John, Jude*);

III.] THE SYNOD OF LAODICEA. 431

The Canons set forth by the Synods which followed the General Council at Nicæa, at Gangra in Paphlagonia, at Antioch in Syria, at Sardica in Thrace, and at Carthage, were chiefly directed to points of ritual and discipline, yet so that in the last Canon of the Synod at Gangra it is said: 'To speak briefly, we desire that what 'has been handed down to us by the divine Scriptures 'and the Apostolic traditions should be done in the 'Church[1].'

Chap. ii.

The Synods which immediately followed this Council disciplinary and not doctrinal.

The first Synod at which the books of the Bible were made the subject of a special ordinance was that of Laodicea in Phrygia Pacatiana; but the date at which the Synod was held, no less than the integrity of the Canon in question, has been warmly debated. In the collections of Canons the Council of Laodicea stands next to that of Antioch, and this order is probably correct. The arguments which have been urged to shew that it was prior to the Council of Nicæa are on the whole of little moment, and the mention of the Photinians in the seventh Canon, no less than the whole character of the questions discussed, is decisive for a later date[2]. A natural confusion of names offers a ready excuse for the contrary opinion. Gratian[3] states that the Laodicene Canons were mainly drawn up by Theodosius;

i. *The Synod of* LAODICEA. *Its date.*

Apocalypse of John;
Epistle of Barnabas;
The Shepherd (a fragment).

Mr Bradshaw has called my attention to the fact that the arrangement of the quires shews that the *Shepherd*, like 4 *Maccabees* in the Old Testament, was treated as a separate section of the volume, and therefore perhaps as an Appendix to the more generally received books.

See also App. D. xx.

[1] *Conc. Gangr.* Can. xxi. f.
[2] The name is omitted in the Latin Version of Isidore, but it is contained in the Greek Text and in the Version of Dionysius Exiguus. Phrygia was not divided into different provinces till after the Council of Sardis, hence the title—Phrygia Pacatiana—points to a date later than 344 A.D. Cf. Spittler, *Werke*, VIII. 68 (ed. 1835).

[3] Grat. *Decr.* Dist. XVI. c. 11: [Synodus] sexta Laodicensis, in qua patres xxxii. statuerunt Canones XLI. (sic ed. 1648; LXIII. ed. Antv. 1573) quorum auctor maxime Theodosius episcopus exstitit.

C.   F F

432 THE AGE OF COUNCILS. [PART

Chap. ii.

c. 363 A.D.

The last Laodicene Canon in the printed editions.

and Theodosius (Theodotus or Theodorus, for the name is variously written) was bishop of Laodicea *in Syria* at the time of the Council of Nicæa. But the statement of Gratian really points to a very different conclusion; for Epiphanius mentions another Theodosius bishop of Philadelphia[1], who is said to have convened a Synod in the time of Jovian for the purpose of condemning certain irregular ordinations[2], and his position coincides admirably with that of the author of our Canons. Internal evidence also supports their identification; nor is it any objection that this Theodosius was an Arian, for the Canons are chiefly disciplinary, and such as could be ratified by orthodox councils; and at the same time that fact explains the omission of all reference to the Nicene Canons, which would otherwise be strange[3].

The date of the Synod of Laodicea (which was in fact only a small gathering of clergy from parts of Lydia and Phrygia[4]) being thus approximately affixed, the question of the integrity of the last Canon, which contains the catalogue of the books of Holy Scripture, remains to be considered. In the printed editions of the Councils the Catalogue stands as an undisputed part of the Greek text, and the whole Canon reads as follows:

---

[1] Epiph. *Hær.* LXXIII. 26.
[2] Philostorg. VIII. 3, 4.
[3] Cf. Pagi, *Crit. ad Baron.* Ann. 314, XXV.; Baron. *Opp.* Tom. VI. (ed. 1738). On the omission of the book of Judith from the Old Testament Canon, said to have been recognised by the Nicene Council, cf. previous page, note 2.
    Beveridge fixes the date of the Synod about the same time (365 A.D.), and supposes that it was summoned in consequence of letters from Valentinian, Valens, and Gratian (Theodor. *H. E.* IV. 6), to the bishops διοικήσεως Ἀσιανῆς, Φρυγίας, Καροφρυγίας Πακατιανῆς, urging them to hold a Synod on some who had been reviving the Homoousian controversy, and also on the choice of men of approved faith for the episcopate (*Pand. Can.* II. 3, p. 193).
[4] Gratian (*l.c.*) says it consisted of 'xxxii. fathers.' Harduin quotes a different version of Gratian's statement from a Parisian Manuscript of Isidore: Laodicensis synodus, in quâ Patres *viginti quatuor* statuerunt Canones LIX., quorum auctor maxime Theodosius episcopus exstitit, subscribentibus Niceta, Macedonio, Anatolio, et cæteris.

III.]   THE SYNOD OF LAODICEA.   433

'Psalms composed by private men (ἰδιωτικούς) must
'not be read (λέγεσθαι) in the Church, nor uncanonical
'(ἀκανόνιστα) books, but only the Canonical [books] of
'the New and Old Testaments.

'How many books must be read (ἀναγινώσκεσθαι);
'Of the Old Testament: 1. The Genesis of the World.
'2. The Exodus from Egypt. 3. Leviticus. 4. Numbers.
'5. Deuteronomy. 6. Jesus the son of Nun. 7. Judges.
'Ruth. 8. Esther. 9. Kings i. ii. 10. Kings iii. iv.
'11. Chronicles i. ii. 12. Esdras i. ii. 13. The Book of
'Psalms cl. 14. The Proverbs of Solomon. 15. Eccle-
'siastes. 16. The Song of Songs. 17. Job. 18. xii.
'Prophets. 19. Esaias. 20. Jeremiah. Baruch. La-
'mentations, and Letter. 21. Ezechiel. 22. Daniel.
'Together xxii. books.'

'Of the New Testament: Four Gospels, according
'to Matthew, Mark, Luke, John. The Acts of the
'Apostles. Seven Catholic Epistles thus: James i.
'Peter i. ii. John i. ii. iii. Jude i. Fourteen Epistles
'of Paul thus: to the Romans i. To the Corinthians
'i. ii. To the Galatians i. To the Ephesians i. To
'the Philippians i. To the Colossians i. To the Thes-
'salonians i. ii. To the Hebrews i. To Timothy i. ii.
'To Titus i. To Philemon i.[1]'

Of this Canon the first paragraph is recognised as
genuine with unimportant variations by every authority;
the second, the Catalogue of the Books itself, is omitted
in various Manuscripts and versions; and in order to
arrive at a fair estimate of its claims to authenticity,
it will be necessary to notice briefly the different forms

Chap. ii.

How far its claims to authenticity are supported by

[1] Cf. App. D. The Canons are variously numbered, but the oldest and best authorities which contain both these paragraphs combine them together as the LIXth Canon. Cf. Spittler, *a. a. O.* 72.

Chap. ii.

1. Greek Manuscripts

with Scholia,

without Scholia.

in which the Canons of the ancient Church have been preserved[1].

The Greek Manuscripts of the Canons may be divided into two classes, those which contain the simple text, and those which contain in addition the scholia of the great commentators. Manuscripts of the second class in no case date from an earlier period than the end of the twelfth century, the era of Balsamon and Zonaras, the most famous Greek canonists. Yet it is on this class of Manuscripts, which contain the Catalogue in question, that the printed editions are based. The earliest Manuscript of the first class with which I am acquainted is of the eleventh century, and one is as late as the fifteenth. The evidence on the disputed paragraph which these Manuscripts afford is extremely interesting. Two omit the Catalogue entirely. In another it is inserted after a vacant space. A fourth contains it on a new page with red dots above and below. In a fifth it appears wholly written in red letters. Three others give it as a part of the last Canon, though headed with a new rubric. In one it appears as a part of the 59th Canon without interruption or break; and in two (of the latest date) numbered as a new Canon[2]. It is

---

[1] The authenticity of the Catalogue has been discussed at considerable length by Spittler (*Sämmtl. Werke*, VIII. 66 ff. ed. 1835), whose essay was published in 1776, and again by Bickell (*Stud. u. Krit.* 1830, pp. 591 ff.). The essay of Spittler seems to me to be much superior to that of his successor in clearness and wideness of view. Spittler regards the Catalogue as entirely spurious; Bickell only allows that it was wanting in some very early copies of the Canons, and supposes that it may have been displaced by the general reception of the Apostolic Canons and Catalogue of Scripture.

[2] The Manuscripts with which I am acquainted are the following:
(α) Cod. Barocc. (Bibl. Bodl.) 26 (7), sæc. xi. ineuntis.
Cod. Misc. (Bibl. Bodl.) 170 (12), sæc. xiv. xv.
These omit the Canon altogether.
(β) Cod. Barocc. (Bibl. Bodl.) 185 (18), sæc. xi. exeuntis.
Gives the Canon after a vacant space.
Cod. Vindob. 56, sæc. xi. On a new page with red dots above and below (Bickell, p. 595).

impossible not to feel that these several Manuscripts mark the steps by which the Catalogue gained its place in the present Greek text; but it may still be questioned whether it may not have thus regained a place which it had lost before. And thus we are led to notice some versions of the Canons which date from a period anterior to the oldest Greek Manuscripts.

The Latin version exists in a threefold form. The earliest (*Versio Prisca*) is fragmentary, and does not contain the Laodicene Canons. But two other versions by Dionysius and Isidore are complete[1]. In the first of these, which dates from the middle of the sixth century, though it exists in two distinct recensions, there is no trace of the Catalogue. In the second, on the contrary, with only two exceptions, as far as I am aware, the Catalògue constantly appears. And though the Isidorian version in its general form only dates from the ninth century, two Manuscripts remain which are probably as old as the ninth century, and both of these contain it[2]. So far then it appears that the evidence of the Latin versions for and against the authenticity of the Cata-

Chap. ii.

2. *The Versions: Latin and*

    Cod. Seld. (Bibl. Bodl.) 48 (10), sæc. xiii. All in red letters.

(γ) Cod. Barocc. (Bibl. Bodl.) 196 (16), anno MXLIII exaratus.

    Cod. Misc. (Bibl. Bodl.) 206, sæc. xi. exeuntis.

    Cod. Cant. (Bibl. Univ. Ee. 4. 29. 22), sæc. xii.

These three give the Catalogue under a rubric ὅσα—διαθήκης, but not as a new Canon.

(δ) Cod. Laud. (Bibl. Bodl.) 39 (21), sæc. xi. ineuntis. As part of Canon 59.

    Cod. Barocc. (Bibl. Bodl.) 205 (18), sæc. xiv. As a new Canon.

    Cod. Barocc. (Bibl. Bodl.) 158 (23), sæc. xv. As a new Canon.

    Cod. Arund. (Brit. Mus.) 533, sæc. xiv. As a new Canon, but all rubricated.

Bandini (*Bibl. Laur.* I. pp. 72, 397, 477) notices several other Manuscripts which contain the Catalogue.

The Manuscripts marked by italics are now I believe quoted on this question for the first time; and for the account of all the Bodleian Manuscripts I am indebted to the kindness of the Rev. H. O. Coxe.

[1] In the account of the Latin versions I have chiefly followed Spittler, *a. a. O.* 98 ff. Cf. Bickell, 601 ff.

[2] Spittler, p. 115. Cf. Bickell, p. 606.

logue is nearly balanced, the testimony of Italy confronting that of Spain.

The Syriac Manuscripts of the British Museum are however more than sufficient to turn the scale. Three Manuscripts of the Laodicene Canons are found in that collection, which are as old as the sixth or seventh century. All of these contain the fifty-ninth Canon, but without any Catalogue. And this testimony is of twofold value from the fact that one of them gives a different translation from that of the other two[1].

Nor is this all: in addition to the direct versions of the Canons, systematic collections and synopses of them were made at various times, which have an important bearing upon the question. One of the earliest of these was drawn up by Martin bishop of Braga in Portugal at the middle of the sixth century. This collection contains the first paragraph of the Laodicene Canon, without any trace of the second; and the testimony which it offers is of more importance, because it was based on an examination of Greek authorities, and those of a very early date, since they did not notice the Councils of Constantinople, Ephesus, and Chalcedon, which were included in the collection of the fifth century[2]. Johannes Scholasticus, a presbyter of Antioch, formed a digest of Canons under different heads about the same time, and this contains no reference to the Laodicene Catalogue, but on the contrary the list of Holy Scriptures is taken

---

[1] The Manuscripts are numbered 14,526; 14,528; 14,529. All of them contain 59 Canons. For the examination of these Manuscripts I am indebted to the kindness of Mr T. Ellis of the British Museum.
The Arabic Manuscript in Rich's collection (7207) is only a fragment. Bickell consulted an Arabic translation at Paris which contained the Laodicene Canons twice, once with and once without the Catalogue (p. 592).

[2] Mart. Brac. *Pref.:* Incipiunt Canones ex orientalibus antiquorum patrum Synodis a venerabili Martino ipso vel ab omni Bracarensi Consilio excerpti vel emendati.

from the last of the Apostolic Canons. The *Nomocanon* is a later revision of the work of Johannes, and contains only the undisputed paragraph; but in a third and later recension the Laodicene and Apostolic Catalogues are both inserted.

On the whole then it cannot be doubted that external evidence is decidedly against the authenticity of the Catalogue as an integral part of the text of the Canons of Laodicea, nor can any internal evidence be brought forward sufficient to explain its omission in Syria, Italy, and Portugal, in the sixth century, if it had been so. Yet even thus it is necessary to account for its insertion in the version of Isidore. So much is evident at once, that the Catalogue is of Eastern and not of Western origin; and, except in details of order, it agrees exactly with that given by Cyril of Jerusalem. Is it then an unreasonable supposition that some early copyist endeavoured to supply, either from the writings of Cyril, or more probably from the usage of the Church which Cyril represented, the list of books which seemed to be required by the language of the last genuine Canon? In this way it is easy to understand how some Manuscripts should have incorporated the addition, while others preserved the original text; and the known tendency of copyists to make their works full rather than pure, will account for its general reception at last.

The later history of the Laodicene Canons does not throw any considerable light on the question of the authenticity of the Catalogue[1]. Though they were originally drawn up by a provincial (and perhaps unorthodox)

---

[1] It is commonly supposed that the Laodicene Canons were ratified at the Council of Chalcedon (451 A.D.): *Conc. Chalc.* Can. 1. But the wording of the Canon is very vague. Justinian by a special ordinance ratified not only the Canons of the four general Councils, of which that of Chalcedon was the last, but also those which they confirmed.

Synod, they were afterwards ratified by the Eastern Church at the Quinisextine Council of Constantinople. But nothing can be concluded from this as to the absence of the list of the Holy Scriptures from the copy of the Canons which was then confirmed. The Canons of the Apostles were sanctioned at the same Council; and though a special reservation was made in approving them, to the effect that the Clementine Constitutions, which they recognised as authoritative, were no longer to be received as Canonical, on account of the interpolations of heretics, no notice was taken of the two Clementine epistles which were also pronounced Canonical at the same time[1]. It is then impossible to press the variations between the Appostolic and Laodicene Catalogues as a conclusive proof that they could not have been admitted simultaneously[2]. The decision of the Council contained a general sanction rather than a detailed judgment. And this is further evident from the differences between the Apostolic and Carthaginian Catalogues which were certainly ratified together[3]. So again at a

---

[1] *Concil. Quinisext.* Can. XXI. The Catalogue of the books of Scripture in the last Apostolic Canon is curious; but as a piece of evidence it is of no value. It was drawn, I believe, from Syrian sources, and probably dates from the sixth century. Cf. App. D.

[2] Though the Catalogues differed in other respects, they coincided in omitting the Apocalypse. Cf. App. D.

[3] The later history of the Canon in the Greek Church, which accepts the decrees of the Quinisextine Council, shews that the ratification of these earlier councils was not supposed to fix definitely (which indeed it could not do) the contents of Holy Scripture. Cyril Lucar (*Confess.* 3) proposed to admit 'such books as 'were recognised by the Synod at 'Laodicea, and by the Catholic and 'orthodox Church,' but he adds to the New Testament 'the Apocalypse 'of the beloved.' There is no Catalogue of the books of Scripture in the *Orthodox Confession*, but the Apocalypse is quoted in it (*Quæst.* 14), and as 'Holy Scripture' (*Quæst.* 73). At the Synod of Jerusalem (A.D. 1672) Cyril was condemned for 'rejecting 'some of the books which the holy 'and œcumenical synods had re-'ceived as Canonical,' but no charge is brought against him for adding to them, so that in this case the Carthaginian and not the Laodicene Catalogue was the standard of reference for the New Testament (*Act. Synod. Hieros.* XVIII. p. 417, Kimmel). In the confession of Dositheus the Greek Church is said to receive 'all the

later time the Laodicene Catalogue was confirmed by a Synod at Aix-la-Chapelle in the time of Charlemagne, and gained a wide currency in the Isidorian version of the Canons. There is however no evidence to shew that there was on this account any doubt in the Western Churches as to the authority or public use of the Apocalypse. But though no argument can be drawn against the authenticity of the Catalogue from the ratification of the Laodicene Canons at Constantinople, that fact leaves the preponderance of evidence against it wholly unaffected. The Catalogue may have been a contemporary appendix to the Canons, but it was not I believe an integral part of the original conciliar text.

It is then necessary to look to the West for the first synodical decision on the Canon of Scripture. Between the years 390 and 419 A.D. no less than six councils were held in Africa, and four of these at Carthage. For a time, under the inspiration of Aurelius and Augustine, the Church of Tertullian and Cyprian was filled with a new life before its fatal desolation. Among the Canons of the third Council of Carthage, at which Augustine was present, is one which contains a list of the books of

Chap. ii.

ii. *The third Council of* CARTHAGE.

'books which Cyril borrowed from 'the Laodicene Council, with the ad- 'dition of those which he called... 'Apocryphal' (Kimmel, p. 467. Cf. *Proleg.* § 11 on the Latin influence supposed to have been exercised on these documents). . In the Confession of Metrophanes Critopulus the Canon of the Old Testament is identical with the Hebrew, that of the New Testament with our own, so that there are 'thirty-three books in 'all, equal in number to the years of 'the Saviour's life.' The Apocrypha is there regarded as useful for its moral precepts, but its canonicity is denied on the authority of Gregory of Nazianzus, Amphilochius, and Johannes Damascenus, but no reference is made to the Laodicene Canon (Kimmel, II. 105 f.). At the Synod of Constantinople a general reference is made to the different Catalogues in the Apostolic Canons and in the Synods of Laodicea and Carthage (Kimmel, II. 225). In the Catechism of Plato and in the authorized Russian Catechism the Old Testament is given according to the Hebrew Canon. On the other hand, the authorized Moscow edition of the Bible contains the Old Testament Apocrypha arranged with the other books (Reuss, § 338).

Holy Scripture. 'It was also determined,' the Canon reads, 'that besides the Canonical Scriptures nothing be 'read in the Church under the title of divine Scriptures. 'The Canonical Scriptures are these: Genesis, Exodus, 'Leviticus, Numbers, Deuteronomy, Joshua the son of 'Nun, Judges, Ruth, four books of Kings, two books 'of Paraleipomena, Job, the Psalter, five books of Solo-'mon, the books of the twelve Prophets, Isaiah, Jere-'miah, Ezechiel, Daniel, Tobit, Judith, Esther, two books 'of Esdras, two books of the Maccabees. Of the New 'Testament: four books of the Gospels, one book of the 'Acts of the Apostles, thirteen Epistles of the Apostle 'Paul, one Epistle of the same [writer] to the Hebrews, 'two Epistles of the Apostle Peter, three of John, one of 'James, one of Jude, one book of the Apocalypse of 'John.' Then follows this remarkable clause: 'Let this 'be made known also to our brother and fellow-priest 'Boniface, or to other bishops of those parts, for the pur-'pose of confirming that Canon, because we have received 'from our fathers that those books must be read in the 'Church.' And afterwards the Canon is thus continued: 'Let it also be allowed that the Passions of Martyrs be 'read when their festivals are kept[1].'

An explanation of the form of this Canon.

Even this Canon therefore is not altogether free from difficulties. The third Council of Carthage was held in the year 397 A.D. in the pontificate of Siricus; and Boniface did not succeed to the Roman chair till the year 418 A.D.; so that the allusion to him is at first sight perplexing. Yet this anachronism admits of a reasonable solution. In the year 419 A.D., after the confirmation of Boniface in the Roman episcopate, the Canons of the African Church were collected and formed into

---

[1] Cf. App. D.

one code. In the process of such a revision it was perfectly natural that some reference should be made to foreign churches on such a subject as the contents of Scripture, which were fixed by usage rather than by law. The marginal note which directed the inquiry was suffered to remain, probably because the plan was never carried out; and that which stood in the text of the general code was afterwards transferred to the text of the original Synod[1].

At this point then the voice of a whole province pronounces a judgment on the contents of the Bible; and the books of the New Testament are exactly those which are generally received at present. But in making this decision the African bishops put aside all notions of novelty. Their decision had been handed down to them by their fathers; and to revert once again from Churches to men, our work would be unfinished without a general review of the principal evidence on the Canon furnished by individual writers from the beginning of the fourth century. Nothing indeed is gained by this for a critical investigation of the subject; for the original materials have been all gathered already. But it is not therefore the less interesting to trace the local prevalence of ancient doubts, and the gradual extension of the Western Canon throughout Christendom.

The evidence of Fathers on the Canon from the fourth century in

Turning towards the Eastern limit of Christian literature we find the ancient Canon of the Peshito still dominant at Antioch, at Nisibis, and probably at Edessa[2].

i. *The Churches of Syria.*

The voluminous writings of Chrysostom, who was at first a presbyter of Antioch and afterwards patriarch of Constantinople, abound in references to Holy Scripture;

1. Antioch. CHRYSOSTOM. † 407 A.D.

---

[1] The Carthaginian Catalogue of the Books of Scripture is found in the Canons of the Council of Hippo (419 A.D.). But mention is made in that of 'fourteen Epistles of Paul' instead of the strange circumlocution given above (*Conc. Hipp.* 36). [2] Cf. supr. p. 241.

he is indeed said to have been the first writer who gave the Bible its present name τὰ βιβλία, *The Books*[1]; but with the exception of one very doubtful quotation from the second Epistle of St Peter[2], I believe that he has nowhere noticed the four Catholic Epistles which are not contained in the Peshito, nor the Apocalypse[3]. It is also in accordance with the same Version that he attributed fourteen Epistles to St Paul, and received the Epistle of St James 'the Lord's brother' with the first Epistles of St Peter and St John[4]. A Synopsis of Scripture which was published by Montfaucon under the name of Chrysostom exactly agrees with this Canon, enumerating 'as the books of the New Testament, fourteen Epistles of St Paul, four Gospels, the book of the Acts, and three of the Catholic Epistles[5].' Theodore, a friend of Chrysostom and bishop of Mopsuestia in Cilicia, wrote commentaries on fourteen Epistles of St Paul; and his remaining fragments contain several quotations from the Epistle to the Hebrews as St Paul's[6]. But Leontius of Byzantium writing at the close of the

---

[1] Suicer, *Thesaurus*, s. v. Comp. p. 182.
[2] *Hom. in Joan.* 34 (al. 33), VIII. p. 230, ed. Par. nova; 2 Pet. ii. 22 (Prov. xxvi. 11). It may be added that there is a clear reference to 2 Pet. ii. 16 in a fragment attributed to Eusebius of Emesa, *Opuscula*, p. 189 (Augusti).
[3] Though Chrysostom nowhere quotes the Apocalypse as Scripture, he must have been acquainted with it. Suidas (s. v. Ἰωάννης) says: δέχεται δὲ ὁ Χρυσόστομος καὶ τὰς ἐπιστολὰς αὐτοῦ τὰς τρεῖς καὶ τὴν Ἀποκάλυψιν. If this be true, it is a singular proof of the inconclusiveness of the casual evidence of quotations. Reuss (p. 188) quotes as from Chrysostom τῶν ἐκκλησιαζομένων οὐ τῶν ἀποκρύφων μὲν ἡ πρώτη ἐπιστολή· τὴν γὰρ δευτέ- ραν καὶ τρίτην οἱ πατέρες ἀποκανονί- ζουσι (*Opp.* VI. 430); but the words are not his though contemporary with him.
[4] It is however very well worth notice that PALLADIUS, a friend of Chrysostom, in a dialogue which he composed at Rome on his life, has expressly quoted the Epistle of St Jude and the third Epistle of St John, and makes an evident allusion to the second Epistle of St Peter. Dial. cc. 18, 20 (ap. Chrysost. *Opp.* T. XIII. pp. 68 C; 79 D; 68 C).
[5] Cf. App. D.
[6] *Comm. in Zachar.* p. 542 (ed. Wegnern, Berl. 1834), οὓς ἐχρῆν αἰσχυνθῆναι γοῦν τοῦ μακαρίου Παύλου τὴν φωνήν...Hebr. i. 7, 8. Cf. Ebed Jesu, ap. Assem. *Bibl. Or.* III. 32. 3.

sixth century states that he rejected 'the Epistle of 'James and the following Catholic Epistles,' by which we must probably understand that he received only the acknowledged first Epistles of St Peter and St John[1]. And though nothing is directly known of his judgment on the Apocalypse, it is at least probable that in respect to this he followed the common opinion of the school to which he belonged. Once again: Theodoret, a native of Antioch and bishop of Cyrus in Syria, used the same books as Chrysostom, and has nowhere quoted the four disputed Epistles or the Apocalypse[2].

Junilius, an African bishop of the sixth century, has given a very full and accurate account of the doctrine on Holy Scripture taught in the schools of Nisibis in Syria, where 'the Divine Law was regularly explained by 'public masters, like Grammar and Rhetoric.' He enumerates all the acknowledged books of the New Testament as of 'perfect authority;' and adds to these the Epistle to the Hebrews as St Paul's, though he places it after the Pastoral Epistles. 'Very many (*quamplu-* '*rimi*),' he says, 'add to the first Epistles of St Peter 'and St John five others, which are called the Canonical 'letters of the Apostles, that is: James, 2 Peter, Jude, '2 and 3 John...' 'As to the Apocalypse of John, there 'is considerable doubt among Eastern Christians[3]...'

---

[1] See also what Cosmas Indicopleustes says of Severian of Gabala (Montf. *Anal. Pp.* p. 135, Venet. 1781). The words of Leontius are: δι' ἣν αἰτίαν (because he rejected the book of Job) αὐτήν τε οἶμαι τοῦ μεγάλου Ἰακώβου τὴν ἐπιστολὴν καὶ τὰς ἑξῆς τῶν ἄλλων ἀποκηρύττει καθολικάς. οὐ γὰρ ἤρκει αὐτῷ κατὰ τῆς παλαιᾶς ἐγχειρεῖν γραφῆς, τὴν Μαρκίωνος ἐξηλωκότι ἀσέβειαν, ἀλλ' ἔδει καὶ κατὰ τῆς νέας αὐτὸν ἀγωνίσασθαι ἵνα ᾖ περιφανεστέρα αὐτῷ ἡ κατὰ τοῦ ἁγίου πνεύματος ἀγωνία (*adv. incorrupt. et Nestor.* § 14. Migne, LXXXVI. p. 1365). Kihn interprets the words τὰς ἑξῆς καθολικάς as I have done; *Theodor. v. Mopsuestia*, § 55.

[2] Cf. Lücke, *Comm. üb. Joh.* I. 348. A Commentary on the Gospels attributed to Victor of Antioch contains references to the Epistle to the Hebrews, and to the Epistles of St James and the first of St Peter. Cf. Lardner, II. c. 122.

[3] The passages are given at length

Chap. ii.
EBED JESU.

At a very much later period Ebed Jesu, a Nestorian bishop of Nisibis in the thirteenth century, has left a catalogue of the writings of the New Testament at the commencement of his summary of ecclesiastical literature. This catalogue exactly agrees with that of the Peshito, including fourteen Epistles of St Paul, and 'three Catholic Epistles ascribed to the Apostles in 'every Manuscript and language;' and it contains no allusion to the other disputed books[1].

3. Edessa.
EPHRAEM SYRUS.
† 378 A.D.

The testimony of Ephraem Syrus is unfortunately uncertain. For while he appears to use all the books of our New Testament in his works, which are preserved only in Greek, I am not aware that there is in the original Syriac text more than one quotation of the Apocalypse, and perhaps an anonymous reference to the second Epistle of St Peter[2].

JOHANNES DAMASCENUS.
† c. 750 A.D.

Johannes Damascenus, the last writer of the Syrian Church whom I shall notice, lived at a time when the Greek element had gained a preponderating influence in the East, and his writings in turn are commonly accepted as an authoritative exposition of the Greek faith. The Canon of the New Testament which he gives[3] contains all the books which we receive now, with the addition of the Canons of the Apostles. This singular insertion admits of a satisfactory explanation from the fact that the Apostolic Canons were sanctioned by the

---

in App. D. For Junilius' view of the Canon in connexion with that of the Antiochene School generally, see Kihn *a. a. O.* §§ 375 ff. Kihn concludes that Junilius gives the Canon of Theodore.

[1] Cf. App. D. It is very remarkable that Ebed Jesu takes no notice of the Apocalypse, since he mentions after a short interval among the works of Hippolytus 'an Apology 'for the Gospel and Apocalypse of 'John, Apostle and Evangelist' (Assem. *Bibl. Orient.* III. 15).

[2] Ephr. Syr. *Opp. Syrr.* II. p. 332 C : Vidit in Apocalypsi sua Johannes librum magnum et admirabilem·et septem sigillis munitum...*ib.* II. p. 342 : Dies Domini fur est (cf. 2 Pet. iii. 10). Cf. Lardner, Pt. II. c. 102.

[3] Cf. App. D.

Quinisextine Council, and their Canonicity might well seem a true corollary from the acknowledgment of their ecclesiastical authority[1].

The Churches of Asia Minor, which are now even more desolate than the Churches of Syria, had lost little of their former lustre in the fourth and fifth centuries. In doctrinal tendency they still mediated between the East and the West. And this characteristic appears in one of two catalogues of the books of the New Testament which have been preserved among the works of Gregory of Nazianzus[2]. After enumerating the four Gospels, the Acts, fourteen Epistles of St Paul, and seven Catholic Epistles, Gregory adds: 'In these you 'have all the inspired books; if there be any book be-'sides these, it is not among the genuine [Scriptures];' and thus he excludes the Apocalypse with the Eastern Church, and admits all the Catholic Epistles with the Western[3]. The second Catalogue which bears the name of Gregory is commonly (and I believe rightly) attributed to his contemporary Amphilochius bishop of Iconium. This extends to a greater length than the former. Beginning with the mention of the four Gospels, of the Acts of the Apostles, and of fourteen Epistles of St Paul, it then continues: 'but some maintain that the 'Epistle to the Hebrews is spurious, not speaking well; 'for the grace [it shews] is genuine. To proceed: what 'remains? Of the Catholic Epistles some maintain that 'we ought to receive seven, and others three only, one

Chap. ii.

ii. *The Churches of Asia Minor.*

The catalogues given by GREGORY *of Nazianzus and by* † *c.* 389 A.D.

AMPHILOCHIUS.

---

[1] The Canons of Carthage were ratified by the Quinisextine Council as well as those of the Apostles and of Laodicea. But the reservation in the Carthaginian decree on the Canonical Books makes the discrepancy between that and the Apostolic Catalogue less remarkable than that between the Laodicene and Apostolic Catalogues. Cf. p. 434.
[2] Both these Catalogues are given in App. D.
[3] COSMAS of Jerusalem, a friend of Johannes Damascenus, gives the same Catalogue (Credner, *Geschichte d. N. T. Kanon*, p. 227).

'of James, and one of Peter, and one of John....The
'Apocalypse of John again some reckon among [the
'Scriptures]; but still the majority say that it is spuri-
'ous. This will be the most truthful Canon of the in-
'spired Scriptures.'

Incidental evidence from Gregory of Nazianzus,

The extant writings of Gregory do not throw much additional light on his views of the Canon. Though he admitted the Canonicity of the seven Catholic Epistles, he does not appear to have ever quoted them by name, and I have only found one or two anonymous references to the Epistle of St James[1]. But on the contrary he once makes an obvious allusion to the Apocalypse, and in another place refers to it expressly with marked respect[2]. This silence of Gregory with regard to the disputed books, though he held them all to be Canonical, at least with the exception of the Apocalypse which he does quote, explains the like silence of Gregory of Nyssa, and of his brother Basil of Cæsarea. Basil refers only once to the Epistle of St James, and once to the Apocalypse as the work of the Evangelist St John[3]. And Gregory twice refers to the Apocalypse as a writing of St John, and a part of Scripture; but makes no allusion to the disputed Catholic Epistles[4]. All these fathers however agree in using the Epistle to the Hebrews as an authoritative writing of St Paul[5].

Gregory of Nyssa, and Basil.

---

[1] Greg. Naz. *Or.* XXVI. 5 (p. 475); James ii. 20. Cf. *Or.* XL. 45.
[2] Greg. Naz. *Or.* XXIX. p. 536; Apoc. i. 8. Cf. *Or.* XL. 45; Apoc. i. 7. *Ib.* Tom. I. p. 516 C (ed. Par. 1609): πρὸς δὲ τοὺς ἐφεστῶντας ἀγγέλους, πείθομαι γὰρ ἄλλους ἄλλης προστατεῖν ἐκκλησίας ὡς Ἰωάννης διδάσκει με διὰ τῆς ἀποκαλύψεως... The Apocalypse was probably in Gregory's opinion excluded from public use in the Church. This is also the interpretation which Reuss places on his evidence (*Hist. du Canon*, 177).
[3] Basil. *Const. Monast.* 26 (Ep. St James); *adv. Eunom.* II. 14 (Apocalypse).
[4] Greg. Nyss. *Or. in Ordin. suam*, I. p. 876 (ed. Par. 1615): ἤκουσα τοῦ εὐαγγελιστοῦ Ἰωάννου ἐν ἀποκρύφοις (in mysterious words) πρὸς τοὺς τοιούτους δι' αἰνίγματος λέγοντος... Apoc. iii. 15. *Adv. Apoll.* 37 (Gallandi, VI. 570 D): τῆς γραφῆς ὁ λόγος (Apoc.).
[5] The works attributed to Cæsarius (Gallandi, VI.) are not the works

But whatever may have been the doubts as to the Canonicity of the Apocalypse which were felt in Asia Minor at the close of the fourth century, they wholly disappeared afterwards. Andrew bishop of Cæsarea at the close of the fifth century wrote a Commentary on it, prefacing his work with the statement that he need not attempt to prove the Inspiration of the book, which was attested by the authority of Papias, Irenæus, Methodius, Hippolytus, and *Gregory the Divine* (of Nazianzus[1]). Arethas, who is supposed to have been a successor of Andrew in the see of Cæsarea, composed another Commentary on the Apocalypse, and adds the name of Basil to the list of the witnesses to its Canonicity given by Andrew[2].

In speaking of the Churches of Syria I omitted to notice that of Jerusalem because it was essentially Greek. Cyril, who presided over it during the middle of the fourth century, has left a catalogue of the books of the New Testament in his Catechetical Lectures which he composed at an early age[3]. In this he includes all the books which we receive, with the exception of the Apocalypse; and at the close of his list he says: 'But let all 'the rest be excluded [from the Canon, and be accounted] 'in the second rank. And all the books which are not 'read in the Churches, neither do thou [my scholar] read 'by thyself, as thou hast heard.' Epiphanius bishop of Constantia (Salamis) in Cyprus was a contemporary and countryman of Cyril. In his larger work against heresies he has given casually a Canon of the New Testament,

Chap. ii

The Apocalypse *received by* ANDREW *of Cæsarea, and by*

ARETHAS.

iii. *The Church of Jerusalem.*

CYRIL.
315—386 A.D.

EPIPHANIUS.
† 403 A.D.

---

of the brother of Basil, but evidently belong to a later age. They contain references to St James (p. 5 D; p. 100 E), to 2 Peter (Πέτρος ὁ κλειδοῦχος τῆς βασιλείας τῶν οὐρανῶν, p. 36 A), and to the Apocalypse (p. 19 E).
[1] *Proleg. ad Comm. in Apoc.* Routh, *Rell. Sacr.* I. p. 15.
[2] Cramer, *Œcum. et Arethæ Comm. in Apoc.* p. 174, ap. Routh, *l.c.* p. 41. Yet the words ὁ ἐν ἁγίοις Βασίλειος are wanting in one Manuscript.
[3] Cyr. *Catech.* IV. 33 (al. 22); cf. App. D.

exactly coinciding with our own[1]; and though he elsewhere mentions the doubts entertained about the Apocalypse, he uses it himself without hesitation as part of 'the spiritual gift of the holy Apostle[2].'

iv. The Church of Alexandria.
ATHANA-SIUS.
† 373 A.D.

The Church of Alexandria remained true to the judgment of its greatest teacher. Athanasius in one of his Festal Epistles has given a list of the books of the New Testament,—'the fountains of salvation,'—exactly agreeing with our own Canon. In addition to these he notices other books, and among them the Teaching of the Apostles and the Shepherd, as useful for young converts, though they were not included in the Canon. The Apocryphal books—the forgeries of heretics—form a third class. But Athanasius takes no notice of any difference of opinion as to the *acknowledged* and *disputed* books: in his judgment both alike were Canonical[3].

CYRIL.
† 444 A.D.
ISIDORE.
† c. 440 A.D.

Cyril of Alexandria and Isidore of Pelusium at the beginning of the fifth century made use of the same books without any addition or reserve. Somewhat earlier Didymus published a commentary on the seven Catholic Epistles, though he states that the second Epistle of St Peter 'was accounted spurious, and not in the Canon, though it was publicly read[4];' and he quoted

DIDYMUS.
† c. 395 A.D.

---

[1] Epiph. *Hær.* LXXVI. 5. App. D.
[2] Epiph. *Hær.* LI. 35: ὁ ἅγιος Ἰωάννης διὰ τοῦ εὐαγγελίου καὶ τῶν ἐπιστολῶν καὶ τῆς Ἀποκαλύψεως ἐκ τοῦ αὐτοῦ χαρίσματος τοῦ ἁγίου μεταδέδωκε. Cf. *ib.* 3.
[3] Athanas. *Ep. Fest.* Tom. I. 767, ed. Bened. 1777. Cf. App. D. The Epistle was written in 367. There is not the least reason to believe that this Canon was designed as a protest against the Canon of Eusebius. It was indeed nothing more than the old Alexandrine Canon. The Catalogue of the Books of Scripture contained in the *Synopsis Sacræ Scripturæ* appended to the works of Athanasius is probably of much later date. It contains all the books in our New Testament. Credner (*Zur Geschichte d. K.* 129 ff.) supposes that it was written not earlier than the 10th century, and based upon the Stichometry of Nicephorus. Cf. p. 450, n. 2.
[4] Did. Alex. p. 1774 ed. Migne (cf. Lücke ad loc.): Non est igitur ignorandum præsentem epistolam esse falsatam (ὡς νοθεύεται, Euseb. *H. E.* II. 23, of the Epistle of St James), quæ licet publicetur (δημο-

the Apocalypse[1]. And in the middle of the fifth century, as has been already seen[2], Euthalius published an edition of the fourteen Epistles of St Paul and of the seven Catholic Epistles, with the help of the Manuscripts which he found in the library of Pamphilus at Cæsarea[3].

After the foundation of Constantinople the new capital assumed in some degree the central position of 'old' Rome; and Rome became more clearly and decidedly the representative of the Western Churches. The Church of Constantinople, like that of Rome in early times, was not fertile in great men. Strangers were attracted to the imperial court, but I do not remember any ecclesiastical writer of Constantinople earlier than Nicephorus and Photius in the ninth century. Chrysostom was trained at Antioch. Cassian had lived in Palestine, Egypt, and Gaul, as well as at Constantinople. Leontius, even if he were a Byzantine by birth, was trained in Palestine, and probably was a bishop of Cyprus. Cassian's works contain quotations from all

σιεύεται, Euseb. *l.c.*) non tamen in Canone est (οὐκ ἐνδιάθηκός ἐστι, Euseb. *H. E.* III. 3).

[1] *In Ps.* xxiii. 10 ἐν τῇ Ἰωάννου Ἀποκαλύψει. *In Ps.* l. 21.

[2] Cf. pp. 394 sqq. There is no evidence to shew what the judgment of Euthalius was on the Apocalypse.

[3] COSMAS INDICOPLEUSTES, an Alexandrian of the sixth century, first a merchant and afterwards a monk, has left a curious work On the World, in which among other digressions he gives some account of the Holy Scriptures (see App. D). He enumerates the four Gospels, the Acts, fourteen Epistles of St Paul, affirming that the Epistle to the Hebrews was originally written in Hebrew and translated into Greek by St Luke or Clement. His account of the Catholic Epistles is obscure and inaccurate. After answering an objection to one of his theories which might be drawn from 2 Peter iii. 12, he proceeds to say that the Church has looked upon them as of doubtful authority, that the Syrians only received three, that no commentator had written upon them. He says particularly that Irenæus only mentioned two, evidently mistaking Euseb. *H. E.* v. 8. Cosm. Indic. *de Mundo*, VII. p. 135, ap. *Anal. Pp.* Venet. 1781. In the works of DIONYSIUS, falsely called the *Areopagite*, which probably belong to the beginning of the sixth century, there is a mystical enumeration of the books of Holy Scripture which includes the Apocalypse. *De eccles. hier.* III. 4.

Chap. ii.

EUTHALIUS.

v. *The Church of Constantinople.*

CASSIAN.
† *c.* 450 A.D.

C.   G G

the Canonical books of the New Testament, except the two shorter Epistles of St John; and there is no reason to suppose that he rejected these. Leontius has left a catalogue of the Apostolic writings, 'received in the 'Church as Canonical,' identical with our own[1]. A catalogue of the books of Scripture, with the addition of the number of verses in each book (Stichometria), is appended to the Chronographia of Nicephorus[2]. This contains all the books of the New Testament, with the exception of the Apocalypse, as 'received by the Church 'and accounted Canonical;' but the Apocalypse is placed among the disputed writings, together with the Apocalypse of Peter, the Epistle of Barnabas, and the Gospel according to the Hebrews[3]. So far then the Canon of Nicephorus coincides with that of Gregory, of Cyril, and of Laodicea, and it is probable that he borrowed it as it stands from some earlier writer. Photius again, who lived a little later than Nicephorus, takes no notice of the Apocalypse, though he certainly received all the other writings of the New Testament. And at a still later time it cannot be shewn that either Œcumenius in Thessaly or Theophylact in Bulgaria looked upon the Apocalypse as Apostolic; but with this partial exception the Canon of Constantinople was complete and pure[4].

---

[1] Cf. App. D.
[2] Credner has examined the Stichometry of Nicephorus (cf. App. D) in connexion with the Festal Letter of Athanasius and the *Synopsis Sacræ Scripturæ* (*Zur Gesch. d. K.* § 3).
[3] I have followed the text of Credner, *a. a. O.* p. 121.
[4] Two later writers of the Greek Church deserve mention as witnessing to the current belief of their times. NICEPHORUS CALLISTI a monk of Constantinople, who wrote an Ecclesiastical History about 1325 A.D., enumerates all the books of the New Testament as we receive them. 'Seven Catholic Epistles,' he says, 'the Church has received of old time '(ἄνωθεν), and reckons them most 'certainly (ὡς μάλιστα) among the 'books of the New Testament...The 'Apocalypse we know to have been 'handed down to the Church. The 'books besides these are spurious 'and falsely named' (*H. E.* II. 45).

In the Western Churches the doubts as to the Epistle to the Hebrews continued to reappear for some time. Isidore of Seville in reviewing the books of the New Testament says that the authorship of the Epistle was considered 'doubtful by very many (*plerisque*) Latin 'Christians on account of the difference of style¹.' But this doubt was rather felt than declared; and its existence is shewn by the absence of quotations from the Epistle, rather than by any open attacks upon its authority. It is not quoted I believe by Optatus of Milevis (Mileum) in Africa, by Phœbadius or Vincent of Lerins in Gaul, nor by Zeno of Verona². Hilary of Rome and Pelagius wrote Commentaries on thirteen Epistles of St Paul; but though they did not comment on the Epistle to the Hebrews, both speak of it as a work of the Apostle³. But the doubt as to the Epistle to the Hebrews was the only one which remained⁴, and the influence of Jerome and Augustine did much to remove it.

It was indeed impossible that the revised Latin Version of Jerome should fail to mould insensibly the

Marginal notes:
Chap. ii. vi. *The Churches of the West. Doubts as to the Epistle to the Hebrews.* † 636 A.D.
c. 370 A.D.
† *c.* 390 A.D. . 425 A.D.
The testimony of JEROME.

LEO ALLATIUS († 1669), keeper of the Vatican Library in the time of Alexander VII., says that 'in his 'time the Catholic Epistles and Apo-'calypse were received as true and 'genuine Scripture, and publicly 'read throughout all Greece like the 'other Scriptures.' Fabr. *Bibl. Gr.* v. App. p. 38.
¹ Isid. *Proem.* §§ 85—109 (v. 155 sqq. ed. Migne). Cf. App. D.
² Pacian has been quoted as omitting all mention of the Epistle, but in fact he quotes it as St Paul's. Pac. *Ep.* III. 13: Apostolus dicit... et iterum...Hebr. x. 1.
³ Pelag. *Comm. in Rom.* i. 17 (Hieron. *Opp.* XI. 649, ed. Migne): Sicut et ipse ad Hebræos perhibens dicit... Hilar. *Comm. in* 2 *Tim.* i.: Nam simili modo et in epistola ad Hebræos scriptum est. Ambr. *Opp.* v. p. 411 (ed. 1567).
⁴ At the Synod at Toledo (671 A.D.) a special decree was made affirming the authority of the Apocalypse: Apocalypsin librum multorum conciliorum auctoritas et synodica sanctorum præsulum Romanorum decreta Johannis evangelistæ esse scribunt, et inter divinos libros recipiendum constituerunt: et quia plurimi sunt qui ejus auctoritatem non recipiant, eumque in ecclesia Dei prædicare contemnant; si quis eum deinceps aut non receperit, aut a Pascha usque ad Pentecosten missarum tempore in ecclesia non prædicaverit, excommunicationis sententiam habebit (*Concil. Tol.* IV. 17). These doubts are not I believe expressed by any Latin father.

judgment of the Western Churches. Jerome, who was well read in earlier fathers, was familiar with the doubts which had been raised as to some of the books of the New Testament, but in his letter to Paulinus, as well as in many other places, he clearly expresses his own conviction of the Canonicity of them all[1]. With regard to the Epistle to the Hebrews and the Apocalypse, he professed 'to be influenced not so much by the custom of 'his own time, as by the authority of the ancients, and 'so he received them both[2].' The Epistles of James and Jude, he says, gained authority in the course of time, having been at first disputed[3]; and he explains

---

[1] Cf. App. D. In his treatise *On Hebrew Names* Jerome enumerates all the books of the New Testament in order, except the second Epistle of St John, which contains no name. The editions mark the names from the *third* Epistle (Diotrephes, Demetrius, Gaius) as belonging to the *second*. Cf. p. 384, n. 1. At the end, after noticing the Apocalypse, Jerome explains some names in the *Epistle to Barnabas*. This book was written about 390 A.D. The treatise *On Illustrious Men* was written in 392 A.D.

[2] Hieron. *Ep. ad Dard.* CXXIX. 3 (414 A.D.): Illud nostris dicendum est hanc epistolam quae inscribitur *ad Hebraeos* non solum ab ecclesiis orientis sed ab omnibus retro ecclesiasticis Graeci sermonis scriptoribus quasi Pauli Apostoli suscipi, licet plerique eam vel Barnabae vel Clementis arbitrentur; et nihil interesse cujus sit, cum ecclesiastici viri sit et quotidie ecclesiarum lectione celebretur. Quod si eam Latinorum consuetudo non recepit inter scripturas Canonicas, nec Graecorum quidem ecclesiae Apocalypsin Joannis eadem libertate suscipiunt; et tamen nos utramque suscipimus, nequaquam hujus temporis consuetudinem sed veterum scriptorum auctoritatem sequentes, qui plerumque utriusque abutuntur testimoniis, non ut interdum de apocryphis facere solent quippe qui et gentilium litterarum raro utantur exemplis, sed quasi Canonicis et ecclesiasticis. This very clear and important passage shews that when Jerome speaks of the 'Epistle to the Hebrews as not reck-'oned among St Paul's' in his letter to Paulinus (394 A.D.), we must suppose that the doubt applies to the authorship and not to the Canonicity of the writing. The distinct and decisive reference to ancient and constant (*ab*utuntur) testimony for the two disputed books deserves careful attention. Cf. *Comm. in Eph. ad init.*

[3] *De Virr. Ill.* 2: Jacobus qui appellatur frater Domini...unam tantum scripsit epistolam, quae de septem Catholicis est, quae et ipsa ab alio quodam sub nomine ejus edita asseritur, licet paulatim tempore procedente obtinuerit auctoritatem.

De Virr. Ill. 4: Judas frater Jacobi parvam quae de septem Catholicis est epistolam reliquit. Et quia de libro Enoch qui Apocryphus est in ea assumit testimonium, a plerisque rejicitur, tamen auctoritatem vetustate jam et usu meruit et inter sanctas scripturas computatur.

the different styles of the first and second Epistles of St Peter by the supposition that the Apostle was forced to employ different 'interpreters' in writing them[1]. The first Epistle of St John was universally received; but the two others, he adds, evidently quoting some earlier writer, are claimed for John the presbyter[2]. Besides the Canonical writings of the New Testament Jerome notices many other ecclesiastical and Apocryphal books, but he never attributes to them Canonical authority[3].

Chap. ii.

The testimony of Jerome may be considered as the testimony of the Roman Church; for not only was he educated at Rome, but his labours on the text of Scripture were undertaken at the request of Damasus bishop of Rome; and later popes republished the Canon which he recognised. Both Innocent[4] and Gelasius[5] pronounced all the books of the New Testament which we now receive, and these only, to be Canonical. And the judg-

and of the Roman Church.

405 A.D.
492—496 A.D.

---

[1] Hieron. *Quæst. ad Hedib.* II. (I. p. 1002, ed. Migne): Habebat ergo [Paulus] Titum interpretem (2 Cor. ii. 12, 13); sicut et beatus Petrus Marcum, cujus evangelium Petro narrante et illo scribente compositum est. Denique et duæ epistolæ quæ feruntur Petri stylo inter se et charactere discrepant structuraque verborum. Ex quo intelligimus diversis eum usum interpretibus. Cf. *de Virr. Ill.* 1: Scripsit [Petrus] duas Epistolas quæ Catholicæ nominantur; quarum secunda a plerisque ejus esse negatur propter styli cum priore dissonantiam. Sed et evangelium juxta Marcum, qui auditor ejus et interpres fuit, hujus dicitur. Libri autem e quibus unus Actorum ejus inscribitur, alius Evangelii, tertius Prædicationis, quartus Apocalypseos, quintus Judicii [*i.e.* the *Shepherd* of Hermas], inter apocryphas scripturas repudiantur.

[2] Scripsit [Johannes] unam epistolam...quæ ab universis ecclesiasticis et eruditis viris probatur. Reliquæ autem duæ...Johannis presbyteri asseruntur. It will be observed that Jerome appeals simply to usage and to the opinion of competent scholars, and not to any formal decision upon the Canon.

[3] Cf. App. B.

[4] Innoc. *ad Exsuperium Tolos.* Cf. App. D. The authenticity of this decretal however is very questionable.

[5] Credner (*Zur Gesch. de K.* § iv.) has examined at great length the triple recension of the famous decretal *On Ecclesiastical Books*. His conclusion briefly is that (1) In its original form it was drawn up in the time of Gelasius, c. 500 A.D. (2) It was then enlarged in Spain, c. 500—700 A.D. (3) Next published as a decretal of Hormisdas (Pope 514—523 A.D.) in Spain, with additions. (4) And lastly variously altered in later times. Credner, *a. a. O.* s. 153. Cf. App. D.

ment which was accepted at Rome was current throughout Italy. Ambrose at Milan, Rufinus at Aquileia[1], and (with some reserve) Philastrius at Brescia[2], confirm the same Canon[3].

The influence of Augustine upon the Western Church was hardly inferior to that of Jerome; and both combined to support the received Canon of the New Testament[4]. Yet even in respect to this their characteristic differences appear. Jerome accepted the tacit judgment of the Church as a whole, and before that laid aside his doubts. Augustine, while receiving as Scripture the same Apostolic writings as Jerome, admitted that the partial rejection of a book detracts from its authority[5]. He thus extended to others a certain freedom of judgment, and even exercised it himself. It is very pro-

---

[1] Ruf. *de Symb. Apost.* § 36. Cf. App. D.

[2] Philastr. *Hær.* LX., LXXXVIII., LXXXIX. Cf. App. D. It is remarkable that while in the former passage he reckons the rejection of the Apocalypse as a heresy, he does not reckon it among the books ordered to be read in Church in § LXXXVIII. He also omits the Epistle to the Hebrews in that section, and in the next section he mentions the variety of custom as to its use.

[3] LUCIFER of Cagliari († 370 A.D.) in Sardinia quotes most of the books of the New Testament, including the Epistle to the Hebrews: Paulus dicit ad Hebræos...Hebr. iii. 5 sqq. (Lucif. *de non Conv. c. Hær.* p. 782 B, ed. Migne). To the testimony of Lucifer may be added that of FAUSTINUS one of his followers, who frequently quotes the Epistle to the Hebrews as St Paul's: Paulus Apostolus...ait in Epistola sua...Hebr. i. 13 (*de Trin.* II. 13. Cf. *ib.* IV. 2; *Lit. Prec. ad Impp.* 27).

CASSIODORUS (or Cassiodorius, b. 468—†c. 560 A.D.), chief minister of Theodoric, in his treatise *De Institutione Divinarum Litterarum* gives three Catalogues of the Holy Scriptures: (1) according to Jerome, (2) according to Augustine, (3) according to the 'ancient translation.' In the two former the Canon of the New Testament of course agrees with our own. In the last he omits the two shorter Epistles of St John, but the evidence of Cod. D has been brought forward to shew that they were included in the *Vetus Latina.* Cf. p. 258, and App. D.

[4] Augustine has given a list of the books of the New Testament exactly agreeing with our present Canon: *de Doctr. Christ.* II. 12, 13. Cf. App. D.

[5] Aug. *l. c.*: Tenebit igitur hunc modum in Scripturis Canonicis, ut eas quæ ab omnibus accipiuntur Ecclesiis Catholicis præponat eis quas quædam non accipiunt: in eis vero quæ non accipiuntur ab omnibus præponat eas quas plures gravioresque accipiunt eis quas pauciores minorisque auctoritatis ecclesiæ tenent.

bable that he did not regard the Epistle to the Hebrews as St Paul's; and at least in his later works he sedulously avoided calling it by the Apostle's name[1]. But while he hesitated as to the authorship of the Epistle, he had no scruples about its Canonicity. And he uses all the other books of the New Testament without reserve, alluding only once, as far as I know, to the doubts about the Apocalypse[2].

The Canon of the New Testament which was supported by the learning of Jerome and the independent judgment of Augustine soon gained universal acceptance wherever Latin was spoken. It was received in Gaul and Spain, and even in Britain and Ireland. Eucherius of Lyons in the fifth century, Isidore of Seville at the close of the sixth century[3], Bede at Wearmouth in the seventh century, and Sedulius in Ireland in the eighth or ninth century, witness to its reception throughout the West. And with the exceptions already noticed, all the evidence which can be gathered from other writers, —from Prudentius in Spain, and from Hilary, Sulpicius, Prosper, Salvian, and Gennadius in Gaul,—confirms their testimony.

From this time the Canon of the New Testament in the West was no longer a problem, but a tradition. If old doubts were mentioned, it was rather as a display of erudition than as an effort of criticism[4].

Chap. ii.

This Canon most widely spread throughout the West,

and undisputed to the era of the Reformation.

---

[1] This is well shewn by Lardner, ch. CXVII. 17. 4. The quotations in the *Opus imperfectum c. Julianum* (written at the close of Augustine's life) are conclusive. Julian himself quotes the Epistle as the work of 'the Apostle' (Aug. *c. Jul.* III. 40; V. 2. 23). Augustine in reply uses the following circumlocutions: quod vidit qui scribens ad Hebræos dixit (I. 48; IV. 104); Sancta scriptura (II. 179); sicut scriptum est (III. 38; IV. 76); cum legas ad Hebræos (III. 151); illius sacræ auctor Epistolæ (VI. 22). Compare (one of his latest works) *Enchiridion*, c. 8, In Epistola ad Hebræos, qua teste usi sunt illustres catholicæ regulæ defensores...

[2] *Serm.* CCXCIX.: Et si forte tu qui ista [Pelagii] sapis hanc Scripturam (Apoc. xi. 3—·12) non accepisti; aut si accipis contemnis...

[3] Cf. App. D.

[4] References are given by Hody,

Chap. ii
The judgment of ALFRIC. † 1006 A.D.

Three typical examples of the mediæval treatment of the New Testament Canon will suffice to shew what was the amount of interest which was felt in it and how the interest was satisfied. The first example is taken from a short Anglo-Saxon treatise on the New Testament written by Alfric, Abbot of Cerne (989 A.D.), and afterwards, as it is supposed, Archbishop of Canterbury[1]. 'There are,' he says[2], '4. books written concerning Christ 'nimselfe, one of them wrote *Mathew*, that followed our 'Sauiour, and was one of his disciples, while heere hee 'liued, and saw his miracles, and after his passion wrote 'thē, such as came to his mind in this book, and in yᵉ 'Hebrew tongue, for their sakes who beleeued on God, 'among yᵉ Iewes. And he is the first Euangelist in this 'volume. *Marke* the Gospeller, who followed *Peter* for 'instruction, and was his own son begotten in the Lord 'by his word, he wrote the second booke from the mouth 'of *Peter*, concerning such things as he learned of his 'doctrine in yᵉ city of *Rome:* as he was entreated by the 'faithfull there beleeuing in God through *Peters* preach-'ing. *Luke* the Euangelist wrote the third booke; who 'from his childhood followed the Apostles and after 'accompanied *Paul* in his travell and learned of him 'the doctrine of the Gospell in sincerity of life : and this 'booke of Christ compiled in *Achæa* and in the Greeke 'tongue, according as he had learned by yᵉ instruction 'of *Paul* and the other Apostles. *Iohn* the Apostle 'began in *Asia*, entreated by the Bishops there, to write 'and yᵗ in Greeke the fourth book, concerning Christ's

---

Credner, and Reuss, *Gesch. d. Heil. Schr.* §§ 328 ff. See also *Bible in the Church*, chapters VIII. IX.

[1] Wright's *Biographia Britannica Literaria*, I. pp. 480 ff.

[2] The translation is that given by W. L'Isle, *A Saxon Treatise concerning the Old and New Testament, written about the time of King Edgar*...London, 1623—republished in 1638 under the title *Divers Ancient Monuments in the Saxon Tongue*...—pp. 24 ff.

'diuinity: and of the deepe mysteries that were reuealed
'vnto him, when he leaned on his louely brest wherin
'was hid the treasure of heauen. These be the 4 waters
'of one welspring, which run from paradise far and wide
'ouer ye people of God. And these 4. Euangelists were
'foresignified by the vision of *Ezechiel. Mathew* in mans
'shape, *Marke* in a lions, *Luke* in a calfs, and Iohn in an
'eagles, for ye mysteries by them signified...

'*Peter* the Apostle wrote two Epistles, but larger
'than are read at Masse, which auaile much to the esta-
'blishing of Faith, and are reckoned in Canon of the
'Bible. So *Iames* the Iust wrote one Epistle of great
'instruction for all men, who obserue any Christianity
'in their life. And *Iohn* ye Euangelist to the honor
'of God compiled three Epistles, which are three
'bookes full of loue in teaching the people. *Iudas* the
'Apostle wrote also an Epistle, not the reprobate
'*Iudas*, who betrayed Iesus; but holy *Iudas* that euer
'followed him. And heere are now 7. bookes of this
'ranke.

'The Apostle *Paul* wrote many Epistles : for Christ
'set him to be a teacher of all nations, and in true since-
'rity he set downe the course of life, which the faithfull
'ought to hold, who betake themselues and their life
'vnto God: fifteene Epistles wrote this one Apostle,
'to the nations by him conuerted vnto the faith: which
'are large books in the Bible, and make much for our
'amendment, if we follow his doctrine, that was teacher
'of the Gentiles. He wrote to the Romans one, to the
'Corinthians two, and one to the Galathians, and one to
'the Ephesians, and one to the Philippians; two to the
'Thessalonians, and one to the Colossians, and one to
'the Hebreues: two to his owne disciple *Timotheus*, and
'one to *Titus*, and one to *Philemon*, and one to the

458 THE AGE OF COUNCILS. [PART

Chap. ii.

'*Laodiceans:* fifteene in all, [sounding] as loud as thun-
'der to [the eares of] faithfull people...
 '*Luke* ye Euangelist, who was a Physitian while he
'liued compiled two books for the health of our soules.
'One of them is the Gospell of Christ, the other is called
'*Actus Apostolorum;* that is in English : the *Acts of*
'*Apostles*, [shewing] what they did while they were
'together, and how afterward they trauelled into farre
'countries as Iesus had commanded them in his holy
'Gospell, that they by their preaching should teach and
'conuert all nations to the faith......
 '*Iohn* liued here longest of them (the Apostles) all,
'and he wrote in his banishment the booke called
'*Apocalypse*, that is, the *Reuelatiō*, which Christ mani-
'fested vnto him by vision in spirit, cōcerning ovr
'Sauiour himselfe and his Church : as also of doomes-
'day and the deuillish Antichrist ; and of the resurrection
'to euerlasting life : And this is the last booke of the
'Bible...
 'All teachers who take not their doctrine and ex-
'amples out of those holy bookes are like those of whom
'Christ himselfe thus said : *Cæcus si cæco ducatum præ-*
'*stet, ambo in foueam cadent :*...but such teachers, as take
'their examples and doctrine from hence, whether it be
'out of the old Testament or the new, are such as Christ
'himselfe againe spake of in these words : *Omnis scriba*
'*doctus in regno cælorum similis est homini patrifamilias,*
'*qui profert de thesauro suo nova et vetera......*'

The Apocry-phal Epistle to the Laodi-cenes.

The history of the Epistle to the Laodicenes[1] which is reckoned by Alfric without hesitation among the Epistles of St Paul forms one of the most interesting episodes in the literary history of the Bible. The earliest

---

[1] The text of the Epistle is given from English Manuscripts in App. E.

III.] THE EPISTLE TO THE LAODICENES. 459

traces of the existence of the present Epistle are found in the sixth century, for there is not the slightest reason to connect the existing Latin compilation which from that date bears the name with the Greek Epistle to the Laodicenes which was current in the second century[1]. In the sixth century the compilation had a wide currency. It is found in the *Speculum* published by Mai, and likewise in the Manuscript of the Vulgate at La Cava, which contain also the interpolated testimony in the Epistle of St John. Towards the middle of the same century it was introduced into a Manuscript of the Latin New Testament which was corrected by the hand of Victor of Capua and is still preserved at Fulda. From this time it occurs very frequently in Western Manuscripts of the Bible, as in the great Gothic Bible of Toledo (8th cent.), in the Book of Armagh[2] (written A.D. 807), in the so-called Charlemagne's Bible of the British Museum (9th cent.), and in many other magnificent copies, as for example the great Bible of the King's Library[3], which seem to have been designed for church use.

One important testimony contributed in all probability very greatly to the popular estimation of the book. Gregory the Great at the close of the sixth century dis-

[1] *Canon Murat.* App. C. It may however be the one which Jerome speaks of in *Catal.* 5: Legunt quidam et ad Laodicenses sed ab omnibus exploditur. The only Greek reference which can be fairly applied to this Latin Epistle is in the Acts of the second Council of Nicæa (787 A.D.), when the circulation of the Epistle of the Western Churches was too general to escape observation even among the Greeks. *Concil.* ii. *Nic. Act.* VI. *Tom.* v.; Mansi, XIII. 293 (Labbé, VII. 475): πρέπον οὖν ἐστι παντὶ χριστιανῷ παρεγγράπτων βίβλων ἀ- κρόασιν ποιουμένῳ ταύτης διαπτύειν καὶ μηδ' ὅλως προσδέχεσθαι. καὶ γὰρ τοῦ θείου ἀποστόλου πρὸς Λαοδικεῖς φέρεται πλαστὴ ἐπιστολὴ ἔν τισι βίβλοις τοῦ ἀποστόλου ἐγκειμένη, ἣν οἱ πατέρες ἡμῶν ἀπεδοκίμασαν ὡς αὐτοῦ ἀλλοτρίαν· καὶ τὸ κατὰ Θωμᾶν Μανιχαῖοι παρεισήγαγον εὐαγγέλιον ὅπερ ἡ καθολικὴ ἐκκλησία ὡς ἀλλότριον εὐσεβῶς ἀποστρέφεται.

[2] But with the note *Sed Hirunumus eam negat esse Pauli.* Betham, *Irish Antiq. Researches,* II. 263.

[3] Brit. Mus. King's I E vii. viii.

tinctly assigned the Epistle to the Apostle Paul, though he admitted its uncanonicity. 'Though he (St Paul) 'wrote,' he says, 'fifteen Epistles, yet the holy Church 'does not hold more than fourteen[1].' As an almost necessary consequence the positive part of his statement was more effectual than the negative limitation of it. If St Paul wrote the letter, it could not fail to be prized by faithful Christians. Another circumstance which favoured the reception of the letter was the supposed reference to it in the Epistle to the Colossians.

To an uncritical age the mere existence of a letter which bore the name of one known to have been sanctioned by Apostolic authority was held to be an adequate proof of its own claims to respect. Haymo bishop of Halberstadt[2] gives expression to this simplicity of faith in a very modest form: 'The Apostle enjoins that 'the Epistle to the Laodicenes (*i.e.* the Latin cento) 'be read to the Colossians, because, though it is very 'short and not reckoned in the Canon, it still has some 'use.' A few generations afterwards John of Salisbury puts forward the argument based upon the assumed reference in the most distinct shape. 'Although the 'Epistle is rejected by all, as Jerome says, yet it was 'written by the Apostle. Nor is this opinion based on 'the conjecture of others, but confirmed by the testi-

---

[1] Gregor. Magn. *Moral.* xxxv. 20, 38 (al. 15, 25), *in Job*, XLII. 16. The reason which Gregory gives for the rejection of the Epistle from the Canon is most instructive and characteristic. Et recte vita sanctæ Ecclesiæ multiplicata per decem et quatuor computatur, quia utrumque Testamentum custodiens et tam secundum legis decalogum quam secundum quatuor Evangelii libros vivens usque ad perfectionis culmen extenditur. Unde et Paulus Apostolus quamvis epistolas quindecim scripserit sancta tamen Ecclesia non amplius quam quatuordecim tenet ut ex ipso Epistolarum numero ostenderet quod doctor egregius legis et evangelii secreta rimatus esset. Why this special Epistle was rejected to render the mystical lesson complete does not appear.

[2] *Comm. in Coloss.* iv.

'mony of the Apostle himself, for he mentions it in his 'Epistle to the Colossians...[1].'

Thus it was that the Apocryphal Epistle passed into the early vernacular translations of the New Testament. It is said that fourteen editions of one or more German versions were printed before Luther's time; and it occurs in the first Bohemian Bible (1488)[2]. It is found also in an Albigensian Version at Lyons, where it occupies its usual place after the Epistle to the Colossians[3]. It was not included by Wycliffe in his Bible, but it is found added to it in some Manuscripts and in two different renderings[4]. One of these may be given, for though the Epistle contains nothing in itself remarkable, the position which it occupies in the history of the Mediæval Canon invests it with a peculiar interest[5].

'*Here bigynneth the epistle to the Laodicenses, which 'is not in the Canon.*

'Poul apostle, not of men, ne by man, but bi Ihesu 'Crist, to the britheren that ben at Laodice, grace to 'ʒou, and pees of God the fadir, and of the Lord Ihesu 'Crist. I do thankyngis to my God bi al my preier, 'that ʒe be dwelling and lastyng in him, abiding the 'biheest in the day of doom. For neithir the veyn spek-'yng of summe vnwise men hath lettide ʒou, the whiche 'wolden turne ʒou fro the treuthe of the gospel, that is 'prechid of me. And now hem that ben of me to the 'profiʒt of truthe of the gospel, God schal make dis-

---

[1] Johan. Sarisb. *Ep.* 143 (ed. Migne).
[2] Anger, *Der Laodicinerbrief*, 152. It is not however found in an earlier edition of the New Testament (1475).
[3] *Revue de Théologie*, Strasb. v. 335.
[4] See p. 462, note.
[5] The text given is from Forshall and Madden, who likewise print the second version, which is also given by Lewis, and after him by Anger *l.c.* This text is found substantially in eight other copies collated by Forshall and Madden and in the imperfect copy taken by Anger from a Dresden Manuscript.

'seruying, and doyng benygnyte of werkis, and helthe 'of euerlasting lijf. And now my boondis ben open, 'which Y suffre in Crist Ihesu, in whiche Y glade and 'ioie. And that is to me euerlastyng helthe, that this 'same thing be doon by ȝoure preirs, and mynystryng 'of the Holi Goost, either by lijf, either bi deeth. For-'sothe to me it is lijf to lyue in Crist, and to die ioie. 'And his mercy schal do in ȝou the same thing, that 'ȝe mown haue the same loue, and that ȝe be of oo will. 'Therfore, ȝe weel biloued britheren, holde ȝe, and do ȝe 'in the dreede of God, as ȝe han herde the presence of 'me; and lijf schal be to ȝou withouten eende. Sotheli 'it is God that worchith in ȝou. And, my weel biloued 'britheren, do ȝe without eny withdrawyng what euer 'things ȝe don. Ioie ȝe in Crist, and eschewe ȝe men 'defoulid in lucre, either foul wynnyng. Be alle ȝoure 'askyngis open anentis God, and be ye stidefast in the 'witt of Crist. And do ȝe tho thingis that ben hool, 'and trewe, and chaast, and iust, and able to be loued; 'and kepe ȝe in herte tho thingis that ȝe haue herd and 'take; and pees schal be to ȝou. Alle holi men greten 'ȝou weel. The grace of oure Lord Ihesu Crist be with 'ȝoure spirit. And do ȝe that pistil of Colocensis to be red 'to ȝou.

'*Here eendith the pistil to Laodicensis*[1].'

Hugo of St Victor.

The progress of thought which brought forth so many noble results in the twelfth century added nothing to the historic appreciation of the Canon of the Bible.

---

[1] Forshall and Madden, IV. pp. 438, 439. 'The Epistle to the Lao-'diceans was excluded as spurious 'both by Wycliffe and Purvey. 'Subsequently however it was trans-'lated together with its argument 'and is found in several Manuscripts 'of the later version, none of which 'appears to have been written early 'in the fifteenth century. Another 'but nearly coeval version of the 'same Epistle occurs in a single 'copy' (*Id.* I. p. xxxii.).

Nay rather the love of symmetry and completeness which prevailed threatened to decide its contents by general principles of arrangement, yet in such a manner as to leave the line of separation between the Holy Scriptures and other books wavering and undefined. Hugo of St Victor may be taken as one of the greatest representatives of his age, and in him this tendency finds a clear expression. 'All divine Scripture,' he says, 'is contained in the two Testaments, that is to say the 'Old and the New. Both Testaments are divided into 'three separate classes [of books]. The Old Testa-'ment contains the Law, the Prophets, the Hagiographa. 'The New Testament the Gospel, the Apostles, the 'Fathers...In the New Testament there are in the First 'Class the Four Gospels. In the Second Class there are 'also four Books, the Acts, the fourteen Epistles of 'Paul combined in one volume, the Canonical [*i.e.* Ca-'tholic] Epistles, the Apocalypse. In the Third Class 'the Decretals hold the first place;...then the writings of 'the holy Fathers.. which are numberless. These writ-'ings of the Fathers are not however reckoned in the 'text of the Divine Scriptures, since in the Old Testa-'ment, as we have said, there are some books which are 'not included in the Canon and yet are read, as the 'Wisdom of Solomon and the like...In these classes how-'ever the harmony of both Testaments is most clearly 'seen. Because as the Law is followed by the Prophets 'and the Prophets by the Hagiographa, so the Gospel 'is followed by the Apostles and the Apostles by the 'Doctors. And it is a result of the marvellous method 'of the divine dispensation, that while the full and per-'fect truth is found in the several Scriptures separately, 'no one of them is superfluous[1].'

Chap. ii.

c. 1097—1141 A.D.

[1] Hugo de S. Vict. *de Scriptura*, 6. The original text is given in App. D.

One more testimony will bring our notice of the Mediæval period to a close. This is taken from a letter of John of Salisbury, the secretary and partisan of Becket, whose devotion to his master in later times when he was raised to the see of Chartres led him to describe himself as bishop 'by the divine favour and the merits 'of St Thomas[1].' The letter was written during his exile in France for Becket's cause, and is addressed to Henry I. Count of Champagne. Henry, who himself took a very active part in the politics of his time, had sent a series of questions to John of Salisbury which throw a strange light upon the studies of the royal statesman. He wished to know what Jerome meant by the 'table of the Sun which was said to have been seen 'by Apollonius,' and what were 'centos from Virgil and 'Homer,' and in the first place of all what John believed to be the number of the books of the Old and New Testaments, and whom he held to be their authors. In reply to this John first refers to the treatise of Cassiodorus upon the subject and then continues in most remarkable words : 'But because my own belief on this 'subject is questioned, I consider that it is not of much 'importance either to me or to others what opinion be 'held. For whether we hold this opinion or that, it 'brings no damage to our salvation. But to indulge in 'a fierce controversy on a subject which is either indif-'ferent in its result or of little moment is as bad as a 'sharp discussion about *goats' wool* between friends. 'Moreover I consider that he rather assails the faith who 'affirms too confidently that which is not certain, than 'one who abstains from a rash decision and leaves in 'uncertainty a subject on which he observes the Fathers

---

[1] Wright, *Biographia Britannica*, II. 235.

'disagree and which he is wholly unable to investigate.
'Nevertheless our opinion can and ought to be more
'inclined to the side which is supported by all or by the
'greater number or the most famous and distinguished
'men...Therefore I follow Jerome...who reckons twenty-
'two books of the Old Testament divided into three
'classes...As for the *Shepherd* [which he mentions] I do
'not know whether it still exists anywhere; but there
'can be no doubt about the reference because Jerome
'and Beda say that they saw and read it. To these are
'added eight volumes of the New Testament, the four
'Gospels, *fifteen* Epistles of Paul embraced in one vo-
'lume, though it is a common and almost universal opi-
'nion that there are only fourteen, ten to churches and
'four to persons, if we must reckon the Epistle to the
'Hebrews among the Epistles of Paul, as Jerome ap-
'pears to do...The fifteenth is that which is written to
'the Church of the Laodicenes, and though, as Jerome
'says, it is rejected by all, yet it was written by the
'Apostle...The seven Canonical Epistles in one volume
'come next; then the Acts in another, and last the
'Apocalypse. And that this is the number of the books
'which are admitted into the Canon of the Holy Scrip-
'tures is a constant and undoubted tradition in the
'Church, which enjoy such authority with all that
'they leave no room for gainsaying or doubt in sound
'minds, because they are written by the finger of God....
'Opinions vary as to the authors, though in the Church
'the opinion has prevailed that they were written by
'those whose names they bear...But why should we
'be anxious, most illustrious Lord, to discuss various
'opinions on the subject, since we are agreed that the
'Holy Spirit is the one author of all Holy Scriptures?
'...It is as if when you were certain of the writer,

Chap. ii.

Chap. ii.

'a question was raised about the pen with which the 'book was written[1].'

Thus the strange freedom of the first words of the mediæval scholar falls back into the devout confession of simple faith. Criticism is silent, but in the language of natural instinct there is an antagonism of thought which is prophetic of future conflict. A desire for liberty has to be reconciled with a desire for trustful repose: the craving for individual conviction with the pious belief in a divine order of history. To assert, to compare, to harmonize these principles was the work of the Reformation, and that in the discussions on the formation and authority of the Bible no less than in the examination of the central doctrines of the Christian belief.

[1] Johan. Sarisb. *Ep.* 143 (ed. Migne). The original text is given in App. D. It may be added that Bp. Pecock affirms very distinctly Jerome's judgment in favour of the exclusive authority of the Hebrew Canon of the Old Testament, and explains how the Apocryphal books came to be added to them. "In the bigynnyng of the chirche, soone after Cristis passioun, writingis dressing men into holynes weren scant...and therfore for deuociown and avidite whiche men in tho daies hadden into goostli techingis thei wroten into her Biblis the book of Philo which is clepid Sapience, and the book of Iesus the sone of Sirak which is clepid Ecclesiastik, and othere mo, for great deinte which Cristen men hadden of tho bokis in tyme of so greet scarsenes of deuoute bokis; not with stonding that thei wisten these seid bokis not be of holi Scripture, as Ierom and othere mo openly witnessen that tho bokis ben not of Holi Scripture. And this oolde deuocioun forto plante the seid bokis into Biblis, whanne euere Biblis weren in writing ceesid not into al tyme after. And ȝit herbi is not the auctorite of tho bookis reised hiȝher then it was bifore; and namelich it cannot be reised therbi so hiȝe, that it be putt bifore gretter evydencis than is the nakid seiyng of hem." (*Repressor*, II. 17, p. 251. Comp. pp. 126, 250.)

CHAPTER III.

THE NEW TESTAMENT IN THE SIXTEENTH CENTURY.

Dixit veritatem, pertulit iniquitatem, allaturus est æquitatem.
AUGUSTINUS.

THE sixteenth century places us again face to face with the combined powers of the East and West[1]. For a time each had gone on fulfilling its own work, but the fall of Constantinople brought them once more into contact. It was not only that 'Greece had arisen from 'the dead with the New Testament in her hand,' but the East had risen with a Bible which was again felt to be a record of real facts, able to quicken faith amidst the conflicts of a world struggling towards a new life. We have already seen generally the part which Palestine and Greece and Rome had to fulfil in the history of the Canon. A work was still reserved for the German races, and when the time came for its accomplishment men were found to do it. Whatever may be thought of some of Luther's special judgments, however hasty and self-willed and imperious they may be, it is impossible to read his comments on Holy Scripture without feeling that he realises its actual historic worth and consequent spiritual meaning in a way which was unknown before. For him the words of Apostles and Prophets are 'living words,'

Chap. iii.
The work of the German races for the Bible.

---

[1] I have ventured to transcribe in this chapter much that is given in the *Bible in the Church*, chap. x.

Chap. iii.

The elements combined in the discussion on the Bible in the 16th century.

An antagonism of principles.

direct and immediate utterances of the Holy Spirit, penetrating to the inmost souls of men, and not mere premisses for arguments or proofs.

This intense sense of the personal character of Holy Scripture, so to speak, springing out of the recognition of its primary historical origin, which found a bold and at times an exaggerated expression in Luther, was more or less characteristic of the whole period. On all sides there was a tendency in the sixteenth century, even when it was repressed, to appeal to history and reason. The mere authority of usage, which at earlier times had been denied only by scholars, was then questioned by many in all classes. The study of Greek had made criticism possible, and laid open the true approach to the investigation of the growth of the Church. But still the real force of historical evidence was as yet imperfectly understood. The materials for testing and tracing to its source a current tradition were still scattered or unknown. And even those who felt most deeply that the Books of the Bible had their origin in human life, among men of like passions with themselves, were yet far removed from a simple and absolute trust in their historical transmission and confirmation by the body to which they were delivered. On the one hand a supposed intuitive perception of the Divine authority of Scripture, immediate and final, was assumed to exist in the individual and to supersede the judgment of the Christian society. On the other an ecclesiastical usage was invested, as it were, with a creative power, by which books which had been deliberately set aside in a second rank were raised to a new dignity as infallible sources of doctrine.

As doctrinal controversy grew wider and keener, the question of the Canon was debated with a vehemence before unknown. To concede to the Church in every age the prerogative of extending by its own power the range of the authoritative sources and tests of doctrine was (as it appeared) to sacrifice the historical basis of a faith once delivered to men. And at the same time the denial of the existence of an absolute living criterion of truth seemed to make it necessary to transfer to the Bible in its collected form every attribute of that infallibility which before had been supposed to reside in the Church or in its earthly head. The collection of Holy Scripture was first narrowed to the strict limits fixed by ancient criticism, at least in the Old Testament, and then step by step it was taken out of the field of historical inquiry. A movement which began by the assertion of the value of historical evidence ended in the suppression of all historical criticism by the later Lutheran and Genevan schools.

The debate guided by feeling more than by criticism.

It is not part of our subject to trace the effects for good and for evil which followed from the general prevalence of this later theory of the Bible in Protestant Churches up to our own time. However repugnant it may be to the wider views of ecclesiastical history which are now opened to us, it would not perhaps be difficult to shew that it fulfilled an important function in preserving a true sense of the Divine authority of Holy Scripture as a whole during a period of transition. If the tendency of the later schools was to reduce the Bible to a mere text-book, the Book itself was in danger of falling to pieces under the free treatment of Luther. At present it is necessary only to notice that the controversy on the Canon in the sixteenth century—the first occasion on which the subject was debated as a question of doctrine in the Catholic Church—was really conducted by feeling rather than by external evidence. The evidence on the subject was not available, even if the disputants could have made use of it. But a more summary method offered itself. In a word the Romanists followed popular usage, regarding the Bible as one only out of many original sources of truth: the Lutherans, or more strictly Luther, judged the written Word by the Gospel contained in it, now in fuller now in scantier measure, to which the Word in man bore witness: the Calvinists, accepting without hesitation the Old Testament from the Jewish Church, and the New Testament from the Christian Church, set up the two records as the outward test and spring of all truth, absolutely complete in itself and isolated from all history.

It would be a fruitful inquiry to follow out the growth and antagonism of the principles involved in these general views: to trace the truth which each embodies and exaggerates: to indicate the influence which partial or faulty teaching on Scripture exercised on other parts of the Christian doctrine in which they were included; and even in the purely historical sketch to which we are now limited a reference to these most interesting questions will give a unity and significance to what might otherwise appear a fragmentary discussion.

§ 1. *The Roman Church.*

At the dawn of the Reformation the great Romanist scholars remained faithful to the judgment on the Canon which Jerome had followed in his translation. And Cardinal Ximenes in the preface to his magnificent Polyglott *Biblia Complutensia*—the lasting monument of the University which he founded at *Complutum* or *Alcala*, and the great glory of the Spanish press—separates the *Apocrypha* from the Canonical books. The books[1],

[1] *Prolog.* III. *b.*

he writes, which are without the Canon, which the Church receives rather for the edification of the people than for the establishment of ecclesiastical doctrines, are given only in Greek, but with a double translation[1].

Cardinal Ximenes spoke only of the disputed books of the Old Testament. His great literary rival went further. Erasmus, in his edition of the New Testament (the first published in the original Greek A.D. 1516) which was dedicated to Leo X., notices the doubts which had been raised as to the controverted books, without pronouncing more than a critical judgment upon them. Thus he distinctly maintains that the *Epistle to the Hebrews* was not written by St Paul, both on the ground of its style, and also from questionable statements on points of doctrine (ch. vi. 6), while he prefaces his criticism with this remark: 'I would wish you, good reader, 'not to consider this Epistle of less value because many 'have doubted whether it is the work of Paul or some 'other writer. Whoever wrote it is worthy of being read 'by Christians on many accounts. And though in ex-'pression it is very widely different from the style of 'Paul, it is most closely akin to the spirit and soul '(*pectus*) of Paul. But while it cannot be shewn conclu-'sively who wrote it, we may gather from very many 'arguments that it was written by some other than Paul.' Again at the close of his Commentary on St James he says:·'The authorship of this Epistle also, although it is 'filled with salutary precepts, was questioned in former 'times. For it does not seem to present in every part 'the dignity and gravity which we look for in an Apo-'stle...For my own part, though I will fight (*digladiabor*)

---

[1] Sixtus Senensis (see p. 479) with an obvious reference to this passage alters it most significantly: 'The 'books which are without the Canon '*of the Hebrews*, which the Church 'reads for edification, are given only 'in Greek, &c.' (*Bibl. S.* IV. *Franciscus Xymenius*.)

Chap. iii.

ERASMUS.
1467—1536
A.D.

His opinion on Hebrews.

The Epistle of St James.

'with no one on the subject, I heartily affirm (*probo et* '*amplector*) the authority of the Epistle. But I am sur-
'prised that on these questions no people are more
'bigoted in their statements than those who cannot tell
'in what language it was originally written....So great
'a man as Jerome was in doubt, and expresses his
'opinion with care. We are reckless in proportion to
'our ignorance.' In like manner he notices the doubts as
to the second Epistle of St Peter and the Epistle of St
Jude, and expressly assigns the second and third Epistles
of St John to the 'Presbyter.' On the *Apocalypse* he
speaks at greater length; and his words are so characteristic that they may be quoted here as a singular
illustration of the manner in which the best scholars of
the sixteenth century approached the criticism of Holy
Scripture[1]. 'St Jerome,' he says, 'bears witness that the
'*Apocalypse* was not received by the Greeks even in his
'time; and moreover that some most learned men had
'assailed the whole substance of the book with severe
'criticisms as a mere romance, on the ground that it pre-
'sents no trace of Apostolic dignity, but contains only
'an ordinary history disguised in symbols. To say no-
'thing at present of these opinions, I have been some-
'what moved by other conjectures and also by the fact
'that the author while writing the Revelation is so anxious
'to introduce his own name: *I John, I John*, just as if
'he were writing a bond and not a book, and that not
'only against the custom of the other Apostles but
'much more against his own custom, since in his Gospel,
'though the subject is less exalted, he nowhere gives his
'own name, but indicates it by slight references, and
'Paul when compelled to speak of his own vision sets
'forth the facts under the person of another. But how

[1] *Nov. Test.* p. 625.

'often does our author when describing most myste-
'rious conversations with Angels introduce the phrase
'*I John*. Further in the Greek Manuscripts which I
'have seen the title is not *of John the Evangelist*, but *of*
'*John the Divine;* not to mention that the style is widely
'different from that of the Gospel and Epistle. For though
'we may admit that there would be little trouble in
'explaining some passages falsely assailed on the ground
'that they are tinged with heretical ideas, these argu-
'ments, I say, would somewhat move me to decline to
'believe that the work belongs to John the Evangelist,
'unless the general consent of the world called me to
'another conclusion, but especially the authority of the
'Church, if at least the Church approves of this work
'with the feeling that she wishes it to be considered
'the work of John the Evangelist and to be held of
'equal weight with the other canonical books....In fact
'I observe that ancient theologians quote passages from
'this book rather for illustration and ornament than
'for the support of a serious proposition. Since even
'among jewels there is some difference; and some
'gold is purer and better than other. In sacred things
'also one thing is more sacred than another. *He who
'is spiritual*, as Paul says, *judges all things, and is judged
'by no one.*'

With this strange conflict of criticism and authority,
with this half-suppressed irony and insinuated doubt,
with this assertion of a final appeal to private judgment,
the great work of Erasmus closes; and it is probable
that the last words best express the freedom of his real
judgment. For some time his notes seem to have been
unchallenged; but the spread of the reformed opinions
directed attention to the statements which they contained in opposition to the current opinion of the Roman

Church. An attack was made upon them before the Theological Faculty of Paris, the Sorbonne, in 1524; and in 1526 the French doctors considered and condemned a large number of propositions which were taken from his New Testament, and the defence which he had previously made. In this censure the Sorbonne declared that 'it was an error of faith to doubt as to the 'author of one of the books' (of the New Testament). 'Though formerly some have doubted about the authors 'of particular books,' the decision runs, 'yet after that 'the Church has received them under the name of such 'authors by its universal usage, and has approved them 'by its judgment, it is not any longer right for a Chris-'tian to doubt of the fact, or to call it in question[1].' This general judgment is then enforced by a special affirmation of the authenticity of the *Epistle to the Hebrews* as St Paul's, *2 Peter*, and the *Apocalypse*, with references to the Councils of Laodicea, Carthage, and the Apocryphal Council at Rome under Gelasius.

Erasmus was the real leader both of the literary and critical schools of the Reformation. His influence extended both to his own Church and to the Protestant Churches of Germany and Switzerland; and opinions which he intimated with hesitation and doubt found

---

[1] Du Plessis, *Collect. Jud. de nov. error.* 1 Jud. iv.; II. 53 ff. *Propositio* I. Non statim dubius est in fide, qui de auctore libri dubitat.
Censura. Hæc propositio temerarie et erronee asseritur, loquendo ut scriptor loquitur de dubio autorum sanctorum librorum novi Testamenti ab Ecclesia sub nomine talium autorum receptorum, cujusmodi sunt autores quatuor librorum Evangeliorum, septem Epistolarum Canonicarum, quatuordecim epistolarum Pauli, actuum Apostolorum et Apocalypsis: nam cum Deus viros illos sanctos *organa sua constituerit in editione talium librorum*, honori eorum detrahit quisquis ab hujusmodi libris nomina eorum aufert, vel in dubium vertit, necnon et a frequenti abducit et fructuosa eorum lectione. Præterea quamvis de autoribus aliquorum hujusmodi librorum a nonnullis olim dubitatum sit, nihilominus *postquam Ecclesia sub nomine talium autorum suo usu universali illos recepit et sua probavit definitione, jam non fas est Christiano dubitare aut in dubium revocare.*

elsewhere a bold expression. To take one example from Romanist scholars, Cardinal Caietan (Jacob [Thomas] de Vio), the adversary of Luther at Augsburg in 1518, gives an unhesitating adhesion to the Hebrew Canon in his *Commentary on all the Authentic Historical Books of the Old Testament*, which was dedicated to Clement VII. 'The whole Latin Church,' he says, 'owes very much 'to St Jerome...on account of his separation of the 'Canonical from the uncanonical books.'

<small>Chap. iii.
Cardinal CAIETAN. 1469—1534 A.D.

1532 A.D. *Ad Clem.* VII. *Pont. Max.*</small>

And the authority of Jerome had equal weight with him in dealing with the Antilegomena of the New Testament. Thus in the preface to his Commentary on the *Epistle to the Hebrews* he writes: 'Since we have re-'ceived Jerome as our rule that we may not err in the 'separation of the Canonical books (for those which he 'delivered as Canonical we hold Canonical, and those 'which he separated from the Canonical books we hold 'without the Canon); therefore as the author of this 'Epistle is doubtful in the opinion of Jerome, the Epistle 'also is rendered doubtful, since unless it is Paul's it is 'not clear that it is Canonical. Whence it comes to pass 'that if anything arise doubtful in faith it cannot be de-'termined from the sole authority of this Epistle. See 'how great mischief an anonymous book creates.' In like manner he quotes Jerome for the doubts entertained as to the authority of *St James*, 2 *Peter*, 2 and 3 *John*, and *St Jude*. Of the three last he expressly says that 'they are of less authority than those which are certainly 'Holy Scripture.' On 2 *Peter* alone he decides favourably, for the argument from style is, he maintains, very fallacious[1]. The *Apocalypse* he dismisses in a sentence.

<small>*The* Disputed Books *of the New Testament.*</small>

---

[1] Infirmum itaque argumentum assumitur: cum unum atque eundem hominem diverso stylo quandoque scribere experientia testetur. Registrum Gregorii tantum dissonat ab aliis scriptis a Gregorio, ut si ex stylo arguendum esset negaretur Gregorii (*Præf. ad 2 Petr.*).

'I confess that I cannot interpret the *Apocalypse* according to the literal sense. Let him interpret it to whom 'God has given the power[1].'

These statements of Cardinal Caietan passed unchallenged during his lifetime, but shortly after his death they were assailed by Catharinus, a vehement controversialist whose life was spent in disputes. Yet Catharinus abandoned the argument from history, and simply took refuge in the decrees of Popes Innocent, Gelasius, and Eugenius, as decisive upon the extent of the Canon[2]. This simple mode of determining the question was unhappily adopted, and probably in part through his influence, at the Council of Trent, in which he played an important part. The Council held its first Session on Dec. 13th, 1545. In the third session (Feb. 4th, 1546) the Nicene Creed was recited and ratified. The subject of Holy Scripture and Tradition was then brought forward for preliminary discussion on Feb. 12th. Four articles taken from the writings of Luther were proposed for consideration or rather for condemnation. Of these the first affirmed that Scripture only (without tradition) was the single and complete source of doctrine; the second that the Hebrew Canon of the Old Testament and the acknowledged books of the New Testament ought alone to be admitted as authoritative. These dogmas were discussed by about thirty divines in four meetings. On the first point there was a general agreement. It was allowed that tradition was a co-ordinate source of doctrine with Scripture. On the

---

[1] Et sic finitur Epistola Judæ: et est finis Commentariorum nostrorum super Novum Testamentum.
Caietæ die 17 Augusti. Anno Domini M.D.XXIX. ætatis autem propriæ sexagesimo primo. Apocalypsim enim fateor me nescire exponere juxta sensum literalem: exponat cui Deus concesserit (*Opera*, T. v. p. 401, ed. 1639).

[2] *Annot. in Comm. Caietani*, Lib. I. (1542).

second there was a great variety of opinion. Some proposed to follow the judgment of Cardinal Caietan and distinguish two classes of books, as, it was argued, had been the intention of Augustine. Others wished to draw the line of distinction yet more exactly, and form three classes, (1) the Acknowledged Books, (2) the Disputed Books of the New Testament, as having been afterwards generally received, (3) the Apocrypha of the Old Testament. A third party wished to give a bare list, as that of Carthage, without any further definition of the authority of the books included in it, so as to leave the subject yet open. A fourth party, influenced by a false interpretation of the earlier papal decrees, and necessarily ignorant of the grave doubts which affect their authenticity, urged the ratification of all the books of the enlarged Canon as equally of Divine authority. The first view was afterwards merged in the second, and on March 8th three minutes were drawn up embodying the three remaining opinions. These were considered privately, and on the 15th the third was carried by a majority of voices. The decree in which it was finally expressed was published on the 8th of April, and for the first time the question of the contents of the Bible was made an absolute article of faith and confirmed by an Anathema. 'The holy œcumenical and general Council of Trent,' so the decree runs, '...following the examples of the 'orthodox Fathers receives and venerates all the books 'of the Old and New Testaments...and also traditions 'pertaining to faith and conduct...with an equal feeling 'of devotion and reverence.' Then follows the list of the books of the Old and New Testaments, including *Tobit, Judith, Wisdom, Ecclesiasticus,* 1 and 2 *Maccabees,* in the same order as the decree of Eugenius IV., and the decree proceeds, 'If however anyone does not

Chap. iii.

Varieties of opinion.

Decree on the Canon of Scripture.

Chap. iii.

'receive the entire books with all their parts as they 'are accustomed to be read in the Catholic Church and 'in the old Latin Vulgate edition (*i.e.* Jerome's with the 'additions) as sacred and Canonical, and knowingly and 'wittingly despises the aforesaid traditions, let him be 'Anathema[1].'

The Decree unprecedented.

This fatal decree, in which the Council, harassed by the fear of lay critics and 'grammarians,' gave a new aspect to the whole question of the Canon, was ratified by fifty-three prelates, among whom there was not one German, not one scholar distinguished for historical learning, not one who was fitted by special study for the examination of a subject in which the truth could only be determined by the voice of antiquity. How completely the decision was opposed to the spirit and letter of the original judgments of the Greek and Latin Churches, how far in the doctrinal equalization of the disputed and acknowledged books of the Old Testament it was at variance with the traditional opinion of the West, how absolutely unprecedented was the conversion of an ecclesiastical usage into an article of belief, will be seen from the evidence which has been already adduced. If historical criticism had made as much advance as grammatical criticism at the time when the decree was enacted, no anathema at least would have been directed against differences of opinion on books or parts of books; for on one point at least scholarship gained the day. It was decided after much discussion that no anathema should be added to the second

---

[1] The words of one remarkable Florentine scholar, Jac. Naclantus, Bishop of Chiozza, are worth quoting. He had taken a decided part in the discussion (Theiner, *Acta Authentica*, i. 59), and when the assent to the decree was required: 'Clodiensis dixit 'hoc verbum tantum: obediam' (Theiner, l. c. 89). A striking speech of Card. Pole given in the same collection (p. 60) deserves study.

part of the decree which affirmed the authority of the Latin Vulgate.

It is unnecessary to continue the history of the Canon in the Romish Church. The attempts which have been made from time to time by Romanist scholars to claim some freedom of opinion on the subject can find no excuse in the terms of the decree. One judgment only will be added, which has considerable interest from the circumstances under which it was pronounced.

The *Bibliotheca Sancta* of the Dominican Sixtus Senensis, which was dedicated to Pius V. as the 'chief 'author of the Index of prohibited books and the purifier 'of Christian literature,' may be taken as the authorised expression of the general views which prevailed in the Council. Sixtus divides the books of the Bible into two classes. The books of the first class (Protocanonical) are those of which there has never been any doubt in the Church, or to use the term which has been already explained the 'acknowledged' books of the Old and New Testaments except *Esther*. The books of the second class—'called Ecclesiastical in former times but now 'Deuterocanonical'—are those which were not generally known till a late period, 'as in the Old Testament *Esther*, '*Tobit*, *Judith*, and *Baruch*, the *Letter of Jeremiah*, the '*Wisdom of Solomon*, *Ecclesiasticus*, the *Additions to* '*Daniel*, 2 *Maccabees*. And in the New Testament in 'like manner, *Mark* xvi. 9—20; *Luke* xxii. 43, 44; *John* 'vii. 53—viii. 11, the *Epistle to the Hebrews*, *James*, 2 '*Peter*, 2 and 3 *John*, *Jude*, *Apocalypse*, and other books 'of the same kind (?), which formerly the ancient Fathers 'of the Church held as Apocryphal and not Canonical, 'and at first permitted to be read only before catechu-'mens (as Athanasius witnesses)...then as (Ruffinus

The statement of SIXTUS SENENSIS. 1566 A.D.

'writes) allowed to be read before all the faithful, not 'for the confirmation of doctrines, but merely for the 'instruction of the people: and...at last willed that they 'should be adopted among the Scriptures of irrefraga- 'ble authority...'

The concessions and claims made in this passage are equally significant. The determination of the books which come within the limits of the Bible is taken out of the domain of historical criticism. It is admitted that for nearly four centuries the Hebrew Canon of the Old Testament was alone received. It is affirmed that the Church has power not only to fix the extent of the Canon, but also to settle questions of text. The field of Biblical study is definitely closed against all free research.

§ 2. *The Saxon School of Reformers.*

Meanwhile a spirit was awakened in Germany which for a time cast a vivid if a partial light upon the Bible as the depository of the Divine teaching transmitted to the Church. The discovery of a Latin Bible, we are told, turned the thoughts of Luther into a new channel. And Luther on his side found in the Bible something which had long been hidden from the world, not as to its doctrine only, but as to its general relation to God and men. The study of the Bible was a life-long passion with him. 'Were I but a great poet,' he said, 'I would write a 'magnificent poem on the utility and efficacy of the Di-'vine word[1].' His judgments on the different Books are given in detail in his Prefaces. These are so full of life, and so characteristic of the man, that they can never lose their interest; and as a whole they form an important chapter in the history of the Bible. His comments

[1] Comp. *Bible in the Church*, pp. 260 ff.

on the Apocrypha have singular vigour and personal appreciation of the value of the several books; nor does he shew less freedom and boldness in dealing with the Antilegomena of the New Testament.

Chap. iii.

For him there is a Gospel within the Gospel, a New Testament within the New Testament. After giving a general summary of the principles of the Christian life, he thus concludes the preface to his first edition of the translation[1]. 'From all this you can rightly judge between 'all the books, and distinguish which are the best. For '*St John's Gospel,* and *St Paul's Epistles,* especially that 'to the *Romans,* and *St Peter's first Epistle,* are the true 'marrow and kernel of all the books; which properly 'also might be the first, and each Christian should be 'counselled to read them first and most, and make them 'as common by daily reading as his daily bread...briefly '*St John's Gospel* and his *first Epistle, St Paul's Epi-* '*stles,* especially those to the *Romans, Galatians, Ephe-* '*sians,* and *St Peter's first Epistle: these*'—the words are emphasized in the original—'*are the books which* '*shew thee Christ, and teach all which it is needful and* '*blessed for thee to know, even if you never see or hear any* '*other book, or any other doctrine.* Therefore is the *Epi-* '*stle of St James* a right strawy Epistle compared with 'them, for it has no character of the Gospel in it.'

Differences in the New Testament.

Agreeably to this general statement Luther placed the *Epistle to the Hebrews, James, Jude,* and the *Apocalypse,* at the end of his translation, after the other books of the New Testament, which he called 'the true and 'certain Capital-books of the New Testament[2]; for these 'four have been regarded in former times in a different 'light.' Of the Epistle to the Hebrews he says that it

He placed some of the disputed books by themselves.

Heb. ii. 3.

[1] *Werke,* ed. Walch, XIV. 104: this is left out in the later editions.
[2] *Ib.* p. 147.

was certainly by a disciple of the Apostles, and not by an Apostle. It was, he thinks, 'put together out of many 'pieces.' The writer 'does not lay the foundation of 'faith, but yet he builds upon it gold, silver, precious 'stones. Therefore even if we find perhaps wood, straw, 'or hay, mingled with it, that shall not prevent us from 'receiving such instruction with all honour; though we 'do not place it absolutely on the same footing as the 'Apostolic Epistles.'

'I admire,' he says, 'the *Epistle of St James*, though 'it was rejected by the ancients, and still hold it as good, 'for this reason that it lays down no teaching of man, and 'presses home the law of God[1]. Yet to express my own 'opinion, without prejudice to any one, I do not hold it to 'be the writing of any Apostle, for these reasons: (1) It 'contradicts St Paul and all other Scripture in giving 'righteousness to works... (2) It teaches Christian peo-'ple, and yet does not once notice the Passion, the 'Resurrection, the Spirit of Christ. The writer names 'Christ a few times; but he teaches nothing of Him, 'but speaks of general faith in God. While it is the 'duty of a true Apostle to preach Christ's Sufferings and 'Resurrection[2]...and therein all true holy books agree, 'that they preach and urge Christ. That too is the 'right touchstone whereby to criticise all books, whether 'they urge Christ or not, for all Scripture testifies of 'Christ...That which does not teach Christ is still not 'Apostolic, even if it were the teaching of St Peter or St 'Paul. Again that which preaches Christ, that were 'Apostolic, even if Judas, Annas, Pilate, and Herod, 'preached it[3].' 'I cannot then place it among the true 'Capital-books; but I will forbid no one to place and

---

[1] *Ib.* p. 148. [2] *Ib.* p. 149.
[3] *Ib.* p. 150.

'elevate it as he pleases; for there are many good say-'ings in it[1].'

The *Epistle of St Jude* is 'indisputably an extract or 'copy from the second Epistle of St Peter[2]....Therefore, 'though I applaud it, it is not an Epistle which can claim 'to be reckoned among the Capital-books, which ought 'to lay the foundation of faith.'

Of the *Apocalypse* he simply says (1534 A.D.)[3] that 'no man ought to be hindered from holding it to be 'a work of St John or otherwise, as he will...[4].' Reckless interpretations had brought it into dishonour. And though it was yet a 'dumb prophecy,' he shews that the true Christian can use it for consolation and warning. 'Briefly, our holiness is in heaven where Christ is, and 'not in the world before our eyes, as some paltry ware 'in the market. Therefore let offence, factions, heresy 'and wickedness, be and do what they may; if only the 'Word of the Gospel remains pure with us, and we hold 'it dear and precious, we need not doubt that Christ 'is near and with us, even if matters go hardest; as we 'see in this Book that through and above all plagues, 'beasts, evil angels, Christ is still near and with His 'saints, and at last overthrows them.'

The freshness and power of Luther's judgments on the Bible, the living sense of fellowship with the spirit which animates them, the bold independence and self-assertion which separate them from all simply critical

---

[1] The edition of 1552 had after these words the following sentence: 'One man is no man in worldly 'things; how then should this single 'writer all alone hold good against 'Paul and all other Scripture?'

[2] He does not notice the doubts raised as to the authority of this Epistle.

[3] Twelve years before he had spoken far more disparagingly of the book. 'For several reasons I hold 'it to be neither Apostolic nor Pro-'phetic...My spirit cannot acquiesce 'in the book:...I abide by the books 'which present Christ clear and pure 'to me.'

[4] *Ib.* p. 152.

conclusions, combined to limit their practical acceptance to individuals. Such judgments rest on no definite external evidence. They cannot be justified by the ordinary rule and measure of criticism or dogma. No Church could rest on a theory which makes private feeling the supreme authority as to doctrine and the source of doctrine. As a natural consequence the later Lutherans abandoned the teaching of their great master on the written Word. For a time the 'disputed' books of the New Testament (Antilegomena) were distinguished from the remainder; but in the early part of the seventeenth century this difference was looked upon as wholly belonging to the past, and towards its close the very letter of the printed text of Scripture was treated by great Lutheran Divines as possessing an inherent and inalienable sanctity beyond the reach of historical discussion. Yet the Lutheran Church has no recognised definition of Canonicity, and no express list of the Sacred Books. The nearest approach to this is in the Lutheran Bible, in which the Apocrypha are placed by themselves and separated distinctly from 'the Holy Scripture.' But on the other hand four of the Antilegomena of the New Testament are in like manner removed from their places in the Latin Bible and placed as a kind of Appendix, though without any special notice. And the detailed judgments which Luther delivered are not more favourable to one class than to the other. To a certain extent therefore the question was left open; and usage alone has determined finally the subordinate position of the Apocrypha to the Old Testament, and elevated the Antilegomena of the New Testament to an equality with the remaining books.

RLSTADT. One attempt however was made to investigate independently the extent of the Canon and the principles on which it was formed. Among the early friends of Luther was Andrew Bodenstein of Karlstadt, who is commonly known by the name of his native town, Archdeacon of Wittenberg. As the Reformation advanced, Luther and Karlstadt were separated by theological differences, and after long sufferings Karlstadt found an honourable retreat in Switzerland. By Bullinger's recommendation he was made professor of theology at Basle and died there in 1541. While he was still working with Luther, in 1520 he published a treatise *On the Canonical Scriptures*, which exhibits a remarkable sense of the real bearings and principles of an investigation into the constitution of the Bible. The book was in advance of the age and appears to have produced no effect at the time. It consists of five parts, (1) On the majesty of Scripture. (2) On the force and strength of Scripture. (3) On the number and order of the Sacred books. (4) On the Catalogues of Jerome and Augustine. (5) A general classification of Scripture. It is with the last division alone that we are now concerned. In this Karlstadt divides all the books of Scripture into three classes of different dignity, almost as Hugo of St Victor had done before him. The first class contains only the *Pentateuch* and the four *Gospels*, 'the clearest 'luminaries of the whole Divine truth.' The second class includes the Prophets according to the Hebrew reckoning, and the acknowledged Epistles of the New Testament (*Paul* 13, *Peter* 1, *John* 1). The third class contains the Hagiographa of the Hebrew Canon and the seven disputed books of the New Testament[1].

This short summary of Karlstadt's results can give

---

[1] The *Acts* is entirely omitted. *Scripturis*, § 136. Yet again in §§ Probably the book was looked upon 65 ff. he appears to pass over the by Karlstadt as an Appendix to St book purposely. Luke's Gospel: see *de Canonicis*

no idea of the breadth and subtlety of many of his remarks. The whole evidence was not before him and consequently he erred in his conclusions; but even as it is, his treatise is not without use in the present day. It was the first clear assertion of the independent supremacy of Holy Scripture, and so far the first enunciation of the fundamental principle of the Reformation. Yet at the same time Karlstadt recognised the historic function of the Church in collecting and ratifying the sacred books. 'Why,' he asks, in reference to Luther's objections to the Epistle of St James, 'if you allow the 'Jews to stamp books with authority by receiving them, 'do you refuse to grant as much power to the Churches 'of Christ, since the Church is not less than the Syna-'gogue?' And though he placed the different books of the Bible in different ranks, yet he drew a broad line between all of them and the traditions or decrees of Christian teachers. 'You see,' he writes, 'kind reader, 'how great is the authority of the Holy Scriptures. 'Whether willingly or unwillingly, you will allow the 'extent of their authority, whose slightest sign all 'other arts and sciences, as far as they affect the mould-'ing of life, revere, regard, dread, adore. Therefore 'rightly the laws of men, the canons of Popes, the cus-'toms of the people, yield to [the Bible] as their mis-'tress, and minister to it.' 'We judge of the opinions 'of all and each from the Sacred Scriptures,' he elsewhere says, 'and therefore we pronounce [the Bible] 'to be the queen and mistress of all and the judge who 'judges all things while she herself is judged by none...' 'The Divine Law, single and alone, is placed beyond 'all suspicion of error, and draws all other laws within 'its dominion, or utterly destroys them if they strive 'against it.'

§ 3. *The Swiss School of Reformers.*

Karlstadt forms a link between the Saxon and Swiss Reformers. While Luther was battling for the one great principle of faith, a more comprehensive movement was begun in Switzerland. Zwingli the foremost of its champions was only a few weeks younger than Luther, and he had not yet heard Luther's name, as he writes, when he began to preach the Gospel. But Zwingli was not contented with the compromise which Luther was willing to make with all that was hallowed by usage, provided it was not positively superstitious. He aimed at forming a strictly logical system based on Scripture only, irrespective of tradition or custom. In this respect he carried out, in intention at least, the principles which Karlstadt had maintained; and the method which he followed became characteristic of the Swiss Churches. The Saxon reformation was in essence conservative: the Swiss reformation was in essence rationalistic.

Zwingli himself does not appear to have discussed the Canon of Scripture. In his notes on the *Epistle to the Hebrews* and *St James* he takes no account of the doubts which had been raised as to their authority. Of the *Apocalypse* alone he declares that he 'takes no account 'of it, for it is not a book of the Bible[1].' While Zwingli was labouring to spread his doctrines at Zurich, his friend Œcolampadius carried on the same work at Basle. In a letter to the Waldenses Œcolampadius explains the views of his party on the Canon. 'In the New 'Testament we receive four *Gospels*, with the *Acts of the* '*Apostles*, and fourteen Epistles of St Paul, and seven

[1] *Werke*, II. 1, p. 169 (ed. Schuler): Us Apocalypsi nemend wir kein kundschaft an, dann es nit ein biblisch buch ist...

'Catholic Epistles, together with the *Apocalypse;* al-'though we do not compare the *Apocalypse*, the Epistles 'of *James* and *Jude,* and 2 *Peter* and 2 and 3 *John* 'with the rest[1].'

This judgment of Œcolampadius may be taken as a fair representation of the feeling in the German Churches of Switzerland. But even before his death, which happened in the same year as that of Zwingli, Farel had begun that movement in the French cantons which under the direction of Calvin influenced more or less the theology of all Western Europe.

CALVIN'S *judgment on the* Antilegomena *of the New Testament.*

With regard to the *Antilegomena* of the New Testament Calvin expresses himself with hardly less boldness than Luther, though practically he followed common usage. He passes over 2 and 3 *John* and the *Apocalypse* in his Commentary without notice, and writes of 1 *John* as simply 'the Epistle of John.' 'I embrace,' he says,

The Epistle to the Hebrews.

'[the Epistle to the *Hebrews*] without doubt among the 'Apostolic Epistles; nor do I doubt but that it was 'through a device of Satan that some have questioned 'its authority...Wherefore let us not allow the Church 'of God and ourselves to be bereft of so great a bless-'ing; but let us vindicate for ourselves the possession of 'it with firmness. We need however feel little anxiety 'as to who wrote it...I cannot myself be brought to 'believe that Paul was the author...The method of in-'struction and style sufficiently shew that the writer

Heb. ii. 3.

'was not Paul, and he professes himself to be one of 'the disciples of the Apostles, which is wholly alien from 'Paul's custom...'

2 Peter.

'The fact that Eusebius says that doubts were for-'merly entertained on it [2 *Peter*] ought not to deter us

---

[1] *Epistola*, Lib. I. p. 3 c, ed. 1548.

'from reading it...I am more moved by the statement
'of Jerome that some, led by the difference of style, did
'not think Peter the author of it. For although some
'likeness with his style can be observed, yet I confess
'that there is an obvious difference which indicates a
'different writer. There are also other plausible con-
'jectures from which we may gather that it was the work
'of some other than Peter...But if it is received as
'Canonical, we must confess that Peter was its author,
'since not only is it inscribed with his name, but the
'writer himself witnesses that he lived with Christ...I
'therefore lay down that if the Epistle be deemed
'worthy of credit it proceeded from Peter, not that he
'wrote it himself, but that some one of his disciples at
'his command included in it what the necessity of the
'times required...Certainly, since the majesty of the
'Spirit of Christ exhibits itself in every part of the
'Epistle, I feel a scruple at rejecting it wholly, however
'much I fail to recognise in it the genuine language of
'Peter.'

Chap. iii.

Of the Epistle of *St James* he speaks more confidently. 'It is known,' he writes, 'from the evidence
'of Jerome and Eusebius, that this Epistle was not
'received formerly without a struggle by many churches.
'There are even at the present day some who do not
'think it worthy of authority. Still I willingly embrace
'it without doubt, because I see no sufficiently good
'reason for rejecting it...Certainly it cannot be required
'of all to treat of the same topic.' And of the Epistle
of *St Jude* he speaks in similar terms: 'Although dif-
'ferent conflicting opinions were entertained about this
'Epistle also among the ancients; still because it is
'useful for reading, and does not contain anything
'foreign to the purity of Apostolic doctrine, while al-

St James.

St Jude.

'ready in former times it gained authority with the best 'writers, I willingly add it to the others.'

In each case a personal and not a critical or historical test was applied. The result could not be long doubtful. The edition of the New Testament which was dedicated by Beza to Queen Elizabeth in the year of Calvin's death, exhibits very clearly the influence which usage exercised in the suppression of the early doubts on the *Antilegomena*. In his preface to the *Epistle to the Hebrews* Beza examines and meets the arguments which had been brought against the belief in its Pauline authorship, and then concludes: 'Let us 'however allow liberty of judgment on this point, pro-'vided only we all agree in this, that this Epistle was 'truly dictated by the Holy Spirit...while it is written 'in so excellent and so exact a method, that (unless we 'can suppose Apollos wrote it, whose learning and elo-'quence combined with the greatest piety are highly 'praised in the Acts) scarcely any one except St Paul 'could have been the writer.' He afterwards notices generally the doubts entertained as to *James*, 2 *Peter*, 2 and 3 *John*, and *Jude*, but sets them aside without discussion. His preface to the *Apocalypse* is far more elaborate. In this he discusses in some detail the objections raised by Erasmus to its Apostolic origin, and pronounces them in general to be severally weak and futile. 'This being the case,' he argues, 'although I do 'not think that we ought to dispute too obstinately as 'to the name of the writer, still I should be inclined to 'assign the book to John the Apostle rather than to any 'one else...If however it were allowed to form a conjec-'ture from the style, I should assign it to no one rather 'than Mark, who also is himself called John. The 'character of this book being similar to and almost iden-

III.] THE REFORMED CONFESSIONS. 491

'tical with that of the Gospel of Mark, not only in words
'but also in general phraseology...Finally, we are led
'to believe that the Holy Spirit was pleased to gather
'into this most precious book those predictions of the
'earlier Prophets which remained to be fulfilled after the
'coming of Christ, and also added some particulars, as
'far as He knew that it concerned us to be acquainted
'with them.'

From what has been said it will appear that the subject of the Canon was not one which excited any marked interest among the chief Swiss reformers. Custom fixed the details of their judgment, and by a gradual process the Bible was more and more removed (as was formally the case in the Romish Church) from the region of history. The idea of Inspiration was substituted for that of Canonicity. The recognition of variety and advance in the records of Revelation was virtually forbidden. The test of authority was placed in individual sentiment, and not in the common witness of the congregation.

Judgments on Scripture in the reformed Confessions.

The progress of thought thus indicated is seen yet more clearly in the public acts of the Reformed Calvinistic Churches. In these also there is a rapid advance from a general assertion of the claims of Holy Scripture to an exact and rigid definition of the character and contents of the Bible. No notice is taken of the limits of the Canon in the Confessions of Faith issued by Zwingli. In the first Confession of Faith at Basle (1534), which is said to have been moulded on the Confession of Œcolampadius, a general reference is made to 'Holy 'Biblical Scripture,' to which every opinion is submitted[1]. In the first Helvetic Confession (1536) Canonical Scripture, that is 'the Word of God, given by the Holy Spirit, 'and set forth by the Prophets and Apostles,' is declared

1523—1530 A.D.

[1] Niemeyer, *Coll. Confess.* p. 104.

to be 'the oldest and most perfect philosophy, which 'alone contains completely all piety and all the rule of 'life¹.' The same general description is found in the Genevan Catechism, published by Calvin in 1545², and in the later Helvetic Confession of 1566³. The Belgian Confession (1561—63), which was influenced in some degree by the English Articles, treats of the Canon at some length. 'We embrace,' it is said, 'Holy Scrip-'ture in those two volumes of the Old and New Testa-'ment, which are called the Canonical Books, about 'which there is no controversy⁴.' Then follows a list of the Hebrew Canon and of the books of the New Testament, as we receive them. 'These books alone,' the next article continues, 'we receive as sacred and 'Canonical, on which our faith can rest, by which it can 'be confirmed and established. And we believe all those 'things which are contained in them, and that not so 'much because the Church receives and approves them 'as Canonical, as because the Holy Spirit witnesses to 'our consciences that they emanated from God; and on 'this account also that they themselves sufficiently wit-'ness to and of themselves approve this their proper 'authority...' 'Moreover we lay down a difference be-'tween these sacred books and those which men call 'Apocryphal, inasmuch as the Church can read the 'Apocryphal books, and take out proof from them so 'far as they agree with the Canonical books; but their 'authority and certainty is by no means such that any 'dogma of Christian faith or religion can certainly be 'established from their testimony...And therefore with 'these divine Scriptures and this truth of God no other

---

¹ Niemeyer, pp. 105, 115.
² *Ib.* p. 159.
³ *Ib.* p. 467.

⁴ *Art.* 3—7, pp. 361—3. Altered afterwards to 'there never was any 'controversy.'

'human writings however holy, no custom, nor multitude, nor antiquity, nor prescription of time, nor succession of persons, nor any councils, no decrees or statutes of men in fine, are to be compared, inasmuch as 'the truth of God excels all things.' Statements to the same general effect, with some verbal agreements, are found in the Articles of the French reformed Church of 1561[1]; but there is this significant difference, that the *Epistle to the Hebrews* is placed in the French catalogue apart from the Epistles of St Paul. The Westminster Assembly, which first met in 1643, followed the same method in dealing with Scripture, and the words of their Confession may be taken as an exact and mature expression of the feelings of the Calvinistic Churches on the subject of the Bible.

'Art. i. ...It pleased the Lord at sundry times and 'in divers manners to reveal Himself and to declare His 'will unto His Church; and...to commit the same 'wholly unto writing; which maketh the Holy Scripture 'to be most necessary; those former ways of God's re-'vealing His will unto His people being now ceased.

'ii. Under the name of Holy Scripture, or the Word 'of God written, are now contained all the books of the 'Old and New Testament, which are these:

'Of the Old Testament, *Genesis...Malachi.*

'Of the New Testament, *The Gospel according to Matthew...The Revelation of John.*

'All which are given by inspiration of God to be the 'rule of faith and life.

'iii. The books commonly called Apocrypha, not 'being of Divine inspiration, are no part of the Canon of 'Scripture; and therefore are of no authority in the

---

[1] Niemeyer, p. 311.

Chap. iii.

The Westminster Confession.

The Humble Advice *of this Assembly of Divines*... pp. 1 ff. ed. 1646.

'Church of God, nor to be any otherwise approved or 'made use of than other human writings.

'iv. The authority of the Holy Scripture, for which 'it ought to be believed and obeyed, dependeth not upon 'the testimony of any man or Church; but wholly upon 'God (who is truth itself) the Author thereof; and there-'fore it is to be received because it is the Word of God.

'v. We may be moved and induced by the testi-'mony of the Church to an high and reverent esteem of 'the Holy Scripture...yet notwithstanding our full per-'suasion and assurance of the infallible truth and Divine 'authority thereof is from the inward work of the Holy 'Spirit bearing witness by and with the Word in our 'hearts.'

The controversies on the text of the Bible, which form a painful episode in the ecclesiastical annals of the seventeenth century, added yet severer precision to definitions like these, which seem sufficiently stringent. The most exact and rigid declaration of the Inspiration of the Bible which is found in any public Confession of Faith was drawn up in the Swiss Declaration of 1675, which forms a characteristic close to this division of our history[1]. 'Almighty God,' thus the articles commence, 'not only provided that His Word, which is a power to 'every one who believes, should be committed to writing 'through Moses, the Prophets, and Apostles, but also has 'watched over it with a fatherly care up to the present 'time, and guarded lest it might be corrupted by the 'craft of Satan or any fraud of man...' Thus the 'He-'brew volume of the Old Testament, which we have 'received from the tradition of the Jewish Church, to 'which formerly the oracles of God were committed, 'and retain at the present day, both in its consonants

[1] Niemeyer, p. 730.

'and in its vowels,—the points themselves, or at least
'the force of the points,—and both in its substance and
'in its words is divinely inspired, so that together with
'the volume of the New Testament it is the single and
'uncorrupted Rule of our faith and life, by whose stand-
'ard, as by a touchstone, all Versions which exist,
'whether Eastern or Western, must be tried, and wher-
'ever they vary be made conformable to it.'

§ 4. *The Arminian School.*

Yet such doctrines as these were not promulgated without opposition. Historical criticism was universally subordinate to doctrinal controversy, but still at times it made itself felt. In this respect the influence of the Arminian School upon the study of Holy Scripture was too great to be neglected in any account of the history of the Canon. The principles which were embodied in their teaching belonged to the dawn of the Reformation, though they only found adequate expression at a later time. Grotius (de Groot) may be taken as their representative, and no one can have used his *Annotations* without feeling that his power of interpreting Scripture, though practically marred by many faults, was yet in several respects far superior to that of his contemporaries. His *Commentary* includes notes on the Old Testament, the Apocrypha, and the New Testament. On the *Antilegomena* of the New Testament he speaks in detail: 'It is most obvious,' he says, 'that the *Epistle* '*to the Hebrews* was not written by St Paul, from the 'difference in style between this Epistle and the Epistles 'of St Paul;' and he then points out various reasons which lead him to attribute it to St Luke. 'Those who 'have rejected the *Epistle of James*...had reasons, but

Chap. iii.

GROTIUS.
1583—1645
A.D.

Præf. ad Hebr.

Votum pro Pace, IV. p. 672.

'not good reasons, for they saw that it was opposed to 'their views: This I remarked, that all might see how 'perilous it is to recede from the general agreement of 'the Church.' 'I believe,' he says, 'that the original 'title of 2 *Peter* was the Epistle of Simeon,' *i.e.* of the successor of James in the bishopric of Jerusalem; 'and 'that the present Epistle was made up of two epistles 'by this primitive bishop, of which the second begins at 'the third chapter.' 'Many of the ancients,' he writes, 'believed that 2 and 3 *John* were not the works of the 'Apostle, with whom Eusebius and Jerome do not dis-'agree; and there are weighty arguments in favour of 'that opinion.' 'I am wholly led to believe that the '*Epistle of Jude* was the work of Judas a bishop of 'Jerusalem in the time of Hadrian.' On the contrary, he maintains that the *Apocalypse* is a genuine work of the Apostle. 'Those early writers believed that it was 'a work of the Apostle John, who justly claim our cre-'dence.' 'I believe however that it was kept in the care 'of the *Presbyter* John, a disciple of the *Apostle,* and 'that therefore it came to pass that it was supposed by 'some to be his work.'

§ 5. *The English Church.*

The history of the Canon in England is clearly reflected in the history of the English translations of the Bible. The work which was begun by Alfric and Wycliffe was brought to a worthy completion in the reign of Henry VIII. and his successors; and the various Bibles which were issued exhibit in details of classification and order the changes of feeling which arose with regard to the *Apocrypha* of the Old and the *Antilegomena* of the New Testament.

The first edition of the New Testament which was printed in English was that of WILLIAM TYNDALE. This probably was completed at Worms in 1525 in two forms, quarto and octavo. A single copy including Matt. i.—xxii. 12 is all that remains of the quarto edition, but this contains after the Prologue a list of the books of the New Testament identical with that of Luther. Twenty-three books (Matthew—3 John) are numbered. The *Epistle to the Hebrews, James, Jude,* and the *Apocalypse,* are placed together at the end without numbers. The *second Epistle of St Peter* and 2 and 3 *John* on the other hand are placed with 1 *Peter* and 1 *John.* The octavo edition of the same date, of which the text has been preserved entire, gives the books in the same order. In the revised edition of 1534, Tyndale added Prologues to the several books in which he notices the same doubts which Luther noticed, except that he is silent on the *Apocalypse,* though he decides generally in favour of the authority of the disputed books. 'Whether [the *Epistle* ' *to the Hebrews*] were Paul's or no I say not, but per- 'mit it to other men's judgments; neither think I it to 'be an article of any man's faith, but that a man may 'doubt of the author[1].' 'But in spite of these doubts 'this Epistle ought no more to be refused for a holy, 'godly, and catholic, than the other authentic Scrip- 'tures[2].' 'Though [the *Epistle of St James*] were refused 'in old time, and denied of many to be the Epistle of a 'very Apostle, and though also it lay not the foundation 'of the faith of Christ...methinketh it ought of right to 'be taken for Holy Scripture[3].' 'As for the *Epistle of* ' *Judas,* though men have and yet do doubt of the author '...I see not but that it ought to have the authority of

Chap. iii.
TYNDALE'S New Testament.

On the disputed books.

---

[1] *Doctrinal Treatises, &c.* p. 521 (ed. Park. Soc.).
[2] *Ib.* p. 523.
[3] *Ib.* p. 525.

'Holy Scripture¹.' In his Prologues to 2 *Peter* and 2 and 3 *John* (like Luther) he does not refer to any doubts as to the Canonicity of the Epistles².

The subsequent editions of the English Bible up to the Authorized Edition of 1611 offer no points of special interest with regard to the history of the Canon of the New Testament³. In the Genevan Bible alone notice is taken in the preface to the Epistle to the Hebrews of the doubts as to whether St Paul wrote it ('as it is 'not like'), but no reference is made to the doubts as to the authority of the other disputed books.

Practically the English Canon of the New Testament was settled by usage. The authoritative teaching of the Church of England in the Articles is not removed beyond all question. In the Articles of 1552 it was affirmed that 'Holy Scripture containeth all things necessary to 'salvation,' but nothing was then said of the books included under that title. In the Elizabethan Articles of 1562 and 1571 a definition was added: 'In the name 'of Holy Scripture we do understand those Canonical 'books of the Old and New Testament of whose autho-'rity was never any doubt in the Church.' Then follows a statement 'Of the names and number of the Canonical 'books,' in which the books of the Old Testament are enumerated at length. A list of the Old Testament Apocrypha is given next, imperfect in the Latin, but complete in the English; and at the end it is said: 'all the books of the New Testament, as they are com-'monly received, we do receive and account them for 'Canonical;' but no list is given⁴. A strict interpreta-

---

¹ *Ib.* p. 531.
² For the general relation of Tyndale's Prologues to Luther's see *History of the English Bible*, pp. 152 ff.
³ The changes with regard to the Apocrypha are given in the *Bible in the Church*, pp. 282 ff.
⁴ Hardwick, *Hist. of the Articles*, App. III. p. 275. The Latin text (1562) only notices the Apocryphal

tion of the language of the Article thus leaves a difference between Canonical books and such Canonical books as have never been doubted in the Church[1]. Nor is it a complete explanation of the omission of a catalogue that the Articles were framed with a special reference to the Church of Rome, with which the Church of England had no controversy as to the New Testament; for the Catalogue of the New Testament books is given, not only in the French and Belgian Articles, which alone of the foreign Confessions contain any list of the books of Scripture, but also in the Westminster Confession and in the Irish Articles[2].

But whatever may be the explanation of this ambiguity,—even if we admit that the framers of our Articles were willing to allow a certain freedom of opinion on a question which was left undecided, not only by the Lutheran, but by many Calvinistic Churches,—there can be no doubt as to the general reception of all the books of the New Testament as they now stand by our chief Reformers. Tyndale in his Prologues notices the doubts as to the Apostolical authority of the Epistles of St Jude and St James and of the Epistle to the Hebrews; but he adds that 'he sees no reason why they should 'not be accounted parts of Holy Scripture[3].' Bishop Jewel rebuts Stapleton's charge that he rejected the Epistle of St James on the authority of Calvin[4]. Bullinger's Decades contain a list of all the books of the New Testament in the 'roll of the Divine Scriptures[5].'

The opinions of the English Reformers.

TYNDALE.

JEWEL.

BULLINGER.

---

books, without distinguishing the Apocryphal *additions* to Esther, Daniel, and Jeremiah.
[1] Some light may be perhaps thrown upon this strange ambiguity, which, as far as I know, is not noticed in any history of the Articles.
[2] *Confes. Fid.* Cap. i.; Niemeyer, II. 1 ff.; Hardwick, *ib.* App. VI.
[3] He makes no preface to the Apocalypse.
[4] Jewel, *Defence of Apology*, Pt. II. ix. 1.
[5] Bullinger, *Decades*, I. p. 54 (ed. Park. Soc.).

Whitaker affirms that our Church receives 'the same 'books of the New Testament and those only, as were 'enumerated at the Council of Trent;' though he notices the doubts of the Lutherans and of Caietan in particular as to the seven Antilegomena[1]. Fulke again in his answer to Martin states that the Holy Scriptures according to the acknowledgment of the English Church are 'all 'and every one of equal credit and authority, as being all inspired of God[2]...' But it is useless to multiply quotations, for I am not aware that the judgment of the English Church as expressed by her theologians has ever varied as to the Canonical authority of any of the books of the New Testament. If she left her sons at liberty to test the worth of their inheritance, they have learnt to value more highly what they have proved more fully. The same Apostolic books as gave life and strength to the early Churches quicken our own. And they are recognised in the same way, by familiar and reverent use, and not by any formal decree.

Conclusion.

Little now remains to be added on a retrospect of the history of the Canon. That whole history is itself a striking lesson in the character and conduct of the Providential government of the Church. The recognition of the Apostolic writings as authoritative and complete was partial and progressive, like the formalizing of doctrine, and the settling of ecclesiastical order. But each successive step was virtually implied in that which preceded; and the principle by which they were all directed was acknowledged from the first.

---

[1] Whitaker, *Disp. on Scripture*, c. xvi. p. 105 (ed. Park. Soc.).

[2] Fulke, *Defence of the Translation of the Bible*, p. 8 (ed. Park. Soc.).

Thus it is that it is impossible to point to any period as marking the date at which our present Canon was determined. When it first appears, it is presented not as a novelty but as an ancient tradition. Its limits were fixed in the earliest times by use rather than by criticism; and this use itself was based on immediate knowledge.

For it is of the utmost importance to remember that the Canon was never referred in the first ages to the authority of Fathers or Councils. The appeal was made not to the judgment of men but to that of Churches, and of those particularly which were most nearly interested in the genuineness of separate writings. And thus it is found that while all the Canonical books are supported by the concurrent testimony of all, or at least of many Churches, no more than isolated opinions of private men can be brought forward in support of the authority of any other writings. For the New Testament Apocrypha can hold a place by the side of the Apostolic books only so long as our view is limited to a narrow range: a comprehensive survey of their general relations shews the real interval by which they are separated.

And this holds true even of those books which are exposed to the most serious doubts. The Canonicity of the second Epistle of St Peter, which on purely historical grounds cannot be pronounced certainly authentic, is yet supported by evidence incomparably more weighty than can be alleged in favour of that of the Epistle of Barnabas, or of the Shepherd of Hermas, the best attested of Apocryphal writings. Nor must it be forgotten that in the fourth century numerous sources of information were still open to which we can no longer have recourse. And how important these may have been for the history of the Canon can be rightly estimated by the results which have followed from some recent discoveries, which have tended without exception to remove specious difficulties and to confirm the traditional judgments of the Church.

But though external evidence is the proper proof both of the authenticity and authority of the New Testament, it is supported by powerful internal testimony drawn from the relations of the books to one another and to the early developments of Christian doctrine. Subjective criticism when used as an independent guide is always uncertain, and often treacherous; but when it is confined to the interpretation and comparison of historic data, it confirms as well as illustrates. And no one perhaps can read the New Testament as a whole, even in the pursuit of some particular investigation, without gaining a conviction of its unity not less real because it cannot be expressed or transferred. But while this must be matter of personal experience, the connexion of the Apostolic writings with the characteristic forms of early doctrine is clearer and more tangible. Something has been said already on this subject, and it offers a wide field for future investigation. For the New Testament is not only a complete spring of Christian truth; it is also a perfect key to the history of the Christian Church.

To the last however it will be impossible to close up every avenue of doubt, and the Canon, like all else that has a moral value, can be determined only with practical and not with demonstrative certainty. But to estimate the comparative value of this proof, let any one contrast the evidence on which we receive the writings of St Paul or St John with that which we regard as satisfactory in the case of the letters of Cicero or Pliny. The result is as striking as it is for the most part unnoticed.

Yet the record of divine Revelation when committed to human care is not, at least apparently, exempted from the accidents and caprices which affect the transmission of ordinary books. And if the evidence by which its authenticity is supported is more complete, more varied, more continuous, than can be brought forward for any other book, it is because it appeals with universal power to the conscience of mankind: because the Church which under the influence of the Spirit first recognised in it the law of its constitution has never failed to seek in it fresh guidance and strength.

Conclusion.

APPENDIX A.

ON THE HISTORY OF THE WORD ΚΑΝΩΝ[1].

Appendix A.
A. The Classical use of κανών.
1. Literally.

THE original meaning of κανών (connected with קָנֶה, κάνη, κάννα, *canna* [*canalis, channel*], *cane, cannon*) is *a straight rod*, as a *ruler*, or rarely the *beam of a balance;* and this with the secondary notion either (1) of keeping anything straight, as the *rods of a shield*, or the rod (*liciatorium*) used in weaving; or (2) of testing straightness, as a *carpenter's rule*, and even improperly a *plumbline*.

2. Metaphorically.

From the sense of literal measurement naturally followed the metaphorical use of κανών (like *regula, norma, rule*) to express that which serves to *measure* or *determine anything;* whether in Ethics, as the good man (Ar. *Eth. Nic.* III. 4, 5); or in Art, as the Doryphorus of Polycletus (ὁ κανών); or in Language, as the 'Canons' of Grammar[2].

With a slight variation in meaning, *great epochs* which served as landmarks of history, were called κανόνες χρονικοί· and κανών was used for a summary account of the contents of a work—the rule, as it were, by which its composition was determined[3].

One instance of the metaphorical use of the word requires special notice. The Alexandrine grammarians spoke of the classic Greek authors, as a whole, as ὁ κανών, the absolute standard of pure language, the perfect model of composition[4].

---

[1] Credner has investigated the early meanings of the word at considerable length, but I cannot accept all his conclusions (*Zur Gesch. d. K.* 3—68).

[2] References for all these meanings are given in the Lexicons.

[3] Cf. Credner, p. 10. To this sense must be referred the *Paschal Canons* of various authors, and the *Eusebian Canons* of the New Testament.

[4] Redepenning, *Origines*, I. 12.

ON THE HISTORY OF THE WORD ΚΑΝΩΝ.

By a common transition in the history of words, κανών as that which measures was afterwards used for that which is so measured. Thus a certain place at Olympia was called κανών, and in late Greek κανών (canon) was used for a fixed tax, as of corn[1]. So also in Music, a canon is a composition in which a given melody is the model on which all the parts are strictly formed.

Appendix A.
3. Passively.

So far we have traced the common use of κανών, and at first sight the application of the word to the collection of classic authors seems to offer a complete explanation of its use in relation to Holy Scripture; but the ecclesiastical history of the word lends no support to such an hypothesis. The word occurs in its literal sense in Judith xiii. 6 (LXX.) for the rod at the head of a couch; and again in Job xxxviii. 5 (Aq.) for a measuring line (קָו, σπαρτίον, LXX. *linea*, Vulg.)[2].

B. The Ecclesiastical use of the word.

1. In the LXX.

In the New Testament it is used in two passages of St Paul's Epistles. In one (Gal. vi. 16, ὅσοι τῷ κανόνι (*regula*, Vulg.) τούτῳ στοιχήσουσι) the abstract idea of the Christian rule of faith is connected by the verb with the primary notion of an outward measure. In the second (2 Cor. x. 13—16, κατὰ τὸ μέτρον τοῦ κανόνος (*regulæ*, Vulg.), κατὰ τὸν κανόνα ἡμῶν, ἐν ἀλλοτρίῳ κανόνι) the transition from an active to a passive sense is very clearly marked.

2. In the New Testament.

In later Christian writers the metaphorical use of κανών is very frequent, both in a general sense (Clem. R. *ad Corinth.* i, ὁ κανὼν τῆς ὑποταγῆς· c. 7, ὁ εὐκλεὴς καὶ σεμνὸς τῆς ἁγίας κλήσεως κανών); and also in reference to a definite rule (*id.* c. 41, ὁ ὡρισμένος τῆς λειτουργίας κανών[3]). One use of the word however rose into peculiar prominence, and is of great importance with regard to the history of Holy Scripture. Hegesippus (cf. pp. 202 sqq.), according to the narration of Eusebius, spoke of those who tried to corrupt the 'sound rule

3. In Patristic writings:
i. Generally:
(a) As a Rule *in the widest sense.*

(β) The Rule *of Truth, whether*

---

[1] Cf. Forcellinus and Du Cange, s. v. Canon.
[2] The word is used by Philo in connexion with παράγγελμα, ὅρος, and νόμος. Credner, ss. 11 f.
[3] Credner (s. 15) thinks that the word even here describes an ideal standard.

Appendix A.	'(τὸν ὑγιῆ κανόνα) of the saving proclamation;' and whether the words be exactly quoted or not, they are fully supported by the authority of subsequent writers[1]. The early fathers, from the time of Irenæus, continually appeal to the *Rule* of Christian teaching,—variously modified in the different phrases the *Rule of the Church*, the *Rule of Truth*, the *Rule of Faith*[2],—in their controversy with heretics; and from the first, as it seems, it was regarded in a double form. At one time it is an
Abstract, or	abstract ideal standard, handed down to successive generations, the inner law, as it were, which regulated the growth and action of the Church, felt rather than expressed, realised
Concrete (*the* Creed).	rather than defined. At another time it is a concrete form, a set creed, embodying the great principles which characterised

[1] In the Clementine Homilies the word κανών is of frequent occurrence. Thus the principle of a duality in nature and Revelation is described as ὁ λόγος τοῦ προφητικοῦ κανόνος, ὁ κανὼν τῆς συζυγίας (*Hom.* II. 15, 18, 33). In like manner mention is made of the 'Rule of the Church' and of the 'Rule of Truth;' and it was by this Rule that apparent discrepancies of Scripture were to be reconciled, by this that the unity of the Jewish nation was preserved (Clem. *ad Jac.* 2 19; Petr. *ad Jac.* 3; Petr. *ad Jac.* 1). Cf. Credner, ss. 17 ff.

[2] Each of these three phrases possesses a peculiar meaning corresponding to the notions of the *Church*, the *Truth*, the *Faith*.

i. Ὁ κανὼν τῆς ἐκκλησίας expresses that Rule or governing principle by which the Church of God in its widest sense is truly held together, and yet gradually unfolded in the different stages of its growth. In early Christian writers it specially described that which was the common ground of the Old and New Testaments. Cf. Clem. Alex. *Strom.* VII. 16. 105; Orig. *de Princ.* IV. 9. But it is no less applied to the peculiar Rule and order of the Christian Church; yet still to that Rule as being one, and not as made up of many rules. Cf. Corn. ap. Euseb. *H. E.* VI. 43. So also we find κανὼν ἐκκλησιαστικὸs in *Synod. Ant.* ap. Routh, *Rell.* III. 291; *Concil. Nic.* Can. 2, 6, &c. And as applied to details, ὁ κανὼν in *Conc. Neocæs.* Can. 14. Cf. Routh, IV. 208. Yet cf. *Syn. Ant.* ap. Routh, III. 505.

ii. Ὁ κανὼν τῆς ἀληθείας. As the Rule of the Church regarded the outward embodiment of divine teaching in a society, so the Rule of Truth had reference to the informing life by which it is inspired. Clem. Alex. VII. 16. For the Christian this Rule was the expression of the fundamental articles of his creed. Cf. Iren. *c. Hær.* I. 9. 4; 22. 1; Novat. *de Trin.* 21; Firm. *Ep.* (Cypr.) LXXV.

iii. Ὁ κανὼν τῆς πίστεως. The Rule of Truth, when viewed in this concrete form, became the Rule of Faith. The phrase first occurs in the letter of Polycrates (Euseb. *H. E.* v. 24), and repeatedly in Tertullian (e.g. *de Vel. Virg.* 1). Credner has discussed these various phrases with his usual care and research; but it is surprising to find a scholar speaking repeatedly of ὁ κανὼν ἐκκλησιαστικός (*a. a. O.* ss. 20—58).

the doctrine and practice of the Catholic Church. Thus Clement speaks of the 'Ecclesiastical Canon' as consisting in the 'harmonious concord of the Law and the Prophets with the 'dispensation (διαθήκη) given to men at the presence of the 'Lord among them[1].' In other words, the Rule which determined the progress of the Church was seen in that principle of unity by which its several parts were bound together, 'in virtue 'of the appropriate dispensations [granted at successive pe-'riods], or rather in virtue of one dispensation adapted to the 'wants of different times[2].' But this principle of unity found a clear expression 'in the one unchangeable rule of faith[3],' the Apostolic enunciation of the great facts of the Incarnation, in which all earlier Revelations and later hopes found their explanation and fulfilment.

At the beginning of the fourth century the word received a still more definite and restricted meaning, without losing the original idea involved in it. The standard of revealed truth was the measure of practice no less than of belief; and Synodical decisions were regarded in detail as 'Canons' of Christian action[4]. In particular the sum of such decisions affecting those specially devoted to the ministry in holy things was the 'Rule' by which they were bound; and they were described simply as 'those included in or belonging to the 'Rule,' just as we now speak of 'ordination' and 'orders[5].'

Appendix A.

(γ) *The* Rule of Discipline.

---

[1] Clem. Alex. *Strom.* VI. 15. 125: κανὼν ἐκκλησιαστικὸς ἡ συνῳδία καὶ ἡ συμφωνία νόμου τε καὶ προφητῶν τῇ κατὰ τὴν τοῦ Κυρίου παρουσίαν παραδιδομένῃ διαθήκῃ. Cf. p. 204, n. 4.
[2] Clem. Alex. *Strom.* VII. 17. 107: κατά τε οὖν ὑπόστασιν κατά τε ἐπίνοιαν κατά τε ἀρχὴν κατά τε ἐξοχὴν μόνην εἶναί φαμεν τὴν ἀρχαίαν καὶ καθολικὴν ἐκκλησίαν, εἰς ἑνότητα πίστεως μιᾶς κατὰ τὰς οἰκείας διαθήκας, μᾶλλον δὲ κατὰ τὴν διαθήκην τὴν μίαν διαφόροις τοῖς χρόνοις, ἑνὸς (τοῦ θεοῦ) τῷ βουλεύματι δι' ἑνὸς (τοῦ κυρίου), συνάγουσαν τοὺς ἤδη κατατεταγμένους, οὓς προώρισεν ὁ θεὸς δικαίους ἐσομένους πρὸ καταβολῆς κόσμου ἐγνωκώς.
[3] Tertull. *de Vel. Virg.* 1.
[4] The ordinances of Gregory of Neo-Cæsarea (c. 262 A.D.) and those of Peter of Alexandria (c. 306 A.D.), taken from his work περὶ μετανοίας (Routh, *Rell. Sacr.* III. 256 ff.; IV. 23 ff.), are called 'Canons,' but it is probable that the title was given to them at a later time. The first Council which gave the name of Canons to its decrees was that of Antioch (341 A.D.): in the earlier Councils they were called δόγματα or ὅροι. Cf. Credner, p. 51 n.
[5] The earliest instance of this use of the word with which I am ac-

Appendix A.

(δ) Canon in a passive sense.

There was a further stage in the history of the word when it assumed a definitely passive meaning, as when applied to the fixed Psalms appointed for festivals, or to the 'Canon,' the invariable element of the Roman Liturgy, in the course of which the dead were commemorated or 'canonized[1].'

ii. As applied to Holy Scripture. The derivatives of κανών were used

Hitherto no instance of the application of the word κανών to the Holy Scriptures has been noticed, and the earliest with which I am acquainted occurs in Athanasius; but the derivatives κανονικός, κανονίζω occur in Origen[2], though these words quainted occurs in the Nicene decrees: Can. 16: πρεσβύτεροι ἢ διάκονοι ἢ ὅλως ἐν τῷ κανόνι ἐξεταζόμενοι. Can. 17: πολλοὶ ἐν τῷ κανόνι ἐξεταζόμενοι. Can. 19:...περὶ τῶν διακονισσῶν καὶ ὅλως τῶν ἐν τῷ κανόνι (al. κλήρῳ) ἐξεταζομένων. Cf. *Conc. Ant.* Can. 6: ὁ αὐτὸς δὲ ὅρος ἐπὶ λαϊκῶν καὶ πρεσβυτέρων καὶ διακόνων καὶ πάντων τῶν ἐν τῷ κανόνι (al. ἐν τῷ κλήρῳ) καταλεγομένων. *Conc. Chalc.* 2: ἢ ὅλως τινὰ τοῦ κανόνος. But this κανών must not be confounded with the κατάλογος though the same persons might be described as *ἐν τῷ καταλόγῳ* and *ἐν τῷ κανόνι*. Thus the two are joined in *Conc. Trull.* 5: μηδεὶς τῶν ἐν ἱερατικῷ καταλόγῳ τῶν ἐν τῷ κανόνι...Again in *Conc. Tol.* III. 5: qui vero *sub canone ecclesiastico* jacuerint... Athanas. (?) *de Virgin.* I. p. 1052: οὐαὶ παρθένῳ τῇ μὴ οὔσῃ ὑπὸ κανόνα. Cf. *Conc. Ant.* 1. The word κανονικοί first occurs in Cyril. (Catech. Pref. 3, cf. *Conc. Laod.* 15; *Conc. Constant.* I. 6), and is found frequently in later writers. Du Cange (s. v.) quotes a passage which illustrates very well the origin of the word: Canonici secundum canones—an earlier writer would have said canonem—regulares secundum regulam vivant.

Bingham (*Antiq.* I. 5, 10) and Credner (p. 56), though with hesitation, identify the κανών and the κατάλογος, but the passages quoted are I think conclusive against the identification.

[1] Cf. Suicer, s. v.

The interchange of κανονικός and καθολικός, not only in the title of the seven Catholic Epistles but elsewhere, is a singular proof of the supposed universality of an authoritative judgment of the Church. Cf. Euseb. *H.E.* III. 5; *Conc. Carthag.* XXIV. (Int. Gr.).

There is a curious account of κανονική—the mathematical basis of music—in Aulus Gellius, *N. A.* XVI. 18; and in other Roman scientific writers the word *canonicus* is used to express that which is determined by definite rules, as the phenomena of the heavens. Cf. August. *de Civ. Dei*, III. 15. 1, and Forcellinus, s. v.

[2] Orig. *de Princ.* IV. 33: in Scripturis Canonicis nusquam ad præsens invenimus. Id. *Prol. in Cantic. s.f.*: Illud tamen palam est multa vel ab apostolis vel ab evangelistis exempla esse prolata et Novo Testamento inserta, quæ in his Scripturis quas Canonicas habemus, nunquam legimus, in apocryphis tamen inveniuntur et evidenter ex ipsis ostenduntur assumpta. Id. *Comm. in Matt.* § 117: In nullo *regulari* libro hoc positum invenitur. Id. *Comm. in Matt.* § 28: Nec enim scimus in libris canonizatis historiam de Janne et Jambre resistentibus Mosi. Just before Rufinus says: Fertur ergo in Scripturis *non manifestis* (*i.e.* apocryphis, as he elsewhere translates the word). The phrase (*Prol. in Cantic. s.f.*) cum

ON THE HISTORY OF THE WORD ΚΑΝΩΝ.

did not come into common use till the beginning of the fourth century. In the interval Diocletian had attempted to destroy the 'Scriptures of the Christian Law;' and as far as his efforts tended to make a more complete separation of authoritative from unauthoritative books, they were likely to fix upon the former a popular and simple title. Yet even after the persecution of Diocletian the word *Canonical* was not universally current. Eusebius I believe nowhere applies it to the Holy Scriptures; and its reappearance in the writings of Athanasius seems to shew that it was originally employed in the school of Alexandria, and thence passed into the general dialect of the Church.

<small>Appendix A.

before the word itself,

but not commonly till after the persecution of Diocletian.</small>

The original meaning of the whole class of words, *Canonical, Canonize, Canon,* in reference to the Scriptures is necessarily to be sought in that of the word first used. But κανονικός, like κανών, was employed both in an active and in a passive sense. Letters which contained rules, and letters composed according to rule, were alike called Canonical[1]; and so the name may have been given to the Apostolic writings either as containing the standard of doctrine or as ratified by the decision of the Church. Popular opinion favours the first interpretation[2]: the prevalent usage of the word however is decidedly in favour of the second. Thus the Latin equivalent of κανονικός,

<small>(α) κανονικός.</small>

---

neque apud Hebræos...amplius *habeatur in Canone*, is probably only a rendering of κανονίζομαι.

Since these words are found in works which survive only in the Latin version, they have been suspected by Redepenning (*Origines*, I. 239) to be due to Rufinus, and not to Origen. Credner follows Redepenning without reserve. But I can see no ground for the suspicion. The fact that in one place we have *regularis* and in another *canonicus* to express the same idea marks an exact translation.

[1] The canonical letter of Gregory of Cæsarea (c. 262 A.D.) is an instance of the first kind (Routh, *Rell.*

Sacr. III. 256 ff.). On the *litteræ formatæ* or *canonicæ*, cf. Bingham, II. 4, 5.

[2] Even Credner has sanctioned this view: 'The Scriptures of the *Canon* (γραφαὶ κανόνος) are,' he says, 'the Scriptures of the Law: those writings are *canonical* which obtain the force of Law: those writings are *canonized* which are included among them' (p. 67). Credner does not quote any instance of the phrase γραφαὶ κανόνος, nor do I know one; but he supports his view by reference to the words *scripturæ legis* in the Acts of Felix (cf. p. 409), and to *litteræ fidei* in Tertullian *de Præscr.* 14.

510   ON THE HISTORY OF THE WORD ΚΑΝΩΝ.

Appendix A.

regularis, points to a passive sense, even though the analogy be imperfect. Ecclesiastics again of every grade were called *Canonici*, as bound by a common rule; and in later times we commonly read of canonical obedience, a canonical allowance, and canonical hours of prayer.

(β) κανονίζω.

The application of κανονίζω (βιβλία κανονιζόμενα, κεκανονισμένα, ἀκανόνιστα) to the Holy Scriptures confirms the belief that they were called *canonical* in a passive sense. In classical Greek the word means to measure or form according to a fixed standard[1]. As in similar terms, the notion of approval was added to that of trial; and those writings might fitly be said to be *canonized* which were ratified by an authoritative rule. Thus Origen says that 'no one should use for the proof of doc-'trine books not included among the canonized Scriptures[2].' Athanasius again speaks of 'books which are canonized (κανονι-'ζόμενα) and have been handed down' from former time[3]. The Canon of [Laodicea] forbade the public reading of 'books 'which had not been canonized (ἀκανόνιστα).' And at a later time we read 'of books used in the Church and which have 'been canonized[4].'

(γ) κανών.
The first use of this word.

The clearest instance in early times of the application of the word κανών to the Scriptures occurs at the end of the enumeration of the books of the Old and New Testaments commonly attributed to Amphilochius. 'This,' he says, 'would 'be the most unerring Canon of the Inspired Scriptures.' The measure, that is, by which the contents of the Bible might be

---

[1] Cf. Arist. *Eth. Nic.* II. 3. 8, κανονίζομεν δὲ καὶ τὰς πράξεις ... ἡδονῇ καὶ λύπῃ. In later times the word was used to express regular grammatical inflexion. Schol. ad Hom. *Odyss.* IX. 347 : τὸ δὲ τῇ πόθεν κα-. νονίζεται ; A very striking instance of the use of the word in this sense, as applied to the substance of Apostolic teaching, is found in the Letter of Ptolemæus to Flora : μαθήσῃ θεοῦ διδόντος ἐξῆς καὶ τὴν τούτου [τοῦ ἀγαθοῦ] ἀρχὴν τε καὶ γέννησιν ἀξιου- μένη τῆς ἀποστολικῆς παραδόσεως ἣν ἐκ διαδοχῆς καὶ ἡμεῖς παρειλήφαμεν, μετὰ καὶ τοῦ κανονίσαι πάντας τοὺς λόγους τῇ τοῦ σωτῆρος διδασκαλίᾳ (*Epist. Ptolem.* ap. Epiph. *Hær.* XXXIII. 7).

[2] Orig. *Comm. in Matt.* § 28 : Nemo uti debet ad confirmationem dogmatum libris qui sunt extra canonizatas scripturas.

[3] Athan. *Ep. Fest.* App. D. The same phrase occurs in Leontius.

[4] Niceph. *Stichometria*, App. D.

tried, and so approximately an index or catalogue of its constituent books[1]. But the use of the word was not confined within these limits. It was natural that the rule of written, no less than of traditional teaching, should be regarded in a concrete form. The ideas of the New Testament and of the Creed grew out of the same circumstances and were fixed by the same authority. Thus Athanasius and later writers speak of books 'without the Canon,' where the Canon is no longer the measure of Scripture, but Scripture itself as fixed and measured, the definite collection of books received by the Church as authoritative. In this sense the word soon found general acceptance. The Canon was the measured field of the theologian, marked out like that of the athlete or of the Apostle by adequate authority.

Appendix A.

But though this was, as I believe, the true meaning of the word, instances are not wanting in which the Scriptures are called a Rule, as being in themselves the measure of Christian truth; for they possess an inherent authority though it was needful that they should be ratified by an outward sanction. At the beginning of the fifth century Isidore of Pelusium calls 'the divine Scriptures the rule of truth[2]'; and it is useless to multiply examples from later ages. Time proved the worth of the Apostolic words. The ideal Rule preceded the material Rule; but after a long trial the Church recognised in the Bible the full enunciation of that law which was embodied in her formularies and epitomized in her Creeds.

Its later meaning.

[1] Amphil. *Iamb. ad Sel.* App. D.
[2] Isid. Pelus. *Ep.* CXIV. ὁ κανὼν τῆς ἀληθείας αἱ θεῖαι γραφαί.

APPENDIX B.

ON THE USE OF APOCRYPHAL WRITINGS IN THE EARLY CHURCH.

Appendix B.
Two classes of writings called Apocryphal.

TWO different classes of writings may be described as Apocryphal in respect to their claims to be admitted among the Canonical Scriptures of the New Testament. The first consists of the scanty remains of the works of the immediate successors of the Apostles: the second of books professing either to be written by Apostles or to contain an authoritative record of their teaching. The history of the first class consequently illustrates the limits by which the idea of Canonicity was bounded; while the history of the second class offers a criterion of the critical tact by which the true and the false were distinguished by the early Church. The two classes together offer an instructive contrast to the New Testament as a whole, no less in their outward fortunes than in their inward character.

i. Writings of Apostolic men.

It would not have been surprising if the writings of the Apostolic Fathers had been invested with something of Apostolic authority, not indeed in accordance with their own claims[1], but by the pardonable reverence of a later age for all those who had looked on the Truth at its dawning. Yet a few questionable epithets alone remain to witness to the existence of such a feeling; and no more than three books of this class obtained a partial ecclesiastical currency, through which they were at first not clearly separated from the disputed writings of the New Testament.

The Epistle of Clement.

The Epistle of Clement, the earliest and best authenticated

[1] Cf. pp. 56 ff.

APOCRYPHAL WRITINGS IN THE EARLY CHURCH. 513

of uncanonical Christian writings, is quoted by Irenæus, by Clement of Alexandria, and by Origen, without anything to shew that they regarded it as an inspired book[1]. Eusebius omits all mention of it in his famous Catalogue of writings which claimed to be authoritative[2]; and though many later writers were acquainted with it, no one I believe favours its reception among the Canonical Scriptures[3].

Appendix B.

The Epistle of Barnabas, in consideration of the name of the 'Apostle,' and of the peculiar character of its teaching, gained a position at Alexandria which it does not appear to have ever held in any other place[4]. It is contained together with the Shepherd in the Sinaitic Manuscript of the Greek Bible. But Eusebius classes it among the 'spurious' books; and Jerome calls it 'Apocryphal[5].'

The Epistle of Barnabas.

The Shepherd of Hermas again, which approximates in form and manner most closely to the pattern of Holy Scriptures, though commonly quoted with respect by the Greek fathers, is expressly stated by Tertullian to have been excluded from the New Testament 'by every Council of the Churches,' Catholic or schismatic[6].

The Shepherd of Hermas.

Nor was it a mere accident that these three writings occupied a peculiar position. They were supposed to be written by men who were honoured by direct Apostolic testimony. But the letters of Polycarp and Ignatius, whose names the New

Honoured in consideration of a supposed Apostolic sanction.

---

[1] Iren. III. 3. 3 (ἱκανωτάτην γραφήν); Clem. Alex. *Strom.* I. 7. 38; IV. 17. 107 (ὁ ἀπόστολος Κλήμης); VI. 8. 65. Cf. *ib.* V. 12. 81. Orig. *de Princ.* II. 3. 6; *Sel. in Ezech.* viii. Cf. *in Joan.* T. VI. 36.

[2] Euseb. *H. E.* III. 25. Cf. p. 415. This is the more remarkable because he elsewhere mentions the Epistle with great respect, cf. iii. 16: μεγάλη καὶ θαυμασία ἐπιστολή. Cf. also *H. E.* VI. 13.

[3] Comp. Lightfoot, pp. 272 ff.

[4] Clem. Alex. *Strom.* II. 6. 31: εἰκότως οὖν ὁ ἀπόστολος Βαρνάβας... *ib.* 7. 35: II. 20. 116: οὔ μοι δεῖ πλειόνων λόγων παραθεμένῳ μάρτυν τὸν ἀποστολικὸν Βαρνάβαν, ὁ δὲ τῶν ἑβδομήκοντα ἦν καὶ συνεργὸς τοῦ Παύλου... Cf. *Strom.* II. 15. 67; *ib.* 18. 84; V. 8. 52; *ib.* 10. 64.

Orig. *c. Cels.* I. 63: γέγραπται ἐν τῇ Βαρνάβα καθολικῇ ἐπιστολῇ. *Comm. in Rom.* I. 24: ...in multis Scripturæ locis... Cf. *de Princ.* III. 2. 4. Comp. App. XX. n.

[5] Euseb. *H. E.* III. 25. Hieron. *de Virr. Ill.* 6: Barnabas Cyprius... epistolam composuit quæ inter apocryphas Scripturas legitur.

[6] Tert. *de Pudic.* 10, 20. Cf. Hieron. *in Hab.* i. (i. 14). The references of Irenæus and Origen to the Shepherd have been noticed already, pp. 385 n. 1, 365 n. 4.

L L 2

Appendix B.

But nowhere publicly received into the Canon.

The writings of the Apostolic Fathers never reckoned Canonical.

Testament does not record, were never put forward as claiming Canonical authority[1]. And thus the high estimation in which the works of Clement and Barnabas and Hermas were held becomes an indirect evidence of the implicit reverence paid to the Apostolic words, and of the Apostolic basis of the Canon.

The usage of the Churches interprets and corrects the judgment of individual writers. The Epistle of Barnabas was read in the time of Jerome, but among the Apocryphal Scriptures, and it is still found in the Sinaitic Manuscript after the Apocalypse. The Epistle of Clement was publicly read in the Church at Corinth and elsewhere[2]; and it also is included (with the second spurious Epistle) in the Alexandrine Manuscript of the Greek Bible[3]; but in this case the book was placed after the Apocalypse; and so in both respects it occupied a position similar to that of the Apocryphal books of the Old Testament, according to the judgment of our own Church. The Shepherd again was long regarded as a book useful for purposes of instruction, and is found not only in the Greek Sinaitic Manuscript, but also in Latin Bibles; but it was definitely excluded from the Canon by Eusebius, Athanasius, and Jerome, who record its partial reception[4]. And in a word, no one of these writings is reckoned among the Canonical books in any Catalogue of the Scriptures[5].

If then it be admitted, and this is the utmost that can be urged, that these books were at one time ranged with the Antilegomena of the New Testament[6], it is evident that they occupied

---

[1] Cf. Hieron. *de Virr. Ill.* 17: [Polyc. ad Phil. Epistola] in conventu Asiæ legitur.

[2] Euseb. *H. E.* III. 16; IV. 23. Hieron. *de Virr. Ill.* 15.

[3] The fact that this is the only copy of the Epistle now in existence is in itself a proof of its comparatively limited circulation.

[4] Euseb. *H. E.* III. 25; Athanas. *Ep. Fest.* T. I. 767.

[5] The Catalogue at the end of the Apostolic Canons may seem an exception to this statement, since it ratifies the two Epistles and Constitutions of Clement; but it has been shewn already that the peculiarities of this Catalogue received no conciliar sanction. Cf. p. 438.

[6] According to the old text of the Stichometry of Nicephorus the Apocalypse is classed with the writings of the Apostolic Fathers as Apocryphal; but the truer text places it with the Apocalypse of Peter, the Gospel according to the Hebrews, and the Epistle of Barnabas, as disputed, while the remaining writings

that position in virtue of a supposed indirect Apostolic autho- | Appendix B.
rity, just as the other books were disputed, because their claims
to Apostolicity were also supposed to be indirect[1]. And it is
equally certain that those who expressed the judgment of the
Church, when a decision was first called for, unanimously excluded them from the Canon, while with scarcely less unanimity
they included in it the Epistles of St James and St Jude, the
Epistle to the Hebrews, and the Apocalypse and shorter Epistles
of St John. The ecclesiastical use of the writings of the Apostolic fathers was partial and reserved from the first, and it
became gradually less frequent till it ceased entirely. Wider
knowledge and longer experience denied to them the sanction
which was accorded to the doubtful books of the New Testament.

Of Apocryphal writings directly claiming Apostolic autho- | ii. *Apocry-phal writings.*
rity, four only deserve particular notice, the Gospel according
to the Hebrews, and the Gospel, the Preaching, and the Apocalypse of St Peter. The Gospel according to the Egyptians[2],
and the Acts of Paul and Thecla, never obtained any marked
authority; and still less so the various Gospels and Acts which
date from the close of the second century, and are popularly
attributed to the inventive industry of Leucius[3].

One passage which occurred in the Gospel according to the | *The Gospel according to the Hebrews.*
Hebrews is found in a letter of Ignatius, who does not how-
ever quote the words as written[4]. Papias again related a story

of the Apostolic Fathers, with some other books, are Apocryphal.
[1] The second Epistle of St Peter is the only exception to this state-ment; and that is beset with pecu-liar historical difficulties on every side.
[2] Clem. Alex. *Strom.* III. 9. 63; *ib.* 13. 93 : πρῶτον μὲν οὖν ἐν τοῖς πα-ραδεδομένοις ἡμῖν τέτταρσιν εὐαγγε-λίοις οὐκ ἔχομεν τὸ ῥητόν, ἀλλ' ἐν τῷ κατ' Αἰγυπτίους. Cf. [Clem.] *Ep.* II. 12. See *Introduction to the Study of the Gospels*, App. C.
[3] Comp. Lardner, *Credibility*, ix. 422 ff.

[4] Ign. *ad Smyrn.* iii. Cf. Jacob-son *l.c.* The general character of the references to the Evangelic nar-rative in Ignatius lends no support to the view that he derived the words directly from any document. Still less is there any valid reason for sup-posing that he derived them from 'the Gospel of the Hebrews' in the (Nazarene) form with which Jerome was acquainted with it. Origen quotes the main phrase from the Teaching of Peter (*de Princ.* Præf. 8). Comp. *Introd. to the Gospels*, App. C. § 16.

Appendix B.

'of a woman accused of many crimes before our Lord, which 'was contained in the Gospel according to the Hebrews,' but the words of Eusebius seem to imply that he did not refer to that book as the source of the narrative[1]. The evangelic quotations of Justin Martyr offer no support to the notion that he used it as a coordinate authority with the Canonical Gospels, but on the contrary distinguish a detail which it contained from that which was written in the Apostolic memoirs[2]. Hegesippus is the first author who was certainly acquainted with it; but there is nothing to shew that he attributed to it any peculiar authority[3]. Clement of Alexandria and Origen both quote the book, but both distinctly affirm that the four Canonical Gospels stood alone as acknowledged records of the Lord's life[4]. Irenæus does not refer to it[5].

The testimony of Eusebius has been already quoted. He reckoned four Gospels only as generally acknowledged. Some Gospels 'brought forward by heretics in the name of Apostles' he rejected peremptorily. But the use which had been made by ecclesiastical writers of 'the Gospel according to the Hebrews' placed it in a different position. He notices, therefore, that according to the opinion of some, it was put in the second division of 'controverted' books, which he calls 'spurious,' in company with the 'Shepherd' and the Epistle of Barnabas[6].

---

[1] Euseb. *H. E.* III. 39. Cf. Routh, *Rell. Sacr.* I. 39.

[2] Cf. pp. 162 ff.

[3] Heges. ap. Euseb. *H. E.* IV. 22; Routh, *Rell. Sacr.* I. 277; supr. pp. 209 f.

[4] Clem. Alex. *Strom.* II. 9. § 45: ᾗ κἂν τῷ καθ' Ἑβραίους εὐαγγελίῳ Ὁ θαυμάσας βασιλεύσαι, γέγραπται, καὶ ὁ βασιλεύσας ἀναπαήσεται. No stress can be laid upon γέγραπται in this connexion where it is not used absolutely.

Orig. *Hom. in Jer.* xv. § 4 (εἴ τις παραδέχεται): *in Joh.* ii. § 6 (ἐὰν δὲ προσίεταί τις). These words taken in connexion with *Hom. in Luc.* I, shew beyond question that Origen did not reckon *the Gospel according to the Hebrews* among 'the four Gospels' (τὰ δὲ τέτταρα μόνα προκρίνει ἡ θεοῦ ἐκκλησία *Hom. in Luc.* i.). See also *in Matt.* T. xv. 14 *Int. Lat.*; and compare Hier. *de Virr. Ill.* 2.

[5] He states indeed that 'the Ebionites used that Gospel only which is 'according to St Matthew' (i. 26, 2; iii. 11, 7). There is no evidence to shew that he knew more than the fact as it had been reported to him. Comp. Euseb. *H. E.* III. 27; nor is there any substantial ground for identifying this Gospel with the Greek 'Gospel according to the Hebrews' of Clement and Origen.

[6] P. 419, *H. E.* III. 25: ἤδη δ' ἐν

WRITINGS IN THE EARLY CHURCH. 517

Epiphanius regarded the 'Hebrew Gospel' as a heretical work based on St Matthew[1]. Jerome has referred to it frequently[2], and he translated it into Greek and Latin, but he nowhere attributes to it any peculiar authority, and calls St John expressly the fourth and last Evangelist[3]. Yet the fact that he appealed to

Appendix B.

τούτοις τινὲς καὶ τὸ καθ''Εβραίους εὐαγγέλιον κατέλεξαν, ᾧ μάλιστα 'Εβραίων οἱ τὸν Χριστὸν παραδεξάμενοι χαίρουσι. The position which the sentence occupies proves that a place among the controverted books was in the judgment of Eusebius the highest and not the lowest place which could be given to the Gospel. Nor is there anything in the words to indicate that it had only 'lately' been reckoned spurious (ἤδη κατέλεξαν); nor yet that it had ever held a place equal to that of the four Gospels. Eusebius quotes a saying from 'the Gospel existing among the Jews 'in the Hebrew language' (*Theoph.* iv. 13. Syr. Lee's trans. p. 234); and again in the Greek remains of the *Theophania* (§ 22, Migne vi. 685) he gives an account of a very interesting version of the parable of the talents from 'the Gospel which has come to 'us in Hebrew characters.' These quotations do not shew, or even tend to shew, that he 'placed' it on the same footing as the four Gospels; though he inclines to the view which is given in the latter place of the Lord's judgment, an opinion which few will share with him. Compare the *Stichometry* of Nicephorus, App. XIX.

[1] This seems to me to be the true interpretation of Epiphanius' confused statements as to the book used by the Ebionites which they called '[the Gospel] according to the He-'brews,' or as he (apparently) wrongly paraphrases afterwards the 'He-'brew [Gospel].' *Hær.* XXX. 3 : δέχονται...τὸ κατὰ Ματθαῖον Εὐαγγέλιον ...καλοῦσι δὲ αὐτὸ κατὰ 'Εβραίους... *Hær.* XXX. 13 : ἐν τῷ γοῦν παρ' οὐτοῖς Εὐαγγελίῳ κατὰ Ματθαῖον ὀνομαζομένῳ οὐχ ὅλῳ δὲ πληρεστάτῳ ἀλλὰ νενοθευμένῳ καὶ ἠκρωτηριασμένῳ,

'Εβραϊκὸν δὲ τοῦτο καλοῦσι...On the other hand he says of the Gospel of the Nazarenes: ἔχουσι τὸ κατὰ Ματθαῖον Εὐαγγέλιον πληρέστατον 'Εβραϊστί (*Hær.* XXIX. 9). Epiphanius is a most untrustworthy guide, but he evidently wished to contrast the two Gospels. As far as he knew (only at second-hand), they were quite distinct books. Neither had any authority as distinct from the Canonical St Matthew, the standard by which they were tried, and the Ebionite Gospel was not only 'mutilated' but also 'corrupted.'

[2] *Dial. adv. Pelag.* III. 2: in Evangelio *juxta Hebræos*, quod Chaldaico quidem Syroque sermone sed Hebraicis litteris scriptum est, quo utuntur usque hodie Nazareni, *secundum apostolos*, sive ut plerique autumant *juxta Matthæum*, quod et in Cæsariensi habetur bibliotheca, narrat historia... Quibus testimoniis si non uteris ad auctoritatem, utere saltem ad antiquitatem, quid omnes ecclesiastici viri senserint. Cf. *de Virr. Ill.* 2; *in Isai.* IV. c. xi.; *id.* XL. c. xl.; *in Ezech.* IV. c. xvi.; *in Mich.* II. c. vii. (quoted with the Song of Solomon, yet with hesitation); *Comm. in Matt.* I. c. vi. 11; *ib.* II. c. xii. 13; *ib.* IV. c. xxvii. 51; *Comm. in Eph.* III. c. v. 4. Credner (*Beitr.* I. 395 ff.) gives these and the remaining passages at length.

[3] As to Jerome's notices of *the Gospel according to the Hebrews* Martianay says rightly (*de Virr. Ill.* ii.): de hoc evangelio multa alibi docet Hieronymus quæ in speciem sibi videntur adversari. The Gospel which he 'translated into Greek and Latin' (*l. c.*) was a copy of *the Gospel according to the Hebrews* used by the Nazarenes (*de Virr. Ill.* iii.). This

Appendix B.

the book as giving the testimony of antiquity furnished occasion for an adversary to charge him with making 'a fifth Gospel[1];' and at a later time, in deference to Jerome's judgment, Bede reckoned it among the 'Ecclesiastical' rather than the 'Apo- 'cryphal writings[2].'

he appears to identify in passing with the *Gospel of the Ebionites* (quo utuntur Nazaræi et Ebionitæ: *in Matt.* xii. 13: comp. *Dial. adv. Pel.* III. 2 quoted above), a casual statement on which no stress can be laid. 'Very 'many' (plerique) held it to be the original (Aramaic) Gospel of St Matthew (quod vocatur a plerisque Matthæi authenticum: *in Matt.* l. c.: comp. note 4), a common way of speaking which explains Jerome's words in *de Virr. Ill.* iii. ipsum Hebraicum [Evangelium Matthæi] habetur usque hodie...and *in Matt.* ii. 5 in ipso Hebraico, where indeed he prefers the reading of the Hebrew copy. So far as I can judge, his treatment of the book does not suggest the idea that he held it to be canonical. The translation which he made was apparently for his own use and not for publication. At least I am not aware that any independent reference to it remains, though Jerome's own quotations attracted considerable attention (note 5). It is worthy of notice that his latest reference (*Dial. adv. Pel.* III. 2, see *n.* 4) is the least precise; and probably expresses some results of later knowledge. Here he assigns to the book the weight of antiquity but not of canonicity in words which recal what he says of Apocrypha of the O. T.: [Ecclesia] legat ad ædificationem plebis non ad auctoritatem Ecclesiasticorum dogmatum confirmandam (*Prol. in Libros Sol.*).

It is hardly worth while to add that Theodoret (*Hær. Tert.* ii. 2) speaks, evidently at second-hand, of the Ebionites as using 'only the Gos- 'pel according to the Hebrews.' Another body, he adds, bearing the same name, used only *the Gospel ac-*

cording to St Matthew (*l. c.*). If his evidence was of independent value it would go to distinguish the Ebionite 'Gospel of St Matthew' from the Ebionite 'Gospel according to the 'Hebrews.' In the next chapter he says that the Nazarenes used 'the 'Gospel according to Peter.' Mr Nicholson (*Gospel according to the Hebrews*, p. 23) reads unaccountably in the first passage τὸ κατὰ 'Εβιωναίους εὐαγγέλιον.

[1] Julian Pelag. ap. August. Op. *imperf.* IV. 88. Theod. Mops. ap. Phot. *Cod.* 177.

[2] Bede *Comm. in Luc. init.* The fragments are collected in the *Introduction to the Study of the Gospels.* App. D. They have been published together with many other 'apocry- 'phal' evangelic fragments by Mr Nicholson (*The Gospel according to the Hebrews*, London, 1879), who has illustrated them by an elaborate Commentary. It is a pleasure to acknowledge the care and labour which he has bestowed upon the work, though the theory which he maintains that 'Matthew wrote *at* '*different times* the canonical Gospel 'and the Gospel according to the 'Hebrews, or at least that large part 'of the latter which runs parallel to 'the former' (p. 104), seems to me to be wholly untenable. The available evidence is far too meagre to furnish a certain view of the relations of the various documents vaguely spoken of as '·the Gospel according 'to the Hebrews,' 'the Hebrew Gos- 'pel,' the Gospel used by the Nazarenes, 'the [Hebrew] Gospel accord- 'ing to St Matthew.' It is quite possible that the Hebrew Gospel of St Matthew was the foundation of the different Aramaic and Greek

WRITINGS IN THE EARLY CHURCH. 519

The Gospel of Peter has been already noticed. How far this Gospel was connected with the 'Preaching of Peter,' which is quoted frequently by Clement of Alexandria[1], and once by Gregory of Nazianzus[2], is very uncertain[3]. There is indeed nothing in the fragments of the Preaching that remain which requires a severer censure than Serapion passed on the Gospel. And it seems very likely that both books contained memoirs of the Apostle's teaching based in a great measure on authentic traditions.

Appendix B.

The Gospel and Preaching of Peter

It has been already shewn that it is uncertain whether the Gospel of Peter was regarded as Canonical at Rhossus[4]; and even if it had been so, the custom of an obscure town, which was at once corrected by superior authority, cannot be set against the silence of the other early Churches, and the condemnation of the book by every later writer who mentions it. In reply to a quotation from the *Doctrine of Peter*, Origen says that we 'must first reply that that book is not reckoned among 'the ecclesiastical books; and next shew that it is not a ge-'nuine writing of Peter nor of any one else who was inspired 'by the Spirit of God;' and Eusebius repeats the same judgment[5]. Nor am I aware that it was ever supposed to be a Canonical book.

not Canonical.

The Canonicity of the Apocalypse of Peter is supported by more important authority. The doubtful testimony of the

The Apocalypse of Peter.

texts, which were variously modified by omissions and traditional accretions. The text of D shews how readily these could gain currency. But no one, I believe, on an impartial examination, could refuse to allow that the fragments which remain of 'the Gospel according to the He-'brews' and the Ebionite and Nazarene Gospels represent as a whole a type of evangelic narrative distinctly later than that of the Canonical narratives; and in the parallels a later type of the common matter.
  [1] Clem. Alex. *Strom.* I. 29. 182; VI. 5. 39 ff.; *ib.* 6. 48; *ib.* 15. 128.
  [2] Greg. Naz. *Ep. ad Cæsar.* I. Credner, *Beitr.* I. 353, 359.

  [3] Some have argued that the Acts, the Preaching, the Doctrine, and the Apocalypse of Peter, the Preaching and Acts of Paul, and the Preaching of Peter and Paul, were only different recensions of the same work. It is perhaps nearer the truth to say that they were all built on a common oral tradition. The variety of titles and forms is in itself a conclusive argument against their general and public reception. Cf. Reuss, § 253.
  [4] Cf. pp. 390 sq.
  [5] Orig. *de Princ.* I. Præf. 8; cf. *Comm. in Joan.* XIII. 17. Euseb. *H. E.* III. 3.

520   APOCRYPHAL WRITINGS IN THE EARLY CHURCH.

Appendix B. Muratorian Canon has been considered before[1]. In addition to this, Clement of Alexandria wrote short notes upon it, as well as upon the Catholic Epistles and upon the Epistle of Barnabas[2]. But the book was rejected by Eusebius[3]. Macarius Magnes twice refers to a passage contained in it (ἐκ περιουσίας) implying that it had no substantial authority in itself[4].

Peculiarities of some Manuscripts of the New Testament. Mention has been made already of the insertion of the two Epistles of Clement and of the Epistle of Barnabas and the Shepherd in the Alexandrine and Sinaitic Manuscripts of the Greek Bible respectively. Two other Greek Manuscripts contain notices of Apocryphal writings which are curious, though they are not of importance.

Cod. Boerner. At the end of the *Codex Boernerianus* (G) a Manuscript of the ninth century, which contains the thirteen Epistles of St Paul with some lacunæ, after a vacant space occur the words: 'The Epistle to Laodiceans 'begins' [προς λαουδακησας (*laudicenses* g.) αρχεται]. This addition is not found in the *Codex Augiensis* (F) which was derived from the same original as G, nor is there any trace of the Epistle itself. Haimo of Halberstadt in the ninth century mentions the Latin cento of Pauline phrases which now bears the title 'as useful though not Canonical[5],' and the inscription in G probably refers to the same compilation.

Cod. Claromont. In the *Codex Claromontanus* (D) again after the Epistle to Philemon there occurs a Stichometry of the books of the Old and New Testament, obviously imperfect and corrupt, and then follows, after a vacant space, the Epistle to the Hebrews. This Stichometry omits the Epistles to the Philippians, both to the Thessalonians, and to the Hebrews; and after mentioning the Epistle of Jude thus concludes: 'The Epistle of Barna-'bas, the Apocalypse of John, the Acts of the Apostles, the 'Shepherd, the Acts of Paul, the Revelation of Peter[6].' But Stichometries are no more than tables of contents; and both the contents and the arrangement of the different books in a Manuscript may have been influenced by many causes.

[1] Cf. p. 218.
[2] Euseb. *H. E.* VI. 14.
[3] *Ib.* III. 23.   [4] IV. 6, 16.
[5] See App. E.
[6] Tischdf. *Cod. Clarom.* p. 468. *Prolegg.* XI. Cf. App. D.

APPENDIX C.

THE MURATORIAN FRAGMENT ON THE CANON.

THE famous fragment on the Canon of the New Testament, which was first published in an unsatisfactory form by Muratori in 1740, has lately been examined by several scholars with the most exact diligence. The collation made by Dr Hertz in 1847 for Baron Bunsen (*Analecta Ante-Nicæna*, I. pp. 137 ff.) and the facsimile traced by Dr Tregelles in 1857 leave absolutely nothing to be desired for a complete knowledge of the text itself[1]. But the general character of the Manuscript in which it occurs has been strangely overlooked, and as this throws considerable light on the fragment itself I copied some pages of the context at Milan this year (1865) by the kind permission of Dr Ceriani, which are now first printed with the Canon. A cursory glance at them will shew what reliance can be placed on the perverse ingenuity of some recent scholars who have not scrupled to affirm that the Canon, so far from being corrupt, is really one of the most correct texts which antiquity has bequeathed to us.

---

[1] Even the most careful transcripts fail in complete accuracy, and I owe to the great kindness of Dr Ceriani the results of a collation of Dr Tregelles' facsimile (made twice) with the original manuscript. These I have added in the notes [1874].

The text has been published again from new collations by Reifferscheid, in the *Transactions of the Imperial Academy, Vienna*, 1871, p. 496 *n*. (republished, *Bibl. Pat. Lat. Ital.* ii. 32 f.), and by Harnack *Zeitschrift für K. G.* iv. 595 ff. The minute variations do not affect the text, and I have retained Dr Ceriani's notes unchanged, for his judgment is not likely to be wrong.

To earlier essays on the fragment may be added those of Harnack, *a. a. O.* iii. 358 ff., Overbeck, *Zur Geschichte d. Kanons*, 1880, 71 ff.; Hilgenfeld, *Ztsch. für Wissensch. Theologie*, 1881, 129 ff. The true understanding of the fragment, or rather fragments, seems to me to depend upon the due recognition of the incompleteness of the text which is commonly overlooked.

Appendix C.

The Manuscript (*Bibl. Ambros.* Cod. 101) in which the Canon is contained was brought from Columban's famous monastery at Bobbio. It may therefore probably be of Irish origin or descent, though there is nothing in the Manuscript itself, as far as I could observe, which proves this to be the case. It was written probably in the eighth (or seventh) century, and contains a miscellaneous collection of Latin fragments, including passages from Eucherius, Ambrose, translations from Chrysostom, and brief expositions of the Catholic Creed. The first sheet ends (p. 9 *b*) abruptly in the middle of a quotation from Eucherius *Liber Formularum Spirit. Intell.* [called in the manuscript *De Nominibus*] cap. vi. beginning *Vir et uxor væ vobis divitibus in Evangelio*, which closes the line. The next sheet (p. 10 *a*) begins at the top without any vacant space whatsoever *quibus tamen interfuit*, and the Canon extends over p. 10 *a*, p. 10 *b*, and p. 11 *a* to within eight lines of the bottom. A little more than half a line is left vacant at the end of the Canon, and then in the next line a new fragment from a Homily of Ambrose commences. It is impossible to tell how much has been lost between the first and second sheets. They probably formed part of the same Manuscript, but the number of lines in the pages of the first sheet is twenty-four, and in those of the second sheet thirty-one. The style of writing is also somewhat different, but not more so I think than is often the case in different parts of the same Manuscript. The sheets have I believe no signature, but I omitted to look carefully for this. It may be added that the pages are generally furnished with a heading, but there is none over those containing the Canon except a simple I on the top of p. 11 *a*.

The Fragment stands exactly thus in the Manuscript[1]:

p. 10 *a*. quibus tamen interfuit et ita posuit.

---

[1] The fragment is of course written wholly in capitals. Some of the letters are larger than others, but it does not appear certain that this is due to anything but the caprice of the scribe and I have neglected to notice the difference. The lines printed in capitals are rubricated in

THE MURATORIAN FRAGMENT ON THE CANON. 523

TERTIO EUANGELII LIBRUM SECANDO* LUCAN
lucas iste medicus post acensum* xpī.
cum eo paulus quasi ut iuris studiosum
secundum adsumsisset numeni suo 5
ex opinione concriset* dnm tamen nec ipse
duidit in carne   et ide pro asequi potuit·
ita et ad natiuitate iohannis incipet dicere
QUARTI EUANGELIORUM. IOHANNIS EX DECIPOLIS
cohortantibus condescipulis et eps suis 10
dixit conieiunate mihi· odie triduo et quid
cuique fuerit reuelatum alterutrum
nobis ennaremus   eadem nocte reue
latum andreae ex apostolis ut recognis
centibus cuntis iohannis suo nomine 15
cunta* discribret* et ideo licit uaria sin
culis euangeliorum libris principia

Appendix C.

    l. 2 T initiale *nigrum* (Ceriani).
    ... sec*u*ndo. [*u* manu dubia, C.]
    l. 3 a*s*censum. [*s* superscriptum manu dubia, C.]
    l. 4 post *studiosum* nullum punctum sed foramen pro directione scripturæ (C).
    l. 6 concri*b*set.
    l. 7 *d* crossed out.
    ... pro*ut*.
    l. 8 post *dicere* foramen non punctum ut l. 4 (C).
    l. 9 *euangeliorum*, rubra omnia et cum puncto rubro post vocem (C).
    l. 16 cun*c*ta. [*c* serius sed vetus, C.]
    ... discrib*e*ret.

the original. In the scanty punctuation I have followed Dr Tregelles' facsimile. [Dr Tregelles has since published the fragments with a very complete commentary (Oxford, 1867), and I owe to him two corrections in the quotation from Ambrose: 11 *b*, 31 *add*. Dei; 12 *a*, 4 cccxviii. for cccviii. 1870.]

    The division of the words cannot be accurately represented. The prepositions are generally written with their cases: e.g. *depassione, deresurrectione*, &c. The *ae* is generally written at length, but three or four times (p. 10 *a* l. 29, p. 10 *b*, l. 8) in a contracted form.

    The words corrected in the Manuscript are marked by an asterisk. The corrections (apparently by the first hand, when it is not otherwise specified) are given below the text.

doceantur nihil tamen differt creden
tium fedei* cum uno ac principali s̄pu de
clarata sint in omnibus omnia de natiui   20
tate de passione de resurrectione
de conuesatione* cum decipulis suis
ac de gemino eius aduentu
primo in humilitate dispectus quod fo*
it secundum potetate* regali   pre   25
clarum quod foturum est. quid ergo
mirum si iohannes tam constanter
sincula etiā in epistulis suis proferam
dicens in semeipsu quæ uidimus oculis
nostris et auribus audiuimus et manus   30
nostrae palpauerunt haec scripsimus
                                  [uobis

p. 10 b. sic enim non solum uisurem sed* auditorem'
sed et scriptorē omnium mirabiliū d̄ni per ordi
nem profetetur acta autē omniū apostolorum
sub uno libro scribta sunt lucas obtime theofi

l. 18 *differt*, sub *t* lineola 1 manu (C).
l. 19 f*i*dei.
l. 22 *conuersatione*.
l. 24 *humilitate*, *u* primo fuit *o*, serius, ut apparet, refectum *u* (C).
ll. 24, 25 The letters *fo* at the end of l. 24 are fairly distinct. Those at the beginning of the next line are almost erased. Dr Tregelles conjectures that the scribe began to write *foturum*, and then discovering his error erased the letters which he had written. [*Quod fo*, omnino intacta, et, linea resumpta, *it* intacta, evanida tamen et maculata: super *fo* autem [linearum vestigia] ut *fu* videatur correctum 1 manu cujus prior pars evanuerit, C.]
l. 25 pote*s*tate.
... post *regali* erasæ duæ literæ (C).
l. 28 *proferam* cum *m* in fine aperte non *t* (C). proferat *sic* (R).
l. 31 *uobis* under the line almost illegible. Dr Tregelles first traced out the true reading. [literæ *us* evanuerunt plene post *u*, ubi *s* connexum cum *a* et partim evanidum, C.]
l. 1 sed *et*.
l. 2 d̄ni, *i* in rasura, manu dubia; videtur fuisse *s* (C).
l. 4 *uno*, pro *o* fuit *u*; manu dubia ex *u* refectum *o* (C).

THE MURATORIAN FRAGMENT ON THE CANON. 525

le conprindit quia sub praesentia eius singula 5
gerebantur sicute* et semote passione petri
euidenter declarat sed* profectione pauli ab* ur
bes* ad spaniā proficescentis epistulæ autem
pauli quae a quo loco uel qua ex causa directe
sint uolentatibus* intellegere ipse declarant > 10
primū omnium corintheis scysmæ heresis in
terdicens deincepsb callætis circumcisione
romanis aūte ornidine* scripturarum sed et*
principium earum e*e* esse xpm intimans
prolexius scripsit de quibus sincolis neces 15
se est ad nobis desputari cum ipse beatus
apostulus paulus sequens prodecessuris sui
iohannis ordinē non nisi *omenati*. semptae*
eccleses* scribat ordine tali a corenthios
prima. ad efesius seconda ad philippinsis* ter 20
tia ad colosensis quarta ad calatas quin
ta ad tensaolenecinsis sexta. ad romanos

Appendix C.

l. 6 sicut*i*, abrasis: relictum *i* (*sicuti*) (C).
l. 7 sed *et*.
... *ab*, *b* manu fortasse prima, refectum ex *d* priori ut videtur (C).
l. 8 *urbe*, erasum *s*.
... *proficescentis*, *e* (prius) scriptum primo, ut apparet, et 1ª manus in actu scriptionis correxit *i* (C).
l. 10 uolentibus. [*e* ex *u* refectum manu dubia: *ta* imperfecte erasa, sed nulla puncta inferius: super initio *t* secundi punctum m. dubia, C.]
l. 13 ordine......*et* erased.
l. 14 post *earum* tres literæ erasæ 1ª et 3ª videntur fuisse *e*, sed media omnino incerta (C).
l. 17 *apostulus*, prius *u* mutatum in *o* manu dubia (C).
... *prodecessuris*, *u* videtur mutatum in *o* manu dubia (C).
l. 18 *nomenati*: *omenatī, litera erasa videtur fuisse *d* non *c*: *n* superius 1ª manu ut videtur (C).
... *semptē*, *a* erasum (C).
l. 19 ecclesi*is*.
l. 20 *efesius*, *u* aperte non *o* (C).
... philippens*es*. [ex *i* in fine factum *e* 1ª manu, C.]
l. 22 Romanus: ex forma potius *us* quam *os* (C).

Appendix C.

septima uerum corentheis* et tesaolecen
sibus* licit* pro correbtione iteretur una
tamen per omnem orbem terrae ecclesia 25
deffusa esse denoscitur et iohannis eni in a͞
pocalebsy licet sept͞e eccleseis scribat
tamen omnibus dicit uer͞u ad filemonem una'
et at tit͞u una   et ad tymoth͞eu duas pro affec
to et dilectione in honore tamen eclesiae ca 30
tholice in ordinatione ecclesiastice

I

p. 11 a. descepline* sc͞ificate sunt fertur etiam ad
laudicensis* alia ad alexandrinos pauli no
mine fincte ad hesem* marcionis et alia plu
ra quae in chatholicam* eclesiam recepi non
potest fel enim cum melle misceri non con 5
cruit epistola sane iude et superscrictio
iohannis duas in catholica habentur et sapi
entia ab amicis salomonis in honor͞e ipsius
scripta   apocalapse etiam iohanis et pe
tri tantum recipemus* quam quidam ex nos 10
tris legi in eclesia nolunt pastorem uero
nuperrim et* temporibus nostris in urbe
roma herma concripsit* sedente cathe

l. 23 cor*i*ntheis, primum *e* manus 1ᵃ instauravit ut *i* eraso ductu inferiori (C).
... t*h*esaolecensibus. [*h* superius manu dubia, C.]
l. 24 lic*e*t. [*e* ex *i* effictum 1ᵃ manu, C.]
p. 11. In fronte I atramento non minio exaratum, et manu dubia (C).
l. 1 d*i*escepline. [ex *e* priori correctum *i* 1ᵃ manu, relicto et *e*, C.]
l. 2 laudicens*e*s. [ex *i* correctum *e* 1ᵃ manu, C.]
l. 3 her*e*sem.
l. 4 catholicam.
l. 10 recip*i*mus.
l. 12 e.
l. 13 con*s*cripsit.

tra urbis romae aeclesiae pio ēps frater*
eius et ideo legi eum quidē oportet se pu   15
plicare uero in eclesia populo neque inter
profe*tas conpletum numero nene* inter
apostolos in finē temporum potest.
arsinoi autem seu ualentini. uel metiad**
nihil in totum recipemus. qui etiam nouū   20
psalmorum librum marcioni conscripse
runt una cum basilide assianum* catafry
cum contitutorem*

ABRHAM NOMERAUIT SERuolus suos uer
naculus et cum trecentis dece et octo   25
uirus* adeptus uictoriam liuerauit nepōte
prouatur diuisionis adfectus quando sic
amabat nepotem ut pro eo nec uellit* decli
nare* periculum quid est nomerauit. hoc
est elegit unde et illud non solū ad scien   30
tiam dei refertur. sed ētiā ad cratia iustorum

p. 11 b. quod in euangelio dicit dn̄s īhs et capilli uestri
omnes nomerati sunt cognouit ergo dn̄s qui
sunt eius eos autem eos* autē* qui non sunt
ipsius non dignatur cognuscere numerauit
cccxviii ut scias non quantitatē numeri sed me   5

l. 14 frat*r*e. [manu dubia, C.]
l. 17 profe*s*tas, *s* erasum (C).
... *neque*. [*nene* sic primo, C.]
l. 19 *metiad*** prius *e* erasione et nova scriptura manu dubia rasuræ fortasse superscriptum : post *d* est manu 1ª, ut apparet, pars superior *i* vel *l* vel *h* : inferius nunc erasum est et manu seriori, ut videtur, inscriptum *e*, quantum apparet, et additum ſ sine puncto (C).
l. 22 assian*o*m. [*u* manu 1ª mutatum in *o*, C.]
l. 23 co*n*stitutorem.
l. 26 uiris.
l. 28 uelli.
l. 29 declinaret.
l. 3 eos autē underlined.

C.   M M

Appendix C.

ritum electionis expressu. eos enim adscuit*
quod* dignus* nomero iudicauit fidelium******
qui in d̄n̄i nostr̄i īh̄u x̄p̄i passionem crederent
ccc enim d* τ greca littera significat. dece
et octo aut̄e summa IH exprimit nomen fidei   10
ergo merito habraham uicit non popoloso
exercito deneque eos quibus quinque regum
arma ceserunt* cum paucis egressus uer
naculis triumfauit sed qui uincit non
debet arorocare* sibi uictoria sed referre   15
deo. hoc abraham docit qui triumpho
homilior factus est non superuior. sacri
ficium denique obtulit decimas dedit
ideoque eum melchisedeh qui interpe
tratione latine dicitur rex iustitiæ rex   20
pacis benedixit erat enim sacerdos sum
mi d̄i qui est rex iustitiæ sacerdos dei
non* cui dicitur tu es sacerdos in aeternū
secondum ordine melcisedeh hoc est dei
filius sacerdos patris qui sui corporis   25
sacrificio patrem nostris repropicia
uit dilectis *nomerauit abraam* seruo
los suos uernaculos et cum cccxviii uiris
adeptus uictoria liuerauit nepotem quid
est nomerauit. hoc est elegit. unde et illud   30
non solum ad scientiā Dei refertur sed
[etiam ad cratia iustorum

p. 12 a. quod in euangelio dicit d̄n̄s īh̄s et capilli uestri
omnes nomerati sunt · cognouit ergo d̄n̄s qui

l. 6 adsc*i*uit.
l. 7 quos dignos.
l. 9 d erased.
l. 13 ces*s*erunt.
l. 15 arrocare.
l. 23 nisi.
l. 27. A late hand in the margin *hic dimite...* abraham.

sunt ipsius . eos autem qui non sunt ipsius non
dignatur cognuscere . nomerauit aute cccxviii
ut scias non quantitate numeri sed meritum
electionis expressum. eos autem sciuit quods*
dignos numero iudicauit fideleium qui in dn̄i
nostri ihu xpi passionem crederent. ccc enim
dece et octo greca littera significat xviii
autem summa IH exprimit nomen fidei.
ergo abraham uicit non populosu exercitu
denique eos quibus v regum arma cesserunt
cum paucis egressus uernaculis trium
phauit . sed qui uincit non debit arrocare
sibi uictoria sed d̄o referri hoc abraham
docit qui triumpho homilior factus est.
non soperior sacrifigium n denique obtu
lit decimas dedit ideoque eum melcisedeh
qui interpetraone latina rex iustitiae
rex pacis benedixit . erat enim sacerdos
summi di qui est rex iustitiae sacerdos d̄i
nisi cu* dicitur tu es sacerdos in aeternum
secondum .ordine melcisedeh hoc est filii
us sacerdus patris qui suis* corporis sacri
ficat patre nostris repropitiauit dilectis
INCIPIT DE EXPOSITIONEM DIUERSARŪ RERŪ

Appendix C.

5

10

15

20

25

INPRIMIS mandragora in genesi genus
pumi simillimum paruo peponis speci
e muel odore...... (Eucher. Lugd. *Instruct.* II. 3.)

The fragment from Ambrose (*De Abrahamo*, I. 3. 15) which
follows the Fragment on the Canon furnishes a fair criterion of
the accuracy to be expected from the scribe. And by a remarkable accident the piece is more than usually instructive,
for the whole fragment is repeated. Thus we have two copies
of the same original and their divergence is a certain index of

l. 6 quos.   l. 22 cui.   l. 24 sui.

THE MURATORIAN FRAGMENT ON THE CANON.

Appendix C.

the inaccuracy of the transcriber which cannot be gainsaid. The second copy differs from the first in the following places:

p. 11 b. 27 nomerauit abraam (Abr. nomerauit).
28 seruolos suos uernaculos (seruolus suos uernaculus).
29 uictoria (uictoriam).
29 *omit* prouatur—periculum (two and a half lines).

p. 12 a. 3 ipsius (eius).
4 nom. autē (*om.* autem).
6 eos autem (eos enim).
6 sciuit (adsciuit).
7 numero (nomero).
7 fideleium (fidelium).
9 dece et octo (d* τ).
11 ergo (ergo merito).
11 abraham (habraham).
11 populosu exercitu (popoloso exercito).
12 denique (deneque).
14 triumphauit (triumfauit).
14 debit (debet).
15 uictoriā (uictoria).
15 dō referri (referre deo).
17 soperior (superuior).
17 sacrifigium (sacrificium).
17 n (?).
18 melcisedeh (melchisedeh).
19 interpetraone (interpetratione).
19 latina (latine).
19 rex (dicitur rex).
23 filii|us (filius).
24 sacerdus (sacerdos).
24 sacrificat (sacrificio).
25 repropitiauit (repropiciauit).

Thus in thirty lines there are thirty unquestionable clerical blunders including one important omission (p. 11^b 29), two other omissions which destroy the sense completely (p. 12^a 11

THE MURATORIAN FRAGMENT ON THE CANON.

merito, 19 *dicitur*), one substitution equally destructive of the sense (p. 12ᵃ 9 *decem et octo* for τ), and four changes which appear to be intentional and false alterations (p. 12ᵃ 6 *scivit*, 11 *populosu exercitu*, 23 *filii*, 25 *sacrificat*). We have therefore to deal with the work of a scribe either unable or unwilling to understand the work which he was copying, and yet given to arbitrary alteration of the text before him from regard simply to the supposed form of words. To these graver errors must be added the misuse of letters (e.g. of *u* for *o* and conversely of *o* for *u*; of *g* for *c*; of *f* for *ph*; of *i* for *e* and conversely of *e* for *i*; of *ei* for *i*; of *u* for *b*; of *c* for *ch*), and the omission of the final *m*.

Nor yet was the actual writer of the Manuscript the only author of errors. It appears from the repetition of one or two obvious mistakes in the repeated fragment that the text from which the copy was made was either carelessly written or much injured. Thus we have in both transcripts *ad cratia, docit, homilior, dilectis* (for *delictis*); and it is scarcely likely that *interpretatione* and *interpetraone* could have been copied severally from a legible original.

On the other hand the text itself as it stands is substantially a good one. The errors by which it is deformed are due to carelessness and ignorance and not to the badness of the source from which it was taken. But these errors are such as in several cases could not be rectified without other authorities for comparison.

In the sheet which precedes the Fragment on the Canon the same phenomena occur. There is in that also the same ignorance of construction: the same false criticism: the same confusion of letters and terminations. If we now apply the results gained from the examination of the context to the Fragment on the Canon, part of it at least can be restored with complete certainty; and part may be pronounced hopelessly corrupt. It has been shewn that a fragment of thirty lines contains three serious omissions and at least two other changes of words wholly destructive of the sense, and it would therefore

Appendix C.

be almost incredible that something of the like kind should not occur in a passage nearly three times as long. Other evidence shews that conjecture would have been unable to supply what is wanting or satisfactorily correct what is wrong in the one case, and there is no reason to hope that it would be happier in the other.

1. Two of the commonest blunders in the Manuscript are the interchange of *u* and *o* and the omission of the final *m*. Of these undoubted examples occur: p. 11^{a}25, 11^{b}9 dece, 11^{b}24 secundum ordine, p. 9^a 22 in mala partem &c., 11^b 11 popoloso exercito, p. 12^a 11 populosu exercitu, p. 12^a 24 sacerdus &c. In the Fragment similar errors occur p. 10^a 2 tertio (-um), secundo (-um); 4 eo (eum); 11 triduo (-um); [23 adventu (-to)]; 24 primo (-um); [foit (fuit)]; 26 foturum; 29 semetipsu (-o); p. 10^b 1 visurem (-orem); 12 circumcisione (-em); 17 apostulus; 20 seconda; 29 affecto; 11^a 6 epistola (elsewhere epistula).

2. The interchange of *e* and *i* (*y*) is even more common. Examples occur: p. 11^b 16 docit; 27 dilectis (delictis); 12^a 14 debit, 15 referri (referre); 11^b 12 deneque; 9^a 11 proxemi. In the Fragment the same error is found in various combinations: p. 10^a 5 numeni (nomine); 8 incipet; 9 iohannis (so l. 15, 10^b 26); 14 recogniscentibus; 16 discriberet, licit; 24 dispectus; p. 10^b 3 profetetur; 5 conprindit; 6 sicute; 8 proficescentis; 11 corintheis; 15 prolexius; 16 desputari; 18 nomenatim; 19 corenthios; 20 philippinses; 21 colosensis; 23 corentheis; 26 deffusa, denoscitur; 27 apocalebsy, eccleseis; p. 11^a 3 heresem; 4 recepi (10, 20 recipimus).

3. The aspirate is also omitted or inserted: p. 8^b 26 talamo; 11^b 11 Habraham; 12^a 18 Melcisedeh. Thus we have in the Fragment p. 10^a 11 odie; p. 10^b 11 scysmae.

4. *C* and *g* are interchanged: p. 11^b 15 arrocare; 31 cratia; 12^a 17 sacrifigium. So in the Fragment 10^a 17 sinculis, 28 sincula; 10^b 15 sincolis (5 singula); 12 callætis; 21 calatas; 11^a 6 concruit; 23 catafrycum.

THE MURATORIAN FRAGMENT ON THE CANON. 533

5. *E* and *ae* are interchanged: p. 9ª 13 consumate iustitiae; p. 9ª 9 audi et vidae. In the Fragment 10ª 25 preclarum; 10ᵇ 9 directe; 10 ipse; 18 semptae͞; 30 eclesiae catholice; 31 eclesiastice descepline; p. 11ª 1 scīficate; 3 fincte, heresem; 6 iude; 14 aeclesiae.

Appendix C.

6. *F* and *ph*: 11ᵇ 14 triumfauit (16 triumpho). So in the Fragment p. 10ᵇ 4 Theofile; 28 Filemonem.

7. Another common interchange is that of *b* and *p* which occurs in the Fragment: p. 10ᵇ 4 scribta, obtime: 24 correbtione; 27 apocalebsy: and conversely 11ª 16 puplicare.

In addition to these changes of letters the repetition of letters and the omission of repeated letters are fruitful sources of error. Of the former there are examples: p. 11ᵇ 15 arorocare, 3 eos autem. In the Fragment both I believe occur. In p. 11ª 6 superscrictio iohannis is an evident mistake for superscripti (or -tæ) iohannis, the *o* (or *io*) having been falsely added from a confusion with the corresponding syllable of the next word. Again in p. 10ª 22 the pronoun suis requires an antecedent and it is extremely likely that $\overline{dni}$ was omitted between the words de natiuitate. So again in p. 10ᵇ 3 profitetur requires se which was probably lost after visorem before sed. It is not unlikely that in p. 11ª 2 alia should be repeated.

One false reading appears to be due to the mechanical assimilation of terminations of which examples occur: p. 12ª 19 interpetraone latina (-ne); 11 populosu exercitu; p. 11ᵇ 11 popoloso exercito. Thus p. 10ᵇ 4 optime Theophile should almost certainly be optime Theophilo. The phrase 'optime Theophile' is found in the Preface to the Gospel and not in the dedication of the Acts, and could not therefore be used as the title of the latter book.

Some forms are mere senseless and unintelligible blunders: 10ª 6 concribset; 10ᵇ 22, 23 Tensaolenecinsis, Thesaolecensibus; 11ª 9 apocalapse. And the inconsistency of the scribe is seen in the variations of spelling the same word: 10ᵇ 11 Corintheis,

THE MURATORIAN FRAGMENT ON THE CANON.

Appendix C.

19 Corenthios, 23 Corentheis; and so with Iohannes and discipulus. But prodecessoris (10ᵇ 17) and finctæ (11ᵃ 3) are probably genuine forms. If then we take account of these errors we shall obtain a text of the Fragment as complete as the conditions of correction will allow. Two or three passages in it will remain which can only be dealt with by conjectures wholly arbitrary and uncertain.

* * * * * * * *

quibus tamen interfuit et ita posuit[1]. Tertium Evangelii librum secundum Lucan Lucas iste medicus post ascensum[2] Christi cum eum Paulus quasi †ut iuris[3] studiosum secundum adsumsisset nomine suo ex opinione[4] conscripsit: Dominum tamen nec ipse uidit in carne, et idem prout assequi potuit, ita et a natiuitate Iohannis incepit dicere*. †Quarti Euangeliorum†[5] Iohannes ex discipulis. Cohortantibus condiscipulis

---

[1] *Et ita*, *i.e.* καὶ οὕτως, even so (as he had heard from St Peter) without addition or omission. Euseb. *H. E.* III. 39. I see no probability whatever in the view advocated by Hesse that the words refer to the last section of St Mark (xvi. 9—20), as containing statements which were not derived from apostolic authority, but due to the Evangelist's own experience (*e.g.* v. 20), a section which Hesse admits to be 'certainly unauthentic.' The phrase 'interesse colloquio' is perfectly good Latin, and the statement that 'Mark recorded what he heard Peter ' relate ' falls in completely with ἕνια γράψας ὡς ἀπεμνημόνευσεν, so that it is needless to seek any other interpretation.

[2] These words evidently refer to the time when St Luke became a teacher and not to the time when he wrote his Gospel, as if the writer thought that St Mark's Gospel was written *before* the Ascension (Hesse, s. 64).

[3] *Ut iuris studiosum secundum*. The words *ut iuris* must be corrupt. *Iuris* might stand for τοῦ δικαίου, but not for τῆς δικαιοσύνης. It has been suggested that it may stand for 'lex,' 'scriptura' (cf. Hesse, p. 75), but hardly, I think, in a translation. *Virtutis* seems to be nearer the sense. The correction of Routh *secum* for *secundum* (cf. Acts xv. 37) is very plausible. If *secundum* is correct it must mean *as assistant, as in the second rank*. [The addition of *sui* makes the reading *itineris [sui] socium secum* quite certain. F. J. A. H.]

[4] The suggestion of [Rönsch] (Hesse s. 80) that *ex opinione* is equivalent to ἐξ ἀκοῆς seems to be most plausible. *Opinio* has the meaning of *rumour* in the silver age. Formerly I supposed that the phrase represented κατὰ τὸ δόξαν with a reference to ἔδοξε κἀμοί (Luke i. 3).

[5] There is an analogy in the Fragment for the change of *Quarti* to *Quartum*. But *Euangeliorum* can hardly be right, and it is probable that the whole clause is corrupt. *Euangeliorum* may be a blunder for *Euangelî librum*, and *conscripsit* may then be supplied from the former

et episcopis suis dixit: Conieiunate mihi hodie triduum, et quid cuique fuerit reuelatum alterutrum¹ nobis enarremus. Eadem nocte reuelatum Andreæ ex apostolis, ut recognoscentibus cunctis, Iohannes suo nomine cuncta describeret. * * * Et ideo² licet uaria singulis Euangeliorum libris principia doceantur nihil tamen differt³ credentium fidei, cum uno ac principali spiritu declarata sint in omnibus omnia de natiuitate, de passione, de resurrectione, de conuersatione cum discipulis suis, ac de gemino eius aduento⁴ *primum in humilitate despectûs, quod fuit, secundum potestate regali præclarum, quod futurum est. * * * Quid ergo mirum si Iohannes tam constanter singula etiam in epistulis suis proferat dicens in semetipsum⁵: *Quæ uidimus oculis nostris, et auribus audiuimus, et manus nostræ palpauerunt, hæc scripsimus*⁶? Sic enim non solum uisorem [se], sed et auditorem, sed et scriptorem omnium mirabilium domini per ordinem profitetur.

Acta autem omnium apostolorum sub uno libro scripta sunt. Lucas optime Theophilo comprendit, quia sub præsentia eius singula gerebantur, sicuti et †semote⁷ passionem Petri euiden-

Appendix C.

---

sentence. But all conjectures are most uncertain, though the stop (in the MS.) after *Evangelium* favours such a conjecture as Hesse adopts... *Evangelii librum secundum Johannem. Johannes ex...*

¹ *Alterutrum.* Let us relate to one another the revelation which we receive. Comp. Acts vii. 26; James v. 16 (Vulgate).

² The whole passage from *Et ideo* —*futurum est* comes in very abruptly and has no connexion with what precedes, which could be expressed by *ideo;* and similarly what follows is not connected with it by *ergo.*

³ *Nihil tamen differt,* οὐδὲν διαφέροι τῇ—πίστει.

⁴ *Aduento.* The relatives and adjectives which follow shew that this was a neuter form answering to *euentum, inuentum,* &c. Possibly it occurs also in Ter. *Phorm.* I. 3, 2.

The addition of *m* is far less likely than the omission of it, or it would be simpler to keep *primo* and read *secundo, præclaro.* If the space at the end of the line indicates an omission, *quorum* would complete the sense.

⁵ *In semetipsum.* καθ' ἑαυτοῦ.

⁶ The quotation from 1 John i. 1 is not verbal, but the word *palpauerunt,* for *contrectauerunt* (*tractauerunt, temptauerunt*) is to be noticed. Tertullian twice quotes the verse with the Vulg. rendering; but Jerome and Victorinus quote *palpauerunt,* and *palpare* represents ψηλαφᾶν in Luke xxiv. 39.

⁷ *Semote...proficiscentis.* This sentence is evidently corrupt. If the general character of the errors of the manuscript had been favourable to the changes it would have been the simplest correction to read *semotâ passione...sed et profectione...*

ter declarat, sed et profectionem Pauli ab urbe¹ ad Spaniam proficiscentis.† * * *

Epistulæ autem Pauli, quæ, a quo loco, uel qua ex causa directæ sint, uolentibus intellegere ipsæ declarant. Primum omnium Corinthiis schisma hæresis² interdicens, deinceps³ Galatis circumcisionem, Romanis autem ordine scripturarum⁴, sed et principium earum esse Christum intimans, prolixius scripsit, de quibus singulis necesse est⁵ a nobis disputari; cum⁶ ipse beatus apostolus Paulus, sequens prodecessoris⁷ sui Iohannis ordinem, nonnisi nominatim septem ecclesiis scribat ordine tali: ad Corinthios (prima), ad Ephesios (secunda), ad Philippenses (tertia), ad Colossenses (quarta), ad Galatas (quinta), ad Thessalonicenses (sexta), ad Romanos (septima). Uerum

proficiscentis, i.e. the narrative was that (in the main) of an eye-witness, as he evidently shews by setting aside without notice events so remarkable as the Martyrdom of Peter and even the last great journey of Paul. Perhaps by reading *semota declarant* a fair sense may be obtained. The personal narrative of St Luke deals with part of the Apostolic history, just as detached allusions clearly point to the Martyrdom of Peter (John xxi. 18, 19); and even the journey of Paul to Spain (Rom. xv. 24 ff.). It is however more likely that some words have been lost at the end of the sentence, such as *significat Scriptura*.

¹ "*Ab urbe* indicates the *Roman* character of the document." Tregelles, p. 40.

² Hesse (s. 158) quotes a parallel future genitive *schismæ* and reads *schismæ hereses*, which, if indeed allowable, is probably to be received.

³ "B after *deinceps* has generally been passed unnoticed; but this seems to be the Greek numeral letter retained by the translator." Tregelles, p. 42.

⁴ *Ordine Scripturarum*, according to the general tenour of the Scriptures. Compare Tregelles, p. 43; who points out that there are more quotations from the Old Testament in the Epistle to the Romans than in all the other Epistles of St Paul together. At the same time it must be noticed that *ordinem* is a very probable correction.

⁵ The reference appears to be to the treatise from which the Fragment is taken.

⁶ The sense of the passage seems to be that a detached discussion of the points raised by the great Epistles is necessary for the whole church, for though St Paul addressed seven churches he distinguished them only by name (nonnisi nominatim), while the typical number seven really marked their unity. Hesse rightly insists on the position of *nominatim*, though I cannot follow his interpretation of this passage.

⁷ St John may be called the 'predecessor' of St Paul, either because he was an Apostle before him (Gal. i. 17, τοὺς πρὸ ἐμοῦ ἀποστόλους), or because the writer of the fragment placed the composition of the Apocalypse before that of the last of St Paul's Epistles to Churches. It seems wholly unreasonable to suppose that the writer placed the composition of St John's *Gospel* (Hesse, s. 98) 'before the beginning of St Paul's literary activity.'

THE MURATORIAN FRAGMENT ON THE CANON. 537

Corinthiis et Thessalonicensibus licet pro correptione iteretur[1], una tamen per omnem orbem terræ ecclesia diffusa esse dinoscitur; et Iohannes enim in Apocalypsi, licet septem ecclesiis scribat, tamen omnibus dicit. Uerum ad Philemonem unam et ad Titum unam, et ad Timotheum duas[2] pro affectu et dilectione; in honore tamen ecclesiæ catholicæ in ordinatione[3] ecclesiasticæ disciplinæ sanctificatæ sunt. Fertur etiam ad Laodicenses, alia ad Alexandrinos, Pauli nomine finctæ ad hæresim[4] Marcionis, et alia plura quæ in catholicam ecclesiam recipi non potest[5]: fel enim cum melle misceri non congruit. Epistula sane Iudæ et superscripti Iohannis duas[6] in Catholica[7] habentur; et Sapientia ab amicis Salomonis in honorem ipsius scripta[8].

Apocalypses etiam Iohannis et Petri tantum recipimus, quam quidam ex nostris legi in ecclesia nolunt. Pastorem uero nuperrime temporibus nostris in urbe Roma Hermas conscripsit, sedente cathedra urbis Romæ ecclesiæ Pio episcopo fratre eius; et ideo legi eum quidem oportet, se publicare[9]

Appendix C.

---

[1] *I.e.* so that the mystical number *seven*, symbolizing the unity of the Church, is apparently lost.

[2] *Duas.* It seems better to change the preceding *una, una* into *unam, unam* than to regard this as a nominative, which however perhaps occurs below. The *tamen* in the following clause implies the opposition of *scripsit* or the like.

[3] Perhaps *in ordinationem* is the better reading. The change, though not absolutely required, is suggested by the character of the MS.

[4] *Ad hæresim, i.e.* πρὸς τὴν αἵρεσιν, *bearing upon,* whether against it or otherwise.

[5] *Recipi non potest, i.e.* παραλαμβάνεσθαι οὐ δυνατόν.

[6] The reading of the MS.: *Superscriptio Ioannis duas* is evidently corrupt. The —*io* is probably due to the *io*— which follows (p. 533). The simplest correction is *superscripti* (or *superscripta*), but *superscriptæ* suits the construction better (ἐπιγε-

γραμμέναι 'Ιωάννου). Hesse's arguments against the use of a nominative *duas* (like *trias*) are strong, and it would probably be better to read *duæ*. [*Duas* does occur in a Pompeian inscription: *Academy,* Jan. 1877, p. 84. 1881.]

[7] *In catholica,* the Catholic Church, Cod. Theod. xvi. 2, 4; if the original reading was not *in catholicis.*

[8] The reference to *Wisdom* in a place where we should expect only the *Antilegomena* of the New Testament, finds a complete parallel in the account which Eusebius gives of Clement of Alexandria (*H. E.* VI. 13), κέχρηται...καὶ ταῖς ἀπὸ τῶν ἀντιλεγομένων γραφῶν μαρτυρίαις, τῆς τε λεγομένης Σολομῶντος. Σοφίας καὶ τῆς'Ιησοῦ τοῦ Σιράχ, καὶ τῆς πρὸς Ἑβραίους ἐπιστολῆς, τῆς τε Βαρνάβα, καὶ Κλήμεντος, καὶ Ἰούδα. Comp. Euseb. *H. E.* v. 8.

[9] *Se publicare, i.e.* δημοσιεύεσθαι.

538 THE MURATORIAN FRAGMENT ON THE CANON.

uero in ecclesia populo, neque inter prophetas, †completum numero[1], neque inter apostolos, in finem temporum potest. Arsinoi autem seu Ualentini, uel †Metiad * * nihil in totum recipimus. Qui etiam nouum psalmorum librum †Marcioni conscripserunt, una cum Basilide, †Assianom Cataphrygum constitutorem[2] * * *

---

[1] *Completum numero.* This appears to be corrupt, for the phrase can scarcely mean 'A collection made up fully in number,' as if *Prophetas* were equivalent to *Corpus Prophetarum* (Volkmar). There is no certain analogy in the fragment for the correction *completo*.

[2] The conclusion is hopelessly corrupt, and evidently was so in the copy from which the Fragment was derived. A. Harnack has endeavoured to shew that '*Mitiadis*' is a correction of '*Tatiani*,' and that the reference is to Tatian's *Diatessaron*. He rewrites the whole passage as follows: Arsinoi autem seu Valentini vel Tatiani nihil in totum recipimus, qui [i.e. Tatianus] etiam novum *Propositionum* librum Marcioni conscripsit. *Zeitschr. f. Luth. Theol.* 1874, pp. 275 ff.; 445 ff. Comp. Leimbach, *id.* 1875, pp. 461 ff.

APPENDIX D.

THE CHIEF CATALOGUES OF THE BOOKS OF THE BIBLE DURING THE FIRST EIGHT CENTURIES.

		No.
A.	Catalogues ratified by Conciliar authority:	
1.	The Laodicene Catalogue	i.
2.	The Carthaginian Catalogue; and	ii.
3.	The Apostolic Catalogue: both ratified at the Quinisextine Council, Can. 2	iii.*a*
	[The Catalogue in the Apostolic Constitutions	iii.*b*]

B. Catalogues proceeding from the Eastern Church:
1. Syria.
    Chrysostom, *Synopsis* .... iv.
    Junilius .... v.
    Johannes Damascenus .... vi.
    Ebed Jesu .... vii.
2. Palestine.
    Melito .... viii.
    Eusebius .... ix.
    Cyril of Jerusalem .... x.
    Epiphanius .... xi.
    [Cod. Alex.] .... xii.
3. Alexandria.
    Origen .... xiii.
    Athanasius .... xiv.
4. Asia Minor.
    Gregory of Nazianzus .... xv.
    Amphilochius .... xvi.
    The 'Sixty Books' .... xvii.

540   CATALOGUES OF BOOKS OF THE BIBLE

Appendix D.

    5. Constantinople.
         Leontius .... xviii.
         Nicephorus .... xix.

    C. Catalogues proceeding from the Western Church:
      1. Africa.
         Stich. ap. Cod. Clarom. .... xx.
         Augustine .... xxi.
      2. Italy.
         Muratorian Canon .... xxii.
         Philastrius .... xxiii.
         Jerome .... xxiv.
         Rufinus .... xxv.
         [Innocent] .... xxvi.
         [Gelasius] .... xxvii.
         Cassiodorus .... xxviii.
      3. France.
         Hilary .... xxix.
      4. Spain.
         Isidore .... xxx.
      5. Mediæval.
         John of Salisbury .... xxxi.
         Hugo of St Victor .... xxxii.

I.[1]

Concilium Laodicenum. 363 A.D.

Can. LIX[2]. (Cf. Bickell, *Stud. u. Krit.* III. SS. 611 ff.; supr. pp. 431 sqq.)

νθ′. Ὅτι οὐ δεῖ ἰδιωτικοὺς ψαλμοὺς λέγεσθαι ἐν τῇ ἐκκλησίᾳ, οὐδὲ ἀκανόνιστα βιβλία, ἀλλὰ μόνα τὰ κανονικὰ τῆς καινῆς καὶ

---

[1] Ea quæ ad *Novum Testamentum* spectant ex libris manuscriptis potissimum hausi, cætera ex impressis.

[2] E cod. Bibl. Univ. Cant. EE. IV. 29. Coll. cod. Arund. 533 Mus. Brit. (Ar.) Dionysius Exig. hæc tantum habet: *Non oportet plebeios psalmos in ecclesia cantari, nec libros præter canonem legi, sed sola sacra volumina novi testamenti vel veteris.* Cui con- sentt. intt. Syrr. Codd. Mus. Brit. 14,526, 14,528, 14,529.

Idem Canon, nisi quod *Baruch Lamentationes et Epistola* omittuntur, habetur in *Capitula Aquisgran.* c. xx. (Mansi, XIII. App. 161, ed. Flor. 1767), hoc titulo præposito: *De libris Canonicis. Sacerdotibus.* Lectt. varr. littera A notavi.

παλαιᾶς[1] διαθήκης. Ὅσα δεῖ βιβλία ἀναγινώσκεσθαι· [2]παλαιᾶς διαθήκης· α´ Γένεσις κόσμου. β´ Ἔξοδος ἐξ Αἰγύπτου. γ´ Λευιτικόν. δ´ Ἀριθμοί. ε´ Δευτερονόμιον. ϛ´ Ἰησοῦς Ναυῆ. ζ´ Κριταί, Ῥούθ. η´ Ἐσθήρ. θ´ βασιλειῶν πρώτη καὶ δευτέρα. ι´ βασιλειῶν τρίτη καὶ τετάρτη. ια´ Παραλειπόμενα, πρῶτον καὶ δεύτερον. ιβ´ Ἔσδρας, πρῶτον καὶ δεύτερον. ιγ´ Βίβλος Ψαλμῶν ἑκατὸν πεντήκοντα. ιδ´ Παροιμίαι Σολομῶντος· ιε´ Ἐκκλησιαστής. ιϛ´[?]Ἄσμα ᾀσμάτων. ιζ´ Ἰώβ. ιη´ Δώδεκα προφῆται. ιθ´ Ἠσαίας. κ´ Ἱερεμίας καὶ Βαρούχ, Θρηνοὶ καὶ Ἐπιστολαί. κα´ Ἰεζεκιήλ. κβ´ Δανιήλ. τὰ δὲ τῆς καινῆς διαθήκης[3]· εὐαγγέλια δ´, κατὰ Ματθαῖον, κατὰ Μάρκον, κατὰ Λουκᾶν, κατὰ Ἰωάννην. πράξεις ἀποστόλων. ἐπιστολαὶ καθολικαὶ ἑπτά· οὕτως[4]· Ἰακώβου α´. Πέτρου α´. β´. Ἰωάννου α´. β´. γ´[5]. Ἰούδα α´. ἐπιστολαὶ Παύλου ιδ´[6]. πρὸς Ῥωμαίους α´· πρὸς Κορινθίους α´. β´· πρὸς Γαλάτας α´· πρὸς Ἐφεσίους α´· πρὸς Φιλιππησίους α´· πρὸς Κολασσαεῖς α´· πρὸς Θεσσαλονικεῖς α´. β´· πρὸς Ἑβραίους α´· πρὸς Τιμόθεον α´. β´· πρὸς Τίτον α´· [7]πρὸς Φιλήμονα α´.

Appendix D.

II.

Can. 39 (ita B. C. Can. 47. Mansi, III. 891. Labbe and Cossart, II. 1409. Cf. supr. pp. 439 seqq.)[8].

Item placuit ut præter Scripturas canonicas nihil in ecclesia legatur sub nomine divinarum Scripturarum. Sunt autem Canonicæ Scripturæ hæ[9]: Genesis, Exodus, Leviticus, Numeri, Deuteronomium, Jesus Naue, Judicum, Ruth, Regnorum libri quatuor, Paralipomenon libri duo, Job, Psalterium Davidicum, Salomonis libri quinque, libri duodecim prophetarum, Jesaias, Jeremias, Ezechiel, Daniel, Tobias, Judith, Esther, Esdræ libri duo, Machabæorum libri duo. Novi autem Testamenti, evangeliorum libri quatuor, Actuum Apostolorum liber unus, Epi-

CONCILIUM CARTHAGINIENSE III. 397 A.D.

---

[1] Ar. τῆς π. καὶ κ.
[2] Ar. al. præm. τῆς.
[3] Bick. al. τὰ δὲ τῆς κ. δ. ταῦτα. τῆς δὲ κ. δ. ταῦτα. Ar.
[4] Bev. om. οὕτως. Ar. om. ἐ. οὗ.
[5] Cod. Cant. α´. β´. Ar. γ.
[6] Bick. + οὕτως.
[7] Bev. Ar. præm. καί.
[8] E cod. Coll. SS. Trin. Cant. B. xiv. 44, sæc. xii. in quo ordo canonum hic est: i.—xxxvii. xlix. xlvii. xlviii. (Placuit—ministri), xlviii. (Quibus—fin.)+xxxviii. &c. Collatis Codd. Mus. Brit. (B.) Cott. Claud. D. 9, sæc. xi.; (C.) Reg. 9 B. xii.
[9] Mansi om. hæ.

542   CATALOGUES OF BOOKS OF THE BIBLE

Appendix D.   stolæ Pauli Apostoli[1] xiii., ejusdem ad Hebræos una, Petri apostoli duæ, Johannis[2] tres, Jacobi i., Judæ i.[3], Apocalypsis Johannis liber unus[4]. [Hoc etiam fràtri et consacerdoti[5] nostro Bonifacio, vel aliis earum partium Episcopis, pro confirmando isto canone innotescat, quia a patribus ista accepimus in ecclesia legenda[6].] Liceat autem[7] legi passiones martyrum cum anniversarii eorum dies celebrantur[8].

III. a.

Can. Apost.   *Can.* LXXXVI. (al. LXXXV.) (Bunsen, *Anal. Ante-Nic.* II. p. 30)[9]: Ἔστω δὲ ὑμῖν πᾶσι κληρικοῖς καὶ λαϊκοῖς βιβλία σεβάσμια καὶ ἅγια· τῆς μὲν παλαιᾶς διαθήκης Μωϋσέως πέντε, Γένεσις, Ἔξοδος, Λευιτικόν, Ἀριθμοί, καὶ Δευτερονόμιον· Ἰησοῦ τοῦ Ναυῆ ἕν· τῶν κριτῶν ἕν· τῆς Ῥοὺθ ἕν· βασιλειῶν τέσσαρα· Παραλειπομένων, τῆς βίβλου τῶν ἡμερῶν, δύο· Ἔσδρα δύο· Ἐσθὴρ ἕν. Ἰουδεὶθ ἕν· Μακκαβαίων τρία· Ἰὼβ ἕν· Ψαλμοὶ ἑκατὸν πεντήκοντα· Σολομῶνος βιβλία τρία, παροιμίαι, ἐκκλησιαστής, ᾆσμα ᾀσμάτων. προφῆται δεκαεέξ· ἔξωθεν δὲ ὑμῖν προσιστορείσθω μανθάνειν ὑμῶν τοὺς νέους τὴν σοφίαν τοῦ πολυμαθοῦς Σειράχ. ἡμέτερα δέ, τουτέστι τῆς καινῆς διαθήκης, εὐαγγέλια τέσσαρα[10], Ματθαίου, Μάρκου, Λουκᾶ, Ἰωάννου· Παύλου ἐπιστολαὶ δεκατέσσαρες· Πέτρου ἐπιστολαὶ δύο· Ἰωάννου τρεῖς· Ἰακώβου μία· Ἰούδα μία[11]. Κλήμεντος ἐπιστολαὶ[12] δύο, καὶ αἱ διαταγαὶ ὑμῖν[13] τοῖς ἐπισκόποις δι' ἐμοῦ Κλή-

---

[1] c. B. C. M. *Pauli ap. ep.*
[2] M. + *apostoli* = B. C.
[3] M. *Judæ apostoli una et Jac. una.*
[4] The collection of Canons ascribed to Isidore adds: *Fiunt igitur libri viginti et septem, ita ut de confirmando isto canone transmarinæ ecclesiæ consulantur*, omitting the alternative clause: *Hoc...legenda;* and no various reading is given. Hardouin gives both clauses. Labbe and Mansi say: Quidam vetustus codex sic habet: *De conf. isto can. transmarin*a *ecclesi*a *consul*atur, adding in a note: '*Fiunt ...de confirmando &c.* Hard.' without making any reference to the change of number or giving any authority for it. The alternative clause shews that the plural is right.
   The best Greek and Latin authorities in *Cod. Eccles. Afric.*, in which the Canon is quoted (*Can.* xxiv.), omit the two Books of the Maccabees.
[5] B. *coepiscopo.*
[6] C. *agenda* vitiose.   [7] C. *etiam.*
[8] B. *dies cel. eor.* C. *dies eor. celebr.*
[9] Hic Catal. integer exstat in Codd. Syrr. (Mus. Brit.) 14,526, 14,527, sæc. vi. vel vii; non autem in MS. Arab. 7207. Dion. Exig. Canones tantum L. vertit.
[10] Syr. + *quæ antea memoravimus.*
[11] Ἰ. μ. om. cod. Bodl. ap. Bev. (Ueltzen.)
[12] Syr. *duæ epp. meæ Clementis.* Comp. Lightfoot, pp. 274 ff.
[13] Bunsen ὑμῶν? err. typ.

μεντος εν οκτώ βιβλίοις προσπεφωνημέναι, ας ου χρή δημοσιεύειν επί πάντων διά τα εν αυταίς μυστικά· και αι πράξεις ημών των αποστόλων.   Appendix D.

III. b.

Lib. II. 57, μέσος δ' ο αναγνώστης εφ' υψηλού τινος εστώς αναγινωσκέτω τα Μωσέως και Ιησού του Ναυή, τα των Κριτών και των Βασιλειών, τα των Παραλειπομένων και τα της Επανόδου· προς τούτοις τα του Ιώβ και του Σολομώνος και τα των εκκαίδεκα προφητών. Ἀνὰ δύο δὲ γενομένων [l. γινομένων] αναγνωσμάτων έτερός τις τους του Δαυίδ ψαλλέτω ύμνους και ο λαός τα ακροστίχια υποψαλλέτω. Μετά τούτο αι πράξεις αι ημέτεραι αναγινωσκέσθωσαν και επιστολαί Παύλου του συνεργού ημών, ας επέστειλε ταις εκκλησίαις καθ' υφήγησιν του αγίου πνεύματος· και μετά ταύτα διάκονος ή πρεσβύτερος αναγινωσκέτω τα ευαγγέλια α εγώ Ματθαίος και Ιωάννης παρεδώκαμεν υμίν και α οι συνεργοί Παύλου παρειληφότες κατέλειψαν υμίν Λυκάς και Μάρκος.   Const. Apost.

IV.

Synopsis Sacr. Script. ap. Chrys. Tom. VI. p. 314 ff. Ed. Bened. Migne, *Patr. Gr.* LVI. 313 f.: Σκοπός...των Διαθηκών είς, των ανθρώπων ή διόρθωσις...μή τοίνυν νομιζέτω τις ξένον είναι νομοθέτου το παλαιάς ιστορίας διηγείσθαι και νόμους αναγράφειν· όπερ γαρ ισχύει νόμος τούτο και η διήγησις του βίου των αγίων. Έστι τοίνυν της παλαιάς το μεν ιστορικόν ως η οκτάτευχος (Genesis, Exodus, Leviticus, Numeri, Deuteronomium, Josue, Judices, Ruth)...Μετ' εκείνο (Ρούθ) αι βασιλείαι αι τέσσαρες...μετά δε τας βασιλείας Έσδρας...(316)...της ουν παλαιάς εστι το μεν ιστορικόν τούτο δή ὃ προειρήκαμεν, το δε συμβουλευτικόν ώς αι τε Παροιμίαι και η του Σειράχ Σοφία και ο Εκκλησιαστής και τα Άσματα των Ασμάτων, το δε προφητικόν ως οι δεκαέξ λέγω προφήται και Ρούθ (?) και Δαυίδ...(318) εστί δε και της καινής βιβλία, αι Επιστολαί αι δεκατέσσαρες Παύλου, τα Ευαγγέλια τα τέσσαρα, δύο μεν των μαθητών του Χριστού Ιωάννου και Ματθαίου· δύο δε Λουκά και Μάρκου· ὧν ο μεν του Πέτρου ο δε του Παύλου γεγόνασι μαθηταί. οι μεν γαρ αυτόπται ήσαν γεγενημένοι, και συγγενόμενοι τω Χριστώ· οι δε παρ' εκείνων τα εκείνων διαδεξάμενοι εις ετέρους

C.   N N

544 CATALOGUES OF BOOKS OF THE BIBLE

Appendix D.

ἐξήνεγκαν· καὶ τὸ τῶν Πράξεων δὲ βιβλίον, καὶ αὐτὸ Λουκᾶ ἱστορήσαντος τὰ γενόμενα· καὶ τῶν καθολικῶν Ἐπιστολαὶ τρεῖς.

V.

JUNILIUS,
Ep. Afric.
c. 550 A.D.

De partibus divinæ legis[1], Lib. I. c. 2 (Galland, xii. 79 seqq. Kihn, *Theodor v. Mopsuestia*, 471 ff.). Species [scripturæ]...aut historia est, aut prophetia, aut proverbialis, aut simpliciter docens.

c. 3. *De historia...Discipulus.* In quibus libris divina continetur historia? *Magister.* In septemdecim. Gen. i. Exod. i. Levit. i. Num. i. Deuter. i. Jesu Nave i. Judicum i. Ruth i. Regum secundum nos iv. secundum Hebræos ii. Evangeliorum iv. secundum Matthæum, secundum Marcum, secundum Lucam, secundum Joannem, Actuum Apostolorum i. *D.* Nulli alii Libri ad divinam Historiam pertinent? *M.* Adjungunt plures: Paralipomenon ii. Job i. Tobiæ[2] i. Esdræ i. Judith i. Hester i. Maccab. ii. *D.* Quare hi libri non inter canonicas scripturas currunt? *M.* Quoniam apud Hebræos quoque super hac differentia recipiebantur, sicut Hieronymus ceterique testantur...

c. 4. *De Prophetia...D.* In quibus libris prophetia suscipitur? *M.* In septemdecim. Psalmorum cl. lib. i. Osee lib. i. Esaiæ lib. i. Joel lib. i. Amos lib. i. Abdiæ lib. i. Jonæ lib. i. Michææ lib. i. Naum lib. i. Habacuc lib. i. Sophoniæ lib. i. Hieremiæ lib. i. Ezechiel lib. i. Daniel lib. i. Aggæi lib. i. Zachariæ lib. i. Malachiæ lib. i. Cæterum de Johannis Apocalypsi apud orientales admodum dubitatur......

c. 5. *De proverbiis...D.* In quibus hæc [proverbialis species] libris accipitur? *M.* In duobus: Salomonis Proverbiorum lib. i. et Jesu filii Sirach lib. i. *D.* Nullus alius liber huic speciei subditur? *M.* Adjungunt quidam librum qui vocatur Sapientiæ et Cantica Canticorum......

[1] Ad Primasium Episcopum (c. 553 A.D.). *Pref.* ...[vidi] quendam Paullum nomine, Persam genere, qui in Syrorum schola in Nisibi urbe est edoctus, ubi divina lex per magistros publicos, sicut apud nos in mundanis studiis Grammatica et Rhetorica, ordine ac regulariter traditur...ejus...regulas quasdam...in duos brevissimos libellos...collegi...

[2] Cf. Kihn, §§ 354 f.

c. 6. *De simplici doctrina...D.* Qui libri ad simplicem doc- [Appendix D.]
trinam pertinent? *M.* Canonici septemdecim[1]; id est;
Eccles. lib. i. Epist. Pauli Apostoli ad Rom. i. ad Corinth.
ii. ad Gal. i. ad Ephes. i. ad Philip. i. ad Coloss. i. ad
Thessal. ii. ad Timoth. ii. ad Titum i. ad Philem. i. ad
Hebr. i.; beati Petri ad gentes prima; et beati Johannis
prima. *D.* Nulli alii libri ad simplicem doctrinam pertinent? *M.* Adjungunt quamplurimi quinque alias quæ
Apostolorum Canonicæ nuncupantur; id est: Jacobi i.
Petri secundam, Judæ unam, Johannis ii.......
c. 7. *De auctoritate Scripturarum. D.* Quomodo divinorum
librorum consideratur auctoritas? *M.* Quia quædam[2]
perfectæ auctoritatis sunt, quædam mediæ, quædam nullius. *D.* Quæ sunt perfectæ auctoritatis? *M.* Quæ
canonica in singulis speciebus absolute numeravimus.
D. Quæ mediæ? *M.* Quæ adjungi a pluribus diximus.
D. Quæ nullius auctoritatis sunt? *M.* Reliqua omnia.
D. In omnibus speciebus hæ differentiæ inveniuntur?
M. In historia et simplici doctrina[3] omnes; nam in prophetia mediæ auctoritatis libri præter Apocalypsim non
reperiuntur; nec in proverbiali specie omnino cassata[4].

VI.

De fide Orthodoxa, IV. 17[5]: ἰστέον δὲ ὡς εἴκοσι καὶ δύο [Johannes
βίβλοι εἰσὶ τῆς παλαιᾶς διαθήκης κατὰ τὰ στοιχεῖα τῆς Ἑβραΐδος Damasce-
φωνῆς· εἴκοσι δύο γὰρ στοιχεῖα ἔχουσιν ἐξ ὧν πέντε διπλοῦνται ὡς nus.
γίνεσθαι αὐτὰ εἴκοσι ἑπτά. διπλοῦν γάρ ἐστι τὸ Χὰφ καὶ τὸ Μὲμ † 750 A.D.]
καὶ τὸ Νοῦν καὶ τὸ Πὲ καὶ τὸ Σαδί. διὸ καὶ αἱ βίβλοι κατὰ τοῦτον
τὸν τρόπον εἴκοσι δύο μὲν ἀριθμοῦνται εἴκοσι ἑπτὰ δὲ εὑρίσκονται
διὰ τὸ πέντε ἐξ αὐτῶν διπλοῦσθαι. Συνάπτεται γὰρ 'Ροὺθ τοῖς
Κριταῖς καὶ ἀριθμεῖται παρ' Ἑβραίοις μία βίβλος· ἡ πρώτη καὶ ἡ
δευτέρα τῶν Βασιλειῶν μία βίβλος· ἡ τρίτη καὶ ἡ τετάρτη τῶν

---

[1] See Kihn; alii *sexdecim.*
[2] i.e. βιβλία. Cf. Kihn, § 377 n.
[3] Gallandii pravam interpunctio-
nem correxi: *doctrina: omnes nam-
que...*
[4] i.e. πάντως ἀποκεκριμμένα. Cf.

Kihn, *l. c.*
[5] Ex edit. Lequien, Paris, 1712;
collata vers. Lat. Joannis Burgun-
dionis (*c.* 1180 A.D.), civis Pisani,
ex codd. Mus. Brit. Reg. 6, B, xii.
(a); 5, D, x. (β); add. 15,407 (γ).

546 CATALOGUES OF BOOKS OF THE BIBLE

Appendix D.

Βασιλειῶν μία βίβλος· ἡ πρώτη καὶ ἡ δευτέρα τῶν Παραλειπομένων μία βίβλος· ἡ πρώτη καὶ ἡ δευτέρα τοῦ Ἐσδρὰ μία βίβλος· οὕτως οὖν συγκεῖνται αἱ βίβλοι ἐν πεντατεύχοις τέτρασι καὶ μένουσιν ἄλλαι δύο ὡς εἶναι τὰς ἐνδιαθέτους βίβλους οὕτως· πέντε νομικάς, Γένεσιν, Ἔξοδον, Λευιτικόν, Ἀριθμοί, Δευτερονόμιον. Αὕτη πρώτη πεντάτευχος ἢ καὶ νομοθεσία. Εἶτα ἄλλη πεντάτευχος τὰ καλούμενα Γραφεῖα παρά τισι δὲ Ἁγιόγραφα ἅτινά ἐστιν οὕτως· Ἰησοῦς ὁ τοῦ Ναυῆ, Κριταὶ μετὰ τῆς Ῥούθ, Βασιλειῶν πρώτη μετὰ τῆς δευτέρας βίβλος μία, ἡ τρίτη μετὰ τῆς τετάρτης βίβλος μία καὶ αἱ δύο τῶν Παραλειπομένων βίβλος μία. Αὕτη δευτέρα πεντάτευχος. Τρίτη πεντάτευχος αἱ στιχήρεις βίβλοι, τοῦ Ἰώβ, τὸ Ψαλτήριον, Παροιμίαι Σολομῶντος, Ἐκκλησιαστὴς τοῦ αὐτοῦ, τὰ Ἄσματα τῶν Ἀσμάτων τοῦ αὐτοῦ. Τετάρτη πεντάτευχος ἡ προφητική, τὸ δωδεκαπρόφητον βίβλος μία, Ἡσαΐας, Ἱερεμίας, Ἰεζηκιήλ, Δανιήλ, εἶτα τοῦ Ἐσδρὰ αἱ δύο εἰς μίαν συναπτόμεναι βίβλον[1], καὶ ἡ Ἐσθήρ. Ἡ δὲ Πανάρετος, τουτέστιν ἡ Σοφία τοῦ Σολομῶντος καὶ ἡ Σοφία τοῦ Ἰησοῦ, ἣν ὁ πατὴρ μὲν τοῦ Σιρὰχ ἐξέθετο Ἑβραϊστὶ Ἑλληνιστὶ δὲ ἡρμήνευσεν ὁ τούτου μὲν ἔγγονος (? ἔκγονος) Ἰησοῦς τοῦ δὲ Σιρὰχ υἱός· ἐνάρετοι μὲν καὶ καλαὶ ἀλλ' οὐκ ἀριθμοῦνται οὐδὲ ἔκειντο ἐν τῇ κιβωτῷ.

Τῆς δὲ νέας διαθήκης εὐαγγέλια[2] τέσσαρα· τὸ[3] κατὰ Ματθαῖον, τὸ κατὰ Μάρκον, τὸ κατὰ Λουκᾶν[4], τὸ κατὰ Ἰωάννην. Πράξεις τῶν ἁγίων ἀποστόλων διὰ Λουκᾶ τοῦ εὐαγγελιστοῦ. Καθολικαὶ[5] ἐπιστολαὶ ἑπτά· Ἰακώβου μία, Πέτρου[6] δύο, Ἰωάννου τρεῖς, Ἰούδα μία. Παύλου ἀποστόλου ἐπιστολαὶ[7] δεκατέσσαρες. Ἀποκάλυψις[8] Ἰωάννου εὐαγγελιστοῦ. Κανόνες τῶν ἁγίων ἀποστόλων[9] διὰ Κλήμεντος.

VII.

Ebed Jesu. † 1318 A.D.

Catal. Libr. omn. Ecclesiasticorum (Assemani, *Bibl. Or.* III. *Pars* I. pp. 3 seqq.).

Prooemium. Virtute auxilii tui Deus,

[1] R. 2428 addit καὶ ἡ Ἰουδίθ (Leq.).
[2] *Evangelistæ* γ.
[3] *quod* sec. M. &c. β. γ.
[4] τὸ κ. Λ. = β.
[5] *Canonicæ* α. *Catholicæ* β. γ.
[6] + *tertius* punctis suppos. γ.
[7] = *epistolæ* γ. sed man. sec. add.
[8] *Apochalypsis* γ.
[9] R. 2428 καὶ ἐπιστολαὶ δύο διὰ Κλήμεντος, sed interpolatum varie huncce codicem esse monuimus (Leq.).

Et precibus omnis justi insignis,
Ac matris celeberrimæ,
Scribere aggredior Carmen admirabile:
In quo Libros Divinos,
Et omnes Compositiones Ecclesiasticas,
Omnium priorum et posteriorum
Proponam Lectoribus.
Nomen Scriptorum commemorabo,
Et quænam scripsere, et qua ratione,
In Deo autem confidens,
En a Moyse initium duco.

Cap. i. Lex quinque Libri,
Genesis, Liber Exodi,
Liber Sacerdotum, Numeri,
Et Liber Deuteronomii.
Dein Liber Josue filii Nun,
Post hunc Liber Judicum,
Et Samuel et Liber Regum
Et Liber Dabarjamin et Ruth.
Et Psalmi David Regis:
Et Proverbia Solomonis et Cohelet:
Et Sirat Sirin et Bar-Sira:
Et Sapientia Magna, et Job.
Isaias, Hosee, Joël,
Amos, Abdias, Jonas,
Michæas, Nahum, Habacuc,
Sophonias, Aggæus, Zacharias,
Malachias, et Hieremias,
Ezechiel, et Daniel:
Judith, Esther, Susanna,
Esdras, et Daniel minor,
Epistola Baruch: et liber
Traditionis seniorum.
Josephi[1] autem scribæ exstant

---

[1] De Flavio Josepho...hic loquitur Sobensis, etsi eum modo cum Æsopo Phryge, modo cum Josepho Gorionide per errorem confundat, ut ex sequentibus palam fit (Assem.).

Appendix D.

    Proverbia[1], et Historia filiorum Samonæ[2].
    Liber etiam Macabæorum[3],
      Et Historia Herodis Regis
      Et liber postremæ desolationis
      Hierosolymæ per Titum.
    Et liber Asiathæ uxoris
      Josephi justi filii Jacob:
    Et liber Tobiæ et Tobith
      Justorum Israelitarum.

Cap. ii. Nunc absoluto Veteri
    Aggrediamur jam Novum *Testamentum*:
    Cujus caput est Matthæus, qui Hebraice
      In Palæstina scripsit.
    Post hunc Marcus, qui Romane
      Loquutus est in celeberrima Roma:
    Et Lucas, qui Alexandriæ
      Græce dixit scripsitque:
    Et Joannes, qui Ephesi
      Græco sermone exaravit Evangelium.
    Actus quoque Apostolorum,
      Quos Lucas Theophilo inscripsit.
    Tres etiam Epistolæ quæ inscribuntur
      Apostolis in omni codice et lingua,
    Jacobo scilicet et Petro et Joanni;
      Et Catholicæ nuncupantur.
    Apostoli autem Pauli magni
      Epistolæ quatuordecim[4]......

Cap. iii. Evangelium, quod compilavit
    Vir Alexandrinus

---

[1] Fabulas Æsopicas intelligit, quas Orientales recentiores Syri Arabesque Josepho Hebræo perperam adscribunt: utrumque enim vocant ܝܘܣܝܦܘܣ *Iosipum*, hoc est Josephum. (Assem.)

[2] i.e. Lib. iv. Maccab.

[3] De opere quod sub nomine *Josephi Gorionidis*...publicatum fuit... loquitur. (Assem.) Equidem ed Librr. Macc. i. ii. interpretor.

[4] *Ep. ad Hebræos* locum ultimum obtinet.

Ammonius qui et Tatianus,
Illudque Diatessaron appellavit.

Cap. iv. Libri quoque quorum Auctores sunt
Discipuli Apostolorum.
Liber Dionysii
Philosophi cælestis.

Cap. v. Et Clementis unius ex septuaginta.. ...

VIII.

Fragm. ap. Euseb. *H. E.* IV. 26. Μελίτων Ὀνησίμῳ τῷ ἀδελφῷ χαίρειν. ἐπειδὴ...καὶ μαθεῖν τὴν τῶν παλαιῶν βιβλίων ἐβουλήθης ἀκρίβειαν πόσα τὸν ἀριθμόν, καὶ ὁποῖα τὴν τάξιν εἶεν ἐσπούδασα τὸ τοιοῦτο πρᾶξαι...ἀνελθὼν οὖν εἰς τὴν ἀνατολὴν καὶ ἕως τοῦ τόπου γενόμενος ἔνθα ἐκηρύχθη καὶ ἐπράχθη καὶ ἀκριβῶς μαθὼν τὰ τῆς παλαιᾶς διαθήκης βιβλία ὑποτάξας ἔπεμψά σοι, ὧν ἐστὶ τὰ ὀνόματα. Μωϋσέως πέντε· Γένεσις, Ἔξοδος, Ἀριθμοί, Λευιτικόν, Δευτερονόμιον· Ἰησοῦς Ναυῆ· Κριταί, Ῥούθ· Βασιλειῶν τέσσαρα· Παραλειπομένων δύο· Ψαλμῶν Δαυΐδ· Σολομῶνος Παροιμίαι ἢ καὶ Σοφία[1]· Ἐκκλησιαστής· Ἆσμα ᾀσμάτων· Ἰώβ. προφητῶν, Ἡσαΐου, Ἱερεμίου, τῶν δώδεκα ἐν μονοβίβλῳ, Δανιήλ, Ἰεζεκιήλ, Ἔσδρας. ἐξ ὧν καὶ τὰς ἐκλογὰς ἐποιησάμην...

IX.

H. E. III. 25. Cf. supr. pp. 414 seqq.

X.

Catech. IV. 33 (22 ed. Mill.) περὶ τῶν θειῶν γραφῶν. ...Φιλομαθῶς ἐπίγνωθι καὶ παρὰ τῆς ἐκκλησίας ποῖαι μέν εἰσιν αἱ τῆς παλαιᾶς διαθήκης βίβλοι, ποῖαι δὲ τῆς καινῆς......πολύ σου φρονιμώτεροι καὶ εὐλαβέστεροι ἦσαν οἱ Ἀπόστολοι καὶ οἱ ἀρχαῖοι ἐπίσκοποι, οἱ τῆς ἐκκλησίας προστάται, οἱ ταύτας παραδόντες· σὺ οὖν τέκνον τῆς ἐκκλησίας μὴ παραχάραττε τοὺς θεσμούς. Καὶ τῆς μὲν παλαιᾶς διαθήκης ὡς εἴρηται τὰς εἴκοσι δύο μελέτα βίβλους, ἃς εἰ φιλομαθὴς τυγχάνεις ἐμοῦ λέγοντος ὀνομαστὶ μεμνῆσθαι σπούδασον. Τοῦ νόμου μὲν γάρ εἰσιν αἱ Μωσέως πρῶται πέντε βίβλοι,

[1] All. καὶ ἡ Σοφία.

Appendix D.

MELITO,
Ep. Sard.
c. 180 A.D.

EUSEBIUS,
† 340 A.D.

CYRILLUS,
Ep. Hierosol. 349.
† 386 A.D.

Appendix D.	Γένεσις, Έξοδος, Λευιτικόν, Αριθμοί, Δευτερονόμιον. Εξής δε Ιησούς υιός Ναυή, και το των Κριτών μετά της Ρουθ βιβλίον έβδομον αριθμούμενον. Των δε λοιπών ιστορικών βιβλίων η πρώτη και η δευτέρα των Βασιλειών μία παρ' Εβραίοις εστί βίβλος, μία δε και η τρίτη και η τετάρτη. Ομοίως δε παρ' αυτοίς και των Παραλειπομένων η πρώτη και η δευτέρα μία τυγχάνει βίβλος, και του Έσδρα η πρώτη και η δευτέρα μία λελόγισται· δωδεκάτη βίβλος η Εσθήρ. Και τα μεν ιστορικά ταύτα. Τα δε στιχηρά τυγχάνει πέντε, Ιώβ, και βίβλος Ψαλμών, και Παροιμίαι, και Εκκλησιαστής, και Άσμα ασμάτων επτακαιδέκατον βιβλίον. Επί δε τούτοις τα προφητικά πέντε· των δώδεκα προφητών μία βίβλος και Ησαίου μία και Ιερεμίου μία μετά Βαρούχ και Θρήνων και Επιστολής, είτα Ιεζεκιήλ και η του Δανιήλ, εικοστηδευτέρα βίβλος της παλαιάς διαθήκης. της δε καινής διαθήκης τα τέσσαρα μόνα ευαγγέλια· τα δε λοιπά ψευδεπίγραφα και βλαβερά τυγχάνει· έγραψαν και Μανιχαίοι κατά Θωμάν ευαγγέλιον, όπερ ευωδία της ευαγγελικής προσωνυμίας επικεχρωσμένον διαφθείρει τας ψυχάς των απλουστέρων. δέχου δε και τας πράξεις των δώδεκα αποστόλων· προς τούτοις δε και τας επτά Ιακώβου και Πέτρου, Ιωάννου και Ιούδα, καθολικάς επιστολάς· επισφράγισμα δε των πάντων και μαθητών το τελευταίον, τας Παύλου δεκατέσσαρας επιστολάς· τα δε λοιπά πάντα κείσθω[1] εν δευτέρω. και όσα μεν εν εκκλησίαις μη αναγινώσκεται, ταύτα μηδέ κατά σαυτόν αναγίνωσκε καθώς ήκουσας......
	XI.
Epiphanius, Ep. Cypr. † c. 403 A.D.	Hæresis VIII. 6. (Dindorf, I. 301 f.) Έσχον δε ούτοι οι Ιουδαίοι άχρι της από Βαβυλώνος αιχμαλωσίας επανόδου βίβλους τε και προφήτας τούτους και προφητών βίβλους ταύτας· πρώτην μεν Γένεσιν, δευτέραν δε Έξοδον...Λευιτικόν...Αριθμούς...Δευτερονόμιον...έκτη βίβλος Ιησού του Ναυή...των Κριτών...της Ρούθ... του Ιώβ...το Ψαλτήριον...Παροιμίαι Σολομώντος...Εκκλησιαστής... το Άσμα των ασμάτων...των Βασιλειών πρώτη...Βασιλειών δευτέρα ...Βασιλειών τρίτη...Βασιλειών τετάρτη...Παραλειπομένων πρώτη ...Παραλειπομένων δευτέρα...το Δωδεκαπρόφητον...Ησαίας...Ιερε-

[1] All. έξω κείσθω.

DURING THE FIRST EIGHT CENTURIES. 551

μίας μετὰ τῶν Θρήνων καὶ Ἐπιστολῶν αὐτοῦ τε καὶ τοῦ Βαρούχ... Appendix D.
Ἰεζεκιήλ...Δανιήλ...Ἔσδρας ά...Ἔσδρας β'...εἰκοστὴ ἑβδόμη
Ἐσθήρ·[1] αὗταί εἰσιν αἱ εἰκοσιεπτὰ βίβλοι αἱ ἐκ θεοῦ δοθεῖσαι τοῖς
Ἰουδαίοις, εἰκοσιδύο δέ εἰσι ὡς τὰ παρ' αὐτοῖς στοιχεῖα τῶν Ἑβραϊ-
κῶν γραμμάτων ἀριθμούμεναι διὰ τὸ διπλοῦσθαι δέκα βίβλους εἰς
πέντε λεγομένας...εἰσὶ δὲ καὶ ἄλλαι παρ' αὐτοῖς δύο βίβλοι ἐν ἀμ-
φιλέκτῳ ἡ Σοφία τοῦ Σιρὰχ καὶ ἡ τοῦ Σολομῶντος, χωρὶς ἄλλων
τινῶν βιβλίων ἐναποκρύφων.

Hæresis LXXVI. *Conf. Act.* v. p. 941; Dindorf, III. 396. Εἰ
γὰρ ἦς ἐξ ἁγίου πνεύματος γεγεννημένος καὶ προφήταις καὶ ἀποστό-
λοις μεμαθητευμένος, ἔδει σε διελθόντα ἀπ' ἀρχῆς γενέσεως κόσμου
ἄχρι τῶν Ἐσθὴρ χρόνων ἐν εἴκοσι καὶ ἑπτὰ βίβλοις παλαιᾶς διαθήκης, εἴκοσι δύο ἀριθμουμένοις, τέτταρσι δὲ ἁγίοις εὐαγγελίοις, καὶ ἐν
τεσσαρσικαίδεκα ἐπιστολαῖς τοῦ ἁγίου ἀποστόλου Παύλου, καὶ ἐν
ταῖς πρὸ τούτων, καὶ σὺν ταῖς ἐν τοῖς αὐτῶν χρόνοις Πράξεσι τῶν
ἀποστόλων, καθολικαῖς ἐπιστολαῖς Ἰακώβου καὶ Πέτρου καὶ Ἰωάννου καὶ Ἰούδα, καὶ ἐν τῇ τοῦ Ἰωάννου Ἀποκαλύψει, ἔν τε ταῖς
Σοφίαις, Σολομῶντός τέ φημι καὶ υἱοῦ Σιράχ, καὶ πάσαις ἁπλῶς
γραφαῖς θείαις......

De Mens. et Pond. 4. Dindorf, IV. 7. Οὕτως γοῦν σύγκειν-
ται αἱ βίβλοι ἐν πεντατεύχοις τέτταρσι καὶ μένουσιν ἄλλαι δύο
ὑστεροῦσαι, ὡς εἶναι τὰς ἐνδιαθέτους βίβλους οὕτως· πέντε μὲν
νομικάς...πέντε στιχήρεις...εἶτα ἄλλη πεντάτευχος τὰ καλούμενα
γραφεῖα παρά τισι δὲ ἁγιόγραφα λεγόμενα, ἅτινά ἐστιν οὕτως,
Ἰησοῦ τοῦ Ναυῆ βίβλος, Κριτῶν μετὰ τῆς Ῥούθ, Παραλειπομένων
πρώτη μετὰ τῆς δευτέρας, Βασιλειῶν πρώτη μετὰ τῆς δευτέρας,
Βασιλειῶν τρίτη μετὰ τῆς τετάρτης. αὕτη τρίτη πεντάτευχος.
ἄλλη πεντάτευχος τὸ Δωδεκαπρόφητον, Ἡσαΐας, Ἱερεμίας, Ἰεζεκιήλ,
Δανιήλ. καὶ αὕτη ἡ προφητικὴ πεντάτευχος. ἔμειναν δὲ ἄλλαι
δύο αἵτινές εἰσι τοῦ Ἔσδρα μία καὶ αὕτη λογιζομένη καὶ ἄλλη
βίβλος ἡ τῆς Ἐσθὴρ καλεῖται. ἐπληρώθησαν οὖν αἱ εἰκοσιδύο
βίβλοι κατὰ τὸν ἀριθμὸν τῶν εἰκοσιδύο στοιχείων παρ' Ἑβραίοις.
αἱ γὰρ στιχήρεις δύο βίβλοι ἥ τε τοῦ Σολομῶντος ἡ Πανάρετος
λεγομένη, καὶ ἡ τοῦ Ἰησοῦ τοῦ υἱοῦ Σιρὰχ ἐκγόνου δὲ τοῦ Ἰησοῦ

[1] εἰκοστὴ ἑβδόμη Ἐσθήρ, Τωβίτ, Ἰουδίθ (Dindf.).

552 CATALOGUES OF BOOKS OF THE BIBLE

Appendix D.

τοῦ καὶ τὴν Σοφίαν Ἑβραιστὶ γράψαντος, ἣν ὁ ἔκγονος αὐτοῦ Ἰησοῦς ἑρμηνεύσας Ἑλληνιστὶ ἔγραψε, καὶ αὗται χρήσιμαι μέν εἰσι καὶ ὠφέλιμοι ἀλλ' εἰς ἀριθμὸν ῥητῶν οὐκ ἀναφέρονται, διὸ οὐδὲ ἐν τῷ Ἀρὼν ἀνετέθησαν, τουτέστιν ἐν τῇ τῆς διαθήκης κιβωτῷ.

XII.

INDEX
Cod. Alex.

Γένεσις κόσμου,
Ἔξοδος Αἰγύπτου,
Λευιτικόν,
Ἀριθμοί,
Δευτερονόμιον,
Ἰησοῦς Ναυῆ,
Κριταί,
Ῥούθ. ὁμοῦ βιβλία ζ'.
Βασιλειῶν α',
Βασιλειῶν β',
Βασιλειῶν γ',
Βασιλειῶν δ',
Παραλειπομένων α',
Παραλειπομένων β'.
ὁμοῦ βιβλία ς'.
Προφῆται ις',
Ὡσηέ α'......
Ἡσαίας ιγ',
Ἱερεμίας ιδ' (add. *Baruch*, *Lament.*, *Epist.*),
Ἰεζεκιὴλ ιε',
Δανιὴλ ις' (cum additamentis),
Ἐσθήρ (cum additamentis),
Τωβίτ,
Ἰουδείθ,
Ἔσδρας α' ἱερεύς (1 Esdras),
Ἔσδρας β' ἱερεύς (Esdras Canonicus, Neemias),
Μακκαβαίων λόγος α',
Μακκαβαίων λόγος β',
Μακκαβαίων λόγος γ',
Μακκαβαίων λόγος δ',

Ψαλτήριον μετ' ᾠδῶν, *Appendix D.*
Ἰώβ,
Παροιμίαι,
Ἐκκλησιαστής,
Ἄσματα ᾀσμάτων,
Σοφία ἡ [ἢ] Πανάρετος,
Σοφία Ἰησοῦ υἱοῦ Σιράχ.
Ἡ Καινὴ Διαθήκη.
Εὐαγγέλια δ'.
Κατὰ Ματθαῖον,
Κατὰ Μάρκον,
Κατὰ Λουκᾶν,
Κατὰ Ἰωάννην.
Πράξεις ἀποστόλων,
Καθολικαὶ ζ',
Ἐπιστολαὶ Παύλου ιδ',
Ἀποκάλυψις Ἰωάννου,
Κλήμεντος ἐπιστολὴ α',
Κλήμεντος ἐπιστολὴ β',
ὁμοῦ βιβλία......
Ψαλμοὶ Σολομῶντος
ιη'.

XIII.

Ap. Euseb. *H. E.* vi. 25. Οὐκ ἀγνοητέον δ' εἶναι τὰς ἐνδια- | ORIGENES.
θήκους βίβλους, ὡς Ἑβραῖοι παραδιδόασιν, δύο καὶ εἴκοσι, ὅσος | † 253 A.D.
ὁ ἀριθμὸς τῶν παρ' αὐτοῖς στοιχείων ἐστίν—εἰσὶ δὲ αἱ εἴκοσι δύο
βίβλοι καθ' Ἑβραίους αἵδε· ἡ παρ' ἡμῖν Γένεσις ἐπιγεγραμμένη...
Ἔξοδος...Λευιτικόν...Ἀριθμοί...Δευτερονόμιον...Ἰησοῦς υἱὸς Ναυῆ
...Κριταί, Ῥούθ...Βασιλειῶν πρώτη δευτέρα...Βασιλειῶν τρίτη τετάρτη...Παραλειπομένων πρώτη δευτέρα...Ἔσδρας πρῶτος δεύτερος...Βίβλος ψαλμῶν...Σολομῶντος Παροιμίαι...Ἐκκλησιαστής...
Ἄσμα ᾀσμάτων...Ἡσαίας...Ἰερεμίας σὺν Θρήνοις καὶ τῇ Ἐπιστολῇ...Δανιήλ...Ἰεζεκιήλ...Ἰώβ...Ἐσθήρ...Ἔξω δὲ τούτων ἐστὶ
τὰ Μακκαβαϊκά......

Cf. supra pp. 358 ff.

XIV.

Ex *Epist. Fest.* xxxix. Ap. Theodorum Balsamonem in *Scholiis* in *Canones*[1]: T. I. 767. Ed. Bened. Par. 1777. Μέλλων δὲ τούτων [sc. τῶν θείων γραφῶν] μνημονεύειν χρήσομαι πρὸς σύστασιν τῆς ἐμαυτοῦ τόλμης τῷ τόπῳ τοῦ εὐαγγελιστοῦ Λουκᾶ, λέγων καὶ αὐτός, Ἐπειδήπερ τινὲς ἐπεχείρησαν ἀνατάξασθαι ἑαυτοῖς τὰ λεγόμενα ἀπόκρυφα καὶ ἐπιμίξαι ταῦτα τῇ θεοπνεύστῳ γραφῇ περὶ ἧς ἐπληροφορήθημεν, καθὼς παρέδοσαν τοῖς πατράσιν οἱ ἀπ' ἀρχῆς αὐτόπται καὶ ὑπηρέται γενόμενοι τοῦ λόγου, ἔδοξε κἀμοὶ προτραπέντι παρὰ γνησίων ἀδελφῶν καὶ μαθόντι ἄνωθεν ἑξῆς ἐκθέσθαι τὰ κανονιζόμενα καὶ παραδοθέντα, πιστευθέντα τε θεῖα εἶναι βιβλία, ἵνα ἕκαστος, εἰ μὲν ἠπατήθη, καταγνῷ τῶν πλανησάντων, ὁ δὲ καθαρὸς διαμείνας χαίρῃ πάλιν ὑπομιμνησκόμενος. ἔστι τοίνυν τῆς μὲν παλαιᾶς διαθήκης βιβλία τῷ ἀριθμῷ τὰ πάντα εἰκοσιδύο· τοσαῦτα γὰρ ὡς ἤκουσα καὶ τὰ στοιχεῖα τὰ παρ' Ἑβραίοις εἶναι παραδέδοται· τῇ δὲ τάξει καὶ τῷ ὀνόματί ἐστιν ἕκαστον οὕτως· πρῶτον Γένεσις, εἶτα Ἔξοδος, εἶτα Λευιτικόν, καὶ μετὰ τοῦτο Ἀριθμοί, καὶ λοιπὸν τὸ Δευτερονόμιον. Ἑξῆς δὲ τούτοις ἐστὶν Ἰησοῦς ὁ τοῦ Ναυῆ καὶ Κριταί, καὶ μετὰ τοῦτο ἡ Ῥούθ, καὶ πάλιν ἑξῆς Βασιλειῶν τέσσαρα βιβλία...μετὰ δὲ ταῦτα Παραλειπομένων α' καὶ β'...εἶτα Ἔσδρας α' καὶ β'...μετὰ δὲ ταῦτα βίβλος Ψαλμῶν καὶ ἑξῆς Παροιμίαι, εἶτα Ἐκκλησιαστὴς καὶ Ἄσμα ἀσμάτων· πρὸς τούτοις ἐστὶ καὶ Ἰὼβ καὶ λοιπὸν Προφῆται, οἱ μὲν δώδεκα εἰς ἓν βιβλίον ἀριθμούμενοι· εἶτα Ἡσαΐας Ἱερεμίας καὶ σὺν αὐτῷ Βαροὺχ Θρῆνοι Ἐπιστολή, καὶ μετ' αὐτὸν Ἰεζεκιὴλ καὶ Δανιήλ· ἄχρι τούτων τὰ τῆς παλαιᾶς διαθήκης ἵσταται. τὰ δὲ τῆς καινῆς οὐκ ὀκνητέον εἰπεῖν· ἔστι γὰρ ταῦτα· Εὐαγγελία τέσσαρα· κατὰ Ματθαῖον, κατὰ Μάρκον, κατὰ Λουκᾶν, κατὰ Ἰωάννην. Εἶτα μετὰ ταῦτα Πράξεις Ἀποστόλων, καὶ ἐπιστολαὶ καθολικαὶ[2] καλούμεναι τῶν ἀποστόλων ἑπτὰ οὕτως· Ἰακώβου μὲν α', Πέτρου δὲ β',

---

[1] Eadem epistola exstat in Vers. Syr. Mus. Brit. (Cod. 12,168, sæc. vii. v. viii.), quam nuper Anglicè reddidit vir reverendus, cui mihi pro singulari ejus humanitate gratiæ agendæ sunt: *The Festal Letters of Athanasius, translated from the Syriac by the Rev. H. Burgess, Ph. D.*, p. 137. Cureton, *Festal Letters of Athanasius*, p. ܠ, 1848. Mai, *Patrum Nova Bibl.* vi. 153 ff.

[2] Syr. om. καθολικαί.

DURING THE FIRST EIGHT CENTURIES. 555

εἶτα Ἰωάννου γ΄, καὶ μετὰ ταύτας Ἰούδα α΄. Πρὸς τούτοις Παύλου ἀποστόλου εἰσὶν ἐπιστολαὶ δεκατέσσαρες, τῇ τάξει γραφόμεναι[1] οὕτως[2]......καὶ πάλιν Ἰωάννου ἀποκάλυψις· ταῦτα πηγαὶ τοῦ σωτηρίου, ὥστε τὸν διψῶντα ἐμφορεῖσθαι τῶν ἐν τούτοις λογίων· ἐν τούτοις μόνοις τὸ τῆς εὐσεβείας διδασκαλεῖον εὐαγγελίζεται. Μηδεὶς τούτοις ἐπιβαλλέτω, μηδὲ τούτων ἀφαιρείσθω τι...ἀλλ' ἕνεκά γε πλείονος ἀκριβείας προστίθημι δὴ τοῦτο γράφων ἀναγκαίως ὡς ὅτι ἔστι καὶ ἕτερα βιβλία τούτων ἔξωθεν οὐ κανονιζόμενα μὲν τετυπωμένα δὲ παρὰ τῶν πατέρων ἀναγινώσκεσθαι τοῖς ἄρτι προσερχομένοις καὶ βουλομένοις κατηχεῖσθαι τὸν τῆς εὐσεβείας λόγον, Σοφία Σολομῶντος καὶ Σοφία Σιρὰχ καὶ Ἐσθὴρ καὶ Ἰουδὶθ καὶ Τωβίας καὶ Διδαχὴ καλουμένη τῶν ἀποστόλων καὶ ὁ Ποιμήν. Καὶ ὅμως, ἀγαπητοί, κἀκείνων κανονιζομένων καὶ τούτων ἀναγινωσκομένων οὐδαμοῦ τῶν ἀποκρύφων μνήμη, ἀλλὰ αἱρετικῶν ἐστιν ἐπίνοια γραφόντων μὲν ὅτε θέλουσιν αὐτὰ χαριζομένων δὲ καὶ προστιθέντων αὐτοῖς χρόνους ἵν' ὡς παλαιὰ προσφέροντες πρόφασιν ἔχωσιν ἀπατᾶν ἐκ τούτου τοὺς ἀκεραίους.

Appendix D.

XV.

Carm. Sect. I. XII. 5 ff. Migne, *Patrol. Gr.* xxvii. 472 ff.; comp. xxxviii. pp. 842 ff. περὶ τῶν γνησίων βιβλίων τῆς θεοπνεύστου γραφῆς.

GREGORIUS NAZIANZENUS.
† 391 A.D.

ὄφρα δὲ μὴ ξείνῃσι νόον κλέπτοιο βίβλοισι
(πολλαὶ γὰρ τελέθουσι παρέγγραπτοι κακότητες)
δέχνυσο τοῦτον ἐμεῖο τὸν ἔγκριτον, ὦ φίλ', ἀριθμόν.
Ἱστορικαὶ μὲν ἔασι βίβλοι δυοκαίδεκα πᾶσαι
τῆς ἀρχαιοτέρης Ἑβραϊκῆς σοφίης.
Πρωτίστη Γένεσις, εἶτ' Ἔξοδος, Λευιτικόν τε
....
Ἡ δ' ἐνάτη δεκάτη τε βίβλοι Πράξεις βασιλήων
καὶ Παραλειπόμεναι. Ἔσχατον Ἔσδραν ἔχεις.
αἱ δὲ στιχηραὶ πέντε ὧν πρῶτός γ' Ἰώβ.
ἔπειτα Δαυίδ· εἶτα τρεῖς Σολομωντίαι
Ἐκκλησιαστὴς Ἄσμα καὶ Παροιμίαι.

[1] Syr. om. γραφόμεναι.   [2] Idem est ordo qui in editt. vulgg.

καὶ πένθ' ὁμοίως πνεύματος προφητικοῦ.

....
....

Ἀρχαίας μὲν ἔθηκα δύω καὶ εἴκοσι βίβλους
τοῖς τῶν Ἑβραίων γράμμασιν ἀντιθέτους·
Ἤδη δ' ἀρίθμει καὶ νέου μυστηρίου.
Ματθαῖος μὲν ἔγραψεν Ἑβραίοις θαύματα Χριστοῦ,
Μάρκος δ' Ἰταλίῃ, Λουκᾶς Ἀχαιΐδι,
Πᾶσι δ' Ἰωάννης κῆρυξ μέγας, οὐρανοφοίτης[1].
Ἔπειτα Πράξεις τῶν σοφῶν ἀποστόλων.
Δέκα δὲ Παύλου τέσσαρές τ' ἐπιστολαί·
Ἑπτὰ δὲ καθολίχ'[2], ὧν Ἰακώβου μία,
Δύω δὲ Πέτρου, τρεῖς δ' Ἰωάννου πάλιν.
Ἰούδα δ' ἐστὶν ἑβδόμη. Πάσας ἔχεις.
Εἴ τις δὲ τούτων ἐκτὸς οὐκ ἐν γνησίοις.

XVI.

Iambi ad Seleucum. Ap. Gregor. Nazianz. *Carm. Sect.* ii. VII. Migne, *Patrol. Gr.* xxxvii. 1593 ff. Cf. Amphiloch. ed. Combef. pp. 130 ff.

Πλὴν ἀλλ' ἐκεῖνο προσμαθεῖν μάλιστά σοι
Προσῆκον, οὐχ ἅπασα βίβλος ἀσφαλὴς
Ἡ σεμνὸν ὄνομα τῆς γραφῆς κεκτημένη.
Εἰσὶν γὰρ εἰσὶν ἔσθ' ὅτε ψευδώνυμοι
Βίβλοι, τινὲς μὲν ἔμμεσοι καὶ γείτονες,
Ὡς ἄν τις εἴποι, τῶν ἀληθείας λόγων.
Αἱ δ' αὖ νόθοι τε καὶ λίαν ἐπισφαλεῖς
Ὡς παράσημα καὶ νόθα νομίσματα,
Ἃ βασιλέως μὲν τὴν ἐπιγραφὴν φέρει,
Κίβδηλα δ' ἐστὶ ταῖς ὕλαις δολούμενα.
Τούτων χάριν σοι τὴν θεοπνεύστων ἐρῶ

---

[1] Metra Gregorius nullo certo ordine commiscet; quod lectores monitos velim, nequis Apocalypsim versu proxime sequenti olim commemoratam fuisse suspicetur.

[2] i.e. καθολικαί. Al. ἑπτὰ δὲ τὰ καθολίχ'... Λουκᾶς, Δεκᾶ, ἑπτᾶ, Ἰουδά et in carm. sequ. ὥρᾰ, Λουκᾶ, relinquere quam corrigere malui.

Βίβλων ἑκάστην, ὡς δ' ἂν εὐκρινῶς μάθῃς
Τὰ τῆς παλαιᾶς πρῶτα διαθήκης ἐρῶ.
Ἡ πεντάτευχος......
Τούτοις Ἰησοῦν προστίθει καὶ τοὺς Κριτάς,
Ἔπειτα τὴν Ῥούθ, Βασιλέων τε τέσσαρας
Βίβλους, Παραλειπομένων δέ γε ξυνωρίδα.
Ἔσδρας ἐπ' αὐταῖς πρῶτος, εἶθ' ὁ δεύτερος.
Ἑξῆς στιχηρὰς πέντε σοι βίβλους ἐρῶ......
Ταύταις προφήτας προστίθει τοὺς δώδεκα......
Μεθ' οὓς προφήτας μάνθανε τοὺς τέσσαρας......
Τούτοις προσεγκρίνουσι τὴν Ἐσθήρ τινες.
Καινῆς Διαθήκης ὥρα μοι βίβλους λέγειν·
Εὐαγγελιστὰς τέσσαρας δέχου μόνους,
Ματθαῖον, εἶτα Μάρκον, ᾧ Λουκᾶν τρίτον
Προσθεὶς ἀρίθμει, τὸν δ' Ἰωάννην χρόνῳ
Τέταρτον, ἀλλὰ πρῶτον ὕψει δογμάτων·
Βροντῆς γὰρ υἱὸν τοῦτον εἰκότως καλῶ,
Μέγιστον ἠχήσαντα τῷ Θεοῦ λόγῳ.
Δέχου δὲ βίβλον Λουκᾶ καὶ τὴν δευτέραν,
Τὴν τῶν καθολικῶν Πράξεων ἀποστόλων.
Τὸ σκεῦος ἑξῆς προστίθει τῆς ἐκλογῆς,
Τὸν τῶν ἐθνῶν κήρυκα, τὸν ἀπόστολον
Παῦλον, σοφῶς γράψαντα ταῖς ἐκκλησίαις
Ἐπιστολὰς δὶς ἑπτά......
Τινὲς δέ φασι τὴν πρὸς Ἑβραίους νόθον,
Οὐκ εὖ λέγοντες· γνησία γὰρ ἡ χάρις.
Εἶεν· τί λοιπόν; καθολικῶν ἐπιστολῶν
Τινὲς μὲν ἑπτά φασιν, οἱ δὲ τρεῖς μόνας
Χρῆναι δέχεσθαι, τὴν Ἰακώβου μίαν,
Μίαν δὲ Πέτρου, τήν τ' Ἰωάννου μίαν,
Τινὲς δὲ τὰς τρεῖς, καὶ πρὸς αὐταῖς τὰς· δύο
Πέτρου δέχονται, τὴν Ἰούδα δ' ἑβδόμην·
Τὴν δ' Ἀποκάλυψιν τὴν Ἰωάννου πάλιν
Τινὲς μὲν ἐγκρίνουσιν, οἱ πλείους δέ γε
Νόθον λέγουσιν. Οὗτος ἀψευδέστατος
Κανὼν ἂν εἴη τῶν θεοπνεύστων γραφῶν......

Appendix D.

XVII.

Hody, *de Textibus*, p. 649 (Cf. cotelier, *Patres Apost.* I. 197; Montfaucon, *Bibl. Coislin.* 193 f. Comp. B. M. Add. 17,469, sæc. xiv. [Dr C. R. Gregory]).·

Περὶ τῶν ξ' βιβλίων καὶ ὅσα τούτων ἐκτός.

α'.	Γένεσις.	λα'.	Ἠσαΐας.
β'.	Ἔξοδος.	λβ'.	Ἰερεμίας.
γ'.	Λευιτικόν.	λγ'.	Ἰεζεκιήλ.
δ'.	Ἀριθμοί.	λδ'.	Δανιήλ.
ε'.	Δευτερονόμιον.	λε'.	Εὐαγγέλιον κατὰ Ματθαῖον.
ς'.	Ἰησοῦς.	λς'.	Κατὰ Μάρκον.
ζ'.	Κριταὶ καὶ Ῥούθ.	λζ'.	Κατὰ Λουκᾶν.
η'.	Βασιλειῶν α'.	λη'.	Κατὰ Ἰωάννην.
θ'.	Βασιλειῶν β'.	λθ'.	Πράξεις τῶν ἀποστόλων.
ι'.	Βασιλειῶν γ'.	μ'.	Ἰακώβου ἐπιστολή.
ια'.	Βασιλειῶν δ'.	μα'.	Πέτρου.
ιβ'.	Παραλειπόμενα ε'.	μβ'.	Πέτρου.
ιγ'.	Ἰώβ.	μγ'.	Ἰωάννου.
ιδ'.	Ψαλτήριον.	μδ'.	Ἰωάννου.
ιε'.	Παροιμίαι.	με'.	Ἰωάννου.
ις'.	Ἐκκλησιαστής.	μς'.	Ἰούδα.
ιζ'.	Ἄσμα ἀσμάτων ε'.	μζ'.	Παύλου πρὸς Ῥωμαίους.
ιη'.	Ἔσδρας.	μη'.	Παύλου πρὸς Κορινθίους.
ιθ'.	Ὠσηέ.	μθ'.	Πρὸς Κορινθίους.
κ'.	Ἀμῶς.	ν'.	Πρὸς Γαλάτας.
κα'.	Μιχαίας.	να'.	Πρὸς Ἐφεσίους.
κβ'.	Ἰωήλ.	νβ'.	Πρὸς Φιλιππησίους.
κγ'.	Ἰωνᾶς.	νγ'.	Πρὸς Κολασσαεῖς.
κδ'.	Ἀβδιοῦ.	νδ'.	Πρὸς Θεσσαλονικεῖς.
κε'.	Ναούμ.	νε'.	Πρὸς Θεσσαλονικεῖς.
κς'.	Ἀμβακούμ.	νς'.	Πρὸς Τιμόθεον.
κζ'.	Σοφονίας.	νζ'.	Πρὸς Τιμόθεον.
κη'.	Ἀγγαῖος.	νη'.	Πρὸς Τίτον.
κθ'.	Ζαχαρίας.	νθ'.	Πρὸς Φιλήμονα.
λ'.	Μαλαχίας.	ξ'.	Πρὸς Ἑβραίους.

DURING THE FIRST EIGHT CENTURIES.

Καὶ ὅσα ἔξω τῶν ξ'.

α'. σοφία Σολομῶντος.	ς'. Μακκαβαίων.
β'. σοφία Σίραχ.	ζ'. Ἐσθήρ.
γ'. Μακκαβαίων.	η'. Ἰουδήθ.
δ'. Μακκαβαίων.	θ'. Τωβίτ.
ε'. Μακκαβαίων.	

Καὶ ὅσα ἀπόκρυφα.

α'. Ἀδάμ.	ιβ'. Σοφονίου ἀποκάλυψις.
β'. Ἐνώχ.	ιγ'. Ζαχαρίου ἀποκάλυψις.
γ'. Λαμέχ.	ιδ'. Ἔσδρα ἀποκάλυψις.
δ'. Πατριαρχαί.	ιε'. Ἰακώβου ἱστορία.
ε'. Ἰωσὴφ Προσευχή.	ις'. Πέτρου ἀποκάλυψις.
ς'. Ἐλδὰμ καὶ Μοδάμ.	ιζ'. Περίοδοι καὶ διδαχαὶ τῶν
ζ'. Διαθήκη Μωσέως.	ἀποστόλων.
[η'. Deest.]	ιη'. Βαρνάβα ἐπιστολή.
θ'. Ψαλμοὶ Σολομῶντος.	ιθ'. Παύλου πρᾶξις (πράξεις).
ι'. Ἠλίου ἀποκάλυψις.	κ'. Παύλου ἀποκάλυψις.
ια'. Ἠσαίου ὅρασις.	κα'. Διδασκαλία Κλήμεντος.

κβ'. Ἰγνατίου διδασκαλία.
[κγ'. Deest. Πολυκάρπου διδασκαλία. *Cod. Coislin.*]
κδ'. Εὐαγγέλιον κατὰ Βαρνάβα (-αν).
Εὐαγγέλιον κατὰ Ματθ. (*i.e.* Ματθίαν).

XVIII.

De Sectis Act. II. (Galland, XII. 625 seqq. Migne, *Patrol. Gr.* LXXXVI. pars I, pp. 1199 ff.)...ἀπαριθμησώμεθα τὰ ἐκκλησιαστικὰ βιβλία. τῶν τοίνυν ἐκκλησιαστικῶν βιβλίων τὰ μὲν τῆς παλαιᾶς εἰσὶ γραφῆς· τὰ δὲ τῆς νέας...τῆς μὲν οὖν παλαιᾶς βιβλία εἰσι κβ'. ὧν τὰ μέν εἰσιν ἱστορικὰ τὰ δὲ προφητικὰ τὰ δὲ παραινετικὰ τὰ δὲ πρὸς τὸ ψάλλειν γενόμενα...τὰ τοίνυν ἱστορικὰ βιβλία εἰσιν ιβ'...ἡ Γένεσις...ἡ Ἔξοδος...οἱ λεγόμενοι Ἀριθμοί...τὸ Λευιτικόν...τὸ Δευτερονόμιον...ταῦτα δὲ τὰ πέντε βιβλία πάντες τοῦ Μωσέως μαρτυροῦσιν εἶναι, τὰ γὰρ ἐφεξῆς οὐδεὶς οἶδε τίνος εἰσί...ἕκτον... Ἰησοῦς τοῦ Ναυῆ...Κριταί...Ῥούθ...τέσσαρες...λόγοι τῶν βασιλειῶν

LEONTIUS.
c. 590 A.D.

560 CATALOGUES OF BOOKS OF THE BIBLE

Appendix D.

ἐν δύο βιβλίοις φερόμενοι...ἑνδέκατόν ἐστιν αἱ Παραλειπόμεναι... δωδέκατόν ἐστιν...ὁ Ἔσδρας...Προφητικὰ δέ εἰσι πέντε...ὁ Ἡσαΐας ...ὁ Ἱερεμίας...ὁ Ἱεζεκιήλ...ὁ Δανιήλ...πέμπτον τὸ δωδεκαπρόφητον λεγόμενον...Παραινετικά εἰσι βιβλία δ΄, ὧν πρῶτον ὁ Ἰώβ· τοῦτο δέ τινες ἐνόμισαν Ἰωσήπου εἶναι σύγγραμμα...αἱ Παροιμίαι Σολομῶντος...ὁ Ἐκκλησιαστής...τὸ Ἄσμα τῶν Ἀσμάτων...εἰσὶ δὲ ταῦτα τὰ τρία βιβλία τοῦ Σολομῶντος· μετὰ ταῦτα ἐστὶ τὸ Ψαλτήριον. καὶ ταῦτα μέν εἰσι τὰ κβ΄ βιβλία τῆς παλαιᾶς· τῆς δὲ νέας ἕξ εἰσι βιβλία, ὧν δύο περιέχει τοὺς τέσσαρας εὐαγγελιστάς· τὸ μὲν γὰρ ἔχει Ματθαῖον καὶ Μάρκον, τὸ δὲ ἕτερον Λουκᾶν καὶ Ἰωάννην. τρίτον ἐστὶν αἱ πράξεις τῶν ἀποστόλων. τέταρτον αἱ καθολικαὶ ἐπιστολαὶ οὖσαι ἑπτά· ὧν πρώτη τοῦ Ἰακώβου ἐστί· ἡ β΄ καὶ ἡ γ΄ Πέτρου· ἡ δ΄ καὶ ε΄ καὶ Ϛ΄ τοῦ Ἰωάννου· ἡ δὲ ζ΄ τοῦ Ἰούδα. καθολικαὶ δὲ ἐκλήθησαν ἐπειδὴ οὐ πρὸς ἓν ἔθνος ἐγράφησαν ὡς αἱ τοῦ Παύλου, ἀλλὰ καθόλου πρὸς πάντα. πέμπτον βιβλίον αἱ ιδ΄ τοῦ ἁγίου Παύλου ἐπιστολαί. ἕκτον ἐστὶν ἡ ἀποκάλυψις τοῦ ἁγίου Ἰωάννου.

Ταῦτά ἐστι τὰ κανονιζόμενα βιβλία ἐν τῇ ἐκκλησίᾳ καὶ παλαιὰ καὶ νέα, ὧν τὰ παλαιὰ πάντα δέχονται οἱ Ἑβραῖοι.

XIX.

Nicephorus.
Patr. Const.
806—814

Cf. Credner, *Zur Gesch. d. K.* ss. 119 ff.[1]

§ i. Ὅσαι εἰσὶ θεῖαι γραφαὶ ἐκκλησιαζόμεναι καὶ κεκανονισμέναι. καὶ ἡ τούτων στιχομετρία οὕτως[2].

α΄. Γένεσις· στίχοι ͵δτ΄.
β΄. Ἔξοδος· στίχοι ͵βω΄.
γ΄. Λευιτικόν· στίχοι ͵βψ΄.
δ΄. Ἀριθμοί· στίχοι ͵γφλ΄.
ε΄. Δευτερονόμιον· στίχοι ͵γρ΄.
Ϛ΄. Ἰησοῦς· στίχοι ͵βρ΄.
ζ΄. Κριταὶ καὶ Ῥούθ· στίχοι ͵βν΄.

[1] Lectt. varr. vers. Lat. Anastasii (c. 870 A.D.) apposui e Cod. Burn. (Mus. Brit.) 284, saec. xii. vel xiii. f. 283.
[2] Cod. Hæ sunt divinæ scripturæ quæ recipiuntur ab ecclesia et canonizantur. Harumque versuum numerus ut subjicitur...Hi autem sunt novi Testamenti.

DURING THE FIRST EIGHT CENTURIES. 561

η'. Βασιλειῶν α' καὶ β'· στίχοι ͵δσμ'.
θ'. Βασιλειῶν γ' καὶ δ'· στίχοι ͵βσγ'.
ι'. Παραλειπόμενα α' καὶ β'· στίχοι ͵εφ'.
ια'. Ἔσδρας α' καὶ β'· στίχοι ͵εφ'.
ιβ'. Βίβλος Ψαλμῶν· στίχοι ͵ερ'.
ιγ'. Παροιμίαι Σολομῶντος· στίχοι ͵αψ'.
ιδ'. Ἐκκλησιαστής· στίχοι φ'.
ιε'. Ἄσμα ἀσμάτων· στίχοι σπ'.
ιϛ'. Ἰώβ· στίχοι ͵αω'.
ιζ'. Ἡσαίας προφήτης· στίχοι ͵γω'.
ιη'. Ἱερεμίας προφήτης· στίχοι ͵δ'.
ιθ'. Βαρούχ· στίχοι ψ'.
κ'. Ἰεζεκιήλ· στίχοι ͵δ'.
κα'. Δανιήλ· στίχοι ͵β'.
κβ'. Οἱ δώδεκα προφῆται· στίχοι ͵γ'.
  Ὁμοῦ τῆς παλαιᾶς διαθήκης βιβλία εἴκοσι δύο.

§ ii. Τῆς νέας διαθήκης.
  α'. Εὐαγγέλιον κατὰ Ματθαῖον· στίχοι ͵βφ'.
  β'. Εὐαγγέλιον κατὰ Μάρκον· στίχοι ͵β'.
  γ'. Εὐαγγέλιον κατὰ Λουκᾶν· στίχοι ͵βχ'.
  δ'. Εὐαγγέλιον κατὰ Ἰωάννην· στίχοι ͵βτ' [1].
  ε'. Πράξεις τῶν ἀποστόλων· στίχοι ͵ν'.
  ϛ'. Παύλου ἐπιστολαὶ ιδ'· στίχοι ͵ετ'.
  ζ'. Καθολικαὶ[2] ζ'. Ἰακώβου α'. Πέτρου β'. Ἰωάννου γ'.
    Ἰούδα α'[3].
  Ὁμοῦ τῆς νέας διαθήκης βιβλία κϛ'·[4].

§ iii. Καὶ ὅσαι ἀντιλέγονται τῆς παλαιᾶς αὐταί εἰσιν.
  α'. Μακκαβαϊκά γ'· στίχοι ͵ζτ'.
  β'. Σοφία Σολομῶντος· στίχοι ͵αρ'.
  γ'. Σοφία υἱοῦ τοῦ Σιράχ· στίχοι ͵βω'.
  δ'. Ψαλμοὶ καὶ ᾠδαὶ Σολομῶντος· στίχοι ͵βρ'.
  ε'. Ἐσθήρ· στίχοι τν'.
  ϛ'. Καὶ Ἰουδήθ· στίχοι ͵αψ'.

Appendix D.

---
[1] Cod. īιDCC.   īCCC.
[2] Cod. + *Epistolæ*.   [4] Cod. *Simul veteris quidem Tes-*
[3] Cod. + *Simul septem: versus no tamenti libri xxii et novi vii.*

O O 2

562 CATALOGUES OF BOOKS OF THE BIBLE

ζ'. Σώσαννα· στίχοι φ'.
η'. Τωβὴτ ὁ καὶ Τωβίας· στίχοι ψ'.
§ iv. Καὶ ὅσαι τῆς νέας ἀντιλέγονται[1].
α'. Ἀποκάλυψις Ἰωάννου· στίχοι ͵αυ'[2].
β'. Ἀποκάλυψις Πέτρου· στίχοι τ'[3].
γ'. Βαρνάβα ἐπιστολή· στίχοι ͵ατξ'[4].
δ'. Εὐαγγέλιον κατὰ Ἑβραίους· στίχοι ͵βϛ'[5].
§ v. Καὶ ὅσα ἀπόκρυφα τῆς παλαιᾶς.
α'. Ἐνώχ· στίχοι ͵δω'.
β'. Πατριάρχαι· στίχοι ͵ερ'.
γ'. Προσευχὴ Ἰωσήφ· στίχοι ͵αρ'.
δ'. Διαθήκη Μωυσέως· στίχοι ͵αρ'.
ε'. Ἀνάληψις Μωυσέως· στίχοι ͵αυ'.
ϛ'. Ἀβραάμ. στίχοι τ'.
ζ'. Ἐλὰδ καὶ Μωδάδ· στίχοι υ'.
η'. Ἐλιὰ προφήτου· στίχοι τιϛ'.
θ'. Σοφονίου προφήτου· στίχοι χ'.
ι'. Ζαχαρίου πατρὸς Ἰωάννου· στίχοι φ'.
κ'. Βαρούχ, Ἀββακούμ, Ἐζεκιὴλ καὶ Δανιὴλ ψευδεπίγραφα.
§ vi. Καὶ ὅσα τῆς νέας ἀπόκρυφα.
α'. ⁶Περίοδος Πέτρου· στίχοι ͵βψν'.
β'. Περίοδος Ἰωάννου· στίχοι ͵βχ'[7].
γ'. Περίοδος Θωμᾶ· στίχοι ͵αψ'.
δ'. Εὐαγγέλιον κατὰ Θωμᾶν· στίχοι ͵ατ'[8].
ε'. Διδαχὴ ἀποστόλων· στίχοι ϛ'.
ϛ'. Κλήμεντος α'. β'. στίχοι ͵βχ'[9].
ζ'. Ἰγνατίου, Πολυκάρπου, [Ποιμένος καὶ] Ἑρμᾶ· στίχοι[10].

[1] Cod. *Et quibus novi contradicitur.*
[2] Cod. ῑv.
[3] Cod. ⲓⲓⲓDCCC.
[4] Cod. ῑCCCVI.
[5] Cod. ῑICC.
[6] Cod. +*Itinerarium Pauli. ver.*
[7] Cod. ⲓⲓD.
[8] Cod. Coisl. ap. Montf. p. 204
ἡ ἀποκάλυψις Ἰωάννου...στίχοι ͵αθ'.
[9] Cod. *Clementis* xxxii.
[10] Cod. *Pastoris....?*

Appendix D.

XX.

Versus Scibtvrarvm Sanctarvm[1]

Cod. Clarom.
Sæc. vii.

	ita Genesis vervs (*sic*)	iiiiD
	Exodvs versvs	iiiDCC
	Leviticvm versvs	iiDCCC
	Nvmeri versvs	iiiDCL
	Devteronomivm ver.	iiiCCC
	Iesv Navve ver.	ii
	Ivdicvm ver.	ii
	Rvd ver.	CCL.
	Regnorvm ver.	
	primvs liber ver.	iiD
	secundvs lib. ver.	ii
	tertivs lib. ver.	iiDC
	qvartvs lib. ver.	iiCCCC
	Psalmi Davitici ver.	D*
	Proverbia ver.	iDC
	Aeclesiastes	DC
	Cantica Canticorvm	CCC
	Sapientia vers.	i
	Sapientia ihv ver.	iiD
	XII Profetae ver.	iiiCX
col. b.	Ossee ver.	DXXX
	Amos ver.	CCCCX
	Micheas ver.	CCCX
	Ioel ver.	XC
	Abdias ver.	LXX
	Ionas ver.	CL
	Navm ver.	CXL

[1] Ex edit. Tischdf. p. 468 sq. Hic index inter Epistolas ad Philem. et ad Hebr. interponitur. Nihil vero est in Græco Cod. textu quod stichometriæ respondeat, quam e codice Latino Scriba Græcus (? Alexandrinus) transtulit. Equidem e Latina, seu potius ex Africana origine deductam esse crediderim, et certe sæculo quarto antiquiorem. Neque aliter censet Tischdf. Proleg. p. xviii.

Appendix D.	Ambacvm ver.	CLX
	Sophonias ver.	CLX
	Aggevs vers.	CX
	Zacharias ver.	DCLX
	Malachiel ver.	CC
	Eseias ver.	iiiDC
	Ieremias ver.	iiiiLXX
	Ezechiel ver.	iiiDC
	Daniel ver.	iDC
	Maccabeorvm sic.	
	lib. primvs ver.	iiCCC
	lib. secvndvs ver.	iiCCC
	lib. qvartvs ver.	i
	Ivdit ver.	iCCC
	Hesdra	iD
p. 496 a.	Ester ver.	i
	Iob ver.	iDC
	Tobias ver.	i
	Evangelia .IIII.	
	Matthevm ver.	iiDC
	Iohannes ver.	ii
	Marcvs ver.	iDC
	Lvcam ver.	iiDCCCC
	Epistvlas Pavli	
	ad Romanos ver.	iXL
	ad Chorintios .I. ver.	iLX
	ad Chorintios .II. ver.	LXX[1]
	ad Galatas ver.	CCCL
	ad Efesios ver.	CCCLXV
	ad Timothevm .I. ver.	CCviii
	ad Timothevm .II. ver.	CCLXXXviiii
	ad Titvm ver.	CXL
	ad Colosenses ver.	CCLi
	ad Filimonem ver.	L

[1] Non dubium est quin h. l. librarius per incuriam scripserit LXX pro iLXX (Tisch. p. 589).

	ad (*sic*) Petrvm prima	CC	Appendix D.
	ad Petrvm .II. ver.	CXL	
col. b.	Jacobi ver.	CCXX	
	Pr. Iohanni Epist.	CCXX	
	Iohanni Epistvla .II.	XX	
	Iohanni Epistvla .III.	XX	
	Ivdæ Epistvla ver.	LX	
	²Barnabæ Epist. ver.	DCCCL	
	Iohannis Revelatio	ICC	
	Actvs Apostolorvm	IIDC	
	²Pastoris versi	IIII	
	²Actvs Pauli ver.	IIIDLX	
	²Revelatio Petri	CCLXX	

XXI.

De Doctr. Christiana, II. 12 (VIII.) (ed. Bened. Par. 1836). Erit igitur divinarum scripturarum solertissimus indagator, qui primo totas legerit notasque habuerit, et si nondum intellectu jam tamen lectione, duntaxat eas quæ appellantur Canonicæ. Nam cæteras securius leget fide veritatis instructus, ne præoccupent imbecillum animum, et periculosis mendaciis atque phantasmatis eludentes præjudicent aliquid contra sanam intelligentiam. In canonicis autem Scripturis, ecclesiarum catholicarum quamplurium auctoritatem sequatur; inter quas sane illæ sint, quæ apostolicas sedes habere et epistolas accipere meruerunt. Tenebit igitur hunc modum in Scripturis Canonicis, ut eas quæ ab omnibus accipiuntur ecclesiis catholicis præponat eis quas quædam non accipiunt; in eis vero quæ non accipiuntur ab omnibus, præponat eas quas plures gravioresque accipiunt eis quas pauciores minorisque auctoritatis

AUGUSTI-
NUS, *Ep.*
Hippon. 355.
† 430 A.D.

---

[1] Hoc nomine, ut videtur, *Ep. ad Hebræos* designatur, cui idem versuum numerus in uno Græco codice tribuitur. Ex Latinis alii DCC alii DCCC versus numerant. Contra Apocryphæ *Barnabæ Epistolæ* in Nice- phori *Stichometria* MCCCLX (MCCCVI) versus tribuuntur.

[2] His quatuor versibus ..manu satis recenti præpositi sunt obeli. (Tisch. p. 589.)

Appendix D.

ecclesiæ tenent. Si autem alias invenerit a pluribus, alias a gravioribus haberi, quanquam hoc facile invenire non possit, æqualis tamen auctoritatis eas habendas puto. 13. Totus autem Canon Scripturarum in quo istam considerationem versandam dicimus, his libris continetur: Quinque Moyseos id est Genesi, Exodo, Levitico, Numeris, Deuteronomio; et uno libro Jesu Nave, uno Judicum, uno libello qui appellatur Ruth, qui magis ad Regnorum principium videtur pertinere, deinde quatuor Regnorum et duobus Paralipomenon non consequentibus sed quasi a latere adjunctis simulque pergentibus. Hæc est historia quæ sibimet annexa tempora continet atque ordinem rerum: sunt aliæ tanquam ex diverso ordine quæ neque huic ordini neque inter se connectuntur, sicut est Job et Tobias et Esther et Judith et Machabæorum libri duo et Esdræ duo, qui magis subsequi videntur ordinatam illam historiam usque ad Regnorum vel Paralipomenon terminatam: deinde Prophetæ in quibus David unus liber Psalmorum, et Salomonis tres Proverbiorum, Cantica Canticorum, et Ecclesiastes. Nam illi duo libri unus qui Sapientia et alius qui Ecclesiasticus inscribitur de quadam similitudine Salomonis esse dicuntur, nam Jesus Sirach eos conscripsisse constantissime perhibetur qui tamen quoniam in auctoritatem recipi meruerunt inter propheticos numerandi sunt. Reliqui sunt eorum libri qui proprie Prophetæ appellantur, duodecim Prophetarum libri singuli, qui connexi sibimet quoniam nunquam sejuncti sunt pro uno habentur; quorum Prophetarum nomina sunt hæc, Osee...... Malachias: deinde quatuor Prophetæ sunt majorum voluminum Isaias, Jeremias, Daniel, Ezechiel. His quadraginta quatuor libris Testamenti Veteris terminatur auctoritas: Novi autem, quatuor libris Evangelii, secundum Matthæum, secundum Marcum, secundum Lucam, secundum Joannem; quatuordecim Epistolis Pauli Apostoli, ad Romanos, ad Corinthios duabus, ad Galatas, ad Ephesios, ad Philippenses, ad Thessalonicenses duabus, ad Colossenses, ad Timotheum duabus, ad Titum, ad Philemonem, ad Hebræos; Petri duabus; tribus Joannis; una Judæ et una Jacobi; Actibus Apostolorum libro uno, et Apocalypsi Joannis libro uno. 14 (ix) In his omnibus libris timentes Deum et pietate mansueti quærunt voluntatem Dei.

Cf. App. C.

XXII.

XXIII.

Hær. LXXXVIII. (Galland, vii. 480 sqq. Migne, *Patr. Lat.* xii. 1199 ff.)...Statutum est ab apostolis et eorum successoribus non aliud legi in ecclesia debere catholica nisi Legem et Prophetas et Evangelia et Actus Apostolorum, et Paulli tredecim epistolas, et septem alias, Petri duas, Joannis tres, Judæ unam, et unam Jacobi, quæ septem Actibus Apostolorum conjunctæ sunt...

Hær. LXXXIX. Sunt alii quoque [hæretici] qui epistolam Paulli ad Hebræos non asserunt esse ipsius, sed dicunt aut Barnabæ esse Apostoli aut Clementis de urbe Roma episcopi; alii autem Lucæ Evangelistæ aiunt; epistolam etiam ad Laodicenses scriptam. Et quia addiderunt in ea quædam non bene sentientes inde non legitur in ecclesia; et si legitur a quibusdam, non tamen in ecclesia legitur populo, nisi tredecim epistolæ ipsius et ad Hebræos interdum...quia factum Christum dicit in ea inde non legitur; de pœnitentia autem propter Novatianos æque.

Hær. LX. ...sunt hæretici qui Evangelium secundum Joannem et Apocalypsim ipsius non accipiunt, et...in hæresi permanent pereuntes ut etiam Cerinthi illius hæretici esse audeant dicere, et Apocalypsim itidem non beati Joannis Evangelistæ et Apostoli sed Cerinthi hæretici...

XXIV.

Prologus Galeatus in libros Samuel et Malachim. Viginti et duas litteras esse apud Hebræos Syrorum quoque et Chaldæorum lingua testatur....Porro quinque litteræ duplices apud Hebræos sunt...unde et quinque a plerisque libri duplices æstimantur, Samuel, Malachim, Dabre-Iamim, Ezras, Jeremias cum Cinoth, id est Lamentationibus suis. Quomodo igitur viginti duo elementa sunt per quæ scribimus Hebraice omne

Appendix D.

quod loquimur et eorum initiis vox humana comprehenditur, ita viginti duo volumina supputantur, quibus quasi litteris et exordiis in Dei doctrina tenera adhuc et lactens viri justi eruditur infantia.

Primus apud eos liber vocatur *Bresith*, quem nos Genesim dicimus. Secundus......Hi sunt quinque libri Mosi quos proprie *Thorath* id est legem appellant.

Secundum Prophetarum ordinem faciunt, et incipiunt ab Jesu filio Nave...Deinde subtexunt...Judicum librum, et in eundem compingunt Ruth...Tertius sequitur Samuel...Quartus....Regum....Quintus Isaias. Sextus Jeremias. Septimus Iezeciel. Octavus liber duodecim Prophetarum...

Tertius ordo Hagiographa possidet; et primus liber incipit ab Job. Secundus a David...Tertius est Salomon, tres libros habens, Proverbia...Ecclesiasten...Canticum Canticorum. Sextus est Daniel. Septimus.. qui apud nos Paralipomenon primus et secundus inscribitur. Octavus Ezras...Nonus Esther.

Atque ita fiunt pariter veteris legis libri viginti duo, id est, Mosi quinque, Prophetarum octo, Hagiographorum novem. Quamquam nonnulli Ruth et Cinoth (Lamentationes) inter Hagiographa scriptitent et libros hos in suo putent numero supputandos, ac per hoc esse priscae legis libros viginti quatuor, quos sub numero viginti quatuor seniorum Apocalypsis Joannes inducit adorantes Agnum et coronas suas prostratis vultibus offerentes......

Hic prologus Scripturarum, quasi galeatum principium omnibus libris quos de Hebræo vertimus in Latinum convenire potest; ut scire valeamus quidquid extra hos est inter Apocrypha esse ponendum. Igitur Sapientia quæ vulgo Salomonis inscribitur, et Jesu filii Sirach liber, et Judith, et Tobias, et Pastor, non sunt in Canone. Machabæorum primum librum Hebraicum reperi. Secundus Græcus est; quod ex ipsa quoque φράσει probari potest...

Ad Paul. Ep. LIII. § 8 (i. p. 548 ed. Migne).

Cernis me Scripturarum amore raptum excessisse modum epistolæ, et tamen non implesse quod volui......Tangam et

Novum breviter Testamentum. Matthæus, Marcus, Lucas, et Johannes, quadriga Domini et verum Cherubim, quod interpretatur scientiæ multitudo, per totum corpus oculati sunt, scintillæ emicant, discurrunt fulgura, pedes habent rectos et in sublime tendentes, terga pennata et ubique volitantia. Tenent se mutuo sibique perplexi sunt, et quasi rota in rota volvuntur, et pergunt quocunque eos flatus Sancti Spiritus perduxerit. Paulus Apostolus ad septem ecclesias scribit, octava enim ad Hebræos a plerisque extra numerum ponitur, Timotheum instruit ac Titum, Philemonem pro fugitivo famulo (Onesimo) deprecatur. Super quo tacere melius puto quam pauca scribere. Actus Apostolorum nudam quidem sonare videntur historiam et nascentis Ecclesiæ infantiam texere; sed si noverimus scriptorem eorum Lucam esse medicum, *cujus laus est in Evangelio*, animadvertemus pariter omnia verba illius animæ languentis esse medicinam. Jacobus, Petrus, Joannes, Judas, Apostoli, septem epistolas ediderunt tam mysticas quam succinctas, et breves pariter et longas: breves in verbis, longas in sententiis, ut rarus sit qui non in earum lectione cæcutiat. Apocalypsis Joannis tot habet sacramenta quot verba. Parum dixi pro merito voluminis. Laus omnis inferior est: in verbis singulis multiplices latent intelligentiæ.

[Appendix D.]

XXV.

Comm. in Symb. Apost. § 36 (Ed. Migne, Paris, 1849)... Hic igitur Spiritus Sanctus est qui in Veteri Testamento Legem et Prophetas, in Novo Evangelia et Apostolos inspiravit. Unde et Apostolus dicit: *omnis scriptura divinitus inspirata utilis est ad docendum.* Et ideo quæ sunt Novi ac Veteris Testamenti volumina, quæ secundum majorum traditionem per ipsum Spiritum Sanctum inspirata creduntur, et ecclesiis Christi tradita, competens videtur hoc in loco evidenti numero, sicut ex patrum monumentis accepimus, designare.

§ 37. Itaque Veteris Testamenti, omnium primo Moysi quinque libri sunt traditi, Genesis, Exodus, Leviticus, Numeri, Deuteronomium. Post hæc Jesus Nave, Judicum simul cum

[RUFINUS]
c. 410 A.D.

Ruth. Quatuor post hæc Regnorum libri quos Hebræi duos numerant; Paralipomenon, qui dierum dicitur liber; et Esdræ duo, qui apud illos singuli computantur, et Hester. Prophetarum vero Esaias, Jeremias, Ezechiel et Daniel: præterea duodecim Prophetarum liber unus. Job quoque et Psalmi David singuli sunt libri. Salomonis vero tres ecclesiis traditi, Proverbia, Ecclesiastes, Cantica Canticorum. In his concluserunt numerum librorum Veteris Testamenti.

Novi vero quatuor Evangelia, Matthæi, Marci, Lucæ, et Joannis. Actus Apostolorum quos describit Lucas. Pauli apostoli epistolæ quatuordecim. Petri apostoli duæ. Jacobi fratris domini et apostoli una. Judæ una. Joannis tres. Apocalypsis Joannis.

Hæc sunt quæ patres intra Canonem concluserunt, et ex quibus fidei nostræ assertiones constare voluerunt.

§ 38. Sciendum tamen est quod et alii libri sunt qui non Canonici sed Ecclesiastici a majoribus appellati sunt, id est Sapientia, quæ dicitur Salomonis, et alia Sapientia, quæ dicitur filii Sirach...Ejusdem vero ordinis libellus est Tobiæ et Judith: et Machabæorum libri.

In Novo vero Testamento libellus qui dicitur Pastoris sive Hermas, qui appellatur Duæ viæ vel Judicium Petri. Quæ omnia legi quidem in ecclesiis voluerunt, non tamen proferri ad auctoritatem ex his fidei confirmandam. Cæteras vero Scripturas Apocryphas nominarunt, quas in Ecclesiis legi noluerunt.

Hæc nobis a patribus tradita sunt, quæ (ut dixi) opportunum visum est hoc in loco designare, ad instructionem eorum qui prima sibi ecclesiæ ac fidei elementa suscipiunt, ut sciant, ex quibus sibi fontibus verbi Dei haurienda sint pocula.

XXVI.

Ad Exsuperium ep. Tolosanum[1] (Galland, Bibl. Pp. viii. 561 seqq.). Hæc sunt ergo[2] quæ desiderata moneri voluisti: Moysi libri quinque...et Jesu Nave, et Judicum, et Regnorum

---

[1] E cod. Coll. SS. Trin. (A) collatis B (cf. p. 541, n. 8) et Cotton. Claud. E, V (D). [2] BD; om. *ergo* A Gall.

libri quatuor simul et Ruth, prophetarum libri sexdecim, Salo- *Appendix D.*
monis libri quinque, Psalterium. Item historiarum, Job liber
unus, Tobiæ unus, Hester unus, Judith unus, Machabeorum
duo, Esdræ duo, Paralipomenon duo. Item Novi Testamenti:
Evangeliorum libri iiii; Pauli Apostoli Epistolæ xiiii: Epistolæ Johannis tres: Epistolæ Petri duæ: Epistola Judæ:
Epistola Jacobi: Actus Apostolorum: Apocalypsis Johannis.
Cætera autem quæ vel sub nomine Matthiæ, sive Jacobi mino-
ris, vel sub nomine Petri et Johannis, quæ a quodam Leucio
scripta sunt, vel sub nomine Andreæ, quæ a Nexocharide[1] et
Leonida philosophis, vel sub nomine Thomæ, et si qua sunt
talia[2], non solum repudianda verum etiam noveris esse dam-
nanda. [Data x kal. Mart. Stilichone ii. et Anthemio virr.
clarr. coss.[3]] (A.D. 405)

XXVII.

Decretum de libris recipiendis et non recipiendis (Credner, *Gelasius.*
Zur Gesch. d. K. p. 192 sqq.). Incipit confirmatio domini
Gelasii Papæ de libris Veteris ac Novi Testamenti.

§ 1. *In principio videlicet quinque libri Moysis.*

   Genesis liber i.
   ......
   Jesu Nave liber i.
   Judicum liber i.
   Ruth liber i.
   Regum libri iv.
   Paralipomenon libri ii.
   Psalmorum cl. liber i.
   Salomonis libri iii.
   Proverbiorum...
   Sapientiæ liber i.
   Ecclesiasticus liber i.

[1] *anexocharide* B.   [2] ABD—*alia* Gall.   [3] om. ABD.

§ 2. *Item Prophetæ numero* xvi.
  Esaiæ liber i....
  Danielis liber i.
  Osee liber i.......
  Malachiæ liber i.

§ 3. *Item Storiarum.*
  Job liber i.
  Tobias liber i.
  Ester liber i.
  Judith liber i.
  Esdra libri ii.
  Machabæorum libri ii.

§ 4. *Item ordo Scripturarum Novi Testamenti, quem Sancta Catholica Romana suscipit et veneratur ecclesia*[1]. Evangeliorum[2] libri iv, id est[3] sec. Matthæum lib. i. sec. Marcum lib. i. sec. Lucam lib. i. sec. Joannem lib. i. Item Actuum Apostolorum liber unus[4].

§ 5. Epistolæ Pauli Apostoli num. xiiii[5].

§ 6. Apocalypsis[6] liber i. Apostolicæ epistolæ[7] numero cum LXX. *eruditissimis episcopis conscripsit.* Equidem, ut verum fatear, librorum ecclesiasticorum et apocryphorum indicem multo majoris auctoritatis esse quam SS. Scripturarum canonem existimo.

---

[1] Recensionum quæ Damasi (D) et Hormisdæ (H) nomina præ se ferunt lectt. varr. apposui; singulas quasque Codd. lectiones Credner dabit. Id vero minime prætermittendum esse credo duos Mus. Brit. codices decretum Gelasii de libris apocryphis continere, nullo librorum S. Scripturæ canone præposito; quorum alter (Cotton. Vesp. B, 13, 12) ita incipit: *Post propheticas et evangelicas scripturas atque apostolicas scripturas vel veteris vel novi testamenti, quas regulariter suscipimus, sancta Romana ecclesia has non prohibet suscipi. Sanctam Synodum Nicænam*... Alter vero (Add. 15,222, sæc. xi.) eundem fere quem Cod. L. (Credner, p. 178) textum exhibet, alio tamen titulo: *Incipit decretum Gelasii papæ quem* (sic) *in urbe Roma*

[2] *Evangelium* D.
[3] om. *id est* H.
[4] D. *Actus Apostolorum liber i.* post Apocalypsim ponit.
[5] Credner, XIII. nulla variatione notata; sed quum quatuordecim in Codd. fere XIIII. scribatur, vereor ne Areval., cujus collationem Cod. A. sequitur, eum in errorem induxerit. *Epp. Pauli* (+*apostoli* H) *numero xiv.* D. H. indice addito.
[6] *Item Apocalypsis Joannis* (+*apostoli* D) *lib. i.* DH.
[7] *Item epistolæ canonicæ* D, *item cann. epp.* H.

vii. Petri apostoli numero[1] ii. Jacobi apostoli numero[1] i. Joannis apostoli iii[2]. Judæ Zelotis[3].

XXVIII.

De instit. div. Litt. cap. xiv[4]. Scriptura Sancta secundum antiquam translationem in Testamenta duo ita dividitur, id est in Vetus et in Novum[5]. In Genesim...Deuteronomium, Jesu Naue...Regum libros quatuor, Paralipomenon libros duos, Psalterium librum unum, Salomonis libros quinque, i.e. Proverbia, Sapientiam, Ecclesiasticum, Ecclesiasten, Canticum Canticorum, Prophetas id est Isaiam...Danielem, Osee...Malachiam qui et Angelus, Job, Tobiam, Esther, Judith, Esdra duos, Machabæorum duos. Post hæc sequuntur Evangelia quatuor[6], id est Matthæi, Marci, Lucæ, Johannis: Actus Apostolorum: Epistolæ Petri ad gentes[7]: Jacobi[8]: Johannis ad Parthos: Epistolæ Pauli ad Romanos una, ad Corinthios[9] duæ, ad Galatas[10] una, ad Philippenses una, ad Ephesios una[11], ad Colossenses una, ad Hebræos una, ad Thessalonicenses[12] duæ, ad Timotheum duæ, ad Titum una[13], ad Philemonem una: Apocalypsis[14] Johannis.

XXIX.

Prol. in Psalm. 15. Migne, *Patr. Lat.* ix. 241. Et ea causa est ut in viginti duos libros lex Testamenti Veteris deputetur, ut cum litterarum numero convenirent. Qui ita secundum traditiones veterum deputantur, ut Moysi sint libri quinque, Jesu Naue sextus, Judicum et Ruth septimus, primus et secundus Regnorum in octavum, tertius et quartus

---

[1] om. *numero* DH.
[2] *Joannis Apost. ep. i. Alterius Joannis Presbyteri ep. ii.* D.
[3] +*epistola i* D. +*apostoli epistola* H.
[4] E cod. Reg. Mus. Brit. 13 A, xxi. 7 (*a*): collatis codd. Cotton. Claud. B, 13, 8 (β); Reg. 10 B, xv. 2 (γ); 5 B, viii. 6 (δ).
Idem divisiones secundum Hieronymum et Augustinum in capitibus proxime præcedentibus tradidit.
[5] Edd. =*in*.
[6] *Evangeliorum quatuor Matthæus*, &c. βγδ; *Evangelistæ quatuor*, edd.
[7] Edd. + *Judæ*. Sed om. αβγδ.
[8] Edd. + *ad duodecim tribus*.
[9] *Chorinthios* γ.
[10] *Galathas* αγδ.
[11] Edd. = *ad Ephesios una* err. typ.? *ad Ephesios duæ* δ.
[12] *Tessalonicenses* γδ.
[13] *ad Tit. una ad Tim. duæ* β.
[14] *Apocalypsin* δ.

Appendix D.

in nonum, Paralipomenon duo in decimum sint, sermones dierum, Esdræ in undecimum, liber Psalmorum in duodecimum, Salomonis Proverbia, Ecclesiastes, Canticum Canticorum in tertium decimum, et quartum decimum et quintum decimum, duodecim autem Prophetæ in sextum decimum, Esaias deinde et Jeremias cum Lamentatione et Epistola; sed et Daniel et Ezekiel et Job et Hester, viginti et duum librorum numerum consumment[1]. Quibusdam autem visum est additis Tobia et Judith viginti quatuor libros secundum numerum Græcarum litterarum connumerare, Romana quoque lingua media inter Hebræos Græcosque collecta; quia his maxime tribus linguis sacramentum voluntatis Dei et beati regni expectatio prædicatur...

XXX.

Isidorus,
Ep. Hispal.
† 636 A.D.

De ordine Librorum S. Scripturæ init.[2] Migne, *Patr. Lat.* lxxxiii. 155 ff.

1. Plenitudo Novi et Veteris Testamenti quam in canone catholica recipit Ecclesia juxta vetustam priorum traditionem ista est.

2. In principio videlicet quinque libri Moysi...

3. Huic succedunt libri Jesu Naue, Judicum et...Ruth...

4. Hos sequuntur quatuor libri Regum. Quorum quidem Paralipomena libri duo e latere annectuntur... 5. Alia sunt volumina quæ in consequentibus diversorum inter se temporum texunt historias, ut Job liber, et Tobiæ, et Esther, et Judith, et Esdræ, et Machabæorum libri duo.

6. Sed hi omnes præter librum Job Regum sequuntur historiam ..

7. Ex quibus quidem Tobiæ, Judith et Machabæorum Hebræi non recipiunt. Ecclesia tamen eosdem inter Canonicas scripturas enumerat.

---

[1] Hæc ex Origene transtulit Hilarius [cf. supra § 13] cujus verba in uno saltem loco parum intellexit, Hebraicum τῶν παραλειπομένων titulum cæteris omissis Latine interpretando. Idem tamen corruptum Origenis textum libro duodecim prophetarum addito supplevit.

[2] E Cod. Reg. (Mus. Brit.) 5 B. viii. (a); coll. Cod. Cotton. Vesp. B. xiii. (b).—Cf. Isid. Procem. §§ 86—109.

8. Occurrunt dehinc Prophetæ, in quibus est Psalmorum liber unus, et Salomonis libri tres, Proverbiorum scilicet, Ecclesiastes et Cantica Canticorum. Duo quoque illi egregii et sanctæ institutionis libelli, Sapientiam dico et alium qui vocatur Ecclesiasticus; qui dum dicantur a Jesu filio Sirach editi, tamen propter quamdam eloquii similitudinem Salomonis titulo sunt prænotati. Qui tamen in Ecclesia parem cum reliquis Canonicis libris tenere noscuntur auctoritatem.

9. Supersunt libri sedecim prophetarum... 11. Hinc occurrit Testamentum Novum, cujus primum Evangeliorum libri sunt quatuor, Matthæus[1] et Marcus, Lucas et Johannes. Sequuntur deinde Epistolæ Pauli apostoli xiiii. id est, ad Romanos, ad Corinthios duæ, ad Galatas[2], ad Ephesios, ad Philippenses[3], et ad Thessalonicenses duæ, ad Colossenses, ad Timotheum duæ, ad Titum vero et ad Philemonem et ad Hebræos singulæ[4] 12. epistolæ, Jacobi apostoli una[5], Petri duæ, Johannis iii.[6] Judæ una[7]. 13. Actus etiam Apostolorum a Luca Evangelista conscriptus; et Apocalypsis Johannis apostoli. Fiunt ergo in ordine utriusque Testamenti libri septuaginta et duo.

14. Hæc sunt enim nova et vetera quæ de thesauro Domini proferuntur, e quibus cuncta sacramentorum mysteria revelantur. Hi sunt duo Seraphim qui in confessione sanctæ Trinitatis jugiter certantes τρὶς ἅγιος hymnum erumpunt.

16. Hæ litteræ sacræ, hi libri integri numero et auctoritate: aliud cum istis nihil est comparandum. Quicquid extra hos fuerit inter hæc sacra et divina nullatenus recipiendum[8].

Appendix D.

---

[1] +*quoque* b.
[2] *Galathas* ab.
[3] *Philipenses* a.
[4] ......ad Hebræos singulæ. 12. Epistolæ quoque Johannis apostoli tres; Petri duæ, Judæ et Jacobi singulæ. 13. Actus etiam Apostolorum et Apocalypsis Johannis (Migne).
[5] om. *una* a.
[6] *iiii or* a.
[7] 'In all the other enumerations of 'the Sacred Books the order of the 'N. T. Books is Gospels, Pauline 'Epistles, Catholic Epistles, Acts, 'Apocalypse, but the order of the 'Catholic Epistles varies strangely in 'the several lists: *Etymol.* vi. 1, § 10, 'Pet. Joh. Jac. Jude; *ib.* vi. 2, §§ '46 f., Pet. Jac. Joh. Jude; *De Eccles.* '*Officiis*, I. 12, § 12, I. 11, § 6, Jac. 'Pet. Joh. Jude.' (Dr E. Abbot.)
[8] *recipienda* b.

XXXI.

Ep. 143, *ad Henricum Comitem Campaniæ.* Migne, *Patr. Lat.* cxcix. 124 ff. Quæsitum vero est quem credam numerum esse librorum Veteris et Novi Testamenti et quos auctores eorum; quid Hieronymus in Epistola ad Paulinum presbyterum de omnibus libris divinæ pagellæ ascripta dicat mensam solis a philosopho Apollonio litteras persequente visam in sabulo; quid item Virgilii centonas et Homeri centonas in eadem dicat Epistola...De primis duabus quæstionibus, de numero scilicet librorum et auctoribus eorum Cassiodorus elegantem composuit librum; sed quia in hac parte fides mea discutitur, mea vel aliorum non multa interesse arbitror quid credatur; sic [si] enim hoc credatur an aliter nullum salutis affert dispendium. In eo autem quod nec obest nec prodest aut in alterutro parum momenti affert acrius litigare; nonne idem est ac si de lana caprina inter amicos acerbius contendatur? Proinde magis fidem arbitror impugnare si quis id de quo non constat pervicacius statuat, quam si a temeraria definitione abstinens id unde patres dissentire videt et quod plane investigare non potest, relinquat incertum. Opinio tamen in alteram partem potest et debet esse proclivior ut quod omnibus aut pluribus aut maxime notis atque præcipuis aut unicuique probato artifici secundum propriam videtur facultatem facilius admittatur, nisi ratio manifesta aut probabilior in his quæ rationi subjecta sunt oppositum doceat esse verum ..

Quia ergo de numero librorum diversas et multiplices patrum lego sententias catholicæ ecclesiæ doctorem Hieronymum sequens, quem in construendo literæ fundamento probatissimum habeo, sicut constat esse viginti duas literas Hebræorum sic viginti duos libros Veteris Testamenti in tribus distinctos ordinibus indubitanter credo...Liber vero Sapientiæ et Ecclesiasticus, Judith, Tobias et Pastor, ut idem pater asserit, non reputantur in Canone, sed neque Machabæorum liber, qui in duo volumina scinditur....Ille autem qui Pastor inscribitur an alicubi sit nescio, sed certum est quod Hieronymus et Beda illum vidisse et legisse testantur. His adduntur Novi Testamenti octo Volumina, scilicet, Evangelium Matthæi Marci Lucæ Ioannis, Epistolæ Pauli quindecim uno volumine comprehensæ, licet sit vulgata et fere omnium communis opinio non esse nisi quatuordecim....Ceterum quindecima est illa quæ ecclesiæ Laodicensium scribitur, et licet, ut ait Hieronymus, ab omnibus explodatur, tamen ab apostolo scripta est. Neque sententia hæc de aliorum præsumitur opinione sed ipsius apostoli testimonio roboratur. Meminit enim ipsius in Epistola ad Colossenses his verbis: *cum lecta fuerit apud vos hæc epistola, facite ut in Laodicensium ecclesia legatur, et ea quæ Laodicensium est legatur vobis.* Sequuntur epistolæ canonicæ septem in uno volumine, deinde Actus Apostolorum in alio et tandem Apocalypsis. Et hunc quidem numerum esse librorum qui in sacrarum scripturarum canonem admittuntur celebris apud ecclesiam et indubitata traditio est, qui tanta apud omnes vigent auctoritate ut contradictionis aut dubietatis locum sanis mentibus non relinquant quin conscriptæ sint digito Dei. Jure ergo et merito cavetur et condemnatur ut reprobus qui in morum verborumque commercio, præsertim in foro fidelium, hujus divini eloquii passim et publice non admittit argentum quod igne Spiritus Sancti examinatum est, purgatum ab omni fæce terrena et macula purgatur septuplum. Istis ergo secure fides incumbat et illis quæ hinc probatum et debitum accipiunt firmamentum, quoniam infidelis et hæreticus est qui eis ausus fuerit refragari.

De librorum vero auctoribus variantur opiniones, licet ista prævaluerit apud ecclesiam eos ab illis esse præscriptos qui in singulorum titulis prænotantur....Sed quæ cura est, serenissime domine, has atque alias in investigatione auctorum discutere, opiniones cum unum omnium sanctarum scripturarum constet esse auctorem Spiritum Sanctum? Nam beatus Gregorius in Moralibus verissime et elegantissime, cum constet libri beati Job, quem exponebat, Spiritum Sanctum esse auctorem, de scriptore libri postmodum quærere habendum esse ac si cum de scriptore certum sit de calamo quo liber scriptus sit dubitetur.

XXXII.

HUGO DE
S. VICTORE.
† 1140 A.D.

De Script. 6. (Migne, *Patr. Lat.* ccxxv. 45.) Omnis divina Scriptura in duobus Testamentis continetur, Veteri videlicet et Novo. Utrumque Testamentum tribus ordinibus distinguitur. Vetus Testamentum continet legem, prophetas, hagiographos. Novum autem Evangelium, apostolos, patres. Primus ordo Veteris Testamenti, id est lex,...Pentateuchum habet....Secundus ordo est prophetarum: hic continet octo volumina....Deinde tertius ordo novem habet libros....Omnes ergo fiunt numero viginti duo. Sunt præterea alii quidam libri ut Sapientia Salomonis, liber Jesu filii Sirach et liber Judith et Tobias et libri Machabæorum, qui leguntur quidem sed non scribuntur in canone. His xxii libris Veteris Testamenti, viii libri Novi Testamenti junguntur. In primo ordine Novi Testamenti sunt iv Evangelia....In secundo similiter sunt quatuor, Actus videlicet Apostolorum, Epistolæ Pauli numero xiv sub uno volumine contextæ, Canonicæ Epistolæ, Apocalypsis. In tertio ordine primum locum habent Decretalia quos Canonicos, i.e. regulares appellamus; deinde sanctorum patrum scripta, i.e. Hieronymi, Augustini, Ambrosii, Gregorii, Isidori, Origenis, Bedæ, et aliorum doctorum, quæ infinita sunt. Hæc tamen scripta patrum in textu divinarum scripturarum non computantur, quemadmodum in Veteri Testamento ut diximus quidam libri sunt qui non scribuntur in Canone et tamen leguntur, ut Sapientia Salomonis et ceteri. Textus igitur divinarum scripturarum quasi totum corpus principaliter xxx libris continetur. Horum xxii in Veteri, viii in Novo Testamento, sicut supra monstratum est, comprehenduntur. Cetera vero scripta quasi adjuncta sunt et ex his præcedentibus manantia. In his autem ordinibus maxime utriusque Testamenti apparet convenientia: quia sicut post legem prophetæ, et post prophetas hagiographi, ita post Evangelium apostoli, et post apostolos doctores ordine successerunt. Et mira quadam divinæ dispensationis ratione actum est, ut cum in singulis

Scripturis plena et perfecta veritas consistat, nulla tamen superflua sit.

Appendix D

XXXIII.

Decretum de Canonicis Scripturis. Sacrosancta œcumenica et generalis Tridentina Synodus, in Spiritu Sancto legitime congregata,...hoc sibi perpetuo ante oculos proponens, ut sublatis erroribus puritas ipsa evangelii et ecclesia conservetur... perspiciensque hanc veritatem et disciplinam contineri in libris scriptis et sine scriptis traditionibus, quæ ab ipsius Christi ore ab Apostolis acceptæ aut ab ipsis apostolis Spiritu Sancto dictante quasi per manus traditæ ad nos usque pervenerunt; orthodoxorum patrum exempla secuta, omnes libros tam Veteris quam Novi Testamenti, cum utriusque unus deus sit auctor; necnon traditiones ipsas tum ad fidem tum ad mores pertinentes, tanquam vel ore tenus a Christo vel a Spiritu Sancto dictatas et continua successione in ecclesia Catholica conservatas, pari pietatis affectu ac reverentia suscipit et veneratur. Sacrorum vero librorum indicem huic decreto adscribendum censuit, ne cui dubitatio suboriri possit, quinam sint qui ab ipsa synodo suscipiuntur. Sunt vero infra scripti. Testamenti veteris, quinque Moysis,...Josue, Judicum, Ruth, quatuor Regum, duo Paralipomenon, Esdræ primus et secundus, qui dicitur Neemias, Thobias, Judith, Hester, Job, Psalterium Davidicum cl psalmorum, Parabolæ, Ecclesiastes, Canticum Canticorum, Sapientia, Ecclesiasticus, Isaias, Hieremias cum Baruch, Ezechiel, Daniel, duodecim prophetæ minores, i. e. Osea...Malachias, duo Machabæorum, primus et secundus. Testamenti novi, quatuor Evangelia,...Actus Apostolorum a Luca evangelista conscripti. Quatuordecim epistolæ Pauli apostoli, ad Romanos,...ad Hebræos. Petri apostoli duæ, Joannis apostoli tres, Jacobi apostoli una, Judæ apostoli una, et Apocalypsis Joannis apostoli. Si quis autem libros ipsos integros cum omnibus suis partibus, prout in ecclesia catholica legi consueverunt, et in veteri vulgata Latina editione habentur, pro sacris et canonicis non susceperit; et traditiones prædictas sciens et prudens contempserit; anathema sit.

Concil. Trident. *Apr.* 8, 1546.

APPENDIX E.

THE EPISTLE TO THE LAODICENES.

THE text of this Epistle is given according to four Manuscripts in the British Museum[1].

A. *Cod. Add.* 11,852. A very valuable Manuscript of St Paul's Epistles, which belonged to the Abbey of St Gall, and was written probably between A.D. 872—884. An inscription at the end of the Capitula of the Epistle to the Romans records the original donation.

> Iste liber Pauli retinet documenta sereni :
> Hartmotus Gallo quem contulit Abba beato.
> Si quis et hunc sancti sumit de culmine Galli,
> Hunc Gallus Paulusque simul dent pestibus amplis.

The text of the Epistle in this Manuscript is perhaps the best which remains. The Epistle stands after that to the Hebrews and has no Capitula.

H. *Harl.* 2833, 31, 1, 2. Sæc. xi. written for the use of the Cathedral of Angers. The Epistle follows the Apocalypse.

C. *Add.* 10,546. Sæc. ix. (known as *Charlemagne's Bible*). The Epistle comes between that to the Hebrews and the Apocalypse.

The text is printed from Cod. Reg. 1 E vii, viii, Sæc. ix, x, in which it appears in its fullest form. I have added readings from the Lambeth manuscripts 3, 4 (L_1) and 1152 (L_2), Sæc. xii, xiii, but I cannot feel sure that the collation is complete.

The italics mark the extent of variation from the printed text; the † an addition to it; the * and ** the first and second hands.

---

[1] The Epistle has been printed with a very complete apparatus by Bp Lightfoot, *Colossians*, pp. 347 ff.

THE EPISTLE TO THE LAODICENES.

Appendix E.

EXPLICIT EPISTOLA AD HEBREOS SCRIPTA. AB URBE ROMA HABET VERSUS DCC. INCIPIUNT CAPITULA IN EPISTOLA AD LAUDICENSES.

I Paulus apostolus pro Laudicensibus domino gratias refert et hortatur eos ut a seductoribus* decipiantur.

II [Quod**?] manifesta vinculat apostoli in quibus lætatur et gaudet.

III Monet Laudicenses apostolus ut sicut sui audierunt præsentiam ita retineant et sine retractatu** faciant.

IIII Hortatur apostolus Laudicenses ut fide sint firmi et que** integra et vera et deo sunt placita faciant. Salutatio fratrum in osculo sancto. EXPLICIUNT CAPITULA INCIPIT EPISTOLA AD LAUDICENSES.

INCIPIT EPISTOLA AD LAUDICENSES[1].

I. PAULUS APOSTOLUS,
non *ab hominibus* neque
per hominem, sed per Ihesum Christum
et Deum patrem omnipotentem
qui suscitavit eum a mortuis,   5
Fratribus qui sunt *Laudiciae:* gratia vobis
et pax a Deo †patre† et Domino *nostro* Ihesu Christo.
Gratias ago *Deo meo et Christo Ihesu* per omnem
orationem meam, quod *estis permanentes*

1 *Incipit* EPISTOLA PAULI AD LAODICENSES. AH.   INCIPIT EPISTOLA AD LAODICENSES C.
2   ab homine A.
4, 5 *om.* ACHL$_2$.
6   Laodiciæ CH.   Laoditiæ*, Laodiciæ** A.
7   Deo et p. L$_2$.
...   patre nostro H.
...   Domino *om.* nostro CHL$_2$.
8   ago Christo per omn. AH.   Deo meo per omn. C.   *om.* et...per L$_2$.
9   perm. estis CHL$_1$L$_2$.

in eo et perseverantes *in operibus* †*ejus speran-* 10
tes promissum in die *judicationis*. Neque
enim destituant vos quorundam *vaniloquia*
insinuantium†; *sed peto ne* vos avertant** a*
a **veritate evangelii quod a me praedicatur.
Et nunc *faciet Deus* ut† qui sunt ex me *ad per-* 15
fectum veritatis evangelii *dei servientes* † et fa-
cientes benignitatem *eorum quae* sunt
salutis vitae æternæ.

II. Et nunc *palam sunt* vincula mea quae pa-
tior in Christo,† *in* quibus laetor *et* gaudeo; 20
et hoc mihi est ad salutem perpetuam, quod ipsum
factum† orationibus vestris† administrante *Spiritu*
Sancto, sive per vitam sive *per* mortem. Est enim mihi
vere vita in Christo et mori gaudium;† et *ipse*
in vobis faciet *misericordiam suam*, ut eandem 25
dilectionem habeatis et sitis unanimes.

 10 op. bonis H. *om*. in op. ejus C.
 10, 11 promissum expectantes CHL$_2$. sp. promissionem A.
 11 judicii CHL$_2$.
 12 *om*. enim ACH. destituunt HL$_2$. destituit C. quorumdam A.
 ... vaniloquentia AC.
 13 insinuantium se A. insanientium H. ut vos av. ACHL$_2$. avartant* A. a *erased*.
 15 Deus faciet A. ut sint A.
 15, 16 in profectum A. ad pfectum H. ad profectum C.
 16 deservientes ACH. des. sint H.
 17 operum quæ AH. operumq. C.
 19 sunt palam A.
 20 in Chr. Ihesu CL$_1$. *om*. in ACHL$_1$. ut gau. C.
 21 michi H. *and v*. 23.
 22 factum est H. et adm. H. et amminstr. C.
 22, 23 sancto spiritu A. spiritum sanctum C.
 23 *om*. per H.
 24 vivere vita CH. vivere A. gau. vel lucrum H. ipsum A. id ipsum C.
 25 misericordia sua A.

THE EPISTLE TO THE LAODICENES.

III. Ergo, dilectissimi, ut *audistis praesentia* mei ita* retinete et facite in timore *Dei*, et erit vobis *pax et* vita in *aeternum;* Est enim Deus qui operatur in *vobis;* et facite sine *retractatu* quaecunque facitis. 30

Appendix E.

IIII. Et quod est†, dilectissimi, gaudete in *Christo*† et praecavete sordidos† in *lucrum*. *Omnes sint* petitiones vestrae palam† *apud* Deum, et estote *sensu firmi in Christo Ihesu*. Et quae *sunt* integra et 35 vera† et *justa et pudica* et amabilia† *et sancta*† facite; et quae audistis et accepistis in corde retinete et erit vobis pax. *Salutate omnes fratres in osculo sancto.* Salutant vos *omnes* sancti *in [Christo Ihesu.* Gratia Domini nostri Ihesu Christi cum spiritu [vestro. Et † facite 40

27 cepistis L_1. praesentiam Domini H. praesentiam A**.
28 *om*. ita CL_1. tim. Domini H.
29 *om*. pax et ACH. in* aeterna (*om*. in**) A.
30 vos C. reatu H. retractatione A. retractu C.
31 quaecumque A.
31, 32 facite et quod est. Dilectissimi C.
32 est optimum AH. Christo Domino L_1. in Domino C.
33 sord. omnes H. in lucro ACH. In omnibus A. *om*. sint H.
34 p. sint H. ante A.
34, 35 firmi in sensu Christi $ACHL_1$.
35 *om*. sunt ACH.
36 vera sunt C. pudica et casta et justa H. pudica et justa et casta A. vera sunt L_1. pudica et justa CL_1. am. sunt H. *om*. et sancta ACH.
38, 39 *om*. salutate—sancto C.
39 sanctos (*for* fratres) A. *om*. omnes C. *om*. in Christo Ihesu ACH.
40 hanc facite H.
40—42 Et facite legi Colosensium vobis. Explicit Epistola ad Laodicenses C.

| Appendix E. | legi Colosensibus *hanc epistolam* et *Colosensibus vos legite*. *Deus autem et pater Domini nostri Ihesu Christi custodiat vos immaculatos in Christo Ihesu, cui est honor et gloria in secula seculorum Amen*

EXPLICIT EPISTOLA AD LAUDICENSES.
INCIPIT PROLOGUS HIERONIMI
IN APOCALYPSIS (*sic*).

41 *om.* hanc epistolam AH.
41, 42 Colosensium vobis AH.   Colosensium vos I$_1$.   Explicit epistola ad Laodicenses. A.   Explicit. H.
42 *om.* Deus autem...to the end AH.

INDEX I.

List of the Authorities quoted in reference to the Canon of the New Testament[1].

Acta Felicis, 413
Æthiopic Version, 371 n.
Africanus, s. Julius
Agrippa Castor, 95
Alexander, Bp of Alexandria, 369 n. 428
ALFRIC, 457
Alogi, 279
Ambrose, Bp of Milan, 454
Ammonius, 325
AMPHILOCHIUS, 445
Anatolius, 369 n.
Ancient Syriac Documents, 246 n.
Andrew, Bp of Cæsarea in Cappadocia, 447
Apelles, 317 n.
Apollinaris, s. Claudius
Apollonius of Ephesus, 382
APOSTOLIC CANONS, 438
— Constitutions, 369
Arabic Version of Erpenius, 244 n.
Archelaus, 396 n.
Arethas, 447
Aristides, 85
Aristides Soph. 405 n.
Aristo of Pella, 94
Arius, 429
Arnobius, 119
Articles, The English, 498
ATHANASIUS, 448, 554
Athenagoras, 118, 229
Auct. adv. Cataphryg. 387
— de Mundo, 380
— adv. Hær. [Hippol.] 378
— Parv. Labyr. 379
— adv. Novat. hær. 374
— de Resurr. [Justin], 171
AUGUSTINE, 454, 565
Aurelius, 374

Bardesanes, 240
Barnabas, 40

Basil, Bp of Cæsarea in Cappadocia, 446
Basilides, 291
Bede, 455
Beza, 490
Bullinger, 499

Cæsarius, 446 n.
Caietan, Cardinal, 475
Caius, 278 n. 378, 407 n.
Calvin, 488
Carpocrates, 296
Carthage, s. Concil.
Cassian, 449
CASSIODORUS, 454
Catharinus, 476
Celsus, 404
Cerdo, 313 n.
Cerinthus, 276
Chrysostom, s. Johannes
Claudius Apollinaris, 227
Clement of Rome, 22
[Clement's] Second Epistle, 179
— Two Epistles to Virgins, 186 n.
Clement of Alexandria, 119, 343, 346 n. 354
Clementine Homilies, 285 ff. 288 ff.
Codex ALEX. (A), 552
— BEZÆ, 176, 259
— Barocc. 558
— Boerner. (G), 520
— CLAROM. (D), 563
— Coislin. (H), 394
Cohortatio ad Græcos [Justin], 171
Commodian, 374
Concil. AQUISGRANENSE, 540 n.
— *Carthaginiense* (256 A.D.), 366 n.
— CARTHAGINIENSE III. 439, 541

---

[1] The authorities which are merely noticed in passing are printed in Italics: those which supply Catalogues of the New Testament in Capitals.

586   INDEX I. LIST OF AUTHORITIES.

Concil. HIEROSOLYMITANUM
        (1672), 438 n.
— HIPPONENSE, 441 n.
— Laodicenum, 431
— *Nicænum*, 429
— Quinisextum, 438
— *Tolosanum*, 451 n.
— TRIDENTINUM, 476, 578
Confessio Belgica, 492
— Gallica, 493
Constantine the Great, 426
Cornelius, 377
Cosmas, 244, 449 n.
Cyprian, 119, 373 f. 386
Cyril, Bp of Alexandria, 448
CYRIL, Bp of Jerusalem, 447, 549
CYRIL LUCAR, 438 n.

Damascenus, s. Johannes
Damasus, 453
Diamper, Synod of, 245
Didachê, The, 63
Didymus, 448
Diognetus, Letter to, 86
DIONYSIUS Areopagita, 449 n.
Dionysius Bar Salibi, 245
Dionysius of Alexandria, 365
Dionysius of Corinth, 188
Dionysius of Rome, 378
Donatists, 413
Dorotheus, 392
Dositheus, 438 n.

EBED JESU, 245, 443, 546
Ebionites, 161 n. 284
Elders quoted by Irenæus, 80
Ephrem Syrus, 241, 244 n. 444
Epiphanes, 297 n.
EPIPHANIUS, 447, 550
Erasmus, 471
Eucherius, 455
EUSEBIUS, Bp of Cæsarea in Palestine, 119, 231, 414
Euthalius, 449
Evangelists in Trajan's time, 82

Faustinus, 454 n.
Firmilian, 386
Fulke, 500

GELASIUS, 453, 571
Gennadius, 455
GREGORY of Nazianzus, 445, 446, 555

Gregory of Neo-Cæsarea, 385
Gregory of Nyssa, 446
Grotius, 495

Hegesippus, 204, 241
Heracleon, 303
Hermas, 193
Hermias, 118
Hesychius, 392 n.
Hierocles, 501
Hilary, Bp of Poictiers, 455, 573
Hilary of Rome, 451
Hippolytus, 380
HUGO of St Victor, 462, 577

Ignatius, 28
INNOCENT I. Bp of Rome, 453, 570
Irenæus, 340, 346 n. 383
ISIDORE, Bp of Seville, 451, 455, 574
Isidore of Pelusium, 448
Isidorus (son of Basilides), 296

JEROME, 451, 567
Jewel, 499
JOHANNES CHRYSOSTOMUS, 441, 543
JOHANNES DAMASCENUS, 444, 545
Johannes Scholasticus, 436
JOHN of Salisbury, 463, 575
Julius Africanus, 368 n.
JUNILIUS, 443, 544
Justin Martyr, 96
Justin the Gnostic, 284 n.

Karlstadt, 485

Lactantius, 119, 372 n.
Latin Versions:
    Vetus Latina, 248
    Vulgate, 263
Leo Allatius, 450
LEONTIUS, 449, 559
Lucian, 405 n.
Lucian of Antioch, 392
Lucifer, 454 n.
Luther, 480

Malchion, 392
Mani, 400
Marcion, 312
Marcosians, 309
Martyrdom of Ignatius, 80 n.
— Polycarp, s. Smyrna
Melito, 220, 549
Memphitic Version, 369

INDEX I. LIST OF AUTHORITIES.

Menander, 276
Methodius, 386
Metrophanes Critopulus, 439 n.
Miltiades, 389 n.
Minucius Felix, 118, 377
Montanus, 399
MURATORIAN CANON, 211

Naassenes, 282
NICEPHORUS, 450, 560
Nicephorus Callisti, 450 n.
Novatus, 377

Œcolampadius, 487
Œcumenius, 487
Ophites, 282
Optatus, 451
Oratio ad Græcos [Justin], 171
Origen, 119, 359
Orthodox Confession, 438 n.

Pacian, 451 n.
Palladius, 442 n.
Pamphilus, 393
Pantænus, 83, 342
Papias, 69
Patripassians, 398
Paul of Samosata, 391
Pelagius, 451
Peratici, 283
Peter Martyr, Bp of Alexandria, 368
PHILASTRIUS, 454, 567
Phileas, 368
Phœbadius, 451
Photius, 450
Pierius, 367
Pinytus, 192
Pistis Sophia, 404 n.
Polycarp, 373
Polycrates, 381
Porphyry, 405
Praxeas, 398
Prosper, 455
Prudentius, 455
Ptolemæus, 306

Quadratus, 84

RUFINUS, 454, 569

Salvian, 455
Saturninus, 293 n.
Sedulius, 455
Serapion, Bp of Antioch, 389

Sethiani, 283
Severian, 443 n.
Sibylline Oracles, 403
Simon Magus, 274
Sixtus Senensis, 479
'Sixty Books,' s. Cod. Barocc.
Smyrna, Epistle of the Church of, 230 n.
Sulpicius, 455
Symmachus, 288 n.
SYNOPSIS S. SCRIPTURÆ ap. Ath. 448 n.
SYNOPSIS S. SCRIPTURÆ ap. Chrys. 442, 543
Syrian Versions :
  Peshito, 236
  Philoxenian, 242 n.
  Harclean, *ib.*

Tatian, 118, 319
Teaching, The, of the Twelve Apostles, 63
Tertullian, 118, 345, 346 n. 371, 373, 374
Testaments of the xii. Patriarchs, 403
Thebaic Version, 369
Theodore, Bp of Mopsuestia, 442
Theodoret, 443
Theodotus, 399
Theodotus Byzant. 311 n.
Theognostus, 368
Theonas, 367
Theophilus, 118, 228, 389
Theophylact, 450
Tichonius, 414 n.
Tyndale, 496, 499

Ulphilas, 429 n.

Valentinus, 298
Victor of Antioch, 443
Victorinus Petaviensis, 372
Vienne and Lyons, Epistle of the Churches of, 339
Vincent of Lerins, 451

Westminster Confession, 493
Whitaker, 500

Ximenes, Cardinal, 470
Xystus, 194 n.

Zeno, 451
Zwingli, 487

INDEX II.

A Synopsis of the Historical Evidence for the Books of the New Testament.

i. *The characteristic teaching of the Apostles.*

  1. The teaching of St PETER.
    Clement of Rome, 24
    Polycarp, 37
  2. The teaching of St JAMES.
    Clement of Rome, 25
    Hermas, 200
  3. The teaching of St JOHN.
    Clement of Rome, 25
    Ignatius, 35
    Letter to Diognetus, 90
    Hermas, 201 f.
    Cerinthus, 277
    Ophites, 283
    Carpocrates, 297
  4. The teaching of St PAUL.
    Clement of Rome, 25
    Ignatius, 33
    Polycarp, 38
    Letter to Diognetus, 90
    Justin Martyr, 168
    Hermas, 200
    Carpocrates, 297
    Marcosians, 309, 310
    Testaments of the xii. Patriarchs, 404

  5. The teaching of the Epistle to the Hebrews.
    Clement of Rome, 26
    Barnabas, 43

ii. *The Catalogues of the Books of the New Testament*[1].

Alfric, 456
Amphilochius, 445, 556
Athanasius, 448, 554
Augustine, 454, 565
Canon Apostol. 542
Canon Murat. 211
Cassiodorus, 573
Cod. Alexandrinus, 552
Cod. Barocc. 558
Cod. Clarom. 563
Concil. Carthag. (Hippo), 440, 541
— [Laod.], 433, 540
— Trident. 578
Cosmas Indicopl. 449 n.
Cyril of Jerusalem, 447, 549
Ebed Jesu, 443, 546
Epiphanius, 447, 550
Eusebius, 414
Gelasius, 453, 571
Gregory Nazianz. 446, 555
Hilary, 573
Hugo of St Victor, 577
Jerome, 451, 567
Innocent I. 453, 570
Johannes Damasc. 444, 545
Isidore of Seville, 455, 574
John of Salisbury, 575
Junilius, 443, 544
Leontius, 449, 559
Nicephorus, 450, 560
Origen, 358, 553
Philastrius, 454, 567
Rufinus, 454, 569
Syn. S. Script. (ap. Chrys.), 543

iii. *The Evidences for the different parts of the New Testament generally.*

  1. *The Gospels.*
    Apostolic Fathers, 52
    Evangelists in Trajan's time, 82

---

[1] The Catalogues which agree with the received Catalogues of the New Testament are marked by Italics.

INDEX II. SYNOPSIS OF HISTORICAL EVIDENCE. 589

Letter to Diognetus, 92
Justin Martyr, 116
Hermas, 201
Muratorian Canon (iv.), 214
Claudius Apollinaris, 227
Peshito (iv.), 244
Carpocrates, 296
[Valentinus, 298]
Ptolemæus (iv.), 306
Marcosians (iv.), 309
Theodotus (iv.), 311 n.
Tatian (iv.), 322
Tertullian (iv.), 346 n.
Clemens Alex. (iv.), ib.
Irenæus (iv.), ib.
Origen (iv.), 358
Celsus (iv.), 404

2. *The Catholic Epistles.*

Seven:
   Pamphilus (?), 394
   Eusebius (?), 415, 424
   Didymus (2 Peter), 448
   Euthalius, 449
   Cassian (om. 2 and 3 John), 449
   Ambrose, 454
Three:
   Peshito, 244
   Chrysostom, 441
Two (1 Peter, 1 John):
   Theodore of Mopsuestia, 442
   Severian of Gabala (?), 443 n.
   = Marcion, 316

3. *The Epistles of St Paul.*

Thirteen (*without Ep. to Hebrews*):
   Canon Murat. 217
   Vetus Latina, 258
   Tertullian, 346 n.
   Clemens Alex. (= Philemon), ib.
   Irenæus (= Philemon), ib.
   Hippolytus (= Philemon), 380
   Cyprian, 372
   Victorinus, ib.
   Caius, 378
Ten (*excluding Pastoral Epp. and Ep. to Hebrews*):
   Basilides, 296
   Marcion, 316

Fourteen:
   Peshito, 244
   Origen (?), 359
   Donatists (? Hebrews), 414
   Eusebius, 416
   Chrysostom, 443
   Euthalius, 449
   Cosmas, 449 n.
   Cassian, 449
   Ambrose, 454

iv. *Special Evidence for separate Books*[1].

The Gospel of St Matthew:
   Barnabas, 51 n.
   Papias, 73
   Seniores ap. Iren. 81
   Pantænus, 83
   Justin Martyr, 113, 132, 140, 154, 157
   Frag. de Resurr. 171
   Dionysius of Corinth, 191
   Hermas, 201 n.
   Hegesippus, 207
   Theophilus, 228
   Athenagoras, 229
   [Simon Magus], 275
   Cerinthus, 277
   Ophites, 283
   Sethiani, 284
   Ebionites, ib.
   Clementine Homilies, 287
   Basilides, 296
   [Valentinus, 300]
   Heracleon, 304
   Ptolemæus, 307
   Marcosians, 308
   Tatian, 321
   Πίστις Σοφία, 404 n.

The Gospel of St Mark:
   Papias, 74
   Justin Martyr, 114
   Frag. de Resurr. 171
   Canon Murat. 214
   Clementine Homilies, 287

The Gospel of St Luke:
   Justin Martyr, 114, 132, 138

---

[1] In the case of the 'acknowledged' books I have not generally carried this later than the beginning of the third century, as at that time all controversy ceases.

Frag. de Resurr. 171
Hegesippus, 207
Canon Murat. 214
Theophilus, 233 n.
Ophites, 283
Basilides, 296
[Valentinus, 300]
Heracleon, 304
Marcion, 315
Epistle of Church of Vienne, 339
Πίστις Σοφία, 402 n.

The Gospel of St John:

[Clement of Rome], 181
Ignatius, 35
Papias, 77
Seniores ap. Iren. 80
Justin Martyr, 151, 167
Frag. de Resurr. 171
Cohort. ad Græcos, 171
Hermas, 201
Hegesippus, 209
Canon Murat. 214
Theophilus, 228
Athenagoras, 229
Claudius Apollinaris, 227
[Simon Magus], 275
Ophites, 283
Peratici, 283
Sethiani, 284
Clementine Homilies, 287
Basilides, 296
[Valentinus, 300]
Heracleon, 304
Ptolemæus, 307
Marcion, 317
Tatian, 321
Epistle of Church of Vienne, 339
Polycrates, 381
Testt. of the xii. Patriarchs, 403
Πίστις Σοφία, 404 n.

The Acts:

Polycarp, 48 n.
Letter to Diognetus, 92
Justin Martyr (?), 169 n.
Cohort. ad Græcos, 171
Hermas, 201
Hegesippus, 207
Canon Murat. 217
Peshito, 244
Theodotus, 311 n.
Epistle of Church of Vienne, 339

Tertullian, 346 n.
Clemens Alex. *ib.*
Irenæus (cf. *c. Hær.* III. 3. 3), *ib.*
= Marcion, 316

Ep. to the Romans:

Clement of Rome, 48 n.
Polycarp, *ib.*
Seniores ap. Iren. 81
Letter to Diognetus, 92
Justin Martyr, 168
Theophilus, 228
Athenagoras, 230
Ophites, 283
Basilides, 296
[Valentinus, 300]
Heracleon, 304
Ptolemæus, 307
Theodotus, 311 n.
Tatian (?), 321
Epistle of Church of Vienne, 339
Πίστις Σοφία, 404 n.

1 *Ep. to the Corinthians:*

Clement of Rome, 48 n.
Ignatius, *ib.*
Polycarp, *ib.*
Seniores ap. Iren. 81
Letter to Diognetus, 92
Justin Martyr, 170
Frag. de Resurr. 171
Cohort. ad Græcos, 171
Hermas, 201
[Hegesippus, 217]
Theophilus, 228
Athenagoras, 230
[Simon Magus, 275]
Ophites, 283
Peratici, 283
Basilides, 296
[Valentinus, 300]
Heracleon, 304
Ptolemæus, 307
Theodotus, 311 n.
Tatian (?), 321
Epistle of Church of Vienne (?), 339

2 *Ep. to the Corinthians:*

Polycarp, 48 n.
Seniores ap. Iren. 81
Letter to Diognetus, 92
Theophilus, 228

[Athenagoras, 230]
Ophites, 283
Sethiani, 284
Basilides, 296

Ep. to the Galatians:
Polycarp, 48 n.
Letter to Diognetus, 92
Orat. ad Græcos, 171
Athenagoras, 230
Ophites, 283
Ptolemæus, 307
Theodotus, 311 n.
Tatian, 322

Ep. to the Colossians:
Justin Martyr, 168
Cohort. ad Græcos, 171
Theophilus, 228
Peratici, 283
Basilides, 296
Ptolemæus, 307
Theodotus, 311 n.

Ep. to the Ephesians:
Clement of Rome, 48 n.
Ignatius, *ib.*
Polycarp (?), *ib.*
Letter to Diognetus, 92
Hermas, 201
Theophilus, 228
Ophites, 283
Basilides, 296
[Valentinus, 300]
Ptolemæus, 307
Marcosians (?), 308
Theodotus, 311 n.
Epistle of Church of Vienne, 339

Ep. to the Philippians:
Polycarp, 48 n.
Ignatius, *ib.*
Letter to Diognetus, 92
Frag. de Resurr. 171
Theophilus, 228
Sethiani, 284
Theodotus, 311
Epistle of Church of Vienne, 339

1 *Ep. to the Thessalonians:*
Ignatius (?), 48 n.
Polycarp (?), *ib.*
Dionysius of Corinth, 192

2 *Ep. to the Thessalonians:*
Polycarp (?), 48 n.
Justin Martyr, 170

1 *Ep. to Timothy:*
Clement of Rome, 48 n.
Polycarp, *ib.*
Barnabas (?), *ib.*
Letter to Diognetus, 92
Frag. de Resurr. 171
Hegesippus (?), 208 n.
Theophilus, 228
Athenagoras (?), 230
Theodotus, 311 n.
Epistle of Church of Vienne, 339

2 *Ep. to Timothy:*
Barnabas (?), 48 n.
Polycarp, *ib.*
Heracleon, 304

Ep. to Titus:
Clement of Rome (?), 48 n.
Letter to Diognetus, 92
Theophilus, 228
Tatian, 321

Ep. to Philemon:
Ignatius (?), 48 n.

Ep. to the Hebrews:
Clement of Rome, 49. Cf. p. 181 n.
Justin Martyr, 170
Pinytus, 192
Peshito, 238 n. 244
Theophilus, 228, 389
Ophites (?), 283
[Valentinus (?) 300]
Pantænus, 355
Clement of Alexandria, *ib.*
Origen, 359, 364
Dionysius of Alexandria, 365
Theognostus, 368
Peter of Alexandria, *ib.*
Alexander of Alex. 368 n. 429
[Tertullian, 371]
Lactantius (?), 372 n.
[Novatus, 377]
Irenæus (?), 384
Gregory Thaumat. 385
Methodius, 387

592 INDEX II. *SYNOPSIS OF HISTORICAL EVIDENCE.*

Synod. Antioch. 391
Pamphilus, 394
Archelaus, 396 n.
Testaments of the xii. Patriarchs, 403 n.
Eusebius, 416, 423
Theodore of Mopsuestia, 442
Pacian, 451
Pelagius, *ib.*
Hilarius Diac. *ib.*
Lucifer, 454 n.
Faustinus, 454 n.
= Vetus Latina (?), 259, 266
= Canon Murat. 218
= Tertullian, 371
= Caius, 318
= Hippolytus, 380
= Marcion, 316
= Cyprian, 372
= Victorinus, *ib.*
= Novatus, 377
= Optatus Mil. 451
= Phœbadius, *ib.*
= Zeno, *ib.*

Ep. of St James:

Clement of Rome, 48 n. Cf. 187
Hermas, 201
Melito (?), 221
Peshito, 244
[Clemens Alex.], 356. Cf. 357
Origen, 361
Dionysius of Alex. 366
[Novatus, 377]
Gregory Thaumat. 385
Eusebius (?), 419, 424
Chrysostom, 442
Basil, 446
= Canon Murat. 219
= Vetus Latina, 265
= Irenæus (?), 384
= Tertullian, 373
= Cyprian, 373
= Theodore of Mopsuestia, 442

First Ep. of St Peter:

[Clement of Rome], 187
Polycarp, 48 n.
Papias, 77
Letter to Diognetus, 91
Hermas, 201
Melito (?), 221

Peshito, 244
Theophilus, 229
Basilides, 296
Marcosians (?), 310
Theodotus, 312 n.
Epistle of Church of Vienne, 339
Tertullian, 263 n. 347 n.
Clemens Alex. *ib.*
Irenæus, *ib.*
Origen, 359

Second Ep. of St Peter:

Clement of Rome. Cf. c. xi.;
 2 Pet. ii. 6—9.
Polycarp (?), 48 n. 329 n.
[Clemens Alex. 355, cf. 358]
Vetus Latina, 264
Origen (?), 362
[Novatus, 377]
Firmilian (?), 386
Theophilus (?), 228 n. 389
Eusebius (?), 415
Ephrem Syrus (?), 444
Palladius, 442 n.
[Melito, 222 n.]
= Peshito, 244
= Irenæus, 384
= Tertullian, 373
= Cyprian, *ib.*
= Hippolytus (?), 380 n.
= Cosmas (?), 449
= Theodore of Mopsuestia (?), 442

First Ep. of St John:

[Clement of Rome], 187
Polycarp, 48 n.
Papias, 77
Letter to Diognetus, 91
Justin, 169
Canon Murat. 218
Peshito, 244
[Valentinus (?), 300]
Epistle of Church of Vienne, 339
Tertullian, 347 n.
Irenæus, *ib.*
Clemens Alex. *ib.*
Origen, 359

Second and Third Epp. of St John:

Canon Murat. (?), 218 f.
Codex Bezæ (Ep. 3), 259
[Clemens Alex.], 355
 Ep. 2, 357

INDEX II. SYNOPSIS OF HISTORICAL EVIDENCE.

Origen (?), 363
Dionysius of Alex. 366
[Tertullian, 373]
[Cyprian, *ib.*]
Alexander of Alex. (Ep. 2), 429
Aurelius (Ep. 2), 374
Irenæus (Ep. 2), 383
Eusebius (?), 419
Tichonius (Ep. 2), 415 n.
Palladius (Ep. 3), 442 n.
= Peshito, 244
= Theodore of Mopsuestia, 442
= Chrysostom (?), 442

Ep. of St Jude:

Canon Murat. 218 f.
Clemens Alex. 355, 357
Origen, 361
Tertullian, 259, 373
Auct. adv. Novat. hær. 374
Caius (?), 380
Malchion, 392
Eusebius (?), 419, 424
Palladius, 442 n.
= Irenæus, 384
= Peshito, 244
= Theodore of Mopsuestia, 442

Apocalypse:

Papias, 77
Justin Martyr, 121, 167
Dionysius of Corinth, 191
Hermas, 201
Canon Murat. 219
Melito, 222
Vetus Latina, 258
Cerinthus, 277
Ophites (?), 284
Marcosians, 311
Tatian, 321

Epistle of Church of Vienne, 339
Tertullian, 347 n. 361, 374
Clemens Alex. 347 n. 357
Irenæus, 347 n. 383
Theophilus, 228, 389
Origen, 359, 363
[Dionysius of Alex. 366]
Victorinus, 372
Cyprian, 374
Commodian, *ib.*
Lactantius, *ib.*
Hippolytus, 380
Apollonius, 382
Methodius, 387
Frag. adv. Cataphr. *ib.*
Theophilus, 389
Pamphilus, 394
Sibylline Oracles, 404
Testt. of the xii. Patriarchs, 403
Lucian, 405 n.
Tichonius, 414 n.
Eusebius (?), 419, 424
Chrysostom (?), 442 n.
Ephrem Syrus, 444
Basil, 446
Gregory of Nyssa, *ib.*
Andrew, 447
Arethas, *ib.*
Epiphanius (?), 447
Athanasius, 448
[Didymus, *ib.*]
Dionysius Areop. 449 n.
= Caius (so said), 278 n. 378, cf. 380
= Dionysius of Alex. 366
= Peshito, 244
= Œcumenius (?), 450
= Theophylact (?), *ib.*
= Concil. Laod. 433
= Amphilochius, 445
= Gregory Nazianz. *ib.*
= Cyril of Jerusalem, 447

THE END.

www.ingramcontent.com/pod-product-compliance
Lightning Source LLC
Chambersburg PA
CBHW052040290426
44111CB00011B/1562